Resource Guide to Accompany Foundations of Behavioral, Social, and Clinical Assessment of Children

Sixth Edition

Jerome M. Sattler
San Diego State University

Jerome M. Sattler, Publisher, Inc.
San Diego

Editorial Services: Sally Lifland and Quica Ostrander, Lifland et al., Bookmakers
Indexers: Jane Hoover and Moriah Cleveland
Interior Design: Quica Ostrander, Sally Lifland, and Jerome M. Sattler
Proofreaders: David N. Sattler, Gail Magin, Patricia L. K. Kelley, and Salvatore Massa
Production Coordinators: Sally Lifland, Jerome M. Sattler, and Kadir Samuel
Compositor: Publishers' Design and Production Services, Inc.
Cover Printer: Edwards Brothers Malloy
Printer and Binder: Edwards Brothers Malloy

This text was set in Times Roman and Helvetica and printed on Utopia Filmcote, with C1S cover paper.

Foundations of Behavioral, Social, and Clinical Assessment of Children, Sixth Edition:
    ISBN: 978-0-9702671-8-4
Resource Guide to Accompany Foundations of Behavioral, Social, and Clinical Assessment of Children, Sixth Edition: ISBN: 978-0-9702671-9-1
Combined *Foundations of Behavioral, Social, and Clinical Assessment of Children, Sixth Edition* and *Resource Guide to Accompany Foundations of Behavioral, Social, and Clinical Assessment of Children, Sixth Edition:* ISBN: 978-0-9702671-2-2

16   15   14   13   12   11   10   9   8   7   6   5   4
Printed in the United States of America

Contents

Table A-1
Background Questionnaire

BACKGROUND QUESTIONNAIRE

FAMILY DATA

Child's name _____ Today's date _____

Birth date _____ Age _____ Sex _____

Home address _____

School _____ Teacher _____

Person(s) filling out this form: ☐ Mother ☐ Father ☐ Stepmother ☐ Stepfather ☐ Caregiver ☐ Other _____

Email address(es) of above person(s) _____

Mother's name _____ Age _____ Education _____

Occupation _____ Phone: Home _____ Business _____

Email address _____

Father's name _____ Age _____ Education _____

Occupation _____ Phone: Home _____ Business _____

Email address _____

Stepmother's name _____ Age _____ Education _____

Occupation _____ Phone: Home _____ Business _____

Email address _____

Stepfather's name _____ Age _____ Education _____

Occupation _____ Phone: Home _____ Business _____

Email address _____

Marital status of parents _____ If separated or divorced, how old was your child when the separation occurred? _____

Who has legal custody of your child? ☐ Mother ☐ Father ☐ Joint

If remarried, how old was your child when the stepparent entered the family? _____

List all people living in the household (use an additional sheet if necessary):

Name	Sex	Relationship to Child	Age
_____	_____	_____	_____
_____	_____	_____	_____
_____	_____	_____	_____
_____	_____	_____	_____
_____	_____	_____	_____

List the name, sex, relationship to child, and age of any brothers, sisters, or other significant people living outside the home: _____
_____
_____

Primary language spoken in the home _____ Other languages spoken in the home _____

What language does your child use to speak with you? _____

What language does your child use to speak with friends? _____

Was your child adopted? ☐ Yes ☐ No If yes, at what age? _____ Does your child know he or she is adopted? ☐ Yes ☐ No

Name of medical coverage group or insurance company (If none, write "none") _____

Name of medical provider _____

If insured, insured's name _____

If referred, who referred you here? _____

(Continued)

Table A-1 *(Continued)*

PRESENTING PROBLEM

Briefly describe your child's current difficulties: _____

_____

_____

_____

How long has this problem been of concern to you? _____

When did you first notice the problem? _____

What seems to help the problem? _____

What seems to make the problem worse? _____

Have you noticed changes in your child's abilities? ☐ Yes ☐ No

If yes, please describe: _____

Have you noticed changes in your child's behavior? ☐ Yes ☐ No

If yes, please describe: _____

Has your child been evaluated or treated for the current problem or similar problems? ☐ Yes ☐ No

If yes, when and by whom? _____

Is your child being treated for a medical illness? ☐ Yes ☐ No

If yes, for what condition is your child being treated? _____

Is your child on any medication at this time? ☐ Yes ☐ No

If yes, please list names of medications: _____

PHYSICAL, SOCIAL, AND BEHAVIORAL CHECKLIST

Place a check next to any behavior or problem that your child *currently* exhibits.

Physical

☐ Has blackouts
☐ Has blank spells
☐ Has coordination problems
☐ Has difficulty catching a ball
☐ Has difficulty running
☐ Has difficulty walking
☐ Has difficulty with balance
☐ Has difficulty with fine-motor coordination
☐ Has difficulty with gross-motor coordination
☐ Has difficulty with hearing
☐ Has difficulty with vision
☐ Has dizziness spells
☐ Has mood swings
☐ Has poor bladder control
☐ Has poor bowel control
☐ Has seizures
☐ Tires easily, has little energy
☐ Other physical problems (describe) _____

Social

☐ Does not get along well with adults
☐ Does not get along well with brothers or sisters
☐ Does not get along well with other children
☐ Does not understand other people's feelings
☐ Has difficulty keeping friends
☐ Has difficulty making friends
☐ Is argumentative

☐ Is more interested in things (objects) than in people
☐ Prefers to be alone
☐ Refuses to share
☐ Other social problems (describe) _____

Behavioral

☐ Bangs head
☐ Bites nails
☐ Blames others for his or her troubles
☐ Breaks objects deliberately
☐ Bullies other children
☐ Clings to others
☐ Complains of aches or pains
☐ Constantly seeks attention
☐ Daydreams frequently
☐ Does not learn from experience
☐ Does not show feelings
☐ Drinks alcohol excessively
☐ Eats inedible objects
☐ Eats poorly
☐ Engages in behavior that could be dangerous to self or others (describe)

_____

☐ Engages in repetitive behavior (describe) _____
☐ Expresses feelings of hopelessness
☐ Expresses feeling that he or she is bad
☐ Fights physically with adults
☐ Fights physically with other children
☐ Fights verbally with adults
☐ Fights verbally with other children

☐ Gets hurt frequently
☐ Gets into trouble with the law (describe) _____
☐ Gives up easily
☐ Has anxiety about going to school
☐ Has anxiety when separated from parents
☐ Has blank spells
☐ Has compulsion about cleanliness—wants to wash all the time
☐ Has difficulty accepting criticism
☐ Has difficulty completing tasks
☐ Has difficulty following directions
☐ Has difficulty learning when faced with distractions
☐ Has difficulty managing tasks
☐ Has difficulty organizing tasks
☐ Has difficulty recognizing that he or she has a drinking problem
☐ Has difficulty resisting peer pressure
☐ Has difficulty waiting turn
☐ Has fear of bathing or showering
☐ Has fear of the bathroom
☐ Has fears at bedtime
☐ Has frequent crying spells
☐ Has frequent temper tantrums
☐ Has low self-esteem
☐ Has many accidents (describe)

_____

☐ Has periods of confusion or disorientation
☐ Has poor attention span
☐ Has poor memory

Table A-1 *(Continued)*

☐ Has trouble making plans
☐ Has trouble sleeping (describe)

_____

☐ Has unusual fears, habits, or mannerisms (describe)

_____

☐ Holds breath
☐ Injures self often
☐ Is a victim of bullying
☐ Is afraid of new situations
☐ Is aggressive (describe)

_____

☐ Is careless
☐ Is clumsy
☐ Is dazed, drugged, or groggy upon return from visiting a parent (in cases of divorce)
☐ Is disobedient
☐ Is disorganized
☐ Is eager to please others
☐ Is easily distracted
☐ Is easily frustrated
☐ Is extremely selfish
☐ Is fearful of strangers
☐ Is fearful of visiting a parent or caregiver (in cases of divorce)

☐ Is fidgety
☐ Is forgetful
☐ Is immature
☐ Is impulsive
☐ Is jealous (describe)

_____

☐ Is nervous or anxious
☐ Is overactive
☐ Is restless
☐ Is sad or unhappy often
☐ Is shy or timid
☐ Is slow to learn
☐ Is stubborn
☐ Is suspicious of other people
☐ Is unusually talkative
☐ Is wary of any physical contact with adults in general
☐ Is withdrawn (describe)

_____

☐ Lies (describe)

_____

☐ Moves slowly
☐ Overeats
☐ Refuses to go to bed
☐ Refuses to sleep alone

☐ Refuses to undress for physical education classes at school
☐ Requires constant supervision
☐ Rocks back and forth
☐ Runs away
☐ Sets fires
☐ Shows anger easily
☐ Shows sexually provocative behavior
☐ Shows wide mood swings
☐ Smokes
☐ Stares into space for long periods
Steals (describe)
☐ Sucks thumb
☐ Takes unnecessary risks
☐ Talks about killing self
☐ Talks about wanting to die
☐ Uses illegal drugs (describe)

_____

☐ Uses legal drugs for recreation (describe) _____

☐ Worries a lot
☐ Yells and calls children names
☐ Other behavioral problems (describe)

_____

_____

LANGUAGE/SPEECH CHECKLIST

Place a check next to any language or speech problem that your child *currently* exhibits.

☐ Does not know names of common objects
☐ Does not make appropriate gestures to communicate
☐ Has difficulty making speech understood
☐ Has difficulty recalling familiar words
☐ Has unusually loud speech
☐ Has unusually soft speech
☐ Is often hoarse

☐ Makes sounds but no words
☐ Mixes up the order of events
☐ Prefers to speak to adults only
☐ Prefers to speak to children only
☐ Prefers to speak to family members only
☐ Responds better to gestures than to words
☐ Seems uninterested in communicating

☐ Speaks in a monotone or exaggerated manner
☐ Speaks in shorter sentences than expected for age
☐ Speaks too fast
☐ Speaks very slowly
☐ Substitutes vague words (e.g., "thing") for specific words
☐ Uses gestures instead of words to express ideas

EDUCATIONAL HISTORY

Place a check next to any educational or school-related behavioral problem that your child *currently* exhibits.

☐ Dislikes school
☐ Forgets to bring homework assignment from school
☐ Forgets to take completed homework to school
☐ Has difficulty asking for help when it is needed
☐ Has difficulty finishing a project on time
☐ Has difficulty following instructions
☐ Has difficulty getting along with other children
☐ Has difficulty getting along with teacher

☐ Has difficulty getting started on his or her homework
☐ Has difficulty keeping notebooks organized
☐ Has difficulty paying attention in class
☐ Has difficulty reading
☐ Has difficulty remembering things
☐ Has difficulty respecting others' rights
☐ Has difficulty sitting still in class
☐ Has difficulty taking notes in class
☐ Has difficulty understanding homework directions
☐ Has difficulty waiting turn in school
☐ Has difficulty with arithmetic

☐ Has difficulty with handwriting
Has difficulty with other subjects (list) _____

_____

☐ Has difficulty with spelling
☐ Has difficulty working independently
☐ Is tired or sleepy in class
☐ Makes careless mistakes
☐ Refuses to do assignments in class
☐ Refuses to do homework
☐ Resists going to school

Did your child attend preschool? ☐ Yes   ☐ No
If yes, at what ages? _____ How often? _____

At what age did your child begin kindergarten? _____ What is his or her current grade? _____

Is your child in a special education class? ☐ Yes   ☐ No
If yes, what type of class? _____

Has your child been held back in a grade? ☐ Yes   ☐ No
If yes, what grade and why? _____

Has your child ever received special tutoring or therapy in school? ☐ Yes   ☐ No
If yes, please describe: _____

Has your child's school performance become worse recently? ☐ Yes   ☐ No
If yes, please describe: _____

Has your child missed a lot of school? ☐ Yes   ☐ No
If yes, please indicate reasons: _____

Has your child been expelled or suspended from school? ☐ Yes   ☐ No
If yes, please indicate reasons: _____

Describe any other problems in school: _____

DEVELOPMENTAL HISTORY

Pregnancy
Did the mother have any problems during pregnancy (for example, unusual bleeding, high blood pressure, an infection, diabetes, serious illness or injury, excessive weight gain, or Rh factor incompability)? ☐ Yes   ☐ No   ☐ Don't know
If yes, what kind of problem? _____

How old was the mother at the time of the baby's birth? _____ Was this a first pregnancy? ☐ Yes   ☐ No   ☐ Don't know
If no, how many times had the mother been pregnant before?_____

During pregnancy, did the mother smoke? ☐ Yes   ☐ No   ☐ Don't know
If yes, how many cigarettes each day? _____

During pregnancy, did the mother drink alcoholic beverages? ☐ Yes   ☐ No   ☐ Don't know
If yes, what alcoholic beverages did she drink? _____

Approximately how much alcohol did the mother consume each day? _____

During which part or parts of pregnancy—1st trimester, 2nd trimester, 3rd trimester—did the mother consume alcohol? _____

Were there times when the mother consumed five or more drinks in one session? ☐ Yes   ☐ No   ☐ Don't know
If yes, during which part or parts of pregnancy—1st trimester, 2nd trimester, 3rd trimester? _____

During pregnancy, did the mother use any prescription, over-the-counter, or recreational drugs? ☐ Yes   ☐ No   ☐ Don't know
If yes, what kind? _____ How often? _____

During pregnancy, was the mother exposed to X-rays or chemicals? ☐ Yes   ☐ No   ☐ Don't know
If yes, what? _____ How often? _____

During pregnancy, was the mother exposed to any infectious diseases? ☐ Yes   ☐ No   ☐ Don't know
If yes, what disease or diseases? _____

During pregnancy, did the mother receive prenatal care? ☐ Yes   ☐ No   ☐ Don't know

Was delivery induced? ☐ Yes   ☐ No   ☐ Don't know

How long was labor? _____ Were forceps used during delivery? ☐ Yes   ☐ No   ☐ Don't know

Was a caesarean section performed? ☐ Yes   ☐ No   ☐ Don't know
If yes, for what reason? _____

Were there any complications associated with the delivery? ☐ Yes   ☐ No   ☐ Don't know
If yes, what kind? _____

Was your child premature? ☐ Yes   ☐ No   ☐ Don't know   If yes, by how many weeks? _____

Was neonatal care needed? ☐ Yes   ☐ No   ☐ Don't know
If yes, what kind of care was required and how long was it needed? _____

Table A-1 *(Continued)*

Infancy

What was your child's birth weight? _____ Were there any defects or complications at birth? ☐ Yes ☐ No ☐ Don't know
If yes, please describe: _____

As an infant, did your child have any feeding problems? ☐ Yes ☐ No ☐ Don't know
If yes, please describe: _____

As an infant, did your child experience any sleeping problems? ☐ Yes ☐ No ☐ Don't know
If yes, please describe: _____

As an infant, did your child need oxygen? ☐ Yes ☐ No ☐ Don't know
If yes, please describe: _____

As an infant, did your child have jaundice? ☐ Yes ☐ No ☐ Don't know
If yes, please describe: _____

As an infant, did your child have infections? ☐ Yes ☐ No ☐ Don't know
If yes, please describe: _____

As an infant, did your child need blood transfusions? ☐ Yes ☐ No ☐ Don't know
If yes, please describe: _____

As an infant, did your child have seizures? ☐ Yes ☐ No ☐ Don't know
If yes, please describe: _____

As an infant, did your child need antibiotics? ☐ Yes ☐ No ☐ Don't know
If yes, please describe: _____

As an infant, did your child experience any other problems? ☐ Yes ☐ No ☐ Don't know
If yes, please describe: _____

As an infant, was your child quiet? ☐ Yes ☐ No ☐ Don't know

As an infant, did your child like to be held? ☐ Yes ☐ No ☐ Don't know

As an infant, was your child alert? ☐ Yes ☐ No ☐ Don't know

As an infant, did your child grow normally? ☐ Yes ☐ No ☐ Don't know
If yes, please describe: _____

As an infant, was your child different in any way from siblings? ☐ Yes ☐ No ☐ Don't know ☐ Not applicable
If yes, please describe: _____

First Years

Place a check next to each phrase that describes your child during his or her first years.

☐ Banged head frequently
☐ Did not babble
☐ Did not enjoy cuddling
☐ Did not smile socially
☐ Did not speak
☐ Did not wave "bye-bye"
☐ Had an excessive number of accidents
☐ Had excessive fears
☐ Had fine-motor problems
☐ Had gross-motor problems

☐ Had peculiar patterns of speech
☐ Had poor eye contact
☐ Had poor sleep patterns
☐ Ignored toys
☐ Preferred to play alone
☐ Was attached to an unusual object (describe) _____
☐ Was colicky
☐ Was constantly into everything
☐ Was difficult to comfort
☐ Was difficult to feed

☐ Was difficult to get to sleep
☐ Was excessively restless
☐ Was exposed to lead
☐ Was insensitive to cold or pain
☐ Was not calmed by being held
☐ Was not interested in other children
☐ Was unaware of painful bumps or falls
☐ Was unusually quiet or inactive
☐ Was very stubborn and challenging

Did your child display any other problems in growth and development during the first few years?
☐ Yes ☐ No ☐ Don't know

If yes, please describe: _____
_____

(Continued)

Developmental Landmarks

The following is a list of infant and preschool behaviors. Please indicate the age at which your child first demonstrated each behavior. If you are not certain of the age but have some idea, write the age followed by a question mark. If you don't remember or don't know the age at which the behavior occurred, write a question mark. If your child has not yet demonstrated the behavior, write an X.

Behavior	Age	Behavior	Age	Behavior	Age
Babbled	_____	Preferred one hand	_____	Showed response to mother	_____
Became toilet trained during day	_____	Put on clothing alone	_____	Smiled	_____
Buttoned clothes	_____	Put several words together	_____	Spoke first word	_____
Crawled	_____	Ran with good control	_____	Stayed dry at night	_____
Drank from cup	_____	Rode tricycle	_____	Stood alone	_____
Fastened zippers	_____	Rode bicycle	_____	Tied shoelaces	_____
Fed self	_____	Rolled over	_____	Took off clothing alone	_____
Held head erect	_____	Said alphabet in order	_____	Used a two-word sentence	_____
Named colors	_____	Sat alone	_____	Walked alone	_____
Played pat-a-cake or peek-a-boo	_____	Showed fear of strangers	_____		

CHILD'S MEDICAL HISTORY

Place a check next to any illness or condition that your child has had and note the approximate age when he or she had the illness or condition.

Illness or condition	Age	Illness or condition	Age	Illness or condition	Age
☐ AIDS	_____	☐ Eczema or hives	_____	☐ Memory problems	_____
☐ Alcohol use	_____	☐ Encephalitis	_____	☐ Meningitis	_____
☐ Allergies	_____	☐ Epilepsy	_____	☐ Mumps	_____
☐ Anemia	_____	☐ Extreme tiredness	_____	☐ Obesity	_____
☐ Asthma	_____	☐ Fainting spells	_____	☐ Paralysis	_____
☐ Bleeding problems	_____	☐ Frequent headaches	_____	☐ Pneumonia	_____
☐ Bone or joint disease	_____	☐ German measles	_____	☐ Polio	_____
☐ Broken bone	_____	☐ Gonorrhea or syphilis	_____	☐ Problems controlling bowels	_____
☐ Cancer	_____	☐ Hay fever	_____	☐ Rheumatic fever	_____
(list type) _____		☐ Hearing problems	_____	☐ Scarlet fever	_____
☐ Chicken pox	_____	☐ Heart disease	_____	☐ Seizures	_____
☐ Convulsions	_____	☐ High blood pressure	_____	☐ Sleeping problems	_____
☐ Diabetes	_____	☐ High fever	_____	☐ Suicide attempt	_____
☐ Difficulty concentrating	_____	☐ HIV	_____	☐ Tuberculosis	_____
☐ Diphtheria	_____	☐ Injuries to head	_____	☐ Urinary tract problems	_____
☐ Dizziness	_____	☐ Jaundice/hepatitis	_____	☐ Vision problems	_____
☐ Drug use	_____	☐ Kidney disease	_____	☐ Vitamin deficiency	_____
☐ Ear infections	_____	☐ Loss of consciousness	_____	☐ Walking problems	_____
☐ Eating disorder	_____	☐ Measles	_____	☐ Whooping cough	_____

Does your child have any illness or disability not covered above? ☐ Yes ☐ No ☐ Don't know If yes, please describe: _____

Has your child been hospitalized? ☐ Yes ☐ No ☐ Don't know If yes, please list reasons: _____

Has your child had any operations? ☐ Yes ☐ No ☐ Don't know If yes, please list reasons: _____

Table A-1 *(Continued)*

Has your child had any accidents? ☐ Yes ☐ No ☐ Don't know If yes, please describe: _____

Has your child been knocked unconscious? ☐ Yes ☐ No ☐ Don't know If yes, please list reasons:_____

Has your child had a brain injury? ☐ Yes ☐ No ☐ Don't know If yes, please list reasons:_____

Has your child had a sport-related
concussion? ☐ Yes ☐ No ☐ Don't know If yes, please describe: _____

Has your child ingested a toxic substance? ☐ Yes ☐ No ☐ Don't know If yes, please list substance: _____

Does your child take any medications? ☐ Yes ☐ No ☐ Don't know If yes, please list the medications and the reason
they are taken: _____

_____

Are your child's immunizations up to date? ☐ Yes ☐ No ☐ Don't know Child's height _____ Child's weight_____

FAMILY MEDICAL HISTORY

Place a check next to any illness or condition that any member of the immediate family has had. When you check an item, please note the family member's relationship to your child.

☐ Alcoholism _____   ☐ Eating disorder _____   ☐ Neurological disease _____
☐ Attention-deficit/   ☐ Emotional problem _____   ☐ Obesity _____
  hyperactivity disorder _____   ☐ Epilepsy _____   ☐ Seizure _____
☐ Blindness _____   ☐ Genetic disorder   ☐ Sleep problems _____
☐ Cancer _____   (list type) _____   ☐ Suicide attempt _____
☐ Deafness _____   ☐ Heart trouble _____   ☐ Violence toward others _____
☐ Depression _____   ☐ Intellectual disability _____ ☐ Other problems (describe)
☐ Developmental problem _____ ☐ Learning disability _____   _____ _____
☐ Diabetes _____   ☐ Lung disease _____   _____ _____
☐ Drug problem _____   ☐ Mental illness _____   _____ _____

OTHER INFORMATION

Child's Activities

What are your child's favorite activities?

1. _____ 2. _____ 3. _____
4. _____ 5. _____ 6. _____

What activities would your child like to engage in more often than he or she does now?

1. _____ 2. _____ 3. _____

What activities does your child like least?

1. _____ 2. _____ 3. _____

What chores does your child do around the house? _____

Has there been any recent change in his or her ability to carry out these chores? ☐ Yes ☐ No ☐ Don't know

If yes, please describe the change: _____

What time does your child usually go to bed on weekdays? _____ On weekends? _____

Trouble with the Law

Has your child ever been in trouble with the law? ☐ Yes ☐ No ☐ Don't know

If yes, please describe briefly: _____

Referral to Child Protective Services or Similar Agency

Has your child ever been referred to Child Protective Services or a similar agency for having been physically abused, sexually abused, emotionally abused, or neglected? ☐ Yes ☐ No ☐ Don't know

If yes, please describe briefly: _____

(Continued)

Table A-1 *(Continued)*

Your Parenting Style[a]

Please check Y (Yes) if the item generally describes how you relate to your child or N (No) if the item does not generally describe how you relate to your child.

1. I usually am responsive to my child's feelings and needs. ☐ Y ☐ N
2. I usually take my child's wishes into consideration before I ask him or her to do something. ☐ Y ☐ N
3. I usually explain to my child how I feel about his or her behavior. ☐ Y ☐ N
4. I usually encourage my child to talk about his or her feelings and problems. ☐ Y ☐ N
5. I usually encourage my child to speak his or her mind freely, even if he or she disagrees with me. ☐ Y ☐ N
6. I usually explain to my child the reasons behind my expectations. ☐ Y ☐ N
7. I usually provide comfort and understanding to my child when he or she is upset. ☐ Y ☐ N
8. I usually compliment my child when he or she does something well. ☐ Y ☐ N
9. I usually consider my child's preferences when I make plans for the family. ☐ Y ☐ N
10. I usually respect my child's opinions and encourage him or her to express them. ☐ Y ☐ N
11. I usually treat my child as an equal member of the family. ☐ Y ☐ N
12. I usually have a warm and intimate relationship with my child. ☐ Y ☐ N
13. When my child asks me why he or she has to do something, I usually tell him or her it is because I said so and I am the parent or because that is what I want. ☐ Y ☐ N

14. I usually punish my child when he or she misbehaves by taking privileges away from him or her (for example, TV, games, visiting friends). ☐ Y ☐ N
15. I usually yell when I disapprove of my child's behavior. ☐ Y ☐ N
16. I usually explode in anger toward my child when he or she misbehaves. ☐ Y ☐ N
17. I usually spank my child when I don't like what he or she does or says. ☐ Y ☐ N
18. I usually use threats as a form of punishment when my child misbehaves. ☐ Y ☐ N
19. I usually punish my child when he or she misbehaves by withholding kisses, hugs, and other forms of emotional expression. ☐ Y ☐ N
20. I usually openly criticize my child when his or her behavior does not meet my expectations. ☐ Y ☐ N
21. I usually find myself struggling to try to change how my child thinks or feels about things. ☐ Y ☐ N
22. I usually point out to my child his or her past behavioral problems to make sure they do not happen again. ☐ Y ☐ N
23. I usually remind my child that I am his or her parent. ☐ Y ☐ N
24. I usually remind my child of all the things I am doing and have done for him or her. ☐ Y ☐ N
25. I usually find it difficult to discipline my child. ☐ Y ☐ N
26. I usually give in to my child when he or she causes a commotion about something. ☐ Y ☐ N
27. I usually spoil my child. ☐ Y ☐ N
28. I usually ignore my child's bad behavior. ☐ Y ☐ N

Which disciplinary techniques are usually effective with your child? _____

_____

For what types of problems are these techniques effective? _____

_____

Which disciplinary techniques are usually ineffective with your child? _____

_____

For what types of problems are these techniques ineffective? _____

_____

Which parent (caregiver) usually administers discipline? _____

Activities Checklist

Place a check next to each activity that your child can do by himself or herself (even if your child does not do the activity regularly).

☐ Clears table
☐ Cooks meals
☐ Does homework alone
☐ Does ironing
☐ Does laundry

☐ Empties garbage
☐ Helps with grocery shopping
☐ Puts clothes away
☐ Sets table
☐ Sews

☐ Unpacks groceries
☐ Washes dishes
☐ Other activities (describe)

_____

_____

Table A-1 *(Continued)*

Child's Responsibilities

Can your child be trusted to care for a pet? ☐ Yes ☐ No ☐ Don't know
If no, why not?_____

Does your child handle his or her personal finances? ☐ Yes ☐ No ☐ Don't know
If no, why not?_____

Does your child take responsibility for his or her personal hygiene? ☐ Yes ☐ No
If no, why not?_____

Is your child's behavior generally age appropriate? ☐ Yes ☐ No

If no, please describe in what ways it is not age appropriate: _____
_____

Other Areas

What do you enjoy doing with your child? _____
_____

What have you found to be the most satisfactory ways of helping your child? _____
_____

What are your child's assets or strengths? _____
_____

Is there any other information that you think may help us in working with your child? _____
_____
_____

What prompted you to seek help at this time? _____
_____

Family Stress Survey

Every family sometimes experiences some form of stress. Please put a check next to any event that you know the family has experienced *in the last 12 months.*

☐ Child changed schools.
☐ Child started drinking alcohol.
☐ Child started having trouble in school.
☐ Child started having trouble with parent (caregiver).
☐ Child started having trouble with sister or brother.
☐ Child started using drugs.
☐ Child was a victim of bullying.
☐ Child was a victim of violence.
☐ Child was bullying other children.
☐ Child's brother died.
☐ Child's close friend moved away.
☐ Child's father died.
☐ Child's mother died.
☐ Child's pet died.

☐ Child's sister died.
☐ Family experienced a natural disaster (describe): _____
☐ Family moved to another city.
☐ Family moved to another part of town.
☐ Family's financial condition changed.
☐ Father lost job.
☐ Grandparent died.
☐ Member of family was accused of child abuse or neglect (describe person's relationship to child):
_____
☐ Mother lost job.
☐ Neighborhood was changing for the worse.

☐ Parent remarried.
☐ Parents divorced.
☐ Parents separated.
☐ Someone in family was in trouble with the law or police (describe person's relationship to child):
_____
☐ Someone in family was seriously injured or became ill (describe person's relationship to child):
_____
☐ Other forms of stress (list): _____
_____
_____
_____

(Continued)

Parent Needs Survey[b]

Listed below are some needs commonly expressed by parents (caregivers). Please put a check next to each item that you feel you need.

☐ A bigger or better house or apartment
☐ A car or other form of transportation
☐ A vacation
☐ Assistance in dealing with problems with friends or neighbors
☐ Assistance in dealing with problems with in-laws or other relatives
☐ Assistance in dealing with problems with my spouse/partner
☐ Assistance in handling other children's jealousy of their brother or sister
☐ Better dental care for my child
☐ Better medical care for my child
☐ Better therapy services for my child
☐ Counseling to help me cope with my situation
☐ Day care so that I can get a job
☐ Health insurance
☐ Help communicating with my child's school

☐ Help with child care
☐ Medical care for myself
☐ More friends who have a child like mine
☐ More information about behavior problems
☐ More information about child development
☐ More information about how I can help my child
☐ More information about my child's abilities
☐ More information about nutrition or feeding
☐ More information about programs that can help my child
☐ More money/financial help
☐ More time for myself
☐ More time to be with my child
☐ More time to be with my spouse
☐ More time to be with other adults

☐ Someone to help with household chores
☐ Someone to talk to about my problems
☐ Someone who can babysit for a day or evening so that I can get away
☐ Someone who can help me feel better about myself
☐ Special equipment to meet my child's needs
☐ Vocational training for myself
☐ Other needs (list): _____
_____
_____
_____
_____
_____
_____
_____
_____

Thank you.

[a] These items are modifications of items included in the Parenting Practices Questionnaire by C. Robinson, B. Mandleco, S. F. Olsen, and C. H. Hart (1995).

[b] These items are modifications of items included in the Parent Needs Survey by M. Seligman and R. B. Darling in *Ordinary Families, Special Children: A Systems Approach to Childhood Disability* (New York, NY: Guilford Press, 1989). The Parent Needs Survey is an instrument designed to identify the priorities and concerns of parents of young children with disabilities. Reprinted and adapted with permission of the publisher and author.

From *Foundations of Behavioral, Social, and Clinical Assessment of Children* (Sixth Edition) by Jerome M. Sattler. Copyright 2014 by Jerome M. Sattler, Publisher, Inc. Permission to photocopy this table is granted to purchasers of this book for personal use only (see copyright page for details).

Table A-2
Personal Data Questionnaire

PERSONAL DATA QUESTIONNAIRE

Please complete this questionnaire as carefully as you can. Please print clearly. All information will be treated confidentially.

Name _____
First   Middle   Last

Address _____
Street

_____
City   State   Zip code

School _____ Grade _____ Age _____ Sex _____ Birth date _____

Phone number _____ Email address_____Today's date _____

SCHOOL INFORMATION

	Name of school	Grades attended	Years attended	Course of study or special classes
Elementary school				
Middle school				
High school				
College				
Other				

Best-liked subjects _____

Least-liked subjects _____

Easiest subjects _____

Hardest subjects _____

Leisure-time (or free-time) activities _____

Hobbies _____

Favorite music group _____

Do you read newspapers or magazines? ☐ Yes ☐ No If yes, which ones? _____

Do you read books? ☐ Yes ☐ No If yes, what types? _____

(If you read books) Approximately how many books have you read in the last month? _____

Do you participate in sports or athletic activities? ☐ Yes ☐ No If yes, which ones? _____

_____

How would you like to be rewarded for getting good grades or for doing things that your parents like? _____

_____

_____

(Continued)

SCHOOL ACTIVITIES

School activity	Number of years of participation	Positions held	Describe activity

Please note any awards received or class offices held: _____

WORK EXPERIENCE

Job held	When	What did you like best about your job?	What did you like least about your job?

FAMILY AND HOME

Name	Does this person live at your home? (yes or no)	Age	Occupation	Years of school
Father				
Mother				
Brothers/Sisters				

HEALTH

Current height _____   Current weight _____

Do you have normal eyesight?   ☐ Yes   ☐ No   If no, do you wear glasses or contacts? ☐ Yes   ☐ No

Do you have normal hearing?   ☐ Yes   ☐ No   If no, do you wear a hearing aid? ☐ Yes   ☐ No

Do you eat a healthy diet?   ☐ Yes   ☐ No   If no, briefly indicate in what way your diet is not healthy: _____

_____

_____

_____

Table A-2 *(Continued)*

Briefly list important factors in your health history, including any serious illnesses or times in the hospital: _____

_____

_____

List any health problems you have now: _____

_____

Are you taking any medications? ☐ Yes ☐ No If yes, list the medications and what you are taking them for: _____

PERSONAL CHARACTERISTICS

Check Y (Yes) if the item describes you fairly well or N (No) if the item does not describe you very well.

1. Absentminded	☐ Y ☐ N	21. Easy-going	☐ Y ☐ N	42. Lonely	☐ Y ☐ N	61. Self-conscious	☐ Y ☐ N
2. Active	☐ Y ☐ N	22. Enthusiastic	☐ Y ☐ N	43. Low in self-		62. Self-disciplined	☐ Y ☐ N
3. Alert	☐ Y ☐ N	23. Excitable	☐ Y ☐ N	esteem	☐ Y ☐ N	63. Serious	☐ Y ☐ N
4. Ambitious	☐ Y ☐ N	24. Extraverted	☐ Y ☐ N	44. Moody	☐ Y ☐ N	64. Shallow	☐ Y ☐ N
5. Anxious	☐ Y ☐ N	25. Fearful	☐ Y ☐ N	45. Nervous	☐ Y ☐ N	65. Shy	☐ Y ☐ N
6. Artistic	☐ Y ☐ N	26. Friendly	☐ Y ☐ N	46. Open to new		66. Sociable	☐ Y ☐ N
7. Ashamed	☐ Y ☐ N	27. Good-natured	☐ Y ☐ N	experiences	☐ Y ☐ N	67. Submissive	☐ Y ☐ N
8. Attentive	☐ Y ☐ N	28. Happy	☐ Y ☐ N	47. Organized	☐ Y ☐ N	68. Sympathetic	☐ Y ☐ N
9. Calm	☐ Y ☐ N	29. Hard-working	☐ Y ☐ N	48. Original	☐ Y ☐ N	69. Talkative	☐ Y ☐ N
10. Careless	☐ Y ☐ N	30. High-strung	☐ Y ☐ N	49. Persevering	☐ Y ☐ N	70. Tense	☐ Y ☐ N
11. Cautious	☐ Y ☐ N	31. Hostile	☐ Y ☐ N	50. Persistent	☐ Y ☐ N	71. Timid	☐ Y ☐ N
12. Cold	☐ Y ☐ N	32. Imaginative	☐ Y ☐ N	51. Pessimistic	☐ Y ☐ N	72. Tough	☐ Y ☐ N
13. Content	☐ Y ☐ N	33. Impatient	☐ Y ☐ N	52. Proud	☐ Y ☐ N	73. Trusting	☐ Y ☐ N
14. Conventional	☐ Y ☐ N	34. Impulsive	☐ Y ☐ N	53. Quarrelsome	☐ Y ☐ N	74. Undependable	☐ Y ☐ N
15. Cooperative	☐ Y ☐ N	35. Inspired	☐ Y ☐ N	54. Quick-tempered	☐ Y ☐ N	75. Unkind	☐ Y ☐ N
16. Critical	☐ Y ☐ N	36. Intelligent	☐ Y ☐ N	55. Quiet	☐ Y ☐ N	76. Warm	☐ Y ☐ N
17. Dependable	☐ Y ☐ N	37. Irritable	☐ Y ☐ N	56. Reserved	☐ Y ☐ N	77. Weak	☐ Y ☐ N
18. Determined	☐ Y ☐ N	38. Jittery	☐ Y ☐ N	57. Responsible	☐ Y ☐ N	78. Witty	☐ Y ☐ N
19. Disorganized	☐ Y ☐ N	39. Lazy	☐ Y ☐ N	58. Sad	☐ Y ☐ N	79. Worrier	☐ Y ☐ N
20. Easily		40. Leader	☐ Y ☐ N	59. Sarcastic	☐ Y ☐ N	80. Unemotional	☐ Y ☐ N
discouraged	☐ Y ☐ N	41. Likeable	☐ Y ☐ N	60. Self-confident	☐ Y ☐ N		

What do you like best about yourself? _____

What do you like least about yourself? _____

Do you use drugs? _____ If yes, what kinds? _____

How often? _____

Do you use alcohol? _____ If yes, what kinds? _____

How often? _____

Do you smoke? _____ If yes, how many cigarettes per day do you smoke? _____

List the stressful events that you have experienced in the past year: _____

_____

HOW I DO THINGS

Check Y (Yes) if the item generally describes how you do things or N (No) if the item does not generally describe how you do things.

1. I usually can find my school supplies when I need them.	☐ Y ☐ N	6. I usually use a planner or calendar.	☐ Y ☐ N
2. I usually remember to do my jobs at home.	☐ Y ☐ N	7. I usually get to classes on time.	☐ Y ☐ N
3. I usually put my books in the same place every day when I come home from school.	☐ Y ☐ N	8. I keep a separate notebook for each class.	☐ Y ☐ N
4. I usually finish a project I start.	☐ Y ☐ N	9. I usually remember to bring my homework back to school.	☐ Y ☐ N
5. I usually think about something before I do it.	☐ Y ☐ N	10. I usually remember to bring home things that I need for studying or for homework.	☐ Y ☐ N

(Continued)

Table A-2 *(Continued)*

---

11. I usually complete tests on time. ☐ Y ☐ N
12. I usually read directions and questions carefully. ☐ Y ☐ N
13. I usually can focus and maintain attention. ☐ Y ☐ N
14. I usually can cope with change or transitions. ☐ Y ☐ N
15. I usually can let go of one activity to attend to another. ☐ Y ☐ N
16. I usually can wait my turn in a game. ☐ Y ☐ N
17. I usually learn from past mistakes or behavior. ☐ Y ☐ N
18. I usually think before I speak or act. ☐ Y ☐ N
19. I usually listen without interrupting others. ☐ Y ☐ N
20. I usually can handle a change in plans. ☐ Y ☐ N
21. I usually can remember lists. ☐ Y ☐ N
22. I usually can stay focused when I study. ☐ Y ☐ N
23. I usually have no difficulty taking notes. ☐ Y ☐ N
24. I usually can write down the important things that the teacher says about a subject. ☐ Y ☐ N
25. I usually have no difficulty writing assignments in class. ☐ Y ☐ N

26. I usually have no difficulty organizing my ideas when I write. ☐ Y ☐ N
27. I usually use a computer without having major problems. ☐ Y ☐ N
28. I usually keep my clothes clean. ☐ Y ☐ N
29. I usually keep my room neat. ☐ Y ☐ N
30. I usually know what to study for tests. ☐ Y ☐ N
31. I usually proofread my written assignment that I do at home. ☐ Y ☐ N
32. I usually have energy to do things. ☐ Y ☐ N
33. I usually am not distracted by surrounding noises. ☐ Y ☐ N
34. I usually can pay attention to a conversation even if more than one other person is talking. ☐ Y ☐ N
35. I usually can handle a task that has several components. ☐ Y ☐ N
36. It is easy for me to come up with a different solution if I get stuck when solving a problem. ☐ Y ☐ N
37. I am full of new ideas. ☐ Y ☐ N
38. I am curious about how things work. ☐ Y ☐ N

STRESS

Check Y (Yes) if the item is something that has recently been causing you stress or N (No) if the item does not generally cause you stress.

1. Adults who don't listen when I talk about problems ☐ Y ☐ N
2. Adults who treat me like a child ☐ Y ☐ N
3. Appearing foolish to others ☐ Y ☐ N
4. Arguments between my parents ☐ Y ☐ N
5. Being abused emotionally or neglected at home ☐ Y ☐ N
6. Being abused physically or subjected to excessive physical punishment at home ☐ Y ☐ N
7. Being abused sexually by an older person ☐ Y ☐ N
8. Being abused sexually by someone close to my age ☐ Y ☐ N
9. Being asked to read aloud or talk in front of the class ☐ Y ☐ N
10. Being bullied by other students ☐ Y ☐ N
11. Being called names by other students ☐ Y ☐ N
12. Being disciplined in school for doing things wrong ☐ Y ☐ N
13. Being hurt physically by other students ☐ Y ☐ N
14. Being ignored by other students ☐ Y ☐ N
15. Being picked out by the teacher for poor work ☐ Y ☐ N
16. Being teased by other students ☐ Y ☐ N
17. Being unable to keep up with others in schoolwork ☐ Y ☐ N
18. Being unable to really talk to my father ☐ Y ☐ N
19. Being unable to really talk to my mother ☐ Y ☐ N
20. Being unable to relate to people my own age ☐ Y ☐ N
21. Classmates' jealousy of my success in school ☐ Y ☐ N
22. Concern about my health ☐ Y ☐ N
23. Cost of books and equipment ☐ Y ☐ N

24. Cost of clothes I need ☐ Y ☐ N
25. Demands by parents on after-school time ☐ Y ☐ N
26. Difficulty in travel to school ☐ Y ☐ N
27. Difficulty with a romantic relationship ☐ Y ☐ N
28. Doubts about my religious beliefs ☐ Y ☐ N
29. Examinations ☐ Y ☐ N
30. Experience with drugs ☐ Y ☐ N
31. Fear of asking teachers about schoolwork ☐ Y ☐ N
32. Feelings of loneliness ☐ Y ☐ N
33. Having other students break something of mine ☐ Y ☐ N
34. Having other students deface my personal property ☐ Y ☐ N
35. Having other students play mean tricks to embarrass me ☐ Y ☐ N
36. Having other students post slander in public places ☐ Y ☐ N
37. Having other students refuse to talk to me ☐ Y ☐ N
38. Having other students steal from me ☐ Y ☐ N
39. Having other students try to extort money from me ☐ Y ☐ N
40. Having other students try to get me into trouble with my friends ☐ Y ☐ N
41. Having rumors spread about me by other students ☐ Y ☐ N
42. Having too many things to study ☐ Y ☐ N
43. Having too much work to prepare for class ☐ Y ☐ N
44. Lack of privacy at home ☐ Y ☐ N
45. Lack of self-confidence ☐ Y ☐ N
46. My mother's drinking ☐ Y ☐ N

Table A-2 *(Continued)*

47. My father's drinking	☐ Y ☐ N	66. Rejection by a group I want to belong to	☐ Y ☐ N
48. My own drinking	☐ Y ☐ N	67. School classes that are too large	☐ Y ☐ N
49. My smoking habit	☐ Y ☐ N	68. Sexual problems	☐ Y ☐ N
50. No place to study at home	☐ Y ☐ N	69. Shortage of money	☐ Y ☐ N
51. No time for leisure activities	☐ Y ☐ N	70. Shyness in social situations	☐ Y ☐ N
52. No time to relax between classes	☐ Y ☐ N	71. Teachers who talk to other students rather than to me	☐ Y ☐ N
53. Nobody to talk to about personal problems	☐ Y ☐ N		
54. Not knowing how to study properly	☐ Y ☐ N	72. Uncertainty about what values are the correct ones	☐ Y ☐ N
55. Parents' divorce or separation	☐ Y ☐ N		
56. Parents who don't understand what it's like to be a student today	☐ Y ☐ N	73. Unemployment of parents	☐ Y ☐ N
		74. Watching so much TV that it affects my homework	☐ Y ☐ N
57. Poor self-concept	☐ Y ☐ N	75. Wishing my parents were richer	☐ Y ☐ N
58. Poor relations with other students	☐ Y ☐ N	76. Worry about entering senior high school	☐ Y ☐ N
59. Pressure from my parents to succeed in life	☐ Y ☐ N	77. Worry about entering middle or junior high school	☐ Y ☐ N
60. Pressure to behave in a way my parents won't approve of	☐ Y ☐ N		
61. Pressure to drink alcohol	☐ Y ☐ N	78. Worry about part-time employment	☐ Y ☐ N
62. Pressure to have sex	☐ Y ☐ N	79. Worry about what others think of me	☐ Y ☐ N
63. Pressure to smoke cigarettes	☐ Y ☐ N	80. Worry that I may not get a good job when I leave school	☐ Y ☐ N
64. Pressure to use drugs	☐ Y ☐ N		
65. Receiving harassing phone calls	☐ Y ☐ N	81. Worry that I won't get into college	☐ Y ☐ N

ALCOHOL AND DRUGS

1. Have you ever ridden in a car driven by someone (including yourself) who had been using alcohol or drugs?	☐ Y ☐ N	6. Have you ever gotten into trouble while using alcohol or drugs?	☐ Y ☐ N
2. Do you ever use alcohol or drugs to relax, feel better about yourself, or fit in?	☐ Y ☐ N	7. Does alcohol or drug use cause your mood to change quickly, such as from happy to sad or sad to happy?	☐ Y ☐ N
3. Do you ever use alcohol or drugs while you are by yourself?	☐ Y ☐ N	8. Do members of your family or friends ever tell you that you should cut down on your drinking or drug use?	☐ Y ☐ N
4. Has anyone ever thought you had a problem with alcohol or drugs?	☐ Y ☐ N		
5. Have you ever forgotten things you did while using alcohol or drugs?	☐ Y ☐ N	9. Does your alcohol or drug use ever make you do something that you would normally not do, such as breaking rules, missing curfew, breaking the law, or having sex with someone?	☐ Y ☐ N

RELATIONSHIP WITH PARENTS

Check Y (Yes) if the item generally describes how you feel about your parents or N (No) if the item does not generally describe how you feel about your parents.

Mother		**Father**	
1. I respect my mother.	☐ Y ☐ N	1. I respect my father.	☐ Y ☐ N
2. I am angry about how my mother treats me.	☐ Y ☐ N	2. I am angry about how my father treats me.	☐ Y ☐ N
3. I am happy when I think about my mother.	☐ Y ☐ N	3. I am happy when I think about my father.	☐ Y ☐ N
4. I love my mother.	☐ Y ☐ N	4. I love my father.	☐ Y ☐ N
5. I am grateful for the things my mother does for me.	☐ Y ☐ N	5. I am grateful for the things my father does for me.	☐ Y ☐ N
6. I am proud of my mother.	☐ Y ☐ N	6. I am proud of my father.	☐ Y ☐ N
7. I care about my mother.	☐ Y ☐ N	7. I care about my father.	☐ Y ☐ N
8. I am confused about my feelings about my mother.	☐ Y ☐ N	8. I am confused about my feelings about my father.	☐ Y ☐ N
9. I am disappointed in or let down by my mother.	☐ Y ☐ N	9. I am disappointed in or let down by my father.	☐ Y ☐ N
10. I am comforted when I think about my mother.	☐ Y ☐ N	10. I am comforted when I think about my father.	☐ Y ☐ N
11. I am close to my mother.	☐ Y ☐ N	11. I am close to my father.	☐ Y ☐ N
12. I appreciate having a mother.	☐ Y ☐ N	12. I appreciate having a father.	☐ Y ☐ N
13. I have positive feelings toward my mother.	☐ Y ☐ N	13. I have positive feelings toward my father.	☐ Y ☐ N
14. I am anxious or nervous about my mother.	☐ Y ☐ N	14. I am anxious or nervous about my father.	☐ Y ☐ N
15. I am upset when I think about my mother.	☐ Y ☐ N	15. I am upset when I think about my father.	☐ Y ☐ N

(Continued)

FAMILY

Check Y (Yes) if the item generally describes your family or N (No) if the item does not generally describe your family.

1. Family members pay attention to each other's feelings. ☐ Y ☐ N
2. My family would rather do things together than with other people. ☐ Y ☐ N
3. We all have a say in family plans. ☐ Y ☐ N
4. Grownups in the family understand and agree on family decisions. ☐ Y ☐ N
5. Grownups in the family compete and fight with each other. ☐ Y ☐ N
6. There is closeness in my family, but each person is allowed to be different. ☐ Y ☐ N
7. We accept each other's friends. ☐ Y ☐ N
8. There is confusion in my family because there is no leader. ☐ Y ☐ N
9. Family members touch and hug each other. ☐ Y ☐ N
10. Family members put each other down. ☐ Y ☐ N
11. We say what we think and feel. ☐ Y ☐ N
12. In my home, we feel loved. ☐ Y ☐ N
13. Even when we feel close, my family is embarrassed to admit it. ☐ Y ☐ N
14. Our happiest times are at home. ☐ Y ☐ N
15. The grownups in my family are strong leaders. ☐ Y ☐ N
16. The future looks good to my family. ☐ Y ☐ N

17. We usually blame one person in my family when things aren't going right. ☐ Y ☐ N
18. Family members go their own way most of the time. ☐ Y ☐ N
19. My family is proud of being close. ☐ Y ☐ N
20. My family is good at solving problems together. ☐ Y ☐ N
21. Family members easily express warmth and caring toward each other. ☐ Y ☐ N
22. It's okay to fight and yell in my family. ☐ Y ☐ N
23. One of the adults in my family has a favorite child. ☐ Y ☐ N
24. When things go wrong, we blame each other. ☐ Y ☐ N
25. Family members would rather do things with other people than together. ☐ Y ☐ N
26. Family members pay attention to each other and listen to what is said. ☐ Y ☐ N
27. We worry about hurting each other's feelings. ☐ Y ☐ N
28. The mood in my family is usually sad and blue. ☐ Y ☐ N
29. We argue a lot. ☐ Y ☐ N
30. One person controls and leads my family. ☐ Y ☐ N
31. My family is happy most of the time. ☐ Y ☐ N
32. Each person takes responsibility for his/her behavior. ☐ Y ☐ N

PLANS

What are your plans for the future? _____

_____

What occupation would you like to have? _____

_____

Are there issues bothering you that you would like to discuss with a professional? ☐ Yes ☐ No   If yes, what are they? _____

_____

ANY OTHER COMMENTS?

_____

_____

_____

_____

Thank you.

Source: The section on stress adapted from Bagley (1992); the section on relationship with parents adapted from Phares and Renk (1998); the section on family adapted from Beavers and Hampson (1990); and the section on alcohol and drugs adapted from Knight, Shrier, Bravender, Farrell, Vander Bilt, and Shaffer (1999).

Table A-3
School Referral Questionnaire

SCHOOL REFERRAL QUESTIONNAIRE

Student's name _____ Grade _____ Sex _____ Date _____

School _____ Teacher's name _____

PRESENTING PROBLEM

Briefly describe student's current problem: _____
_____
_____

How long has this problem been of concern to you? _____

When did you first notice the problem? _____

What seems to help the problem? _____

What seems to make the problem worse? _____

Have you noticed changes in the student's abilities? ☐ Yes ☐ No

If yes, please describe: _____

Have you noticed changes in the student's behavior? ☐ Yes ☐ No

If yes, please describe: _____

Has the student been evaluated or treated for the current problem or similar problems? ☐ Yes ☐ No

If yes, when and by whom? _____

What are the student's current school grades? _____
_____

What do you want to learn from this evaluation? _____
_____

CHECKLIST

Directions: Place a check mark next to each item that accurately describes the student. If you can't evaluate an item, please write a question mark next to the box by the item number.

Cognitive

☐ 1. Has poor comprehension of material
☐ 2. Has poor short-term memory for verbal stimuli
☐ 3. Has poor short-term memory for nonverbal stimuli
☐ 4. Has limited attention span
☐ 5. Has difficulty understanding oral directions
☐ 6. Has difficulty understanding written directions
☐ 7. Has difficulty following a sequence of directions
☐ 8. Misunderstands material presented at a fast rate
☐ 9. Has difficulty recalling story sequences
☐ 10. Has difficulty understanding teacher when he or she moves around the room
☐ 11. Has difficulty being adaptable
☐ 12. Has difficulty reasoning abstractly
☐ 13. Has difficulty conceptualizing material
☐ 14. Uses problem-solving strategies inefficiently
☐ 15. Learns very slowly
☐ 16. Has poor long-term memory
☐ 17. Forgets newly learned skills

Language/Academic

☐ 18. Has difficulty decoding words
☐ 19. Has poor reading comprehension
☐ 20. Has poor expressive language
☐ 21. Has poor listening comprehension
☐ 22. Uses gestures instead of words
☐ 23. Has difficulty rapidly naming objects
☐ 24. Has difficulty rapidly reading words
☐ 25. Has speech impairment
☐ 26. Has difficulty producing rhymes
☐ 27. Has difficulty recognizing similar phonemes
☐ 28. Has difficulty arranging phonemes into words
☐ 29. Has difficulty using verbal coding as an aid in memory
☐ 30. Has difficulty using verbal coding as an aid in rehearsal
☐ 31. Has poor grammar
☐ 32. Has poor math computation skills
☐ 33. Has limited math problem-solving skills
☐ 34. Does not retain math facts

(Continued)

Table A-3 *(Continued)*

☐ 35. Has poor spelling
☐ 36. Has fluctuating performance
☐ 37. Has difficulty writing compositions
☐ 38. Does not know names of common objects

Perceptual/Motor

☐ 39. Has poor auditory perception
☐ 40. Has poor visual perception
☐ 41. Has poor tactile discrimination
☐ 42. Has poor handwriting
☐ 43. Has clumsy and awkward movements
☐ 44. Has poor speech communication
☐ 45. Has difficulty putting objects in correct sequence
☐ 46. Has difficulty remembering sequence of objects
☐ 47. Has right-left confusion
☐ 48. Has poor gross-motor coordination
☐ 49. Has poor fine-motor coordination
☐ 50. Moves slowly
☐ 51. Has slumped posture
☐ 52. Has rigid, tense posture
☐ 53. Has atypical, inappropriate posture

Behavioral

☐ 54. Avoids doing work in class
☐ 55. Gives up easily
☐ 56. Has difficulty beginning tasks on time
☐ 57. Has difficulty completing tasks on time
☐ 58. Asks questions constantly
☐ 59. Is impulsive
☐ 60. Has trouble starting and continuing tasks
☐ 61. Has difficulty changing from one assignment to another
☐ 62. Shifts often to other activities
☐ 63. Has difficulty working independently
☐ 64. Has difficulty playing quietly
☐ 65. Is easily distracted
☐ 66. Doesn't seem to listen
☐ 67. Shows aggressive behavior
☐ 68. Shows disruptive behavior
☐ 69. Talks excessively
☐ 70. Interrupts others often
☐ 71. Speaks out of turn (often blurts out answers)
☐ 72. Makes comments not related to topic being discussed
☐ 73. Has difficulty remaining seated
☐ 74. Fidgets often when seated
☐ 75. Fails to return on time to class
☐ 76. Has limited persistence
☐ 77. Fails to do homework
☐ 78. Loses homework
☐ 79. Seeks attention constantly
☐ 80. Is unorganized
☐ 81. Uses immature vocabulary
☐ 82. Is slow to complete tasks
☐ 83. Behaves inappropriately
☐ 84. Uses drugs or alcohol
☐ 85. Hurts others
☐ 86. Is cruel to animals
☐ 87. Talks about suicide

☐ 88. Destroys others' property
☐ 89. Is out of chair when supposed to be doing work
☐ 90. Has constant and repetitive behavior
☐ 91. Speaks slowly
☐ 92. Shouts or yells for no apparent reason
☐ 93. Has hallucinations
☐ 94. Stutters
☐ 95. Injures self often
☐ 96. Bites nails
☐ 97. Bangs head
☐ 98. Holds breath
☐ 99. Does not tolerate changes in routine
☐ 100. Wanders aimlessly around room
☐ 101. Daydreams
☐ 102. Is often sleepy or lethargic
☐ 103. Tires easily
☐ 104. Tells lies
☐ 105. Steals
☐ 106. Has numerous physical complaiints
☐ 107. Is often tardy
☐ 108. Is frequently absent
☐ 109. Has poor eye contact
☐ 110. Requires constant supervision
☐ 111. Engages in dangerous behaviors
☐ 112. Has been suspended in the past
☐ 113. Prefers not to try new activities
☐ 114. Fails to use free time appropriately

Social

☐ 115. Is immature
☐ 116. Is stubborn
☐ 117. Has low self-esteem
☐ 118. Is socially isolated
☐ 119. Is not popular
☐ 120. Has difficulty communicating interests
☐ 121. Has difficulty accepting criticism
☐ 122. Has limited social perceptiveness
☐ 123. Gives in to peer pressure
☐ 124. Is uncooperative
☐ 125. Has poor skills on playground
☐ 126. Is overly compliant
☐ 127. Is selfish
☐ 128. Seems suspicious of other people
☐ 129. Refuses to share
☐ 130. Shows sexually provocative behavior
☐ 131. Blames others for problems
☐ 132. Has difficulty seeking help
☐ 133. Has difficulty accepting help from teacher
☐ 134. Has difficulty accepting help from peers
☐ 135. Does not get along with other children
☐ 136. Does not offer opinions and answers when asked
☐ 137. Does not enjoy group activities
☐ 138. Does not show concern for others' feelings and property
☐ 139. Resolves conflicts by shouting, fighting, or intimidating others
☐ 140. Has difficulty making constructive contributions during group activities

Table A-3 *(Continued)*

☐ 141. Avoids others completely
☐ 142. Has anger management problems
☐ 143. Displays inappropriate humor
☐ 144. Seeks to manipulate others
☐ 145. Is rigid and opinionated
☐ 146. Has unusual interest in sensational violence
☐ 147. Is fascinated with violence-filled entertainment
☐ 148. Bullies other children
☐ 149. Is the victim of bullying

Affect/Motivation

☐ 150. Is easily frustrated
☐ 151. Shows anger quickly
☐ 152. Has limited motivation
☐ 153. Is often anxious
☐ 154. Is depressed or unhappy
☐ 155. Has low interest in schoolwork
☐ 156. Is self-critical
☐ 157. Is overexcitable
☐ 158. Is hyperactive
☐ 159. Has temper tantrums
☐ 160. Has unusual fears
☐ 161. Is easily annoyed
☐ 162. Frequently cries
☐ 163. Is tense and fearful
☐ 164. Seldom shows emotion
☐ 165. Is shy or timid
☐ 166. Is upset by changes in routine

☐ 167. Has wide mood swings
☐ 168. Appears to feel hopeless
☐ 169. Has difficulty recognizing that he or she has a problem

Self-Care Skills

☐ 170. Has poor personal hygiene
☐ 171. Has disheveled and unclean personal appearance
☐ 172. Fails to dress appropriately for weather
☐ 173. Has poor table manners in cafeteria
☐ 174. Engages in self-stimulating behaviors

Physical Health

☐ 175. Has vision problems
☐ 176. Has hearing problems
☐ 177. Has dental problems
☐ 178. Complains of headaches
☐ 179. Complains of stomach pains
☐ 180. Complains of fatigue
☐ 181. Is overweight
☐ 182. Is underweight
☐ 183. Complains of loss of appetite
☐ 184. Has a physical disability (describe: _____)
☐ 185. Has a chronic illness (describe: _____)
☐ 186. Has other physical health problems (describe: _____)

ASSETS

Please list the child's assets or strengths in each of the following areas.

Cognitive _____

Language/academic _____

Perceptual/motor _____

Behavioral _____

Social _____

Affect/motivation _____

Self-care skills _____

OTHER COMMENTS

Please list any other psychological, behavioral, or social problems the child has. _____

_____

Please list anything else about the child that you think may be helpful. _____

_____

Thank you.

Table B-1
Semistructured Interview Questions for a Child or Adolescent of School Age

Introduction

1. Hi! I'm Dr. [Ms., Mr.] _____. How are you today?
2. When you don't understand a question that I ask, please say "I don't understand." When you tell me that, I'll try to ask it better. OK?
3. Please tell me how old you are.
4. When is your birthday?
5. What is your address?
6. And what is your telephone number?

Information About Problem

7. Has anyone told you why you are here today?
   (If yes, go to question 8; if no, go to question 10.)
8. Who told you?
9. What did he [she] tell you?
10. Tell me why *you* think you are here.
    (If child mentions a problem or a concern, explore it in detail. Ask questions 11 to 40, as needed. If the child does not mention a problem or concern, go to question 41.)
11. Tell me about [cite problem child mentioned].
12. When did you first notice [cite problem]?
13. How long has it been going on?
14. (If relevant) Where does [cite problem] happen?
15. (If needed) Does it occur at home . . . at school . . . when you're traveling . . . at a friend's house?
16. (If relevant) When does the problem happen?
17. (If needed) Does it happen when you first get up in the morning . . . during the day . . . at night before bedtime . . . at mealtimes? . . . Does it happen when you are with your mother . . . your father . . . brothers and sisters . . . other children . . . other relatives . . . the whole family together . . . friends . . . at school?
18. (If relevant) How long does the problem last?
19. How often does [cite problem] occur?
20. (If relevant) Do your brothers and sisters also have [cite problem]?
21. (If yes) Is your [cite problem] worse than or not as bad as theirs?
22. In what way?
23. What happens just before [cite problem] begins?
24. What happens just after [cite problem] begins?
25. What makes [cite problem] worse?
26. What makes [cite problem] better?
27. What do you do when you have [cite problem]?
28. What seems to work best?
29. What do you think caused [cite problem]?
30. Was anything happening in your family when [cite problem] first started?
31. (If needed) Did your parents get separated or divorced . . . you move to another city or school . . . your dad or mom lose a job . . . someone in your family go into the hospital?
32. (If some event occurred) How did you feel when [cite event] happened?
33. How do your parents help you with [cite problem]?
34. (If relevant) How do your brothers and sisters help you with [cite problem]?
35. And your friends, do they help in any way?
36. Have you seen anybody for help with [cite problem]?
    (If yes, go to question 37; if no, go to question 41.)

37. Whom did you see?
38. What kind of help did you get?
39. Has it helped?
40. (If needed) In what way?

School

41. Let's talk about school. What grade are you in?
42. What is your teacher's name [are your teachers' names]?
43. How do you get along with your teacher[s]?
44. Who is your favorite teacher?
45. Tell me about him [her].
46. Who is the teacher you like the least?
47. Tell me about him [her].
48. What subjects do you like best?
49. What is it about these subjects that you like?
50. And what subjects do you like least?
51. What is it about these subjects that you don't like?
52. What grades are you getting?
53. Are you in any activities at school?
54. (If yes) What activities are you in at school?
55. How do you get along with your classmates?
56. Tell me how you spend a usual day at school.

Attention and Concentration at School

57. Do you have any trouble following what your teacher says [teachers say]?
58. (If yes) What kind of trouble do you have?
59. Do you daydream a lot when you are in class?
60. (If yes) Tell me about that.
61. Can you complete your assignments, or are you easily distracted?
62. (If distracted) What seems to distract you?
63. Do you have trouble sitting still or staying in your seat at school?
64. (If yes) Tell me about the trouble you're having.
65. Do you find it hard to sit still for a long time and do you need a lot of breaks while studying?
66. Do you like to leave your studies to go see what's going on, get a drink, or change rooms or positions?
67. (If yes) Tell me more about that.
68. Do you have any trouble copying what your teacher writes on the blackboard?
69. (If yes) What kind of trouble do you have?
70. Do you have any trouble remembering things?
71. (If yes) Tell me about the trouble you're having.
72. How is your concentration?
73. Do you like to keep at your work until it's done?
74. Tell me more about that.
75. Do you have trouble taking notes in class?
76. (If yes) Tell me about the trouble you're having.
77. Do you have trouble taking tests?
78. (If yes) Tell me about the trouble you're having.

Home

79. Now let's talk about your home. Who lives with you at home?
    (Many questions from 80 to 117 assume that the child lives in a family with two caregivers. Ask those questions that apply to the child or modify them as needed—for example, substituting "stepmother" for "mother" or "sister" for "brothers and sisters."

Table B-1 *(Continued)*

80. Tell me a little about [cite persons child mentioned].
81. (If needed) What does your father do for work?
82. (If needed) What does your mother do for work?
83. Tell me what your home is like.
84. Do you have your own room at home?
    (If no, go to question 85; if yes, go to question 87.)
85. Whom do you share your room with?
86. How do you get along?
87. What chores do you do at home?
88. How do you get along with your father?
89. What does he do that you like?
90. What does he do that you don't like?
91. How do you get along with your mother?
92. What does she do that you like?
93. What does she do that you don't like?
    (If child has one or more siblings, go to question 94 and modify questions as appropriate; if child has no siblings, go to question 101.)
94. How do you get along with your brothers and sisters?
95. What do they do that you like?
96. What do they do that you don't like?
97. What do you argue or fight with your brothers and sisters about?
98. What does your mother or father do when you argue or fight with your brothers and sisters?
99. Do your parents treat you and your brothers and sisters the same?
100. (If no) Tell me about that.
101. Are there rules you must follow at home?
102. Tell me about those.
103. When you get in trouble at home, who disciplines you?
104. Tell me about how your father [mother] disciplines you.
105. How do your parents tell you or show you that they like what you have done?
106. When you have a problem, whom do you talk to about it?
107. How does he [she] help you?
108. Do you think your parents are worried about you?
109. (If yes) What are their worries about you?
110. Is there anyone else in your family whom you are close to, like a grandparent or other relative?
111. (If yes) Tell me about him [her, them].
112. Do you spend much time at home alone?
113. (If yes) Tell me about that.
114. Does your family eat meals together?
115. (If yes) Tell me about the meals you eat together.
116. (If needed) How often do you eat meals together?
117. In general, how would you describe your family?

Interests

118. Now let's talk about what you like to do. What hobbies and interests do you have?
119. What do you do in the afternoons after school?
120. What do you do in the evenings on school days?
121. Tell me what you usually do on Saturdays and Sundays.
122. Do you play any sports?
123. (If yes) Tell me what sports you play.
124. Of all the things you do, what do you like doing best?
125. And what do you like doing least?

126. Do you belong to any group like the Boy Scouts [Girl Scouts] or a church group?
127. (If yes) Tell me about the group you belong to.
128. How much TV do you watch in a day?
129. Would you like to watch more TV?
130. (If yes) About how much more would you like to watch?
131. What are your favorite programs?
132. What do you like about them?
133. Do you play games on a PlayStation or some similar system?
     (If yes, go to question 134; if no, go to question 137.)
134. Where do you play these games?
135. How many hours a day do you play them?
136. What are your favorite games?
137. Do you like music?
138. (If yes) What kind of music—what are your favorite groups?

Friends

139. Do you have friends?
     (If yes, go to question 140; if no, go to question 149.)
140. Tell me about your friends.
     (Ask questions 141 to 148, as needed.)
141. What do you like to do with your friends?
142. Are you spending as much time with your friends now as you used to?
143. When you are with your friends, how do you feel?
144. How are your friends treating you?
145. Who is your best friend?
146. Tell me about him [her].
147. What do you like to do together?
148. How many of your friends do your parents know?
     (Go to item 150.)
149. Tell me about not having friends.

Mood/Feelings

150. Tell me about how you've been feeling lately.
151. Do you have different feelings in the same day?
152. (If yes) Tell me about these different feelings.
153. Have you been feeling more nervous over the past couple of days, as though you can't relax?
154. (If yes) Tell me about that.
155. Nearly everybody feels happy at times. What kinds of things make you feel happiest?
156. And sometimes people feel sad. What makes you feel sad?
157. What do you do when you're sad?
158. Sometimes children [teenagers] begin to get less pleasure from things that they used to enjoy. Has this happened to you?
159. (If yes) Tell me about that.
160. Have there been times lasting more than a day when you felt very cheerful in a way that was different from your normal feelings?
161. (If yes) Tell me about these feelings.
162. Almost everybody gets angry at times. What kinds of things make you angriest?
163. What do you do when you are angry?
164. Do you ever get into fights?
165. (If yes) Tell me about the fights.

(Continued)

Table B-1 *(Continued)*

Fears/Worries

166. Most children [teenagers] get scared sometimes about some things. What do you do when you are scared?
167. Tell me what scares you.
168. Does anything else scare you?
169. Are you startled by noises?
170. (If yes) Tell me more about that.
171. Do you have any special worries?
172. (If yes) Tell me about what you are worried about.

Self-Concept

173. What do you like best about yourself?
174. Anything else?
175. Tell me about the best thing that ever happened to you.
176. What do you like least about yourself?
177. Anything else?
178. Tell me about the worst thing that ever happened to you.
179. If you had a child of the same sex as you, in what ways would you want the child to be like you?
180. How would you want the child to be different from you?

Somatic Concerns

181. Tell me how you feel about your body.
182. Have you been feeling that way lately?
183. Do you have any problems with not having enough energy to do the things you want to do?
184. (If yes) Tell me what problems you're having.
185. Tell me how you feel about eating.
186. Are you having problems sleeping enough?
187. (If yes) Tell me about your problems getting enough sleep. (Go to question 190.)
188. Are you sleeping too much?
189. (If yes) Tell me about your problems with sleeping too much.
190. Tell me about your health.
191. (If needed) Have you been sick a lot?
192. (If yes) Tell me about that. (Follow up as needed.)
193. Do you ever get headaches?
194. (If yes) Tell me about them.
195. (If needed) How often do you get them? . . . What do you usually do?
196. Do you get stomachaches?
197. (If yes) Tell me about them.
198. (If needed) How often do you get them? . . . What do you usually do?
199. Do you get any other kinds of body pains?
200. (If yes) Tell me about them.
201. Do you have any trouble seeing things?
202. (If yes) Tell me about the trouble you're having seeing.
203. Do you have any trouble hearing things?
204. (If yes) Tell me about the trouble you're having hearing.
205. Do you take medicine every day?
     (If yes, go to question 206; if no, go to question 210.)
206. What do you take the medicine for?
207. What medicine do you take?
208. How often do you take the medicine?
209. How does the medicine make you feel?

Obsessions and Compulsions

210. Some children [teenagers] have thoughts that they think are silly or unpleasant or do not make sense, but these thoughts keep repeating over and over in their minds. Have you had thoughts like this?
211. (If yes) Tell me about these thoughts.
212. Some children [teenagers] are bothered by a feeling that they have to do something over and over even when they don't want to do it. For example, they might keep washing their hands or checking over and over again whether the door is locked or the stove is turned off. Is this a problem for you?
213. (If yes) Tell me about it.

Thought Disorder

214. Do you ever hear things no one else hears that seem funny or unusual?
215. (If yes) Tell me about them.
216. (If a voice) What does it say? . . . How often do you hear it? . . . How do you feel about the voice? . . . What do you usually do when you hear it?
217. Do you ever see things no one else sees that seem funny or unreal?
218. (If yes) Tell me about them.
219. (If needed) How often do you see them? . . . How do you feel about them? . . . What do you usually do when you see them?
220. Do you ever feel as if someone's spying on you or plotting to hurt you?
221. (If yes) Tell me about these feelings.
222. Does your thinking seem to speed up or slow down at times?
223. (If yes) Tell me about that.
224. Is it hard for you to make decisions?
225. (If yes) Tell me about that.
226. Is it hard for you to concentrate on your reading?
227. (If yes) Tell me about that.
228. Is it hard for you to understand people when they talk?
229. (If yes) Tell me about that.
230. Does it seem as if your thoughts are getting more mixed up or jumbled lately?
231. (If yes) Tell me more about that.
232. Have you had experiences that seemed odd or frightening to you?
233. (If yes) Tell me about them.

Memories/Fantasy

234. What's the first thing you can remember from the time you were a little baby?
235. How old were you then?
236. Tell me about your dreams.
237. Do you ever have the same dream over and over again?
238. (If yes) Tell me about that.
239. Who are your favorite television characters?
240. Tell me about them.
241. What animals do you like best?
242. Tell me what you like about these animals.
243. What animals do you like least?
244. Tell me what you don't like about these animals.
245. What is your happiest memory?
246. What is your saddest memory?
247. If you could change places with anyone in the whole world, who would it be?

Table B-1 *(Continued)*

248. Tell me about that.
249. If you could go anywhere you wanted to right now, where would you go?
250. Tell me about that.
251. If you could have three wishes, what would they be?
252. What things do you think you might need to take with you if you were to go to the moon and stay there for six months?

Aspirations

253. What do you plan on doing when you're grown up?
254. Do you think you will have any problem doing that?
255. If you could do anything you wanted when you became an adult, what would it be?
    (If interviewee is an adolescent, go to questions following question 258.)

Concluding Questions

256. Do you have anything else that you would like to tell me about yourself?
257. Do you have any questions that you would like to ask me?
258. Thank you for talking with me. If you have any questions or if you want to talk to me, please call me or ask your teacher to let me know. Here is my card.

ADDITIONAL QUESTIONS FOR ADOLESCENTS

Jobs

1. Do you have an after-school job or a summer job?
2. (If yes) Tell me about your job.

Sexual Relations

3. Do you have a special girlfriend [boyfriend]?
4. (If yes) Tell me about her [him].
5. Have you had any sexual experiences?
6. (If yes) Tell me about them.
7. Do you have any sexual concerns?
8. (If yes) Tell me about them.
9. Are you concerned about getting a sexual disease?
10. Tell me about that.
11. Are you sexually active now?
    (If yes, go to question 12; if no, go to question 17 if adolescent is a female or question 51 if adolescent is a male.)
12. Tell me about your sexual activity.
13. Do you use birth control?
    (If yes, go to question 14; if no, go to question 16.)
14. What type?
15. (If needed) Do you [Does your partner] use a condom?
    (If adolescent is a female, go to question 17; if adolescent is a male, go to question 51.)
16. Tell me about not using birth control.
    (If adolescent is a female, go to question 17; if adolescent is a male, go to question 51.)

Questions for Adolescent Females Only

17. Have you ever been pregnant?
    (If yes, go to question 18; if no, go to question 86.)
18. Tell me about it.
    (Ask questions 19 to 50, as needed.)
19. How many times have you been pregnant?

(Ask questions 20 to 50 for each pregnancy, as needed.)
20. How old were you when you became pregnant [the first time, the second time, etc.]?
21. Did you have the baby?
    (If yes, go to question 22; if no, go to question 44.)
22. When was the baby born?
23. Did you have a boy or a girl?
24. How is the child?
25. Who helped you during the pregnancy?
26. Did you see a doctor for care during your pregnancy?
27. Were there any problems during your pregnancy?
28. And were there any complications while you were in labor?
29. And during delivery, were there any problems?
30. Did you have any problems soon after the baby was born?
31. How did you feel during the pregnancy?
32. How do you feel about your baby?
33. How did your family react to your being pregnant?
34. And how did the baby's father react to your being pregnant?
35. Are you raising the baby?
    (If yes, go to question 36; if no, go to question 40.)
36. What is it like being a mother?
37. What kind of help are you getting?
38. Does the baby's father contribute money?
39. Does the baby's father see the baby?
    (Go to question 86.)
40. Who is raising the baby?
41. How do you feel about that?
42. (If needed) Do you ever see the baby?
43. (If yes) Tell me about that.
    (Go to question 86.)
44. What happened during your pregnancy that you didn't have the baby?
    (If interviewee had an abortion, go to question 45; otherwise, go to question 86.)
45. Tell me about the abortion.
    (Ask questions 46 to 50, as needed.)
46. What were your feelings about the abortion before you had it?
47. And how did you feel afterwards?
48. What would having a baby have meant for your future?
49. Would your family have helped you if you had had the baby?
50. Tell me about that.
    (Go to question 86.)

Questions for Adolescent Males Only

51. Have you ever gotten anyone pregnant?
    (If yes, go to question 52; if no, go to question 86.)
52. Tell me about it.
    (Ask questions 53 to 55, as needed.)
53. How many times have you gotten someone pregnant?
    (Ask questions 54 to 85, as needed, for each time interviewee got someone pregnant.)
54. How old were you when you got someone pregnant [the first time, the second time, etc.]?
55. Did she have the baby?
    (If yes, go to question 56; if no, go to question 81.)

Table B-1 *(Continued)*

56. When was the baby born?
57. Was the baby a boy or a girl?
58. How is the child?
59. Who helped the mother during the pregnancy?
60. Did she see a doctor for care during her pregnancy?
61. Were there any problems during her pregnancy?
62. And were there any problems while she was in labor?
63. And during her delivery, were there any problems?
64. And were there any problems soon after the baby was born?
65. How did she feel during her pregnancy?
66. How did she feel about the baby?
67. And how did you react to her being pregnant?
68. Do your parents know that you got someone pregnant?
69. (If yes) How did your parents react to her being pregnant?
70. Who is raising the baby?
    (If the baby is being raised by the mother or by someone else the father knows, go to question 71; if the baby is being raised by the father, go to question 76; if the baby was given up for adoption, go to question 78.)
71. How is the baby doing?
72. Do you see the baby?
73. (If yes) Tell me about that.
74. Do you contribute financially to the baby's support?
75. Tell me about that.
    (Go to question 86.)
76. How is the baby doing?
77. What is it like being a father?
    (Go to question 86.)
78. How do you feel about the baby being adopted?
79. Is there anything else you want to tell me about your feelings about the adoption?
80. (If yes) Go ahead.
    (Go to question 86.)
81. What happened during her pregnancy that she didn't have the baby?
    (If she had an abortion, go to question 82; otherwise, go to question 86.)
82. Tell me about the abortion.
    (Ask questions 83 to 85, as needed.)
83. What were your feelings about the abortion before it was performed?
84. And how did you feel afterwards?
85. What would having a baby have meant for your future?
    (Go to question 86.)

Eating Habits
86. Now I'm going to ask some questions about your eating habits. Tell me about what you eat.

87. Tell me where you usually eat your meals.
88. Tell me when you usually eat your meals.
89. Have you ever gone on eating binges—that is, eaten an abnormally large amount of food over a short period of time?
90. (If yes) Tell me about these eating binges.
91. Has there ever been a time when people gave you a hard time about being too thin or losing too much weight?
92. (If yes) Tell me about that.
93. Has there ever been a time when people gave you a hard time about being too fat or gaining too much weight?
94. (If yes) Tell me about that.

Drug/Alcohol Use
95. Do your parents drink alcohol?
96. (If yes) Tell me about their drinking.
97. (If needed) How much do they drink? . . . How frequently do they drink? . . . Where do they drink?
98. Do your friends drink alcohol?
99. (If yes) Tell me about their drinking.
100. Do you drink alcohol?
101. (If yes) Tell me about your drinking.
102. Was there ever a time when you drank too much?
103. (If yes) Tell me about the time[s] when you drank too much.
104. Has anyone in your family—a friend, a doctor, or anyone else—ever said that you drank too much?
105. (If yes) Tell me about that.
106. Has alcohol ever caused problems for you?
107. (If yes) Tell me about that.
108. Do your parents use drugs?
109. (If yes) Tell me about the drugs they use.
110. (If needed) How much of the drugs do they take? . . . How frequently do they take them?
111. Do your friends use drugs?
112. (If yes) Tell me about the drugs they use.
113. Do you use drugs?
114. (If yes) Tell me about the drugs you use.
115. Have you or has anyone else ever thought that you used drugs too much?
116. (If yes) Tell me about that.
117. Do your friends huff or use aerosols or inhalants?
118. (If yes) Tell me about that.
119. Have you ever huffed or used aerosols or inhalants?
120. (If yes) Tell me about that.
    (Go back to questions 256–258 in the main interview.)

Table B-2
Semistructured Interview Questions for an Older Child or Adolescent in a Mental Status Evaluation

1. Hi! I'm Dr. [Ms., Mr.] _____. I'd like to ask you some questions. OK?

General Orientation to Time, Place, and Person
2. What is your name?
3. How old are you?
4. What is today's date?
5. What day of the week is it?
6. What is the season?
7. What time of day is it?
8. Where are you?
9. What is the name of the state we are in?
10. What is the name of this city?
11. What is the name of this place?

Recent and Remote Memory
12. And your telephone number is . . . ?
13. What is your address?
14. What grade are you in?
15. What is my name?
16. What did you have for breakfast?
17. What did you do in school [at the hospital, at home] yesterday?
18. Who is the president of the United States?
19. Who was the president before him?
20. (If relevant) Where did you live before you moved to [cite city]?
21. Name three major cities in the United States.
22. What are two major news events that happened in the last month?
23. How did you get to this hospital [clinic, office]?
24. What is your father's name?
25. What is your mother's name?
26. When is your birthday?
27. Where were you born?

28. What school do you go to?
29. (If relevant) When did you finish elementary school?
30. (If relevant) When did you finish high school?

Immediate Memory
31. Say these numbers after me: 6-9-5 . . . 4-3-8-1 . . . 2-9-8-5-7.
32. Say these numbers backwards: 8-3-7 . . . 9-4-6-1 . . . 7-3-2-5-8.
33. Say these words after me: pencil, chair, stone, plate.

Insight and Judgment
34. What does this saying mean: "Too many cooks spoil the broth"?
35. What does this saying mean: "A stitch in time saves nine"?
36. How are a banana, a peach, and a pear alike?
37. How are a bicycle, a wagon, and a car alike?

Reading, Writing, and Spelling
38. Read these words. (Give interviewee a piece of paper with the following words on it: pat, father, setting, intervention.)
39. Now write these same words. (Give interviewee a blank piece of paper on which to write; show the same words as in question 38 for the interviewee to copy.)
40. Spell these words aloud: spoon . . . cover . . . attitude . . . procedure.

Arithmetical Concentration
41. (For children between 7 and 12 years) Subtract by 3s, starting with 30.
42. (For adolescents) Subtract by 7s, starting with 50.

Concluding Questions
43. Are there any questions that you would like to ask me?
44. (If yes) Go ahead.
45. Thank you for talking with me. If you have any questions or if you want to talk to me, please call me. Here is my card.

Table B-3
Semistructured Interview Questions for an Older Child or Adolescent with Depression

Introduction

1. Hi! I'm Dr. [Ms., Mr.] _____. I'd like to talk to you about how you're getting along. OK?
2. When you don't understand a question that I ask, please say "I don't understand." When you tell me that, I'll try to ask it better. OK?

Dysphoric Mood

3. Tell me how you're feeling.
   (If needed, ask questions 4 through 24; otherwise, go to directions preceding question 25.)
4. I'm going to name some feelings and reactions. Please tell me if you often feel this way. OK?
5. Sad. Do you feel sad?
6. (If yes) Tell me about feeling sad.
7. Lonely. Do you feel lonely?
8. (If yes) Tell me about feeling lonely.
9. Unhappy. Do you feel unhappy?
10. (If yes) Tell me about feeling unhappy.
11. Hopeless. Do you feel hopeless?
12. (If yes) Tell me about feeling hopeless.
13. Depressed. Do you feel depressed?
14. (If yes) Tell me about feeling depressed.
15. Pessimistic. Do you feel pessimistic?
16. (If yes) Tell me about feeling pessimistic.
17. Do you get moody?
18. (If yes) Tell me about the times you get moody.
19. Do you get easily annoyed?
20. (If yes) Give me some examples of what annoys you.
21. Do you cry easily?
22. (If yes) Tell me about the times you cry easily.
23. Are you hard to please?
24. (If yes) Give me some examples of how you are hard to please.
    (Ask questions 25 to 32 separately for each feeling or reaction mentioned by interviewee, as needed.)
25. In the last week, how often have you felt [cite feeling or reaction]?
26. When did you first notice being troubled by [cite feeling or reaction]?
27. Does this feeling ever go away for some time—say, for a few days or weeks?
28. (If yes) How do you feel when [cite feeling or reaction] goes away?
29. How does [cite feeling or reaction] start—does it start suddenly, or is there a slow build-up of feelings?
30. Is your [cite feeling or reaction] connected in some way with what you are doing at a particular time?
31. (If yes) Tell me about that.
32. Do you have any idea about why this [cite feeling or reaction] comes about?
33. Has anything happened to you lately that might be important to mention now?
34. When do you feel best during the day?
35. When do you feel worst during the day?
36. How much change do you notice in the way you feel from day to day?

37. (If relevant) When you are feeling really down, is there anything that can cheer you up?
38. (If yes) Tell me what can cheer you up.

Self-Deprecatory Ideation

39. How do you feel about yourself?
    (Ask questions 40 to 53, as needed.)
40. Do you feel that you are worthless?
41. (If yes) Tell me about your feelings of being worthless.
42. Do you feel that you are useless?
43. (If yes) Give me some examples of how you feel useless.
44. Do you feel that you are dumb or stupid?
45. (If yes) Give me some examples of when you feel dumb or stupid.
46. Do you feel that you are ugly?
47. (If yes) Tell me about your feelings of being ugly.
48. Do you feel guilty?
49. (If yes) Give me some examples of when you feel guilty.
50. Do you feel that you are to blame for something that happened?
51. (If yes) Tell me about your feelings.
52. Do you believe that you are being harassed or picked on?
53. (If yes) Tell me about these feelings of being harassed or picked on.
54. Do you feel that you want to die?
55. (If yes) Tell me about these feelings of wanting to die.
56. Have you thought about committing suicide?
57. (If yes) Tell me about these thoughts.
58. Have you attempted suicide?
59. (If yes) Tell me about your suicide attempt[s].
60. Have you thought about running away from home?
61. (If yes) Tell me about these thoughts of wanting to run away from home.

Aggressive Behavior (Agitation)

62. Do you think that you're difficult to get along with?
63. (If yes) Give me some examples of how you're difficult to get along with.
64. Do you argue a lot with anyone?
    (If yes, go to question 65; if no, go to question 67.)
65. Who do you argue with?
66. What do you argue about?
67. Do you have trouble getting along with people in authority, such as teachers, the school principal, or the police?
    (If yes, go to question 68; if no, go to question 70.)
68. Who do you have trouble getting along with?
69. Give me some examples of the trouble you have getting along with [cite person or persons named by interviewee].
70. Do you get into fights with people?
    (If yes, go to question 71; if no, go to question 73.)
71. Who do you fight with?
72. What do you fight about?
73. Do you feel angry sometimes?
    (If yes, go to question 74; if no, go to question 76.)
74. What do you feel angry about?
75. What do you do when you feel angry?

Table B-3 *(Continued)*

Sleep Disturbances

76. Do you need more sleep than usual lately?
77. (If yes) Tell me about that.
78. Do you have trouble sleeping?
79. (If yes) Tell me about your trouble sleeping.
80. (If needed) How many nights this week have you had trouble falling asleep?
81. Are you restless when you sleep?
82. (If yes) Tell me about your restlessness when you sleep.
83. Is it hard for you to wake up in the morning?
84. (If yes) Tell me about the difficulty you have waking up in the morning.

Change in School Performance and Attitude

85. How do you feel about school?
86. Has your attitude toward school changed recently?
87. (If yes) How has your attitude toward school changed?
88. Do you daydream in school?
89. (If yes) Give me some examples of when you daydream.
90. Do you have trouble concentrating in school?
91. (If yes) Tell me about your trouble concentrating in school.
92. How have your grades been?
93. Do you have a good memory or a poor memory for your schoolwork?
94. (If poor) Give me some examples of your poor memory for schoolwork.
95. Do you find that you usually get your homework done?
96. (If no) Tell me about that.
97. Have there been changes recently in your ability to do your schoolwork?
98. (If yes) Tell me about these changes.
99. Have you ever refused to go to school?
100. (If yes) Tell me about that.

Diminished Socialization

101. How are you getting along with your friends?
102. Do you have any close friends you can talk to?
103. Tell me about that.
104. Have there been any changes in your relationships with your friends?
105. (If yes) Tell me about these changes.
106. And how about school? How do you get along with other students at school?
107. (If needed) Have you lost interest in doing things with other people?
108. (If yes) Tell me about that.

109. How much time do you spend alone?
110. And how do you feel when you are alone?
111. Do you feel a need to be alone?
112. (If yes) Tell me about that.

Somatic Complaints

113. Tell me about your health.
      (Ask questions 114 to 121, as needed.)
114. Do you get headaches?
115. (If yes) Tell me about your headaches.
116. Do you get pains in your stomach?
117. (If yes) Tell me about the pains in your stomach.
118. Do you get muscle aches or pains?
119. (If yes) Tell me about your muscle aches or pains.
120. Do you have any other pains or physical problems?
121. (If yes) Tell me about these pains or physical problems.

Loss of Usual Energy

122. Have you lost interest in doing things, like your hobbies?
123. (If yes) Give me some examples of your loss of interest.
124. Do you feel as though you have less energy to do things?
125. (If yes) Give me some examples of your loss of energy.
126. Have you stopped doing anything you used to do?
127. (If yes) Tell me about that.
128. Do you often feel tired?
129. (If yes) Give me some examples of your feeling tired.
130. Is there anything you look forward to?
131. (If yes) Tell me what you look forward to.

Unusual Change in Appetite and/or Weight

132. Has there been a change in your appetite?
133. (If yes) Tell me about the change in your appetite.
      (If needed, ask questions 134 to 137.)
134. Have you had to force yourself to eat?
135. (If yes) Tell me about that.
136. Do you find yourself eating too much?
137. (If yes) Tell me about that.
138. Has there been a change in your weight?
139. (If yes) Tell me about the change in your weight.

Concluding Questions

140. Is there anything else you would like to talk about or tell me?
141. (If yes) Go ahead.
142. Is there anything you would like to ask me?
143. (If yes) Go ahead.
144. Thank you for talking to me. If you have any questions or if you want to talk to me, please call me. Here is my card.

Note. With modifications, these questions also could be used with a parent. You would need to substitute the child's name for "you" or "your" and make the appropriate grammatical changes. If interviewee expresses suicidal thoughts, consider asking the questions in Table B-4 in this Appendix.
Source: Adapted from Weinberg, Rutman, Sullivan, Penick, and Dietz (1973) and Wilson, Spence, and Kavanagh (1989).

Table B-4
Semistructured Interview Questions for an Older Child or Adolescent Who May Be Suicidal

Introduction

1. Hello. I'm Dr. [Ms., Mr.] _____. I'd like to talk with you about how you're getting along. OK?
2. When you don't understand a question that I ask, please say "I don't understand." When you tell me that I'll try to ask it better. OK?

Changes in Behavior and Feelings

3. Have you noticed any changes in the way you're feeling or acting recently?
   (If yes, go to question 4; if no, go to question 42 or ask questions 5 to 41, as needed.)
4. What changes have you noticed?
   (Ask questions 5 to 41, as needed.)
5. Do you feel that life is pretty hopeless?
   (If yes, go to question 6; if no, go to question 8.)
6. In what way?
7. What has happened to make you feel that life is hopeless?
8. Do you often feel so frustrated that you just want to lie down and quit trying altogether?
9. (If yes) Tell me more about that.
10. Do you ever feel that you are worthless?
11. (If yes) Tell me about these feelings.
12. Have you become quieter recently?
13. (If yes) Tell me about that.
14. Do you find yourself losing interest in things?
15. (If yes) What are you losing interest in?
16. And do you tend to stay by yourself?
17. (If yes) Tell me about that.
18. And how about crying—do you find yourself crying often?
19. (If yes) Tell me about that.
20. Do you find that you are blaming yourself for bad things that have happened?
21. (If yes) What do you blame yourself for?
22. Do you blame yourself for family problems?
23. (If yes) What family problems do you blame yourself for?
24. Have you become more irritable lately?
25. (If yes) Tell me about that.
26. Do you find that you get angry very easily?
27. (If yes) Tell me about that.
28. Have you been worried about losing your mother or father? [If applicable, add other close relatives, such as sister or brother.]
29. (If yes) Tell me about your worries.
30. Have you been worried about losing a close friend?
31. (If yes) Tell me about your worries about losing a close friend.
32. Have you recently changed the way you eat?
33. (If yes) In what way?
34. Have your sleep patterns recently changed?
35. (If yes) In what way?
36. Have your school grades recently changed?
37. (If yes) In what way?
38. Has your personality changed in any way recently?
39. (If yes) In what way?
40. Have you begun to use drugs or alcohol recently?
41. Tell me about that.

Actions Suggestive of Loss of Interest in Living

42. Have you recently given away possessions that are very special to you?
43. (If yes) What have you given away?
44. Have you done anything to hurt yourself?
45. (If yes) Tell me what you have done.
46. Do you tend to do dangerous things these days?
47. (If yes) What sorts of things are you doing?
48. Have you eaten or drunk anything that might harm you?
49. (If yes) What have you eaten or drunk?
50. Have you done anything that might cause you to die?
51. (If yes) What have you done?
52. Have you written anything that you think might be the last thing you will ever write?
53. (If yes) What have you written?

Traumatic Events

54. Have you been seriously sick recently?
55. (If yes) Tell me about your illness.
56. Has someone close to you been hospitalized?
57. (If yes) Tell me about his [her] hospitalization.
58. Have you lost a pet recently?
59. (If yes) Tell me about how you lost your pet.
60. Did you recently end a relationship with a good friend?
61. (If yes) Tell me about that.
62. Has someone close to you died recently?
63. (If yes) Tell me about who died.
64. Has anyone in your family attempted or committed suicide?
   (If yes, go to question 65; if no, go to question 67.)
65. Who was it?
66. Please tell me about it.
67. Have any of your friends attempted or committed suicide?
   (If yes, go to question 68; if no, go to question 70.)
68. Who was it?
69. Please tell me about it.
70. Is there anyone else you like or admire who has attempted or committed suicide?
   (If yes, go to question 71; if no, go to question 73.)
71. Who was it?
72. Please tell me about it.
73. Is there anything else that has happened to you or to someone close to you that you are concerned about?
74. (If yes) Tell me about what happened.

Preoccupation with Death

75. Do you think about dying?
76. (If yes) What do you think about?
77. Do you dream about dying?
78. (If yes) What do you dream about?
79. Have you ever seen a dead person?
80. (If yes) Tell me about that.
81. Do you dream about any of your relatives who are dead?
82. (If yes) What do you dream about?
83. What do you think happens to people when they die?
84. How would others feel if you were dead?
85. Does the idea of endless sleep appeal to you?
86. (If yes) Tell me more about that.

Table B-4 *(Continued)*

Family

87. How does your family feel about the way you have been feeling?
88. How are you getting along with your parents?
89. Do your parents fight a lot?
    (If yes, go to question 90; if no, go to question 92.)
90. What do they fight about?
91. How does their fighting make you feel?
92. Do your parents give you the help and encouragement you feel you need?
93. Do you feel pressured to do more or better than you are able to?
94. (If yes) Tell me about that.
95. (If appropriate) How have you been getting along with your sisters [brothers]?
96. Has anyone in your family been abused?
97. (If yes) Tell me about that.
98. Is there anyone in your family who is seriously ill?
    (If yes, go to question 99; if no, go to question 102.)
99. Who is ill?
100. What illness does she [he] have?
101. How do you feel about her [his] being ill?

Thoughts and Actions Related to Suicide

102. Have you recently thought about killing yourself?
     (If yes, ask questions 103 through 111, as needed; if no, go to question 112.)
103. How much do you want to die?
104. How serious are you about wanting to die?
105. Do you have a plan for how you will kill yourself?
     (If yes, go to question 106; if no, go to question 110.)
106. Tell me about your plan.
107. Do you have a way to carry out your plan?
108. (If needed) Do you think about using a gun, a knife, pills, or some other method?
109. (If yes) Tell me about that.
110. How do you think your family and friends would feel if you tried to take your life?
111. Tell me about that.
112. Have you wished that you were dead?
113. (If yes) Tell me about that.
114. Have you talked to anyone about killing yourself?
115. (If yes) Tell me about that.
116. Have you ever tried to commit suicide?
     (If yes, go to question 117; if no, go to question 123.)
117. Tell me about your suicide attempt.
     (Ask questions 118 to 122, as needed.)
118. What happened?
119. When did it happen?
120. Who found you?
121. What happened after he [she] found you?
122. How do you feel about what you did?
123. Do you want to live?
124. Tell me about how you feel about living.
125. Have you thought about hurting someone else in addition to hurting yourself?
     (If yes, go to question 126; if no, go to question 128.)
126. Who is this person?
127. What have you thought about doing to him [her]?

Concluding Questions

128. What are your future plans?
129. Is there anything else you would like to tell me?
130. (If yes) Go ahead.
131. How does talking about all this make you feel?
132. Can anyone do anything to make you feel better?
133. Tell me about that.
134. Do you have anyone you can talk to about your problems?
135. (If yes) Who is that?
136. Is there anything else you would like to talk about?
137. (If yes) Go ahead.
138. Is there anything you would like to ask me?
139. (If yes) Go ahead.
140. Can you promise me that you won't hurt yourself at least until you meet with me again?
     (If yes, go to question 144; if no, go to question 141.)
141. Because you can't promise me that you won't hurt yourself, I must call your parents [or appropriate authorities]. Please wait here until I call them. (Call parents or appropriate authorities.) Is there anything else you would like to discuss?
     (If yes, go to question 142; if no, go to question 143.)
142. Go ahead.
     (Go to question 144.)
143. Your parents [or cite representative of appropriate agency] will be here soon. Thank you for talking with me. If you have any questions or if you want to talk to me, please call me. Here is my card. (End interview.)
144. Thank you for talking with me. If you have any questions or if you want to talk to me, please call me. Here is my card.

Note. With modifications, these questions also could be used with a parent. You would need to substitute the child's name for "you" or "your" and make the appropriate grammatical changes.
Source: Adapted, in part, from Pfeffer (1986).

Table B-5
Semistructured Interview Questions for an Adolescent or Older Child Being Screened for Alcohol Abuse or Dependence

Introduction
1. Hi. I'm Dr. [Ms., Mr.] _____. I'd like to talk to you about how you're getting along. OK?
2. When you don't understand a question that I ask, please say "I don't understand." When you tell me that, I'll try to ask it better. OK?

Background Information
3. Tell me about your being here today.
   (If the adolescent does not mention problems with alcohol, go to question 4; if the adolescent does mention problems with alcohol, go to question 5.)
4. I understand that you are drinking alcohol. Is that right?
   (If the adolescent acknowledges alcohol use, go to question 5. If the adolescent refuses to acknowledge that he or she has a problem with alcohol, you may not be able to continue with this interview. Instead, consider asking the questions in Table B-1 in this Appendix that focus on general issues associated with adolescent adjustment. Begin with item 7.)
5. Tell me about your drinking.
   (Ask questions 6 to 28, as needed.)
6. What do you drink?
7. How much do you drink?
8. How often do you drink?
9. At what times during the day do you drink?
10. Do you ever drink just after you get up in the morning?
11. (If yes) Tell me about that.
12. Can you stop drinking after you've had one or two drinks if you want to?
13. (If needed) Where do you do your drinking?
14. Are you alone when you drink, or are you with other people?
15. (If with others) Tell me something about the people you drink with.
16. How do you get the alcohol?
    (If purchased, go to question 17; if not purchased, go to question 20.)
17. Who buys the alcohol for you?
18. Do you give this person money to buy the alcohol?
19. Where do you get the money to buy the alcohol?
20. How old were you when you first started drinking?
21. What did you drink when you first started?
22. How much did you drink at that time?
23. Have you ever been drunk?
    (If yes, go to question 24; if no, go to question 26.)
24. Tell me about the times you have been drunk.
25. How old were you the first time you ever drank enough to get drunk?
26. How has your drinking changed since you first began to drink?
27. Do you think you are losing control over your drinking?
28. (If yes) Tell me about that.

Symptoms and Related Issues
29. Do you ever have hangovers?
30. (If yes) Tell me about the times you get hangovers.
31. Have you ever had blackouts while drinking—that is, have you ever drunk enough that you couldn't remember the next day what you said or did?

32. (If yes) Tell me about your blackouts.
33. Have you ever had the shakes after cutting down on your drinking or when you stopped drinking?
    (If yes, go to question 34; if no, go to question 37.)
34. Tell me about when you had the shakes.
35. How often have you had the shakes?
36. And what did you do about the shakes?
37. Have you ever had health problems because of your drinking, such as liver disease or stomach problems?
38. (If yes) Tell me about them.
39. Have you ever made any rules about drinking, like not drinking before 5 o'clock in the evening or never drinking alone?
40. (If yes) Tell me about them.
41. Have you ever continued to drink when you were in a situation that might be made worse by drinking, such as when you were taking medicine that was not supposed to be used with alcohol?
42. (If yes) Tell me about these times.
43. Have you ever gone on binges where you kept drinking for a couple days or more without sobering up?
44. (If yes) Tell me about these times.
45. Have your parents said anything to you about your drinking?
    (If yes, go to question 46; if no, go to question 49.)
46. What did they say?
47. When did they say this to you?
48. And what did you do about it?
49. Have other people said anything to you about your drinking?
    (If yes, go to question 50; if no, go to question 52.)
50. What did they say?
51. And what did you do about it?

Reasons for Drinking
52. People have different reasons for drinking. What reasons do you have for drinking?
53. (If needed) Is it because you like the taste . . . you are celebrating special occasions . . . your friends drink . . . you feel nervous and tense . . . you are upset . . . you feel lonely or sad . . . you want to get high? Are there other reasons?
54. Does alcohol ever allow you to do things that you wouldn't do if you weren't drinking?
55. (If yes) Tell me about these things.
56. Have you ever felt bad or guilty about your drinking?
57. (If yes) Tell me about your feelings.

Problems as a Result of Drinking
58. Have you ever gotten into fights while drinking?
59. (If yes) Tell me about these times.
60. Have you ever been arrested because of your drinking?
61. (If yes) Tell me about that.
62. (If adolescent has a driver's license) Have you ever been arrested for drunk driving?
63. (If yes) Tell me about that.
64. Have you ever had an accident because of drinking?
65. (If yes) Tell me about that.

Table B-5 *(Continued)*

66. Have you ever had school troubles because of drinking—like missing too much school, coming in late for classes, or not paying attention in class?
67. (If yes) Tell me about these times.
68. (If relevant) Have you ever had trouble on a job because of drinking—like missing work or coming in late for work?
69. (If yes) Tell me about these times.
70. Have you lost any friends because of your drinking?
71. (If yes) Tell me about what happened.
72. Has there ever been a period of your life when you could not go on with your daily activities unless you had something to drink?
73. (If yes) Tell me about that.

Family and Friends
74. Does your father drink alcohol?
75. (If yes) Tell me about that.
76. Does your mother drink alcohol?
77. (If yes) Tell me about that.
78. (If relevant) Do any of your sisters and brothers drink alcohol?
79. (If yes) Tell me about that.
80. Does anyone else in the family drink alcohol?
81. (If yes) Who?
82. Do your friends drink alcohol?
(If yes, go to question 83; if no, go to question 85.)
83. Tell me about their drinking.
84. When you are drinking with your friends, do you ever try to drink a bit extra and hide it from them?
85. Does anyone in your family use drugs?
86. (If yes) Tell me about that.
87. Do your friends use drugs?
88. (If yes) Tell me about that.
89. Do you also use drugs?
90. (If yes) Tell me about the drugs you use.

Attempts to Seek Help
91. Have you ever felt the need to cut down on your drinking?
92. (If yes) Tell me about that.
93. Have you ever talked to your parents . . . your friends . . . your doctor . . . your clergyperson . . . your teachers . . . any other professional about drinking too much?
(If yes, go to question 94; if no, go to question 97.)

94. Tell me about who you talked to.
95. What did you say?
96. And what did he [she, they] say?
97. Have you ever tried to stop drinking?
98. (If yes) Tell me about the times when you tried to stop drinking.
99. Do you think you have a drinking problem?
100. (If yes) Tell me about that.
101. Have you ever been in an alcohol treatment program? (If yes, go to question 102; if no, go to question 104.)
102. Tell me about when you were in the program.
103. Did it help?
104. What is your goal—what would you like to see happen with regard to your drinking right now?

Attitude Toward Treatment
(If the adolescent has said that he or she has a problem with alcohol, go to question 105; if not, go to question 109.)
105. Do you want help for your problem?
(If yes, go to question 106; if no, go to question 109.)
106. What kind of help do you want?
107. How long do you think it will take to gain control over your drinking?
108. Are you prepared to work with people who are trained to help you?
109. If you did not drink alcohol, what would you miss most about it?
110. And what would be the best thing about not drinking alcohol?
111. How would your friends react if you did not drink alcohol?
112. And how would your family react if you did not drink alcohol?
113. How then do you see the role of alcohol in your life—that is, what part should alcohol play in your life?

Concluding Questions
114. Is there anything else you would like to tell me about your alcohol use?
115. (If yes) Go ahead.
116. Do you have any questions that you would like to ask me?
117. (If yes) Go ahead.
118. Thank you for talking with me. (Tell the interviewee what will happen next, as needed.) If you have any questions or if you want to talk to me, please call me. Here is my card.

Note. With modifications, these questions also could be used with a parent. You would need to substitute the child's name for "you" or "your" and make the appropriate grammatical changes. Table B-6 in this Appendix contains a semistructured interview useful for inquiring about drug use.
Source: Adapted, in part, from Robins and Marcus (1987).

Table B-6
Semistructured Interview Questions for an Adolescent or Older Child with a Drug Abuse Problem

Introduction

1. Hi! I'm Dr. [Ms., Mr.] _____. I'd like to talk to you about how you're getting along. OK?
2. When you don't understand a question that I ask, please say "I don't understand." When you tell me that, I'll try to ask it better. OK?

Background Information

3. Tell me about your being here today.
   (If the adolescent does not mention problems with drug use, go to question 4; if the adolescent does mention problems with drug use, go to question 5.)
4. I understand that you are using drugs. Is that right?
   (If the adolescent acknowledges drug use, go to question 5. If the adolescent refuses to acknowledge that he or she has a problem with drugs, you may not be able to continue with this interview. Instead, consider asking the questions in Table B-1 in this Appendix that focus on general issues associated with adolescent adjustment. Begin with item 7.)
5. Tell me about the drug[s] you use.
6. Where do you get it [them]?
7. How much does it cost?
8. About how much money do you spend each week on [cite drug]?
9. How do you pay for it?
10. Are you having financial problems because of your drug use?
11. (If yes) Tell me about that.
12. Have you ever done things you otherwise wouldn't do to get [cite drug]?
13. (If yes) Tell me about that.
14. (If needed) What do you do to get [cite drug]?
15. Do you have trouble turning down [cite drug] when it is offered to you?
16. Tell me about that.
17. Does the sight, thought, or mention of [cite drug] trigger urges and cravings for it?
18. (If yes) Tell me about that.
19. Do you think about [cite drug] much of the time?
20. (If yes) Tell me about these thoughts.
21. Do you have any concerns about your drug use?
22. (If yes) Tell me about your concerns.
23. (If needed) Are you frightened by the strength of your drug habit?

Exposure to Drugs

24. Does anyone else in your family drink alcohol too much or use drugs?
25. (If yes) Tell me about that.
26. Do any of your friends regularly use alcohol or drugs?
27. (If yes) Tell me about that.
28. Do any of your friends sell or give drugs to other kids?
29. (If yes) Tell me about that.
30. When did you first learn about [cite drug]?
31. Who told you about [cite drug]?
32. What did he [she] tell you?
33. How old were you when you first tried [cite drug]?
34. Where were you when you first tried [cite drug]?

35. Was anyone else there?
36. (If yes) Tell me about who was there.
37. How much [cite drug] did you take?
38. How did you feel after you took [cite drug]?
39. As you look back on your first experience with [cite drug], do you have any thoughts about the experience now?

Drug Usage

40. How old were you when you first started using [cite drug] regularly?
41. How do you go about taking [cite drug]?
42. (If needed) Do you smoke it . . . eat or swallow it . . . inject it . . . snort it . . . inhale it?
43. How much [cite drug] do you take?
   (If drug is injected, go to question 44; if not, go to question 46.)
44. Do you use a sterile needle?
45. Do you share needles with other people?
46. Where are you when you take [cite drug]?
47. (If needed) Do you take it at home . . . at school . . . in the park . . . at friends' houses . . . in other places?
48. At what times during the day do you take [cite drug]?
49. Are you with anyone else when you take [cite drug]?
50. (If yes) Tell me about whom you're with.
51. About how many times have you used [cite drug]?
52. When was the last time you used [cite drug]?
53. How often do you use [cite drug]?
54. (If needed) On the average, how many days per week do you use [cite drug]?
55. How long have you been doing this?
56. Do you tend to use all the [cite drug] that you have on hand, even though you want to save some for another time?
57. Was there a particular time when you realized that you had begun to use [cite drug] more often?
   (If yes, go to question 58; if no, go to question 60.)
58. When was that?
59. Why do you think you started to use [cite drug] more often?
60. How do you feel when you don't have [cite drug]?
61. What do you do about it when you don't have [cite drug]?
62. Did you ever find you needed larger amounts of [cite drug] because you couldn't get high on the amount you were using?
63. (If yes) Tell me more about that.
64. (If needed) When did that begin to happen?
65. Would you use even more [cite drug] if you could get it?
66. Have you ever woken up the morning after taking [cite drug] and found you couldn't remember a part of what happened the night before, even though your friends tell you that you didn't pass out?
67. Do you often wish you could keep taking [cite drug] even after your friends have had enough?
68. (If yes) Tell me about that.

Drug Binges

69. Do you go on drug binges—that is, use a drug or drugs continually for a period of time?
   (If yes, go to question 70; if no, go to question 77.)
70. How many times have you gone on binges?

Table B-6 *(Continued)*

71. When was the last time you went on a binge?
72. What was happening in your life at that time?
73. How long does a binge last?
74. How much [cite drug] do you take during a binge?
75. How do you feel during the binge?
76. How do you feel after the binge?

Attempts to Stop Drug Usage

77. Has a friend or member of your family ever gone to anyone for help about your drug use?
78. (If yes) Tell me about that.
79. Have you ever attended Alcoholics Anonymous or Narcotics Anonymous meetings?
80. (If yes) Tell me about what happened.
81. Have you ever tried to stop taking [cite drug]? (If yes, go to question 82; if no, go to question 89.)
82. What did you do to try to stop taking [cite drug]?
83. How long did you go without taking [cite drug]?
84. What happened that you started taking [cite drug] again?
85. About how many times have you tried to stop taking [cite drug]?
86. What happened when you tried to stop?
87. (If needed) Did you have withdrawal symptoms—that is, did you feel sick because you stopped or cut down on [cite drug]?
88. (If yes) Tell me about your symptoms.
89. Do you have any idea why you haven't stopped using [cite drug]?
90. (If yes) Tell me about that.
91. Have you ever tried to limit your drug use to only certain times or certain situations?
92. (If yes) Tell me about that.

Symptoms Associated with Drug Usage

93. Do you have any health problems because of using [cite drug]? (If yes, go to question 94; if no, go to question 97.)
94. Tell me about your health problems.
95. Have you ever gone to a doctor about these problems?
96. (If yes) What did the doctor do?
97. How is your appetite?
98. Have you gained or lost weight recently?
99. (If yes) Tell me about that.
100. Tell me about what you ate yesterday and today.
101. Is that the usual amount you eat?
102. (If no) How did that differ from what you would eat other times?
103. When you are taking [cite drug] regularly, do you miss meals?
104. (If yes) Tell me more about that.
105. Have you ever been hospitalized for using [cite drug]?
106. (If yes) Tell me about that.
107. Have you ever overdosed on a drug?
108. (If yes) Tell me about that.
109. Has your use of [cite drug] caused you to miss school . . . do poorly in school . . . get into trouble with your teacher or principal . . . get into an accident . . . lose control . . . get the shakes or become depressed . . . get into trouble with your family . . . get into trouble with your

friends . . . get into trouble with the police . . . have sex with someone . . . be sexually abused by someone?
110. (If yes to any of the above) Tell me about how you happened to [name problem] and the role [cite drug] played. (Ask this question for each behavior mentioned by interviewee.)
111. Do people who don't know about the drug use tell you that your behavior or personality has changed?
112. Have your parents talked to you about your drug use?
113. Tell me about that.
114. (If adolescent has a driver's license) Do you ever drive a car when you're high on [cite drug]?
115. (If yes) Tell me about that.
116. (If needed) Have you neglected your schoolwork or any important responsibilities because of your drug habit?
117. (If yes) Tell me about that.
118. Have your values and priorities changed because of your drug use?
119. (If yes) Tell me about that.
120. Do you feel guilty or ashamed for using [cite drug]?
121. Do you like yourself less for using [cite drug]?
122. Do you tend to spend time with certain people or go to certain places because you know that [cite drug] will be available?
123. Do you have any strange or scary feelings or thoughts when you use [cite drug]?
124. (If yes) Tell me about them.
125. Do you find yourself lying and making excuses because of your drug use?
126. (If yes) Tell me about that.
127. Do you ever deny or downplay the severity of your drug problem?
128. Has taking [cite drug] interfered with your life or activities?
129. (If yes) Tell me about how taking [cite drug] has interfered.
130. Have you been spending less time with "straight" people since you've been using more [cite drug]?

Reasons for Taking Drugs

131. People have different reasons for taking drugs. What reasons do you have?
132. (If needed) Is it because you like the feeling it gives you . . . you need it to have a good time . . . you're afraid of being bored or unhappy without it . . . it makes you feel less nervous or tense . . . you feel lonely and sad . . . your friends take drugs . . . you feel you couldn't function well without it?
133. Have your reasons for taking [cite drug] changed since you began using it?
134. (If yes) Tell me about that.

Involvement with Other Drugs

135. Do you drink alcohol or use any other drugs in addition to [cite drug]? (If yes, go to question 136; if no, go to question 141.)
136. Tell me about what you take or drink.
137. How does it make you feel?
138. Do you do it at the same time you use [cite drug]?
139. (If yes) Are you concerned about how these drugs [the drugs and alcohol] interact with each other?
140. (If yes) Tell me about your concerns.

(Continued)

Table B-6 *(Continued)*

Attitude Toward Treatment

141. Do you think you have a problem with drugs?
    (If yes, go to question 142; if no, go to question 146.)
142. Do you want help for your problem?
    (If yes, go to question 143; if no, go to question 146.)
143. What kind of help do you want?
144. How long do you think it will take to gain some control over your drug use?
145. Are you prepared to work with people trained to help you?
146. If you became drug free, what would you miss most about [cite drug]?
147. And if you became drug free, what would be the best thing about being clean?

148. How would your friends react if you became clean?
149. And how would your family react if you became clean?

Concluding Questions

150. Is there anything else you'd like to tell me about your drug use?
151. (If yes) Go ahead.
152. Do you have any questions that you would like to ask me?
153. (If yes) Go ahead.
154. Thank you for talking with me. If you have any questions or if you want to talk to me, please call me. Here is my card.

Note. With modifications, these questions also could be used with a parent. You would need to substitute the child's name for "you" or "your" and make the appropriate grammatical changes. Table B-5 in this Appendix contains a semistructured interview useful for inquiring about alcohol abuse or dependence.

Source: Adapted, in part, from Roffman and George (1988) and Washton, Stone, and Hendrickson (1988).

Table B-7
Semistructured Interview Questions for a Child or Adolescent with a Learning Disability

Introduction

1. Hi! I'm Dr. [Ms., Mr.] _____. I'd like to talk to you about how you are getting along. OK?
2. When you don't understand a question that I ask, please say "I don't understand." When you tell me that, I'll try to ask it better. OK?

Attitude Toward School

3. How are you getting along in school?
4. What do you like about school?
5. What don't you like about school?
6. What are your favorite subjects?
7. What are your least favorite subjects?
8. Which subjects are easiest for you?
9. Which subjects are hardest for you?
10. Now I'd like to talk to you about some specific subjects. OK?

Reading

11. How well can you read?
12. Do you like to read?
13. Tell me about that.
14. When you read, do you make mistakes like skipping words or lines, reading the same lines twice, or reading letters backwards?
15. (If needed) Tell me about the mistakes you make when you read.
16. Do you find that you can read each line of every paragraph but, when you finish the page or chapter, you don't remember what you've just read?
17. Do you understand and remember better when you read aloud or when you read silently?

Writing

18. How good is your handwriting?
19. Do you find that you cannot write as fast as you think?
20. (If yes) Do you run one word into another when you're writing because you're thinking of the next word rather than the one you're writing?
21. How good is your spelling?
22. Tell me about that.
23. How good is your grammar?
24. Tell me about that.
25. How good is your punctuation?
26. Tell me about that.
27. Do you know how to type on a computer?
28. (If yes) Does using a computer make writing easier for you?
29. Tell me about that.
30. Do you have difficulty copying from the chalkboard?
31. Tell me about that.
32. Do you have difficulty taking notes when the teacher lectures?
33. Tell me about that.

Math

34. Do you know the multiplication tables?
35. (If no) Tell me about that.
36. When you do math, do you make mistakes like writing "21" when you mean to write "12," mixing up columns of numbers, or adding when you mean to subtract?

37. Tell me about the mistakes you make when you do math.
38. Do you sometimes start a math problem but halfway through forget what you were trying to do?

Sequencing

39. When you speak or write, do you sometimes find it hard to get everything in the right order—do you maybe start in the middle, go to the beginning, and then jump to the end?
40. Do you have trouble saying the alphabet in order?
41. (If yes) Tell me about that.
42. Do you have to start from the beginning each time you say the alphabet?
43. Do you have trouble saying the days of the week in order?
44. (If yes) Tell me about that.
45. Do you have trouble saying the months of the year in order?
46. (If yes) Tell me about that.

Abstraction

47. Do you understand jokes when your friends tell them?
48. (If no) Tell me about that.
49. Do you sometimes find that people seem to say one thing yet tell you that they meant something else?
50. (If yes) Tell me about that.

Organization

51. What does your notebook look like?
52. (If needed) Is it pretty neat and organized, or is it a mess, with papers in the wrong place or falling out?
53. Is it hard for you to organize your thoughts or to organize the facts you're learning into the bigger idea that the teacher is trying to teach you?
54. Can you read a chapter and answer the questions at the end of the chapter but still not be sure what the chapter is about?
55. (If yes) Tell me about that.
56. Do you have trouble planning your time so that things get done on time?
57. (If yes) Tell me about that.
58. What does your bedroom at home look like?

Memory

59. How is your memory?
60. Has it changed in any way?
    (Ask questions 61 to 64, as needed.)
61. Do you find that you can learn something at night but, when you go to school the next day, you don't remember what you learned?
62. When talking, do you sometimes forget what you are saying halfway through?
63. (If yes) What do you do when this happens?
64. (If needed) Do you cover up by saying things like "Whatever," "Oh, forget it," or "It's not important"?

Language

65. When the teacher is speaking in class, do you have trouble understanding or keeping up?
66. (If yes) Tell me about that.
67. Do you sometimes misunderstand people and, therefore, give the wrong answer?

(Continued)

Table B-7 *(Continued)*

68. (If yes) When does this tend to happen?
69. Do you sometimes lose track of what people are saying?
70. (If yes) Does this sometimes cause you to lose your concentration in class?
71. Do you sometimes have trouble organizing your thoughts when you speak?
72. (If yes) Tell me about that.
73. Do you sometimes have a problem finding the word you want to use?
74. (If yes) When this happens, what do you do?

Study Habits
75. Now I'd like to ask you about your learning and study habits. Tell me about what happens when you study.
76. Do you learn better alone, with one friend, or in a group?
77. Tell me more about that.
78. When you study, do you like to have adults help you, only help you if you ask them to, or leave you alone?
79. Tell me about that.

Time Rhythm
80. At what time of day do you learn best?
81. (If needed) Do you learn best early in the morning, right before lunch, after lunch, after school, or right before bedtime?
82. After you wake up in the morning, how long does it take you to feel really awake?
83. Do you sometimes have trouble staying awake after lunch or dinner?
84. (If yes) Tell me more about that.
85. Do you like to get up early?
86. If you stay up late, do you feel "foggy" the next day—as if your head were in a cloud?
87. What time do you usually go to bed?
88. How long does it usually take you to fall asleep?

Environment
89. Where is the best place for you to study?
90. Tell me more about that.
91. Do you like to study in a room with bright lighting or low lighting?
92. Do you think you feel cold or hot more often than other people?
93. (If yes) Tell me about that.
94. Do you like the room you're in to be warm or cool?

Attention and Concentration
95. Do you prefer noise or silence when you are studying?
96. Can you study if you hear a radio or television in the background?
97. Are you distracted if you hear people talking or children playing?
98. Do you like to study with music playing?
99. (If yes) What kind of music?
100. Do you daydream a lot when you are in class?
101. (If yes) Tell me about that.
102. Do you have trouble sitting still or staying in your seat at school?
103. (If yes) Tell me about the trouble you're having.

104. And at home, do you have trouble sitting still or staying in your seat?
105. (If yes) Tell me about that.
106. How is your concentration?
107. Can you complete your assignments, or are you easily distracted?
108. (If distracted) What seems to distract you?
109. Do you like to leave your studies to go see what's going on, get a drink, or change rooms or positions?
110. (If yes) Tell me more about that.
111. Do you like to keep at your work until it's done?
112. Tell me more about that.

Study Habits
113. Do you like to eat, chew gum, or have a drink while you are studying?
114. (If yes) How does it help?
115. Do you overeat while you are studying?
116. (If yes) How does it help?
117. Do you have any nervous habits while you're studying, such as chewing your fingernails or a pencil?
118. (If yes) Tell me about your habits.

Motivation
119. How important is it for you to get good grades?
120. Tell me about that.
121. Do you think your grades are important to your parents?
122. Tell me about that.
123. Do you think your grades are important to your teachers?
124. Tell me about that.
125. When you try to get good grades, is it more to please adults or to please yourself?
126. Tell me about that.
127. Do you think that getting a good education is important?
128. Tell me about that.
129. Do you think reading is important for more things in life than just school?
130. Tell me about that.
131. Do you let things go until the last minute?
132. Tell me about that.
133. Do you feel responsible for your learning?
134. Tell me about that.
135. How do you feel when you don't do well in school?
136. How do you feel when you turn in an assignment late?
137. How do you feel when you don't finish an assignment?
138. Do you like solving problems on your own, or do you prefer being told exactly what is expected and how to do it?
139. Do you get upset easily when you are learning?
140. (If yes) Tell me about that.
141. Do you like to learn and find out things, even when you aren't in school and don't have to?
142. Tell me about that.
143. How do you feel when someone criticizes your schoolwork?
144. Tell me about that.
145. Do you usually try to do your very best in school?
146. Tell me about that.

Table B-7 *(Continued)*

Anxiety

147. Do you think that you worry more about school or tests than other kids do?
148. (If yes) Tell me about that.
149. Do you feel shaky when the teacher asks you to read aloud, get up in front of the class, or write on the board?
150. (If yes) Tell me about that.
151. How do you feel about surprise tests?

Concluding Questions

152. Is there anything else you would like to tell me or talk about?
153. (If yes) Go ahead.
154. Do you have any questions that you would like to ask me?
155. (If yes) Go ahead.
156. Thank you for talking with me. If you have any questions or if you want to talk to me, please call me. Here is my card

Note. With modifications, these questions also could be used for a parent. You would need to substitute the child's name for "you" or "your" and make the appropriate grammatical changes.
Source: Adapted from Dunn and Dunn (1977) and Silver (1992).

Table B-8
Semistructured Interview Questions for an Older Child or Adolescent with Tramautic Brain Injury

These questions supplement those in Table B-1 in this Appendix.

Introduction

1. Hi, I'm Dr. [Ms., Mr.] _____. I'm going to be asking you some questions. When you don't understand a question that I ask, please say "I don't understand." When you tell me that, I'll try to ask it better. OK?
2. Has anyone told you why you are here today?
   (If yes, go to question 3; if no, go to question 5.)
3. Who told you?
4. What did he [she, they] tell you?
   (Go to question 6.)
5. Tell me why you think you are here. (If interviewee doesn't know, explain to her or him that you want to find out how she or he is getting along or something similar.)

General Problems

6. Please tell me anything you can about how you are getting along.
7. (If needed) Are you having any problems?
   (If child says that he or she is having problems, go to question 8; otherwise, go to question 19.)
8. Tell me about [cite problems mentioned by child].
9. How do you feel about [cite problems]?
10. What changes have you noticed since [cite problems] began?
11. In what situations do you have the most difficulty with [cite problems]?
12. What do you do in these situations?
13. Is there anything that helps?
14. (If yes) How does it help?
15. What kind of help would you like?
16. How do your parents feel about the problems you are having?
17. How do your friends feel about the problems you are having?
18. And how do your teachers feel about the problems you are having?

Specific Current Problems and Complaints

19. I'm going to name some areas in which you may have problems. If you have problems or complaints in any of these areas, please let me know by saying yes. After we finish the list, we'll go back to the beginning and I'll ask you more about these problems. OK?

   (*If the child previously told you about a problem, do not mention it again now.* Pause after you name each problem or complaint. From time to time, remind the child of the task by prefacing the name of the problem with "Are you having a problem with . . . ?" or "Do you have any complaints about . . . ?")

   General Physical Problems
   • bowel or bladder control
   • seizures
   • headaches

   • dizziness
   • pain
   • sleeping
   • numbness
   • loss of feeling
   • blackouts
   • muscle strength
   • endurance
   • coordination

   Sensory-Motor Problems
   • seeing
   • hearing
   • smelling
   • speaking
   • balance
   • movements you can't control or stop
   • doing things too fast or too slowly
   • standing
   • walking
   • running
   • drawing
   • handwriting
   • eating
   • dressing
   • bathing
   • recognizing objects
   • building or constructing things
   • hearing ringing sounds
   • changes in taste
   • tingling in your fingertips or toes

   Cognitive Problems
   • thinking
   • planning
   • concentrating
   • remembering
   • paying attention
   • understanding directions
   • giving directions
   • learning
   • judging
   • reading
   • writing stories, poems, and other things
   • spelling
   • doing simple arithmetic problems
   • understanding what is read to you
   • handling money
   • finding your way around
   • organizing things
   • changing from one activity to another

   Psychosocial-Affective Problems
   • keeping up with your responsibilities at home
   • staying interested in things
   • getting along with other children
   • getting along with friends and family members

Table B-8 *(Continued)*

- getting along with teachers
- controlling your temper
- feeling sad
- feeling anxious
- showing initiative
- realizing that another person is upset
- controlling your laughter
- being inconsiderate of others
- being impatient
- being inflexible
- becoming angry without cause
- changing moods easily
- being irritable
- being aggressive
- being uncooperative
- being negative
- lying
- stealing
- having to do things exactly the same way each time
- changes in your personality
- recognizing problems in yourself
- being insecure
- visiting friends
- keeping friends
- going shopping

Language and Communication Problems
- talking too much
- talking too little
- using the right word
- using peculiar words
- saying embarrassing things
- reversing what you hear
- defining words
- naming objects that are shown to you
- counting
- naming the days of the week
- repeating names
- carrying on a conversation
- recognizing mistakes that you make in speaking or writing or reading
- using the telephone
- looking up telephone numbers
- remembering telephone numbers
- watching television

Consciousness Problems
- feeling disoriented
- feeling that you are losing your body
- feeling that some unknown danger is lurking
- doing things that you are unaware of
- starting to do one thing and then finding yourself doing something else
- feeling that the size of your hands or feet or head is changing

(If the child responded "yes" to any of the above problems, go to question 20; otherwise, go to question 24.)

20. You told me that you have a problem with [cite area]. Tell me more about your difficulty with [cite area]. (Repeat for each problem.)
21. Which problems bother you most?
22. How do you deal with these problems?
23. How do your parents deal with these problems?

Accident or Injury
24. I'd like to learn about the accident [injury]. Please tell me about it.
    (Ask questions 25 to 36 as needed.)
25. What happened?
26. What were you doing at the time of the accident [injury]?
27. Who else was involved in the accident [injury]?
28. Were you unconscious?
    (If yes, go to question 29; if no, go to question 31.)
29. How long were you unconscious?
30. Where did you wake up?
31. What kind of treatment did you get?
32. How did the treatment help?
33. What kind of treatment are you receiving now?
34. What was your behavior like right after the accident [injury] happened?
35. What was your behavior like several days later?
36. And what is your behavior like now?

Adjustment to Brain Injury and Typical Activities
37. Have you noticed any changes since the accident [injury] in how you are getting along with your parents?
38. (If yes) Tell me what you have noticed.
39. (If relevant) Have you noticed any changes since the accident [injury] in how you are getting along with your brothers and sisters?
40. (If yes) Tell me what you have noticed.
41. Have you noticed any changes since the accident [injury] in how you are getting along with your friends?
42. (If yes) Tell me what you have noticed.
43. Have there been any changes in your schoolwork since the accident [injury]?
44. (If yes) Tell me about the changes in your schoolwork.
45. (If relevant) Have there been any changes in your work habits since the accident [injury]?
46. (If yes) Tell me about the changes in your work habits.

Concluding Questions
47. Is there anything else that you want to tell me or that you think I should know?
48. (If yes) Go ahead.
49. Do you have any questions that you would like to ask me?
50. (If yes) Go ahead.
51. Thank you for talking with me. If you have any questions, if you want to talk to me, or if you think of anything else you want to tell me, please call me. Here is my card.

Note. With modifications, these questions also could be used with a parent of a child with traumatic brain injury. You would need to substitute the child's name for "you" or "your" and make the appropriate grammatical changes.

Table B-9
Semistructured Interview Questions for a Parent of a Child Who May Have a Psychological or Educational Problem or Disorder

Some of the questions in this table (for example, those dealing with peer relationships, interests and hobbies, and academic functioning) are not applicable to infants, and other questions (for example, those dealing with academic functioning) are not applicable to toddlers. Therefore, use your judgment in selecting appropriate questions to use. This table can be used in conjunction with Table B-10 in this Appendix, which contains additional questions concerning specific areas of child development in infancy and the toddler/preschool years. At the end of this table are additional questions that you can use to inquire about adolescents.

Introduction
1. Hi! I'm Dr. [Ms., Mr.] _____. I'd like to talk to you about [cite child's name]'s adjustment and functioning. OK?

Parent's Perception of Problem Behavior
2. Please tell me your concerns about [cite child's name].
3. (If needed) Can you describe these concerns a little more?
4. Is there anything else that you are concerned about?
5. What concerns you most?
6. Let's discuss [cite problem] in more detail. How serious do you consider [cite problem] to be?
7. When did you first notice [cite problem]?
8. How long has [cite problem] been going on?
9. Where does [cite problem] occur?
10. (If needed) Tell me about how [cite child's name] behaves at school . . . in stores or other public places . . . in a car . . . at friends' houses . . . with visitors at home.
11. When does [cite problem] occur?
12. (If needed) Does it happen in the morning . . . in the afternoon . . . at bedtime? . . . Does it occur when [cite child's name] is with you . . . his [her] father [mother] . . . his [her] brothers and sisters . . . other children . . . other relatives?
13. How long does [cite problem] last?
14. How often does [cite problem] occur?
15. What happens just before [cite problem] begins?
16. What happens just after [cite problem] begins?
17. What makes [cite problem] worse?
18. What makes [cite problem] better?
19. What do you think is causing [cite problem]?
20. Was anything significant happening in your family when [cite problem] first started?
21. (If needed) For example, had you recently separated or divorced . . . moved to another city or school district . . . had financial problems . . . dealt with the serious illness of a family member?
22. (If some event occurred) What was [cite child's name]'s reaction to [cite event]?
23. How does [cite child's name] deal with [cite problem]?
24. Do any other children in your family also have [cite problem]?
25. (If yes) How does [cite child's name]'s [cite problem] compare with theirs?
26. Has [cite child's name] been evaluated or received any help for [cite problem]?
(If yes, go to question 27; if no, go to question 29.)

27. What type of evaluation or help has he [she] received?
28. And what progress has been made?
29. Why do you think [cite child's name] has [cite problem]?
30. How do you deal with [cite problem]?
31. How successful has it been?
32. How do family members react to [cite child's name]'s [cite problem]?
33. Are any of the other problems you mentioned, such as [cite problem], of particular concern to you now?
(If yes, repeat questions 6 to 32 as needed.)

Home Environment
34. Tell me what your home is like.
35. Where does [cite child's name] sleep?
36. Where does [cite child's name] play?
37. Who lives at your home?
38. (If needed) Do you have a husband [wife] or partner?
39. (If relevant) Tell me about your husband [wife, partner].

Neighborhood
40. Tell me about your neighborhood.
41. Do you know your neighbors?
42. (If yes) What do you think of your neighbors?
43. (If needed) How do you get along with them?

Sibling Relations (if relevant)
44. How does [cite child's name] get along with his [her] brothers and sisters?
45. What do they do that [cite child's name] likes?
46. What do they do that [cite child's name] dislikes?
47. How do they get along when you aren't around?
48. Do you think the children behave differently when you are there?

Peer Relations
49. Does [cite child's name] have friends?
(If yes, go to question 50; if no, go to question 60.)
50. Tell me about [cite child's name]'s friends.
51. (If needed) About how many friends does he [she] have?
52. (If needed) What are their ages?
53. How does he [she] get along with his [her] friends?
54. What does [cite child's name] do with his [her] friends?
55. How does he [she] get along with friends of the opposite sex?
56. Do you approve of his [her] friends?
57. Does [cite child's name] usually go along with what his [her] friends want to do, or is [cite child's name] more likely to do what he [she] wants to do?
58. Does [cite child's name] have a problem keeping friends?
59. (If yes) Tell me about that.
(Go to question 64.)
60. Tell me about [cite child's name]'s not having friends.
61. Does [cite child's name] have opportunities to meet other children?
62. (If needed) Tell me more about that.
63. Does [cite child's name] seem to want to have friends?
64. How do other children react to [cite child's name]?

Table B-9 *(Continued)*

Child's Relations with Parents and Other Adults

65. How does [cite child's name] get along with you?
66. What does [cite child's name] do with you on a regular basis?
67. How does [cite child's name] express his [her] affection for you?
68. What are the good times like for [cite child's name] and you?
69. What are the bad times like for [cite child's name] and you?
70. Are there times when both you and [cite child's name] end up feeling angry or frustrated with each other?
71. (If yes) Tell me more about that.
    (If there are other adults in the household, repeat questions 65 to 71 for each adult, substituting the adult's name, and then go to question 72; otherwise, go to question 78.)
72. When something is bothering [cite child's name], whom does he [she] confide in most often?
73. Who is responsible for discipline?
74. Who is most protective of [cite child's name]?
75. Do you have any concerns about how other adults interact with [cite child's name]?
76. (If yes) Tell me about your concerns.
77. (If needed) About whom do you have concerns?
78. Does [cite child's name] listen to what he [she] is told to do?
79. How is [cite child's name] disciplined?
80. Which techniques are effective?
81. Which are ineffective?
82. What have you found to be the most satisfactory ways of helping your child?
83. How do you express your affection for [cite child's name]?

Child's Interests and Hobbies

84. What does [cite child's name] like to do in his [her] spare time?
85. What types of games does [cite child's name] like to play?
86. How skilled is [cite child's name] at sports or other games?
87. Is [cite child's name] involved in any extracurricular activities?
88. (If yes) Tell me about that.
89. What does [cite child's name] like to do alone . . . with friends . . . with family members?
90. What activities does [cite child's name] like least?
91. How much television does [cite child's name] watch each day?
92. Do you think that is an acceptable amount of television?
93. (If no) Tell me about that.
94. What are his [her] favorite programs?
95. How do you feel about the programs he [she] watches?
96. Does [cite child's name] play video or computer games?
97. (If yes) How much time does [cite child's name] spend each day playing these games?
98. Do you think that is an acceptable amount of time?
99. (If no) Tell me about that.
100. (If needed) And how about listening to music? Does [cite child's name] listen to music?
     (If yes, go to question 101; if no, go to question 103.)
101. What kind of music does [cite child's name] listen to?
102. How do you feel about the music [cite child's name] listens to?

Child's Routine Daily Activities

103. How does [cite child's name] behave when he [she] wakes up?
104. What changes occur in [cite child's name]'s behavior during the course of a day?
105. (If needed) Does he [she] become more fidgety or restless as the day proceeds, or does he [she] become more calm and relaxed?
106. Does [cite child's name] do household chores?
107. (If yes) What chores does he [she] do?
108. What does [cite child's name] do before bedtime?
109. How does [cite child's name] behave when he [she] goes to bed?

Child's Cognitive Functioning

110. How well does [cite child's name] learn things?
111. Does [cite child's name] seem to understand things that are said to him [her]?
112. Does [cite child's name] seem to be quick or slow to catch on?
113. Does [cite child's name] stick with tasks that he [she] is trying to learn?

Child's Academic Functioning

114. How is [cite child's name] getting along in school?
115. What does he [she] like best about school?
116. What does he [she] like least about school?
117. What grades does [cite child's name] get?
118. What are [cite child's name]'s best subjects?
119. What are [cite child's name]'s worst subjects?
120. Are you generally satisfied with [cite child's name]'s achievement in school?
121. (If no) Tell me what you're not satisfied about.
122. How does [cite child's name] feel about his [her] schoolwork?
123. How does [cite child's name] get along with the other children at school?
124. How does [cite child's name] get along with his [her] teacher[s]?
125. What do you think of [cite child's name]'s school?
126. What do you think of [cite child's name]'s teacher[s]?
127. What do you think of the principal of the school?
128. Has [cite child's name] ever repeated a grade or attended a readiness or transition class?
129. (If yes) Tell me about that.
130. Has any teacher recommended special help or special education services for [cite child's name]?
     (If yes, go to question 131; if no, go to question 136.)
131. Tell me about the help that was recommended.
132. Please describe what help, if any, he [she] has received.
133. Does [cite child's name] attend a special class?
134. Have you needed to attend specially scheduled parent-teacher meetings because of [cite child's name]'s behavior?
135. (If yes) What did you learn at the meeting[s]?

Child's Behavior

136. Tell me about [cite child's name]'s attention span.
137. What kind of self-control does [cite child's name] have?
138. How well does [cite child's name] follow directions?
139. Tell me about [cite child's name]'s activity level.
140. Is [cite child's name] impulsive?
141. (If yes) Tell me about his [her] impulsiveness.

Child's Affective Life

142. What kinds of things make [cite child's name] happy?
143. What makes him [her] sad?
144. What does [cite child's name] do when he [she] is sad?
145. What kinds of things make [cite child's name] angry?
146. What does [cite child's name] do when he [she] is angry?
147. What kinds of things make [cite child's name] afraid?
148. What does [cite child's name] do when he [she] is afraid?
149. What kinds of things does [cite child's name] worry about?
150. What kinds of things does [cite child's name] think about a lot?
151. What sorts of things does [cite child's name] ask questions about?
152. How does [cite child's name] typically react to a painful or uncomfortable event, such as when he [she] gets an injection or has to take pills?
153. How does [cite child's name] feel about himself [herself]?
154. How does [cite child's name] behave when faced with a difficult problem?
155. What makes [cite child's name] frustrated?
156. What does [cite child's name] do when he [she] is frustrated?
157. Does [cite child's name] ever become annoyed when you try to help him [her] with something?
158. (If yes) Tell me about that.
159. What things does [cite child's name] do well?
160. What things does [cite child's name] really enjoy doing?
161. Tell me what [cite child's name] is really willing to work to obtain.
162. What do you do when [cite child's name] is sad . . . is angry . . . is afraid . . . worries a lot . . . is in pain?

Child's Motor Skills

163. Tell me about [cite child's name]'s ability to do things that require small motor movements, such as turning pages of a book, using scissors, and folding paper.
164. Tell me about [cite child's name]'s general coordination, such as his [her] ability to walk, jump, skip, and roll a ball.

Child's Health History

165. I'd like to ask you about [cite child's name]'s health history. What common childhood illnesses has [cite child's name] had?
166. And has [cite child's name] had any serious illnesses?
167. (If yes) Tell me about them.
168. (As needed) When did the illness start? . . . What was the treatment? . . . Was the treatment successful?
169. Has he [she] had any surgical procedures?
170. (If yes) Tell me about them.
171. How would you describe [cite child's name]'s usual state of health?
172. Do you believe that [cite child's name] has been growing adequately?
173. (If no) Tell me more about that.
174. How is [cite child's name]'s hearing?
175. How is [cite child's name]'s vision?
176. Did [cite child's name] ever have any serious accidents or injuries?
177. (If yes) Tell me about them.
178. Did [cite child's name] ever go to an emergency room for an accident or illness?
179. (If yes) Tell me about it.

180. Did [cite child's name] ever need any stitches?
181. (If yes) Tell me about it.
182. Has [cite child's name] ever had any broken bones?
183. (If yes) Tell me about it.
184. Did [cite child's name] ever swallow anything dangerous?
185. (If yes) Tell me about what happened.
186. Does [cite child's name] have any allergies?
187. (If yes) Tell me about them.
188. What immunizations has [cite child's name] had?
189. Does [cite child's name] eat well?
190. (If no) Tell me about that.
191. Does [cite child's name] sleep well?
192. (If no) Tell me about that.
193. Does [cite child's name] have nightmares or other sleep problems?
194. (If yes) Tell me about that.
195. Does [cite child's name] have problems with bowel or bladder control?
196. (If yes) Tell me about that.
197. Does [cite child's name] take any medicine regularly? (If yes, go to question 198; if no, go to question 204.)
198. What medicine does he [she] take regularly?
199. What does [cite child's name] take the medicine for?
200. Does [cite child's name] report any side effects from taking the medicine? (If yes, go to question 201; if no, go to question 204.)
201. What are the side effects?
202. Have you discussed them with your doctor?
203. (If yes) What did the doctor say?

Family

204. Tell me about your family. Does anyone in your immediate or extended family have any major problems?
205. (If yes) Tell me about them.
206. (If relevant) How are you getting along with your husband [wife, partner]?
207. (If relevant) In your opinion, how does your relationship with your husband [wife, partner] affect [cite child's name]'s problem?
208. Have you or members of your family had any serious medical or psychological difficulties?
209. Has anyone in the family whom [cite child's name] was close to died?
210. (If yes) Tell me about that.
211. How about a close friend? Have any of [cite child's name]'s friends died?
212. (If yes) Tell me about that.
213. Has the family lost a pet?
214. (If yes) Tell me about the loss.
215. Has anyone in your family been the victim of a crime?
216. (If yes) Please tell me about what happened.
217. Have you recently changed your place of residence?
218. (If yes) Tell me about your move.
219. (If relevant) Has [cite child's name]'s caregiver recently changed?
220. (If yes) Tell me about that.
221. Have any members of your family had a problem similar to [cite child's name]'s problem?
222. (If yes) Tell me about that.
223. Has anyone in the family shown a major change in behavior within the past year?

Table B-9 *(Continued)*

224. (If yes) Tell me about that.
225. (If needed) Do any members of your family have a problem with drugs or alcohol?
226. (If yes) Tell me about that.
227. Do you have any concern that [cite child's name] may have been physically abused or sexually abused?
228. (If yes) Tell me about your concern.

Parent's Expectations

229. Do you think that [cite child's name] needs treatment, special education, or special services?
230. (If yes) What do you expect such services to do for [cite child's name]?
231. What are your goals for [cite child's name]?
232. How would your life be different if [cite child's name]'s problems were resolved?
233. (If relevant) Do you desire treatment for your own difficulties? (If there are other adult members of the household, go to question 234; otherwise, go to instructions following question 239.)
234. Who in the family is most concerned about [cite child's name]'s problem?
235. Who is least concerned?
236. Who is most affected by the problem?
237. Who is least affected?
238. How does your view of [cite child's name]'s problem compare with that of [cite other adult members of household]?
239. How does your view about what should be done to help [cite child's name] compare with that of [cite other adult members of household]? (Before concluding the interview with questions 240–244), ask the questions at the end of this table about the development of an adolescent or those in Table B-10 in this Appendix about the development of an infant or toddler/preschooler, as needed.)

Concluding Questions

240. Overall, what do you see as [cite child's name]'s strong points?
241. And overall, what do you see as [cite child's name]'s weak points?
242. Is there any other information about [cite child's name] that I should know?
243. Where do you see [cite child's name] five years from now?
244. Thank you for talking with me. If you have any questions or if you want to talk to me, please call me. Here is my card.

Additional Questions About Adolescent's Development

1. Is [cite child's name] involved in any dating activities?
2. (If yes) What kind of dating activities?
3. Are there any restrictions on his [her] dating activities?
4. (If yes) How does he [she] feel about them?
5. Have you talked with [cite child's name] about sexual behaviors? (If yes, go to question 6; if no, go to question 10.)
6. Tell me what you've talked about.
7. What kinds of sexual concerns does [cite child's name] have?
8. Do you and [cite child's name] agree or disagree about appropriate sexual behavior?
9. Tell me about that.
10. So far as you know, does [cite child's name] use drugs? (If yes, go to question 11; if no, go to question 20.)
11. Tell me about his [her] drug use. (Ask questions 12 to 19, as needed.)
12. What kind of drugs does [cite child's name] use?
13. How does [cite child's name] get the drugs?
14. How does [cite child's name] pay for the drugs?
15. Has [cite child's name] ever gotten into trouble because of his [her] drug use?
16. (If yes) Tell me about that.
17. Has [cite child's name] received any treatment for his [her] drug use?
18. (If yes) Tell me about the treatment he [she] has received.
19. Is there anything else you want to tell me about [cite child's name]'s drug use?
20. So far as you know, does [cite child's name] drink alcohol? (If yes, go to question 21; if no, go to question 30.)
21. Tell me about his [her] drinking. (Ask questions 22 to 29, as needed.)
22. What kind of alcohol does [cite child's name] drink?
23. How does [cite child's name] get the alcohol?
24. (If relevant) How does [cite child's name] pay for the alcohol?
25. Has [cite child's name] ever gotten into trouble because of his [her] drinking?
26. (If yes) Tell me about that.
27. Has [cite child's name] received any treatment for his [her] use of alcohol?
28. (If yes) Tell me about the treatment he [she] has received.
29. Is there anything else you want to tell me about [cite child's name]'s drinking?
30. Does [cite child's name] get high by using other substances besides drugs or alcohol? (If yes, go to question 31; if no, go to question 240 in main interview.)
31. What does [cite child's name] use to get high?
32. Tell me about that. (Ask questions 33 to 39, as needed.)
33. How does [cite child's name] get [cite substance]?
34. (If relevant) How does [cite child's name] pay for [cite substance]?
35. Has [cite child's name] ever gotten into trouble because of his [her] use of [cite substance]?
36. (If yes) Tell me about that.
37. Has [cite child's name] received any treatment for his [her] use of [cite substance]?
38. (If yes) Tell me about the treatment he [she] has received.
39. Is there anything else you want to tell me about [cite child's name]'s use of [cite substance]? (Go to question 240 in main interview.)

Note. If you want to obtain information about other problems, repeat questions 7 through 33 in the main interview. Any responses given to questions in this interview can be probed further. If you want to ask additional questions about maternal obstetric history, pregnancy, or labor and delivery or if you suspect that the parent has minimal parenting skills, see Table B-10 in this Appendix.

Table B-10
Semistructured Interview Questions to Obtain a Detailed Developmental History from a Mother Covering Her Child's Early Years and to Evaluate Parenting Skills

The questions in this semistructured interview supplement those in Table B-9 in this Appendix, which should be used first. You then have the choice of following up in areas related to infancy and toddler/preschool years. The questions are designed not only to obtain information about the child but also to evaluate parenting skills. Select the questions that you believe are applicable to the specific case and that complement those in Table B-9. If you want information about the mother's obstetric history, you might say, for example, "I'd now like to get some more information about [cite child's name]'s development. I would first like to learn about the time before [cite child's name] was born." If you decide to begin the semistructured interview with another section, use an appropriate introduction. Sections that pertain specifically to infants or toddlers/preschoolers are so identified in the section headings.

Maternal Obstetric History
1. How old were you when [cite child's name] was born?
2. Have you had any other pregnancies?
   (If yes, go to question 3; if no, go to question 9.)
3. Tell me about them. (Pay particular attention to miscarriages, abortions, and premature births and their outcomes.)
4. How many living children do you have?
5. (If more than one child) How old are they now?
6. (If any child died) How did your child die?
7. (If needed) Tell me about what happened.
8. (If needed) How old was your child when he [she] died?
9. I'd like to talk to you about your pregnancy with [cite child's name]. What was your pregnancy like?
   (Ask questions 10 to 13, as needed.)
10. Was it planned?
11. (If yes) How long did it take you to become pregnant?
12. Did you have any illnesses or problems during pregnancy? (Pay particular attention to vaginal bleeding, fevers, rashes, hospitalizations, weight gain, weight loss, vomiting, hypertension, proteinuria [the presence of an excess of protein in the urine; also called albuminuria], preeclampsia [a toxemia of late pregnancy characterized by hypertension, albuminuria, and edema], general infections, and urinary tract infections.)
13. Were any sonograms performed?
   (If yes, go to question 14; if no, go to question 16.)
14. How many were performed?
15. What did it [they] show?
16. Was your blood type incompatible with that of [cite child's name]?
17. (If yes) Tell me about that.
18. Did you take any medications or street drugs during pregnancy?
19. (If yes) What did you take? (Any of the following may affect the development of the fetus: prescription drugs; over-the-counter pills; cocaine/crack; marijuana/pot; hallucinogens, such as LSD, PCP, DMT, mescaline, and mushrooms; stimulants, such as uppers, speed, amphetamines, crystal, crank, and Dexedrine; tranquilizers, such as downers, Valium, Elavil, Quaaludes, Stelazine, barbiturates, and

thorazine; and opiates, such as morphine, Demerol, Percodan, codeine, Darvon, Darvocet, heroin, and methadone. If the mother mentions one of these or any other drug that may affect the fetus, go to question 20; if not, go to question 25.)
20. How often did you take it?
21. When during your pregnancy did you take it?
22. How did it make you feel?
23. Did you tell your health care provider that you were taking [cite drug]?
24. (If yes) Tell me about that.
25. Did you drink alcohol during your pregnancy?
   (If yes, go to question 26; if no, go to question 32.)
26. What did you drink?
27. How often did you drink alcohol?
28. And how much did you drink each time?
29. When during your pregnancy did you start drinking?
30. Did you drink throughout your pregnancy?
31. Did you tell your health care provider that you were drinking alcohol during your pregnancy?
32. Did you smoke cigarettes during your pregnancy?
   (If yes, go to question 33; if no, go to question 39.)
33. Tell me about that.
34. How many cigarettes did you smoke each day?
35. When during your pregnancy did you start smoking?
36. Did you smoke throughout your pregnancy?
37. Did you tell your health care provider that you were smoking during your pregnancy?
38. (If yes) Tell me about that.
39. Did you have x-rays taken during your pregnancy?
40. (If yes) Tell me about them.
41. Were you exposed to chemicals or other potentially harmful substances during your pregnancy?
42. (If yes) Tell me about what you were exposed to.
43. Did you see a health care provider during your pregnancy?
   (If yes, go to question 44; if no, go to question 46.)
44. What kind of health care provider did you see during your pregnancy?
45. How many visits did you make?
   (Go to question 47.)
46. Why didn't you see a health care provider?
47. Did you see anyone else for care during your pregnancy?
48. (If yes) Tell me about whom you saw.
49. Overall, was your pregnancy with [cite child's name] a good experience or a bad experience?
50. Tell me about your answer.
51. In general, how would you rate your health during your pregnancy with [cite child's name]?
52. Tell me about your answer.

Labor, Delivery, Infant's Condition at Birth, and Immediate Postpartum Period for Mother
1. Now I'd like to talk to you about your labor and delivery. Tell me about your labor and delivery.
   (Ask questions 2 to 15, as needed.)
2. What were your thoughts and feelings during labor?
3. Was [cite child's name] born on time?

Table B-10 *(Continued)*

4. (If early) How early was [cite child's name] born?
5. (If late) How late was [cite child's name] born?
6. How long did the labor last?
7. What kind of delivery did you have?
8. (If needed) Was it normal . . . breech . . . cesarean . . . forceps . . . induced?
9. (If delivery was cesarean, forceps, or induced) Why was this type of delivery needed?
10. How did the delivery go?
11. (If needed) Were there any complications at delivery?
12. (If yes) Tell me about them.
13. Were you given anything for pain during labor?
14. (If yes) Tell me about it.
15. Were labor and delivery what you expected?
16. What were your first impressions of your new baby?
17. Was the baby's father present during delivery?
18. (If yes) What were his first impressions of the new baby?
19. How was [cite child's name] right after he [she] was born?
20. What was [cite child's name]'s weight at birth?
21. What was [cite child's name]'s length at birth?
22. What was [cite child's name]'s skin color?
23. Did [cite child's name] cry soon after birth?
24. Do you know [cite child's name]'s Apgar score?
25. (If yes) What was it?
26. Did you want to hold [cite child's name] right away?
27. Were you allowed to hold [cite child's name]?
28. (If father was present) Was the baby's father allowed to hold [cite child's name]?
29. Did you have any physical problems immediately after [cite child's name] was born?
30. (If yes) Tell me about them.
31. Did you have any psychological problems after [cite child's name] was born?
32. (If yes) Tell me about them.
33. Did you have a rooming-in arrangement with the baby? (If yes, go to question 34; if no, go to question 35.)
34. What was it like to have the baby in the room with you? (Go to question 36.)
35. Why didn't you have a rooming-in arrangement?
36. Did [cite child's name] have any health problems following birth?
37. (If yes) Tell me about them.
38. Was [cite child's name] in a special care nursery in the hospital for observation or treatment? (If yes, go to question 39; if no, go to question 47.)
39. Tell me about the reason [cite child's name] was in a special care nursery.
40. Did you visit [cite child's name] when he [she] was in the special care nursery?
41. Did you feed [cite child's name] when he [she] was in the special care nursery?
42. How did you feel about having [cite child's name] stay in the special care nursery?
43. And how many days old was [cite child's name] when he [she] went home from the special care nursery? (If the father is in the picture, go to question 44; if not, go to question 47.)
44. Did the baby's father visit [cite child's name] when he [she] was in the special care nursery?

45. Did the baby's father feed [cite child's name] when he [she] was in the special care nursery?
46. How did the baby's father feel about having [cite child's name] stay in the special care nursery?
47. How did you spend your time in the first few days at home with [cite child's name]?
48. After the first few days, how much time did you spend at home with [cite child's name]?
49. Was [cite child's name] breastfed or bottlefed?
50. How did that go? (If the father is in the picture, go to question 51; if not, end this section.)
51. Did [cite child's name]'s father also spend time with him [her]?
52. What was their relationship like at this time?
53. (If needed) How did he feel about the baby?
54. Did the baby's father help you during this time?
55. Tell me about that.

Infant's Attachment

1. When [cite child's name] came home from the hospital, what was it like to have him [her] home?
2. Did you feel you knew the baby?
3. Tell me about that.
4. Did you feel the baby knew you?
5. Tell me about that.
6. How were [cite child's name]'s first few weeks of life at home?
7. Did [cite child's name] have any problems?
8. (If needed) Did [cite child's name] have problems with eating . . . drinking . . . sleeping . . . alertness . . . irritability?
9. (If yes) Tell me about [cite child's name]'s problems. (Inquire about the types of problems, their severity, what the parent did, treatment, outcomes, and so forth.)
10. Was it easy or difficult to comfort [cite child's name]?
11. How did you go about comforting [cite child's name]?
12. Was [cite child's name] too good—that is, did he [she] demand little or no care?
13. (If yes) What did you think about this?
14. Was [cite child's name] alert as a baby?
15. (If no) Tell me about how [cite child's name] reacted.
16. What was [cite child's name]'s mood generally?
17. How well did he [she] adjust to new things or routines?
18. How did he [she] respond to new people?
19. Was he [she] cuddly or rigid?
20. Was he [she] overactive or underactive?
21. Did he [she] engage in any tantrums . . . rocking behavior . . . head banging?
22. Did [cite child's name] develop a regular pattern of eating and sleeping?
23. (If no) Tell me about that.
24. Were there any surprises during [cite child's name]'s first weeks of life at home?
25. What was most enjoyable about taking care of [cite child's name]?
26. And what was least enjoyable about taking care of [cite child's name]?
27. What was most difficult about taking care of [cite child's name]?

28. What was easiest about taking care of [cite child's name]?
29. How did you feel about [cite child's name] during his [her] first few weeks of life at home?
30. (If father is in the picture) How did his [her] father feel about [cite child's name] during his [her] first few weeks of life?
31. (If other children in family) How did the other children in the family react to [cite child's name]?
32. (If needed) Did the other children show any signs of jealousy?
33. (If yes) How did they demonstrate their jealousy, and how did you [you and your husband, you and the baby's father] handle the jealousy?
34. Did you have confidence in yourself as a parent during the first six months of [cite child's name]'s life?
35. Tell me about that.
36. What kind of adjustments did you [you and your family] have to make?
37. How did your extended family react to [cite child's name]?

Infant's Responsiveness (if infant is focus of interview)
1. Does [cite child's name] respond to your voice?
2. When you pick [cite child's name] up, does he [she] become quiet?
3. Does [cite child's name] smile?
4. Does [cite child's name] look at you when you try to talk to or play with him [her]?
5. (If no) What does [cite child's name] do instead?
6. What sounds does [cite child's name] make?
7. Does [cite child's name] reach out and grasp a person's face or finger?
8. Can [cite child's name] tell the difference between strangers and familiar people?
9. Does [cite child's name] play with other people?
10. How does [cite child's name] respond to new people?
11. How does [cite child's name] respond to being in a new place?
12. How often does [cite child's name] want to be held?
13. Does [cite child's name] like physical contact, such as when you gently touch his [her] face, hands, and arms?
14. Is there any physical activity that [cite child's name] seems to enjoy especially?

Infant's Crying, Adjustment to Caregiving Situation, Behavior in Public, and Unusual Behavior (if infant is focus of interview)
1. When does [cite child's name] cry?
2. What do you do when [cite child's name] cries?
3. Why do you think [cite child's name] cries?
4. (If needed) When [cite child's name] cries, does it usually mean that something is really wrong or is it that something is bothering him [her] only a little bit and he [she] wants attention?
5. Can you tell the difference between the types of crying [cite child's name] does?
6. (If yes) How?
7. (If no) What does he [she] do that makes it difficult to know what his [her] crying means?
8. With whom do you leave [cite child's name] when you go out?
9. How do you feel about leaving [cite child's name]?
10. Do you leave [cite child's name] at a day care center, at somebody's house, or at your house with a sitter during any part of the week?
    (If yes, go to question 11; if no, go to question 28.)
11. Where do you leave him [her]?
12. Tell me about the reason you leave [cite child's name] there.
13. (If day care center or someone's house) How did you find out about [cite place where child is cared for]?
14. Are you satisfied with the way [cite child's name] is cared for there?
15. How is [cite child's name] getting along at [cite place where child is cared for]?
16. (If needed) Is [cite child's name] having any problems there?
17. (If yes) Tell me about them.
18. (If needed) How does [cite child's name] get along with the child care provider[s]?
19. (If needed) How does [cite child's name] get along with the other children?
20. Do you have a chance to talk regularly about [cite child's name] with the person[s] taking care of him [her]?
21. How long does it take you to get to [cite place where child is cared for]?
22. How does [cite child's name] act when you leave him [her] at [cite place where child is cared for]?
    (If behavior is not satisfactory, go to question 23; if behavior is satisfactory, go to question 27.)
23. How do you feel when [cite child's name] acts this way?
24. Does [cite child's name] always show that he [she] is upset in the same way?
25. What do you do to quiet [cite child's name] when he [she] is upset?
26. Does it help?
27. How does [cite child's name] react when you pick him [her] up from [cite place where child is cared for]?
28. How do you feel about taking [cite child's name] out in public?
29. How does [cite child's name] behave when he [she] is outside the home?
30. How does [cite child's name] react when you take him [her] to a friend's home?
    (If there are problems or concerns, go to question 31; otherwise, go to question 33.)
31. How do you handle these problems?
32. What seems to work best?
33. Does [cite child's name] have any unusual behaviors?
    (If yes, go to question 34; if no, end this section.)
34. What unusual behaviors does [cite child's name] have?
35. How often does [cite child's name] exhibit [cite unusual behavior]?
36. What is most likely to bring on [cite unusual behavior]?
37. What situations seem to make [cite child's name]'s [cite unusual behavior] worse?
38. What do you do at these times?
39. What works best?
40. Is there any connection between what [cite child's name] eats and [cite unusual behavior]?
41. How do you feel about taking care of [cite child's name] when he [she] behaves in this way?

Table B-10 *(Continued)*

Infant's Play, Language, Communication, and Problem-Solving Skills (if infant is focus of interview)
1. What does [cite child's name] play?
2. What toys does [cite child's name] like to play with?
3. What is [cite child's name]'s favorite toy?
4. Does [cite child's name] like to do the same activity over and over again?
5. What sounds does [cite child's name] make?
6. How long has he [she] been making these sounds?
7. In which situations does [cite child's name] make sounds?
8. (If needed) Does he [she] make sounds early in the morning in his [her] crib . . . while riding in the car . . . when other children are around . . . when playing by himself [herself] . . . when adults are talking . . . when someone is talking on the phone . . . when in a quiet room?
9. At what times during the day does [cite child's name] make the most sounds?
10. What is happening at these times?
11. Does [cite child's name] seem to be trying to tell you something as he [she] babbles or makes sounds?
12. (If yes) Do you have any idea what [cite child's name] is trying to say when he [she] makes sounds?
13. How does [cite child's name] let you know that he [she] wants something?
14. How does [cite child's name] let you know how he [she] feels?
15. (If relevant) About how many words does [cite child's name] understand?
16. (If relevant) Tell me about [cite child's name]'s ability to gesture or point.
17. Do you ever hear [cite child's name] making sounds a few minutes after an adult speaks to him [her]?
18. Was there a time when [cite child's name] made more sounds or babbled more?
    (If yes, go to question 19; if no, go to question 21.)
19. When did he [she] babble more?
20. How long has it been since he [she] stopped babbling as much?
21. Has [cite child's name] had any recent illness with fever and earache?
22. Is [cite child's name] exhibiting any other behavior that concerns you?
23. (If yes) What is this behavior?
24. Have there been any changes or stressful events in your home recently?
25. (If yes) Tell me about them.
26. Does [cite child's name] say any words?
27. (If yes) How old was [cite child's name] when he [she] spoke his [her] first words?
28. How does [cite child's name] use his [her] hands, eyes, and body to solve problems?
29. Tell me about [cite child's name]'s attention span.

Infant's Motor Skills (if infant is focus of interview)
(Note that these questions are arranged in developmental sequence. If the child has not mastered a motor skill, it is unlikely that he or she will be able to perform the next motor skill. Therefore, you can stop your inquiry after you find that the child has not mastered a skill.)

1. Can [cite child's name] roll over?
   (If yes, go to question 2; if no, go to question 3.)
2. How old was he [she] when he [she] first rolled over?
   (Go to question 4.)
3. What progress is [cite child's name] making toward rolling over?
4. Can [cite child's name] crawl?
   (If yes, go to question 5; if no, go to question 6.)
5. How old was he [she] when he [she] began to crawl?
   (Go to question 7.)
6. What progress is [cite child's name] making toward crawling?
7. Can [cite child's name] sit up?
   (If yes, go to question 8; if no, go to question 9.)
8. How old was he [she] when he [she] first sat up?
   (Go to question 10.)
9. What progress is [cite child's name] making toward sitting up?
10. Can [cite child's name] pull himself [herself] up to a standing position?
    (If yes, go to question 11; if no, go to question 13.)
11. How old was he [she] when he [she] first pulled himself [herself] up to a standing position?
12. Does [cite child's name] sometimes remain standing for a short time after he [she] has pulled himself [herself] up?
    (Go to question 14.)
13. What progress is he [she] making toward pulling himself [herself] up to a standing position?
14. Can [cite child's name] walk?
    (If yes, go to question 15; if no, go to question 16.)
15. How old was he [she] when he [she] first walked?
    (Go to question 18.)
16. What progress is he [she] making toward walking?
17. (If needed) Does [cite child's name] seem to want to move and explore on his [her] own?
18. In what situations is [cite child's name] most active physically?
19. (If needed) Is he [she] most active when someone plays with him [her] . . . when other children are around . . . when he [she] is outdoors?
20. Tell me about [cite child's name]'s ability to do things that require small-motor movements, such as his [her] ability to grasp things, pick things up, hold onto things, and release things.
21. Is [cite child's name] able to transfer small objects from hand to hand?
22. Does [cite child's name] help you hold his [her] bottle?
23. Is [cite child's name] able to follow an object or face with his [her] eyes?
24. Does [cite child's name] use his [her] eyes to examine his [her] hands?
25. Does [cite child's name] reach for objects?

Infant's Temperament and Activity Level (if infant is focus of interview)
1. How would you describe [cite child's name] to someone who did not know him [her] well?
2. What moods does [cite child's name] have?
3. How would you describe [cite child's name]'s activity level?

(Continued)

Table B-10 *(Continued)*

---

4. Are there times when [cite child's name] engages in quiet activities?
5. (If yes) Tell me about these times.
6. When does [cite child's name] get overexcited?
7. When [cite child's name] gets overexcited, what do you do to calm him [her] down?
8. What kinds of comforting make [cite child's name] feel better?
9. How does [cite child's name] respond to new situations?
10. How does [cite child's name] respond to being separated from you?
11. (If relevant) And how does [cite child's name] respond to being separated from his [her] father?
12. (If child has trouble separating) How long does [cite response] last?
13. What do you do to help [cite child's name] with difficult changes?
14. (If responses to questions in this section do not give you the information you want about the child's temperament, ask more direct questions, such as the following.) Would any of the following terms be helpful in describing [cite child's name]—even-tempered . . . moody . . . independent . . . clinging . . . stubborn . . . flexible . . . active . . . calm . . . happy . . . sad . . . serious . . . carefree?
15. (If yes to any of the above) Please give me an example of why you would say [cite child's name] is [cite term].

Infant's Eating (if infant is focus of interview)
1. I'd like to learn about [cite child's name]'s eating. How is [cite child's name] eating?
2. What does [cite child's name] like to eat?
3. Is [cite child's name] a messy eater?
4. (If yes) Tell me about that.
5. How does [cite child's name] let you know that he [she] is hungry?
6. How does [cite child's name] show that he [she] likes certain foods?
7. How does [cite child's name] show his [her] dislike for certain foods?
8. Is [cite child's name] able to tolerate most foods?
9. Does [cite child's name] like warm foods or cold foods?
10. Does [cite child's name] like foods with any special flavors . . . special smells . . . special colors?
11. What does [cite child's name] seem to enjoy about being fed?
12. (If needed) Does [cite child's name] enjoy having you pay attention to him [her] . . . being at eye level with you while he [she] is in the high chair . . . having you talk to him [her] while he [she] eats . . . playing with the spoon?
13. What meals does [cite child's name] eat during the day?
14. What snacks does [cite child's name] eat during the day?
15. Are there certain times during the day when [cite child's name] makes excessive demands for food?
   (If yes, go to question 16; if no, go to question 18.)
16. At what times does this happen?
17. Do you think [cite child's name] is truly hungry, or is he [she] just asking for attention?
18. Does [cite child's name] skip meals and not ask to eat?
19. (If yes) Tell me about that.

20. Does [cite child's name] eat when you do or at different times?
21. (If at different times) Tell me about the reason [cite child's name] eats at different times.
22. How often does [cite child's name] see adults in the family eat?
23. Does [cite child's name] eat what he [she] is given at mealtimes?
24. Does [cite child's name] have any problems with eating?
25. (If yes) What are the problems?
26. Does [cite child's name] drink from a cup or bottle?
27. (If yes) Does [cite child's name] have any problems with drinking from a cup [bottle]?
28. (If yes) What are the problems?
   (If child has problems with eating, drinking, or both, go to question 29; otherwise, end this section.)
29. How do you handle the problems?
30. Do those methods work?
31. (If father is in the picture) What does [cite child's name]'s father think about how you handle the problems?

Infant's Sleeping (if infant is the focus of the interview)
1. How is [cite child's name] sleeping at night?
2. About how many hours of sleep does he [she] get at night?
3. Tell me what happens at night before bedtime.
4. (If needed) Does [cite child's name] go to sleep on his [her] own, or does he [she] need to be rocked, patted, or given some other kind of help from you?
5. Does [cite child's name] take a daytime nap or naps?
   (If yes, go to question 6; if no, go to question 9.)
6. Around what time[s] does he [she] nap?
7. And for how long?
8. Is there any connection between the amount of time he [she] sleeps during the day and his [her] sleeping at night?
9. Do you think that [cite child's name] is tired enough at bedtime to go to sleep easily?
10. What kind of routine do you have at night for putting [cite child's name] to bed?
11. What parts of the nighttime routine do you think [cite child's name] likes?
12. What parts of the nighttime routine do you think [cite child's name] dislikes?
13. What parts of the routine do you like?
14. And what parts of the routine do you dislike?
15. Does [cite child's name] wake up during the night?
   (If yes, go to question 16; if no, go to question 23.)
16. How often does [cite child's name] wake up during the night?
17. About what time does [cite child's name] wake up?
18. How does [cite child's name] act when he [she] wakes up?
19. (If needed) Does he [she] moan . . . scream . . . whimper occasionally . . . call you?
20. What do you do when [cite child's name] wakes up during the night?
21. What seems to work the best?
22. Have you noticed any changes in [cite child's name]'s behavior during the daytime since he [she] began to wake up at night?
23. Have you noticed any signs of physical discomfort, such as teething, earache, congestion from a cold, or general fussiness, during the day?

Table B-10 *(Continued)*

24. (If yes) What have you noticed?
25. Have there been any changes recently in your home or in the child's routine related to bedtime?
26. (If yes) Tell me about these changes.
27. Does anyone share [cite child's name]'s bedroom?
28. (If yes) Who shares his [her] bedroom?
29. Does [cite child's name] have any difficulties falling asleep?
30. (If yes) Tell me about them.
31. Does [cite child's name] have his [her] own bed?
32. (If no) With whom does [cite child's name] sleep?
33. When does [cite child's name] usually go to bed?
34. How do you know when [cite child's name] is tired?

Toddler's/Preschooler's Personal-Social-Affective Behavior
(if toddler/preschooler is focus of interview)
1. Does [cite child's name] take turns?
2. Can [cite child's name] point to body parts on a doll?
3. Can [cite child's name] name his [her] own body parts?
4. Can [cite child's name] identify himself [herself] in a mirror?
5. Does [cite child's name] use words like *I, me,* and *them* correctly?
6. Does [cite child's name] feed himself [herself]?
7. Does [cite child's name] use a spoon or a fork?
8. Does [cite child's name] imitate things you do, like sweeping the floor and making the bed?
9. Does [cite child's name] play with a doll and do such things as feed, hug, and scold the doll?
10. How does [cite child's name] handle common dangers, such as hot stoves, electrical outlets, sharp knives, crossing the street, and the like?
11. How does [cite child's name] behave when he [she] plays with another child?
12. Does [cite child's name] share his [her] toys?
    (If yes, go to question 13; if no, go to question 15.)
13. What toys does he [she] share?
14. And with whom does he [she] share them?
    (Go to question 16.)
15. What have you done to help him [her] learn how to share?
16. Does [cite child's name] have temper tantrums?
    (If yes, go to question 17; if no, go to question 26.)
17. Tell me about the temper tantrums.
18. What sets off the temper tantrums?
19. Are the temper tantrums more frequent at certain times of the day than at other times?
20. (If yes) Tell me about these times.
21. Where do the temper tantrums occur?
22. What happens when [cite child's name] has a temper tantrum?
23. How do you feel about the temper tantrums?
24. How do you deal with [cite child's name]'s temper tantrums?
25. Which methods seem to be most effective?
26. How does [cite child's name] get along with other children?
27. Is [cite child's name] stubborn at times?
    (If yes, go to question 28; if no, go to question 31.)
28. In what way is [cite child's name] stubborn?
29. How do you handle his [her] stubbornness?
30. Has it worked?
31. Does [cite child's name] hit, bite, or try to hurt other children?
    (If yes, go to question 32; if no, go to question 36.)

32. How does he [she] hurt other children?
33. Why do you think he [she] acts this way?
34. How do you handle these situations?
35. What seems to work best?
36. Does [cite child's name] have any fears?
    (If yes, go to question 37; if no, go to question 46.)
37. What fears does he [she] have?
38. What kinds of situations tend to make [cite child's name] fearful?
39. Are these unfamiliar situations or familiar ones?
40. What does [cite child's name] do when he [she] is fearful?
41. How long has [cite child's name] been fearful?
42. What do you do when [cite child's name] shows fear?
43. How does it work?
44. Have you found that some methods are more effective than others?
45. (If yes) Tell me about them.
46. How do you handle [cite child's name]'s demands for your attention?
47. What situations seem to cause [cite child's name] to demand your attention?
48. What kinds of things does [cite child's name] seem to want when he [she] asks for attention?
49. Does he [she] demand your attention for a long time, or will a short time do?
50. Have you noticed any changes during the past few months in how much attention [cite child's name] has demanded?
51. (If yes) Tell me about the changes you've noticed.
52. How does [cite child's name] react when he [she] meets new people?
53. How do you feel about [cite child's name]'s behavior when he [she] meets new people?
54. (If needed) Is there anything you can do to make [cite child's name] more comfortable when he [she] meets new people?
55. When does [cite child's name] cry?
56. What do you do when [cite child's name] cries?
57. Why do you think [cite child's name] cries?
58. (If needed) When [cite child's name] cries, does it usually mean that something is really wrong or is it that something is bothering him [her] only a little bit and he [she] wants attention?
59. How can you tell the difference between the types of crying [cite child's name] does?
60. Does [cite child's name] play with his [her] genitals?
    (If yes, go to question 61; if no, go to question 66.)
61. When does [cite child's name] play with his [her] genitals?
62. (If needed) Does this occur during any particular situation[s]?
63. (If yes) In what situation[s] does he [she] play with his [her] genitals?
64. How do you feel about his [her] doing this?
65. And what do you do when you find [cite child's name] playing with his [her] genitals?
66. What kinds of activities does [cite child's name] seem to be interested in?
67. What does [cite child's name] like to do on his [her] own?
68. Are you having any difficulties getting [cite child's name] to perform daily routines, such as washing hands . . . dressing . . . picking up clothes . . . putting away toys?

(Continued)

Table B-10 *(Continued)*

69. Does [cite child's name] let you do things *with* him [her]?
70. Tell me about that.
71. Does [cite child's name] let you do things *for* him [her]?
72. Tell me about that.
73. How does [cite child's name] get along with adults?
74. Is [cite child's name] interested in people?
75. Tell me more about that.
76. How does [cite child's name] spend his [her] time during a typical weekday?
77. And on weekends, how does [cite child's name] spend his [her] time?
78. How does [cite child's name] feel about himself [herself]?
79. (If there are other siblings in family) How does [cite child's name] compare with his [her] sisters and brothers?
80. Is [cite child's name] interested in animals?
81. Tell me more about that.
82. Is [cite child's name] generally interested in things?
83. (If no) Tell me more about that.
84. At what time of the day is [cite child's name] most active?
85. When [cite child's name] needs to do things, like get dressed or put things away, does he [she] do them too fast, too slowly, or at just about the right pace?
    (If too fast, go to question 86; if too slowly, go to question 90; otherwise, go to question 94.)
86. What happens when you try to make [cite child's name] move more slowly?
87. What other things does [cite child's name] do too fast?
88. (If needed) Does [cite child's name] eat too fast . . . get ready for bed too fast?
89. Are you concerned that [cite child's name] may be hyperactive?
    (Go to question 94.)
90. What happens when you try to make [cite child's name] move faster?
91. What other things does [cite child's name] do slowly?
92. (If needed) Does he [she] eat slowly . . . get ready for bed slowly?
93. Are you concerned that [cite child's name] may be generally slow?
94. How does [cite child's name] react when his [her] play is interrupted?
95. How does [cite child's name] let you know when he [she] wants to keep doing an activity longer than you had planned?
96. Does [cite child's name] have any unusual behaviors?
    (If yes, go to question 97; if no, end this section.)
97. What unusual behaviors does [cite child's name] have?
98. How often does [cite child's name] exhibit [cite unusual behavior]?
99. What is most likely to bring on [cite unusual behavior]?
100. What situations seem to make [cite child's name]'s [cite unusual behavior] worse?
101. What do you do at these times?
102. What works best?
103. Is there any connection between what [cite child's name] eats and [cite unusual behavior]?
104. How do you feel about taking care of [cite child's name] when he [she] behaves in this way?

Toddler's/Preschooler's Play and Cognitive Ability (if toddler/preschooler is focus of interview)

1. How does [cite child's name] occupy himself [herself] during the day?
2. What does [cite child's name] like to play?
3. How would you describe [cite child's name]'s play?
4. (If needed) Is it quiet play . . . active play? . . . Does he [she] build things . . . color?
5. What toys or other objects does [cite child's name] play with?
6. What kinds of things does [cite child's name] do with the toys or other objects that he [she] plays with?
7. What toys seem to be particularly interesting to [cite child's name]?
8. And how does [cite child's name] play with the toys he [she] especially likes?
9. Is [cite child's name] interested in exploring objects?
10. (If yes) Tell me more about what [cite child's name] does.
11. What happens when [cite child's name] is left on his [her] own to play?
12. How long does [cite child's name] usually stay with an activity?
13. Does [cite child's name] seem to play better at certain times of the day than at others?
14. What is particularly distracting to [cite child's name]?
15. In what situations does [cite child's name] get the most out of his [her] play?
16. How does [cite child's name] let you know what he [she] is interested in?
17. Tell me more about that.
18. (If relevant) Can [cite child's name] find his [her] toys when they are mixed up with those of his [her] brothers and sisters?
19. Is [cite child's name] more interested in watching others play than in playing himself [herself]?
20. Do you think that [cite child's name]'s play is about the same as that of other children of his [her] age?
21. (If no) In what way is it different?
22. What changes have you noticed over the last few months in the way [cite child's name] plays?
23. Where does [cite child's name] play at home?
24. (If needed) Does he [she] play in different rooms?
25. Does he [she] have enough space to play?
26. (If no) What have you done to get more space for [cite child's name] to play in?
27. How long does [cite child's name] stay in his [her] own room to play?
28. Is this amount of time OK with you?
29. Does [cite child's name] prefer playing alone or with someone?
30. With whom does he [she] like to play?
31. Does [cite child's name] engage in any pretend play?
32. (If needed) Does he [she] play house . . . play school . . . play doctor?
33. Does [cite child's name] have any imaginary friends?
34. (If yes) Who are they?
35. How does [cite child's name]'s play change when an adult plays with him [her]?
36. What kinds of things does [cite child's name] like to do with you?

Table B-10 *(Continued)*

37. How does [cite child's name] react when you try to show him [her] how to use a toy?
38. How much fun is [cite child's name] to play with?
39. Have you ever wondered whether [cite child's name] enjoys playing with you?
40. Tell me about that.
41. How much time do you spend playing with [cite child's name]?
42. Does having [cite child's name]'s toys underfoot in the house bother you?
43. (If yes) Tell me about that.
44. Does [cite child's name] look at you when you try to talk to or play with him [her]?
45. (If no) What does he [she] do instead?
46. Is [cite child's name] responsive to you?
47. Is [cite child's name] responsive to other adults?
48. Does [cite child's name] like physical contact, such as when you gently touch his [her] face, hands, and arms?
49. (If no) Tell me about that.
50. Is there any physical activity that [cite child's name] seems to enjoy especially?
51. Does [cite child's name] like doing the same activity over and over again?
52. Does [cite child's name] like to spin objects?
53. (If yes) Tell me about that.
54. Does [cite child's name] play outdoors?
    (If yes, go to question 55; if no, go to question 60.)
55. Where does he [she] play outdoors?
56. (If needed) Do you take [cite child's name] to any parks or playgrounds?
57. How does [cite child's name] react when you take him [her] outdoors to play?
58. Does [cite child's name] behave differently outdoors than indoors?
59. (If yes) In what way?
60. Does [cite child's name] seem to be in constant motion?
61. (If yes) How do you handle that?
62. Tell me about [cite child's name]'s ability to pay attention.
63. Does [cite child's name] like to put puzzles together?
64. Tell me about that.
65. Can [cite child's name] construct things out of blocks?
66. Tell me about that.

Toddler's/Preschooler's Adjustment to Caregiving Situation
(if toddler/preschooler is focus of interview)

1. Do you leave [cite child's name] at a day care center, at preschool, at somebody's house, or at your house with a sitter during any part of the week?
   (If yes, go to question 2; if no, go to question 20.)
2. Where do you leave him [her]?
3. Tell me about the reason you leave [cite child's name] there.
4. How do you feel about leaving [cite child's name]?
5. (If day care center, preschool, or someone's house) How did you find out about [cite place where child is cared for]?
6. Are you satisfied with the way [cite child's name] is cared for there?
7. How is [cite child's name] getting along at [cite place where child is cared for]?

8. (If needed) Is [cite child's name] having any problems there?
9. (If yes) Tell me about them.
10. (If needed) How does [cite child's name] get along with the caregiver[s]?
11. (If needed) How does he [she] get along with the other children?
12. Do you have a chance to talk regularly about [cite child's name] with the person[s] taking care of him [her]?
13. How long does it take you to get to [cite place where child is cared for]?
14. How does [cite child's name] act when you leave him [her] at [cite place where child is cared for]?
    (If behavior is not satisfactory, go to question 15; if behavior is satisfactory, go to question 19.)
15. How do you feel when [cite child's name] acts this way?
16. Does [cite child's name] always show that he [she] is upset in the same way?
17. What have you done to try to help him [her]?
18. Does it help?
19. How does [cite child's name] react when you pick him [her] up from [cite place where child is cared for]?
20. How do you feel about taking [cite child's name] out in public?
21. How does [cite child's name] behave when he [she] is outside the home?
22. How does [cite child's name] react when you take him [her] to a friend's home?
    (If there are problems or concerns, go to question 23; otherwise, end section.)
23. How do you handle these problems?
24. What seems to work best?

Toddler's/Preschooler's Self-Help Skills
(if toddler/preschooler is focus of interview)

1. Is [cite child's name] toilet trained?
   (If yes, go to question 2; if no, go to question 5.)
2. How old was [cite child's name] when he [she] was toilet trained?
3. Does [cite child's name] have toilet accidents once in a while?
   (If yes, go to question 4; if no, go to question 13.)
4. Tell me about the toilet accidents [cite child's name] has.
   (Go to question 13.)
5. Have you begun to toilet train [cite child's name]?
   (If no, go to question 6; if yes, go to question 7.)
6. At what age do you think [cite child's name] should be toilet trained?
   (Go to question 13.)
7. Tell me how it's going.
   (Ask questions 8 to 12, as needed.)
8. Are you having any problems with the toilet training?
9. (If yes) Tell me about the problems you're having.
10. What training methods are you using?
11. What did [cite child's name] do to make you think that he [she] was ready to be toilet trained?
12. (If needed) Did he [she] come to you to be changed? . . . Was he [she] interested in watching others in the bathroom . . . imitating others . . . staying dry?

Table B-10 *(Continued)*

13. Tell me about how [cite child's name] dresses and undresses himself [herself].
    (Ask questions 14 to 17, as needed.)
14. What clothing can [cite child's name] put on?
15. What clothing can [cite child's name] take off?
16. (If child is older than 4 years) Can [cite child's name] tie his [her] shoes?
17. How much supervision does [cite child's name] need in dressing and undressing?
18. Tell me about [cite child's name]'s bath time.
19. (If needed) Does [cite child's name] wash himself [herself]?
20. Does [cite child's name] wash his [her] hands when necessary, such as when he [she] is dirty or after he [she] goes to the toilet?
21. (If no) Tell me about [cite child's name]'s not washing his [her] hands when necessary.
22. Does [cite child's name] brush his [her] teeth?
23. (If no) Tell me about [cite child's name]'s not brushing his [her] teeth.
24. Does [cite child's name] brush or comb his [her] hair?
25. (If no) Tell me about [cite child's name]'s not brushing or combing his [her] hair.

Toddler's/Preschooler's Language, Communication, Speech, Comprehension, and Problem-Solving Skills
(if toddler/preschooler is focus of interview)
1. Does [cite child's name] talk?
   (If yes, go to question 2; if no, go to question 20.)
2. When did [cite child's name] begin to talk?
3. Does [cite child's name] have any problems with his [her] speech?
4. (If yes) Tell me about [cite child's name]'s problems with speech.
5. (If needed) Is [cite child's name] having problems speaking clearly . . . forming grammatically correct sentences . . . saying the right words in order . . . stuttering?
6. About how many words can [cite child's name] say?
7. What kinds of words does [cite child's name] usually say?
8. Does [cite child's name] have any pet phrases?
9. (If yes) What are they?
10. Does [cite child's name] use action words?
11. Can [cite child's name] speak in sentences?
12. (If yes) How old was [cite child's name] when he [she] first combined words to make sentences?
13. Did [cite child's name] have any problems with speech in the past?
14. (If yes) Tell me about that.
15. Do you understand what [cite child's name] says?
16. (If no) Tell me more about that.
17. Do other people understand [cite child's name]'s speech?
18. (If no) Tell me more about that.
19. What kinds of things does [cite child's name] talk about?
    (Go to question 25.)
20. How is [cite child's name] able to tell you about what he [she] needs?
21. (If needed) Does [cite child's name] make any sounds?
22. (If yes) Tell me about the sounds that [cite child's name] makes.
23. Did [cite child's name] ever talk?

24. (If yes) Tell me about when he [she] talked.
25. Does [cite child's name] understand most things that are said to him [her]?
26. (If no) What problems does [cite child's name] have in understanding things that are said to him [her]?
27. Can [cite child's name] follow directions?
28. (If no) What problems does [cite child's name] have in following directions?

Toddler's/Preschooler's Motor Skills
(if toddler/preschooler is focus of interview)
1. Tell me about [cite child's name]'s ability to do things that require small motor movements, such as his [her] ability to grasp things, pick up things, hold onto things, and release things.
2. (If needed) Tell me about [cite child's name]'s ability to open doors . . . turn pages in a book . . . use scissors to cut paper . . . fold paper . . . build objects with blocks . . . use pencils . . . use crayons . . . draw . . . copy circles or squares . . . screw things . . . unscrew things . . . button . . . tie shoes . . . use a zipper . . . play with Lego-type toys . . . print letters.
3. What types of toys are most frustrating to [cite child's name]?
4. Tell me about [cite child's name]'s other motor skills, such as his [her] ability to walk, run, jump, skip, and play ball.
5. (If needed) Tell me about [cite child's name]'s ability to walk up steps . . . walk down steps . . . hop . . . roll a ball . . . throw a ball . . . climb . . . ride a tricycle . . . use a slide . . . use a jungle gym.

Questions for Pregnant Mother About Toddler's/Preschooler's Acceptance of the Arrival of a New Baby
(if toddler/preschooler is focus of interview)
1. How do you think [cite child's name] will handle the coming of the new baby?
2. What do you think will be most difficult for [cite child's name] to handle?
3. What might you do to help [cite child's name] adjust to the new baby?
4. Have you told [cite child's name] about the new baby?
   (If yes, ask questions 5 and 6; if no, end this section.)
5. What did you say to him [her]?
6. And how did he [she] react?

Questions About the Family Environment and Family Relationships
1. I'd now like to ask you about life at home. OK?
2. How does [cite child's name] get along with you?
3. (For older child) How did [cite child's name] get along with you when he [she] was younger?
4. Who else lives at home?
   (If father or other adult male is in the picture, go to question 5; otherwise, go to directions before question 7.)
5. How does [cite child's name] get along with [cite name of father or other adult male]?
6. With whom does [cite child's name] get along better, you or [cite name of father or other adult male]?
   (If child has siblings, go to question 7; otherwise, go to directions before question 12.)

Table B-10 *(Continued)*

7. How does [cite child's name] get along with his [her] sisters and brothers?
   (Ask questions 8 to 11, as needed.)
8. What situations tend to cause conflict between [cite child's name] and the other children?
9. What do you do when the children argue?
10. What have you found that works?
11. What do you think would happen if you let the children settle their arguments themselves—except when you thought that one child might hurt another?
    (If mother has a husband or partner, go to question 12; otherwise, go to question 14.)
12. How are you getting along with your husband [partner]?
13. (If needed) Is there anything bothering you about your relationship with your husband [partner]?
14. Do any relatives live in your home?
    (If yes, go to question 15; if no, go to question 18.)
15. How are things working out with your mother-in-law [father-in-law, mother, father, etc.] staying at your home?
16. Are there any problems with having her [him, them] there?
17. How does [cite child's name] get along with her [him, them]?
18. Do any relatives live nearby?
    (If yes, go to question 19; if no, end section.)
19. Where do they live?
20. How does [cite child's name] get along with them?

Questions to Evaluate Parent's Ability to Set Limits and Discipline Child
1. How do you make [cite child's name] mind you?
2. Do you feel that you are spoiling [cite child's name]?
3. Tell me about your answer.
4. Does anyone tell you that you are spoiling [cite child's name]?
5. (If yes) Tell me about that.
6. Do you believe that [cite child's name] acts spoiled?
7. (If yes) In what ways does he [she] act spoiled?
8. Do you ever give in to [cite child's name]?
   (If yes, go to question 9; if no, go to question 14.)
9. Give me some examples of how you give in to [cite child's name].
10. How often do you give in to [cite child's name]?
11. How do you feel about giving in?
12. Which things are you sorry you gave in to?
13. Which of the things you gave in to do you feel are disruptive to the family?
14. Do you believe that you are too easy with [cite child's name], too strict, or just about right?
15. Tell me about that.
16. Which of [cite child's name]'s behaviors are particularly irritating to you?
17. In which areas would you most like to set limits?
18. What things won't you let [cite child's name] do?
19. Overall, how satisfied are you with [cite child's name]'s behavior?
20. Are there times when [cite child's name] doesn't mind you or gets into trouble?
    (If yes, go to question 21; if no, go to question 32.)

21. Tell me about these times.
22. (If needed) What kind of trouble does [cite child's name] get into?
23. What do you do when [cite child's name] doesn't mind or gets into trouble?
24. (If relevant) How does [cite child's name] react when he [she] is punished?
25. Which methods of discipline work best?
26. Which methods don't work?
27. How do you feel when you have to discipline [cite child's name]?
28. What problems are you most concerned about?
29. What does [cite child's name] do that makes you most angry?
30. Does [cite child's name] usually understand what is expected of him [her]?
31. How do you expect [cite child's name] to behave?
32. What does [cite child's name] do that leads you to think that he [she] can live up to your expectations?
    (If the child's father or stepfather or any other adult male lives at home or has visitation rights, go to question 33, substituting the appropriate name for "father" as necessary; otherwise, end this section.)
33. What about [cite child's name] makes his [her] father most angry?
34. What does his [her] father discipline him [her] for?
35. How does his [her] father discipline him [her]?
36. Does his method work?
37. How does [cite child's name]'s father feel when he has to discipline him [her]?
38. How does [cite child's name] respond to his [her] father's discipline?
39. Do you and [cite child's name]'s father agree about how to discipline him [her]?
40. (If no) How do you handle the disagreements?
41. How do you feel about what [cite child's name]'s father does when he is angry with him [her]?
42. Do you do anything about your feelings?

Environmental Safeguards and Neighborhood
1. What have you done to make the house safe for [cite child's name] and to keep him [her] from getting into things?
2. (If needed) Have you put covers on electric outlets? . . . Have you put safety latches on any drawers or cupboards that contain cleaning products or other poisons, knives, guns, or other dangerous things?
3. Does [cite child's name] get into things at home that he [she] is not supposed to?
   (If yes, go to question 4; if no, go to question 8.)
4. What does he [she] get into?
5. Have you been teaching [cite child's name] not to get into these things?
6. (If yes) How has it been going?
7. How do you feel when [cite child's name] wants to get into everything he [she] sees?
8. Does [cite child's name] ever break things?
   (If yes, go to question 9; if no, go to question 11)
9. How do you feel when this happens?

(Continued)

Table B-10 *(Continued)*

10. And what do you do when he [she] breaks things?
11. Does [cite child's name] seem to understand when you tell him [her] not to touch objects?
12. (If yes) Do you think that he [she] can remember not to get into things?
13. Which objects seem to be particularly attractive to [cite child's name]?
14. Why do you think [cite child's name] likes them so much?
15. How do you stop [cite child's name] when he [she] is about to do something dangerous?
16. How long have you lived in your present house [apartment]?
17. How do you like living there?
18. (If needed) Tell me about that.
19. How do you get along with your neighbors?
20. (If needed) Tell me about that.
21. Are there any problems in the neighborhood?
22. (If yes) Tell me about them.

Mother's Resources and Occupation
1. Do you have any living relatives?
   (If yes, go to question 2; if no, go to question 8.)
2. Tell me who your living relatives are.
3. How often do you see your relatives?
4. And how do you get along?
5. Do they give you help when you need it?
   (If yes, go to question 6; if no, go to question 8.)
6. Which relatives give you help when you need it?
7. How do they help you?
8. Do you have any close friends?
   (If yes, go to question 9; if no, go to question 12.)
9. Tell me about them.
10. Have you ever turned to them for help?
11. (If yes) And how did they respond?
12. To whom would you turn for help if your family needed it?
13. Do you have someone to talk to when you have a problem or are feeling frustrated and upset?
14. Tell me about it.
15. Do you have medical insurance?
16. (If no) How do you plan to take care of any hospitalizations?
17. Have you been in contact with any social agencies?
18. (If yes) Tell me about your contacts.
19. Are you a member of a religious group?
20. (If yes) Tell me about the group.
21. Do you have a job outside of the home?
   (If yes, go to question 22; if no, go to instructions following question 24.)
22. What is your occupation?
23. How do you like your job?
24. (If needed) Tell me more about that.
   (If father is in the picture, go to question 25; otherwise, end this section.)
25. What is [cite child's name]'s father's occupation?
26. And how does [cite child's name]'s father like his job?
27. (If needed) Tell me more about that.

Mother Who Stays at Home
1. What do you enjoy about being a full-time parent?
2. What do you find most difficult about being a full-time parent?

3. What made you decide to be a full-time parent?
4. (If needed) What were you doing before your child was [children were] born?
5. Are you occasionally able to get out of the house with [cite child's name]?
6. Are you able to get some time for yourself on a regular basis?
7. Tell me about your answer.
8. (If needed) Do you get a babysitter occasionally and go out by yourself or with a friend [with your husband]?
9. Do you know other parents with young children in the neighborhood?
10. (If yes) Have you worked out any cooperative babysitting arrangements with them?

Spending Time with Child (for mother who works)
1. How much time do you spend with [cite child's name]?
2. How do you feel about the amount of time you spend with [cite child's name]?
3. How do you spend time with [cite child's name] before you go to work?
4. And when you come home, how do you spend time together?
5. And on weekends, how do you spend time together?
6. Which times seem to be the most enjoyable for you and [cite child's name]?
7. Which times seem to be the most rushed and tense for you and [cite child's name]?
8. How do you feel about taking care of [cite child's name] when you return home from work?
9. What do you usually do when you pick [cite child's name] up after work?
10. Do you have any time alone when you come home after work?
11. How do you deal with [cite child's name] if he [she] cries and fusses in the evening?
12. How do you get [cite child's name] to relax when you get home after work?
13. How do you get to relax when you get home after work?

Family Medical History
1. I'd like to know about your health history. Have you had any serious illnesses, accidents, or diseases?
2. (If yes) Tell me about them.
3. (As needed) How was the diagnosis established? . . . Tell me about the course of your illness, its treatment, and the prognosis.
   (If father is in the picture, go to question 4; otherwise, go to question 7 if child has siblings or end section if child does not have siblings.)
4. And how about [cite child's name]'s father—has he had any serious illnesses, accidents, or diseases?
5. (If yes) Tell me about them.
6. (As needed) How was the diagnosis established? . . . Tell me about the course of his illness, its treatment, and the prognosis.
   (If child has siblings, go to question 7; otherwise, end section.)

Table B-10 *(Continued)*

7. And [cite child's name]'s sisters and brothers—have they had any serious illnesses, accidents, or diseases?
8. (If yes) Tell me about them.
9. (As needed) How was the diagnosis established? . . . Tell me about the course of the illness, its treatment, and the prognosis.

General Questions About Infant or Toddler/Preschooler and Mother

1. We've covered a lot of areas. Before we finish, I have just a few more questions I'd like to ask you. OK?
2. What experiences did you have with young children before you had a child?
3. What do you like about being a parent?
4. What do you dislike about being a parent?
5. Is being a parent what you expected?
6. Tell me about that.
7. (If needed) What about being a parent is as you expected? What is different from what you expected?
8. What would make it easier for you to be a parent?
9. What about [cite child's name] gives you the most pleasure?
10. What kinds of things do you do together that are fun?
11. Do you have quiet times when you relax together?
12. (If yes) Tell me about them.
    (If mother has other children, go to question 13; otherwise, go to the instructions before question 15.)
13. Do you spend about the same amount of time with [cite child's name] as you do with the other children?
14. (If no) Tell me about that.
    (If child's father or stepfather or any other adult male lives at home or has visitation rights, go to question 15, substituting the appropriate name for "father" as necessary; otherwise, go to question 19.)
15. What kinds of things does [cite child's name] do with his [her] father?

16. How much time do they spend together?
    (If father has other children, go to question 17; otherwise, go to question 19.)
17. Is this about the same amount of time as he spends with the other children in the family?
18. (If no) Tell me about that.
19. In general, does [cite child's name] act like other children of his [her] age?
20. (If no) In what way doesn't he [she] act like other children of his [her] age?
21. Is there anything else about [cite child's name] that you would like to tell me?
22. (If yes) Go ahead.
23. Is [cite child's name] having any problems that we didn't discuss?
24. (If yes) What are they?
25. (If not asked previously) Do you have any reason to think that [cite child's name] is under any particular stress at this time?
26. (If yes) Tell me about that.
27. (If not asked previously) Have there been any changes in the home or in the child's routine recently?
28. (If yes) Tell me about that.
29. Have you discussed your concerns about [cite child's name]'s problems with a health care provider?
30. (If yes) What did the health care provider say?
31. Is there anything else about your role as a parent that you would like to tell me?
32. (If yes) Go ahead.
33. Do you have any questions that you would like to ask me?
34. (If yes) Go ahead.
35. Thank you for talking with me. If you have any questions or if you want to talk to me, please call me. Here is my card.

Note. This table is designed for interviewing mothers about their young children. With some alterations, it also could be used to interview fathers or other caregivers. Use Table B-13 in this Appendix to interview a parent who has a child with a pervasive developmental disorder.
Source: Adapted from Bromwich (1981) and Ferholt (1980).

Table B-11
Semistructured Interview Questions for a Parent Regarding a Brief Screening of Her or His Preschool-Age Child

1. Hi! I'm Dr. [Ms., Mr.] _____. I'd like to talk to you about [cite child's name]. Tell me a little bit about him [her].
2. Please tell me what [cite child's name] has been doing and learning lately.
3. How well do you think [cite child's name] is doing now?
4. Do you have any concerns about [cite child's name]'s health?
5. (If yes) What are your concerns?
6. Are you concerned about [cite child's name]'s general physical coordination or his [her] ability to run, climb, or do other motor activities?
7. (If yes) What are your concerns?
8. How well does [cite child's name] seem to understand things that are said to him [her]?
9. How well does [cite child's name] let you know what he [she] needs?
10. How would you describe [cite child's name]'s speech?
11. Does [cite child's name] speak in sentences?
12. Does [cite child's name] have any unusual speech behaviors?
    (If yes, go to question 13; if no, go to question 15.)
13. Tell me what seems to be unusual about his [her] speech.
14. (If needed) Is [cite child's name]'s speech intelligible?
15. Do you have any concerns about [cite child's name]'s behavior?
16. (If yes) What are your concerns?
17. How well does [cite child's name] get along with other children . . . with adults . . . with his [her] brothers or sisters . . . with you [you and your spouse]?
18. How well does [cite child's name] feed himself [herself] . . . dress himself [herself] . . . go to the toilet by himself [herself]?
19. Is there anything else about [cite child's name] that you wonder or worry about?
20. Did [cite child's name] have any difficulties during his [her] first two years of life?
21. (If yes) Tell me about that.
22. Does [cite child's name] have any problems that we did not cover?
23. Do you have any questions that you would like to ask me?
24. (If yes) Go ahead.
25. Thank you for talking with me. If you have any questions or if you want to talk to me, please call me. Here is my card.

Note. You can use probing questions to follow up on any problem areas mentioned by the parent.
Source: Adapted from Lichtenstein and Ireton (1984).

Table B-12
Semistructured Interview Questions for a Parent Regarding How Her or His Preschool-Age or Elementary School–Age Child Spends a Typical Day

Introduction

1. Hi! I'm Dr. [Ms., Mr.] _____. I'd like to know how [cite child's name] spends a typical day. I'll be asking you about how [cite child's name] spends the morning, afternoon, and evening. OK? Let's begin.

Early Morning

2. What time does [cite child's name] usually wake up?
3. Does [cite child's name] wake up by himself [herself]?
4. How do you know [cite child's name] is awake?
5. What does [cite child's name] do after he [she] wakes up?
6. Where are the other members of the family at that time?
7. What is [cite child's name]'s mood when he [she] wakes up?
8. How does [cite child's name] get along with other members of the family right after he [she] wakes up?
9. When does [cite child's name] get dressed?
10. Does [cite child's name] dress himself [herself]?
11. (If no) What kind of help does [cite child's name] need?
    (Go to question 13.)
12. Can [cite child's name] manage buttons . . . manage zippers . . . tie his [her] shoes?
13. Does [cite child's name] choose his [her] own clothes?
14. Are there any conflicts over dressing?
15. (If yes) Tell me about that.

Breakfast

16. Does [cite child's name] usually eat breakfast?
    (If yes, go to question 17; if no, go to question 22.)
17. When does [cite child's name] usually eat breakfast?
18. What does [cite child's name] usually have for breakfast?
19. With whom does [cite child's name] eat breakfast?
20. Are there any problems at breakfast?
21. (If yes) Tell me about them.
    (Go to question 23.)
22. Tell me about [cite child's name]'s not eating breakfast.

Morning

23. What does [cite child's name] do after breakfast [in the morning]?
24. (If needed) Does [cite child's name] go to a day care center or preschool, a regular school, or a sitter's house, or does he [she] stay at home?
    (For children who stay at home, go to question 25; for children who go to a sitter's house, go to question 30; for children who go to a day care center or preschool, go to question 43; for children who go to a regular school, go to question 78.)

Stays at Home

25. Who is at home with [cite child's name]?
26. (If parent stays at home with child) How do you feel about being at home with him [her] during the day?
27. How does [cite child's name] spend his [her] time at home?
28. Does [cite child's name] have any problems at home during the day?
29. (If yes) Tell me about them.
    (Go to question 107.)

Goes to Sitter's House

30. Tell me about the sitter who watches [cite child's name].

31. How long does it take you to get to the sitter's house?
32. What time does [cite child's name] go there?
33. What time does [cite child's name] leave the sitter's?
34. How many other children are at the sitter's house when [cite child's name] is there?
35. (If one or more children) Tell me about the other children.
36. (If needed) How old are the other children at the sitter's?
37. How does [cite child's name] like it at the sitter's?
38. What kinds of things does [cite child's name] do there?
39. How is [cite child's name] doing at the sitter's?
40. Are you satisfied with [cite child's name]'s care at the sitter's?
41. (If no) Tell me about why you're not satisfied.
42. What changes have you noticed in [cite child's name]'s behavior since he [she] has been at the sitter's?
    (Go to question 107.)

Goes to Day Care Center or Preschool

43. Tell me about the day care center [preschool] that [cite child's name] goes to.
44. How long does it take you to get there?
45. What time does [cite child's name] go there?
46. What time does [cite child's name] leave the center [preschool]?
47. How old are the other children at the center [preschool]?
48. How many children are in [cite child's name]'s group?
49. And how many caregivers are in [cite child's name]'s group?
50. How does [cite child's name] like it at the center [preschool]?
51. What kinds of things does [cite child's name] do there?
52. How is [cite child's name] doing at the center [preschool]?
53. Are you satisfied with the center [preschool]?
54. (If no) Tell me about why you're not satisfied.
55. What changes have you noticed in [cite child's name]'s behavior since he [she] has been at the center [preschool]?
56. How did you decide to send [cite child's name] to this center [preschool]?
57. Have you met with [cite child's name]'s teacher?
58. (If yes) Tell me what you learned in talking with the teacher.
    (Go to question 61.)
59. Do you believe that you need to meet with [cite child's name]'s teacher?
60. (If yes) Tell me about why you want to meet with [cite child's name]'s teacher.
61. Do you participate in any activities at the center [preschool]?
62. (If yes) Tell me about them.
63. Is [cite child's name] having any problems at the center [preschool]?
    (If yes, go to question 64; if no, go to question 107.)
64. Tell me about [cite child's name]'s problem[s].
65. What is being done about it [them]?
66. Is anything being accomplished?
67. (If needed) Have you discussed the problem[s] with the teacher?
68. (If answer to question 67 is yes) What did the teacher say?
69. How do you feel about how the center [preschool] is handling the problem[s]?

(Continued)

70. Has [cite child's name] had problems in a center [preschool] before?
(If yes, go to question 71; if no, go to question 74.)
71. Tell me about them.
72. What did you do about the problems then?
73. How were the problems resolved?
74. (If relevant) Have any of your other children had problems in a center [preschool]?
75. (If answer to question 74 is yes) Tell me about that.
76. Is there anything you would like to ask me about [cite child's name]'s problem[s] at the center [preschool]?
77. Is there anything you think I might do to help you with [cite child's name]'s problem[s] at the center [preschool]?
(Go to question 107.)

Goes to Regular School
78. Tell me about [cite child's name]'s school.
79. How is [cite child's name] doing at school?
80. What are [cite child's name]'s best subjects?
81. What are his [her] poorest subjects?
82. What activities does [cite child's name] like best at school?
83. How does [cite child's name] get along with the other children?
84. How does [cite child's name] get along with the teachers?
85. Are you satisfied with the school?
86. (If no) Tell me about that.
87. How did you decide to send [cite child's name] to this school?
88. Have you met with [cite child's name]'s teacher?
89. (If yes) Tell me what you learned in talking with the teacher.
(Go to question 92.)
90. Do you believe that you need to meet with [cite child's name]'s teacher?
91. (If yes) Tell me about why you want to meet with [cite child's name]'s teacher.
92. Are you involved in any school activities?
93. Tell me about them.
94. Is [cite child's name] having any problems at school?
(If yes, go to question 95; if no, go to question 101.)
95. Tell me about [cite child's name]'s problem[s].
96. What is being done about it [them]?
97. Is anything being accomplished?
98. (If needed) Have you discussed the problem[s] with the teacher?
99. (If answer to question 98 is yes) What did the teacher say?
100. How do you feel about how the school is handling the problem[s]?
101. Has [cite child's name] had problems in school before?
(If yes, go to question 102; if no, go to question 107.)
102. Tell me about them.
103. What did you do about the problems then?
104. How were the problems resolved?
105. Is there anything you would like to ask me about [cite child's name]'s problem[s] at school?
106. Is there anything you think I might do to help you with [cite child's name]'s problem[s] at school?

Lunch
107. When does [cite child's name] usually eat lunch?

108. What does [cite child's name] usually have for lunch?
109. Does [cite child's name] usually eat his [her] lunch?
110. Who eats with [cite child's name] at lunchtime?
111. Are there any problems at lunchtime?
112. (If yes) Tell me about the problems.

Afternoon
113. How does [cite child's name] spend his [her] afternoons?
114. Are there any problems in the afternoon?
115. (If yes) Tell me about them.

Related Areas
(Ask about any of the following areas, as needed.)
116. Before we get to supper and the end of the day, I'd like to ask you about [cite child's name]'s eating, friends, play activities, TV watching, and behavior outside the home. Let's first turn to [cite child's name]'s eating. OK?

Eating
117. How is [cite child's name]'s diet in general?
118. What are [cite child's name]'s likes and dislikes in food?
119. What is [cite child's name]'s behavior like when he [she] refuses to eat something?
120. How do you handle that kind of situation?
121. What does [cite child's name] usually have for snacks?
122. Are there any problems about snacks?
123. (If yes) Tell me about them.

Friends
124. Tell me about [cite child's name]'s friends.
125. (If needed) How old are they?
126. Where do the children play?
127. What do they do together?
128. How do they get along?
129. Are they able to take turns and share toys?
130. (If no) Tell me about that.
131. Who supervises them?
132. What kind of supervision do they need?

Play Activities
133. Does [cite child's name] ride a tricycle or bicycle?
134. (If yes) How well does [cite child's name] ride the tricycle [bicycle]?
135. Is [cite child's name] reckless in his [her] play?
136. (If yes) Tell me about that.
137. Does [cite child's name] have any fears about climbing?
138. (If yes) Tell me about that.
139. What are some of [cite child's name]'s favorite toys?
140. What does [cite child's name] like to do with them?
141. Is [cite child's name] able to play alone?
142. Tell me about that.

TV Watching
143. Does [cite child's name] watch television?
(If yes, go to question 144; if no, go to question 154.)
144. What TV programs does [cite child's name] watch?
145. How much time does [cite child's name] spend watching television in an average day?
146. Does anyone in the family watch television with him [her]?
147. Does [cite child's name] watch any adult shows?
148. (If yes) Which adult shows does he [she] watch?

Table B-12 *(Continued)*

149. Has [cite child's name] ever been frightened by any shows?
150. (If yes) Tell me about that.
151. How did you handle his [her] fear?
152. Do you supervise [cite child's name]'s TV viewing?
153. Tell me about that.

Behavior Outside the Home

154. I'd like to know how [cite child's name] gets along when you go out, such as to a store, friend's house, church or synagogue or mosque, or restaurant. First, does [cite child's name] go shopping with you? (If yes, go to question 155; if no, go to question 159.)
155. How does [cite child's name] behave in the stores?
156. Does [cite child's name] like to choose things to buy?
157. What happens if [cite child's name] wants things he [she] cannot have?
158. How do you handle it?
159. How does [cite child's name] behave at a friend's house?
160. And how does [cite child's name] behave at church or synagogue or mosque, if you attend?
161. And how does [cite child's name] behave if you go to a restaurant?

Supper

162. When does [cite child's name] usually eat supper?
163. What does [cite child's name] usually have for supper?
164. Does [cite child's name] usually eat all his [her] food?
165. Who eats with [cite child's name] at supper?
166. Are there any problems at suppertime?
167. (If yes) Tell me about them.

Evening

168. What does [cite child's name] usually do in the evening?
169. When does [cite child's name] usually go to bed?
170. Does [cite child's name] have any routines associated with going to bed?
171. (If yes) Tell me about them.
172. Does [cite child's name] have any problems around bedtime?
173. (If yes) Tell me about them.
174. How much sleep does [cite child's name] usually get?
175. Does [cite child's name] sleep through the night? (If no, go to question 176; if yes, go to question 179.)
176. How often does [cite child's name] wake up?
177. What does [cite child's name] do when he [she] wakes up?
178. How do you handle it?
179. Where does [cite child's name] sleep?
180. Does [cite child's name] share a room with anyone?
181. (If yes) With whom?
182. How does that arrangement work out?

Concluding Questions

183. Is there anything that we have left out about how [cite child's name] spends a typical day?
184. (If yes) Please tell me about that.
185. Is there anything that you would like to ask me?
186. (If yes) Go ahead.
187. Thank you for talking with me. If you have any questions or if you want to talk to me, please call me. Here is my card.

Source: Adapted from Ferholt (1980).

Table B-13
Semistructured Interview Questions for a Parent of a Child Who May Have an Autism Spectrum Disorder

The questions in this table primarily apply to children who are at least toddlers (ages 1 to 3 years). If the child is an infant, use only those questions that are appropriate.

Introduction

1. Hi! I'm Dr. [Ms., Mr.] _____. I'd like to get from you as complete a picture of [cite child's name]'s development as possible. OK?

Developmental History

2. Did you [the mother] experience any problems during your [her] pregnancy?
3. (If yes) Tell me about the problems.
4. Did you [the mother] experience any difficulties during labor and delivery?
5. (If yes) Tell me about those difficulties.
6. After [cite child's name] was born, did you sometimes wonder whether he [she] might have problems?
7. (If needed) Did you sometimes wonder whether he [she] might be deaf or blind?
8. (If yes) Tell me what you were concerned about.
9. Do you recall when [cite child's name] sat unassisted for the first time?
10. (If yes) When was that?
11. Do you recall how old [cite child's name] was when he [she] took his [her] first steps?
12. (If yes) When was that?
13. How would you describe [cite child's name]'s emotional responses during infancy?

Social Behavior as Infant

14. Now please tell me how [cite child's name] responded to you when he [she] was an infant.
    (Ask questions 15 to 22, as needed.)
15. Was [cite child's name] overly rigid when you held him [her]?
16. Was [cite child's name] ever overly limp when you held him [her]?
17. Did [cite child's name] seem to resist being held closely?
18. Did [cite child's name] seem indifferent to being held?
19. Did [cite child's name] look at you when you spoke to him [her]?
20. Did [cite child's name] enjoy playing peek-a-boo?
21. Was [cite child's name] content to be alone?
22. (If no) Did [cite child's name] cry and demand attention if he [she] was left alone?
23. And now please tell me how [cite child's name] responded to other adults.
    (Ask questions 24 to 27, as needed.)
24. Was [cite child's name] frightened of other people?
25. (If yes) Tell me more about that.
26. Did [cite child's name] withdraw from people?
27. (If yes) Tell me more about that.

Social Behavior as Toddler, Preschooler, or School-Age Child

28. How does [cite child's name] interact with you now?
    (Ask questions 29 to 51, as needed.)

29. Does [cite child's name] look at you while you are playing with him [her]?
30. (If no) What does he [she] do?
31. Does [cite child's name] look at you when you are talking to him [her]?
32. (If no) What does he [she] do?
33. Does [cite child's name] make direct eye contact with you?
34. Does [cite child's name] point with his [her] finger to show you things or to ask for things?
35. What does [cite child's name] do when you smile at him [her]?
36. Does [cite child's name] look through you as if you weren't there?
37. Does [cite child's name] seem to be hard to reach or in his [her] own world?
38. (If yes) Give me some examples.
39. Does [cite child's name] bring you things to show you?
40. Does [cite child's name] want you for comfort when he [she] is sick or hurt?
41. (If no) Tell me more about that.
42. Does [cite child's name] enjoy being held or cuddled?
43. Does [cite child's name] enjoy being bounced on your knee or swung?
44. Does [cite child's name] hug or kiss you back when you hug or kiss him [her]?
45. Does [cite child's name] come to you for a kiss or hug on his [her] own, without your asking him [her] to?
46. Does [cite child's name] enjoy being kissed?
47. Is [cite child's name] particular about when or how he [she] likes affection?
48. (If yes) Give me some examples of this.
49. Does [cite child's name] go limp when you hold or hug him [her]?
50. Does [cite child's name] pull away from you when you are being affectionate with him [her]?
51. And how does [cite child's name] interact with other adults? (Ask questions 52 to 57, as needed.)
52. Does [cite child's name] ignore people who try to interact with him [her]?
53. (If yes) Tell me more about that.
54. Does [cite child's name] actively avoid looking at people during interactions with them?
55. (If yes) Tell me more about that.
56. Does [cite child's name] look at people more when they are far away than when they are interacting with him [her]?
57. Does [cite child's name] make direct eye contact with people other than you?

Peer Interactions

58. Now I'd like to talk to you about how [cite child's name] gets along with other children. Please tell me about that.
    (Ask questions 59 to 68, as needed.)
59. Does [cite child's name] prefer to play alone rather than with other children?
60. Does [cite child's name] like to watch other children while they are playing?
61. Will [cite child's name] ever join in play with other children?

Table B-13 (Continued)

62. Do other children invite [cite child's name] to play with them?
63. Does [cite child's name] play games with other children in which they each take turns?
64. (If yes) What games does he [she] play with other children?
65. Does [cite child's name] enjoy playing with other children?
66. How does [cite child's name] show his [her] feelings toward other children?
67. Does [cite child's name] seem to be interested in making friends with other children?
68. (If yes) How does [cite child's name] show this interest?

Affective Responses

69. Now I'd like to ask you about [cite child's name]'s feelings. Does [cite child's name] seem to understand how others are feeling?
70. Please give me some examples.
71. Does [cite child's name] seem to understand the expressions on people's faces?
72. Is it difficult to tell what [cite child's name] is feeling from his [her] facial expressions?
73. (If yes) What makes it hard to tell?
74. Does [cite child's name] smile during his [her] favorite activities?
75. Does [cite child's name] smile, laugh, and cry when you expect him [her] to?
76. Do [cite child's name]'s moods change quickly, without warning?
77. (If yes) Please give me some examples of these changes.
78. Does [cite child's name] become very frightened of harmless things?
79. (If yes) What does he [she] become frightened of?
80. Does [cite child's name] laugh for no obvious reason?
81. Does [cite child's name] cry for no obvious reason?
82. Does [cite child's name] shed tears when he [she] cries?
83. Does [cite child's name] make unusual facial expressions?
84. (If yes) Please describe them.

Communication Ability

85. Now I'd like to talk to you about [cite child's name]'s language. Does [cite child's name] currently speak or attempt to speak?
    (If yes, go to question 86; if no, go to question 92.)
86. Tell me about his [her] speech.
87. Does [cite child's name] repeat words or phrases spoken by others?
88. Does [cite child's name] refer to himself [herself] as "you" or by his [her] name?
89. Does [cite child's name] have any problems when he [she] speaks?
90. (If yes) Tell me about those.
91. Overall, how would you describe [cite child's name]'s language abilities?
    (Go to question 100.)
92. Has he [she] ever spoken in the past?
    (If yes, go to question 93; if no, go to question 100.)
93. When did [cite child's name] speak in the past?
94. What did he [she] say?
95. How old was [cite child's name] when he [she] stopped speaking?

96. Did anything happen at the time he [she] stopped speaking?
97. (If yes) Tell me about what happened.
98. What did you think when [cite child's name] stopped speaking?
99. Tell me about that.
100. In addition to talking, there are lots of other ways that children can communicate their needs and wants, such as making sounds, pointing, or gesturing. Does [cite child's name] communicate by any other method?
101. (If yes) Tell me about that.
102. Does [cite child's name] have a range of facial expressions?
103. (If yes) Tell me about them.
104. Does [cite child's name] nod or shake his [her] head, clearly meaning yes or no?
105. Does he [she] use other gestures such as "thumbs up" to indicate success or approval?
106. Can you understand what [cite child's name] is trying to communicate?
107. Can other people understand him [her]?
108. Does [cite child's name] become frustrated when he [she] tries to communicate?
109. (If yes) What does [cite child's name] do when he [she] is frustrated?
110. Does [cite child's name] respond when you say his [her] name?
111. Does [cite child's name] understand what you say to him [her]?
112. How can you tell?
113. Does [cite child's name] seem interested in the conversations other people are having?
114. (If yes) Tell me more about that.
115. Does [cite child's name] follow simple directions, such as "Get your coat"?
116. Does [cite child's name] respond to only one word in a sentence rather than to the whole meaning of the sentence?
117. (If yes) Please give me some examples of this.
118. Does [cite child's name] take some speech literally? For example, would [cite child's name] think that the saying "It's raining cats and dogs" literally meant that cats and dogs were falling from the sky?
119. Does [cite child's name] listen to you when you read him [her] short stories?
120. Do you ever send [cite child's name] out of the room to get one object?
121. Could [cite child's name] be sent to get two or three things?
122. Can [cite child's name] follow a sequence of commands, such as "First do this, then this, then this"?
123. Can [cite child's name] understand the past tense . . . the future tense . . . the present tense?
124. Does [cite child's name] have any problems with spatial words, such as *under, in,* or *above?*
125. Does [cite child's name] understand better if instructions are sung to a tune instead of spoken?
126. Do you have to point or use gestures to help [cite child's name] understand what you say?

(Continued)

127. (If yes) Please give me some examples of what you do.
128. Does [cite child's name] understand that a nod or a shake of the head means yes or no?
129. Does [cite child's name] understand your different tones of voice?
130. Please give me some examples.
131. Does [cite child's name] understand other gestures you use?
132. Please give me some examples.
133. When you point to something, does [cite child's name] look in the direction you point?

Using Senses and Responding to Environment
134. Now I'd like to ask you about the way [cite child's name] uses his [her] senses and how he [she] responds to the environment. First, how does he [she] react to painful events, such as falling down or bumping his [her] head?
135. Is [cite child's name] overly sensitive to being touched?
136. (If yes) How does he [she] show this?
137. Does [cite child's name] examine objects by sniffing or smelling them?
138. (If yes) Please give me some examples of this.
139. Does [cite child's name] put inedible objects in his [her] mouth?
140. (If yes) What are some of the inedible objects he [she] puts in his [her] mouth?
141. Does [cite child's name] examine objects by licking or tasting them?
142. (If yes) Please give me some examples of this.
143. Is [cite child's name] overly interested in the way things feel?
144. (If yes) Tell me about this.
145. Does [cite child's name] enjoy touching or rubbing certain surfaces?
146. (If yes) Give me some examples of this.
147. Is [cite child's name] oversensitive to sounds or noises?
148. (If yes) Give me some examples of his [her] oversensitivity.
149. Does [cite child's name] cover his [her] ears at certain sounds?
150. (If yes) Please give me some examples of when he [she] does this.
151. Does [cite child's name] become agitated or upset at sudden or loud noises?
152. (If yes) Give me some examples of when this happens.
153. Does it seem to you that [cite child's name] does not hear well?
154. (If yes) Tell me more about this.
155. Does [cite child's name] ever ignore loud noises?
156. (If yes) Give me some examples of when he [she] ignores loud noises.
157. Does [cite child's name] stare into space for long periods of time?
158. (If yes) When might he [she] do this?
159. Is [cite child's name] overly interested in looking at small details or parts of objects?
160. (If yes) Please give me some examples of this.
161. Does [cite child's name] hold objects close to his [her] eyes to look at them?

162. Is [cite child's name] overly interested in watching the movements of his [her] hands or fingers?
163. Is [cite child's name] overly interested in watching objects that spin?
164. (If yes) Give me some examples of what he [she] likes to watch spin.
165. Is [cite child's name] overly interested in looking at lights or shiny objects?
166. (If yes) Give me some examples of this.
167. Is [cite child's name] overly sensitive to bright lights?
168. (If yes) Tell me more about this.
169. Does [cite child's name] look at things out of the corners of his [her] eyes?
170. (If yes) Give me some examples of this.
171. Does [cite child's name] do things without looking at what he [she] is doing?
172. (If yes) Give me some examples of what he [she] does without looking.
173. Is [cite child's name] aware of dangers, such as from hot or sharp objects?
174. Tell me about that.

Movement, Gait, and Posture
175. The next topic I'd like to cover is the way [cite child's name] moves and uses his [her] body. First, does [cite child's name] walk?
(If yes, go to question 176; if no, go to question 183.)
176. How does [cite child's name] walk?
177. (If needed) Does he [she] walk with swinging arms . . . on tip toe . . . oddly and awkwardly . . . gracefully?
178. Can [cite child's name] walk upstairs without help?
179. Can [cite child's name] walk downstairs without help?
180. Is [cite child's name] able to climb well?
181. Can [cite child's name] pedal a tricycle or a bicycle?
182. Can [cite child's name] run as well as other children of his [her] age?
183. Is [cite child's name]'s posture odd or awkward in any way?
184. (If yes) In what way is his [her] posture odd or awkward?
185. Can [cite child's name] copy other people's movements?
186. Does [cite child's name] wave goodbye?
187. Does [cite child's name] clap his [her] hands?
188. Are [cite child's name]'s movements easy, or are they stiff and awkward?
189. How easily does he [she] learn gymnastic exercises, dances, or miming games?
190. Does he [she] confuse up/down, back/front, or right/left when trying to imitate others?
191. How does he [she] behave when excited?
192. Does excitement cause [cite child's name] to move his [her] whole body, including face, arms, and legs?
193. Does [cite child's name] spin or whirl himself [herself] around for long periods of time?
194. (If yes) Tell me more about that.
195. Does [cite child's name] rock back and forth for long periods of time?
196. (If yes) Tell me more about that.
197. Does [cite child's name] move his [her] hands or fingers in unusual or repetitive ways, such as flapping or twisting them?

Table B-13 (Continued)

198. (If yes) Please give me some examples.
199. How well does [cite child's name] use his [her] fingers?
200. Tell me about that.
201. Does [cite child's name] move his [her] body in unusual or repetitive ways?
202. (If yes) Please give me some examples.
203. Would you say that [cite child's name] is more active or less active than other children of his [her] age?
204. Tell me about that.

Need for Sameness

205. Now I'd like to talk to you about [cite child's name]'s flexibility in adapting to change. Tell me how [cite child's name] responds when something out of the ordinary happens and his [her] routines must be changed.
206. Does [cite child's name] insist on certain routines or rituals, such as wearing only certain clothes or types of clothing?
207. (If yes) Tell me more about that.
208. Does [cite child's name] become upset if changes are made in his [her] daily routines?
209. (If yes) Please give me some examples of how he [she] becomes upset.
210. Does [cite child's name] become upset if his [her] belongings are moved or disturbed?
211. (If yes) Please give me some examples of how he [she] becomes upset.
212. Does [cite child's name] become upset if changes are made in the household—for example, if furniture is moved?
213. (If yes) Please give me some examples of how he [she] becomes upset.
214. Does [cite child's name] have certain favorite objects or toys that he [she] insists on carrying around?
215. (If yes) Tell me more about that.
216. Does [cite child's name] become upset when things don't look right, such as when the rug has a spot on it or books on a shelf lean to the side?
217. (If yes) Please give me some examples of this.
218. Does [cite child's name] become upset when he [she] is interrupted before he [she] has finished doing something?
219. (If yes) Give me some examples of this.
220. Does [cite child's name] become agitated or upset by new people, places, or activities?
221. (If yes) Please give me some examples of this.
222. Does [cite child's name] insist on performing certain activities over and over again?
223. (If yes) Tell me more about these activities.
224. Does [cite child's name] become upset when he [she] puts on new clothes?
225. (If yes) Tell me more about that.
226. Does [cite child's name] have certain mealtime rituals, such as eating from only one specific plate?
227. (If yes) Tell me about [cite child's name]'s mealtime rituals.
228. Does [cite child's name] have unusual food preferences, such as foods of a certain color or texture?
229. (If yes) Please give me some examples of what foods he [she] prefers.

Play and Amusements

230. Now I'd like to talk to you about [cite child's name]'s play. What kinds of games does [cite child's name] play?
231. Does [cite child's name] ever pretend to do things, such as pretending to feed himself [herself] with pretend food?
232. Does [cite child's name] enjoy playing simple hide-and-seek games with you?
233. Does [cite child's name] like to play with toys?
234. Does [cite child's name] roll things along the floor?
235. How many blocks can [cite child's name] use to build a tower?
236. Can [cite child's name] put puzzles together?
237. (If yes) How large a puzzle—how many pieces—can he [she] put together?
238. Does [cite child's name] make things with Legos, Tinker Toys, or similar toys?
239. (If yes) Can [cite child's name] follow the printed diagrams that come with such toys?
240. Does [cite child's name] use toys in unusual ways, such as spinning them or lining them up over and over again?
241. (If yes) Tell me how he [she] uses toys in unusual ways.
242. Is [cite child's name] destructive with toys?
243. (If yes) Tell me about that.
244. Does [cite child's name] play with toys or other objects in exactly the same way each time?
245. Does [cite child's name] imitate what you do when you play with him [her]?
246. (If yes) Tell me about that.
247. Does [cite child's name] imitate what other children do in their play?
248. (If yes) Tell me about that.
249. Does [cite child's name] engage in make-believe play?
250. (If needed) Does he [she] pretend to be a cowboy [cowgirl], policeman [policewoman], or doctor while acting out an imaginary game?
251. (If yes) Tell me about that.
252. Does [cite child's name] play with cars or trains as if they were real, such as by putting cars into a garage or moving trains around on a track?
253. Does [cite child's name] play with toy animals, dolls, or tea sets as if they were real?
254. Does [cite child's name] kiss the toy animals and dolls, put them to bed, hold tea parties for them, or play school with them?
255. Does [cite child's name] engage in imaginative play with other children, such as pretending to be doctor and nurse, mother and father, or teacher and student?
256. Does [cite child's name] take an active part, contributing to the play fantasy, or is he [she] always passive?
257. Does [cite child's name] join in cooperative play that does not incorporate fantasy, such as tag, hide-and-seek, ball games, and table games?
258. What types of outings does [cite child's name] enjoy?
259. What does [cite child's name] watch on television?
260. How long does [cite child's name] watch at a time?
261. How much time does [cite child's name] spend watching television each day?
262. What are [cite child's name]'s favorite shows?

(Continued)

Table B-13 *(Continued)*

263. Does [cite child's name] enjoy listening to music?
264. (If yes) What kind of music does [cite child's name] like?
265. Can [cite child's name] sing in tune?
266. Can [cite child's name] play a musical instrument?
267. (If yes) What instrument?

Special Skills

268. I'd like to learn whether [cite child's name] is especially good at something. Does he [she] have any special skills?
269. (If yes) Tell me about his [her] skills.
270. (If needed) We talked earlier about working with puzzles. Now can you tell me whether [cite child's name] has an unusual talent for assembling puzzles?
271. (If answer to question 270 is yes) Tell me about that.
272. Does [cite child's name] show any unusual abilities in music?
273. (If yes) Tell me about his [her] unusual abilities in music.
274. Does [cite child's name] have a very good memory?
275. (If yes) Tell me about his [her] memory.

Self-Care

(Modify the following questions based on the child's age.)

276. Now I'd like to talk to you about how [cite child's name] can take care of himself [herself]. First, does [cite child's name] have to be fed, or can he [she] feed himself [herself] with his [her] fingers, a spoon, a spoon and a fork, or a knife and a fork?
277. Does [cite child's name] need a special diet?
278. (If yes) Tell me about his [her] special diet.
279. Can [cite child's name] help himself [herself] to food when at the table?
280. Can [cite child's name] cut a slice of bread from a loaf?
281. How good are [cite child's name]'s table manners?
282. Does [cite child's name] have any problems with chewing?
283. Does [cite child's name] drink from a cup?
284. Does [cite child's name] dribble?
285. Can [cite child's name] wash and dry his [her] hands?
286. Can [cite child's name] bathe himself [herself] without help?
287. Is [cite child's name] aware when his [her] hands or face is dirty?
288. Can [cite child's name] dress himself [herself]?
289. (If yes) Tell me what [cite child's name] can do.
290. Can [cite child's name] undress himself [herself]?
291. (If yes) Tell me what [cite child's name] can do.
292. Can [cite child's name] brush or comb his [her] own hair?
293. Can [cite child's name] brush his [her] own teeth?
294. Is [cite child's name] concerned if his [her] clothes are dirty or untidy?
295. What stage has [cite child's name] reached in his [her] toilet training in the daytime?
296. (If dry during the day) And at nighttime, does [cite child's name] stay dry?
297. (If answer to question 296 is no) Tell me more about this.
298. Can [cite child's name] get objects that he [she] wants for himself [herself]?
299. Does [cite child's name] look for things that are hidden?
300. Does [cite child's name] climb on a chair to reach things?
301. Can [cite child's name] open doors?

302. Can [cite child's name] open locks?
303. Is [cite child's name] aware of the danger of heights or of deep water?
304. Is [cite child's name] aware that traffic is dangerous?
305. Does [cite child's name] know how to cross a street safely?
306. How much does [cite child's name] have to be supervised?
307. Is [cite child's name] allowed to go alone into another room . . . outside . . . in the neighborhood . . . farther away?
308. (If child is older than 11 or 12 years) Can [cite child's name] travel on a bus or train alone?

Sleep

309. Let's talk now about [cite child's name]'s sleeping habits. What are [cite child's name]'s sleeping habits? (Ask questions 310 to 319, as needed.)
310. What time does [cite child's name] go to sleep?
311. Does [cite child's name] have any rituals before going to sleep?
312. (If yes) Tell me about them.
313. Does [cite child's name] have any problems going to sleep?
314. (If yes) Tell me about them.
315. About how many hours of sleep does [cite child's name] get at night?
316. Does [cite child's name] take a daytime nap or naps?
317. (If yes) Around what time[s] does he [she] nap?
318. For how long?
319. What time does [cite child's name] get up in the morning?

Behavior Problems

(Modify the following questions based on the child's age.)

320. Let's talk now about [cite child's name]'s behavior. Does [cite child's name] run away or wander?
321. (If yes) Tell me about that.
322. Is [cite child's name] destructive with toys or other things?
323. (If yes) Tell me about that.
324. Does [cite child's name] have severe temper tantrums?
325. (If yes) Tell me about them.
326. (If needed) When do they occur? . . . Where do they occur? . . . How long do they last?
327. Does [cite child's name] hurt other children by biting, hitting, or kicking them?
328. (If yes) Give me some examples of how [cite child's name] hurts other children.
329. Does [cite child's name] try to hurt adults by biting, hitting, or kicking them?
330. (If yes) Give me some examples of how [cite child's name] tries to hurt adults.
331. How does [cite child's name] behave in public?
332. (If needed) Does [cite child's name] grab things in shops . . . scream in the street . . . make nasty remarks . . . feel people's clothing, hair, or skin . . . do anything else that is annoying?
333. Does [cite child's name] resist whatever you try to do for him [her]?
334. Does [cite child's name] automatically say "no" to any suggestion?

Table B-13 *(Continued)*

335. Is [cite child's name] generally aggressive?
336. (If yes) Tell me about his [her] aggressiveness.
337. Is [cite child's name] generally manipulative?
338. (If yes) Tell me about that.
339. Does [cite child's name] comply with rules or requests?
340. (If no) Tell me about how he [she] responds to rules or requests.
341. Does [cite child's name] hurt himself [herself] on purpose, such as by banging his [her] head, biting his [her] hand, or hitting or deeply scratching any part of his [her] body?
342. (If yes) Please give me some examples.
343. How would you describe [cite child's name]'s overall behavior at home?

School and Learning Ability

344. (If relevant) Now I'd like to talk about school. Does [cite child's name] go to school?
    (If yes, go to question 345; if no, go to question 349. Modify questions 349 to 361 based on the child's age.)
345. Where does [cite child's name] go to school?
346. How is [cite child's name] doing in school?
347. What subjects does [cite child's name] study in school?
348. (If subjects named) Tell me about how [cite child's name] is doing in these subjects.
349. Tell me about [cite child's name]'s ability to recognize objects in pictures.
350. (If needed) What kinds of pictures does [cite child's name] recognize?
351. Tell me about [cite child's name]'s ability to read.
352. (If needed) What kinds of things does [cite child's name] read?
353. Tell me about [cite child's name]'s ability to write.
354. (If needed) What does [cite child's name] write?
355. Tell me about [cite child's name]'s ability to do arithmetic.
356. (If needed) What kind of arithmetic problems can [cite child's name] do?
357. Can [cite child's name] tell time?
358. Does [cite child's name] know the days of the week?
359. Does [cite child's name] know the months of the year?
360. Does [cite child's name] know dates?
361. Can [cite child's name] draw?

Domestic and Practical Skills

(Modify the following questions based on the child's age.)

362. Now let's talk about how [cite child's name] functions at home. Does [cite child's name] have any chores to do around the house?
363. (If yes) Tell me about what [cite child's name] does. (Ask question 364 as needed.)
364. Does [cite child's name] help set the table . . . clean the table . . . straighten up his [her] room . . . wash his [her] clothes . . . help with washing dishes . . . use a vacuum cleaner . . . help with shopping . . . help prepare food . . . cook . . . knit or sew . . . do woodwork . . . do any other kind of craft . . . help with gardening?

Concluding Questions

365. Is there anything else you would like to discuss?
366. (If yes) Go ahead.
367. Does [cite child's name] have any problems that we didn't discuss?
368. (If yes) Tell me about them.
369. Do you have any questions that you would like to ask me?
370. (If yes) Go ahead.
371. Thank you for talking with me. If you have any questions later or if you want to talk to me, please call me. Here is my card.

Source: Adapted from Schreibman (1988), Stone and Hogan (1993), and Wing (1976). Permission to use questions from the "Parent Interview for Autism" was obtained from W. L. Stone.

Table B-14
Semistructured Interview Questions for a Family

1. Hi! I'm Dr. [Ms., Mr.] _____. In order to try to work out the problems you're having as a family, I'd like to hear from everyone about what's going on. OK?
2. (Looking at each of the family members present) Would you like to tell me why you are here today?

Perception of Problem

3. What do you see as the problem? (Obtain each family member's view, if possible.)
4. When did the problem start?
5. How did the problem start?
6. What is the problem like now?
7. How has the problem affected all of you? (Obtain each member's view, if possible.)
8. How have you dealt with the problem? (Obtain each member's view, if possible.)
9. To what degree have your attempts been successful?
10. Have you had any previous professional help?
    (If yes, go to question 11; if no, go to question 15.)
11. What kind of help did you receive?
12. What do you think about the help you received?
13. Was it successful?
14. Tell me in what ways it was successful [unsuccessful].

Description of Family

15. What words would you use to describe your family?
16. How do you think other people would describe your family?
17. What's it like when you are all together?
18. (Looking at the other family members) What kind of a person is [cite father's name]?
19. (Looking at the other family members) What kind of a person is [cite mother's name]?
20. (Looking at the other family members) What kind of son is [cite each son's name in turn]?
21. (Looking at the other family members) What kind of daughter is [cite each daughter's name in turn]?
22. Do you agree with the description of yourself given by the other family members? (Obtain a response from each member.)
23. Which parent deals more with the children?
24. Do the children have any specific chores to do at home?
25. Are these arrangements satisfactory and fair?
26. (If no) How could they be better?
27. Do you find it easy to talk with others in your family? (Obtain a response from each member; explore any difficulties, including who is involved and what the problem is.)
28. What's it like when you discuss something together as a family?
29. Who talks the most?

30. Who talks the least?
31. Does everybody get a chance to have a say?
32. Do you find you have to be careful about what you say in your family? (Obtain a response from each member.)
33. Who are the good listeners in your family?
34. Is it helpful to talk things over with the family, or does it seem to be a waste of time?
35. Is it easy to express your feelings in your family?
36. Do you generally know how the others in your family are feeling?
37. How can you tell how they are feeling?
38. How much time do you spend together as a family?
39. What sorts of things do you do together?
40. Who does what with whom?
41. Is this okay with everybody?
42. Who is closest to whom in the family?
43. How are decisions made in your family?
44. Is this satisfactory?
45. (If no) What would be preferable?
46. Do you have disagreements in your family?
    (If yes, go to question 47; if no, go to question 52.)
47. Who has disagreements?
48. What are they about?
49. What are the disagreements like?
50. What happens?
51. Do they get worked out?
52. What kind of work do you do, Mr. [cite father's last name]?
53. What kind of work do you do, Mrs. [cite mother's last name]?
54. (Indicating the children) Do any of you have jobs?
55. (If yes) What kind of work do you do?

Extended Family

56. Are there any other relatives or close friends living at home or nearby?
    (If yes, go to question 57; if no, go to question 59.)
57. Who are they?
58. How do all of you get along with them [him, her]?

Concluding Questions

59. How might each of you change in order to improve the family situation?
60. Is there anything else that you would like to discuss?
61. (If yes) Go ahead.
62. Are there any questions that any of you would like to ask me?
63. (If yes) Go ahead.
64. Thank you for talking with me. If you have any questions or if you want to talk to me, please call me. Here is my card.

Source: This table is based on the Family Assessment Interview, which was prepared by Dr. Peter Loader for the Family Research Programme at Brunel–The University of West London. Work related to the interview schedule was published by Kinston and Loader (1984).

Table B-15
Semistructured Interview Questions for a Teacher of a Child Referred for School Difficulties

Introduction

1. Hi! I'm Dr. [Ms., Mr.] _____. Please tell me why you referred [cite child's name].
2. Before we talk about these problems, I'd like to ask you about how [cite child's name] functions in some general areas. Does [cite child's name] have any auditory problems that you have noticed?
3. Does he [she] have any problems in the visual area . . . in the motor area . . . with speech . . . with attention . . . with concentration . . . in getting along with other children . . . in getting along with you or other teachers?
4. How about [cite child's name]'s energy level? Does he [she] tire easily?
5. And how is [cite child's name]'s motivation?
6. How does [cite child's name] handle assignments that require organization . . . that require planning . . . that require independent effort?
7. Does [cite child's name] attend class regularly?
8. (If no) Tell me about that.
9. Does [cite child's name] arrive in class on time, or is he [she] frequently late?
10. (If late) Do you know why he [she] is late?
11. Tell me about how [cite child's name] does his [her] homework.
    (If academic problems are important, go to question 12 and then go to specific sections for problems in reading, mathematics, spelling, use of language, attention and memory, perception, and motor skills. If child has primarily behavioral problems, go to question 134. If needed, ask questions from both the academic and behavioral sections. To conclude the interview after you inquire about the child's academic and/or behavioral problems, go to question 183.)

Academic Problems

12. What types of academic problems is [cite child's name] having in the classroom?

Reading Difficulties

13. What types of reading difficulties does [cite child's name] have?
    (Ask questions 14 to 23, as needed.)
14. Does [cite child's name] have any problems with silent reading . . . oral reading . . . reading comprehension . . . reading speed . . . endurance . . . listening?
15. Does [cite child's name] have difficulty reading single letters . . . words . . . sentences . . . paragraphs . . . stories?
16. How accurately does [cite child's name] seem to hear sounds in words?
17. Does [cite child's name] have difficulty with specific parts of words, such as prefixes, suffixes, middle sound units, vowels, or consonants?
18. How does [cite child's name] go about attacking words?
19. Does [cite child's name] have receptive difficulties, such as difficulty in understanding what he [she] reads?
20. Does [cite child's name] have expressive difficulties, such as difficulty in telling you about what he [she] has read?

21. Is there a discrepancy between [cite child's name]'s silent and oral reading?
22. (If yes) Tell me about the discrepancy.
23. What do you think should be done to help [cite child's name] master reading skills?

Mathematics Difficulties

24. What types of mathematical difficulties does [cite child's name] have?
25. Tell me about [cite child's name]'s problem with [cite mathematical difficulty].
26. (Include only relevant items, based on the child's grade level and the information obtained in questions 24 and 25.) Does [cite child's name] have difficulty with addition . . . subtraction . . . multiplication . . . division . . . memorization or recall of number facts . . . word problems . . . oral problems . . . fractions . . . decimals . . . percents . . . measurement concepts such as length . . . area . . . liquid measures . . . dry measures . . . temperature . . . time . . . money . . . exponents . . . numerical reasoning . . . numerical application . . . story problems . . . algebra . . . geometry?
27. Is [cite child's name] careless when he [she] does mathematical problems?
28. Is [cite child's name] impulsive when he [she] does mathematical problems?
29. Is [cite child's name] unmotivated when he [she] does mathematical problems?
30. What do you think should be done to help [cite child's name] master mathematical skills?

Spelling Difficulties

31. What types of spelling difficulties does [cite child's name] have?
32. Tell me more about [cite child's name]'s problem with [cite spelling difficulty].
33. (If needed) Does [cite child's name] tend to insert extra letters . . . omit letters . . . substitute one letter for another one . . . spell phonetically . . . reverse sequences of letters . . . put letters in the wrong order?
34. What do you think should be done to help [cite child's name] master spelling skills?

Language Skill Difficulties

35. What types of language difficulties does [cite child's name] have?
36. Tell me more about [cite child's name]'s problem in [cite language skill difficulty].
    (Ask questions 37 to 49, as needed.)
37. Does [cite child's name] have oral expressive language difficulties?
38. (If yes) Tell me about them.
39. Does [cite child's name] have difficulty speaking in complete sentences . . . using correct words in speaking . . . writing expressive language?
40. (If yes) Tell me about his [her] difficulties.
41. Does [cite child's name] have difficulty with writing complete sentences . . . using correct words in writing . . . generating

(Continued)

Table B-15 *(Continued)*

ideas . . . grammar . . . punctuation . . . writing organized compositions?

42. How would you compare [cite child's name]'s oral and written language?

43. Does [cite child's name] have difficulty using nonverbal gestures or signs?

44. Does [cite child's name] have difficulty speaking?

45. (If yes) What kinds of difficulties does he [she] have speaking?

46. (If needed) Does [cite child's name] have problems with pronunciation . . . speed of talking . . . vocal tone . . . intonation?

47. Does [cite child's name] have receptive language difficulties, such as difficulty understanding what others say . . . what he [she] reads . . . gestures?

48. How well does [cite child's name] recognize pictures . . . environmental sounds . . . nonverbal signs?

49. What do you think should be done to help [cite child's name] master language skills?

Attention and Memory Difficulties

50. What types of attention and/or memory difficulties does [cite child's name] have?

51. Tell me more about [cite child's name]'s problem with [cite attention and/or memory difficulty].
(Ask questions 52 to 92, as needed.)

General Attention

52. Under what conditions does [cite child's name] have difficulty attending to things?

53. Is [cite child's name] able to concentrate for an amount of time that is appropriate for his [her] chronological age?

54. Can [cite child's name] focus on a specific task?

55. Is [cite child's name] able to sustain attention for the duration of a typical assignment?

56. Is [cite child's name] distractible?

57. (If yes) Tell me about that.

58. Does [cite child's name] talk excessively . . . have difficulty working or playing quietly . . . often fail to finish things or follow through . . . often seem not to listen . . . often act before thinking . . . excessively shift from one activity to another?

59. Does [cite child's name] have difficulty organizing work . . . often lose things necessary for activities at school or home, such as toys, pencils, books, or assignments?

60. Does [cite child's name] need a lot of supervision?

61. Does [cite child's name] call out in class or blurt out answers?

62. Is [cite child's name] able to filter out surrounding noises—such as pencil sharpening or noises in the hall—so that he [she] can concentrate on the assigned task?

63. Does [cite child's name] stare into space for relatively long periods of time . . . doodle frequently?

64. Can [cite child's name] sit still for a long period of time?

65. (If no) Tell me what he [she] does.

66. Can [cite child's name] sit still for a short period of time?

67. (If no) Tell me what he [she] does.

68. Does [cite child's name] repeatedly say "What" or "Huh"?

69. Does [cite child's name] seek quiet places to work . . . become very upset in noisy, crowded places?

70. Is [cite child's name] constantly in motion?

71. How tolerant of frustration is [cite child's name]?

72. Is [cite child's name] impulsive in his [her] behavior?

Auditory Attention

73. How does [cite child's name] attend to sounds . . . lectures . . . class discussions?

74. Can [cite child's name] shift his [her] attention from one sound to another?

75. Does [cite child's name] have difficulty maintaining his [her] focus on sounds?

76. (If yes) Are there any specific types of sounds that he [she] has difficulty focusing on?

77. Is it easier for [cite child's name] to attend to rhythmic sounds, like music, than to spoken language sounds?

78. Does [cite child's name] mistake words he [she] hears, like *rat* for *ran*?

79. Does [cite child's name] attend better when you speak slowly to him [her]?

Auditory Memory

80. Does [cite child's name] have a good memory for things that happened recently . . . for things that happened in the distant past . . . for present events?

81. Can [cite child's name] recall people's names easily?

82. Does [cite child's name] have difficulty learning telephone numbers . . . addresses . . . the alphabet?

83. Does [cite child's name] call common objects, such as buttons and zippers, by their correct names?

84. Does [cite child's name] hesitate to name objects when he [she] is asked to do so?

85. Does [cite child's name] often ask to have questions repeated?

Visual Attention

86. How does [cite child's name] attend to visual stimuli?

87. (If needed) How does he [she] attend to . . . pictures . . . words in print . . . TV presentations . . . movie presentations . . . information on a computer screen?

Visual Memory

88. Does [cite child's name] remember things that he [she] saw recently . . . things that he [she] saw in the distant past . . . present events?

89. Can [cite child's name] recall the names of people he [she] has seen?

90. Does [cite child's name] have difficulty associating names with pictures?

91. Does [cite child's name] have difficulty recognizing letters . . . numbers . . . shapes?

92. What do you think should be done to help [cite child's name] master attention and memory skills?

Perceptual Difficulties

93. What types of perceptual difficulties does [cite child's name] have?

94. Tell me more about [cite child's name]'s problem with [cite perceptual difficulties].
(Ask questions 95 to 111, as needed.)

95. Does [cite child's name] have difficulty with auditory perception?

Table B-15 (Continued)

96. Does he [she] have difficulty with localizing sounds . . . identifying sounds . . . distinguishing between sounds . . . auditory sequencing . . . sound blending . . . figure-ground identification of sounds—that is, identifying only the most important sounds and ignoring other potentially useful sounds?
97. Does [cite child's name] have difficulty with visual perception?
98. Does he [she] have difficulty with identifying visual stimuli . . . matching forms . . . discriminating figure from ground—that is, identifying only the key letter, shape, or form on a page . . . recognizing letters or words in different forms, such as lowercase versus uppercase or standard type versus italics?
99. Does [cite child's name] have difficulty with spatial perception?
100. Does he [she] have difficulty recognizing the position or location of an object on a page . . . in a room . . . in a building . . . on the playground?
101. Does [cite child's name] have difficulty with appreciating relative sizes . . . depth perception . . . perspective . . . recognizing whether objects differ in size?
102. Does [cite child's name] have difficulty distinguishing right from left?
103. Which modality—visual or auditory—does [cite child's name] prefer?
104. Does [cite child's name] prefer to look at pictures or at graphs?
105. Does [cite child's name] prefer making oral or written presentations?
106. Does [cite child's name] seem to have difficulty processing visual information . . . auditory information?
107. Can [cite child's name] copy material from a chalkboard . . . from an overhead . . . from dictation?
108. Can [cite child's name] keep his [her] place on a page while reading?
109. Can [cite child's name] find his [her] way around a school building?
110. Can [cite child's name] open his [her] locker?
111. What do you think should be done to help [cite child's name] master perceptual skills?

Motor Skill Difficulties
112. What types of motor difficulties does [cite child's name] have?
113. Tell me more about [cite child's name]'s problem with [cite motor difficulties].
(Ask questions 114 to 133, as needed.)
114. Does [cite child's name] have gross-motor problems?
115. (If yes) Please describe them.
116. Do they involve walking . . . running . . . sitting . . . throwing . . . balance?
117. Does [cite child's name] have fine-motor problems?
118. (If yes) Tell me about them.
119. Do they involve drawing . . . handwriting . . . coloring . . . tracing . . . cutting . . . pencil grip . . . hand dexterity?
120. Tell me more about these problems.
121. (If there are handwriting problems) Does [cite child's name] have problems in sequencing, such as transposing

letters . . . spatial orientation, such as placing a letter of one word at the end of the preceding word (for example, writing "goh ome" for "go home") . . . writing letters or words on the same line . . . writing letters of appropriate size?
122. Does [cite child's name] scrawl?
123. Does [cite child's name] make tiny compressed letters?
124. Are [cite child's name]'s papers messy or neat?
125. How would you compare how [cite child's name] writes on a spelling test with how he [she] writes spontaneously?
126. Is [cite child's name] able to clearly write single letters . . . uppercase letters . . . lowercase letters . . . words . . . sentences . . . paragraphs . . . short stories or themes?
127. Is [cite child's name]'s problem in remembering shapes or in reproducing letter shapes?
128. Does [cite child's name] have visual-motor integration difficulties?
129. (If yes) Tell me about them.
130. What do you think should be done to help [cite child's name] master motor skills?
131. Can [cite child's name] type?
132. (If yes) How well does [cite child's name] type?
133. Does [cite child's name] do better with a word processor than with handwriting?

Behavioral Difficulties
134. Now I'd like to talk with you about [cite child's name]'s behaviors that bother you most. I'd like to discuss these behaviors, when they occur, how often they occur, and what occurs in your classroom that might influence the behaviors. I also would like to discuss some other matters related to [cite child's name] that will help us develop useful interventions. Please describe exactly what [cite child's name] does that causes you concern.
135. Which behaviors bother you most?
136. Which behaviors, in order of most to least pressing, would you like to work on now?
137. Let's look into the first problem in more detail. How serious is the problem behavior?
138. How long has it been going on?
139. When does the problem behavior occur?
140. (If needed) Does it occur when the children are just arriving at school . . . at their desks in the classroom . . . in small groups . . . at recess . . . at lunch . . . on a field trip . . . at an assembly? . . . Does it occur on a particular day of the week?
141. What classroom activity is generally taking place at the time the problem behavior occurs?
142. (If needed) Does the problem occur when the child is . . . working on a reading assignment . . . working on a math assignment . . . working on a history assignment . . . working on a writing assignment . . . working on a spelling assignment . . . working on an art assignment . . . working on a music assignment . . . working on a social studies assignment. . . involved in a lecture. . . in unstructured play . . . doing independent work . . . interacting with you . . . interacting with other children?
143. How does the problem behavior affect the other children in the class?

Table B-15 *(Continued)*

144. How long does the problem behavior last?
145. How often does the problem behavior occur?
146. How many other children in the class also have this problem?
147. How does the level of [cite child's name]'s problem behavior compare with that of other children in the class who show the same behavior?
148. What happens just before the problem behavior begins?
149. What happens just after the problem behavior begins?
150. What makes the problem behavior worse?
151. What makes the problem behavior better?

Teacher's Reactions to Problem Behavior and Child
152. What do you do when the problem behavior occurs?
153. What does [cite child's name] do then?
154. What have you done that has been even partially successful in dealing with the problem behavior?
155. What do you think is causing the problem behavior?
156. What is your reaction to [cite child's name] in general?

Child's Relationship with Peers
157. How does [cite child's name] get along with his [her] classmates?
158. Does [cite child's name] have many friends?
159. Do the children include [cite child's name] in their games and activities?
160. Is [cite child's name] disliked by other children?
161. (If yes) Tell me why other children dislike [cite child's name].
162. How do other children contribute to [cite child's name]'s problem?
163. What do they do when [cite child's name] engages in the problem behavior?
164. How do other children help reduce the problem behavior?
165. How do other children react to [cite child's name] in general?
166. (If relevant) How do other teachers perceive and react to [cite child's name]?

Child's Social-Interpersonal Difficulties
(If social-interpersonal difficulties were not discussed, use this section.)
167. Does [cite child's name] have social and interpersonal problems?
168. (If yes) Tell me more about [cite child's name]'s problem in [cite social-interpersonal difficulties].
(Ask questions 169 to 176, as needed. Whenever there is a yes response, you might say "Please tell me more about that.")
169. Does [cite child's name] cry easily . . . give up easily . . . fly into a rage with no obvious cause . . . fear trying new

games or activities . . . lie or cheat in games . . . have problems with losing . . . show overcontrolling tendencies . . . prefer the company of younger children . . . prefer to be alone?
170. Does [cite child's name] have difficulty waiting for his [her] turn in games or group situations?
171. Does [cite child's name] fight, hit, or punch other children?
172. Does [cite child's name] frequently interrupt other children's activities?
173. Is [cite child's name] bossy, always telling other children what to do?
174. Does [cite child's name] tease other children or call them names?
175. Does [cite child's name] refuse to participate in group activities?
176. Does [cite child's name] lose his [her] temper often and easily?

Teacher's Expectations and Suggestions
177. For what part of the day is [cite child's name]'s behavior acceptable?
178. What do you consider to be an acceptable level of frequency for the problem behavior?
179. What expectations do you have for [cite child's name]?
180. What suggestions do you have for remedying the problem behavior?
181. What would you like to see done?
182. How would your life be different if [cite child's name]'s problems were resolved?

Child's Strengths
183. What are [cite child's name]'s strengths?
184. In what situations does [cite child's name] display these strengths?
185. How can these strengths be used in helping [cite child's name]?

Teacher's View of Child's Family
186. How much contact have you had with [cite child's name]'s family?
187. What impressions do you have about [cite child's name]'s family?

Concluding Questions
188. Are there any questions that you would like to ask me?
189. (If yes) Go ahead.
190. Thank you for talking with me. If you have any questions or if you want to talk to me further, please call me. Here is my card.

Note. Questions 137 through 151 can be repeated for additional problem areas.
Source: Some questions in this table were adapted from McMahon and Forehand (1988) and Witt and Elliott (1983).

Table B-16
Semistructured Interview Questions for a Student About Bullying at School

General Questions About Bullying

1. Hi! I'm Dr. [Ms., Mr.] _____. I'm going to ask you some questions about your school, how you feel in school, and how you feel about going to school. Okay?
2. How do students treat each other at your school?
3. How do students treat teachers at your school?
4. How do teachers treat students at your school?
5. How do teachers treat each other at your school?
6. Are racial, ethnic, cultural, and religious beliefs respected at your school? (If no) Tell me in what way they are not respected.
7. Do the teachers at your school respect differences among students? (If no) Tell me in what way differences are not respected.
8. Do the administrators at your school, like the principal and vice-principal, respect differences among students? (If no) Tell me in what way differences are not respected.
9. Are students at your school respectful of others' sexual orientation? (If no) Tell me in what way they are not respectful. (If needed) Is your school safe for lesbians, gays, and students who question their sexual orientation? (If no) Tell me in what way your school is not safe for these students.
10. Are male teachers at your school respectful of female students? (If no) Tell me in what way the female students are not respected.
11. Are female teachers at your school respectful of male students? (If no) Tell me in what way the male students are not respected.
12. Are male teachers at your school respectful of male students? (If no) Tell me in what way the male students are not respected.
13. Are female teachers at your school respectful of female students? (If no) Tell me in what way the female students are not respected.
14. Are students and faculty at your school respectful of students with disabilities? (If no) Tell me in what way students with disabilities are not respected.
15. How safe do you feel in your classroom? (If not safe) Tell me about your feelings.
16. How safe do you feel on the playground? (If not safe) Tell me about your feelings.
17. How safe do you feel in the cafeteria? (If not safe) Tell me about your feelings.
18. How safe do you feel in the bathroom? (If not safe) Tell me about your feelings.
19. How safe do you feel in the hallways? (If not safe) Tell me about your feelings.
20. How safe do you feel in the locker rooms? (If not safe) Tell me about your feelings.
21. (If applicable) How safe do you feel on the school bus? (If not safe) Tell me about your feelings.
22. How safe do you feel going to and from school? (If not safe) Tell me about your feelings.
23. What does "bullying" mean to you?
24. Have you ever been bullied? (If yes) Tell me about that.
25. Have you ever been scared to go to school because you were afraid of being bullied? (If yes) Tell me about it. (If needed) What have you tried to do about it?
26. Have you ever been cyberbullied by means of text messages, pictures or photos, video clips, phone calls, e-mails, instant messages, or comments in a chat room or on a website? (If yes) Tell me about it. (If needed) How did you feel when it happened?

Questions About Ways to Prevent Bullying

1. What do you think needs to happen at your school to stop bullying?
2. Would you be willing to tell someone if you had been bullied? (If yes) Tell me about that. (If no) Tell me why not.
3. Is your school doing anything to try to prevent bullying? (If yes) Tell me what your school is doing. (If needed) Tell me about the school's rules and programs against bullying.
4. What do you think you and your friends could do to help stop bullying?
5. What do you think your parents could do to help stop bullying?

Concluding Questions

1. Is there anything else you would like to tell me? (If yes) Go right ahead.
2. Thank you for talking with me. If you have any questions or if you want to talk to me, please call me. Here is my card.

Additional Questions as Needed

1. Has anyone at school hit, kicked, pushed, or hurt you? (If yes) Tell me about it. (If needed) How did you feel when it happened?
2. Has anyone at school made sexual comments to you that bothered you? (If yes) Tell me about it. (If needed) How did you feel when it happened?
3. Has anyone spread mean rumors about you? (If yes) Tell me about it. (If needed.) How did you feel when it happened?
4. Has anyone told your friends not to like you anymore? (If yes) Tell me about it. (If needed) How did it make you feel?
5. Has anyone stared at you in a mean way? (If yes) Tell me about it. (If needed) How did it make you feel?
6. Has anyone gossiped about you or told lies about you? (If yes) Tell me about it. (If needed) How did it make you feel?
7. Have other students ever turned away when you walked up to them? (If yes) Tell me about it. (If needed) How did it make you feel?
8. Do you ever feel left out of activities? (If yes) Tell me about it. (If needed) How do you feel when it happens?
9. Has anyone forced you to give up lunch money, food, a drink, or a snack? (If yes) Tell me about it. (If needed) How did you feel when it happened?

Source: Delaware Attorney General (n.d.) and U.S. Department of Health and Human Services (2003a).

Table B-17
Semistructured Interview Questions for a Victim of Bullying

1. Hi! I'm Dr. [Ms., Mr.] _____. I understand that you have been bullied. Tell me about what happened. Take your time.
2. How did it make you feel?
3. Who did the bullying? (If needed) A boy or a girl? An older student at your school?
4. Tell me about this student.
5. When did it happen?
6. Where did it happen?
7. Did anyone else see what happened? (If yes) Who saw what happened? Did he [she] do anything? (If yes) What did he [she] do?
8. Did you tell a teacher or someone else on the school staff about what happened? (If yes) What did he [she] do? (If no) Tell me why you did not tell a teacher or another school staff member about what happened.
9. Why do you think the other student [students] bullied you?
10. Did you talk to your parents about what happened? (If yes) What did they say or do? Did it help? (If no) Tell me why you did not tell your parents.
11. Did you talk to a friend about what happened? (If yes) What did he [she] do? Did it help? (If no) Tell me why you did not tell a friend.
12. Have you ever been bullied before this time? (If yes) Tell me about the other time. (Ask follow-up questions as needed: When? Who did it? What happened afterward?)
13. You know that what happened was not your fault. [Name of student who bullied] should not have done that. What can I do to help?
14. Is there anything else you would like to tell me? (If yes) Go ahead.
15. You will hear from someone on the school staff about what will happen next. Thank you for coming and talking with me. I know it hasn't been easy.

Table B-18
Semistructured Interview Questions for a Student Who Has Witnessed Bullying

1. Hi! I'm Dr. [Ms., Mr.] _____. I understand that you saw [cite student's name] being bullied. What did you see happening? (Ask questions 2 to 4 as needed.)
2. When did it happen?
3. Where did it happen?
4. Who did the bullying?
5. What did you do?
6. What was your reason for doing this?
7. How did it make you feel when you saw a student at your school being bullied by other students?
8. Did anyone else see what was happening? (If yes) Who else saw it? What did he [she, they] say or do?
9. Did you tell a teacher or anyone else on the school staff about what happened? (If yes) Whom did you tell? (If no) Tell me why you did not tell a teacher or another member of the school staff.
10. (If applicable) Are you aware that the school has an anonymous tip line for reporting incidents of bullying or any other incidents of concern?
11. What would you do if you saw it happening again?

Additional Questions as Appropriate

12. I'd like to talk with you about other times that you may have seen someone bullied. Okay? Have you seen anyone at school [or on the school bus] hit, kick, push, or otherwise hurt another student? (If yes) Let's talk about what happened.
13. What did you do?
14. What was your reason for doing this?
15. How did it make you feel to see what happened?
16. Have you heard anyone at school [or on the school bus] make sexual comments to another student that bothered you? (If yes) Let's talk about what happened.
17. What did you do?
18. What was your reason for doing this?
19. How did it make you feel to hear the comments?
20. Have you heard about anyone spreading mean rumors about another student? (If yes) Let's talk about what happened.
21. What did you do?
22. What was your reason for doing this?

23. How did it make you feel when you heard the rumors?
24. Have you seen any other student being deliberately left out of activities? (If yes) Let's talk about what happened.
25. What did you do?
26. What was your reason for doing this?
27. How did it make you feel to see what happened?
28. Have you seen anyone forcing another student to give up lunch money, food, a drink, or a snack? (If yes) Let's talk about what happened.
29. What did you do?
30. What was your reason for doing this?
31. How did it make you feel to see what happened?
32. Have you seen anyone bully another student by means of text messages, pictures or photos, video clips, phone calls, e-mails, instant messages, or comments in a chat room or on a website? (If yes) Let's talk about what happened.
33. What did you do?
34. What was your reason for doing this?
35. How did it make you feel to see what happened?
36. Have you seen other students encourage a bully? (If yes) Let's talk about what happened.
37. What did you do?
38. What was your reason for doing this?
39. How did it make you feel to see what happened?
40. Have you seen other students stand up for a victim of bullying? (If yes) Let's talk about what happened.
41. What did you do?
42. What was your reason for doing this?
43. How did it make you feel to see what happened?
44. Have you noticed anything else about how other students respond to bullying at your school? (If yes) Tell me what you have noticed.

Concluding Questions

45. Is there anything else that you would like to talk about? (If yes) Go ahead.
46. Thank you for talking with me. If you have any questions or if you want to talk to me, please call me. Here is my card.

Table B-19
Semistructured Interview Questions for a Student Who Has Bullied Another Student

1. Hi! I'm Dr. [Ms., Mr.] _____. I understand that you may have bullied another student. Please tell me about that.

Additional Questions

2. Did you know [cite other student's name] before this incident took place? (If yes) How long have you known each other?
3. Have you had difficulties with [cite other student's name] in the past? (If yes) What kind of difficulties?
4. Now let's discuss the incident in more detail. What happened?
5. When did it take place?
6. Where did it take place?
7. Who was involved?
8. What part did you play?
9. Was anyone else involved? (If yes) Who else was involved? What part did they play?
10. Did anyone else see what happened? (If yes) Who saw it? And how would they describe the incident?
11. Did this take place more than once? (If yes) Tell me about the other times.
12. How would someone else who witnessed the other incident describe your actions?
13. Would you do the same thing again or act differently? Tell me about that.
14. Do you understand what was wrong about what you did?
15. How do you feel about what you did?
16. Have you thought about how your actions or words could have hurt this student's feelings? (If yes) Tell me about that.
17. How would you feel if this student did or said these things to you?
18. How do you think you could be more sensitive to whether your actions might hurt someone else?
19. What do you think your parents will say when they learn about what you have done? (Ask questions 20 to 29 as relevant.)
20. Have you been involved in anything like this before with anyone else? (If yes) Tell me about the other times.
21. Have you hit, kicked, pushed, or done anything else to hurt other students in school, on the school bus, walking to or from school, or in some other place? (If yes) Tell me about that. (If needed) What was your reason for doing this?
22. Have you said mean things or spread rumors about another student at school? (If yes) Tell me about that. (If needed) What was your reason for doing this?
23. Have you teased other students or called them names in ways that might make them feel bad? (If yes) Tell me about that. (If needed) What was your reason for doing this?
24. Have you made sexual comments to other students who you know are likely to be bothered by your comments? (If yes) Tell me about that. (If needed) What was your reason for doing this?
25. Have you ever bullied another student through text messaging? (If yes) Tell me about that. (If needed) What was your reason for doing this?
26. Have you ever bullied another student by sending pictures or photos or video clips electronically? (If yes) Tell me about that. (If needed) What was your reason for doing this?
27. Have you ever bullied another student in a phone call? (If yes) Tell me about that. (If needed) What was your reason for doing this?
28. Have you ever bullied another student in an e-mail? (If yes) Tell me about that. (If needed) What was your reason for doing this?
29. Have you ever bullied another student by any other electronic means such as in a chat room, in an instant message, or on a website? (If yes) Tell me about that. (If needed) What was your reason for doing this?

Concluding Questions

30. Is there anything else that you would like to discuss?
31. I will get back to you soon on what will happen next. But meanwhile, do not do anything to hurt another student or to make him or her feel bad. Be aware that your future behaviors will be closely monitored. Okay?
32. Thank you for talking with me. If you have any questions or if you want to talk to me, please call me. Here is my card.

Table B-20
Asking the Right Questions About a School's Anti-Bullying Policies

The following are some critical questions that you should ask in evaluating bullying at your school. The answers to these and other questions, although not always readily available, will help you guide your school in choosing an appropriate set of responses to bullying.

The School

1. Does the school administration believe that the school has a problem with bullying?
2. Is the school administration aware of the long-term harm associated with bullying and chronic victimization?
3. Is the school administration aware of the different types of behavior that constitute bullying?
4. Does the school administration know how often bullying occurs on the campus each year?
5. How does the school's level of bullying compare with that of other schools?
6. What insights do teachers have about bullying? Can they identify some of the reasons bullying occurs?
7. Does the school have a policy to guide teachers and other staff members in handling incidents of bullying? If so, what is the policy? Is it applied fairly to all students? Do parents know about the school's policy? And does it include a procedure to follow in reporting bullying?
8. Who are the key personnel at the school who handle incidents of bullying (e.g., counselor, school psychologist, vice-principal, nurse, social worker)? Do they take seriously all incidents of bullying?
9. Does a member of the school staff meet with the parents of students involved in bullying incidents?
10. Are students aware of how to report bullying?
11. Does the school have an anonymous tip line or tip box?
12. Does the school provide training on bullying to the school staff?
13. Do teachers hold regular classroom meetings with their students to discuss issues related to bullying and peer relations?
14. Has the school engaged parents and other members of the community in bullying prevention?

Offenders

1. How are incidents of bullying handled?
2. How does the school identify bullies? Are adequate records kept? Are school counselors (or other professionals) in the loop?
3. Where do bullies operate at the school?
4. When does bullying occur at those locations?
5. Are those who supervise the locations during times when bullying occurs trained to identify bullying incidents and handle them appropriately?
6. Given that most bullying occurs in areas where there are no teachers, is the current method for identifying bullies adequate?
7. Is there increased adult supervision in "hot spots" for bullying?
8. What are the consequences for bullying at the school? Are they applied consistently?
9. Does a member of the school staff meet with students who bully their peers to reinforce school rules against bullying, administer appropriate consequences for bullying behaviors, and make them aware that future behaviors will be closely monitored?
10. Does the bullying stop as a result of the meeting between the student and the staff member? How is this determined?

Victims and Victimization

1. Does the school know all students who are possible victims of bullying?
2. How does the school identify victims? Given that most victims and witnesses do not report bullying, is the current system for identifying victims adequate? Who are the chronic victims? What has the school done to protect them?
3. What are the most common forms of bullying at the school?
4. Does the school policy address them?
5. Does the school have a policy regarding the role of bystanders in reporting bullying? If so, is the policy having the desired effect?

Source: Adapted from Sampson (2009).

Table B-21
Semistructured Interview Questions for a Student Who May Pose a Threat

1. Hi! I'm Dr. [Ms., Mr.] _____. What is your understanding of why you have been asked to meet with me?
2. We are concerned about [behavior that has been reported]. Tell me about that.
3. Why do you think we at school are concerned about what happened [specific event]?
4. In order to help me better understand this situation and be able to help you, I am going to ask you some more questions. Okay?

Social and Peer Factors

5. What do you typically do after school?
6. Do you have any hobbies or interests? (If yes) Tell me about them.
7. Are you involved with any groups or teams outside of school? (If yes) Tell me about the groups [teams]. (If no) Tell me why you are not involved with any group or team.
8. What are your favorite movies?
9. Favorite video games?
10. Favorite TV shows?
11. Favorite music groups?
12. Favorite Internet sites?
13. Who are your friends?
14. How long have you been friends with them?
15. Do you have a best friend? (If yes) How long have you been best friends?
16. Have you had a problem with any of your friends recently? (If yes) Tell me about that.
17. How would you describe the students at your school?
18. Are there any groups of students that you don't get along with? (If yes) Who are they?
19. How would your classmates describe you?
20. Is that an accurate description?
21. Do you feel they misunderstand you? (If yes) Tell me about that.
22. Do you get teased or picked on by other children? (If yes, ask questions 23–25; if no, go to question 26.)
23. Tell me about that.
24. Do you get teased in school? (If yes) What do you get teased about there?
25. Do you get teased outside of school? (If yes) What do you get teased about there?
26. Have you recently broken up with a girlfriend [boyfriend]? (If yes) What happened?
27. Have you recently ended a good friendship? (If yes) What happened?
28. Have you been pulling away from your friends? (If yes) Tell me about that.
29. Have you been feeling isolated recently? (If yes) Tell me about that.

Family, School, and Environmental Situations

30. Are you close to your parents? (Following any answer) Tell me about that.
31. Do they listen to you?
32. What do your parents do (occupation)?
33. What are their work hours like?
34. Do you do any family activities together? (If yes) What do you typically do? How often?
35. Have you experienced any changes recently in your family life? (If yes) Tell me about the changes.
36. Do you think your parents treat you fairly? (Following any response) Tell me about that.
37. Do your parents ever punish you? (If yes) Usually for what reasons? How do your parents typically punish you? (If needed, provide examples such as time out, grounding, hitting, or taking away TV.)
38. Do your parents supervise what you watch on TV? (If yes) How do you feel about that?
39. Do your parents supervise your access to the Internet? (If yes) How do you feel about that?
40. Does anyone in your family seem very sad or angry? (If yes) Tell me about that.
41. Have you ever used any drugs or alcohol? (If yes) What drugs [alcohol]? How often?
42. Do you have difficulty in school? (If yes) Tell me about that.
43. How important is it to you to do well in school?
44. How do your parents react to your school performance?

History of Violent or Aggressive Behavior

45. Have you ever hurt an animal on purpose? (If yes) Tell me about that.
46. Do you ever pick on younger or smaller children? (If yes) Tell me about that.
47. Have you ever purposely hurt anyone? (If yes) Tell me about that. (If no) How close have you ever come to hurting anyone?
48. Have you thought about hurting someone or wished you could hurt someone? (If yes) How often do you have those thoughts?
49. Do you get into fights? (If yes) Tell me about that. (If needed) In school? Outside of school?
50. Do you feel that it is necessary to get back at someone who hurts you or does something to you that you don't like? (If yes) Tell me about that.
51. Did you ever harass anyone in the past? (If yes) Tell me about that. (If needed) What made you stop doing that?
52. Have you ever been in trouble with the police? (If yes) What happened?

Depression and Other Emotional Concerns

53. Do you ever feel sad, upset, or depressed? (If yes) What kinds of things make you feel that way?
54. Do you ever feel that no one cares about you or loves you? (If yes) Tell me about that.
55. Do you get angry often? (If yes) Give me some examples of what makes you angry.
56. Do you often argue with other people? (If yes) Tell me about the arguments.
57. Do you have any difficulty sleeping? (If yes) Tell me about that.

Table B-21 *(Continued)*

58. Do you have any difficulty eating? (If yes) Tell me about that.
59. Do you have any difficulty concentrating on your work? (If yes) Tell me about that.
60. Do you ever feel lonely? (If yes) Tell me about these feelings.
61. Do you prefer to stay by yourself? (If yes) Tell me why you prefer to stay by yourself.
62. Do you blame yourself for things that go wrong? (Following any response) Tell me about that.
63. How do you handle stress?
64. How do you handle anger?

Suicidal Fantasies or Actions
65. Have you ever thought of hurting yourself? (If yes) Tell me about that.
66. Have you ever wished or tried to kill yourself? (If yes) Tell me about that. (If needed) What made you decide not to kill yourself?

Evaluation of Threat-Related Behaviors
67. Are you angry at anyone now? (If yes) Who is making you angry? (If needed) What is the reason you are angry?
68. Have you recently been angry at anyone? (If yes) Who made you angry? Are you still angry at [cite person's name]? (If yes) Tell me more about that.
69. Are you thinking about hurting anyone? (If yes, go to question 70; if no, go to question 80.)
70. Whom are you thinking about hurting?
71. When do you think you might hurt [cite person's name]?
72. Where do you think you might do this?
73. How long have you been thinking this way?
74. Are you able to control these thoughts about hurting [cite person's name]?
75. Do you think you would be able to stop yourself from hurting [cite person's name] if you wanted to?
76. What steps have you taken to carry out your plan?
77. Have you conducted a rehearsal or practice exercise? (If yes) What exactly did you do to practice? How did that make you feel?

78. Have you told anyone else about your desire to harm [cite person's name] or your plan to do so? (If yes) Whom did you tell? What did you tell him [her]?
79. Have you threatened [cite person's name] or taken any kind of action against him [her]?
80. How do you think others view you when you make a threat or behave aggressively?
81. Do you have access to a weapon? (If yes) What type of weapon? Where is the [type of weapon] located? Have you shown it to anyone?
82. Have you ever brought a weapon to school? (If yes) What did you bring to school? When did you bring it? What was your reason for bringing it?
83. Did you show it to anyone or tell anyone you had it on you? (If yes) Whom did you show it to or tell about having it?
84. Do you foresee any changes in your life that could make things better? (Following any response) Tell me about that.
85. Do you foresee any changes that could make things get worse? (Following any response) Tell me about that.

Identification of Support Resources and Interview Closure
86. Whom do you have to talk to or assist you when you have problems?
87. Are there any steps that you think the school, your parents, or you could take to make things better for you? (If yes) What steps could be taken and by whom? (If no) Why not?
88. Given where things stand right now, what are you thinking about or planning to do at this point? (Follow up on appropriate leads.)
89. Thank you for coming. (Close with a statement that describes short-term next steps and concrete examples of available resources, such as "I'll need to contact your parents to talk about . . ." or "I'm going to make an appointment for you to meet with the vice-principal, who will talk to you about . . . .")

Note: Notify the school administrator, the threat coordinator (if one is designated), or law enforcement if you believe that the threat to harm another person is credible or imminent. Also see Table L-19 in the Resource Guide for a checklist of risk factors for potential violence.
Source: Biller, Glassman, Roosa, Schneller, and Venezia (2008).

Table C-1
Classroom Observation Checklist

CLASSROOM OBSERVATION CHECKLIST

Child's name: _____   Teacher's name: _____

Age: _____ Grade level: _____ Class: _____   School: _____

Observer's name: _____   Time: Begin _____ End _____ Date: _____

Directions: Check Yes, No, or NA (not applicable or not observed) for each item.

Classroom Layout	Yes	No	NA
1. Seating arrangement is appropriate	☐	☐	☐
2. Room is accessible for students with disabilities	☐	☐	☐
3. Noise level is acceptable	☐	☐	☐
4. Appearance overall is pleasant	☐	☐	☐
5. Appearance overall is organized	☐	☐	☐
6. Room is not overcrowded	☐	☐	☐
7. Desks and furniture are arranged to maximize space or enhance instruction	☐	☐	☐
8. Air quality is good	☐	☐	☐
9. Odors are minimal	☐	☐	☐
10. Room is hazard free	☐	☐	☐
11. Temperature is comfortable	☐	☐	☐
12. Lighting is adequate	☐	☐	☐
13. Students are physically comfortable	☐	☐	☐
14. Classroom is attractive to students	☐	☐	☐
15. Maximum use is made of bulletin board and wall space	☐	☐	☐
16. All students can see presentation of instruction	☐	☐	☐
17. Distractions are minimal	☐	☐	☐
18. High-traffic areas are free from congestion	☐	☐	☐
19. Students are not seated in high-traffic or congested areas	☐	☐	☐
20. Equipment and books are up-to-date	☐	☐	☐
21. Frequently used materials are easily accessible	☐	☐	☐
22. Students know where materials/books/assignments belong	☐	☐	☐
23. Students can see teacher and teacher can see students at all times	☐	☐	☐

Organization of Instruction	Yes	No	NA
24. Directions for activities are clear	☐	☐	☐
25. Directions for assignments are clear	☐	☐	☐
26. Assignments are posted clearly	☐	☐	☐
27. Homework assignments are written on board or overhead	☐	☐	☐
28. Materials are prepared ahead of time	☐	☐	☐
29. Materials are distributed efficiently	☐	☐	☐
30. There is a plan in place for interruptions and unexpected events	☐	☐	☐
31. Time is well planned, leaving little down time	☐	☐	☐

Behavioral Considerations	Yes	No	NA
32. Clear expectations are communicated regarding acceptable behavior	☐	☐	☐
33. Expectations regarding behavior are posted clearly	☐	☐	☐
34. Rules are phrased positively and are realistic	☐	☐	☐
35. A variety of reinforcers are used	☐	☐	☐
36. Ratio of positive to negative statements in class is high	☐	☐	☐
37. Students are clear about positive and negative consequences	☐	☐	☐
38. Effective classroom management techniques are used	☐	☐	☐
39. Rules are aligned with schoolwide behavioral expectations	☐	☐	☐
40. Desired behaviors are reinforced appropriately	☐	☐	☐
41. Students take responsibility for their behavior	☐	☐	☐
42. Teacher takes appropriate action when a student is not engaged	☐	☐	☐
43. Transitions between activities are smooth and without confusion	☐	☐	☐
44. Transitions in and out of the classroom are clearly defined	☐	☐	☐

Teacher's Instructional Strategies	Yes	No	NA
45. Uses whole group, small group, and independent work effectively	☐	☐	☐
46. Paces lecture appropriately	☐	☐	☐
47. Monitors students' attention to lesson continually	☐	☐	☐
48. Uses age-appropriate activities	☐	☐	☐
49. Adapts instructional level to students' skill levels and needs	☐	☐	☐
50. Has effective beginning and end routines	☐	☐	☐
51. States purposes of lesson clearly	☐	☐	☐
52. Summarizes previous lesson clearly	☐	☐	☐
53. Uses up-to-date and interesting materials and examples	☐	☐	☐
54. Uses strategies that capture and maintain students' interest	☐	☐	☐
55. Varies instructional tools and methods	☐	☐	☐
56. Introduces and explains new concepts clearly	☐	☐	☐

Table C-1 *(Continued)*

Teacher's Instructional Strategies *(Cont.)*	Yes	No	NA
57. Repeats key concepts as needed	☐	☐	☐
58. Makes frequent use of comprehension checks that require students to demonstrate their understanding	☐	☐	☐
59. Encourages students to understand, ask questions, and interpret ideas from diverse perspectives	☐	☐	☐
60. Summarizes discussion periodically	☐	☐	☐
61. Demonstrates a good knowledge of the subject matter	☐	☐	☐
62. Demonstrates mastery of grammar, punctuation, and spelling	☐	☐	☐
63. Gives appropriate consideration to students with special needs	☐	☐	☐
64. Uses questioning effectively	☐	☐	☐
65. Gives appropriate feedback in a timely manner	☐	☐	☐
66. Responds adequately to students' questions	☐	☐	☐
67. Responds appropriately to diversity issues and to cultural differences during lesson	☐	☐	☐
68. Ends lesson with appropriate closure and review focusing on main objectives of lesson	☐	☐	☐
69. Directs students on how to prepare for next class	☐	☐	☐
70. Gives homework assignments clearly	☐	☐	☐

Teacher's Influence on Social Climate

	Yes	No	NA
71. Projects a friendly, positive attitude	☐	☐	☐
72. Listens to what students have to say	☐	☐	☐
73. Demonstrates rapport with students	☐	☐	☐
74. Invites students to be risk-takers without fear of ridicule	☐	☐	☐
75. Provides students with opportunities for success	☐	☐	☐
76. Provides students with opportunities to interact	☐	☐	☐

Teacher's Influence on Social Climate *(Cont.)*	Yes	No	NA
77. Demonstrates effective communication skills	☐	☐	☐
78. Resolves conflicts appropriately	☐	☐	☐
79. Provides an overall safe, nonthreatening environment	☐	☐	☐
80. Shows respect at all times	☐	☐	☐
81. Uses humor appropriately and avoids sarcasm	☐	☐	☐

Teacher's Personal and Professional Characteristics

	Yes	No	NA
82. Displays enthusiasm	☐	☐	☐
83. Displays confidence	☐	☐	☐
84. Displays flexibility	☐	☐	☐
85. Displays empathy	☐	☐	☐
86. Begins and ends class on time	☐	☐	☐
87. Dresses appropriately and is well groomed	☐	☐	☐
88. Speaks clearly and audibly	☐	☐	☐
89. Matches facial expressions to spoken words	☐	☐	☐
90. Interacts positively with students	☐	☐	☐
91. Treats all students in an equitable manner	☐	☐	☐

Students' Behavior[a]

	Yes	No	NA
92. Are serious and eager to learn	☐	☐	☐
93. Attend to class lecture or engage in class assignment	☐	☐	☐
94. Ask appropriate questions	☐	☐	☐
95. Participate in class activities	☐	☐	☐
96. Participate in class discussion	☐	☐	☐
97. Ask for help or assistance as needed	☐	☐	☐
98. Volunteer to answer questions	☐	☐	☐
99. Behave appropriately during lesson	☐	☐	☐
100. Interact with teacher appropriately	☐	☐	☐
101. Interact with other students appropriately	☐	☐	☐

Comments: _____

[a] Ratings should pertain to majority of students in the class.
Source: Adapted from Career Special Technical Populations (n.d.); Purdue University, School of Education (2002).
From *Foundations of Behavioral, Social, and Clinical Assessment of Children* (Sixth Edition) by Jerome M. Sattler. Copyright 2014 by Jerome M. Sattler, Publisher, Inc. Permission to photocopy this appendix table is granted to purchaser of this book for personal use only (see copyright page for details).

Table C-2
Observation Checklist for Rating a Child in a Classroom

OBSERVATION CHECKLIST FOR RATING A CHILD IN A CLASSROOM

Child's name: _____   Teacher's name: _____

Age: _____ Grade level: _____ Class: _____   School: _____

Observer's name: _____   Time: Begin _____ End _____ Date: _____

Directions: PART A: Check Yes, No, or NA. PART B: Check one box using the following scale:

1	2	3	4	5	NA
Never	Seldom	Sometimes	Frequently	Always	Not applicable or Not observed

PART A

Appearance — Check one: Yes No NA
1. Is dressed appropriately ☐ ☐ ☐
2. Is of appropriate weight ☐ ☐ ☐
3. Is underweight ☐ ☐ ☐
4. Is overweight ☐ ☐ ☐
5. Looks tired ☐ ☐ ☐
6. Has bruises ☐ ☐ ☐

Preparation for Class
7. Was on time to class ☐ ☐ ☐
8. Had homework ☐ ☐ ☐
9. Had needed materials ☐ ☐ ☐

PART B

Activity Level — Check one: 1 2 3 4 5 NA
1. Has appropriate activity level ☐ ☐ ☐ ☐ ☐ ☐
2. Is hyperactive ☐ ☐ ☐ ☐ ☐ ☐
3. Is lethargic ☐ ☐ ☐ ☐ ☐ ☐

Attention
4. Is attentive ☐ ☐ ☐ ☐ ☐ ☐
5. Is inattentive ☐ ☐ ☐ ☐ ☐ ☐
6. Is easily distracted ☐ ☐ ☐ ☐ ☐ ☐

Effort/Motivation
7. Has appropriate motivation ☐ ☐ ☐ ☐ ☐ ☐
8. Gives up easily ☐ ☐ ☐ ☐ ☐ ☐
9. Works carelessly ☐ ☐ ☐ ☐ ☐ ☐
10. Is hesitant to begin working ☐ ☐ ☐ ☐ ☐ ☐
11. Shows apathetic behavior ☐ ☐ ☐ ☐ ☐ ☐
12. Works slowly ☐ ☐ ☐ ☐ ☐ ☐
13. Has difficulty working independently ☐ ☐ ☐ ☐ ☐ ☐
14. Does not complete assignments on time ☐ ☐ ☐ ☐ ☐ ☐

Fine-Motor Skills
15. Builds with blocks ☐ ☐ ☐ ☐ ☐ ☐
16. Uses scissors ☐ ☐ ☐ ☐ ☐ ☐
17. Colors appropriately ☐ ☐ ☐ ☐ ☐ ☐
18. Manipulates buttons ☐ ☐ ☐ ☐ ☐ ☐

Temperament — Check one: 1 2 3 4 5 NA
19. Has appropriate temperament ☐ ☐ ☐ ☐ ☐ ☐
20. Is sullen ☐ ☐ ☐ ☐ ☐ ☐
21. Is withdrawn ☐ ☐ ☐ ☐ ☐ ☐
22. Is agitated ☐ ☐ ☐ ☐ ☐ ☐
23. Is angry ☐ ☐ ☐ ☐ ☐ ☐
24. Is anxious ☐ ☐ ☐ ☐ ☐ ☐
25. Is confused ☐ ☐ ☐ ☐ ☐ ☐
26. Is easily upset ☐ ☐ ☐ ☐ ☐ ☐

Speech
27. Has difficulty modulating voice ☐ ☐ ☐ ☐ ☐ ☐
28. Mispronounces words ☐ ☐ ☐ ☐ ☐ ☐
29. Speaks slowly and haltingly ☐ ☐ ☐ ☐ ☐ ☐
30. Has difficulty saying initial sounds ☐ ☐ ☐ ☐ ☐ ☐
31. Stutters ☐ ☐ ☐ ☐ ☐ ☐
32. Speaks too loudly ☐ ☐ ☐ ☐ ☐ ☐
33. Speaks too softly ☐ ☐ ☐ ☐ ☐ ☐
34. Does not participate in discussions ☐ ☐ ☐ ☐ ☐ ☐

Language
35. Uses appropriate language ☐ ☐ ☐ ☐ ☐ ☐
36. Invents words ☐ ☐ ☐ ☐ ☐ ☐
37. Uses vague, imprecise language ☐ ☐ ☐ ☐ ☐ ☐
38. Has difficulty staying on topic ☐ ☐ ☐ ☐ ☐ ☐
39. Has difficulty explaining things ☐ ☐ ☐ ☐ ☐ ☐
40. Has limited vocabulary ☐ ☐ ☐ ☐ ☐ ☐
41. Has poor grammar ☐ ☐ ☐ ☐ ☐ ☐
42. Confuses similar-sounding words ☐ ☐ ☐ ☐ ☐ ☐
43. Has difficulty understanding directions ☐ ☐ ☐ ☐ ☐ ☐
44. Has difficulty understanding concepts ☐ ☐ ☐ ☐ ☐ ☐
45. Has difficulty generalizing ☐ ☐ ☐ ☐ ☐ ☐
46. Has difficulty understanding figurative language ☐ ☐ ☐ ☐ ☐ ☐

Reading
47. Reads appropriately ☐ ☐ ☐ ☐ ☐ ☐
48. Has difficulty identifying sounds ☐ ☐ ☐ ☐ ☐ ☐
49. Has difficulty blending sounds into words ☐ ☐ ☐ ☐ ☐ ☐
50. Has difficulty reading regular words ☐ ☐ ☐ ☐ ☐ ☐

Table C-2 *(Continued)*

Reading *(Cont.)*	Check one: 1 2 3 4 5 NA
51. Has difficulty reading irregular words	☐ ☐ ☐ ☐ ☐ ☐
52. Has difficulty reading sentences	☐ ☐ ☐ ☐ ☐ ☐
53. Reads too slowly	☐ ☐ ☐ ☐ ☐ ☐
54. Reads too quickly	☐ ☐ ☐ ☐ ☐ ☐
55. Has difficulty retelling what has been read	☐ ☐ ☐ ☐ ☐ ☐
56. Has difficulty with comprehension	☐ ☐ ☐ ☐ ☐ ☐

Writing

	Check one: 1 2 3 4 5 NA
57. Writes appropriately	☐ ☐ ☐ ☐ ☐ ☐
58. Resists writing	☐ ☐ ☐ ☐ ☐ ☐
59. Writes slowly	☐ ☐ ☐ ☐ ☐ ☐
60. Writes too quickly	☐ ☐ ☐ ☐ ☐ ☐
61. Has difficulty with handwriting	☐ ☐ ☐ ☐ ☐ ☐
62. Has difficulty with pencil grasp	☐ ☐ ☐ ☐ ☐ ☐

Composition

	Check one: 1 2 3 4 5 NA
63. Has poor grammar	☐ ☐ ☐ ☐ ☐ ☐
64. Has poor spelling	☐ ☐ ☐ ☐ ☐ ☐
65. Has poor punctuation	☐ ☐ ☐ ☐ ☐ ☐
66. Has poor content	☐ ☐ ☐ ☐ ☐ ☐
67. Has poor organization	☐ ☐ ☐ ☐ ☐ ☐

Relationship with Teacher

	Check one: 1 2 3 4 5 NA
68. Shows appropriate behavior	☐ ☐ ☐ ☐ ☐ ☐
69. Shows uncooperative behavior	☐ ☐ ☐ ☐ ☐ ☐
70. Shows angry behavior	☐ ☐ ☐ ☐ ☐ ☐
71. Shows hostile behavior	☐ ☐ ☐ ☐ ☐ ☐
72. Is argumentative	☐ ☐ ☐ ☐ ☐ ☐
73. Withdraws from teacher	☐ ☐ ☐ ☐ ☐ ☐
74. Seeks too much attention	☐ ☐ ☐ ☐ ☐ ☐

Relationship with Teacher *(Cont.)*

	Check one: 1 2 3 4 5 NA
75. Does not follow teacher's instructions	☐ ☐ ☐ ☐ ☐ ☐
76. Interrupts teacher	☐ ☐ ☐ ☐ ☐ ☐

Relationship with Other Children

	Check one: 1 2 3 4 5 NA
77. Shows appropriate behavior	☐ ☐ ☐ ☐ ☐ ☐
78. Avoids interactions	☐ ☐ ☐ ☐ ☐ ☐
79. Interacts poorly	☐ ☐ ☐ ☐ ☐ ☐
80. Interrupts other children	☐ ☐ ☐ ☐ ☐ ☐
81. Waits for other children to initiate interactions	☐ ☐ ☐ ☐ ☐ ☐
82. Has difficulty sharing	☐ ☐ ☐ ☐ ☐ ☐
83. Has difficulty dealing with group pressure	☐ ☐ ☐ ☐ ☐ ☐
84. Is rejected by other children	☐ ☐ ☐ ☐ ☐ ☐
85. Has difficulty responding to teasing	☐ ☐ ☐ ☐ ☐ ☐
86. Fights with other children	☐ ☐ ☐ ☐ ☐ ☐
87. Bullies other children	☐ ☐ ☐ ☐ ☐ ☐
88. Is a victim of bullying by other children	☐ ☐ ☐ ☐ ☐ ☐
89. Seeks attention by joking or clowning	☐ ☐ ☐ ☐ ☐ ☐

Other Behaviors

	Check one: 1 2 3 4 5 NA
90. Daydreams	☐ ☐ ☐ ☐ ☐ ☐
91. Stares	☐ ☐ ☐ ☐ ☐ ☐
92. Is disorganized	☐ ☐ ☐ ☐ ☐ ☐
93. Picks at parts of body	☐ ☐ ☐ ☐ ☐ ☐
94. Has unpredictable behavior	☐ ☐ ☐ ☐ ☐ ☐
95. Talks out of turn	☐ ☐ ☐ ☐ ☐ ☐
96. Sucks thumb	☐ ☐ ☐ ☐ ☐ ☐
97. Has poor motor control	☐ ☐ ☐ ☐ ☐ ☐

Comments: _____
_____
_____
_____

Table C-3
Observation Protocol Combining Interval and Event Recording

OBSERVATION PROTOCOL

Referred child (RC): _____   Teacher's name: _____

Comparison child (CC): _____   School: _____

Observer's name: _____   Time: Begin _____ End _____ Date: _____

Interval recording method: _____   Grade level: _____ Class: _____

Interval length: _____   Activity[a]: _____

Interval recording behavior: _____   Event recording behavior: _____

Interval	Interval recording		Event recording		Interval	Interval recording		Event recording		Interval	Interval recording		Event recording	
	RC	CC	RC	CC		RC	CC	RC	CC		RC	CC	RC	CC
1					21					41				
2					22					42				
3					23					43				
4					24					44				
5					25					45				
6					26					46				
7					27					47				
8					28					48				
9					29					49				
10					30					50				
11					31					51				
12					32					52				
13					33					53				
14					34					54				
15					35					55				
16					36					56				
17					37					57				
18					38					58				
19					39					59				
20					40					60				

SUMMARY

Interval recording	Total number of intervals	% of intervals
Referred child		
Comparison child		

Event recording	Total number of events	% of events
Referred child		
Comparison child		

[a] Activity can refer to independent seatwork, small group activity, large group activity, group instruction, free time, or something else.
Source: Adapted from Adams-Wells Special Services Cooperative (n.d.).
From *Foundations of Behavioral, Social, and Clinical Assessment of Children* (Sixth Edition) by Jerome M. Sattler. Copyright 2014 by Jerome M. Sattler, Publisher, Inc. Permission to photocopy this appendix table is granted to purchaser of this book for personal use only (see copyright page for details).

Table C-4
Interval Recording Form

INTERVAL RECORDING FORM

Referred child (RC): _____   Teacher's name: _____
Comparison child (CC): _____   School: _____
Observer's name: _____   Time: Begin _____ End _____ Date: _____
Interval recording method: _____   Grade level: _____ Class: _____
Interval length: _____   Activity[a]: _____

BEHAVIOR CODES

O = On-task—Looking at teacher, at another speaker, or at a work area in front of him or her; participating in class discussions; following teacher's directions; working quietly at desk; behaving appropriately in other ways.
V = Verbal off-task—Talking out, singing, talking to classmates, making noises, whistling.
M = Motor off-task—Engaging in bodily movement; hitting; kicking; playing with clothes, objects, foot, or finger; tapping pencil; rocking; moving up on knees.
P = Passive off-task—Staring blankly, looking out of window or into hallway, watching peers, watching clock, putting head on desk, sleeping.
S = Out-of-seat—Being out of seat without permission.

Interval	Behavior code		Comment	Interval	Behavior code		Comment
	RC	CC			RC	CC	
1				11			
2				12			
3				13			
4				14			
5				15			
6				16			
7				17			
8				18			
9				19			
10				20			

SUMMARY

Behavior	Referred child		Comparison child	
	Total number of intervals	% of intervals	Total number of intervals	% of intervals
O = On-task				
V = Verbal off-task				
M = Motor off-task				
P = Passive off-task				
S = Out-of-seat				

Note. The number of intervals can be increased as needed.
[a] Activity can refer to independent seatwork, small group activity, large group activity, group instruction, free time, or something else.
Source: Adapted from Adams-Wells Special Services Cooperative (n.d.).
From *Foundations of Behavioral, Social, and Clinical Assessment of Children* (Sixth Edition) by Jerome M. Sattler. Copyright 2014 by Jerome M. Sattler, Publisher, Inc. Permission to photocopy this appendix table is granted to purchaser of this book for personal use only (see copyright page for details).

Table C-5
Classroom Observation Code: A Modification of the Stony Brook Code

---

GENERAL INSTRUCTIONS FOR USING
THE CLASSROOM OBSERVATION CODE

1. This observation coding system is used to record behaviors that occur during structured didactic teaching and/or during periods of independent work under teacher supervision. Behaviors that occur during free play periods, snack time, etc., are not recorded. In addition, observers should not code behaviors in the following situations: a) whenever the child is out of seat at the teacher's request to hand out or collect materials, read in front of the class, work at the blackboard, or wait in line to have work checked; b) whenever the child receives individualized instruction from the teacher; c) whenever there is no assigned task, including instances in which the child is not required to initiate a new task after completion of assigned work; and d) whenever the teacher leaves the room.

2. Observers must be aware of the specific task assigned to the child and must note the particular class activity on the observation sheet. In addition, observers must be familiar with the general rules in each classroom. These rules, obtained from the teacher, are used as guidelines for employing this coding system. For example, a child who leaves his or her seat to sharpen a pencil without asking the teacher will be scored as "Gross Motor–Standing" (*GMs*) only if this behavior requires teacher permission. (*See* the Classroom Observation Code Observer Data Sheet: Classroom Rules.)

3. When a behavior category is observed, *circle* the respective symbols on the coding sheet. If no behavior category is observed, then code "Absence of Behavior" (*AB*); draw a slash through this particular symbol.

4. In coding a particular category, it is essential that the observer be familiar with the timing requirements of each of the behavior categories. That is, non-timed categories are coded as soon as they occur within a 15-second interval, with only the first occurrence noted. Timed categories are coded only if the child engages in behavior for more than 15 consecutive seconds. For example, a child is scored as "Off-Task" in interval 2 if the behavior began in interval 1 and continued uninterrupted throughout interval 2. Continue coding the behavior in subsequent intervals as long as the behavior continues, uninterrupted, throughout these intervals. Each box on the observation coding sheet corresponds to a 15-second interval.

5. Any time the child leaves the room for more than one full interval without permission, those interval boxes on the coding sheet should be crossed out. (*See* "Non-Compliance" and "Off-Task" for further details.)

6. Each coding sheet is divided into two 4-minute blocks. Observe each child for a total of 16 minutes, alternating 4-minute observations on each child.

I. Interference—Symbol: *I*

Purpose: This category is intended to detect any verbal or physical behaviors or noises that are disturbing to others; the purpose here is to detect a discrete and distinct behavior that does not necessarily persist.

Timing: This category is coded as a Discrete, Non-Timed Behavior.

Description:

A. Interruption of the teacher or another student during a lesson or quiet work period.

Examples:

1. Calling out during a lesson when the teacher or another student has the floor (includes ooh's and ahh's when raising hand).

2. Initiating discussion with another child during a work period.

Note:

1. "Interference" is coded immediately within the interval in which it first occurs.

2. If the child initiates a conversation that overlaps two intervals, code *I* only in the first interval.

3. If conversation stops and then starts anew in the next interval, code that interval as *I* if conversation is initiated by the target child.

4. In most classrooms a child is scored as *I* if he or she calls out an answer to the teacher's question. However, *I* is *not* coded in classrooms where calling out answers is permitted.

5. If the child engages in a conversation overlapping two intervals that is initiated by another child, do *not* code *I* in either interval.

6. Do *not* score the child as *I* if there is uncertainty as to whether the child initiated conversation or is only responding to another child.

7. Do *not* score the child as *I* if there is uncertainty as to whether or not a sound (e.g., "ooh") was made by the child.

B. Production of Sounds

Examples:

1. Vocalizations: e.g., screams, whistles, calls across room, coughs, sneezes, or loud yawns.

2. Noises other than vocalization: slamming or banging objects, tapping ruler, foot tapping, hand clapping, etc.

Note: Do not code *I* if a sound is made accidentally (e.g., the child drops a book, knocks over a chair, etc.).

C. Annoying Behavior: This behavior refers to nonverbal interruption. The child interrupts another child during a teacher-directed or independent work lesson.

Examples:

1. Tapping lightly or making gentle physical movements or gestures toward another child.

2. Sitting on another's desk when that child is present at the desk.

3. Moving or lifting another's desk when the owner is present.

D. Clowning.

Examples:

1. Mimicking the teacher or another child.

2. Kicking an object across the floor.

3. Engaging in or organizing games and other inappropriate activities during a work period (e.g., playing kickball in the class, throwing and catching a ball).

4. Showing off his or her own work when not called on by the teacher.

Table C-5 (Continued)

5. Making animal imitations.

6. Calling out a wildly inappropriate answer or making an obviously inappropriate public statement.

7. Shooting paper clips, airplanes, spitballs, etc. (If aimed at someone, this behavior is coded as "Aggression," *A*.)

8. Standing on a desk, chair, or table when not requested to do so by the teacher, or in any other inappropriate situation.

9. Posturing (child acts to characterize an action, an object, or another person).

10. Dancing in the classroom.

11. Play-acting.

12. Making mock threats. (If this does not occur in a clowning situation, then it is coded instead as "Threat or Verbal Aggression," *AC*.)

Note: If clowning involving vigorous gross-motor movements (e.g., running, dancing) occurs while the child is out of chair, then code both *I* and "Gross Motor–Vigorous" (*GMv*).

II. Off-Task—Symbol: *X*

Purpose: This category is intended to monitor behaviors when the child, *after* initiating the appropriate task-relevant behavior, attends to stimuli other than the assigned work.

Timing: This category is coded as Timed Behavior.

Description:

A. Manipulation and/or attending to objects, people, or parts of the body to the total exclusion of the task for one full interval following the interval in which the behavior began.

Examples:

1. The child plays with a pencil for one full interval after the interval in which the behavior was initially seen, without visual orientation toward the assigned task.

2. The child engages in extended conversation when he or she is supposed to be working.

3. The child does a task other than the assigned one (e.g., reads a different book). It is therefore essential that the observer be aware of the classroom situation and the specific assigned task.

Note:

1. When the child is doing something under the desk or where the observer can't see and is not attending to the task, assume the behavior is inappropriate and code *X*.

2. If the teacher is conducting a lesson at the board such that the child is required to look at the teacher or the board, score the child as *X* if he or she does not look at the teacher and/or the board at any time during the interval after the interval in which he or she first looked away.

3. If the teacher or another student is lecturing, reading a story, issuing instructions, etc., such that the child's task is to listen to the speaker, then code *X* if the child, by his or her behavior, indicates that he or she is not listening (e.g., head down on the desk, doodling in book, looking in book, etc.). Do *not* code *X* if the child looks at the speaker at any time during the interval.

4. Do *not* code *X* if the child shows any visual orientation to the task. Do *not* code *X* if there is uncertainty as to his or her visual orientation.

5. Do *not* code *X* if the child, by his or her behavior, indicates that he or she is listening (e.g., the child looks at the speaker's subject matter).

6. Do *not* code *X* if the child plays with or manipulates an object while attending to the task.

B. Code as *X* those instances when the child is allowed to leave his or her seat (e.g., to throw something in the trash) but remains away from the seat for more than five consecutive intervals following the interval in which he or she first left the seat.

Example:

Leaves Seat	Out of Seat	Out of Seat	Out of Seat	Out of Seat	Out of Seat	Out of Seat
1	2	3	4	5	6	7

Interval 7 is coded as *X* and "Out-of-Chair" (*OC*). Continue coding *X* and *OC* as long as the child remains away from his or her desk. If the child engages in task-relevant behavior while out of seat (e.g., attends to a teacher lesson), then stop coding *X* but continue coding *OC*.

Note:

1. If after initiating the task the child leaves the classroom for more than one full interval without permission, code *X* and indicate that the child is out of the room by crossing out the interval box. Continue coding *X* as long as the child remains out of the room.

2. Do *not* code *X* if the child stops working and it is not clear whether he or she has completed the task. However, put a dot above the interval in which there is uncertainty. If the teacher then confirms that the child was off-task (e.g., she says: "Why aren't you working?"), then go back and code these "dotted" intervals as *X*. If the teacher gives no indication, do not code *X*.

3. Do *not* code *X* in any interval that has been coded as "Solicitation" (*S*).

III. Non-Compliance—Symbol: *NC*

Purpose: This category is intended to monitor behaviors that reflect a failure on the part of the child to follow teacher instructions.

Timing: This category is coded as a Timed Behavior.

Description: The child fails to initiate appropriate behavior in response to a command or request from the teacher. It is to be distinguished from "Off-Task" (*X*), which is coded when the child, *after initiating* task-relevant behavior, ceases this task-relevant behavior.

Example: After a command has been given by the teacher (e.g., "Copy the words on the board into your notebook"), the child has one full interval after the interval in which the command was given to initiate the behavior. If the child has not complied, begin coding *NC* and continue coding *NC* for each full interval in which the child fails to initiate the task.

Note:

1. When the teacher gives a specific command, write "T.C." above the interval box in which the teacher finished giving the command.

2. If the child indicates that he or she is carrying out the teacher's command (e.g., the child looks for his or her notebook), then allow the child *five* full intervals to comply. If after this time period he or she has not initiated task-relevant behavior (e.g., copying words), then begin coding *NC*.

(Continued)

Table C-5 *(Continued)*

3. If before initiating the task the child leaves the classroom for more than one full interval without permission, code *NC* and cross out the interval box. Continue coding *NC* as long as the child remains out of the room.

4. The teacher will often issue commands that are not task-related, but are instead related to the handling of materials (e.g., "Put down your pencils," "Put away your book"). If the child has not complied by the end of the first full interval following the interval in which the command was given, then code that interval as *NC*. Do *not* continue coding *NC*. If the teacher repeats the same commands, then note "T.C." and begin to time the child to see if he or she complies.

5. A teacher may issue more than one command (e.g., "Put down your pencils and look at the board"). The child should *not* be scored as *NC* if he or she looks at the board but does not put down his or her pencil. Therefore, do not code *NC* if the child follows the more salient, task-related aspect of the teacher's command. The child should be scored as *NC* if he or she does *not* follow the more salient command (i.e., "look at the board").

6. The teacher will often tell the class to take out a textbook and begin working independently on a particular page. Do *not* code *NC* if the child begins working in the book on the wrong page.

7. A child may not have a book in school or may be unable to find it. Give the child *five* full intervals to attempt to find the appropriate materials. If at the end of this time interval the child has not informed the teacher that he or she doesn't have the book (homework, crayons, etc.), then begin coding *NC* until he or she notifies the teacher.

Situations that arise in the classroom can make it difficult to decide whether a child is non-compliant or off-task. The following guidelines should be useful in clarifying some of these situations.

8. During a classroom lesson the teacher will often issue commands that are *specific to the ongoing lesson.* In these instances, a child who had been working on the lesson but who does not follow the new command should be scored as *X* rather than *NC*. For example, during a math lesson, the children have been working in their math workbooks. They have been following the teacher's directions and have worked on specific math examples. The teacher tells them to "Do example 10." The child has been working all along but does not do example 10. If the required time interval elapses and the child has not begun work on this example, he or she should be scored as *X*.

9. The following situation should be coded as *NC* and not "Off-Task" (*X*). During a classroom lesson, the teacher instructs the children to work on or direct their attention to a task different from the one on which they had been working. For example, during a math lesson, the children have been working in their math workbooks. The teacher now shifts the focus of the math lesson and instructs the children to work on set theory using colored blocks. If the child does not follow these instructions within the required time interval, he or she should be scored as *NC*.

IV. Minor Motor Movement—Symbol: *MM*

Purpose: There are two aspects to this category, both of which are intended to monitor behaviors of the child that are indicative of restlessness and fidgeting.

Timing: This category is coded as Discrete, Non-Timed Behavior.

Description: Minor motor movements refer to buttock movements and rocking movements of the child while he or she is in the seat and/or to buttock movements while he or she is in *non-erect* positions while out of seat.

A. The child engages in in-seat movements such that there is an *observable* movement of the lower buttock(s)—i.e., that part of the buttock(s) that is in contact with the seat of the chair.

Examples: The following pertain to movements of one or both buttocks.

1. Sliding in seat.
2. Twisting, turning, wiggling, etc.—coded only when accompanied by buttock movement.
3. Lifting one or both buttocks off the seat.
4. Buttock movements while kneeling or squatting in seat.

B. The child produces rocking movements of his or her body and/or chair. Body rocking movements are defined as *repetitive* movements (at least two complete back-and-forth movements) from the waist up in a back-and-forth manner. Movements of the chair are also coded as *MM* when the child lifts two chair legs off the floor.

Note:

1. Do *not* code *MM* if the child makes *just one* forward-leaning movement or *just one* backward-leaning movement. However, if this movement is accompanied by an observable buttock movement, then *MM* should be coded.

2. Code as *MM any* movement that takes the child from a seated position into a kneeling, squatting, or crouching position, either in or out of the seat.

3. If the child is kneeling in or out of his or her seat or *leaning* over a desk or table, then code as *MM* any observable movements of the lower and/or upper buttocks—i.e., that area from the upper thigh to the hip.

4. If the child goes from a standing to a kneeling or squatting position, code *MM*.

5. Do *not* code *MM* if the physical set-up is such that the child *must* move in order to work on a task. There are *two* specific situations where minor motor movements should not be coded.

(a) The position of the child's desk requires that he or she move in order to work on a task—for example, the child faces the side of the room and the blackboard is in front. In this situation, the child *must* move his or her buttocks in order to copy from the board.

(b) While the child is working on a task that requires his or her visual attention (e.g., copying from the board, watching the teacher), the child's view is obstructed, requiring him or her to move in order to maintain visual contact.

6. Do *not* code *MM* if the child moves from a standing or kneeling position to a sitting position in the chair.

V. Gross-Motor Behavior

Purpose: There are two aspects of this category which are intended to monitor motor activity that results in the child's leaving his or her seat and/or engaging in vigorous motor activity.

Timing: This category is coded as a Discrete, Non-Timed Behavior.

Table C-5 *(Continued)*

A. Gross Motor–Standing—Symbol: *GMs*

Description: GMs refers to motor activity that results in the child's leaving his or her seat and standing on one or both legs (on the floor, chair, or desk) in an erect or semi-erect position such that the child's body from the waist up is *at least* at a 135-degree angle with the floor.

Note:

1. Do *not* code *GMs* when the child has permission, specific or implied, to leave his or her seat (e.g., to sharpen a pencil, throw something away, get materials, go to the board, go to the teacher's desk, etc.). If the child leaves his or her seat without permission, then code *GMs*.

2. Do *not* code *GMs* if the physical set-up is such that the child *must* move in order to work on a task. For example, while the child is working on a task that requires his or her visual attention (e.g., copying from the board, watching a demonstration), the child's view is obstructed, requiring him or her to stand up in order to maintain visual contact.

3. If it is not clear whether the child had to stand up, then code *GMs*.

B. Gross Motor–Vigorous—Symbol: *GMv*

Description: This is coded when the child engages in vigorous motor activity *while not seated at his or her desk* or when the child *leaves* his or her seat in a sudden, abrupt, or impulsive manner.

Examples:

1. Jumping up out of seat.
2. Running away from seat.
3. Running in the classroom.
4. Crawling across the floor.
5. Twirling.
6. Acrobatics.
7. Swinging between two seats or desks.

VI. Out-of-Chair Behavior—Symbol: *OC*

Purpose: This category is intended to monitor extended out-of-seat behavior.

Timing: This category is coded as a Timed Behavior.

Description: The child remains out of chair for one full interval after the interval in which he or she first left the seat.

Note:

1. *OC* is coded for each complete interval that the child remains out of chair, irrespective of whether the child is standing, sitting, or kneeling on the floor or roaming around the classroom.

2. If while being coded as *OC* the child kneels or squats (out-of-chair) or sits on the floor, then code this movement as "Minor Motor Movement" (*MM*) and continue to code *OC*. Any buttock movements that occur while the child is seated on the floor are coded as *MM*. *OC* is discontinued only when the child sits or kneels in a chair—be it his or her own or someone else's.

3. If the child is out of a chair getting materials, sharpening a pencil, getting a drink of water, throwing something away, etc. (when these are permitted behaviors), then allow the child a maximum of five full intervals after the interval in which he or she first left the seat to complete this task. After these five intervals, if the child is still out of chair, then begin coding *OC*. If the child is *not working* during this period, then also score him or her as "Off-Task" (*X*).

4. If fewer than five intervals have elapsed and the child has obtained his or her goal (e.g., gotten a book, thrown something away, etc.), then allow him or her one full interval to return to his or her seat. If at the end of that interval he or she has not returned to the seat, then code that interval as *OC*

5. It is essential to be familiar with classroom rules regarding leaving seat with and without permission.

VII. Physical Aggression—Symbol: *A*

Purpose: This category is intended to measure physical aggression directed at another person or destruction of other's property. This behavior is coded regardless of the accuracy of the intended assault.

Timing: This category is coded as a Discrete, Non-Timed Behavior.

Description:

A. The child makes a forceful movement directed at another person, either directly or by utilizing an object as an extension of the hand.

Examples:

1. Blocking someone with arms or body; tripping, kicking, or hitting another person.
2. Throwing objects at another person.
3. Pinching, biting.

Note:

1. In all of the above examples, even if the child misses his or her goal, the behavior should be coded as *A*.

2. Code *A* even when the physical aggression is initiated by another child and the target child defends himself or herself. However, this should be noted on the coding sheet.

B. Destruction of others' materials or possessions or school property.

Examples:

1. Tearing or crumpling others' work.
2. Breaking crayons, pencils, or pens of others.
3. Misusing others' books (ripping out pages, writing in them, etc.).
4. Writing on another child or on another child's work.
5. Writing on a school desk.
6. Writing in a school textbook.

Note:

1. Code *A* even if the owner of the material is not at his or her desk.

2. If the child engages in *continuous* destructive behavior (e.g., writes on a desk or in a school textbook for several consecutive intervals), then code *A* only in the first interval in which the behavior occurs. If the child *interrupts* this destructive behavior and then returns to it, then code *A* anew.

C. Grabbing material in a sudden manner.

Examples:

1. The child grabs a book out of the hands of another child.
2. The child grabs his or her own material from another child.

Note:

Exclude casually taking material out of another's hand.

(Continued)

Table C-5 *(Continued)*

VIII. Threat of Verbal Aggression—Symbol: to children = *AC*, to teacher = *AT*

Purpose: This category is intended to monitor verbalizations or physical gestures of children that are abusive or threatening.

Timing: This category is coded as a Discrete, Non-Timed Behavior.

Description:

A. The child uses abusive language and gestures to children

Examples:

1. The child curses at another, says "shut up" to another.

2. The child sticks out his or her tongue at another, makes a threatening gesture, etc.

3. The child threatens others.

4. The child teases others, criticizes others.

5. The child bullies others.

B. When asked to do something by the teacher, the child directly states, "No I won't; I'm not going to do that." This should be coded as "Interference" (*I*) and *AT*. Do *not* code "Solicitation" (*S*).

C. The child answers the teacher back when a reply is not acceptable.

Example:

The teacher states, "We are not going outside today." The child calls back in a defiant manner, "Why not? I want to."

IX. Solicitation of Teacher—Symbol: *S*

Purpose: This category monitors behaviors directed toward the teacher. It is important to note that this behavior is coded only when initiated by the target child.

Timing: This category is coded as a Discrete, Non-Timed Behavior.

Description: Behaviors directed at obtaining the teacher's attention.

Examples:

1. Leaving seat and going up to the teacher. (This would be coded as *S* and "Gross Motor–Standing" (*GMs*); if the child speaks to the teacher, "Interference" (*I*) is also coded.)

2. Raising hand.

3. Calling out to the teacher.

Note:

1. These behaviors are coded as *S* whether or not the teacher recognizes the child.

2. When a child calls out to the teacher by mentioning the teacher's name or directs a question or statement specifically to the teacher while the teacher is attending to another child or addressing the class, then the behavior is coded as both *S* and "Interference" (*I*).

3. If the child says "ooh," "ahh," etc., while raising his or her hand in response to the teacher's question, code this as "Interference" (*I*) but *not S*.

4. If the observation begins while a teacher-child interaction is taking place, assume that the teacher initiated the interaction and do *not* code *S*.

5. If the child raises his or her hand in order to solicit the teacher and keeps the hand raised for more than one interval, code *S only* in the first interval in which the behavior occurred.

6. "Solicitation" and "Interference"(*I*) are coded if the child calls out an answer to the teacher when another child has the floor.

7. "Solicitation" is *not* coded if the child raises his or her hand in response to a teacher's question.

8. "Solicitation" is *not* coded if the child calls out in response to a teacher's question. In most classrooms, "Interference" (*I*) is coded if the child calls out an answer to a teacher's question.

X. Absence of Behavior—Symbol: *AB*

If no inappropriate behaviors as defined by the above categories occur in an interval, then code *AB*.

Table C-5 (Continued)

CLASSROOM OBSERVATION CODE
OBSERVER DATA SHEET: CLASSROOM RULES

Child A: _____ Seat: _____

Child B: _____ Seat: _____

School: _____ Teacher: _____ Room #: _____ Date: _____

1. Must a child always raise his or her hand before asking or answering questions?

   a) During a teacher-conducted lesson   _____

   b) During independent work   _____

   c) Comments _____

2. May a child engage in conversation with other children?

   a) During a teacher-conducted lesson   _____

   b) During independent work   _____

   c) Comments _____

3. Must a child work after completion of assigned task?   _____

   a) On what? _____

   b) Can this be done out of his or her assigned seat?   _____

4. May a child leave the room without permission?   _____

5. May a child leave his or her seat without permission to

   a) sharpen a pencil_____   e) get materials _____

   b) throw something away _____   f) stand while working_____

   c) get a drink _____   g) other _____

   d) speak to the teacher_____

6. Other classroom rules: _____

   _____

(Continued)

Table C-5 *(Continued)*

CLASSROOM OBSERVATION CODE
SCORING SHEET

	1		2		3		4		5		6		7		8	
A	X	I A	X	I A	X	I A	X	I A	X	I A	X	I A	X	I A	X	I A
	NC	AC	NC	AC	NC	AC	NC	AC	NC	AC	NC	AC	NC	AC	NC	AC
	MM	AT	MM	AT	MM	AT	MM	AT	MM	AT	MM	AT	MM	AT	MM	AT
	GMs	GMv	GMs	GMv	GMs	GMv	GMs	GMv	GMs	GMv	GMs	GMv	GMs	GMv	GMs	GMv
	OC	S	OC	S	OC	S	OC	S	OC	S	OC	S	OC	S	OC	S
		AB		AB		AB		AB		AB		AB		AB		AB

	1		2		3		4		5		6		7		8	
B	X	I A	X	I A	X	I A	X	I A	X	I A	X	I A	X	I A	X	I A
	NC	AC	NC	AC	NC	AC	NC	AC	NC	AC	NC	AC	NC	AC	NC	AC
	MM	AT	MM	AT	MM	AT	MM	AT	MM	AT	MM	AT	MM	AT	MM	AT
	GMs	GMv	GMs	GMv	GMs	GMv	GMs	GMv	GMs	GMv	GMs	GMv	GMs	GMv	GMs	GMv
	OC	S	OC	S	OC	S	OC	S	OC	S	OC	S	OC	S	OC	S
		AB		AB		AB		AB		AB		AB		AB		AB

	1		2		3		4		5		6		7		8	
C	X	I A	X	I A	X	I A	X	I A	X	I A	X	I A	X	I A	X	I A
	NC	AC	NC	AC	NC	AC	NC	AC	NC	AC	NC	AC	NC	AC	NC	AC
	MM	AT	MM	AT	MM	AT	MM	AT	MM	AT	MM	AT	MM	AT	MM	AT
	GMs	GMv	GMs	GMv	GMs	GMv	GMs	GMv	GMs	GMv	GMs	GMv	GMs	GMv	GMs	GMv
	OC	S	OC	S	OC	S	OC	S	OC	S	OC	S	OC	S	OC	S
		AB		AB		AB		AB		AB		AB		AB		AB

	1		2		3		4		5		6		7		8	
D	X	I A	X	I A	X	I A	X	I A	X	I A	X	I A	X	I A	X	I A
	NC	AC	NC	AC	NC	AC	NC	AC	NC	AC	NC	AC	NC	AC	NC	AC
	MM	AT	MM	AT	MM	AT	MM	AT	MM	AT	MM	AT	MM	AT	MM	AT
	GMs	GMv	GMs	GMv	GMs	GMv	GMs	GMv	GMs	GMv	GMs	GMv	GMs	GMv	GMs	GMv
	OC	S	OC	S	OC	S	OC	S	OC	S	OC	S	OC	S	OC	S
		AB		AB		AB		AB		AB		AB		AB		AB

Abbreviations: X = Off-Task; NC = Non-Compliance; MM = Minor Motor Movement; GMs = Gross Motor–Standing; OC = Out-of-Chair; I = Interference; A = Physical Aggression; AC = Threat of Verbal Aggression to Children; AT = Threat of Verbal Aggression to Teacher; GMv = Gross Motor–Vigorous; S = Solicitation of Teacher; AB = Absence of Behavior.

Observer_____ Date _____ Time _____

Source: Reprinted, with changes in notation, with permission of the authors from H. Abikoff and R. Gittelman, "Classroom Observation Code: A Modification of the Stony Brook Code," *Psychopharmacology Bulletin*, 1985, *21*, pp. 901–909.
From *Foundations of Behavioral, Social, and Clinical Assessment of Children* (Sixth Edition) by Jerome M. Sattler. Copyright 2014 by Jerome M. Sattler, Publisher, Inc. Permission to photocopy this appendix table is granted to purchasers of this book for personal use only (see copyright page for details).

Table C-6
Playground Observer Impression Form

PLAYGROUND OBSERVER IMPRESSION FORM

Child's name: _____   Teacher's name: _____

Age: _____ Grade level: _____ Class: _____   School: _____

Observer's name: _____   Time: Begin _____ End _____ Date: _____

Directions: PART A: Check Yes, No, or NA. PART B: Check one box using the following scale:

1	2	3	4	5	NA
Never	Seldom	Sometimes	Frequently	Always	Not applicable or Not observed

PART A

Appearance — Check one (Yes No NA)

1. Is dressed appropriately ☐ ☐ ☐
2. Weight is appropriate ☐ ☐ ☐
3. Is underweight ☐ ☐ ☐
4. Is overweight ☐ ☐ ☐
5. Looks tired ☐ ☐ ☐
6. Has bruises ☐ ☐ ☐

PART B

Physical Ability — Check one (1 2 3 4 5 NA)

7. Has appropriate activity level ☐ ☐ ☐ ☐ ☐ ☐
8. Walks appropriately ☐ ☐ ☐ ☐ ☐ ☐
9. Runs appropriately ☐ ☐ ☐ ☐ ☐ ☐
10. Jumps appropriately ☐ ☐ ☐ ☐ ☐ ☐
11. Kicks appropriately ☐ ☐ ☐ ☐ ☐ ☐
12. Throws a ball appropriately ☐ ☐ ☐ ☐ ☐ ☐
13. Skips appropriately ☐ ☐ ☐ ☐ ☐ ☐
14. Catches a ball appropriately ☐ ☐ ☐ ☐ ☐ ☐
15. Climbs playground equipment ☐ ☐ ☐ ☐ ☐ ☐
16. Maintains balance ☐ ☐ ☐ ☐ ☐ ☐
17. Maneuvers around environment safely ☐ ☐ ☐ ☐ ☐ ☐

Relationship with Other Children

18. Takes turns appropriately ☐ ☐ ☐ ☐ ☐ ☐
19. Cooperates with other children ☐ ☐ ☐ ☐ ☐ ☐
20. Engages in reciprocal conversations ☐ ☐ ☐ ☐ ☐ ☐
21. Joins in play ☐ ☐ ☐ ☐ ☐ ☐
22. Is rejected by other children ☐ ☐ ☐ ☐ ☐ ☐
23. Withdraws from other children ☐ ☐ ☐ ☐ ☐ ☐
24. Shows concern when another child is hurt ☐ ☐ ☐ ☐ ☐ ☐
25. Takes on a leadership role ☐ ☐ ☐ ☐ ☐ ☐
26. Is popular with other children ☐ ☐ ☐ ☐ ☐ ☐
27. Argues with other children ☐ ☐ ☐ ☐ ☐ ☐

Relationship with Other Children *(Cont.)* — Check one (1 2 3 4 5 NA)

28. Hits or pushes other children ☐ ☐ ☐ ☐ ☐ ☐
29. Displays physical affection with other children ☐ ☐ ☐ ☐ ☐ ☐
30. Is bossy ☐ ☐ ☐ ☐ ☐ ☐
31. Helps other children ☐ ☐ ☐ ☐ ☐ ☐
32. Initiates interactions with other children ☐ ☐ ☐ ☐ ☐ ☐
33. Disrupts group interactions ☐ ☐ ☐ ☐ ☐ ☐
34. Is a victim of verbal aggression ☐ ☐ ☐ ☐ ☐ ☐
35. Is a victim of physical aggression ☐ ☐ ☐ ☐ ☐ ☐
36. Is a victim of bullying ☐ ☐ ☐ ☐ ☐ ☐
37. Bullies other children ☐ ☐ ☐ ☐ ☐ ☐
38. Plays mostly alone ☐ ☐ ☐ ☐ ☐ ☐
39. Plays mostly next to (but not with) another child ☐ ☐ ☐ ☐ ☐ ☐
40. Spends most of the time with male children ☐ ☐ ☐ ☐ ☐ ☐
41. Spends most of the time with female children ☐ ☐ ☐ ☐ ☐ ☐

Temperament

42. Has mood swings ☐ ☐ ☐ ☐ ☐ ☐
43. Is animated, jovial, or happy ☐ ☐ ☐ ☐ ☐ ☐
44. Is depressed, sad, or down ☐ ☐ ☐ ☐ ☐ ☐
45. Is easy to anger ☐ ☐ ☐ ☐ ☐ ☐
46. Is detached or distant ☐ ☐ ☐ ☐ ☐ ☐
47. Is shy ☐ ☐ ☐ ☐ ☐ ☐
48. Is passive ☐ ☐ ☐ ☐ ☐ ☐
49. Is assertive ☐ ☐ ☐ ☐ ☐ ☐

Behavior

50. Follows teacher's directions ☐ ☐ ☐ ☐ ☐ ☐
51. Has a short attention span ☐ ☐ ☐ ☐ ☐ ☐
52. Is disciplined by teacher ☐ ☐ ☐ ☐ ☐ ☐
53. Destroys equipment ☐ ☐ ☐ ☐ ☐ ☐

Table C-7
Checklist for Observing Children's Play

CHECKLIST FOR OBSERVING CHILDREN'S PLAY

Child's name: _____   Teacher's name: _____

Age: _____ Grade level: _____ Class: _____   School: _____

Observer's name: _____   Time: Begin _____ End _____ Date: _____

Directions: Check each item that applies to the target child.

Solitary Play	*Parallel Play*	*Group Play*
Functional play ☐ 1. Target child makes faces and dances while watching self in mirror. ☐ 2. Target child lies on back in the middle of the floor. ☐ 3. Target child spins truck wheels with fingers. ☐ 4. Target child runs around in a circle. ☐ 5. Other _____	*Functional play* ☐ 1. Target child and another child sit at a table and draw, but there is no interaction between the two. ☐ 2. Target child and another child push a button, open a door, and ring bells on a busy box, but they do not attend to each other's actions as they play. ☐ 3. Other _____	*Functional play* ☐ 1. Target child and another child are engaged in imitative behavior involving touching each other, smiling, and laughing. ☐ 2. Other _____
Constructive play ☐ 1. Target child pushes car along a track. ☐ 2. Target child plays with puzzle pieces. ☐ 3. Target child places toy people in cars. ☐ 4. Target child plays with robot and punches button on robot. ☐ 5. Target child builds building using blocks. ☐ 6. Target child constructs an object with Legos. ☐ 7. Other _____	*Constructive play* ☐ 1. Target child and another child paint together at a table, target child tells the other child that he or she is making a rainbow, and they trade paints. ☐ 2. Target child and another child sit at a table, and each makes his or her own construction out of Legos. ☐ 3. Target child and another child sit at a table working on a puzzle but do not interact. ☐ 4. Other _____	*Constructive play* ☐ 1. Target child and another child exchange objects or offer objects to each other. ☐ 2. Target child throws a ball and waits for another child to retrieve it. ☐ 3. Target child and another child shovel sand into a toy truck and then dump the sand into a large pile. ☐ 4. Other _____
Dramatic play ☐ 1. Target child plays alone with puppets. ☐ 2. Target child plays in housekeeping area. ☐ 3. Other _____	*Dramatic play* ☐ 1. Target child and another child are close to each other and play with puppets, but target child takes on the role of the puppet and the other child plays separately by just manipulating the puppet. ☐ 2. Other _____	*Dramatic play* ☐ 1. Target child and another child pretend to order pizza. Target child is the customer, and the other child has a puppet who manages the restaurant. Target child gives his or her order. ☐ 2. Target child and another child pretend to be dressed up. Target child begins to leave area, and the other child says, "Don't go without your hat." ☐ 3. Other _____
Games-with-rules play ☐ 1. Target child plays a board game and adheres to the rules. ☐ 2. Other _____	*Games-with-rules play* ☐ 1. Target child and another child play on the same game board, but they do not play together. ☐ 2. Other _____	*Games-with-rules play* ☐ 1. Target child and another child play ball under a self-imposed, strict set of rules. ☐ 2. Other _____

Note. See Table 9-3 (p. 302) in *Foundations of Behavioral, Social, and Clinical Assessment of Children, Sixth Edition* for a definition of each type of play.
Source: Adapted from Guralnick and Groom (1988).

Table C-8
Social Competence Observation Schedule

Category	Description
Interacting with Peers	
1. Passively accepts aggression or domination from peer (Factor I)	Child allows another to boss, push, hit, or grab things from him or her without retaliation of any kind
2. Communicates in a positive way with peer (Factor I)	Child shows natural communication with peers; child appears at ease and comfortable in the situation
3. Is involved in cooperative activity with peer (Factor II)	Child voluntarily becomes involved with one or more children in an activity not required by the teacher
4. Shows successful leadership activity (Factor I)	Child initiates activity and makes suggestions that are followed by peers
5. Bosses or bullies peer—verbal (Factor II)	Child tells others what or what not to do, commands others
6. Exhibits physical aggression against peer (Factor II)	Child engages in aggression involving actual physical contact
Interacting with Teacher	
7. Clings to teacher (Factor I)	Child constantly stays by teacher's side or, for example, holds on to teacher's hand or clothes
8. Tenses or withdraws in response to teacher's approach (Factor I)	Child tenses body or moves farther away when approached by teacher
9. Communicates feelings to teacher in positive way (Factor I)	Child makes a positive statement to the teacher that is not related to classroom activities
10. Volunteers ideas or suggestions to teacher (Factor I)	Child makes suggestions or gives ideas during formal, teacher-directed classroom activities
11. Seeks attention of teacher while latter is interacting with another child (Factor II)	Child calls out to teacher, grabs teacher's arm, or performs similar actions when teacher is involved with another child
12. Exhibits physical aggression toward teacher (Factor II)	Child hits, kicks, or bites teacher
13. Seeks teacher attention—negative (Factor II)	Child uses inappropriate behavior to seek teacher's attention
14. Follows teacher request for help (Factor II)	Child follows teacher's directions willingly and immediately
15. Follows teacher suggestion regarding play activity (Factor II)	Child accepts and follows teacher's ideas or suggestions during informal, free activity
16. Exhibits other cooperative interactions with teacher (Factor II)	—
Child Is Alone	
17. Quietly listens to peer or teacher (Factor I)	Child is attentive to teacher while latter is giving instruction, reading a story, or performing a similar activity or when peer talks to him or her
18. Daydreams, stares into space, has blank look (Factor I)	Child has tuned out what is happening in the classroom, is unaware of what is going on, and looks sad
19. Puts things away carefully (Factor I)	—
20. Appears alone, confused, and bewildered (Factor I)	Child's face registers confusion; child appears not to understand or know how to organize or carry out an activity
21. Cries or screams—frightened (Factor I)	Child cries or screams to express some emotion other than, for example, anger or humiliation
22. Wanders aimlessly (Factor I)	—
23. Engages in task in positive manner (Factor II)	Child is actively involved in carrying out task sanctioned by teacher; he or she is concentrating, alert, and interested
24. Engages in task in negative manner (Factor II)	Child resists instructions, destroys an object, or engages in similar negative behaviors
25. Throws temper tantrum (Factor II)	Child screams or kicks

(Continued)

Table C-8 *(Continued)*

Category	Description
Child Is Alone *(Continued)*	
26. Exhibits inappropriate verbal activity (Factor II)	Child expresses anger or frustration through words or gestures
27. Exhibits inappropriate gross-motor activity (Factor II)	Child runs around room, throws objects, jumps, or performs similarly inappropriate gross-motor activity
28. Exhibits other isolated negative behavior (Factor I)	—

Note. Factor I refers to Interest-Participation vs. Apathy-Withdrawal and Factor II refers to Cooperation-Compliance vs. Anger-Defiance. Items 2, 3, 4, 9, 10, 14, 15, 16, 17, 19, and 23 are given 1 point, while items 1, 5, 6, 7, 8, 11, 12, 13, 18, 20, 21, 22, 24, 25, 26, 27, and 28 are given −1 point.

This schedule was designed to parallel the two teacher-judgment measures developed by Martin Kohn (the Social Competence Scales and the Problem Checklist). For additional information about the schedule, see Ali Khan and R. D. Hoge, "A Teacher-Judgment Measure of Social Competence: Validity Data," *Journal of Consulting and Clinical Psychology*, 1983, *51*, 809–814.

Source: Reprinted, with changes in notation, by permission of R. D. Hoge.

Table C-9
Preschool Children's Social, Behavioral, and Motor Competence Checklist

PRESCHOOL CHILDREN'S SOCIAL, BEHAVIORAL, AND MOTOR COMPETENCE CHECKLIST

Child's name: _____ Teacher's name: _____

Age: _____ Grade level: _____ Class: _____ School: _____

Observer's name: _____ Time: Begin _____ End _____ Date: _____

Directions: Check one box using the following scale:

Rating scale:	1	2	3	4	5
	Never	Sometimes	Usually	Often	Always

Characteristics	Check one					
Social Behavior	1	2	3	4	5
The child					
1. Is happy.	☐	☐	☐	☐	☐
2. Comes to program willingly.	☐	☐	☐	☐	☐
3. Copes with rebuffs or other disappointments adequately.	☐	☐	☐	☐	☐
4. Displays a capacity for humor.	☐	☐	☐	☐	☐
5. Engages in positive interactions with other children (e.g., smiles, waves, nods).	☐	☐	☐	☐	☐
6. Elicits a positive response when approaching others.	☐	☐	☐	☐	☐
7. Expresses wishes and preferences clearly (e.g., gives reasons for actions).	☐	☐	☐	☐	☐
8. Asserts own rights and needs appropriately.	☐	☐	☐	☐	☐
9. Resolves social problems with peers.	☐	☐	☐	☐	☐
10. Is not easily intimidated by bullying.	☐	☐	☐	☐	☐
11. Bullies other children.	☐	☐	☐	☐	☐
12. Is cooperative (e.g., shares, takes turn, responsive to others' needs).	☐	☐	☐	☐	☐
13. Is aggressive (e.g., kicks, shakes, grabs, spits, pushes, bites, scratches).	☐	☐	☐	☐	☐
14. Is invited by other children to join them in play, friendship, and work.	☐	☐	☐	☐	☐
15. Is named by other children as someone they are friends with or like to play and work with.	☐	☐	☐	☐	☐
16. Is aware of feelings of others and helps and comforts others.	☐	☐	☐	☐	☐
17. Makes relevant contributions to ongoing activities.	☐	☐	☐	☐	☐
18. Has one or more friends.	☐	☐	☐	☐	☐
19. Negotiates and compromises with others appropriately.	☐	☐	☐	☐	☐
20. Accepts and enjoys peers and adults who have special needs.	☐	☐	☐	☐	☐
21. Accepts and enjoys peers and adults who belong to ethnic groups other than his or her own.	☐	☐	☐	☐	☐
22. Shows appropriate response to new adults (e.g., friendly, approaches them cheerfully).	☐	☐	☐	☐	☐
Classroom Behavior					
The child					
23. Listens attentively when teacher is reading to group.	☐	☐	☐	☐	☐
24. Works quietly on tasks.	☐	☐	☐	☐	☐
25. Completes projects on time.	☐	☐	☐	☐	☐
26. Follows teacher's directions.	☐	☐	☐	☐	☐
27. Waits until teacher has finished asking a question before answering.	☐	☐	☐	☐	☐
28. Controls attention and resists distraction.	☐	☐	☐	☐	☐
29. Follows a sequence of directions.	☐	☐	☐	☐	☐
30. Tackles new tasks confidently.	☐	☐	☐	☐	☐
31. Persists in the face of difficulties.	☐	☐	☐	☐	☐
32. Monitors progress and seeks help appropriately.	☐	☐	☐	☐	☐
33. Is aware of own strengths and weaknesses.	☐	☐	☐	☐	☐
34. Speaks about future planned activities.	☐	☐	☐	☐	☐

(Continued)

Table C-9 *(Continued)*

Characteristics	Check one				
Social Behavior	1	2	3	4	5
The child					
35. Makes reasoned choices and decisions.	☐	☐	☐	☐	☐
36. Asks questions and suggests answers.	☐	☐	☐	☐	☐
37. Adopts previously heard language for own purposes.	☐	☐	☐	☐	☐
38. Initiates activities.	☐	☐	☐	☐	☐
39. Enjoys solving problems.	☐	☐	☐	☐	☐
Motor Behavior					
The child					
40. Engages in physical activity and play.	☐	☐	☐	☐	☐
41. Walks smoothly over objects.	☐	☐	☐	☐	☐
42. Balances well.	☐	☐	☐	☐	☐
43. Runs and jumps appropriately.	☐	☐	☐	☐	☐
44. Tracks a ball easily.	☐	☐	☐	☐	☐
45. Throws a ball well.	☐	☐	☐	☐	☐
46. Catches a ball easily.	☐	☐	☐	☐	☐
47. Uses crayons well.	☐	☐	☐	☐	☐
48. Uses pens and pencils well.	☐	☐	☐	☐	☐
49. Cuts out shapes easily.	☐	☐	☐	☐	☐
50. Carries objects well.	☐	☐	☐	☐	☐

Source: Adapted in part from McClellan and Katz (2001) and Whitebread, Coltman, Pasternak, Sangster, Grau, Bingham, Almeqdad, and Demetriou (2009).

Table D-1
Self-Monitoring Form for Recording Stressful Situations

SELF-MONITORING QUESTIONNAIRE

Name: _____

Directions: Complete the following items for each situation that made you unhappy.

Date	Describe situation	What happened before?	What happened after?	Who else was there?	What were you feeling and thinking?	Stress rating[a]

[a]Rate how much stress you were feeling on a scale from 1 to 10, with 1 = the least intense stress and 10 = the most intense stress.
Note. This form can be expanded to include 7 days.
From *Foundations of Behavioral, Social, and Clinical Assessment of Children* (Sixth Edition) by Jerome M. Sattler. Copyright 2014 by Jerome M. Sattler, Publisher, Inc. Permission to photocopy this appendix table is granted to purchaser of this book for personal use only (see copyright page for details).

Table D-2
Self-Monitoring Form for Recording Daily Exercise

EXERCISE LOG

Name: _____

Directions: Complete the following items about your daily exercise.

Date	What kinds of exercise did you do?	What time of day did you exercise?	How many minutes did you exercise?	Who else was there?	How much did you exert yourself?[a]	How much did you enjoy yourself?[b]	What problems did you have while exercising?

[a]Use a scale from 1 to 10, with 1 = No exertion and 10 = Completely exhausted.
[b]Use a scale from 1 to 10, with 1 = Did not enjoy at all and 10 = Really enjoyed.
Note. This form can be expanded to include 7 days.
From *Foundations of Behavioral, Social, and Clinical Assessment of Children* (Sixth Edition) by Jerome M. Sattler. Copyright 2014 by Jerome M. Sattler, Publisher, Inc. Permission to photocopy this appendix table is granted to purchaser of this book for personal use only (see copyright page for details).

Table D-3
Self-Monitoring Form for Recording Attention

RECORDING FORM

Name: _____   Date: _____

Directions: Circle **Yes** each time you were paying attention to the teacher when you heard the tone, and circle **No** if you weren't paying attention to the teacher when you heard the tone.

1. Yes No	6. Yes No	11. Yes No	16. Yes No
2. Yes No	7. Yes No	12. Yes No	17. Yes No
3. Yes No	8. Yes No	13. Yes No	18. Yes No
4. Yes No	9. Yes No	14. Yes No	19. Yes No
5. Yes No	10. Yes No	15. Yes No	20. Yes No

From *Foundations of Behavioral, Social, and Clinical Assessment of Children* (Sixth Edition) by Jerome M. Sattler. Copyright 2014 by Jerome M. Sattler, Publisher, Inc. Permission to photocopy this appendix table is granted to purchaser of this book for personal use only (see copyright page for details).

Table D-4
Student's Diary Form for Describing a Target Behavior

STUDENT DIARY

Name: _____   Date: _____

1. Did you have any problems today? (Circle one) Yes   No
   If you circled Yes, please complete the following items.
2. Describe the problem.

_____

_____

3. What happened before the problem began?

_____

_____

4. What happened after the problem began?

_____

_____

5. What did you do about the problem?

_____

_____

6. What did your teacher do about the problem?

_____

_____

7. What did the other students in the class do about the problem?

_____

_____

8. Why do you think the problem happened?

_____

_____

9. Describe anything else about the problem that you think is important.

_____

_____

Table D-5
Self-Monitoring Form for Recording Target Behavior

RECORDING FORM

Name: _____   Date: _____

Behavior to record: Out of seat

Directions: Fill in one circle each time you were out of your seat when you were not supposed to be out of your seat.

Morning   O O O O O O O O O O O O O O O O O O O O O O O O O O O O O

Afternoon   O O O O O O O O O O O O O O O O O O O O O O O O O O O O O O

Note. The target behavior can be changed as needed. The form also can be changed to show specific time periods if needed.
From *Foundations of Behavioral, Social, and Clinical Assessment of Children* (Sixth Edition) by Jerome M. Sattler. Copyright 2014 by Jerome M. Sattler, Publisher, Inc. Permission to photocopy this appendix table is granted to purchaser of this book for personal use only (see copyright page for details).

Table D-6
Self-Monitoring Form for Recording Intensity of Reaction

RECORDING FORM FOR FEELINGS

Name: _____

Directions: Three times each day—once in the morning, once in the afternoon, and once at night—complete the sadness graph. In the column that indicates the time when you record your answer, put an X in the square opposite the number that says how you feel. Use the following scale:

1 = I do not feel sad.
2 = I feel a little sad.
3 = I feel somewhat sad.
4 = I feel very sad.
5 = I feel extremely sad.

Day: _____   Date: _____

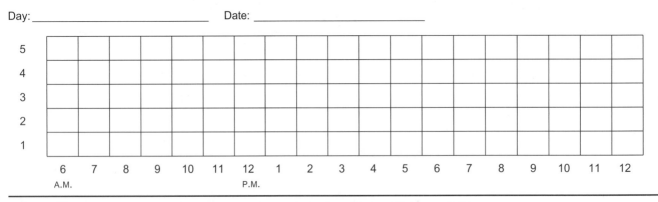

Note. This form can be used for any type of emotion or pain. Adapted from Allen and Matthews (1998).
From *Foundations of Behavioral, Social, and Clinical Assessment of Children* (Sixth Edition) by Jerome M. Sattler. Copyright 2014 by Jerome M. Sattler, Publisher, Inc. Permission to photocopy this appendix table is granted to purchaser of this book for personal use only (see copyright page for details).

Table D-7
Self-Monitoring Form for Recording Homework Assignments

RECORDING FORM FOR HOMEWORK

Name: _____   Date: _____

Class: _____   Teacher: _____

Directions: Circle Y (Yes), N (No), or NA (Not applicable) after each question.

Questions	Circle One		
1. Did you read the homework assignment sheet in class?	Y	N	NA
2. Did you put the homework assignment sheet in your notebook or write the homework assignment in your notebook in class?	Y	N	NA
3. Did you ask questions when you did not understand the homework assignment?	Y	N	NA
4. Did you take home the homework assignment sheet or your notes about the homework assignment?	Y	N	NA
5. Did you take home the books you needed to do the homework?	Y	N	NA
6. Did you complete the homework at home?	Y	N	NA
If you said "no" to question 6, leave questions 7 and 8 blank. If you said "yes" to question 6, go to question 7.			
7. If you completed the homework, did you bring it to class?	Y	N	NA
If you said "no" to question 7, leave question 8 blank. If you said "yes" to question 7, answer question 8 if you have a work folder in class.			
8. If you brought the homework to class, did you file it in your work folder?	Y	N	NA

Source: Adapted from Trapani and Gettinger (1996).

Table D-8
Self-Monitoring Form for Younger Children for Recording Behavior in Two Categories

RECORDING FORM

Name: _____   Date: _____

Directions:
If you were paying attention to your school work or teacher when the tone sounded, put an X on this face:

If you were *not* paying attention to your school work or teacher when the tone sounded, put an X on this face:

1.
2.
3.
4.
5.
6.
7.
8.
9.
10.

Note. This form can be used for any off-task behavior.
From *Foundations of Behavioral, Social, and Clinical Assessment of Children* (Sixth Edition) by Jerome M. Sattler. Copyright 2014 by Jerome M. Sattler, Publisher, Inc. Permission to photocopy this appendix table is granted to purchaser of this book for personal use only (see copyright page for details).

Table D-9
Self-Monitoring Form for Younger Children for Recording Behavior in Five Categories

RECORDING FORM

Name: _____   Date: _____

Directions: Put an X on the face that shows what you were doing when the tone sounded. Here is what the faces mean.

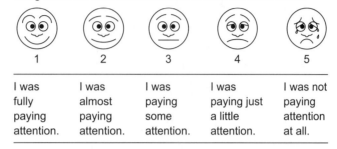

1	2	3	4	5
I was fully paying attention.	I was almost paying attention.	I was paying some attention.	I was paying just a little attention.	I was not paying attention at all.

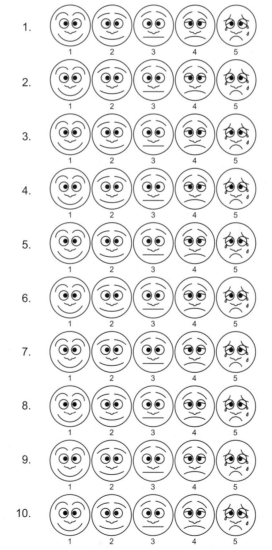

Appendix E
***DSM-5* Disorders That May Be Evident in Childhood and Early Adulthood**

Disorder	Brief Description
Neurodevelopmental Disorders	
Intellectual Disability	A disability characterized by deficits in general mental abilities and impairment in adaptive functioning in comparison to an individual's age, gender, and socioculturally matched peers; deficits have an onset during the developmental period.
Global Developmental Delay	A delay in development characterized by failure to meet expected developmental milestones in several areas of intellectual functioning; applicable to children under 5 years of age whose functioning level cannot be assessed reliably.
Communication Disorders	A group of disorders that reflect persistent difficulties in language, speech, and communication.
Autism Spectrum Disorder	A disorder characterized by persistent impairment in reciprocal social communication and social interaction along with restricted and repetitive patterns of behavior, interests, or activities that are present from early childhood and limit everyday functioning.
Attention-Deficit/Hyperactivity Disorder	A disorder characterized by a persistent pattern of inattention and/or hyperactivity-impulsivity that interferes with functioning to a degree that is inconsistent with developmental level and that negatively affects social, academic, and occupational activities.
Specific Learning Disorder	A disorder characterized by persistent difficulties in learning to read, write, spell, perform arithmetical calculations, or develop mathematical reasoning skills during the formal years of schooling.

Motor Disorders
  Developmental Coordination Disorder
 	
  Tourette's Disorder
 	
  Persistent Motor or Vocal Tic Disorder
  Provisional Tic Disorder
	A disorder characterized by motor performance that is substantially below what would be expected given the child's chronological age and previous opportunities for skill acquisition.
	A disorder characterized by multiple motor tics or one or more vocal tics (sudden, rapid, recurrent, nonrhythmic motor movements or vocalizations).
	A disorder characterized by single or multiple motor tics or vocal tics, but not both motor and vocal tics.
	A disorder characterized by single or multiple motor tics and/or vocal tics.

Schizophrenia Spectrum and Other Psychotic Disorders	
Delusional Disorder	A disorder characterized by one or more delusions that last for at least one month.
Brief Psychotic Disorder	A disorder characterized by delusions, hallucinations, disorganized speech, and/or grossly disorganized or catatonic behavior; the symptoms are not culturally sanctioned.
Schizophreniform Disorder	A disorder characterized by some of the same symptoms as in schizophrenia, but episodes are briefer.
Schizophrenia	A disorder characterized by delusions, hallucinations, disorganized speech, disorganized or catatonic behavior, and/or negative symptoms (e.g., diminished emotional expression or avolition [general lack of drive or motivation to pursue meaningful goals]).
Schizoaffective Disorder	A disorder characterized by an uninterrupted period of illness during which some symptoms of schizophrenia are present along with either a major depressive or a manic episode.
Substance/Medication-Induced Psychotic Disorder	A disorder characterized by delusions and/or hallucinations associated with substance use or with a medication.
Psychotic Disorder Due to Another Medical Condition	A disorder characterized by hallucinations or delusions due to another medical condition.

Appendix E *(Continued)*	
Disorder	*Brief Description*
Catatonia Associated with Another Mental Disorder	A disorder characterized by the presence of catatonia along with another mental disorder such as a neurodevelopmental disorder, psychotic disorder, bipolar disorder, or depressive disorder.
Catatonic Disorder Due to Another Medical Disorder	A disorder characterized by the presence of catatonia that is attributed to the physiological effects of another medical condition.
Bipolar and Related Disorders	
Bipolar I Disorder	A disorder characterized by a distinct period of abnormally and persistently elevated expansive or irritable mood and abnormally and persistently increased goal-directed activity or energy lasting at least one week.
Bipolar II Disorder	A disorder characterized by recurring mood episodes consisting of one or more major depressive episodes and at least one hypomanic episode.
Cyclothymic Disorder	A disorder characterized by a chronic, fluctuating mood disturbance with hypomanic and depressive symptoms.
Substance/Medication-Induced Bipolar and Related Disorder	A disorder characterized by abnormally and persistently elevated expansive or irritable mood and abnormally increased activity or energy associated with ingestion of a substance.
Bipolar Disorder Due to Another Medical Condition	A disorder characterized by abnormally and persistently elevated expansive or irritable mood and abnormally increased activity or energy that is a direct physiological consequence of another medical condition.
Depressive Disorders	
Disruptive Mood Dysregulation Disorder	A disorder characterized by severe recurrent temper outbursts grossly out of proportion in intensity or duration to the situation; applicable to children between the ages of 6 and 18 years.
Major Depressive Disorder	A disorder characterized by a depressed mood most of the day and nearly every day, markedly diminished interest or pleasure in all or most activities, significant weight loss, insomnia, psychomotor agitation, fatigue, feelings of worthlessness, difficulty concentrating, and recurrent thoughts of death.
Persistent Depressive Disorder (Dysthymia)	A disorder characterized by a depressed mood for most of the day; symptoms, however, do not meet the full criteria for a major depressive episode.
Premenstrual Dysphoric Disorder	A disorder characterized by mood lability, irritability, and dysphoria (an emotional state involving anxiety, depression, or unease) before menstruation.
Substance/Medication-Induced Depressive Disorder	A disorder characterized by a depressed mood or markedly diminished interest or pleasure in most activities soon after substance intoxication or withdrawal or after exposure to a medication.
Depressive Disorder Due to Another Medical Condition	A disorder characterized by a depressed mood or markedly diminished interest or pleasure in most activities that is a direct consequence of another medical condition.
Anxiety Disorders	
Separation Anxiety Disorder	A disorder characterized by developmentally inappropriate excessive fear or anxiety concerning separation from home or attachment figures.
Selective Mutism	A disorder characterized by a failure to initiate speech or respond when spoken to by others, except in the presence of immediate family members at home.
Specific Phobia	A disorder characterized by marked fear of or anxiety about a specific object or situation.

(Continued)

Appendix E *(Continued)*	
Disorder	***Brief Description***
Social Anxiety Disorder	A disorder characterized by marked fear of or anxiety about social situations where scrutiny by others is possible.
Panic Disorder	A disorder characterized by recurrent unexpected panic attacks followed by persistent concern about additional panic attacks and their consequences.
Agoraphobia	A disorder characterized by marked fear or anxiety about public transportation, open spaces, enclosed places, standing in a line, being in a crowd, or being outside of the home alone.
Generalized Anxiety Disorder	A disorder characterized by excessive anxiety and worry about events or activities.
Substance/Medication-Induced Anxiety Disorder	A disorder in which symptoms of a panic or an anxiety disorder develop during or soon after substance intoxication or withdrawal or after exposure to a medication.
Anxiety Disorder Due to Another Medical Condition	An anxiety disorder due to a physiological effect of another medical condition.
Obsessive-Compulsive and Related Disorders	
Obsessive-Compulsive Disorder	A disorder characterized by obsessions, compulsions, or both.
Body Dysmorphic Disorder	A disorder characterized by preoccupation with one or more perceived defects or flaws in physical appearance that either are not observable to others or appear slight to them.
Hoarding Disorder	A disorder characterized by persistent difficulties discarding or parting with possessions, regardless of their actual value.
Trichotillomania (Hair-Pulling) Disorder	A disorder characterized by recurrent pulling out of one's own hair that results in hair loss.
Excoriation (Skin Picking) Disorder	A disorder characterized by recurrent picking at one's own skin that results in skin lesions.
Substance/Medication-Induced Obsessive-Compulsive and Related Disorder	A disorder characterized by symptoms of obsessive-compulsive and related disorders that develop after substance intoxication, substance withdrawal, or exposure to a medication capable of producing the symptoms.
Obsessive-Compulsive and Related Disorder Due to Another Medical Condition	A disorder characterized by symptoms of obsessive-compulsive and related disorders that are attributable to another medical condition.
Trauma- and Stressor-Related Disorders	
Reactive Attachment Disorder	A disorder characterized by markedly disturbed and developmentally inappropriate attachment behaviors, such as rarely turning to an attachment figure for comfort, support, protection, and nurturance.
Disinhibited Social Engagement Disorder	A disorder characterized by culturally inappropriate, overly familiar behavior with strangers.
Posttraumatic Stress Disorder	A disorder characterized by clinically significant distress or impairment in social, occupational, or other important areas of functioning due to exposure to actual or threatened death, serious injury, or sexual violation; applicable to children older than 6 years, adolescents, and adults.
Acute Stress Disorder	A disorder characterized by a range of distress symptoms due to exposure to actual or threatened death, serious injury, or sexual violation.
Adjustment Disorder	A disorder characterized by the development of emotional or behavioral symptoms in response to one or more identifiable stressors.

Appendix E *(Continued)*	
Disorder	***Brief Description***
Dissociative Disorders	
Dissociative Identity Disorder	A disorder characterized by two or more distinct personality states resulting in a disruption of identity.
Dissociative Amnesia	A disorder characterized by inability to recall important autobiographical information, usually of a traumatic or stressful nature, that is inconsistent with ordinary forgetting.
Depersonalization/Derealization Disorder	A disorder characterized by persistent or recurrent experiences of depersonalization, derealization, or both.
Somatic Symptom Disorders	
Somatic Symptom Disorder	A disorder in which distressing somatic symptoms result in significant disruption of daily life.
Illness Anxiety Disorder	A disorder characterized by preoccupation with having or acquiring a serious medical illness.
Conversion Disorder	A disorder characterized by impairments in voluntary motor or sensory function, with or without apparent impairment of consciousness; symptoms are incompatible with a recognized neurological or medical condition.
Psychological Factors Affecting Other Medical Condition	A disorder in which psychological or behavioral factors adversely affect a medical condition by exacerbating or delaying recovery, interfering with treatment, increasing health risks, or influencing the underlying pathophysiology and thereby leading to an exacerbation of symptoms.
Factitious Disorder	A disorder characterized by falsification of physical or psychological signs and symptoms in oneself or others with whom one is associated.
Feeding and Eating Disorders	
Pica	A disorder characterized by persistent eating of nonnutritive and nonfood substances.
Rumination Disorder	A disorder characterized by repeated regurgitation of food, which may be re-chewed, re-swallowed, or spit out.
Avoidant/Restrictive Food Intake Disorder	A disorder characterized by a disturbance in eating or feeding behavior leading to a failure to meet appropriate nutritional and/or energy needs.
Anorexia Nervosa	A disorder characterized by (a) a restriction of energy intake relative to one's requirements, (b) an intense fear of gaining weight, and (c) a disturbance in self-perceived weight or shape.
Bulimia Nervosa	A disorder characterized by recurrent episodes of binge eating together with inappropriate behaviors designed to prevent weight gain (e.g., self-induced vomiting, use of laxatives, fasting, excessive exercise).
Binge-Eating Disorder	A disorder characterized by recurrent episodes of binge eating; the binge eating is not associated with inappropriate behaviors designed to prevent weight gain.
Elimination Disorders	
Enuresis	A disorder characterized by repeated involuntary or intentional voiding of urine in bed or clothes.
Encopresis	A disorder characterized by involuntary or intentional expulsion of feces in inappropriate places.

(Continued)

Appendix E *(Continued)*	
Disorder	*Brief Description*
Sleep-Wake Disorders	
Insomnia Disorder	A disorder characterized by difficulty initiating sleep or returning to sleep without caregiver intervention, early-morning awakening with inability to return to sleep, nonrestorative sleep, prolonged resistance to going to bed and/or bedtime struggles, and significant distress or impairment in daytime functioning associated with loss of sleep.
Hypersomnolence Disorder	A disorder characterized by excessive sleepiness despite sleeping at least 7 hours and recurrent periods of sleep or lapses into sleep within the same day.
Narcolepsy	A disorder characterized by recurrent daytime naps or lapses into sleep.
Obstructive Sleep Apnea Hypopnea	A breathing-related sleep disorder characterized by repeated episodes of upper airway obstruction during sleep.
Central Sleep Apnea	A disorder characterized by (a) episodes of frequent arousal and awakening during sleep, (b) insomnia, and (c) awakening short of breath five or more times per hour of sleep.
Sleep-Related Hypoventilation	A disorder characterized by episodes of decreased respiration associated with elevated CO_2 levels and resulting in insomnia or sleepiness.
Circadian Rhythm Sleep-Wake Disorder	A disorder characterized by a persistent or recurrent pattern of sleep disruption due to an alteration of the circadian system (daily cycle of biological activity based on a 24-hour period) and resulting in sleepiness, insomnia, or both.
Non-Rapid Eye Movement Sleep Arousal Disorder	A disorder characterized by recurrent episodes of incomplete awakening from sleep accompanied by sleepwalking or sleep terrors.
Nightmare Disorder	A disorder characterized by repeated occurrences of extended, extremely dysphoric, and well-remembered dreams, usually involving efforts to avoid threats to survival, security, or physical integrity.
Rapid Eye Movement Sleep Behavior Disorder	A disorder characterized by repeated episodes of arousal during sleep associated with vocalization and/or complex motor behaviors that may cause distress or impairment in social, occupational, or other areas of functioning.
Restless Legs Syndrome	A disorder characterized by an urge to move the legs, usually accompanied or caused by uncomfortable and unpleasant sensations in the legs.
Substance/Medication-Induced Sleep Disorder	A disorder characterized by a severe sleep disturbance that occurs during or soon after substance intoxication or after withdrawal from or exposure to a medication capable of producing the symptoms.
Sexual Dysfunctions	
A heterogeneous group of disorders characterized by a disturbance in the ability to respond sexually or to experience sexual pleasure.	
Gender Dysphoria	
Gender Dysphoria in Children	A disorder characterized by a marked incongruence between a child's experienced or expressed gender and his or her assigned gender.
Gender Dysphoria in Adolescents or Adults	A disorder characterized by a marked incongruence between an adult's experienced or expressed gender and his or her assigned gender.

Appendix E *(Continued)*	
Disorder	***Brief Description***
Disruptive, Impulse-Control, and Conduct Disorders	
Oppositional Defiant Disorder	A disorder characterized by a pattern of angry and irritable moods, argumentative and defiant behavior, or vindictiveness.
Intermittent Explosive Disorder	A disorder characterized by recurrent behavioral outbursts resulting from a failure to control aggressive impulses.
Conduct Disorder	A disorder characterized by a repetitive and persistent pattern of behavior in which the basic rights of others or major age-appropriate societal norms or rules are violated.
Pyromania	A disorder characterized by multiple episodes of deliberate and purposeful fire setting.
Kleptomania	A disorder characterized by recurrent failure to resist impulses to steal items that are not needed for personal use or for their monetary value.
Substance Use and Addictive Disorders	
Alcohol-Related Disorders	A group of disorders characterized by consumption of alcohol in high amounts that leads to physical and psychological impairments; includes alcohol use disorder, alcohol intoxication, and alcohol withdrawal.
Caffeine-Related Disorders	A group of disorders characterized by consumption of caffeine in high dosages that leads to agitation, distress, and related symptoms; includes caffeine intoxication and caffeine withdrawal.
Cannabis-Related Disorders	A group of disorders characterized by use of cannabis that leads to significant impairment in social and interpersonal relations and failure to fulfill major obligations at work, school, or home; includes cannabis use disorder, cannabis intoxication, and cannabis withdrawal.
Hallucinogen-Related Disorders	A group of disorders characterized by use of phencyclidine (PCP, or "angel dust") or other compounds in high dosages that leads to clinically significant impairment or distress, including feelings of separation from mind and body, social and interpersonal problems, placing oneself in physically hazardous situations, and failing to meet obligations at school, home, or work; includes phencyclidine use disorder, phencyclidine intoxication, and hallucinogen persisting perception disorder.
Inhalant-Related Disorders	A group of disorders characterized by use of a hydrocarbon-based inhalant substance that leads to clinically significant impairment or distress, including missing work or school and interpersonal problems; includes inhalant use disorder and inhalant intoxication.
Opioid-Related Disorders	A group of disorders characterized by use of opioids that leads to clinically significant impairment or distress, including coma, slurred speech, impairment in attention or memory, participation in drug-related crimes, marital difficulties, unemployment, and irregular employment; includes opioid use disorder, opioid intoxication, and opioid withdrawal.
Sedative-, Hypnotic-, or Anxiolytic-Related Disorders	A group of disorders characterized by use of sedatives, hypnotic agents, or anxiolytic substances that leads to clinically significant impairment or distress, including slurred speech, uncoordination, unsteady gait, nystagmus, cognitive dysfunction, coma, interpersonal difficulties, anxiety, insomnia, somatic complaints, school absences, and termination of participation in sports; includes sedative, hypnotic, or anxiolytic use disorder; sedative, hypnotic, or anxiolytic intoxication; and sedative, hypnotic, or anxiolytic withdrawal.
Stimulant-Related Disorders	A group of disorders characterized by use of an amphetamine-type substance, cocaine, or other stimulants that leads to clinically significant impairment or distress, including tachycardia, pupillary dilation, elevated or lowered blood pressure, perspiration or chills, nausea or vomiting, weight loss, psychomotor agitation, muscular weakness, confusion, interpersonal problems, and failure to participate in recreational, social, or employment activities; includes stimulant use disorder, stimulant intoxication, and stimulant withdrawal.

(Continued)

Appendix E *(Continued)*	
Disorder	*Brief Description*
Tobacco-Related Disorders	A group of disorders characterized by excessive use of tobacco that leads to clinically significant impairment or distress, including a strong craving to use tobacco; failure to fulfill obligations at school, home, or work; social or interpersonal problems; placing oneself in situations where smoking is physically hazardous; and medical problems such as coughing, shortness of breath, and accelerated skin aging; includes tobacco use disorder and tobacco withdrawal.
Unknown Substance Disorders	A group of disorders characterized by use of a substance not classified under other categories that leads to clinically significant impairment or distress; includes other (or unknown) substance use disorder, other (or unknown) substance intoxication, and other (or unknown) substance withdrawal.
Gambling Disorder	A disorder characterized by problematic gambling behavior that leads to clinically significant impairment or distress.
Neurocognitive Disorders	
Delirium	A disorder characterized by disturbances in attention and cognition that develop over a short period of time as a direct physiological consequence of another medical condition, substance intoxication or withdrawal, exposure to a toxin, or multiple etiologies.
Major Neurocognitive Disorder Due to Traumatic Brain Injury	A disorder characterized by a traumatic brain injury that causes loss of consciousness, posttraumatic amnesias, disorientation and confusion, and neurological symptoms; also present are significant declines in complex attention, executive functions, learning and memory, language, perceptual-motor functioning, and social cognition.
Mild Neurocognitive Disorder Due to Traumatic Brain Injury	A disorder characterized by a traumatic brain injury that causes loss of consciousness, posttraumatic amnesias, disorientation and confusion, and neurological symptoms; also present are modest declines in complex attention, executive functions, learning and memory, language, perceptual-motor functioning, and social cognition.
Major Neurocognitive Disorder Due to HIV Infection	A disorder due to infection by the human immunodeficiency virus (HIV) that results in significant declines in complex attention, executive functions, learning and memory, language, perceptual-motor functioning, and social cognition.
Mild Neurocognitive Disorder Due to HIV Infection	A disorder due to infection by the human immunodeficiency virus (HIV) that results in modest declines in complex attention, executive functions, learning and memory, language, perceptual-motor functioning, and social cognition.
Major Neurocognitive Disorder Due to Another Medical Condition	A disorder that, based on evidence from the history, physical examination, or laboratory findings, appears to be the consequence of another medical condition and that leads to significant declines in complex attention, executive functions, learning and memory, language, perceptual-motor functioning, and social cognition.
Mild Neurocognitive Disorder Due to Another Medical Condition	A disorder that, based on evidence from the history, physical examination, or laboratory findings, appears to be the consequence of another medical condition and that leads to modest declines in complex attention, executive functions, learning and memory, language, perceptual-motor functioning, and social cognition.
Major Neurocognitive Disorder Due to Multiple Etiologies	A disorder that, based on evidence from the history, physical examination, or laboratory findings, appears to be the consequence of one or more etiological processes, excluding use of substances, and that leads to significant declines in complex attention, executive functions, learning and memory, language, perceptual-motor functioning, and social cognition.
Mild Neurocognitive Disorder Due to Multiple Etiologies	A disorder that, based on evidence from the history, physical examination, or laboratory findings, appears to be the consequence of one or more etiological processes, excluding use of substances, and that leads to modest declines in complex attention, executive functions, learning and memory, language, perceptual-motor functioning, and social cognition.

Appendix E *(Continued)*	
Disorder	*Brief Description*
Personality Disorders	
Paranoid Personality Disorder	A disorder characterized by a pattern of pervasive distrust and suspiciousness of others.
Schizoid Personality Disorder	A disorder characterized by a pervasive pattern of detachment from social relationships and a restricted range of expression of emotions.
Schizotypical Personality Disorder	A disorder characterized by (a) a pervasive pattern of social and interpersonal deficits marked by acute discomfort with close relationships, (b) cognitive and perceptual distortions, and (c) eccentricities of behavior.
Antisocial Personality Disorder	A disorder characterized by a pervasive pattern of disregard for and violation of the rights of others.
Borderline Personality Disorder	A disorder characterized by a pervasive pattern of deficits in interpersonal relations, self-image, and emotions and marked by impulsivity.
Histrionic Personality Disorder	A disorder characterized by a pervasive pattern of excessive emotionality and attention seeking.
Narcissistic Personality Disorder	A disorder characterized by a pervasive pattern of grandiosity, need for admiration, and lack of empathy.
Avoidant Personality Disorder	A disorder characterized by a pervasive pattern of social inhibition, feelings of inadequacy, and hypersensitivity to negative evaluation.
Dependent Personality Disorder	A disorder characterized by a pervasive and excessive need to be taken care of that leads to submissive and clinging behavior and fears of separation.
Obsessive-Compulsive Personality Disorder	A disorder characterized by a pervasive pattern of preoccupation with orderliness, perfectionism, and mental and interpersonal control.
Personality Change Due to Another Medical Condition	A disorder characterized by a personality disturbance, representing a change from a previous personality pattern, that, based on evidence from the history, physical examination, or laboratory findings, appears to be the direct physiological consequence of another medical condition.
Paraphilic Disorders	
Voyeuristic Disorder	A disorder characterized by recurrent and intense sexual arousal obtained from observing an unsuspecting individual who is naked, in the process of disrobing, or engaging in sexual activity.
Exhibitionistic Disorder	A disorder characterized by recurrent and intense sexual arousal obtained from exposing one's genitals to an unsuspecting individual.
Frotteuristic Disorder	A disorder characterized by recurrent and intense sexual arousal obtained from touching or rubbing against a nonconsenting person.
Sexual Masochism Disorder	A disorder characterized by recurrent and intense sexual arousal obtained from being humiliated, beaten, bound, or otherwise made to suffer.
Sexual Sadism Disorder	A disorder characterized by recurrent and intense sexual arousal obtained from the physical or psychological suffering of another individual.
Pedophilic Disorder	A disorder characterized by recurrent and intense sexually arousing fantasies, sexual urges, or behaviors involving a prepubescent or early pubescent child or children.
Fetishistic Disorder	A disorder characterized by recurrent and intense sexual arousal obtained either from the use of nonliving objects or from a highly specific focus on one or more nongenital body parts.

(Continued)

Appendix E *(Continued)*	
Disorder	*Brief Description*
Transvestic Disorder	A disorder characterized by recurrent and intense sexual arousal obtained from cross-dressing.
Other Mental Disorders	
Other Specified Mental Disorder Due to Another Medical Condition	A disorder characterized by symptoms of a mental disorder due to another medical condition that cause distress or impairment in social, occupational, or other areas of functioning; symptoms, however, do not meet the full criteria of a specific mental disorder.
Unspecified Mental Disorder Due to Another Medical Condition	A disorder characterized by symptoms of a mental disorder due to another medical condition that cause distress or impairment in social, occupational, or other areas of functioning; symptoms, however, do not meet the full criteria of a specific mental disorder, and the clinician chooses not to specify the reasons that the criteria are not met.

Note. Appendix E summarizes the major *DSM-5* disorders applicable to children and young adults, but does not include all *DSM-5* disorders. *This appendix should not be used to arrive at a DSM-5 diagnosis.*
Source: Adapted from *DSM-5* (American Psychiatric Association, 2013).

Table F-1
Functional Behavioral Assessment Recording Form

FUNCTIONAL BEHAVIORAL ASSESSMENT RECORDING FORM

Name of student: _____   Date: _____

Sex: _____   Age: _____   School: _____

Date of birth: _____   Examiner/Teacher: _____

Problem Behavior

1. Describe the problem behavior. _____

2. Describe other behaviors that might be related to the problem behavior. _____

3. Where is the problem behavior most likely to happen? _____

4. Where is the problem behavior least likely to happen? _____

5. At what time of day is the problem behavior most likely to happen? _____

6. At what time of day is the problem behavior least likely to happen? _____

7. When does the problem behavior stop? _____

8. Does the problem behavior escalate gradually or quickly? _____

9. How intense is the problem behavior? _____

10. How often does the problem behavior occur? _____

11. Who is present when the problem behavior occurs? _____

12. Is anyone present who ordinarily would not be there? If so, who is this person? _____

13. Is anyone absent who is usually in the setting? If so, who is absent? _____

14. How long does the problem behavior last? _____

15. When did the problem behavior first start? _____

16. Has the frequency of the problem behavior increased or decreased recently? _____

17. When was the last time the problem behavior occurred? _____

18. What, if any, medical problems may have caused, maintained, or worsened the problem behavior? _____

Events Preceding the Problem Behavior (Antecedent Events)

1. Describe what usually happens before the problem behavior begins. _____

2. Describe characteristics of the setting where the problem behavior takes place. _____

(Continued)

Table F-1 *(Continued)*

3. What activities are most likely to produce the problem behavior? _____
    _____

4. What activities are least likely to produce the problem behavior? _____
    _____

5. What classroom activities usually take place prior to the problem behavior? _____
    _____

6. What is the pace of the classroom activity before the problem behavior takes place? _____
    _____

7. Describe the student's mood before the problem behavior takes place. _____
    _____

8. Describe events in the student's life that might have affected his or her behavior. _____
    _____

9. Describe challenges at home (e.g., daily routines or family conflicts) and inside and outside of school (e.g., relationships with
    peers and neighbors) that may contribute to the problem behavior._____
    _____

Events Following the Problem Behavior (Consequent Events)

1. Describe what the teacher does and how he or she reacts to the problem behavior._____
    _____

2. Describe what other students do and how they react to the problem behavior._____
    _____

3. Describe what the administrator does and how he or she reacts to the problem behavior._____
    _____

4. Describe what other individuals do and how they react to the problem behavior. _____
    _____

5. Describe the consequences associated with the problem behavior. _____
    _____

6. How much time elapses between when the student engages in the problem behavior and when others respond?_____
    _____

7. Describe how the student usually reacts after the problem behavior takes place._____
    _____

8. What actions seem to decrease the problem behavior once it begins? _____
    _____

9. How long does it usually take to get the student back to the scheduled activity? _____
    _____

10. How do the intensity, duration, and frequency of the problem behavior interfere with the student's learning? _____
    _____

Interventions

1. Are crisis intervention procedures needed to ensure safety and de-escalation of the student's behavior, and, if so, what
    procedures should be used?_____
    _____

2. What potential cognitive and motivational resources does the student have for coping with the problem behavior? _____
    _____

3. What functions do you believe are served by the problem behavior? _____
    _____

4. Describe the student's attitudes about the class, teacher, and school. _____
    _____

5. Describe the student's attitudes about his or her parents, siblings, and other relatives. _____
    _____

Table F-1 (Continued)

6. Describe the teacher's, parents', and other concerned individuals' levels of understanding of the problem behavior. _____

7. Describe the student's, family's, school's, and community's strengths and resources for change. _____

8. What replacement behaviors need to be taught (including social skills, problem-solving skills, and communication skills) in order to reduce or eliminate the problem behavior?_____

9. What are some positive strategies for diminishing the problem behavior and promoting skills the student needs to function more effectively? _____

10. What are some positive strategies for changing the environment to prevent the problem behavior from occurring? _____

11. Describe other factors that should be considered in designing the behavioral intervention plan. _____

12. Describe strategies that should be used to facilitate the transfer of behavior changes across environments. _____

13. Describe the interventions needed to maintain and generalize the use of socially acceptable alternative behaviors over time and across settings. _____

From *Foundations of Behavioral, Social, and Clinical Assessment of Children* (Sixth Edition) by Jerome M. Sattler. Copyright 2014 by Jerome M. Sattler, Publisher, Inc. Permission to photocopy this table is granted to purchasers of this book for personal use only (see copyright page for details).

Table F-2
Functional Behavior Assessment Brief Recording Form

FUNCTIONAL BEHAVIORAL ASSESSMENT BRIEF RECORDING FORM

Name of student:_____   Date:_____

Sex:_____   Age:_____   School:_____

Date of birth:_____   Examiner:_____

A—Antecedents (Describe what happened before the problem behavior occurred)	B—Behavior (Describe what the child did)	C—Consequences (Describe what happened after the problem behavior occurred)

Table F-3
Checklist of Possible Antecedent Events, Behaviors, and Consequent Events

CHECKLIST OF POSSIBLE ANTECEDENT EVENTS, BEHAVIORS, AND CONSEQUENT EVENTS

Name of student: _____ Date: _____

Sex: _____ Age: _____ School:_____

Date of birth: _____ Examiner/Teacher:_____

Directions: Check as many antecedent events, behaviors, and consequent events that apply.

ANTECEDENT EVENTS

Environmental Variables
☐ Activity
(Describe) _____
☐ Alone
☐ With others
☐ Auditorium
☐ Bus
☐ Bus stop
☐ Cafeteria
☐ Classroom
☐ Computer room
☐ Dressing room
☐ Gym
☐ Hallway
☐ Library
☐ Locker room
☐ Playground
☐ Restroom
☐ Special classroom
(Describe) _____
☐ Study hall
☐ Walkway
☐ Workshop room
(Describe) _____
☐ Beginning of school day
☐ End of school day
☐ Middle of school day
☐ Time of day _____
☐ Unstructured time
☐ Change of activity
☐ Change of routine
☐ Change of class
☐ Circle group activity
☐ Class examination
☐ Eating lunch
☐ End of preferred activity
☐ Independent seat work
☐ Individual assignment
☐ Large group instruction
☐ Lecture
☐ Playing games on the playground
(Describe) _____
☐ Small-group work

☐ Subject being taught
(Describe) _____
☐ Teacher's aide present
☐ Transition of subject matter (routine)
☐ Transition (unexpected)
☐ Watching children play on playground
☐ Working on a computer
☐ Lighting
(Describe) _____
☐ Materials being used
(Describe) _____
☐ Noise level
(Describe) _____
☐ Number of adults present _____
☐ Number of students present _____
☐ Room temperature
(Describe) _____
☐ Seating arrangement
(Describe) _____
☐ Staff member present
☐ Other
_____
_____

Personal Events
☐ Activity too long
☐ Alcohol use
☐ Arguing with parents before school
☐ Arguing with peer
☐ Attention withdrawn
☐ Becoming upset
☐ Change in diet
☐ Change in medications
☐ Drug use
☐ Engaging in horseplay
☐ Failing a test
☐ Family stress
(Describe) _____
☐ Fatigue
☐ Favorite activity taken away
☐ Favorite food taken away
☐ Favorite toy or device taken away
☐ Fear of failure

☐ Fear of ridicule by peer
☐ Fear of ridicule by teacher
☐ Harassment by peer
☐ Hunger
☐ Illness
(Describe) _____
☐ Increase in sensory stimulation
(Describe) _____
☐ Not knowing what is required on an assignment
☐ Not taking medications
☐ Parent not home
☐ Peer interrupts student
☐ Peer intimidates student
☐ Peer rejects student
☐ Peer teases student
☐ Receiving test results
☐ Sleep problems
☐ Social conflict
☐ Start of nonpreferred activity
☐ Teacher asks student to do a boring assignment
☐ Teacher asks student to participate in an activity
☐ Teacher asks student to perform a general task
☐ Teacher asks student to perform a long assignment
☐ Teacher denies student's request for an activity
☐ Teacher denies student's request for an item
☐ Teacher doesn't pay attention to student
☐ Teacher doesn't spend time with student
☐ Teacher interrupts student
☐ Teacher reprimands student
☐ Teacher spends time with student
☐ Teacher talks to another student
☐ Teacher teases student
☐ Warning by teacher
☐ Other
_____
_____

(Continued)

Table F-3 *(Continued)*

BEHAVIORS

- ☐ Alcohol use
- ☐ Assaulting others
- ☐ Banging head
- ☐ Biting
- ☐ Bullying
- (Describe) _____
- ☐ Crying
- ☐ Cyberbullying
- (Describe) _____
- ☐ Defying authority
- ☐ Destroying or damaging property
- ☐ Displaying psychotic symptoms
- (Describe) _____
- ☐ Disrespectful to staff
- ☐ Disrespectful to peer
- ☐ Disrupting class
- ☐ Drug use
- ☐ Engaging in inappropriate sexual behavior
- (Describe) _____
- ☐ Engaging in self-stimulating behavior
- (Describe) _____
- ☐ Failing to complete assignment

- ☐ Failing to follow directions
- ☐ Fighting
- ☐ Grabbing
- ☐ Kicking
- ☐ Late for class
- ☐ Leaving class without permission
- ☐ Loud talking
- ☐ Marking up walls
- ☐ Noncompliant behavior
- (Describe) _____
- ☐ Out of seat
- ☐ Physically aggressive to peer
- ☐ Physically aggressive to teacher
- ☐ Pulling others
- ☐ Pushing others
- ☐ Refusing to stay seated
- ☐ Refusing to work
- ☐ Running away
- ☐ Screaming
- ☐ Self-injury
- (Describe) _____
- ☐ Stealing
- ☐ Stereotypic behavior

- ☐ Talking out of turn
- ☐ Teasing
- ☐ Threatening others physically
- ☐ Threatening others verbally
- ☐ Throwing temper tantrums
- ☐ Throwing things
- ☐ Truant
- ☐ Using profane language
- ☐ Vandalism
- (Describe) _____
- ☐ Violating school rules
- (Describe) _____
- ☐ Violating weapons prohibitions
- (Describe) _____
- ☐ Whining
- ☐ Withdrawing
- ☐ Yelling
- ☐ Other
- _____
- _____
- _____

CONSEQUENT EVENTS

- ☐ Activity changed
- ☐ After-school detention
- ☐ Conference with student
- ☐ Demands on student lessened
- ☐ Given additional assignments
- ☐ Given an alternative activity
- ☐ Given an alternative educational placement
- ☐ Given desired food
- ☐ Given desired toy
- ☐ Given requested activity
- ☐ Increase in attention
- ☐ In-school suspension
- ☐ Loss of privileges

- ☐ Lunch detention
- ☐ Note to parents
- ☐ Out-of-school suspension
- ☐ Peer mediation
- ☐ Peers' negative attention
- ☐ Peers' positive attention
- ☐ Physical comfort
- ☐ Physical restraint
- ☐ Planned ignoring
- ☐ Referral to counselor
- ☐ Removal to another room
- ☐ Seat changed
- ☐ Sent home
- ☐ Sent to nurse

- ☐ Sent to office
- ☐ Structured warning
- ☐ Teacher-parent conference
- ☐ Teacher praise
- ☐ Teacher reprimand
- ☐ Teacher-student conference
- ☐ Teacher warning
- ☐ Telephone call to parents
- ☐ Time out
- ☐ Withdrawal of attention
- ☐ Other
- _____
- _____
- _____

Table G-1
Structured Observation of Academic and Play Settings (SOAPS)

INSTRUCTIONS FOR STRUCTURED OBSERVATION OF ACADEMIC AND PLAY SETTINGS

To conduct the observation, you will need two tables (or desks) and chairs, a popular toy (e.g., hand-held videogame), five double-sided worksheets, and three copies of the recording form. Before the child enters the room, place the five double-sided worksheets on one table (or desk) and the toy on a nearby table (or desk). The room should be equipped with a one-way mirror or with a mounted camera for observing the child from an adjacent room.

Bring the child into the room and say, "This is our classroom. Here is your table. Let me show you some worksheets and how to do them." Help the child do a sample item at the top of each worksheet. Then say, "There are too many problems here for you to complete them all. But while I am gone for 15 minutes, I want you to do as many of them as you can. Keep working, don't leave your chair, and don't play with the toy over there. I'll be next door to make sure you're okay. I'll let you know when the 15 minutes are over. You can begin now." Then leave the room.

Use a 5-second time interval to record five behaviors: attention, sitting, fidgeting, noisy, and toy play. Note that the first two behaviors are appropriate behaviors and the last three are inappropriate behaviors. Make an audiotape that gives you prompts indicating the beginning of each interval. Record the following: "Begin 1 [5 seconds], Begin 2 [5 seconds], Begin 3, . . . , Begin 60."

In each of the five behavior code columns on the recording form, circle the code that represents the behavior observed during each interval. Three recording forms are needed for each 15-minute session.

After the session, record the number of intervals in which the child was on-task. Convert the number of on-task intervals to a percentage (divide by 60). A general rule is that a minimum of 80% on-task behavior is expected for elementary-age children. Also record the number of worksheet items correctly completed.

Definitions of Coded Behaviors

1. *Attention* (Attending = AT; Not Attending = /AT). Code Attention when the child's eyes are focused on one of the assigned worksheets. Momentary shifts in focus away from a worksheet as well as obvious scribbling and clear lack of engagement with the task are coded as Not Attending (off-task).

2. *Sitting* (Sitting = SI; Not Sitting = /SI). Code Sitting when the child is sitting in the chair or when the child's weight is supported by the chair (e.g., when the child is sitting on his or her legs on the chair or when the child stands on the chair).

3. *Fidgeting* (Fidgeting = FI; Not Fidgeting = /FI). Code Fidgeting when the child makes any repetitive movement that is not directed to the completion of worksheet items (e.g., tapping a pencil on the table).

4. *Noisy* (Noisy = NO; Not Noisy = /NO). Code Noisy when the child makes an audible vocalization, even if the vocalization is low in volume or is unintelligible (e.g., whispering, singing, yelling).

5. *Toy Play* (Toy Play = TO; Not Toy Play = /TO). Code Toy Play when the child plays with the toy or when the child is looking at the toy and is within arm's reach of it.

(Continued)

Table G-1 *(Continued)*

RECORDING FORM FOR STRUCTURED OBSERVATION OF ACADEMIC AND PLAY SETTINGS

Name: _____   Date: _____   School: _____

Sex: _____   Grade: _____   Birth date: _____   Teacher: _____

Intervals on-task: AT_____/60 = _____%; SI_____/60 = _____%; /FI_____/60 = _____%; /NO_____/60 = _____%; /TO_____/60 = _____%

No. of items completed correctly: 1_____; 2_____; 3_____; 4_____; 5_____; 6_____; 7_____; 8_____; 9_____; 10_____

Interval	Attention		Sitting		Fidgeting		Noisy		Toy Play	
1	AT	/AT	SI	/SI	FI	/FI	NO	/NO	TO	/TO
2	AT	/AT	SI	/SI	FI	/FI	NO	/NO	TO	/TO
3	AT	/AT	SI	/SI	FI	/FI	NO	/NO	TO	/TO
4	AT	/AT	SI	/SI	FI	/FI	NO	/NO	TO	/TO
5	AT	/AT	SI	/SI	FI	/FI	NO	/NO	TO	/TO
6	AT	/AT	SI	/SI	FI	/FI	NO	/NO	TO	/TO
7	AT	/AT	SI	/SI	FI	/FI	NO	/NO	TO	/TO
8	AT	/AT	SI	/SI	FI	/FI	NO	/NO	TO	/TO
9	AT	/AT	SI	/SI	FI	/FI	NO	/NO	TO	/TO
10	AT	/AT	SI	/SI	FI	/FI	NO	/NO	TO	/TO
11	AT	/AT	SI	/SI	FI	/FI	NO	/NO	TO	/TO
12	AT	/AT	SI	/SI	FI	/FI	NO	/NO	TO	/TO
13	AT	/AT	SI	/SI	FI	/FI	NO	/NO	TO	/TO
14	AT	/AT	SI	/SI	FI	/FI	NO	/NO	TO	/TO
15	AT	/AT	SI	/SI	FI	/FI	NO	/NO	TO	/TO
16	AT	/AT	SI	/SI	FI	/FI	NO	/NO	TO	/TO
17	AT	/AT	SI	/SI	FI	/FI	NO	/NO	TO	/TO
18	AT	/AT	SI	/SI	FI	/FI	NO	/NO	TO	/TO
19	AT	/AT	SI	/SI	FI	/FI	NO	/NO	TO	/TO
20	AT	/AT	SI	/SI	FI	/FI	NO	/NO	TO	/TO
21	AT	/AT	SI	/SI	FI	/FI	NO	/NO	TO	/TO
22	AT	/AT	SI	/SI	FI	/FI	NO	/NO	TO	/TO
23	AT	/AT	SI	/SI	FI	/FI	NO	/NO	TO	/TO
24	AT	/AT	SI	/SI	FI	/FI	NO	/NO	TO	/TO
25	AT	/AT	SI	/SI	FI	/FI	NO	/NO	TO	/TO
26	AT	/AT	SI	/SI	FI	/FI	NO	/NO	TO	/TO
27	AT	/AT	SI	/SI	FI	/FI	NO	/NO	TO	/TO
28	AT	/AT	SI	/SI	FI	/FI	NO	/NO	TO	/TO
29	AT	/AT	SI	/SI	FI	/FI	NO	/NO	TO	/TO
30	AT	/AT	SI	/SI	FI	/FI	NO	/NO	TO	/TO
31	AT	/AT	SI	/SI	FI	/FI	NO	/NO	TO	/TO
32	AT	/AT	SI	/SI	FI	/FI	NO	/NO	TO	/TO
33	AT	/AT	SI	/SI	FI	/FI	NO	/NO	TO	/TO
34	AT	/AT	SI	/SI	FI	/FI	NO	/NO	TO	/TO
35	AT	/AT	SI	/SI	FI	/FI	NO	/NO	TO	/TO
36	AT	/AT	SI	/SI	FI	/FI	NO	/NO	TO	/TO
37	AT	/AT	SI	/SI	FI	/FI	NO	/NO	TO	/TO
38	AT	/AT	SI	/SI	FI	/FI	NO	/NO	TO	/TO
39	AT	/AT	SI	/SI	FI	/FI	NO	/NO	TO	/TO
40	AT	/AT	SI	/SI	FI	/FI	NO	/NO	TO	/TO
41	AT	/AT	SI	/SI	FI	/FI	NO	/NO	TO	/TO
42	AT	/AT	SI	/SI	FI	/FI	NO	/NO	TO	/TO
43	AT	/AT	SI	/SI	FI	/FI	NO	/NO	TO	/TO
44	AT	/AT	SI	/SI	FI	/FI	NO	/NO	TO	/TO
45	AT	/AT	SI	/SI	FI	/FI	NO	/NO	TO	/TO
46	AT	/AT	SI	/SI	FI	/FI	NO	/NO	TO	/TO
47	AT	/AT	SI	/SI	FI	/FI	NO	/NO	TO	/TO
48	AT	/AT	SI	/SI	FI	/FI	NO	/NO	TO	/TO
49	AT	/AT	SI	/SI	FI	/FI	NO	/NO	TO	/TO
50	AT	/AT	SI	/SI	FI	/FI	NO	/NO	TO	/TO
51	AT	/AT	SI	/SI	FI	/FI	NO	/NO	TO	/TO
52	AT	/AT	SI	/SI	FI	/FI	NO	/NO	TO	/TO
53	AT	/AT	SI	/SI	FI	/FI	NO	/NO	TO	/TO
54	AT	/AT	SI	/SI	FI	/FI	NO	/NO	TO	/TO
55	AT	/AT	SI	/SI	FI	/FI	NO	/NO	TO	/TO
56	AT	/AT	SI	/SI	FI	/FI	NO	/NO	TO	/TO
57	AT	/AT	SI	/SI	FI	/FI	NO	/NO	TO	/TO
58	AT	/AT	SI	/SI	FI	/FI	NO	/NO	TO	/TO
59	AT	/AT	SI	/SI	FI	/FI	NO	/NO	TO	/TO
60	AT	/AT	SI	/SI	FI	/FI	NO	/NO	TO	/TO

Table G-1 *(Continued)*

WORKSHEETS FOR STRUCTURED OBSERVATION OF ACADEMIC AND PLAY SETTINGS

Note that each of the following worksheets is a condensed version and needs to be expanded to fill an 8½-by-11-inch page.

Name: _____ 1

Date: _____

FILL IN THE EMPTY BOXES

P	V	R	N	O	Z	B	U	H	X
1	2	3	4	5	6	7	8	9	10

V	P	Z	O	H	R	B	Z	N	X	U	R	Z	V

R	O	B	H	P	V	N	Z	U	X	R	U	Z	X

N	H	O	X	P	Z	R	B	H	P	V	R	U	B

O	X	Z	V	B	U	X	P	O	N	B	R	H	P

Z	P	B	R	U	V	N	Z	H	X	P	O	B	N

B	V	U	N	H	P	R	X	Z	H	U	V	N	X

U	R	H	O	X	P	Z	B	U	X	H	N	O	Z

2

FILL IN THE EMPTY BOXES

@	%	#	*	$	!	¢	=	?	+
1	2	3	4	5	6	7	8	9	10

$	¢	#	@	+	=	!	*	%	?	*	@	+	$

=	%	$	!	¢	#	?	!	@	+	*	?	%	#

$	%	+	¢	@	%	#	!	?	=	!	¢	@	*

=	$	#	*	¢	+	?	=	!	%	+	=	¢	#

@	+	$	*	=	$	#	%	+	?	!	¢	#	@

¢	+	=	%	@	?	!	$	*	#	?	%	@	=

+	¢	#	*	!	$	+	!	%	@	#	=	?	*

3

MARK OUT ALL OF THE A'S THAT YOU SEE

G K A B P L A

T R C A L J V A A L W Q P F

Q W R A N C K A F W T D V P

O E X S H A W Z N L P D A I

K A P T A D W Q L H N B F A

G F A B K Y U S A D A C D F

A J X W N D A N W A C Y S L

T H X A M V D E A H L I A N

F G A D R A U O P Q S A D R

P K T A Y D R A T A W N A A

J A G N U S R T A N C A R U

4

MARK OUT ALL OF THE H'S THAT YOU SEE

K J Y H U P N

U R E C N H T R S U N G A J

H H M W S T R H O Y T H K P

R D H S W P O U H R D G H F

N H I L S H B D V M H X A T

L S Y C H W M H D N S X J A

F D C A D G S Y T J B A F G

A F V N H L Q W D A T P A K

I A D P L N Z W A H S X B O

T Y J H L Y E S E L S N E O

Y U I R F G N M B C V D H H

(Continued)

Table G-1 (Continued)

FILL IN THE EMPTY BOXES

R	X	S	U	Z	Q	T	E	G	H
1	2	3	4	5	6	7	8	9	10

U	E	R	G	X	H	G	T	S	Q	E	Z	T	H

X	E	U	Z	R	T	S	X	Q	H	R	G	Z	Q

S	Z	R	H	Q	T	U	X	G	S	E	U	R	T

E	S	X	G	Q	U	H	Z	T	H	U	R	E	Z

S	X	E	Q	G	R	T	Z	U	H	G	X	Q	S

E	T	H	X	R	U	Q	G	S	Z	S	H	E	X

Q	U	R	T	G	Z	X	H	E	S	T	G	R	Z

FILL IN THE EMPTY BOXES

Q	W	R	T	Y	P	S	D	F	G
1	2	3	4	5	6	7	8	9	10

T	D	Q	F	W	G	F	S	R	P	D	Y	S	G

W	D	T	Y	Q	S	R	W	P	G	Q	F	Y	P

R	Y	Q	G	P	S	T	W	F	R	D	T	Q	S

D	R	W	F	P	T	G	Y	S	G	T	Q	D	Y

R	W	D	P	F	Q	S	Y	T	G	F	W	P	R

D	S	G	W	Q	T	P	F	R	Y	R	G	D	W

P	T	Q	S	F	Y	W	G	D	R	S	F	Q	Y

MARK OUT ALL OF THE 4'S THAT YOU SEE

2 5 6 8 4 3 0 4

4 5 6 8 4 4 9 0 3 1 5 4 6 7

6 7 3 2 4 8 1 4 0 9 8 5 4 4

7 5 4 6 8 4 9 0 7 4 5 7 3 2

4 4 9 8 0 6 4 5 7 3 7 3 7 4

3 7 5 4 8 0 1 2 4 4 4 7 5 4

2 3 7 5 6 8 9 0 7 5 6 8 9 0

5 8 9 4 6 5 2 1 0 3 0 9 8 4

5 7 6 8 9 0 1 2 3 7 5 8 9 0

4 6 5 7 4 8 9 0 3 2 7 1 6 9

0 9 2 3 6 4 7 8 1 4 5 6 2 9

MARK OUT ALL OF THE 3'S THAT YOU SEE

3 7 1 9 0 3 2 5

3 2 9 6 4 0 1 3 8 4 3 9 0 2

7 3 5 2 9 7 6 4 5 3 1 2 5 4

0 5 7 8 3 1 4 2 4 6 8 7 3 5

9 5 2 8 0 4 3 7 4 1 3 6 0 5

6 8 3 3 5 1 8 5 3 9 2 9 4 3

9 4 3 5 2 3 6 6 3 9 0 1 9 4

8 4 1 0 6 4 3 2 7 3 9 0 6 4

7 5 2 7 3 9 0 8 3 1 5 3 6 7

6 2 3 1 6 8 9 3 5 7 2 6 0 4

5 3 6 1 7 9 2 5 4 3 0 7 3 8

Table G-1 *(Continued)*

9

FILL IN THE EMPTY BOXES

Y	O	I	C	D	J	T	B	L	S
1	2	3	4	5	6	7	8	9	10

I	D	T	B	L	O	Y	S	J	C	T	L	D	I

B	O	C	L	Y	S	O	J	C	B	J	Y	L	T

I	T	D	Y	L	S	O	J	C	B	J	Y	L	T

Y	D	O	J	I	S	C	T	L	B	I	Y	S	D

J	L	O	B	S	Y	I	L	T	D	C	B	J	O

D	T	S	L	Y	J	I	C	B	O	L	I	Y	S

L	C	Y	D	J	I	B	S	O	T	C	D	O	B

10

FILL IN THE EMPTY BOXES

B	C	N	R	Z	J	P	K	A	G
1	2	3	4	5	6	7	8	9	10

P	J	N	R	C	G	A	B	Z	K	N	C	J	P

R	G	K	C	A	B	J	P	Z	N	G	R	K	B

P	N	J	A	C	B	G	Z	K	R	Z	A	C	N

A	J	B	Z	P	B	K	N	C	R	P	A	G	J

Z	K	G	B	R	P	A	C	N	J	K	R	Z	G

J	N	B	C	A	Z	P	K	R	G	C	P	A	B

C	K	A	J	Z	P	R	B	G	N	K	J	G	R

Source: Adapted from Roberts, Milich, and Loney (1984). Worksheets reproduced, with changes in notation, with permission from Mary Ann Roberts.

Table G-2
ADHD Questionnaire

ADHD QUESTIONNAIRE

Child's name: _____   Name of person filling out form: _____

Age: _____   Grade: _____   School: _____   Date: _____

Directions: Please read each item and check either Y (Yes) or N (No). If you check Yes, please answer the questions in the last three columns for that item. Be sure to indicate whether you are using years or months for your answers.

Behavior	*Check one*	*How old was the child when you first noticed the behavior?*	*How long has the behavior persisted?*	*In what settings does the child show this behavior (such as home, playground, school, or work)?*
1. Often fails to give close attention to details or makes careless mistakes in schoolwork, work, or other activities	☐ Y ☐ N			
2. Often has difficulty sustaining attention in tasks or play activities	☐ Y ☐ N			
3. Often does not seem to listen when spoken to directly	☐ Y ☐ N			
4. Often does not follow through on instructions and fails to finish schoolwork, chores, or duties in the workplace	☐ Y ☐ N			
5. Often has difficulty organizing tasks and activities	☐ Y ☐ N			
6. Often avoids, dislikes, or is reluctant to engage in tasks that require sustained mental effort (such as schoolwork or homework)	☐ Y ☐ N			
7. Often loses things necessary for tasks or activities, such as toys, school assignments, pencils, or books	☐ Y ☐ N			
8. Often is easily distracted by extraneous stimuli	☐ Y ☐ N			
9. Often is forgetful in daily activities	☐ Y ☐ N			
10. Often fidgets with hands or feet or squirms in seat	☐ Y ☐ N			
11. Often leaves seat in classroom or in other situations in which remaining seated is expected	☐ Y ☐ N			
12. Often runs about or climbs excessively in situations in which it is inappropriate	☐ Y ☐ N			
13. Often has difficulty playing or engaging in leisure activities quietly	☐ Y ☐ N			
14. Often is "on the go" or acts as if "driven by a motor"	☐ Y ☐ N			
15. Often talks excessively	☐ Y ☐ N			
16. Often blurts out answers before questions have been completed	☐ Y ☐ N			
17. Often has difficulty awaiting turn	☐ Y ☐ N			
18. Often interrupts or intrudes on others (e.g., butts into conversations or games)	☐ Y ☐ N			

Source: Adapted from American Psychiatric Association (2013).

Table G-3
DSM-5 Checklist for Attention-Deficit/Hyperactivity Disorder

DSM-5 CHECKLIST FOR ATTENTION-DEFICIT/HYPERACTIVITY DISORDER

Child's name: _____   Parent's name: _____

Age: _____   Grade: _____   School: _____   Date: _____

Directions: Check Y (Yes) or N (No) for each item.

Symptoms	Check one	
1. Inattention		
a. Often fails to give close attention to details or makes careless mistakes in schoolwork, work, or other activities	☐ Y	☐ N
b. Often has difficulty sustaining attention in tasks or play activities	☐ Y	☐ N
c. Often does not seem to listen when spoken to directly	☐ Y	☐ N
d. Often does not follow through on instructions and fails to finish schoolwork, chores, or duties in the workplace	☐ Y	☐ N
e. Often has difficulty organizing tasks and activities	☐ Y	☐ N
f. Often avoids, dislikes, or is reluctant to engage in tasks that require sustained mental effort	☐ Y	☐ N
g. Often loses things necessary for tasks or activities	☐ Y	☐ N
h. Often is easily distracted by extraneous stimuli	☐ Y	☐ N
i. Often is forgetful in daily activities	☐ Y	☐ N
2. Hyperactivity and Impulsivity		
a. Often fidgets with hands or feet or squirms in seat	☐ Y	☐ N
b. Often leaves seat in classroom or in other situations in which remaining seated is expected	☐ Y	☐ N
c. Often runs about or climbs excessively in situations in which it is inappropriate	☐ Y	☐ N
d. Often has difficulty playing or engaging in leisure activities quietly	☐ Y	☐ N
e. Often is "on the go" or acts as if "driven by a motor"	☐ Y	☐ N
f. Often talks excessively	☐ Y	☐ N
g. Often blurts out answers before a question has been completed	☐ Y	☐ N
h. Often has difficulty awaiting turn	☐ Y	☐ N
i. Often interrupts or intrudes on others	☐ Y	☐ N

(Continued)

Table G-3 (Continued)

DSM-5 Diagnostic Criteria	Check one	
A. A persistent pattern of inattention and/or hyperactivity-impulsivity that interferes with functioning or development, as characterized by (1) and/or (2) below:	☐ Y	☐ N
1. Inattention a. Six or more symptoms (five if individual is age 17 or older) from the list of symptoms in Section 1 (Inattention) on the prior page have been present for at least 6 months to a degree that is inconsistent with developmental level and have had a direct negative effect on social and academic/occupational activities.	☐ Y	☐ N
b. Symptoms are not solely a manifestation of oppositional behavior, defiance, hostility, or failure to understand tasks or instructions.	☐ Y	☐ N
If a and b are checked Y (Yes), criteria are fulfilled for Inattention.		
2. Hyperactivity and Impulsivity a. Six or more symptoms (five if individual is age 17 or older) from the list of symptoms in Section 2 (Hyperactivity and Impulsivity) on the prior page have been present for at least 6 months to a degree that is inconsistent with developmental level and have had a direct negative effect on social and academic/occupational activities.	☐ Y	☐ N
b. Symptoms are not solely a manifestation of oppositional behavior, defiance, hostility, or failure to understand tasks or instructions.	☐ Y	☐ N
If a and b are checked Y (Yes), criteria are fulfilled for Hyperactivity and Impulsivity.		
B. Several inattentive or hyperactive-impulsive symptoms were present prior to age 12 years.	☐ Y	☐ N
C. Several inattentive or hyperactive-impulsive symptoms are present in two or more settings.	☐ Y	☐ N
D. There is clear evidence that the symptoms interfere with or reduce the quality of social, academic, or occupational functioning.	☐ Y	☐ N
E. The symptoms do not occur exclusively during the course of schizophrenia or another psychotic disorder and are not better explained by another mental disorder.	☐ Y	☐ N

If above items A through E are checked Y (Yes), criteria are fulfilled for diagnosis of attention-deficit/hyperactivity disorder.

Specify presentation (check one):
☐ Combined presentation   ☐ Predominantly inattentive presentation   ☐ Predominantly hyperactive/impulsive presentation

Check if in partial remission ☐

Specify current severity (check one):
☐ Mild   ☐ Moderate   ☐ Severe

Source: Based on *DSM-5* (American Psychiatric Association, 2013).
From *Foundations of Behavioral, Social, and Clinical Assessment of Children* (Sixth Edition) by Jerome M. Sattler. Copyright 2014 by Jerome M. Sattler, Publisher, Inc. Permission to photocopy this appendix table is granted to purchasers of this book for personal use only (see copyright page for details).

Table H-1
Informal Tests of Word Prediction Abilities

CLOZE PROCEDURES

Name: _____   Date: _____

Sex: _____   Grade: _____   School: _____

Birth date: _____   Teacher: _____

Score (number correct): Task 1 _____ , Task 2 _____ , Task 3 _____ , Task 4 _____ , Task 5 _____ , Task 6 _____ .

Task	*Procedure and Examples*
1. Auditory Cloze with Oral Response Child is required to complete a spoken sentence or phrase orally with a word that is both semantically and syntactically correct. This is a good beginning task for children, regardless of age, because it defines the prediction abilities necessary for the subsequent tasks.	*Directions:* Say: "I am going to say a sentence that has a word missing. I want you to complete the sentence with a word that makes the most sense. For example, if I say *An airplane flies in the* _____ [pause], you could say *sky* or *air.* Do you have any questions? [Answer any questions.] Here is the first sentence." Administer all six items, but stop testing if the child becomes frustrated. Score the child's responses as 1 (correct) or 0 (incorrect). Give credit for any reasonable response. 1. Maria went to the lake to _____. (fish, swim, relax, etc.) 2. John used his money to buy some _____. (candy, clothes, food, etc.) 3. A horse can run very _____. (fast, quickly, slowly, etc.) 4. On a lonely farm in the country lived a man and his _____. (wife, child, donkey, etc.) 5. Mr. Cook was going to the _____ to get some eggs. (barn, store, market, shop, etc.) 6. Ray finished picking up the trash and walked back to the _____. (house, store, barn, etc.)
2. Auditory Cloze, Initial Grapheme, and Oral Response Child is presented with a spoken phrase or sentence with a single word omitted and is given the initial grapheme of the missing word. The prediction now involves an added constraint; not only must the response be semantically and syntactically acceptable, but it must also begin with the indicated grapheme. This task, unlike the auditory cloze, requires familiarity with letters and with oral response words.	*Directions:* Say: "I am going to say a sentence that has a word missing. The sentence will also have the first letter of the missing word. I want you to complete the sentence with a word that begins with that letter and makes the most sense. For example, if I say *In the morning I put on my shoes and s_____* [make the first *sound* of the missing word], you could say *socks* or *shirt.* Do you have any questions? [Answer any questions.] Here is the first sentence." Administer all six items, but stop testing if the child becomes frustrated. Score the child's responses as 1 (correct) or 0 (incorrect). Give credit for any reasonable response that begins with the appropriate letter. 1. My kitten drinks m_____. (milk) 2. Today, the mailman brought a l_____. (letter) 3. Sandy put the small rock in his p_____. (pocket, pack) 4. Last night for supper we had potatoes and b_____. (bread, beef, bacon, etc.) 5. The alligator was hiding in the w_____ of the swamp. (water, weeds) 6. When the car stopped, the old man got out and k_____ it. (kicked)

(Continued)

Table H-1 *(Continued)*

Task	Procedure and Examples
3. Visual Cloze with Alternatives and Oral Response Child selects, from two alternatives, the more appropriate word to complete the written sentence. This task, which assesses use of semantic and syntactic cues, relies heavily on a child's ability to read the target sentence and the alternatives. A child may err on this task even though he or she has adequate word prediction ability. The chance factor is much higher on this task than on the others.	*Directions:* Say: "I am going to show you a sentence and I want you to read it silently. When you come to the part that has two words in parentheses, tell me which word makes the most sense. For example, look at this sentence. [Show child this sentence: *The dog chased the (pat, cat).*] The word that makes the most sense is *cat.* Do you have any questions? [Answer any questions.] Here is the first sentence." Administer all six items, but stop testing if the child becomes frustrated. Score the child's responses as 1 (correct) or 0 (incorrect). Give credit only if the child chooses the correct word. 1. Mary can hit the (dill/ball). 2. Sam picked some (fingers/flowers) from his garden. 3. An old lady was in her (house/horse). 4. Kim will (come/came) home after the ballgame. 5. Because she was mad, Mom said, "Go to your room and don't come (out/our)." 6. On the way to school, Tim stopped to pick up a (life/leaf).
4. Visual Cloze with Oral Response Child is required to complete a written sentence orally with a word that is both semantically and syntactically correct. Odd responses may be based on a miscue of one of the words in the item, not on a misapplication of semantic and syntactic constraints. Scoring should be based on both semantic and syntactic acceptability.	*Directions:* Say: "I am going to show you a sentence that has a word missing. Read the sentence silently and then tell me what missing word makes the most sense. For example, look at this sentence. [Show child this sentence: *At night I go to _____ .*] You could say *sleep* or *bed.* Do you have any questions? [Answer any questions.] Here is the first sentence." Administer all six items, but stop testing if the child becomes frustrated. Score the child's responses as 1 (correct) or 0 (incorrect). Give credit for any reasonable response. 1. Run as fast as you _____. (can, want, etc.) 2. The baby was very _____. (happy, sad, etc.) 3. At breakfast Max spilled milk all over the _____. (table, floor, kitchen, etc.) 4. A red bird built a nest in the _____. (tree, chimney, etc.) 5. The dog is old, but he still _____. (runs, eats, etc.) 6. Every day I eat a big bowl of cereal _____ breakfast. (for, at)
5. Visual Cloze with Written Response Child is presented with a written phrase or sentence with a word omitted and is required to write an appropriate word in the space provided. Scoring should be based primarily on both semantic and syntactic acceptability.	*Directions:* Say: "I am going to show you a sentence that has a word missing. Read the sentence silently and then print on the blank line a word that makes the most sense. For example, look at this sentence. [Show child this sentence: *My mother likes to _____.*] You could print the word *cook* or *read* or *sew* here [point to the blank line]. Do you have any questions? [Answer any questions.] Here is the first sentence." Administer all six items, but stop testing if the child becomes frustrated. Score the child's responses as 1 (correct) or 0 (incorrect). Give credit for any reasonable response. 1. The boy kicked the _____. (ball, dog, car, etc.) 2. One day a _____ ran off the road. (car, bike, motorcycle, etc.) 3. I wanted to see if I could _____ fudge. (make, cook, etc.) 4. The duck flew over the water, and soon we could not _____ him. (see, find, etc.) 5. Once upon a time there was a king who was so _____ they called him King Charming. (nice, beautiful, charming, etc.) 6. Texas Dan was the best cowboy around, and he could _____ a bucking bronco. (ride)

Table H-1 *(Continued)*	
Task	*Procedure and Examples*
6. Visual Cloze, Initial Grapheme, and Written Response Child is presented with a written sentence with a word omitted and is required to write an appropriate word using the grapheme shown. Providing the initial grapheme limits the range of acceptable responses. Some children give responses that meet the initial grapheme criterion but that do not follow the semantic and syntactic cues.	*Directions:* Say: "I am going to show you a sentence that has a word missing. The sentence will also have the first letter of the missing word. Read the sentence silently. I want you to complete the sentence by printing the rest of the missing word that makes the most sense. For example, look at this sentence. [Show child this sentence: *The lion was in a cage at the z____* .] You could print the rest of the word *zoo* here like this. [Print *oo* on the blank line.] Do you have any questions? [Answer any questions.] Here is the first sentence." Administer all six items, but stop testing if the child becomes frustrated. Score the child's responses as 1 (correct) or 0 (incorrect). Give credit for any reasonable response. 1. The girl eats the h_____. (hotdog, hamburger, etc.) 2. Peter named his dog B_____. (Bill, Boy, Ben, etc.) 3. My bike is r_____ and white. (red) 4. Mary didn't want her little brother playing w_____ her toys. (with) 5. Where could I go if I wanted t_____ hide? (to) 6. The artist could draw the most beautiful p_____ of flowers. (picture)

Note. Record the child's response. Also note if the child makes (a) no response, (b) an incorrect response that was related to the theme, or (c) an incorrect response that was not related to the theme. If the child gives more than one word, ask for a single word.

Source: Adapted from Allington (1979). The six items for each procedure were obtained from R. L. Allington, personal communication, April 1982.

Table H-2
Strip Initial Consonant Task

STRIP INITIAL CONSONANT TASK

Name: _____   Date: _____

Sex: _____ Grade: _____   School: _____

Birth date: _____   Teacher: _____

Score (number correct): _____

As you present each sample and item, speak clearly and distinctly and emphasize the key word.

Say, "Listen carefully. I am going to say a word. If you take away the first sound of the word I say, you will find a new word. First, I'll show you how to do it. *Ball.* If you take away the first sound, the new word is *all.* Now let's try another." Give Sample Item 1.

Sample Item 1
Say, "Tell me what the new word is when you take away the first sound in *cat.* What is the new word when you take away the first sound?"

If the child succeeds, say, "That's right" and go to Sample Item 2.

If the child fails, say, "If you take away the first sound from the word *cat,* the new word is *at.*" Repeat Sample Item 1. Say, "*Cat.* What is the new word when you take away the first sound?"

If the child succeeds, say, "That's right" and go to Sample Item 2.

If the child fails, say, "If you take away the first sound from the word *cat,* the new word is *at.*" Proceed to Sample Item 2.

Sample Item 2
Say, "Let's try another one. What is the new word when you take away the first sound from the word *task*?"

If the child succeeds, say, "That's right" and go to Test Item 1.

If the child fails, say, "If you take away the first sound from the word *task,* the new word is *ask.*" Repeat Sample Item 2. Say, "What is the new word when you take away the first sound from the word *task*?"

If the child succeeds, say, "That's right" and go to Test Item 1.

If the child fails, say, "If you take away the first sound from the word *task,* the new word is *ask.*" Proceed to Test Item 1.

Test Items
Say, "If you take away the first sound in *pink,* what is the new word?" If necessary, repeat these instructions before you say each new word. Do not correct any answers or indicate whether they are correct. Give all nine items.

1. pink
2. man
3. nice
4. win
5. bus
6. pitch
7. call
8. hit
9. pout

Source: Adapted from Stanovich, Cunningham, and Cramer (1984).
From *Foundations of Behavioral, Social, and Clinical Assessment of Children* (Sixth Edition) by Jerome M. Sattler. Copyright 2014 by Jerome M. Sattler, Publisher, Inc. Permission to photocopy this appendix table is granted to purchaser of this book for personal use only (see copyright page for details).

Table H-3
Phonological Memory Test

PHONOLOGICAL MEMORY TEST

Name:_____   Date:_____

Sex:_____   Grade:_____   School:_____

Birth date:_____   Teacher:_____

Score (number correct): Words_____   Nonwords_____

Directions

Word directions: "I am going to say some words. After I say each word, you say it. Let's try one for practice: *big.* Now you say it. . . . OK. Here is the first word. . . . Now you say it." Introduce each item with "Here is the next word." If needed, also say: "Now you say it."

Nonword directions: "I am going to say some made-up words. After I say each made-up word, you say it. Let's try one for practice: *kek.* Now you say it. . . . OK. Here is the first made-up word. . . . Now you say it." Introduce each item with "Here is the next word." If needed, also say: "Now you say it."

Words	Nonwords
1. Arm _____	16. Grall_____
2. Hate_____	17. Nate_____
3. Pot_____	18. Mot _____
4. Bird _____	19. Plurd _____
5. Pull _____	20. Tull _____
6. Rabbit _____	21. Rubid_____
7. Letter_____	22. Diller _____
8. Driver_____	23. Grindle_____
9. Picture_____	24. Fannock _____
10. Button _____	25. Yennet_____
11. Newspaper _____	26. Brastering _____
12. Alphabet _____	27. Dopelate _____
13. Holiday _____	28. Kannifer_____
14. Elephant _____	29. Tumperine_____
15. Potato _____	30. Parrazon _____

Source: Adapted from Gathercole and Adams (1993).
From *Foundations of Behavioral, Social, and Clinical Assessment of Children* (Sixth Edition) by Jerome M. Sattler. Copyright 2014 by Jerome M. Sattler, Publisher, Inc. Permission to photocopy this appendix table is granted to purchaser of this book for personal use only (see copyright page for details).

Table H-4
Phonological Oddity Task

PHONOLOGICAL ODDITY TASK

Name: _____   Date: _____

Sex: _____   Grade: _____   School: _____

Birth date: _____   Teacher: _____

Score (number correct): Test 1 _____ Test 2 _____ Test 3 _____

Speak clearly and distinctly, at an even pace, and emphasize the four key words in each item or example.

TEST 1. FIRST SOUND DIFFERENT

Say, "Listen carefully. I am going to say four words. One of the words begins with a different sound from the other words. Here is an example. If I say *bag, nine, beach, bike,* the word that begins with a different sound is *nine.* Now you try one." Give Sample Item 1.

Sample Item 1

Say, "Which word begins with a different sound from the other words: *rat, roll, ring, pop*?"

If the child passes, say, "That's right" and go to Sample Item 2.

If the child fails, say, "*rat, roll, ring, pop.* The word that has a different beginning sound is *pop.*" Repeat Sample Item 1. Say, "Which word begins with a different sound from the other words: *rat, roll, ring, pop*?"

If the child passes, say, "That's right" and go to Sample Item 2.

If the child fails, say, "*rat, roll, ring, pop.* The word that has a different beginning sound is *pop.*" Go to Sample Item 2.

Sample Item 2

Say, "Let's try another one. Which word has a different beginning sound: *nut, sun, sing, sort*?"

If the child passes, say, "That's right" and go to Test Item 1.

If the child fails, say, "*nut, sun, sing, sort.* The word that has a different beginning sound is *nut.*" Repeat Sample Item 2. Say, "Which word has a different beginning sound: *nut, sun, sing, sort*?"

If the child passes, say, "That's right" and proceed to Test Item 1.

If the child fails, say, "*nut, sun, sing, sort.* The word that has a different beginning sound is *nut.*" Proceed to Test Item 1.

Test Items

Give Test Items 1 through 8. Say, "Which word has a different beginning sound?" Then say the four words. If necessary, repeat the instructions before each item. Do not correct any answers or indicate whether they are correct. Introduce each item with "Here are the next four words."

1. not no nice *son*
2. ball bite *dog* beet
3. girl *pat* give go
4. *yes* run rose round
5. cap *jar* coat come
6. hand hut *fun* here
7. *cat* tan time ton
8. luck like look *arm*

TEST 2. MIDDLE SOUND DIFFERENT

Say, "Listen carefully. I am going to say four words. One of the words has a different sound in the middle from the other words. Here is an example. If I say *tap, cap, tell, hat,* the word that has a different sound in the middle is *tell.* Now you try one." Give Sample Item 1.

Sample Item 1

Say, "Which word has a different sound in the middle from the other words: *mop, hop, tap, pop*?"

If the child passes, say, "That's right" and go to Sample Item 2.

If the child fails, say, "*mop, hop, tap, pop.* The word that has a different sound in the middle is *tap.*" Repeat Sample Item 1. Say, "Which word has a different sound in the middle from the other words: *mop, hop, tap, pop*?"

If the child passes, say, "That's right" and go to Sample Item 2.

If the child fails, say, "*mop, hop, tap, pop.* The word that has a different sound in the middle is *tap.*" Go to Sample Item 2.

Sample Item 2

Say, "Let's try another one. Which word has a different middle sound: *pat, fit, bat, cat*?"

If the child passes, say, "That's right" and go to Test Item 1. If the child fails, say, "*pat, fit, bat, cat.* The word that has a different middle sound is *fit.*" Repeat Sample Item 2. Say, "Which word has a different middle sound: *pat, fit, bat, cat*?"

If the child passes, say, "That's right" and proceed to Test Item 1.

If the child fails, say, "*pat, fit, bat, cat.* The word that has a different middle sound is *fit.*" Proceed to Test Item 1.

Test Items

Give Test Items 1 through 8. Say, "Which word has a different middle sound?" Then say the four words. If necessary, repeat the instructions before each item. Do not correct any answers or indicate whether they are correct. Introduce each item with "Here are the next four words."

1. lot cot pot *hat*
2. fun *pin* bun gun
3. *hug* dig pig wig
4. red fed *lid* bed
5. wag rag bag *leg*
6. fell *doll* well bell
7. dog fog *jug* log
8. fish dish wish *mash*

Table H-4 (Continued)

TEST 3. LAST SOUND DIFFERENT

Say, "Listen carefully. I am going to say four words. One of the words has a different sound at the end from the other words. Here is an example. If I say *fog, tag, pig, let*, the word that ends with a a different sound is *let*. Now you try one." Give Sample Item 1.

Sample Item 1

Say, "Which word has a different sound at the end from the other words: *hat, mat, fan, cat*?"

If the child passes, say, "That's right" and go to Sample Item 2.

If the child fails, say, "*hat, mat, fan, cat.* The word that has a different ending sound is *fan*." Repeat Sample Item 1. Say, "Which word has a different sound at the end from the other words: *hat, mat, fan, cat*?"

If the child passes, say, "That's right" and go to Sample Item 2.

If the child fails, say, "*hat, mat, fan, cat.* The word that has a different ending sound is *fan*." Go to Sample Item 2.

Sample Item 2

Say, "Let's try another one. Which word has a different ending sound: *doll, hop, pop, top*?"

If the child passes, say, "That's right" and go to Test Item 1.

If the child fails, say, "*doll, hop, pop, top.* The word that has a different ending sound is *doll*." Repeat Sample Item 2. Say, "Which word has a different ending sound: *doll, hop, pop, top*?"

If the child passes, say, "That's right" and proceed to Test Item 1.

If the child fails, say, "*doll, hop, pop, top.* The word that has a different ending sound is *doll*." Proceed to Test Item 1.

Test Items

Give Test Items 1 through 8. Say, "Which word has a different ending sound?" Then say the four words. If necessary, repeat the instructions before each item. Do not correct any answers or indicate whether they are correct. Introduce each item with "Here are the next four words."

1. sun run *tub* fun
2. *hen* peg leg beg
3. fin *sit* pin win
4. map cap gap *jam*
5. cot hot *fox* pot
6. fill *pig* hill mill
7. *peel* weed seed feed
8. pack lack *sad* back

Source: Adapted from Bradley (1980) and Stanovich, Cunningham, and Cramer (1984).
From *Foundations of Behavioral, Social, and Clinical Assessment of Children* (Sixth Edition) by Jerome M. Sattler. Copyright 2014 by Jerome M. Sattler, Publisher, Inc. Permission to photocopy this appendix table is granted to purchaser of this book for personal use only (see copyright page for details).

Table H-5
List of Regular Words, Irregular Words, and Nonsense Words

Regular Words		Irregular Words		Nonsense Words	
Grade 2	Grade 3	Grade 2	Grade 3	Grade 2	Grade 3
up	best	was	glisten	lopeb	fidot
it	nostril	does	pleasure	pilk	peb
am	napkin	learn	prove	sut	ipcrot
crop	rid	one	doubtful	nintred	kaxin
went	scalpel	gone	honest	noxtof	stum
at	spun	lawn	lawn	skep	polt
ran	disc	work	shove	sopog	fisc
hand	drank	among	realm	lin	glin
silk	complex	early	gentle	sifton	cospim
tax	demanded	flood	cough	lemp	lemp
top	piano	there	pigeon	ig	hintred
dog	rustic	right	cupboard	tipik	gix
man	hundred	any	fought	flontel	yentop
pen	colt	sugar	rough	marpi	oxitac
get	custom	nothing	hour	lut	pontflact

Source: Adapted from Freebody and Byrne (1988).

From *Foundations of Behavioral, Social, and Clinical Assessment of Children* (Sixth Edition) by Jerome M. Sattler. Copyright 2014 by Jerome M. Sattler, Publisher, Inc. Permission to photocopy this appendix table is granted to purchaser of this book for personal use only (see copyright page for details).

Table H-6
Auditory Analysis Test

AUDITORY ANALYSIS TEST

Name: _____   Date: _____

Sex: _____   Grade: _____   School: _____

Birth date: _____   Teacher: _____

Score (number correct): _____

Directions: Show the child the top half of a sheet of 8½ × 11-inch paper on which pictures of a cow and a boy's head are shown side by side. Say: "Say *cowboy.*" After the child responds, cover the picture of the boy and say: "Now say it again, but without *boy.*" If the response is correct (*cow*), expose the bottom half of the sheet on which drawings of a tooth and a brush are shown side by side. Say: "Say *toothbrush.*" After the child responds, cover the picture of the tooth and say: "Say it again, but without *tooth.*"

If the child fails either demonstration item, teach the task by repeating the demonstration procedures with the pictures. If the child again fails to make correct responses to both items, discontinue testing.

If both responses are correct, withdraw the picture sheet and proceed with the test. Say: "Say *birthday.*" Wait for a response, and then say: "Now say it again, but without *day.*" Continue with the test. Always pronounce the specific sound (*not the letter name*) of the item to be omitted. If the child has a speech articulation problem, take this into consideration when you score the response. If the child fails an item, repeat the item. If there is still no response, record a score of 0 and give the next item. *Discontinue after four consecutive scores of 0.*

Circle the items that the child correctly segments; record incorrect responses on the blank line following the item. Note that the correct responses for all items are real words, except for items 26, 30, and 33.

Items

A. cow(boy) _____   20. (t)rail _____

B. (tooth)brush _____   21. (sh)rug _____

  1. birth(day) _____   22. g(l)ow _____

  2. (car)pet _____   23. cr(e)ate _____

  3. bel(t) _____   24. (st)rain _____

  4. (m)an _____   25. s(m)ell _____

  5. (b)lock _____   26. Es(ki)mo _____

  6. to(ne) _____   27. de(s)k _____

  7. (s)our _____   28. Ger(ma)ny _____

  8. (p)ray _____   29. st(r)eam _____

  9. stea(k) _____   30. auto(mo)bile _____

10. (l)end _____   31. re(pro)duce _____

11. (s)mile _____   32. s(m)ack _____

12. plea(se) _____   33. phi(lo)sophy _____

13. (g)ate _____   34. s(k)in _____

14. (c)lip _____   35. lo(ca)tion _____

15. ti(me) _____   36. cont(in)ent _____

16. (sc)old _____   37. s(w)ing _____

17. (b)reak _____   38. car(pen)ter _____

18. ro(de) _____   39. c(l)utter _____

19. (w)ill _____   40. off(er)ing _____

Table H-7
Yopp-Singer Test of Phoneme Segmentation

YOPP-SINGER TEST OF PHONEME SEGMENTATION

Name: _____   Date: _____

Sex: _____   Grade: _____   School: _____

Birth date: _____   Teacher: _____

Score (number correct): _____

Directions: "We're going to play a word game. I'm going to say a word, and I want you to break the word apart. Do this by telling me each sound in the word in order. For example, if I say *old*, you should say /o/-/l/-/d/. [Be sure to say the sounds, not the letters, in the word.] Let's try a few together."

Practice items: *ride, go, man.* Assist the child in segmenting these items as necessary.

Circle the items that the child correctly segments. Record incorrect responses on the blank line following the item.

Items

1. dog _____   12. lay _____
2. keep _____   13. race _____
3. fine _____   14. zoo _____
4. no _____   15. three _____
5. she _____   16. job _____
6. wave _____   17. in _____
7. grew _____   18. ice _____
8. that _____   19. at _____
9. red _____   20. top _____
10. me _____   21. by _____
11. sat _____   22. do _____

Source: Adapted from Yopp (1995).
From *Foundations of Behavioral, Social, and Clinical Assessment of Children* (Sixth Edition) by Jerome M. Sattler. Copyright 2014 by Jerome M. Sattler, Publisher, Inc. Permission to photocopy this appendix table is granted to purchaser of this book for personal use only (see copyright page for details).

Table H-8
Informal Writing Inventory

INFORMAL WRITING INVENTORY

Name: _____ School: _____

Sex: _____ Grade: _____ Teacher: _____

Birth date: _____ Date: _____ Title of assignment: _____

Guidelines

A. Content

1. Development of Ideas—Does the writer have a theme or message to convey? Does the entire composition relate to these basic ideas? Are the ideas well developed?

2. Overall Organization—Are paragraphs and sentences logically ordered? Is there a thesis statement in the first paragraph? Do topic sentences follow the thesis statement? Do supporting details follow topic sentences?

3. Comprehensibility—Is the message clear? Is the writing easy to understand? Will the reader have questions? Are gaps present?

4. Paragraph Development—Does each paragraph have a main idea? Do the sentences in the paragraphs relate to each other? Are sentences logically ordered?

5. Sentence Construction—Are all of the sentences complete (absence of fragments)? Does each sentence contain a single idea (absence of run-on sentences)?

6. Types of Sentences—What kinds of sentences are included (compound, complex, simple, declarative, interrogative)? Do sentences contain too few or too many words?

7. Use of Words—Are the words descriptive/vague, complex/simple, appropriate/inappropriate, formal/informal? Are words omitted or parts omitted from or added to words?

8. Length—Is the passage too long or too short? Does the length reflect a reasonable effort?

B. Grammar

9. Subject-Verb Agreement—Do subjects and verbs agree?

10. Verb Tense—Is the correct verb tense used?

11. Pronoun Antecedents—Do pronouns and antecedents agree?

12. Use of Adjectives/Adverbs—Are adjectives and adverbs used properly?

13. Syntax—Is the sentence structure correct (e.g., parallelism, use of modifiers)?

14. Consistency of Tense—Is the tense appropriate and consistent across sentences and paragraphs?

C. Mechanics

15. Capitalization—Are capital letters used appropriately? If not, what types of words need to be capitalized (e.g., proper nouns, first word in a sentence)?

16. Punctuation—Is correct punctuation used? If not, what types of punctuation are needed (e.g., periods, commas, apostrophes)?

17. Spelling—Is the spelling generally correct? What types of spelling problems occurred? Did the writer have problems with difficult or easy words?

18. Handwriting—Is the handwriting generally neat and readable, with adequate spacing and consistent letter size?

	Evaluation (check one)				
Area	*Excellent*	*Adequate*	*Fair*	*Poor*	*Comments*
A. Content					
1. Development of Ideas					
2. Overall Organization					
3. Comprehensibility					
4. Paragraph Development					
5. Sentence Construction					
6. Types of Sentences					
7. Use of Words					
8. Length					

(Continued)

Table H-8 *(Continued)*

Area	Excellent	Adequate	Fair	Poor	Comments
B. Grammar					
9. Subject-Verb Agreement					
10. Verb Tense					
11. Pronoun Antecedents					
12. Use of Adjectives/Adverbs					
13. Syntax					
14. Consistency of Tense					
C. Mechanics					
15. Capitalization					
16. Punctuation					
17. Spelling					
18. Handwriting					

Source: Adapted from Billingsley (1998).

Table H-9
Diagnostic Spelling Test

DIAGNOSTIC SPELLING TEST

Directions: Give the child a sheet of paper and a pencil with an eraser. Say: "I am going to say some words, and then I want you to spell each one. I will say the word first and then use it in a sentence. Here is the first word." Say the first word in List 1 or List 2, as appropriate; then follow the word with its corresponding sentence. On the blank line following the sentence, record the child's response.

List 1 (grades 2 and 3)		Response	List 2 (grade 4 and higher)		Response
Word	*Illustrative Sentence*		*Word*	*Illustrative Sentence*	
1. not	He is *not* here.	_____	1. flower	A rose is a *flower*.	_____
2. but	Mary is here, *but* Joe is not.	_____	2. mouth	Open your *mouth*.	_____
3. get	*Get* the wagon, John.	_____	3. shoot	John wants to *shoot* his toy gun.	_____
4. sit	*Sit* down, please.	_____	4. stood	We *stood* under the roof.	_____
5. man	Father is a tall *man*.	_____	5. while	We sang *while* we marched.	_____
6. boat	We sailed our *boat* on the lake.	_____	6. third	We are in the *third* grade.	_____
7. train	Tom has a new toy *train*.	_____	7. each	*Each* child has a pencil.	_____
8. time	It is *time* to come home.	_____	8. class	Our *class* is reading.	_____
9. like	We *like* ice cream.	_____	9. jump	We like to *jump* rope.	_____
10. found	We *found* our lost ball.	_____	10. jumps	Mary *jumps* rope.	_____
11. down	Do not fall *down*.	_____	11. jumped	We *jumped* rope yesterday.	_____
12. soon	Our teacher will *soon* be here.	_____	12. jumping	The girls are *jumping* rope now.	_____
13. good	He is a *good* boy.	_____	13. hit	*Hit* the ball hard.	_____
14. very	We are *very* happy to be here.	_____	14. hitting	John is *hitting* the ball.	_____
15. happy	Jane is a *happy* girl.	_____	15. bite	Our dog does not *bite*.	_____
16. kept	We *kept* our shoes dry.	_____	16. biting	The dog is *biting* on the bone.	_____
17. come	*Come* to our party.	_____	17. study	*Study* your lesson.	_____
18. what	*What* is your name?	_____	18. studies	He *studies* each day.	_____
19. those	*Those* are our toys.	_____	19. dark	The sky is *dark* and cloudy.	_____
20. show	*Show* us the way.	_____	20. darker	This color is *darker* than that one.	_____
21. much	I feel *much* better.	_____	21. darkest	This color is the *darkest* of three.	_____
22. sing	We will *sing* a new song.	_____	22. afternoon	We may play this *afternoon*.	_____
23. will	Who *will* help us?	_____	23. grandmother	Our *grandmother* will visit us.	_____
24. doll	Make a dress for the *doll*.	_____	24. can't	We *can't* go with you.	_____
25. after	We play *after* school.	_____	25. doesn't	Mary *doesn't* like to play.	_____
26. sister	My *sister* is older than I.	_____	26. night	We read to Mother last *night*.	_____
27. toy	I have a new *toy* train.	_____	27. brought	Joe *brought* his lunch to school.	_____
28. say	*Say* your name clearly.	_____	28. apple	An *apple* fell from the tree.	_____
29. little	Tom is a *little* boy.	_____	29. again	We must come back *again*.	_____
30. one	I have only *one* book.	_____	30. laugh	Do not *laugh* at other children.	_____
31. would	*Would* you come with us?	_____	31. because	We cannot play *because* of the rain.	_____
32. pretty	She is a *pretty* girl.	_____	32. through	We ran *through* the yard.	_____

Note: See Table H-10 for the elements tested in the Diagnostic Spelling Test.
Source: Reprinted and adapted from *Teacher's Guide for Remedial Reading* by William Kottmeyer, © 1959, with permission of The McGraw-Hill Companies, pp. 88–89.
From *Foundations of Behavioral, Social, and Clinical Assessment of Children* (Sixth Edition) by Jerome M. Sattler. Copyright 2014 by Jerome M. Sattler, Publisher, Inc. Permission to photocopy this appendix table is granted to purchaser of this book for personal use only (see copyright page for details).

Table H-10
Elements Tested in the Diagnostic Spelling Test

List 1 (grades 2 and 3)		List 2 (grade 4 and higher)	
Word	**Element Tested**	**Word**	**Element Tested**
1. not 2. but 3. get 4. sit 5. man	Short vowels	1. flower 2. mouth	ow-ou spellings of ou sound, er ending, th spelling
6. boat 7. train	Two vowels together	3. shoot 4. stood	Long and short oo, sh spelling
8. time 9. like	Vowel-consonant-e	5. while	wh spelling, vowel-consonant
10. found 11. down	ow-ou spelling of ou sound	6. third	th spelling, vowel before r
12. soon 13. good	Long and short oo	7. each	ch spelling, two vowels together
14. very 15. happy	Final y as short i	8. class	Double final consonant, c spelling of k sound
16. kept 17. come	c and k spellings of the k sound	9. jump 10. jumps 11. jumped 12. jumping	Addition of s, ed, ing; j spelling of soft g sound
18. what 19. those 20. show 21. much 22. sing	wh, th, sh, ch, and ng spellings, ow spelling of long o	13. hit 14. hitting	Doubling final consonant before ing
23. will 24. doll	Doubled final consonant	15. bite 16. biting	Dropping final e before ing
25. after 26. sister	er spelling	17. study 18. studies	Changing final y to i before ending
27. toy	oy spelling of oi sound	19. dark 20. darker 21. darkest	er, est endings
28. say	ay spelling of long a sound	22. afternoon 23. grandmother	Compound words
29. little	le ending	24. can't 25. doesn't	Contractions
30. one 31. would 32. pretty	Nonphonetic spellings	26. night 27. brought	Silent gh
		28. apple	le ending
		29. again 30. laugh 31. because 32. through	Nonphonetic spellings

Note. See Table H-9 for the list of sentences.
Source: Reprinted and adapted from *Teacher's Guide for Remedial Reading* by William Kottmeyer, © 1959, with permission of The McGraw-Hill Companies, p. 90.

Table H-11
Informal Assessment of Arithmetic

Number System

Say: "I am going to say some numbers, and I want you to tell me what number comes next. Here is the first one." Introduce the next four items with "Here is the next one."

1. 1, 2, 3, 4, 5,
2. 2, 4, 6, 8,
3. 1, 5, 9, 13,
4. 63, 65, 67,
5. 100, 200, 300,

Counting

6. Say: "Count by tens starting with 10 and stop when I tell you. Go ahead; count by tens starting with 10." Stop the child after he or she says the fifth number.

7. Say: "Count by tens starting with 14 and stop when I tell you. Go ahead; count by tens starting with 14." Stop the child after he or she says the fifth number.

Writing Numbers from Oral Presentation

Say: "Write these numbers using this pencil. Here is the first number." Introduce the next four items with "Here is the next number." Give the child a blank sheet of paper on which to write the numbers.

8. 39
9. 400
10. 658
11. 303
12. 550

Reading Numbers

Say: "I am going to show you some numbers. I want you to tell me what the numbers are. Here is the first one." Make five 3 × 5 cards, one for each number. Show each card to the child.

13. 18
14. 40
15. 300
16. 509
17. 842

Addition

Say: "I would like you to do the following problems. Use this pencil to write your answers. Go ahead." Point to problems 18 to 25 or reproduce them on a separate piece of paper.

18.	4 +45	22.	17 + 22
19.	6 +2	23.	23 + 3
20.	8 +9	24.	47 +36
21.	6 +7	25.	439 +596

Subtraction

Say: "Now, I would like you to do the following problems. Use this pencil to write your answers. Go ahead." Point to problems 26 to 35 or reproduce them on a separate piece of paper.

26.	6 −5	31.	46 − 12
27.	9 −2	32.	87 −49
28.	16 − 8	33.	65 −17
29.	14 − 3	34.	504 −383
30.	34 −13	35.	300 −177

Multiplication

Say: "Now, I would like you to do the following problems. Use this pencil to write your answers. Go ahead." Point to problems 36 to 43 or reproduce them on a separate piece of paper.

36.	6 ×4	40.	43 × 2
37.	9 ×0	41.	28 × 5
38.	4 ×1	42.	56 ×22
39.	7 ×6	43.	19 ×10

Division

Say: "Now, I would like you to do the following problems. Use this pencil to write your answers. Go ahead." Point to problems 44 to 50 or reproduce them on a separate piece of paper.

44.	8 ÷ 4	48.	64 ÷ 7
45.	9 ÷ 3	49.	109 ÷ 5
46.	54 ÷ 6	50.	78 ÷ 46
47.	100 ÷ 2		

Table H-12
Stories for Meaningful Memory Recall

Directions: Say: "I am going to read a story. Listen carefully. When I am through, tell me the story that I read to you." Give the child 1 point for each unit recalled correctly; exact wording or order is not important. Also consider how the child organizes various elements in the story, what particular features the child recalls in the story, and what features the child distorts in the story. Do not read the numbers. They represent each important element in the story.

STORIES

Bozo Story

1) Once there were three 2) thieves 3) named 4) Bozo, 5) Tommy, and 6) Frank. 7) Bozo 8) was their leader. 9) They were good 10) friends and 11) went everywhere 12) together. 13) One night the 14) three of them 15) sneaked 16) through 17) a window 18) into 19) a house 20) on a hill. 21) There were trees 22) around the house. 23) Suddenly a 24) light 25) came on 26) in another 27) room. 28) They quickly 29) climbed 30) out 31) of the window. 32) Bozo and 33) Tommy 34) ran 35) down 36) the hill. 37) The other thief 38) climbed 39) a tree. 40) When a man 41) came 42) to the door of the house, 43) he could see 44) no one.

Airplane Story

1) The airplane 2) was coming in 3) for a landing. 4) It was 5) full 6) of people. 7) Suddenly, 8) the airplane 9) leaned 10) far to 11) the left 12) side. 13) All of the passengers 14) were afraid. 15) The pilot 16) did not know 17) what was wrong 18) so he landed the plane 19) very carefully. 20) As he landed, 21) one wing of the plane 22) scraped 23) the ground. 24) The passengers 25) and the pilot 26) climbed out 27) and looked 28) at the plane. 29) To their surprise, 30) a large 31) group 32) of birds 33) was sitting 34) on the wing of the plane.

Linda Story

1) Linda 2) was playing 3) with her new 4) doll 5) in front 6) of her house. 7) Suddenly, 8) she heard 9) a strange 10) sound 11) coming from under 12) the porch. 13) It was the flapping 14) of wings. 15) Linda ran 16) inside 17) the house and 18) grabbed 19) a shoe 20) box 21) from the closet. 22) She found 23) some sheets 24) of paper 25) and cut 26) the paper 27) into pieces 28) and put them 29) in the box. Linda 30) gently 31) picked up 32) the helpless 33) animal 34) and took it 35) with her. 36) Her teacher 37) knew what to do.

Source: Reprinted with permission of E. H. Bacon and D. C. Rubin, unpublished material. These stories were used in research by Bacon and Rubin (1983).

Table H-13
Questions to Help You Learn About a Child's Attitude Toward Reading and Writing

ATTITUDE TOWARD READING AND WRITING

Name: _____ Date: _____

Sex: _____ Grade: _____ School: _____

Birth date: _____ Teacher: _____

Reading

1. How did you learn to read? _____

2. Who helped you learn to read? _____

3. What did they do to help you? _____

4. Who is the best reader you know? _____

5. Why do you think he or she is the best? _____

6. Are you a good reader? _____

7. How do you know? _____

8. Do you like to read? _____

9. When do you read? _____

10. What is your favorite book? _____

11. What is the last book you read? _____

12. When did you read it? _____

13. When you are reading alone and you come to a word you don't know, what do you do? _____

    _____

14. Why do you read? _____

15. Tell me three words that describe how you feel about reading. _____

16. How do you decide what you will read? _____

17. Who is your favorite author? _____

18. Do you like to be read to? _____

19. How many books have you read over the past 6 months? _____

Writing

20. Tell me three words that describe how you feel about writing. _____

21. How did you learn to write? _____

22. Why do you write? _____

23. Are you a good writer? _____

24. What makes a good writer? _____

25. When do you write? _____

26. What do you like to write about? _____

27. How much have you written over the past 6 months? _____

28. (If appropriate) Tell me about what you have written. _____

29. When you have a writing assignment, how do you usually go about completing it? _____

(Continued)

Table H-13 *(Continued)*

30. Is there anything else that you do? _____

31. Do you like to write? _____

32. Tell me about that. _____

33. How good is your writing? _____

34. Tell me about that. _____

35. What are some things you think about before you write? _____

36. What are some things you do before you write? _____

37. Once you've written your assignment, what do you usually do? _____

38. Some writers make an outline before they begin writing. Do you do that? _____

39. What do you do after your first draft is completed? _____

40. (If needed) Do you edit the first draft? _____

41. (If yes) Tell me what you do when you edit it. _____

Source: Adapted from Deshler, Ellis, and Lenz (1996), Farnan and Kelly (1991), and Mather and Gregg (2003).
From *Foundations of Behavioral, Social, and Clinical Assessment of Children* (Sixth Edition) by Jerome M. Sattler. Copyright 2014 by Jerome M. Sattler, Publisher, Inc. Permission to photocopy this appendix table is granted to purchaser of this book for personal use only (see copyright page for details).

Table H-14
Sentence Completion Technique for Children Who May Have Learning Problems

SENTENCE COMPLETION TECHNIQUE FOR CHILDREN WHO MAY HAVE LEARNING PROBLEMS

Name: _____ Date: _____

Sex: _____ Grade: _____ School: _____

Birth date: _____ Teacher: _____

Directions: Say: "I am going to start a sentence. Then I'd like you to finish it any way you want. Here is an example. If I say, 'When I am tired. . . ,' you can say, 'I go to bed,' 'I take a nap,' 'I sit down,' or anything else that you can think of. OK? Let's try the first one."

Reading

1. When reading in class, I become nervous if _____.

2. Reading is easiest when _____.

3. Jobs that require reading are _____.

4. My favorite reading activity is _____.

5. If I couldn't read, _____.

6. My favorite place to read is _____.

7. If I could do any type of reading, I would _____.

8. Reading reminds me of _____.

9. The worst place to read is _____.

10. Jobs that do not require reading are _____.

11. If you asked people what they thought of reading, most would say _____.

12. I would be less nervous about reading if _____.

13. The person with whom I would like to read is _____.

Mathematics

14. When doing mathematics in class, I become nervous if _____.

15. Mathematics is easiest when _____.

16. Jobs that require mathematics are _____.

17. My favorite mathematics activity is _____.

18. If I couldn't do mathematics, _____.

19. My favorite place to do mathematics is _____.

20. If I could do any type of mathematics, I would _____.

21. Mathematics reminds me of _____.

22. The worst place to do mathematics is _____.

23. Jobs that do not require mathematics are _____.

24. If you asked people what they thought of mathematics, most would say _____.

25. I would be less nervous about mathematics if _____.

26. The person with whom I would like to do mathematics is _____.

(Continued)

Table H-14 *(Continued)*

Spelling

27. When doing spelling in class, I become nervous if _____.

28. Spelling is easiest when _____.

29. Jobs that require spelling are _____.

30. My favorite spelling activity is _____.

31. If I couldn't spell, _____.

32. My favorite place to do spelling is _____.

33. If I could do any type of spelling, I would _____.

34. Spelling reminds me of _____.

35. The worst place to do spelling is _____.

36. Jobs that do not require spelling are _____.

37. If you asked people what they thought of spelling, most would say _____.

38. I would be less nervous about spelling if _____.

39. The person with whom I would like to do spelling is _____.

Writing

40. When doing writing in class, I become nervous if _____.

41. Writing is easiest when _____.

42. Jobs that require writing are _____.

43. My favorite writing activity is _____.

44. If I couldn't write, _____.

45. My favorite place to do writing is _____.

46. If I could do any type of writing, I would _____.

47. Writing reminds me of _____.

48. The worst place to do writing is _____.

49. Jobs that do not require writing are _____.

50. If you asked people what they thought of writing, most would say _____.

51. I would be less nervous about writing if _____.

52. The person with whom I would like to do writing is _____.

General

53. The best time for me to do homework is _____.

54. When I start my homework, I _____.

55. At home, I study _____.

56. When I finish my homework, I _____.

57. My favorite subject is _____.

58. My least favorite subject is _____.

59. I think school is _____.

Source: Adapted from Giordano (1987).

Table H-15
Reading Study Skills Questionnaire

READING STUDY SKILLS QUESTIONNAIRE

Name: _____   Class: _____

Date: _____   Teacher's name: _____

School: _____

Directions: Read each question and put a check mark in the box for Y (Yes), N (No), or DK (Don't Know).
Try to answer each question. Thank you.

	Check one

	Yes	No	Don't Know
Part 1. *When I have a reading assignment, I usually . . .*			
1. preview the material by reading the heading and one or two sentences.	☐ Y	☐ N	☐ DK
2. think about what I already know about this topic.	☐ Y	☐ N	☐ DK
3. think about how much time it might take me to complete it.	☐ Y	☐ N	☐ DK
4. think about how much of the assignment I want to read on the first day.	☐ Y	☐ N	☐ DK
5. think about what the rest of the material might be about after I read the first few sentences.	☐ Y	☐ N	☐ DK
6. think about what might be easy to learn as I look it over.	☐ Y	☐ N	☐ DK
7. think about what might be difficult to learn as I look it over.	☐ Y	☐ N	☐ DK
8. ask myself who the main characters in the story are as I read it.	☐ Y	☐ N	☐ DK
9. ask myself what a paragraph is about after I have read the paragraph.	☐ Y	☐ N	☐ DK
10. think about how what I am reading relates to what I already know about the topic.	☐ Y	☐ N	☐ DK
Part 2. *When I am reading an assignment, I usually . . .*			
11. use a dictionary (either a book or a dictionary on a computer) to look up words that I don't know.	☐ Y	☐ N	☐ DK
12. know when I need to give more attention to some parts of the assignment than to other parts.	☐ Y	☐ N	☐ DK
13. get someone to help me with the assignment when I am having difficulty with it.	☐ Y	☐ N	☐ DK
14. wonder how each paragraph fits in with the paragraphs that came before and after it.	☐ Y	☐ N	☐ DK
Part 3. *After I finish a reading assignment, I usually . . .*			
15. think about whether it turned out the way I thought it would.	☐ Y	☐ N	☐ DK
16. ask myself whether the material made sense.	☐ Y	☐ N	☐ DK
17. think about whether I need to reread parts of it.	☐ Y	☐ N	☐ DK
18. think about how the people in the story would look if they were real.	☐ Y	☐ N	☐ DK
19. try to summarize what I read.	☐ Y	☐ N	☐ DK
20. think about what I have learned.	☐ Y	☐ N	☐ DK
21. think about how what I learned fits in with other information I know about the topic.	☐ Y	☐ N	☐ DK

Table H-16
Self-Evaluation of Note-Taking Ability

SELF-EVALUATION OF NOTE-TAKING ABILITY

Name: _____   Class: _____

Date: _____   Teacher's name: _____

School: _____

Directions: Use the following rating scale to evaluate your ability to take notes:

1 I don't do this very well.
2 I'm barely OK at this.
3 I'm OK at this.
4 I do this well.
5 I do this very well.

Circle one number for each item. Thank you.

When I take notes, I usually . . .	Circle one				
1. write fast enough.	1	2	3	4	5
2. pay attention.	1	2	3	4	5
3. am able to make sense of the notes after the lecture.	1	2	3	4	5
4. know what information is important to write down.	1	2	3	4	5
5. understand what the teacher is saying.	1	2	3	4	5
6. see the overheads clearly.	1	2	3	4	5
7. see the notes that the teacher writes on the board clearly.	1	2	3	4	5
8. hear the teacher clearly.	1	2	3	4	5
9. use my notes to study for tests.	1	2	3	4	5
10. find my notes helpful when I study.	1	2	3	4	5

Source: Adapted from Deshler, Ellis, and Lenz (1996).
From *Foundations of Behavioral, Social, and Clinical Assessment of Children* (Sixth Edition) by Jerome M. Sattler. Copyright 2014 by Jerome M. Sattler, Publisher, Inc. Permission to photocopy this appendix table is granted to purchaser of this book for personal use only (see copyright page for details).

Table H-17
Self-Monitoring Procedure to Improve Reading Comprehension

SELF-MONITORING PROCEDURE TO IMPROVE READING COMPREHENSION

Be aware of what you understand when you are reading.
Identify the parts of the passage that you do not understand.
Use the following strategies to help you with any problems that you have in understanding the passage.

Strategy 1:
Applying Prior Knowledge
As you look over the reading passage, ask yourself: "What do I already know about this topic?" _____

_____

Strategy 2:
Identifying Difficult Passages
As you read, identify where you might be having difficulty. Ask yourself:

"What part of the reading passage didn't I understand?" _____

"What word or words confused me or were unfamiliar to me?" _____

Then you might say:

"This is not making sense because _____."

"This is not what I expected because _____."

"This doesn't connect to what I already read because _____."

Strategy 3:
Dealing with Difficult Sentences or Passages
If you come to a difficult sentence or passage, try the following things.

A. Ask yourself: "What do I think the author is trying to say?" You can answer this by
- rereading the passage
- reviewing your previous ideas about the passage and relating these ideas to the ideas that confuse you
- replacing a word or words you don't know with ones that you do know and think would make sense and then looking up any difficult words in a dictionary (or online)
- changing your ideas to match the new information you obtain
- asking someone for help

B. Say the following to yourself:
"Maybe I'd better _____."

"Something I could do is _____."

"Since I don't understand this word, a good strategy would be to _____."

"First I saw _____ , but now I see _____."

"What I thought this was about no longer makes sense because _____."

"I need to revise my thinking by _____."

"Maybe I need to consider _____."

C. Look back through the text to see if the author mentioned this idea or material before. If so, ask yourself: "What did the author say about it?" _____

_____

D. Look forward in the text for information that might help you resolve any problems. Ask yourself: "Are there any charts or graphics in the reading material that might help me better understand the passage?" _____

_____

(Continued)

Table H-17 *(Continued)*

Strategy 4:
Making Predictions
Make predictions about what will come next. This will help you gain a better understanding of the passage. Correct and revise your predictions as you gain new information from the text. You could say:

"I'm guessing that _____ will happen next."

"I bet that _____."

"I wonder if _____."

Strategy 5:
Using Your Own Experiences
Use your own experience to consider how you might apply what you are reading to your life. You could say:

"This is like _____."

"This reminds me of _____."

"This could help me with _____."

"This is helping me to think about plans for _____."

Strategy 6:
Creating Images
Think about the sensory and physical details in the passage and expand on them by creating images or scenes in your mind. For example, you might visualize an expression on a character's face or the room the characters are in. As you read, develop and adapt these images. You could say:

"In my mind's eye, _____."

"I imagine _____."

"I see _____."

"I have a picture of _____."

Strategy 7:
Concluding Thoughts
After you finish reading the passage, ask yourself the following questions:

"Who are the main characters?" _____

"What is the setting of the story?" _____

"What is the story about?" _____

"What are the problems or conflicts in the story?" _____

"How does the story end?" _____

"What did I learn after reading this passage?" _____

Source: Gusinger (2009) and Wilhelm (2001).

Table H-18
Checklist of Problems Associated with Learning Disabilities

CHECKLIST OF PROBLEMS ASSOCIATED WITH LEARNING DISABILITIES

Name: _____ Date: _____

	Check one	
Cognitive/Academic	Y	N
1. Difficulty connecting letters to their sound	☐	☐
2. Difficulty expressing ideas in writing	☐	☐
3. Difficulty following directions	☐	☐
4. Difficulty keeping place when reading	☐	☐
5. Difficulty learning alphabet	☐	☐
6. Difficulty remembering sounds that letters make	☐	☐
7. Difficulty rhyming words	☐	☐
8. Difficulty spelling	☐	☐
9. Poor encoding of phonological information in long-term memory	☐	☐
10. Poor grammatical understanding	☐	☐
11. Poor listening skills	☐	☐
12. Poor mathematical skills	☐	☐
13. Poor memory of basic mathematical facts	☐	☐
14. Poor number sense	☐	☐
15. Poor phonological awareness	☐	☐
16. Poor reading comprehension	☐	☐
17. Poor recognition of letters and numerals	☐	☐
18. Poor verbal expression	☐	☐
19. Poor vocabulary	☐	☐
20. Reading slowly	☐	☐
21. Reading with limited fluency	☐	☐
Information-Processing/Executive Functions		
1. Difficulty detecting inadequacies in reading materials	☐	☐
2. Difficulty generalizing	☐	☐
3. Difficulty identifying critical content of reading materials	☐	☐
4. Difficulty identifying critical information needed to solve problems	☐	☐
5. Difficulty recognizing when more information is needed to solve problems	☐	☐
6. Difficulty recognizing whether tasks have been performed correctly	☐	☐
7. Difficulty retelling story in order	☐	☐
8. Difficulty self-monitoring	☐	☐
9. Difficulty shifting attention	☐	☐
10. Difficulty sustaining attention	☐	☐
11. Difficulty with labeling	☐	☐
12. Difficulty with verbal rehearsal	☐	☐
13. Difficulty with clustering	☐	☐
14. Difficulty with chunking	☐	☐
15. Difficulty with selective attention	☐	☐
16. Difficulty with self-regulation	☐	☐
17. Difficulty working under time constraints	☐	☐
18. Poor cognitive strategies	☐	☐
19. Poor independent work habits	☐	☐

	Check one	
Information-Processing/Executive Functions *(Cont.)*	Y	N
20. Poor organizational skills	☐	☐
21. Poor planning skills	☐	☐
22. Poor processing skills	☐	☐
23. Poor retrieval of encoded information	☐	☐
24. Poor study skills	☐	☐
Perceptual		
1. Confuses math symbols	☐	☐
2. Delayed development of consistent hand preference	☐	☐
3. Difficulty hearing slight difference between words	☐	☐
4. Difficulty in interpreting facial expressions and body language	☐	☐
5. Difficulty in perceiving figure-ground relationship	☐	☐
6. Difficulty pronouncing words	☐	☐
7. Difficulty in temporal sequencing	☐	☐
8. Difficulty memorizing auditory and visual stimuli	☐	☐
9. Difficulty with cross-modal sensory integration	☐	☐
10. Difficulties with visual and auditory perception	☐	☐
11. Misreads numbers	☐	☐
12. Poor attention span	☐	☐
13. Poor fine-motor coordination	☐	☐
14. Poor revisualization	☐	☐
15. Poor spatial perception	☐	☐
16. Poor speech articulation	☐	☐
17. Poor visual organization	☐	☐
18. Reverses numbers	☐	☐
Social-Behavioral		
1. Acting-out behavior	☐	☐
2. Anxiety	☐	☐
3. Depression	☐	☐
4. Destructiveness	☐	☐
5. Difficulty following social rules of conversation	☐	☐
6. Difficulty making friends	☐	☐
7. Difficulty with conflict management	☐	☐
8. Disorganized behavior	☐	☐
9. Disruptiveness	☐	☐
10. Distractibility	☐	☐
11. Hyperactivity	☐	☐
12. Immaturity	☐	☐
13. Impulsiveness	☐	☐
14. Irritability	☐	☐
15. Low expectations for future achievement	☐	☐
16. Low self-esteem	☐	☐
17. Minimal confidence in ability to influence learning outcomes	☐	☐
18. Mischievousness	☐	☐
19. Poor self-image	☐	☐

Source: Geary (2004); Hallahan and Mercer (2002); Kavale and Forness (1996); Lerner (2003); Maehler and Schuchardt (2011); Mazzocco, Feigenson, and Halberda (2011); National Dissemination Center for Children with Disabilities (2011b); Siegler (1998); Singh, Singh, and Singh (2011); and Vellutino, Fletcher, Snowling, and Scanlon (2004).

Table I-1
Teacher and Parent Recommendation Form for Children Who Are Gifted and Talented

TEACHER AND PARENT RECOMMENDATION FORM
FOR CHILDREN WHO ARE GIFTED AND TALENTED

Child's name: _____   Date: _____

Age: _____   Sex: _____   Grade: _____   School: _____

Name of person filling out form: _____

Directions: Please check the box that represents your rating of each characteristic.

Rating scale:	1	2	3	4	5
	Never	Sometimes	Usually	Often	Always

Characteristic	Check one	Characteristic	Check one

Learning Style — (1 2 3 4 5)
1. Has outstanding memory ☐☐☐☐☐
2. Pays attention to details ☐☐☐☐☐
3. Has excellent reasoning ability ☐☐☐☐☐
4. Is intellectually curious ☐☐☐☐☐
5. Learns things rapidly ☐☐☐☐☐
6. Is a keen and alert observer ☐☐☐☐☐
7. Shows complex thought processes ☐☐☐☐☐
8. Has the capacity for seeing unusual relationships ☐☐☐☐☐
9. Has an advanced vocabulary and communication skills ☐☐☐☐☐
10. Achieves well above grade level in several subjects ☐☐☐☐☐
11. Reads a great deal ☐☐☐☐☐
12. Asks unusual questions for age ☐☐☐☐☐
13. Has good insight into cause-and-effect relations ☐☐☐☐☐
14. Makes valid generalizations about events, people, or objects ☐☐☐☐☐
15. Quickly perceives similarities, differences, and anomalies ☐☐☐☐☐
16. Is skeptical, critical, and evaluative ☐☐☐☐☐

Motivation
17. Has a high energy level ☐☐☐☐☐
18. Is nonconforming and independent ☐☐☐☐☐
19. Is persistent in completing tasks ☐☐☐☐☐
20. Is resourceful in finding answers ☐☐☐☐☐
21. Becomes absorbed in tasks when interested ☐☐☐☐☐
22. Requires little external motivation when work is exciting ☐☐☐☐☐
23. Strives toward perfection ☐☐☐☐☐
24. Enjoys intellectual pursuits ☐☐☐☐☐
25. Is concerned about social and moral issues ☐☐☐☐☐

Interests — (1 2 3 4 5)
26. Has strong interest in some artistic activity ☐☐☐☐☐
27. Has strong interest in some academic area ☐☐☐☐☐
28. Has strong interest in some sport or physical activity ☐☐☐☐☐

Leadership Characteristics
29. Is self-confident ☐☐☐☐☐
30. Enjoys taking on responsibility ☐☐☐☐☐
31. Expresses self well ☐☐☐☐☐
32. Adapts well to new situations ☐☐☐☐☐
33. Stimulates others ☐☐☐☐☐
34. Organizes people and events ☐☐☐☐☐
35. Recognizes skills and abilities of others ☐☐☐☐☐
36. Articulates ideas clearly ☐☐☐☐☐
37. Gives directions clearly and effectively ☐☐☐☐☐
38. Exercises authority reliably and responsibly ☐☐☐☐☐
39. Is looked to by others when something must be decided ☐☐☐☐☐
40. Has an advanced sense of justice and fairness ☐☐☐☐☐

Creativity
41. Shows emotional sensitivity ☐☐☐☐☐
42. Generates a large number of ideas and solutions to problems ☐☐☐☐☐
43. Is imaginative ☐☐☐☐☐
44. Has a preference for novelty ☐☐☐☐☐
45. Is open-minded and receptive to new ideas ☐☐☐☐☐
46. Has a sense of humor and can laugh at himself or herself ☐☐☐☐☐
47. Is a risk-taker and adventurous ☐☐☐☐☐

Table I-2
Parent and Teacher Recommendation Form for Preschool Children Who Are Gifted and Talented

PARENT AND TEACHER RECOMMENDATION FORM
FOR PRESCHOOL CHILDREN WHO ARE GIFTED AND TALENTED

Child's name: _____ Date: _____

Age: _____ Sex: _____ Grade: _____ School: _____

Name of person filling out form: _____

Directions: Please check one box using the following scale:

Rating scale:	1	2	3
	Not true	Somewhat true	Very true

Characteristic	Check one		
Developmental Characteristics	1	2	3
1. Showed unusual alertness in infancy	☐	☐	☐
2. Showed advanced progression through the early developmental milestones	☐	☐	☐
3. Understood directions, such as right and left, at an early age	☐	☐	☐
4. Showed early interest in time	☐	☐	☐
5. Learned to read before age 5 years	☐	☐	☐
6. Showed early interest in numbers	☐	☐	☐
Learning Style			
7. Has outstanding memory and can carry out complex instructions to do several things in succession	☐	☐	☐
8. Has a long attention span	☐	☐	☐
9. Has an advanced vocabulary and communication skills	☐	☐	☐
10. Uses metaphors or analogies	☐	☐	☐
11. Makes up songs or stories spontaneously	☐	☐	☐
12. Makes interesting shapes or patterns with blocks, board shapes, or other material	☐	☐	☐
13. Puts together difficult puzzles	☐	☐	☐
14. Understands abstract or complex concepts	☐	☐	☐
15. Masters a new skill, concept, song, or rhyme with unusual speed	☐	☐	☐
16. Uses language to exchange ideas	☐	☐	☐
17. Takes apart and reassembles things with unusual skill	☐	☐	☐
18. Remembers and makes mental connections between past and present experiences	☐	☐	☐
Personality			
19. Demonstrates a preference for novelty	☐	☐	☐
20. Shows curiosity and asks many questions	☐	☐	☐
21. Modifies language when talking to less mature children	☐	☐	☐
22. Has a sense of humor	☐	☐	☐
23. Becomes absorbed in one kind of activity	☐	☐	☐
24. Is persistent and sticks to a task	☐	☐	☐
25. Displays great interest or skill in ordering or grouping objects	☐	☐	☐
26. Shows sensitivity to the needs or feelings of other children or adults	☐	☐	☐
27. Shows unusual attentiveness to features of the home or preschool environment	☐	☐	☐
28. Uses verbal skills to handle conflict or to influence other children's behavior	☐	☐	☐
29. Prefers to play with older children or with adults	☐	☐	☐
30. Is able to look after himself or herself	☐	☐	☐
31. Wanted to do things for himself or herself at an early age	☐	☐	☐

Source: Adapted, in part, from Roedell (1980b) and Silverman (1997).

Table I-3
Checklist for Identifying Children Who Are Creative

CHECKLIST FOR IDENTIFYING CHILDREN WHO ARE CREATIVE

Child's name: _____   Date: _____

Age: _____   Sex: _____   Grade: _____   School: _____

Name of person filling out form: _____

Directions: Please check one box using the following scale:

Rating scale:	1	2	3	4	5
	Never	Sometimes	Usually	Often	Always

Characteristic	Check one (1 2 3 4 5)	Characteristic	Check one (1 2 3 4 5)
1. Concentrates intensely	☐☐☐☐☐	26. Has an internal locus of control	☐☐☐☐☐
2. Defers judgment	☐☐☐☐☐	27. Is intuitive	☐☐☐☐☐
3. Shows above-average intellectual ability	☐☐☐☐☐	28. Displays inventiveness	☐☐☐☐☐
4. Is adaptable	☐☐☐☐☐	29. Has little tolerance for boredom	☐☐☐☐☐
5. Shows aesthetic appreciation	☐☐☐☐☐	30. Makes unusual associations between ideas	☐☐☐☐☐
6. Asks provocative questions	☐☐☐☐☐	31. Needs a supportive climate	☐☐☐☐☐
7. Is attracted to the complex and mysterious	☐☐☐☐☐	32. Displays nonconformism	☐☐☐☐☐
8. Is committed to completing tasks	☐☐☐☐☐	33. Is open to experience	☐☐☐☐☐
9. Shows curiosity	☐☐☐☐☐	34. Is original	☐☐☐☐☐
10. Delights in beauty of theory	☐☐☐☐☐	35. Is playful	☐☐☐☐☐
11. Desires to share products and ideas	☐☐☐☐☐	36. Provides multiple solutions	☐☐☐☐☐
12. Is eager to resolve disorder	☐☐☐☐☐	37. Seeks new, unusual, or unconventional associations among items of information	☐☐☐☐☐
13. Has extensive knowledge background	☐☐☐☐☐	38. Sees that solutions generate new problems	☐☐☐☐☐
14. Is flexible	☐☐☐☐☐	39. Is looked to by others when something must be decided	☐☐☐☐☐
15. Has good memory	☐☐☐☐☐	40. Has self-confidence	☐☐☐☐☐
16. Shows attention to detail	☐☐☐☐☐	41. Has a sense of mission	☐☐☐☐☐
17. Has a high energy level	☐☐☐☐☐	42. Has a sense of wonder	☐☐☐☐☐
18. Displays humor (perhaps bizarre)	☐☐☐☐☐	43. Is sensitive	☐☐☐☐☐
19. Is idiosyncratic	☐☐☐☐☐	44. Has a tolerance for ambiguity and conflict	☐☐☐☐☐
20. Is imaginative	☐☐☐☐☐	45. Is unconventional	☐☐☐☐☐
21. Improvises	☐☐☐☐☐	46. Is willing to face social ostracism	☐☐☐☐☐
22. Generates and develops ideas	☐☐☐☐☐	47. Displays a willingness to take risks	☐☐☐☐☐
23. Is independent	☐☐☐☐☐		
24. Shows ingenuity	☐☐☐☐☐		
25. Has insight into complex topics or ideas	☐☐☐☐☐		

Source: Characteristics obtained, in part, from Ford and Ford (1981).
From *Foundations of Behavioral, Social, and Clinical Assessment of Children* (Sixth Edition) by Jerome M. Sattler. Copyright 2014 by Jerome M. Sattler, Publisher, Inc. Permission to photocopy this table is granted to purchasers of this book for personal use only (see copyright page for details).

Table J-1
Observation Form for Recording Behaviors That May Reflect Autism Spectrum Disorder and Positive Behaviors

OBSERVATION FORM FOR RECORDING BEHAVIORS THAT MAY REFLECT AUTISM SPECTRUM DISORDER AND POSITIVE BEHAVIORS

Child's name: _____   Examiner's name: _____

Age: _____ Sex: _____ Grade: _____ School: _____ Date: _____

Directions: Place an X in a box to indicate that the behavior was observed during that period. For "Other," write in the name of the behavior.

	Period									Total
	1	2	3	4	5	6	7	8	9	
Sensory Modulation										
1. Covers ears with hands										
2. Peers at objects or people from the corner of eye										
3. Looks closely at hands										
4. Stares										
5. Rubs surfaces										
6. Sniffs objects or people										
7. Sniffs hands										
8. Switches light on and off										
9. Locks and unlocks door										
10. Spins objects for a long time										
11. Does not respond to name										
12. Other:										
13. Other:										
Motility										
1. Flaps hands										
2. Turns head often										
3. Flicks or wiggles finger										
4. Grimaces										
5. Whirls or spins										
6. Walks on toes										
7. Darts or lunges										
8. Assumes peculiar postures										
9. Rocks body										
10. Jumps repetitively										
11. Runs aimlessly										
12. Bangs head										
13. Taps back of hand often										
14. Other:										
15. Other:										
General Behavior										
1. Rubs objects over lips										
2. Claps hands										
3. Mouths hands										
4. Lacks appropriate facial expressions										
5. Resists change										
6. Has tantrums										
7. Displays self-injurious behavior										
8. Displays rigidity										
9. Insists on sameness										
10. Over- or underreactive to sensory input										
11. Has difficulty processing sensory information										
12. Other:										
13. Other:										

(Continued)

Table J-1 (*Continued*)

	Period									Total
	1	*2*	*3*	*4*	*5*	*6*	*7*	*8*	*9*	*Total*
Relation to Examiner										
1. Rarely makes eye contact										
2. Does not smile in response to smiles of examiner										
3. Does not respond to his or her name when called										
4. Turns face away when called										
5. Grabs objects										
6. When speaking, speaks only about own interests or to request items										
7. Makes inappropriate attempts at contact										
8. Ignores examiner										
9. Asks the same questions repeatedly										
10. Does not share a toy or activity										
11. Other:										
12. Other:										
Relation to Toys										
1. Uses toys inappropriately										
2. Uses toys ritualistically										
3. Spins toys inappropriately										
4. Plays nonfunctionally with parts of toys										
5. Lets toys fall out of hand										
6. Throws toys inappropriately										
7. Ignores toys										
8. Uses toys in a restricted manner (with few combinations and in few constructive ways)										
9. Lines up toys in an obsessive manner										
10. Other:										
11. Other:										
Language										
1. Is nonverbal										
2. Speaks only to self										
3. Speaks too loudly or too quietly										
4. Shows immediate echolalia										
5. Shows delayed echolalia										
6. Reverses pronouns										
7. Uses words in a peculiar fashion										
8. Has difficulty initiating or sustaining conversation										
9. Gives tangential details when answering questions										
10. Other:										
11. Other:										
Positive Behavior										
1. Shows examiner a toy										
2. Asks examiner to play with him or her										
3. Asks examiner questions										
4. Asks examiner for help										
5. Engages in pretend play[a]										
6. Takes turns rolling or throwing the ball										
7. Uses gestures										
8. Directs facial expressions to examiner										
9. Other:										
10. Other:										

[a] Examples are pretending to talk on the phone, fly a helicopter, cook, and feed a doll.

Source: Adapted from Adrien, Ornitz, Barthelemy, Sauvage, and LeLord (1987) and Filipek et al. (1999).

Table J-2
Modified Checklist for Autism in Toddlers (M-CHAT)

MODIFIED CHECKLIST FOR AUTISM IN TODDLERS

Child's name: _____   Parent's name: _____

Child's age: _____   Date: _____

Directions: Please fill out the following checklist about how your child **usually** is. Please try to answer every question. If the behavior is rare (for example, you've seen it once or twice), please answer as if the child did not do it by checking N (No). If the behavior is not rare, please check Y (Yes).

Behavior	Check one	
1. Does your child enjoy being swung or bounced on your knee?	☐ Y	☐ N
2. Does your child take an interest in other children?	☐ Y	☐ N
3. Does your child like climbing on things, such as stairs?	☐ Y	☐ N
4. Does your child enjoy playing peek-a-boo or hide-and-seek?	☐ Y	☐ N
5. Does your child sometimes pretend, for example, to talk on the phone or take care of dolls, or pretend other things?	☐ Y	☐ N
6. Does your child sometimes use his [her] index finger to point, to ask for something?	☐ Y	☐ N
7. Does your child sometimes use his [her] index finger to point, to indicate interest in something?	☐ Y	☐ N
8. Can your child play properly with small toys—such as cars or bricks—without just mouthing, fiddling, or dropping them?	☐ Y	☐ N
9. Does your child sometimes bring objects over to you to show you something?	☐ Y	☐ N
10. Does your child look you in the eye for more than a second or two?	☐ Y	☐ N
11. Does your child sometimes seem oversensitive to noise (for example, plugging ears)?	☐ Y	☐ N
12. Does your child smile in response to your face or your smile?	☐ Y	☐ N
13. Does your child imitate you (for example, if you make a face, will your child imitate it)?	☐ Y	☐ N
14. Does your child respond to his [her] name when you call?	☐ Y	☐ N
15. If you point to a toy across the room, does your child look at it?	☐ Y	☐ N
16. Does your child walk?	☐ Y	☐ N
17. Does your child look at things you are looking at?	☐ Y	☐ N
18. Does your child make unusual finger movements near his [her] face?	☐ Y	☐ N
19. Does your child try to attract your attention to his [her] own activity?	☐ Y	☐ N
20. Have you ever wondered if your child is deaf?	☐ Y	☐ N
21. Does your child understand what people say?	☐ Y	☐ N
22. Does your child sometimes stare at nothing or wander with no purpose?	☐ Y	☐ N
23. Does your child look at your face to check your reaction when faced with something unfamiliar?	☐ Y	☐ N

Source: Adapted from Robins, Fein, Barton, and Green (2001).
From *Foundations of Behavioral, Social, and Clinical Assessment of Children* (Sixth Edition) by Jerome M. Sattler. Copyright 2014 by Jerome M. Sattler, Publisher, Inc. Permission to photocopy this table is granted to purchasers of this book for personal use only (see copyright page for details).

Table J-3
Autism Spectrum Disorder Questionnaire for Parents

AUTISM SPECTRUM DISORDER QUESTIONNAIRE FOR PARENTS

Child's name: _____   Parent's name: _____

Age: _____ Sex: _____ Grade: _____ School: _____ Date: _____

Directions: Please read each item and check either Y (Yes) or N (No). If you check "Yes," please answer the questions in the two columns to the right of that item. Be sure to indicate whether you are using years or months in your answers.

Behavior	*Check one*	*Age of the child when behavior first noticed*	*How long has the behavior persisted?*
1. Makes little eye contact when talking to others	☐ Y ☐ N		
2. Peers at objects from the corner of the eye	☐ Y ☐ N		
3. Did not wave bye-bye as an infant	☐ Y ☐ N		
4. Does not smile socially	☐ Y ☐ N		
5. Does not respond to sounds or names	☐ Y ☐ N		
6. Shows extreme distress at small changes or during times of transition	☐ Y ☐ N		
7. Does not spontaneously share experiences with other people	☐ Y ☐ N		
8. Prefers to play alone rather than with other children	☐ Y ☐ N		
9. Ignores children or adults who are trying to interact with him or her	☐ Y ☐ N		
10. Does not seem to understand how others are feeling	☐ Y ☐ N		
11. Seems to live in a world of his or her own	☐ Y ☐ N		
12. Did not babble as an infant	☐ Y ☐ N		
13. Has difficulty taking turns speaking or starting a conversation	☐ Y ☐ N		
14. Has peculiar patterns of speech (such as odd tone or volume)	☐ Y ☐ N		
15. Repeats other people's phrases over and over again	☐ Y ☐ N		
16. Speaks in a repetitive and stereotyped way	☐ Y ☐ N		
17. Speaks, but confuses the word "I" with the word "you"	☐ Y ☐ N		
18. Makes up new words that do not make sense and cannot be corrected	☐ Y ☐ N		
19. Does not engage in imaginative play or use toys in pretend play	☐ Y ☐ N		
20. Plays with toys in rigid or repetitive ways	☐ Y ☐ N		
21. Has strong attachments to unusual objects (such as sticks or pieces of paper) rather than to more typical toys (such as teddy bears or dolls)	☐ Y ☐ N		
22. Has a narrow and intense focus on a particular topic (for example, train schedules) or skill (for example, memorizing phone numbers)	☐ Y ☐ N		
23. Is preoccupied with things being done in a certain way (for example, insists on always drinking from the same cup or following the same route) and becomes upset if changes are made in his or her daily routines	☐ Y ☐ N		

Table J-3 *(Continued)*

Behavior	Check one	Age of the child when behavior first noticed	How long has the behavior persisted?
24. Becomes upset if things don't look right (such as a stain on a tablecloth), if something is out of place, or if there is a change in the way things are arranged or done	☐ Y ☐ N		
25. Does the same thing over and over again with his or her body (such as rocking, clapping hands, flapping arms, running aimlessly, walking on toes, spinning, or doing other odd movements)	☐ Y ☐ N		
26. Does the same thing over and over again with objects (such as opening and closing doors, flipping the tops of trash cans, turning a light switch on and off, flicking strings, transferring water from one container to another, or spinning objects)	☐ Y ☐ N		
27. Is overly interested in looking at small objects or parts of objects	☐ Y ☐ N		
28. Does not use his or her index finger to point or to ask for something	☐ Y ☐ N		
29. Has a rigid preference for certain foods	☐ Y ☐ N		
30. List any other unusual behavior: _____			

Table J-4
Checklist of Possible Signs of an Autism Spectrum Disorder

CHECKLIST OF POSSIBLE SIGNS OF AN AUTISM SPECTRUM DISORDER

Child's name: _____ Clinician's name: _____

Age: _____ Sex: _____ Grade: _____ School: _____ Date: _____

Directions: Check Y (Yes) or N (No) for each item.

Social-Emotional Reciprocity   Check one
1. Does not smile socially   ☐ Y ☐ N
2. Is not interested in being held   ☐ Y ☐ N
3. Has difficulty in normal back-and-forth conversation   ☐ Y ☐ N
4. Fails to initiate or respond to social interactions   ☐ Y ☐ N
5. Does not respond to sounds or names   ☐ Y ☐ N
6. Cannot tell you what he or she wants   ☐ Y ☐ N

Nonverbal Communicative Behaviors Used for Social Interaction
1. Does not integrate verbal and nonverbal communication   ☐ Y ☐ N
2. Did not wave bye-bye as an infant   ☐ Y ☐ N
3. Has an expressionless face   ☐ Y ☐ N
4. Makes little eye contact when talking to others   ☐ Y ☐ N

Developing, Maintaining, and Understanding Relationships
1. Has difficulty adjusting behavior to suit various social contexts   ☐ Y ☐ N
2. Does not engage in imaginative play   ☐ Y ☐ N
3. Has difficulty making friends   ☐ Y ☐ N
4. Has no interest in making friends   ☐ Y ☐ N

Stereotyped or Repetitive Motor Movements, Use of Objects, or Speech
1. Lines things up obsessively   ☐ Y ☐ N
2. Has odd movement patterns   ☐ Y ☐ N
3. Displays immediate echolalia   ☐ Y ☐ N
4. Displays delayed echolalia   ☐ Y ☐ N
5. Uses idiosyncratic phrases   ☐ Y ☐ N
6. Uses language in a stereotyped and repetitive way   ☐ Y ☐ N

Insistence on Sameness, Inflexible Adherence to Routines, or Ritualized Patterns of Verbal or Nonverbal Behavior
1. Shows extreme distress at small changes   ☐ Y ☐ N
2. Has difficulty with transitions   ☐ Y ☐ N
3. Has rigid thinking patterns   ☐ Y ☐ N
4. Displays rituals on greeting others   ☐ Y ☐ N
5. Has a rigid preference for certain foods   ☐ Y ☐ N

Highly Restricted, Fixated Interests That Are Abnormal in Intensity or Focus   Check one
1. Has strong attachment to or preoccupation with unusual objects   ☐ Y ☐ N
2. Has excessively circumscribed or perseverative interests   ☐ Y ☐ N

Hyperreactivity or Hyporeactivity to Sensory Input or Unusual Interest in Sensory Aspects of the Environment
1. Is indifferent to pain   ☐ Y ☐ N
2. Is indifferent to temperature   ☐ Y ☐ N
3. Has adverse responses to sounds   ☐ Y ☐ N
4. Has adverse responses to textures   ☐ Y ☐ N
5. Smells objects excessively   ☐ Y ☐ N
6. Touches objects excessively   ☐ Y ☐ N
7. Is visually fascinated by lights   ☐ Y ☐ N
8. Is visually fascinated by movement   ☐ Y ☐ N

Language Development and Communication
1. Said a few words early but does not now   ☐ Y ☐ N
2. Did not babble by 12 months   ☐ Y ☐ N
3. Had no single words by 16 months   ☐ Y ☐ N
4. Had no two-word spontaneous phrases (in contrast to echolalic phrases) by 24 months   ☐ Y ☐ N
5. Speaks too formally or in a "robotic" way   ☐ Y ☐ N

Physiological Concerns
1. Shows loss of skills   ☐ Y ☐ N
2. Has poor muscle tone   ☐ Y ☐ N
3. Has frequent ear infections   ☐ Y ☐ N
4. Has difficulty sleeping or unusual sleep patterns   ☐ Y ☐ N
5. Has frequent gastrointestinal problems   ☐ Y ☐ N
6. Has seizures   ☐ Y ☐ N

Other Concerns or Symptoms
_____
_____
_____
_____
_____

Table J-5
DSM-5 Checklist for Autism Spectrum Disorder

DSM-5 CHECKLIST FOR AUTISM SPECTRUM DISORDER

Child's name: _____ Clinician's name: _____

Age: _____ Sex: _____ Grade: _____ School: _____ Date: _____

Directions: Check Y (Yes) or N (No) for each item.

Symptoms	Check one
A. Social Communication and Social Interaction	
1. Deficits in social-emotional reciprocity	☐ Y ☐ N
2. Deficits in nonverbal communicative behaviors used for social interaction	☐ Y ☐ N
3. Deficits in developing, maintaining, and understanding relationships	☐ Y ☐ N

Specify severity of social communication impairments (check one):

☐ Level 1—requiring support   ☐ Level 2—requiring substantial support   ☐ Level 3—requiring very substantial support

B. Restricted, Repetitive Patterns of Behavior, Interests, or Activities	
1. Stereotyped or repetitive motor movements, use of objects, or speech	☐ Y ☐ N
2. Insistence on sameness, inflexible adherence to routines, or ritualized patterns of verbal or nonverbal behavior	☐ Y ☐ N
3. Highly restricted, fixated interests that are abnormal in intensity or focus	☐ Y ☐ N
4. Hyperreactivity or hyporeactivity to sensory input or unusual interest in sensory aspects of the environment	☐ Y ☐ N

Specify severity of restricted, repetitive patterns of behavior (check one):

☐ Level 1—requiring support   ☐ Level 2—requiring substantial support   ☐ Level 3—requiring very substantial support

Diagnostic Criteria

A. All three items in part A are present.	☐ Y ☐ N
B. At least two of the four items in part B are present.	☐ Y ☐ N
C. Symptoms are present during early developmental period.	☐ Y ☐ N
D. Symptoms cause clinically significant impairment in social, occupational, or other important areas of current functioning.	☐ Y ☐ N
E. The disturbance is not better explained by intellectual disability or global developmental delay.	☐ Y ☐ N

If "Yes" is checked for diagnostic criteria A through E, criteria are fulfilled for a diagnosis of autism spectrum disorder.

Specify if the disorder occurs:

☐ With intellectual impairment   ☐ Without intellectual impairment

☐ With language impairment   ☐ Without language impairment

Specify any known medical or genetic condition or environmental factor: _____

Specify any accompanying neurodevelopmental, mental, or behavioral disorder: _____

Specify if the disorder occurs:

☐ With catatonia   ☐ Without catatonia

Source: Adapted from *DSM-5* (American Psychiatric Association, 2013).
From *Foundations of Behavioral, Social, and Clinical Assessment of Children* (Sixth Edition) by Jerome M. Sattler. Copyright 2014 by Jerome M. Sattler, Publisher, Inc. Permission to photocopy this table is granted to purchasers of this book for personal use only (see copyright page for details).

Handout K-1
Handout for Parents: Guidelines for Working with Children with Special Needs

INTRODUCTION

This handout provides general guidelines for parents who have children with special needs. You are not expected to follow every suggestion, and some suggestions may not apply to your child. You should consider your child's age, sex, language competency, type of special needs, and severity of disability in applying these suggestions. At the end are tips particularly for parents of children with brain injury, a visual impairment, a hearing loss, and an autism spectrum disorder, as well as tips for avoiding or dealing with a substance-induced disorder and tips for parents of children who are gifted and talented.

GENERAL SUGGESTIONS

Supporting Your Child

1. Let your child know that you're there for him or her—offer your full support. This will help make your child feel worthwhile and valued.
2. Remember that your role as a parent changes as your child grows older and develops.
3. Encourage your child to share his or her thoughts and feelings with you, and listen attentively and empathically to your child. Acknowledge any difficulties, pain, or sadness that your child is feeling. Make it clear that you are genuinely concerned about his or her feelings and that you care about and value your child. Reassure your child that things will get better.
4. Don't try to talk your child out of his or her symptoms.
5. Reinforce your child's appropriate behavior with verbal praise (for example, "Great job listening to all the directions!") and nonverbal gestures (for example, smiles and pats on the back).
6. Plan for one-on-one time with your child each day. As little as 10 to 15 minutes every day will let your child know that he or she is special to you. Follow your child's lead during this special time.
7. Plan family activities that your child enjoys.
8. Don't give up if your child shuts you out at first; talking to others may be difficult for children with special needs.
9. Give advice when your child needs it or when he or she asks for it.
10. Give your child reasonable alternatives rather than ultimatums.
11. If your child has other caregivers, make sure that they are familiar with your child's daily routines.
12. Provide good nutrition, because a good diet can help your child.
13. Anticipate problems and try to avoid them whenever possible.
14. If your child is reluctant to go to school or refuses to go, find out why and help your child return to school as quickly as possible. You may have to consider a shorter school day temporarily. Work with the teacher, special education team, school psychologist, school counselor, school social worker, or school nurse on these efforts.
15. If your child is able to do so, encourage him or her to keep a diary of the times when a problem occurred, how he or she was feeling at that time, and what happened. If writing is difficult, your child may choose to use an audio or video recorder to preserve this information, or draw pictures depicting what happened and how he or she felt.
16. Always steer your child away from dangerous situations and remove your child from situations that trigger inappropriate behavior.
17. Be an advocate for your child when he or she needs community services.
18. If you have a preschool child,
    - Help your child understand what it means to play fair, share toys, and tell the truth.
    - Encourage your child to ask questions if he or she does not understand what you are saying.
    - Use times when your child becomes frustrated at play as opportunities to strengthen his or her problem-solving skills. For example, if a tower of blocks keeps collapsing, work together to find a solution.
19. Always speak honestly with your child about his or her behavior and challenges, about how to improve his or her behavior, and about how to cope with the challenges.
20. Recognize that your child may experience setbacks in his or her development. Be patient and support your child during these difficult times. Setbacks are also opportunities for learning.

Reducing Your Child's Stress

1. Schedule periods for rest and relaxation and try to avoid letting your child become fatigued.

2. Plan ahead to be sure that your child is not overtired or hungry during shopping trips and other outings.
3. Teach your child how to relax. Relaxation techniques include deep breathing, counting to 10, and visualizing a soothing place. Schedule some time when your child can engage in calm activities, such as listening to music, taking a bath, and reading.
4. Minimize sources of stress and anxiety at home and at other places.
5. If your child gets distracted easily at home, identify quiet places where distractions are reduced. You may need to turn off televisions, radios, stereos, cell phones, and computer speakers.
6. Note whether anything in the environment—for example, noise, temperature, or smells—seems to cause your child discomfort. If so, try to reduce these sources of stress.
7. If an activity is taking a long time or is upsetting your child, stop the activity so that your child doesn't feel too much stress. Try to gradually increase your child's tolerance for the activity by continuing it a bit longer each time and then rewarding your child if he or she stays with the somewhat longer activity.

Helping Your Child Fall Asleep

1. Keep regular bedtime hours and provide some quiet time before your child goes to sleep.
2. Reduce stimulating activities about 1 hour before bedtime by encouraging your child to read, color, or play quietly.
3. Establish a consistent and relaxing bedtime routine that lasts between 20 and 30 minutes before your child goes to sleep, and avoid exposing the child to scary stories or TV shows during this time.
4. Do not give your child anything containing caffeine in the 6 hours before bedtime. In general, it is beneficial to minimize your child's caffeine consumption.
5. Avoid feeding your child a big meal close to bedtime.
6. Cuddle your child for a few minutes before he or she goes to bed, unless your child is uncomfortable with hugs.
7. Make sure that your child is comfortable before he or she goes to sleep (for example, clothes and blankets should not restrict movement, and the bedroom shouldn't be too warm or too cold).
8. Encourage your child to fall asleep with a favorite object such as a blanket or stuffed animal, if needed.
9. If your child is a worrier, give him or her a flashlight, a spray bottle filled with "monster spray" (water), or a large stuffed animal for protection.
10. Play quiet, soothing music in the background or use white noise (like an electric fan) as your child is falling asleep, if needed.
11. Try to ensure that your child gets plenty of sleep every night.

Strengthening Your Child's Self-Esteem

1. Instill confidence in your child. For example, help your child understand his or her strengths and weaknesses, make your child feel special, encourage your child to make friends and to be helpful to others, and encourage and praise your child for his or her accomplishments and effort.
2. Encourage your child to develop interests that will build his or her self-esteem.

3. Compliment your child when he or she behaves appropriately, and provide guidance and constructive feedback whenever needed.
4. Support your child in any activity in which he or she experiences success.
5. Help your child use his or her strengths to compensate for weaknesses.
6. Teach your child self-advocacy skills, such as learning to ask for help or for something he or she needs.

Recognizing Signs of Suicide

1. Take signs of depression and suicidal ideation very seriously. Respond quickly if your child tells you that he or she is thinking about death or suicide. It is important to evaluate the extent of the danger. Children at the highest risk for committing suicide in the very near future have a specific suicide plan, the means to carry out the plan, a time schedule for doing it, and an intention to do it. Signs of suicidal thinking include the following:
   - New or more extensive thoughts of suicide
   - Talking overtly or obliquely about suicide
   - Trying to commit suicide
   - New or worsening signs of depression
   - New or worsening signs of anxiety
   - New or worsening signs of agitation
   - New or worsening signs of irritability
   - Aggressive, angry, or violent behavior
   - New or worsening signs of anger
   - Panic attacks
   - Giving away prized possessions
   - Sudden improvement in mood
   - Acting on dangerous impulses
   - Other unusual changes in behavior
2. If you think that your child might be suicidal, seek professional help immediately by calling a 24-hour crisis hotline, your health care provider, or 911.

TALKING TO YOUR CHILD

1. Keep lines of communication open with your child. Try to be logical, organized, clear, concise, and concrete in your communications.
2. Orient your child to time, place, and other types of information, as needed.
3. Look at your child when you speak to him or her.
4. Speak slowly and distinctly.
5. Use concrete language; avoid jargon, double meanings, sarcasm, and idiomatic language.
6. Don't tease your child if teasing upsets him or her.
7. Guide your child to listen for specific information. If needed, gradually increase the amount of information you give to your child.
8. Learn to read your child's nonverbal cues.
9. If your child has difficulty communicating, be patient. Increase communications gradually and systematically. If needed, help your child learn to communicate using gestures, sign language, picture boards, and/or communication devices. Work on communication early, and be consistent in order to help your child improve. Better communication will help relieve frustration and may lead to

better behavior. A speech and language pathologist can help improve your child's communication.

10. Establish a system of verbal or nonverbal signals to cue your child to attend, respond, or alter his or her behavior.

11. Allow time for your child to process your instructions or comments.

12. Accompany verbal instructions and gestures with written instructions; when possible, use visual cues along with verbal communications.

13. Be sure that your words match your nonverbal behavior.

14. Make sure that you have your child's attention before you give him or her directions.

15. Break complex instructions down into small, specific steps.

16. Repeat instructions as needed.

17. Limit the number of choices you give your child.

HELPING YOUR CHILD PERFORM ACTIVITIES

1. Help your child learn organizational and time management skills.

2. Encourage your child to make a weekly calendar and to carry a written log of activities, a schedule of classes, a list of assignments and due dates, and a list of classroom locations.

3. Encourage your child to use a calculator, audio recorder, computer, and other devices to help him or her do school assignments.

4. Encourage your child to develop word-processing skills.

5. Allow your child as much time as needed to complete homework assignments and chores.

6. Encourage your child to write in an address book the phone numbers of friends and relatives, their street addresses, and their e-mail addresses.

7. Encourage your child to write letters once a week, either on paper or electronically, to a few members of your extended family.

8. Encourage your child to keep a list of items to purchase from the store.

9. Encourage your child to monitor his or her behavior. For example, put the date at the top of a sheet of paper and the numbers 1 to 20 on the side of the paper, and tell your child to put a check mark beside the next number each time he or she performs the desired behavior, beginning with number 1.

10. Encourage your child to participate in activities that may help him or her overcome limitations.

11. Plan activities around your child's physical and emotional capabilities, skills, and interests. These activities might include reading, drawing, or cooking by himself or herself; playing a musical instrument alone or in a band; helping you or another family member cook; playing a board game or card game with you, another member of the family, or a friend; or playing an appropriate video game alone or with a family member or a friend.

12. Explain the difference between the demands of new situations and those of old ones.

13. Alert your child to what you expect him or her to do shortly before it is time to do it. This will help your child feel more informed. For example, tell your child that you will be leaving a friend's house in 5 minutes, instead of giving your child only a moment's notice. This gives your child time to finish whatever he or she is doing with the friend.

14. Use reinforcements—such as watching a TV show, playing a favorite game, visiting a store, or earning tokens or points exchangeable for something your child wants—to motivate your child to perform needed activities.

15. Encourage your child to focus on one day at a time.

INCREASING YOUR CHILD'S SOCIAL SKILLS

1. Help your child develop good social skills. For example, encourage your child to display good manners and be courteous, be considerate of the feelings of others, share toys, use words rather than hitting someone when he or she is mad, be gentle when touching people and pets, apologize if he or she hurts another child's feelings, and appreciate other children's strengths and differences. Praise your child when he or she shows good social skills. Also, set a positive example for your child by greeting people warmly and resolving conflicts by discussing them. Finally, you can try one or both of the following activities. Watch a movie or television show together with your child and discuss the dialogue, facial expressions, and body language of the actors. Or, present your child with an opening vignette (for example, a short episode or story) involving a social situation and ask him or her to provide an ending. Then discuss what your child said and discuss other possible endings.

2. Help your child develop good communication skills. For example, talk to your child whenever possible. Encourage your child to maintain eye contact during conversations, not to let his or her mind wander or daydream when talking to someone, to think twice before speaking to avoid inappropriate comments, not to monopolize discussions, to let others finish speaking before he or she begins to talk, and to begin and end a conversation politely. Praise your child when he or she shows good communication skills.

3. Teach your child how to interact with others by showing and explaining how you handle social situations.

4. Encourage your child to become involved in activities that provide a healthy outlet for stored-up energy and stress.

5. Find opportunities in your community for activities such as Boy Scouts or Girl Scouts, recreation center activities, clubs, and sports. These will help your child build social skills as well as have fun.

6. Encourage your child to play with other children, to attend birthday parties, to participate in after-school activities, and to participate in other social situations. However, do not force your child to play with other children or to participate in group activities unless he or she is ready to do so. It is often easier for children to interact one on one than with a large group.

7. Supervise your child's social interactions with his or her friends.

8. If your child is of preschool age, provide structured activities for him or her with one or two friends.

9. Teach your child how to identify other people's nonverbal communication (facial expressions, gestures).

10. Help your child learn to tell whether he or she is communicating well by observing other people's reactions.

11. Make adjustments in your child's after-school commitments, based on his or her abilities and needs. Don't feel compelled to follow a rigid schedule of after-school activities for your child. Select activities that you believe your child can handle. For example, if your child is easily distracted, have him or her join a club that has a few members rather than a club with many members. If your child feels tired after school, allow him or her to rest at home rather than going out to play a vigorous game. Use your best judgment in making adjustments.

USING TEACHING STRATEGIES WITH YOUR CHILD

1. Find out what skills your child is learning at school, and find ways for your child to apply those skills at home.
2. Use teaching methods that are most likely to get a positive response from your child. For example, set reasonable expectations, use a pleasant and calm voice, use language that your child understands, teach one activity at a time, break down the activity into small steps, check to see whether your child understands what you are saying, listen to your child, redirect your child when he or she engages in challenging behavior, give your child choices, model appropriate behavior, be consistent, show respect for your child, and follow through on your promises. Understand that mistakes are inevitable, use them as opportunities to teach and assist your child, and emphasize the positive aspects of your child's learning, even if he or she is not completely successful. Reward effort, not perfection.
3. Use intensive, repetitive training to make routines automatic.
4. Teach new skills when your child is at his or her best—for example, when he or she is rested and in a good mood.
5. Use concrete objects along with words when you are teaching your child. For example, use plastic letters to teach reading, utensils to teach table manners, and toy cars, airplanes, trains, and trucks to teach about transportation. Allow your child to touch the objects, because touching them may make it easier for your child to learn.
6. Teach vocabulary words by showing your child a flash card with a photo of the object and the name of the object on the same side of the card. (Or, show the actual object along with a flash card that names it.) This technique is especially helpful if your child does not speak.
7. Help your child learn to understand cause-and-effect relationships.
8. Correct your child's errors by showing him or her what to do.
9. Encourage your child's curiosity.
10. Help your child classify and categorize objects.
11. Provide stimulation and model good language skills.
12. Help your child comprehend and remember long units of language. For example, use short sentences first and then gradually increase their length or number, speak slowly, repeat phrases or sentences, and, when necessary, use pictures to illustrate the meaning of a passage.
13. If your child does not read, read to him or her and encourage him or her to look at the book or other reading material as you read.
14. Encourage early mathematics and number activities.

15. Encourage your child to listen to music and to develop a sense of rhythm.
16. Teach your child simple time concepts (for example, morning/afternoon/evening, before/after).
17. Judiciously use teaching strategies you find in Internet resources.

HELPING YOUR CHILD BECOME INDEPENDENT

1. Encourage independence in your child. For example, help your child learn daily care skills, such as dressing, feeding himself or herself, using the bathroom, and grooming.
2. Give your child jobs and reasonable responsibilities at home, keeping in mind your child's age, attention span, and abilities.
3. Start with very easy daily care tasks and jobs, and increase the difficulty of these tasks and jobs in very small steps.
4. Involve your child in establishing rules and regulations, planning daily schedules, and organizing family activities whenever possible.
5. Encourage your child to undertake new challenges that you believe he or she can meet.
6. Encourage your child to develop the skills needed to become an independent lifelong learner. For example, encourage your child's curiosity and initiative. At dinner or before bed, you and your child can talk about what each of you learned that day. It can be something that you or your child learned from a book, TV, or the Internet or something that your child learned at school. Encourage your child to go to the local library, use the Internet to obtain information, learn a new skill (such as playing a musical instrument, dancing, or playing a sport), and ask questions when he or she is unsure of something. Help your child manage time wisely. Also help your child with homework, especially if your child is in the early grades.

HELPING YOUR CHILD REGULATE HIS OR HER BEHAVIOR

1. Create a home environment that is stable and organized. Store things as close as possible to where they are used, and have "a place for everything, and everything in its place."
2. To the extent possible, develop and maintain a predictable, consistent daily schedule of activity that takes both your child's needs and your own needs into consideration. For example, set up regular times for meals, homework, TV, getting up, and going to bed, and stick to the schedule. Prepare your child for any changes.
3. If needed, post lists and reminders about the routines in key places around the house. For example, you might keep a list of things that your child needs to bring to school by the front door or in your child's backpack.
4. Reduce dangers, temptations, and distractions in your child's physical environment.
5. Follow a style of parenting that is neither too permissive nor too authoritarian.
6. Help your child identify any sources of stress and anxiety, and try to remove or reduce these stresses. For example, prepare your child for transitions, changes in routine, and

the like. If your child has attention problems, provide additional structure.

7. Set reasonable expectations for your child, and adjust your expectations to fit your child's abilities.

8. Set reasonable, age-appropriate rules and limits on your child's behavior. Be sure that your child knows what will happen if he or she does not follow the rules and that you follow through with all consequences consistently.

9. Determine the behaviors or events that take place before, during, and after unwanted or undesirable behaviors. This may better enable you to understand your child's behavior and avoid problems.

10. Be alert to any signs that your child is reaching his or her frustration level.

11. Find strategies to help your child calm down when he or she is frustrated, such as taking extra time to respond or taking a deep breath.

12. Minimize sources of stress that your child might face at home and with his or her friends.

13. Don't let your child perform any actions that might hurt another person; instead, redirect your child to an acceptable activity.

14. Avoid overstimulating your child.

15. Avoid overloading your child with information.

16. Allow your child to rest as needed.

17. Remain calm when your child acts impulsively or shows other poorly regulated behaviors. These behaviors may be brought out when your child is tired or stressed, when there are changes in routine, or when the environment is overly stimulating or demanding.

18. Allow and encourage your child to take a break when needed.

19. Use rewards, including praise and other motivational techniques (like placing gold stars on a calendar), to help your child complete difficult tasks and sustain effort. Always bring attention to the positives. For example, acknowledge successes frequently ("You did a great job cleaning up your room" or "You handled that situation well and were able to work things out with your brother"). Reward your child with privileges (sitting next to a parent in the car) and special activities (a trip to the park or a family picnic) for meeting behavioral goals. Determine what rewards will be most effective with your child, and always follow through with promised rewards.

20. When your child misbehaves, talk to him or her about it if you think it is appropriate. Ask your child to tell you about the situation and about what happened. Clarify any details, if needed. Then ask your child why he or she misbehaved and what he or she could have done instead.

21. Use time-outs as a consequence for inappropriate behavior.

22. Create a daily chart on which points or tokens are given as rewards for appropriate behavior and/or points or tokens are taken away as consequences for inappropriate behavior.

23. Increase your child's overall coping skills because these skills will lead to better regulation of behavior and help him or her gain a sense of independence. For example, encourage your child to remain calm and rational when other children do undesirable things, ignore trivial negative behaviors of others, and practice relaxation techniques in

difficult situations (for example, relaxing his or her body, doing deep breathing, or imagining a calming and relaxing scene). Prepare your child for changes so that he or she will have time to adjust (for example, moving to a new house, entering a new school, or taking a trip).

24. Provide adequate opportunities for your child to exercise control over events in his or her life. This will help your child develop a sense of competence and a desire to regulate and be responsible for his or her behavior.

25. Be an advocate for your child, but don't overprotect him or her. Hold your child accountable for his or her behavior and achievements.

HELPING YOUR CHILD BECOME MORE RESILIENT

1. Convey to your child that you love him or her for who he or she is, not for what he or she can achieve. The sense of security that comes from believing that one is unconditionally accepted is a strong basis for self-confidence.

2. Show that you appreciate your child's persistence as much as his or her achievements, but do not falsify your judgments simply to make your child feel good.

3. Always treat your child with respect, as you would like to be treated. Never humiliate him or her. This can severely undermine your child's confidence and capacity to deal constructively with others.

4. Encourage your child to develop interest in healthy activities and to master skills that he or she enjoys. Mastery of a skill brings self-respect and a sense of potency. Practicing that skill can help your child forget or feel less overwhelmed by any unhappy things happening in his or her life.

5. Recognize that everyone at times needs emotional support. Help your child to make friends, and be a good friend yourself.

6. Help your child to think constructively about difficulties that he or she encounters. Show your child how to put things into perspective—to view difficulties and setbacks as challenges rather than as catastrophes.

7. Help your child learn to value courage.

WORKING WITH HEALTH CARE PROVIDERS

1. Work with the health care team to understand your child's special needs. Don't be shy about asking questions. Tell them what you know or think and ask them about your child's condition.

2. Keep lines of communication open with your child's health care provider.

3. Track changes in your child's condition, and call your health care provider if symptoms seem to worsen.

4. Talk to your health care provider about your child's treatment plan and treatment options, such as one-on-one talk therapy, family support services, group or family therapy, educational classes, behavior management techniques, and medication. Make suggestions, if you want to.

5. In discussing medication as an option, consider the following issues:
   - Is my child's condition severe enough to justify drug treatment?

- Is medication the best option for treating my child's condition?
- What is the best drug, and what is the appropriate dosage?
- What are the side effects and risks of the medication?
- Can my child tolerate any unwanted side effects of the medication?
- Are there any foods or other substances that my child would need to avoid?
- How might this medication interact with other medications that my child is taking?
- How long would my child have to take this medication?
- Would my child have difficulty withdrawing from the medication?
- Would my child's condition return if he or she stopped taking the medication?
- Should I try non-drug treatments first for my child's condition?
- How much time would a course of therapy for my child take?
- What self-help strategies might help my child's condition?
- If my child takes medication, should he or she pursue therapy as well?

6. Make sure that your child takes medications according to the health care provider's instructions. Do not skip or alter the dose or stop administering the medication when the child feels better. Always check with your health care provider before you discontinue your child's medication before the prescribed time.

7. If your child has been prescribed medication, watch for any possible side effects, such as nausea, anxiety, irritability, restlessness, dizziness, weight gain or loss, tremors, sweating, difficulty sleeping (insomnia), fatigue, dry mouth, diarrhea, constipation, headaches, stomach upset, depressed mood, anger, drowsiness, tics (abnormal movements, eye blinking, lip biting, arm jerking, vocal sounds), decreased appetite, or irregular heartbeat. Ask your health care provider which side effects should be reported immediately and which can be discussed at the next appointment.

WORKING WITH SCHOOL PERSONNEL

1. Inform the staff at your child's school about your child's condition and sign a release form authorizing your health care provider to share information about your child with the school.

2. If your child takes medicine, inform the school staff and tell them about any possible side effects associated with the medications that your child is taking.

3. If your child has any side effects associated with medications, see if the school can accommodate them. Here are some examples of accommodations:
   - If your child has diarrhea, ask the teacher to give him or her a permanent pass to leave the classroom as needed.
   - If your child is frequently thirsty, ask the teacher to allow him or her to have a water bottle.

- If your child is excessively hungry, ask the teacher to allow him or her to have snacks in school (perhaps at the nurse's office).
- If your child has visual difficulties, ask the teacher to reduce the length of reading assignments or to assign someone to read the material to your child and to write your child's answers for an assignment or test.
- If your child has a sleep disturbance, ask the teacher to allow your child to arrive late or leave early, to walk around during class, to sit in a bright area of the room, or to take a short nap.
- If your child occasionally seems to lose control, ask the teacher to allow him or her to go for a walk or perform a vigorous activity (like washing the whiteboard) to help him or her regain a sense of stability or balance.

4. Work in partnership with the school staff to identify any learning, social, or emotional problems that your child may have.

5. Work with the school staff to develop an educational plan to address your child's needs.

6. Notify school personnel of the best method for communicating with you (for example, e-mail, phone, or mail).

7. If your child is returning to school after a prolonged absence, ask school personnel to test your child as soon as possible. Testing will identify your child's current level of performance, how that level compares with his or her past performance, and what interventions are needed.

8. Meet with your child's teacher, if possible, before school starts. If you cannot meet with the teacher, prepare a one-page description of your child's strengths and weaknesses and the best way to contact you, and give it to the teacher before school starts. Include any helpful information, such as your child's signs of stress, what triggers your child's stress, how to reduce your child's stress, and other challenges that the teacher might face.

9. Remain in close contact with school personnel throughout the school year to discuss how your child is adjusting to school and what steps are needed to improve his or her performance. Work with the staff to identify a "safe" place where your child may go to escape from a stressful situation. Notify them of any changes in your child's treatment that might reflect on his or her school performance. You want to keep lines of communication open.

10. Establish a collaborative relationship with school personnel and look for opportunities to show them your appreciation and support.

11. Volunteer your time to assist with activities in your child's classroom or in the school's media center, computer center, labs, or library.

12. Consult with the school psychologist, counselor, social worker, and/or nurse at your child's school as needed.

PREPARING YOUR CHILD FOR SCHOOL

1. Establish or re-establish "school-year" home routines a few weeks prior to the beginning of a school year. This might mean having your child go to bed earlier, wake up earlier, or follow morning routines for getting ready to go to school.

2. Establish homework routines by having your child do quiet activities at a specific time and place every day. Encourage your child to read, write in a journal, solve a crossword puzzle, or perform another similar activity at this time.

3. If your child will be attending a new school, orient your child to the school by visiting it with your child several times over the summer so that he or she becomes familiar with the layout; check with the principal (or designated staff member) to get permission. Even if your child is returning to the same school he or she attended previously, consider visiting it a few times during the summer. When your child knows his or her class schedule, practice routines that he or she will be following when school begins—for example, going from one class to another and going to the bus stop, homeroom, locker room, cafeteria, auditorium, and bathrooms.

4. Help your child become accustomed to school clothes by giving him or her a chance to wear the school uniform, if one is required, or to wear other school clothes a few times before the school year begins.

5. Invite one child from your child's class to your home a week or two before school starts. Consider enlisting the help of a parent of a child without special needs to encourage his or her child to act as a peer buddy for your child.

WORKING WITH YOUR CHILD'S SIBLINGS

1. Explain the condition of your child with special needs to his or her siblings.

2. Recognize that your child's siblings may be concerned about their role in the family, the extent of their brother's or sister's special needs, the prognosis, and the changes taking place in the family dynamics and structure.

3. Give your child's siblings as much attention as they need; don't neglect or ignore them.

4. Don't expect your child's siblings to compensate for what your child with special needs lacks.

5. Be sure that your expectations for your child's siblings are realistic. It's easy to forget sometimes that they are children first; you cannot expect them to handle difficult situations like little adults.

6. Don't allow your child's siblings to take on excessive chores and responsibilities. This might lead to feelings of resentment toward you and their sibling with special needs.

7. Praise your child's siblings when they do something you want them to do. Let them know specifically what it was that you liked. For example, you can say, "I liked the way you played with your brother today while I was fixing dinner."

8. Don't expect too much too soon from your child's siblings when they interact with the child with special needs. Progress often comes in short, sometimes halting steps. Don't be surprised by occasional setbacks, and be sure to give corrections in a gentle, positive manner.

9. Keep the lines of communication open, paying attention to the feelings underlying what your children tell you. Let them know that their observations, concerns, and suggestions are valued and worthy of discussion.

10. Remember that your child's siblings will have occasional negative feelings toward their sibling with special needs—such as jealousy and resentment—and that these feelings are normal and best approached with understanding, not with shame or guilt.

11. Show your child's siblings how you want them to behave. There is no substitute for a positive example, especially when it is coupled with the opportunity to practice appropriate behavior under the watchful eye of a warm, supportive parent.

12. If your child's siblings begin to obtain lower school grades, be ill more frequently than usual, have tantrums, or show regressive behavior, explore with them the possible reasons for the changes and try to improve the situation. Obtain professional help, if needed.

BECOMING A MORE EFFECTIVE PARENT

1. Take care of yourself by eating right, getting enough sleep, and making time to enjoy things. Taking the time you need to relax will help to ensure that you can maintain the energy needed to help your child with special needs and your other children.

2. Stay calm, speak in a calm voice, and maintain control of yourself. You cannot force your child to behave the way you want, but you can control your own behavior.

3. Act the way you want your child to act. Be a good role model.

4. Recognize that your child has gifts as well as limitations and that, while your child may be a challenge, he or she has much to contribute to society.

5. Learn about strategies for managing your child's behavior by consulting books and the Internet or by talking to a mental health professional.

6. Pay attention to your child's mental health. If needed, consider taking your child for therapy. Therapy can help your child deal with frustration, feel better about himself or herself, and get along better with other children.

7. Obtain therapy for yourself if the difficulty of raising your child begins to feel overwhelming and limits your ability to be a good parent.

8. Talk to other parents whose children have similar special needs. Parents can share practical advice and provide emotional support for each other.

9. Be open with other members of the family about your child with special needs and invite them to ask questions and share their feelings. Enlist the aid of siblings, and give them ongoing praise for helping the child with special needs. If siblings (or any other family member) constantly criticize the child with special needs or interfere with your efforts to work with him or her, consider asking your health care provider for advice.

10. Keep a positive attitude about whatever success your child has in improving his or her condition. Recognize that small successes can make a difference in the quality of his or her life.

11. Be patient and understanding. Living with a child with special needs can be difficult and draining. At times, you are likely to experience frustration, depression, anxiety, exhaustion, rejection, despair, aggravation, or other negative emotions. Remember that your child is not being difficult on purpose; his or her outbursts are not deliberate and are not intended to embarrass or annoy you. Your

child may be experiencing feelings of inadequacy, helplessness, and rejection, so do your best to stay optimistic and to provide an atmosphere of compassion and consistency.

TIPS PARTICULARLY FOR PARENTS OF CHILDREN WITH BRAIN INJURY

General Suggestions

1. Learn about traumatic brain injuries, including sports-related injuries.
2. Ask your child's health care provider to explain your child's injuries and condition.
3. When your child returns to school, be sure that the school has a copy of the medical report, including the report from rehabilitation services.
4. Keep in touch with your child's teacher and ask for weekly progress reports. In turn, inform the teacher of your child's progress at home.
5. Keep the home environment predictable and familiar.
6. Provide structure and routine.
7. Prepare your child for changes, giving logical explanations when possible.
8. Pay attention to sensory input from the environment (noise, temperature, and smells) and how they may affect your child.

Understanding Your Child

1. Encourage your child to share his or her thoughts and feelings with you.
2. Focus on your child's strengths.
3. Recognize that your child may not be able to do things that he or she did before the injury and try to find alternative ways to accomplish the same goals.
4. Allow your child to do things at his or her own pace.
5. Set limits on your child's behavior as needed.
6. Help your child understand his or her injury and what rehabilitation will be needed.

Handling Emotions and Avoiding Overstimulation

1. Be alert to any signs that your child is reaching his or her frustration level.
2. Understand that your child's outbursts are not deliberate and are not intended to embarrass you.
3. Find strategies to help your child calm down when frustrated, such as taking extra time to respond or taking a deep breath.
4. Minimize sources of stress that your child might face at home and with his or her friends.
5. Don't let your child perform any actions that might hurt another person; instead, redirect your child to an acceptable activity.
6. Avoid overstimulating your child.
7. Avoid overloading your child with information.

Talking to Your Child

1. Speak slowly and distinctly.
2. Look at your child when you speak to him or her.
3. Use concrete language; avoid jargon, double meanings, sarcasm, nicknames, and teasing.
4. Guide your child to listen for specific information.

5. Gradually increase the amount of information you give your child.
6. Learn to read your child's nonverbal cues.
7. Encourage your child to communicate on his or her own.
8. Establish a system of verbal or nonverbal signals to cue your child to attend, respond, or alter his or her behavior.
9. Provide clear, logical, organized, and concrete instructions.
10. Accompany verbal instructions with written instructions.
11. Increase communication activities gradually and systematically.
12. Make sure that you have your child's attention before you give him or her directions.
13. Break complex instructions down into small, specific steps.
14. Repeat instructions as needed.
15. Help your child remember longer pieces of information. For example, have your child visualize each item on a list to be recalled (perhaps visualizing milk, cheese, and oranges in a refrigerator).
16. Limit the number of choices you give your child.
17. Check whether your child understands your communications. If necessary, ask your child to repeat the information in his or her own words.

Helping Your Child Perform Activities

1. Help your child learn organizational and time management skills.
2. Encourage your child to make a weekly calendar and to carry a written log of activities, a schedule of classes, a list of assignments and due dates, and a list of classroom locations.
3. Have your child use sticky notes to help him or her remember tasks. Your child can also use a digital voice reminder, a digital assistant, a cell phone, or a pager.
4. Encourage your child to use a calculator, audio recorder, computer, and other devices to help him or her do school assignments.
5. Encourage your child to develop word processing skills.
6. Allow your child as much time as needed to complete homework assignments and chores.
7. Encourage your child to pace himself or herself and not to take on too much.
8. Encourage your child to write in an address book the phone numbers of friends and relatives, their street addresses, and their e-mail addresses; to make a list of items to purchase from the store; or to write letters to members of your extended family.
9. Encourage your child to keep his or her desk clear of things that are not being used.
10. Encourage your child to monitor his or her behavior. For example, put the date at the top of a sheet of paper and the numbers 1 to 20 on the side of the paper, and tell your child to put a check mark beside the next number each time he or she performs the desired behavior, beginning with number 1.
11. Encourage your child to participate in programs that may help him or her overcome limitations and build self-esteem.
12. Plan activities around your child's physical and emotional capabilities and interests.
13. Assign your child jobs around the house, fitted to his or her ability.

14. Encourage your child to lead a normal life within the limits of his or her ability.
15. Provide your child with advance notice when there will be changes in his or her schedule.
16. Explain the difference between the demands of new situations and those of old ones.
17. Alert your child to what you expect him or her to do shortly before it is time to do it. This will help your child feel more informed. For example, tell your child that you will be leaving a friend's house in 5 minutes, instead of giving your child only a moment's notice. This gives your child time to finish whatever he or she is doing with the friend.
18. Encourage your child to focus on one day at a time.
19. Keep distractions to a minimum at home.

Increasing Your Child's Social Skills

1. Serve as a role model for your child for good social behavior.
2. Give your child a choice about whether to participate in social activities, but encourage him or her to have friends.
3. Supervise your child's social interactions with his or her friends.
4. If your child is of preschool age, provide structured activities for him or her with one or two friends.
5. Teach your child how to identify other people's facial expressions.
6. Allow your child to become independent to the extent that this is possible.
7. Provide praise and awards as appropriate.
8. Instill confidence in your child. For example, help your child understand his or her strengths and weaknesses, make your child feel special, help your child develop his or her skills in things that he or she enjoys, encourage your child to make friends and to be helpful to others, and encourage and praise your child for his or her accomplishments and effort.

TIPS PARTICULARLY FOR PARENTS OF CHILDREN WITH A VISUAL IMPAIRMENT

1. Recognize that your child will need to use senses other than vision to acquire information and to navigate the environment. Help your child make use of any residual vision for these tasks.
2. Be sure that your home has adequate lighting and that the rooms are not cluttered. This is especially important if your child has low vision.
3. Give your child extra attention and make a conscious effort to expand his or her experiences from infancy on. This will help your child learn skills that children who are sighted develop by watching and imitating people.
4. Encourage your child who has low vision to use various tools, as appropriate, such as eyeglasses or contact lenses, a magnifying device, a slant board for bringing material closer, dark-line paper, a large-print calculator, a hat or visor to decrease glare from overhead lights or the sun, colored overlays to provide better contrast for printed material, a tape recorder, or a Braille writer. Consult with a teacher of children with visual impairments for additional suggestions.

5. If possible, use the latest assistive technology to help your child. Examples include a voice terminal service to access the Internet, computer software that provides auditory information, a talking dictionary, visual enhancement technology such as a video magnifier or closed-circuit television system (CCTV), and a talking global positioning system. Consult with a teacher of children with visual impairments for additional suggestions.
6. Give your child clear instructions, descriptions, and explanations, and repeat them as often as needed. Use directional words and name places, as in "Walk to the kitchen and turn right to get to the refrigerator." If you are teaching your child to hop, say, "Stand on your left foot, raise your right foot, jump in the air, and land on your left foot."
7. Provide direct experiences for your child. For example, let your child touch a pet to learn about the pet. Or, invite your child to help you bake cookies in order to learn about the connection between baking and eating cookies. Your child may need to be taught explicitly that small toys often represent full-size objects.
8. Help your child make sense of the information that he or she receives from different sources. You can do this by describing the connections between the sources of information. For example, help your child understand the terms "heavy" and "light" by giving him or her heavy and light objects to hold.
9. Recognize that in unfamiliar settings your child may become more anxious and experience a lack of confidence. Help him or her adjust to new surroundings.
10. Teach your child the skills he or she needs to become independent. Depending on your child's age and level of independence, these skills may include maintaining personal hygiene, feeding himself or herself, dressing, grooming, cooking, shopping, orienting himself or herself, and maintaining mobility. Don't fall into the habit of doing everything for your child. Also, give your child the time that he or she needs to complete tasks, because it probably will take longer for him or her to perform tasks than it does for children who are sighted. Children often learn self-help skills by watching others; because your child has little or no ability to do this, these skills are likely to take longer to develop. Finally, your child may be hesitant to explore because of fear of the unknown, and your job is to diminish his or her fear. Consult with an orientation and mobility specialist, who can help your child learn to travel independently.
11. Encourage your child to play with other children. Remember that your child may have some difficulty interacting with other children because he or she misses subtle cues and facial expressions that are helpful in social interactions.

TIPS PARTICULARLY FOR PARENTS OF CHILDREN WITH A HEARING LOSS

1. If your health care provider recommends hearing aids, a cochlear implant, or an auditory brainstem implant, discuss the benefits and limitations of each procedure with your health care provider and with your family.

2. Make sure that your child uses any appropriate assistive technology devices that have been recommended for him or her and that they are in good working order; keep rechargeable batteries charged and buy replacement batteries in advance. Examples of assistive listening devices are infrared systems, FM systems, loop systems, personal amplifiers, and 3-D headphones. Environmental alert devices include visual alert signalers and remote receivers, wake-up alarm systems, and car alert systems. Other technologies that may be recommended include computer-assisted note-taking, speech recognition software, telecommunication devices for the deaf (TDDs or TTYs), amplified telephones, visual beep indicator programs, and closed-captioning decoders.

3. Look at your child when you speak to him or her, and be sure that your child, in turn, is watching you.

4. Maintain a pleasant facial expression, unless, of course, you need to discipline your child or show an emotion such as sadness or disappointment.

5. Speak distinctly and slowly, without exaggerating or distorting your lip movements, particularly if your child has some hearing ability or speech-reading ability.

6. Use short, simple sentences.

7. Use gestures and pointing while you talk.

8. Emphasize key words in your phrases.

9. If you need to repeat yourself, rephrase if at all possible.

10. When you are reading to your child, make sure that lights do not shine in his or her eyes or create a glare on the materials.

11. Do not turn away from your child in the middle of a sentence.

12. Be sure that no obstructions block your child's view of your lips.

13. Do not chew gum, smoke a cigarette, put your hand on your chin, cover your mouth, or do anything else that might impede speech reading.

14. Don't talk while the child's attention is directed elsewhere.

15. If your child is learning to sign, learn to sign yourself. You may find it easier to learn from a video than from a book.

16. Encourage your child to play with other children.

TIPS PARTICULARLY FOR PARENTS OF CHILDREN WITH AN AUTISM SPECTRUM DISORDER

Helping Your Child with Speech and Language

1. Use your child's name to gain his or her attention.

2. Let your child know when an activity will be over. For example, say, "You have 5 minutes left to watch television."

3. Use literal—rather than metaphorical or figurative—language, except when you are specifically working to increase your child's comprehension of figurative language, such as idioms, multi-meaning words, jokes, and teasing. Say, for example, "Take off your shoes and put on your slippers" instead of "Change into your slippers," because your child may take the latter remark literally and not understand it. Choose colloquial expressions carefully, because your child might interpret them literally. To help your child understand colloquial sayings, collect the more common ones in a notebook and describe what each one means. For example, for the saying "I am hungry as a

horse," you can write, "I am very hungry." Be as a concrete as possible.

4. Avoid giving your child lengthy oral instructions. If necessary, give one direction at a time.

5. Don't demand that your child maintain eye contact with you when you are speaking with him or her, but teach your child how to maintain eye contact and work at his or her pace.

6. Give your child some time to respond before repeating or rephrasing what you said, in order to allow for possible auditory processing difficulties.

7. Present material visually as well as orally.

8. Limit use of vague words like "maybe," "we'll see," or "later." Say, for example, "We will do that after dinner tonight" or "I will give you an answer at lunchtime," instead of "Maybe we will do that later."

9. Make your instructions positive—say what to do rather than what not to do. Say, for example, "Put your toys in the toy box" instead of "Don't leave your toys on the floor."

10. Accompany your verbal communication with nonverbal behaviors. For example, if you say, "Please drink your milk," point to the cup and move your hand to your mouth as if you were holding a cup.

11. If your child is able to speak, ask him or her to repeat what you said when you want to check on his or her understanding of your communication.

12. Use simple commands rather than questions. Say, for example, "Tell me the name of the animal from which we get milk" rather than "Where do we get milk?"

13. Provide straightforward and complete instructions. Say, for example, "Ask your father where he put the baseball tickets, and then come and tell me his answer" instead of "Ask your father about the tickets."

14. Use specific questions rather than open-ended questions. Say, for example, "What happened at the softball game today?" rather than "How was school?"

15. Arrange to have your child learn alternative means of communication, such as sign language, if he or she does not speak, and consider learning sign language yourself. You can also use electronic communication devices, such as voice synthesizers and computers programmed with spoken language.

Using Effective Socialization Strategies

1. Keep your promises; try not to make promises that you may not be able to keep.

2. Help your child understand what is expected of him or her in social situations.

3. Don't talk about your child in front of him or her, unless you include your child in the conversation.

4. Be consistent in your rules of social behavior.

5. Do not expect your child to understand emotional pleas.

6. Learn what is likely to cause your child to react negatively, and try to minimize these occurrences.

7. Prime your child for new situations by explaining in advance what you expect will happen. For example, before you move into a new house, visit it with your child and try to involve your child in packing belongings before the move.

8. Help your child learn about appropriate social interactions. For example, discuss with your child how words and

actions affect other people. Your child may need to be taught to recognize the effect of his or her actions on others. If he or she says something offensive, let him or her know that "words hurt, just like getting punched in the arm hurts." Encourage your child to stop and think about how another person might feel before he or she acts or speaks.

9. Encourage your child to play with other children who do not have disabilities, including playing board games and card games, under your supervision.

10. Help your child learn how to take turns while playing games with other children and then teach him or her how to take turns in social conversations.

11. Work with other children to help them learn to accept your child.

Sensory Considerations

1. Keep in mind that your child may engage in disruptive behavior as a reaction to aversive or overwhelming sensory stimuli. For example, the ticking of a clock can seem like the beating of a drum, the breeze from an open window can feel like a tremendous gust, the smell of food from the kitchen can make your child feel sick, and the bright sunshine pouring through the windows may be almost blinding to your child. This sensory overload may make focusing difficult and frustrating. To cope with the frustration, your child might choose to tap a pencil on a desk repeatedly (or engage in some other disruptive behavior). What appears to be disruptive behavior may be a way for your child to cope with the sensory overload.

2. Evaluate the forms of sensory stimulation in your home, and try to assess how the home environment affects your child. If possible, make appropriate modifications.

3. Limit your child's exposure to sensory stressors such as noisy places, disliked food, or disliked clothing.

4. Eliminate visual distractions such as excessive light, movements, reflections, or background patterns. Eliminate fluorescent lights if your child dislikes them. Encourage your child to keep only necessary items on his or her desk.

5. Eliminate auditory distractions such as noisy fans and loudspeakers.

6. Eliminate textures that seem to be aversive.

7. Make sure that the temperature in the house is comfortable for the child.

8. Watch for signs of anxiety and stress due to sensory or emotional overload. For example, notice if your child puts his or her hands over his or her ears, plugs his or her ears, squeezes a body part, or engages in repetitive behaviors, like rocking or hand/finger twisting.

9. Create a "quiet space" in your home, where your child can go to escape from stressful situations. In this area you can have objects that are calming to your child, such as Koosh balls, books, and a bean bag chair.

10. Have a "fiddle basket" containing small items (for example, small Koosh balls, Bend Bands, FiddleLinks, and clothespins) for your child to use when he or she is anxious.

11. Teach your child relaxation techniques to use when he or she is anxious, such as "Take a big breath" or "Count to 10." You can write these down on cards for your child to carry with him or her and look at when needed.

Using Effective Behavioral Strategies

1. Remember that your child cannot help the way that he or she behaves; it is not his or her fault or anyone else's fault.

2. Tell your child about the behaviors that you want him or her to do in the order in which they should be done. Say, for example, "First get your toothbrush, then put the toothpaste on your toothbrush, and then brush your teeth."

3. Use reinforcers—such as watching a TV show, playing a favorite game, visiting a store, or earning tokens or points exchangeable for something your child wants—to motivate your child to perform needed activities. Change reinforcers regularly so that the items or activities you choose do not lose their ability to motivate your child.

4. When you offer a reward, choose one that you know your child will like. If you don't know, ask your child about what he or she likes. Then make sure that it is available and use it without delay after your child performs the desired behavior.

5. Replace unwanted behavior with a favorite activity; in other words, use distraction when needed.

6. Sing to your child to improve his or her attention.

7. Teach your child coping skills that are not disruptive to other children, like squeezing a squishy ball in his or her hand.

8. Don't assume that your child is misbehaving in order to get attention. It may be that his or her behavior is a reaction to a feeling of fear. Your child may be fearful because he or she is having difficulty controlling his or her environment or because the environment seems unpredictable. Therefore, provide an environment with clear structure and routine and post the child's daily schedule somewhere in your home where the child can readily see it.

9. Your child may have difficulty with transitions; he or she may get "stuck" and have difficulty moving from one activity to another. If needed, coach your child through the transition. Also consider using visual schedules, discussing upcoming activities, and role playing. Appropriate strategies to use depend on your child's age and abilities.

10. When your child is frustrated, try to remain calm and help him or her regain composure.

Using Effective Teaching Strategies

1. Use teaching methods that are most likely to get a positive response from your child. For example, set reasonable expectations, use a pleasant and calm voice, use language that your child understands, teach one activity at a time, break down the activity into small steps, check to see whether your child understands what you are saying, listen to your child, redirect your child when he or she engages in challenging behavior, give your child choices, model appropriate behavior, be consistent, show respect for your child, and follow through on your promises. Understand that mistakes are inevitable, use them as opportunities to teach and assist your child, and emphasize the positive aspects of your child's learning, even if he or she is not completely successful. Reward effort, not perfection.

2. Design a color-coding system with your child for his or her daily planner. This will help your child keep track of due dates for assignments and activities.

3. Give your child a written checklist to help keep him or her focused and "on task." Encourage your child to complete each step listed on the checklist in sequential order.

4. Modify worksheets as needed. For example, you may need to include fewer problems per sheet; larger, highly visual space for responding; and a box next to each question to be checked when the question has been completed.

5. Have your child make an "Assignments to Be Completed" folder as well as a "Completed Assignments" folder for activities that you and he or she did at home.

6. If your child has visual processing problems, reduce contrast on reading materials by using black print on colored paper. Try colors such as tan, light blue-gray, or light green, but experiment with other colors as needed. Avoid bright yellow, because this color might hurt your child's eyes.

7. Teach your child generalization skills by using several examples to illustrate a point. For example, if you want to teach your child not to run across the street, use several locations to teach this principle.

8. Use physical objects, such as blocks, to teach number concepts.

9. Teach your child how to type if he or she has poor handwriting.

10. Incorporate your child's special interests into the games or activities you engage in with him or her. For example, if your child likes trucks, use toy trucks as aids in teaching him or her reading and mathematics.

11. Try to establish a connection between your child's interests and the area of study. For example, if your child is fascinated with baseball, have him or her read a biography of a famous baseball player and write a report. Math skills could be taught by having your child look at baseball statistics.

12. Start with only two options in teaching your child to make choices.

13. Don't ask your child to look and listen at the same time if he or she is unable to process visual and auditory input simultaneously.

14. If your child is staring off into space or doodling, don't assume that he or she is not listening; doodling or staring may actually help your child better focus on what you are presenting. Simply ask your child a question to check if he or she is listening.

15. If your child repeats the same question over and over, despite having heard the answer to the question, write the answer on a sheet of paper. Then whenever your child asks the same question, point to the paper with the written answer.

16. Use a touch screen tablet for learning, communication, and play.

17. Use closed captions on the television set to teach your child reading. Recording your child's favorite program with captions is helpful, because you can show the program again and stop it as needed.

18. Use an LCD monitor if the flicker from a CRT monitor annoys your child.

Helping Your Child with School

1. If your child often fails to bring a required object to school (for example, a pencil), put a picture of the object (the pencil) on the cover of his or her notebook.

2. If your child fails to finish assignments, maintain a list at home of assignments to be completed.

3. Don't scold your child when he or she fails to carry out a task, but instead work out a way to avoid the problem in the future.

4. If your child will be attending a new school, orient your child to the school by visiting it with your child several times over the summer so that he or she becomes familiar with the layout; check in with the principal (or designated staff member) to get permission. Even if your child is returning to the same school he or she attended previously, consider visiting it a few times during the summer. When your child knows his or her class schedule, practice routines that he or she will be following when school begins—for example, going from one class to another and going to the bus stop, homeroom, locker room, cafeteria, auditorium, and bathrooms.

5. Help your child become accustomed to school clothes by giving him or her a chance to wear the school uniform, if one is required, or to wear other school clothes a few times before the school year begins.

TIPS FOR AVOIDING OR DEALING WITH A SUBSTANCE-INDUCED DISORDER

1. Maintain good communication with your child.

2. Insist on meeting your child's friends and becoming acquainted with them.

3. Set clear rules about curfew in cooperation with your child and enforce the rules consistently.

4. Set clear rules for your child about attendance at parties, those held at your home and elsewhere.

5. Be alert to signs of a substance-induced disorder (excessive alcohol or drug use), such as the following:

PHYSICAL AND HEALTH CHANGES

- Bloodshot eyes, extremely large or small pupils, watery eyes, blank stares, or involuntary movements of the eyeball (*nystagmus*)
- Deterioration in physical appearance, rapid weight loss, unexplained injuries such as cuts or bruises, unusual breath or body odors, slurred speech, unsteady gait, tremors, fast heart rate, extremely dry mouth, nausea or vomiting, complaints of *tinnitus* (ringing in the ears) or *paresthesias* (sensations such as prickling, burning), dramatic fluctuations in appetite
- Chronic coughing, sniffing, or black phlegm
- Needle tracks on various parts of the body or perforated nasal septum
- Skin boils, skin sores, or nasal bleeding

EMOTIONAL CHANGES

- Extremes of energy and tiredness, sleep difficulties or excessive sleep, or fatigue
- Changes in social activities or relationships with friends, ranging from extreme social confidence to lack of interest in things that used to provide pleasure
- Poor judgment

- Irresponsibility with money
- Restlessness, manic behavior, or panic attacks
- Feelings of depression, anxiety, or euphoria
- Emotional lability, decreased impulse control, violent behavior, or hyperactivity
- Marked distortion in sense of time, feelings of *depersonalization* (your child thinks that things around him or her are not real or that he or she is observing himself or herself from outside his or her body), paranoia, delusions, visual distortions, or hallucinations

FAMILY AND SCHOOL CHANGES

- Starting arguments with family members, breaking family rules, missing curfews, or withdrawing from interactions with family members (for example, spending time alone behind closed doors)
- Decreased interest in school, negative attitudes toward school, drop in school grades, increased absences from school, or disciplinary problems in school

6. Seek immediate professional help for your child when he or she shows indications of a substance-induced disorder.
7. Cooperate fully with any treatment program. Remember that relapse is common, and be prepared to respond to any relapses by continuing treatment.
8. Monitor your own use of alcohol and other drugs and remember that you are an important role model for your child.

TIPS FOR PARENTS OF CHILDREN WHO ARE GIFTED AND TALENTED

Teaching Your Child to Be a Productive Member of Society

1. Teach your child to accept children with diverse abilities. Everyone has value.
2. Involve your child in the kinds of nonacademic activities that can shape a child's life. For example, encourage your child to join a club, band, debating team, sport team, yearbook committee, school newspaper, theater group, or cheerleading squad; take an art, music, drama, cooking, photography, woodworking, auto repair, or martial arts class; and/or participate in intramural sports or scouting.
3. Teach your child to help others and make a positive contribution to the world.
4. Teach your child to respect other cultures, religions, and life styles.
5. Teach your child to respect teachers or other adults.
6. Teach your child that first impressions are important.
7. Model respect for others, honest communication, and personal accountability.
8. Discuss current events.
9. Encourage independence through responsible behavior.
10. Show your child how to effect change through positive action.

Nurturing and Recognizing Your Child's Special Interests and Talents

1. Identify your child's interests and talents.

SIGNS OF LEADERSHIP ABILITY

Your child
- Is organized and organizes others.
- Is self-confident.

- Is well liked by others.
- Can stimulate and arouse others.
- Recognizes the skills and abilities of others.
- Interacts with others easily.
- Can articulate the goals of a group.
- Articulates ideas clearly.
- Listens to others empathetically.
- Understands how groups function.
- Gives directions clearly and effectively.
- Exercises authority reliably and responsibly.
- Supports others in a group when appropriate.

GENERAL SIGNS OF VISUAL/PERFORMING ARTS ABILITY

Your child
- Is outstanding in some expressive or performing art, such as visual arts, music, drama, or some physical activity.
- Expresses himself or herself in creative ways.
- Has high standards.
- Is critical of his or her own work.
- Is a keen observer.
- Willingly tries different media and/or techniques.
- Is well informed about his or her particular field of interest.
- Has an outstanding sense of spatial relationships.
- Has good motor coordination.
- Desires to produce original work.

SIGNS OF VISUAL ARTS ABILITY

Your child
- Draws a variety of objects.
- Expresses depth in drawings.
- Uses good proportion in drawings.
- Treats art seriously and pursues it in his or her spare time.
- Shows originality in art.
- Uses art to express feelings and experiences.
- Is interested in other people's art.
- Likes to model three-dimensional objects using clay, soap, or other materials.

SIGNS OF MUSICAL ABILITY

Your child
- Has a good sense of rhythm.
- Discriminates musical and other sounds well.
- Understands musical relationships.
- Shows tonal memory.
- Responds readily to rhythm, melody, and harmony.
- Uses music to express feelings and experiences.
- Makes up original tunes.
- Enjoys dance and dramatic activities with musical elements.

SIGNS OF DRAMATIC ARTS ABILITY

Your child
- Readily shifts into the role of another character.
- Uses voice to reflect changes in mood.
- Demonstrates understanding of conflict when acting out a dramatic event.
- Communicates feelings by means of facial expressions, gestures, and bodily movements.
- Enjoys evoking emotional responses from listeners.
- Has the ability to dramatize feelings and experiences.

- Brings a dramatic situation to a climax with a well-timed ending when telling a story.

SIGNS OF PHYSICAL ABILITY

Your child

- Enjoys participation in various athletic activities.
- Handles his or her body with outstanding coordination, precision, ease, and poise for age.
- Has a high energy level.
- Excels in endurance, strength, movement, and rhythm.
- Has good manipulative skills.
- Is highly competitive.
- Likes to work with tools, machines, and motors.
- Practices at length.
- Is eager to use his or her special abilities.
- Strives for improved performance.
- Is challenged by difficult athletic activities.

2. Nurture your child's passions, strengths, interests, and creative forms of expression.
3. Make music and art a part of your life and your child's life.
4. Find a healthy balance between school and outside activities.

Nurturing a Positive Parent-Child Relationship

1. Value your child's individuality; children who are gifted can be very different from one another.
2. Know your child's friends.
3. Encourage open, two-way communication and really listen.
4. Know the difference between encouragement and support and "pushing."
5. Don't over-schedule your child.
6. Don't expect adult behavior from a child.
7. Never underestimate your child's potential for growth, but be reasonable.
8. Allow your child to fail, and teach him or her that much can be learned through mistakes. Model "safe risk-taking."
9. Tolerate "safe" rebellion.
10. Offer choices rather than ultimatums.
11. Set clear and consistent expectations and consequences.
12. Always try to maintain a sense of humor.
13. Don't be intimidated by having a child who is gifted. You still need to be in charge.
14. Remember that a child who is gifted is often his or her own worst critic.
15. Enjoy your child who is gifted.

Monitoring Your Child's Education

1. Request an appropriately challenging curriculum.
2. Know your child's teachers and whether they have high expectations and are willing to modify instruction for bright learners.
3. Volunteer for school activities unrelated to your child's specific needs.
4. Help organize curriculum-related field trips, guest speakers, and topic displays.
5. Offer supportive assistance to your child's teachers.
6. Participate on school committees involving gifted children.
7. Keep a home file of school documents and a portfolio of your child's work.
8. At home, help your child develop good study habits and time management skills.

9. Teach your child that from Monday through Friday, school receives top priority.
10. Teach your child how to "play the game" and work within the system without giving up creativity and individuality.
11. Ask for the school's assistance in career guidance and postsecondary planning for your high school student.
12. Start saving early for postsecondary education.

Helping Your Child Navigate Through Life

1. Teach your child to do his or her best and not to make comparisons.
2. Encourage your child to work hard and play hard.
3. Encourage a love of reading.
4. Connect your child to your family heritage.
5. Let your child know that sometimes life is difficult and that it is okay to seek help.
6. Provide opportunities for your child to exercise responsible choices.
7. Help your child set goals.
8. Teach your child to seek more than one solution.
9. Teach your child that some failure is inevitable and acceptable.
10. Teach your child to challenge himself or herself.
11. Teach your child that alone time is not lonely time.
12. Teach your child that quality, not quantity, counts.

REFERENCES

Austega's Gifted Service. (n.d.). *Characteristics checklist for gifted children*. Retrieved from http://austega.com/gifted/9-gifted/22-characteristics.html

Boyse, K. (2004). *Non-verbal learning disability (NLD or NVLD)*. Retrieved from http://www.med.umich.edu/1libr/yourchild/nld.htm

Boyse, K. (2009). *ADHD: What parents need to know*. Retrieved from http://med.umich.edu/yourchild/topics/adhd.htm

Boyse, K. (2010). *Sleep problems*. Retrieved from http://www.med.umich.edu/yourchild/topics/sleep.htm

Grandin, T. (2002). *Teaching tips for children and adults with autism*. Retrieved from http://www.autism.org/temple/tips.html

Ives, M., & Munro, N. (2001). *Caring for a child with autism: A practical guide for parents*. London, England: Jessica Kingsley.

Johnson, D. J. (2000). *Helping young children with learning disabilities at home*. Retrieved from http://www.ldonline.org/article/Helping_Young_Children_with_Learning_Disabilities_at_Home

Johnson, J. A. (n.d.). *Teaching students with Aspergers syndrome: Tips for teachers and parents*. Retrieved from http://hubpages.com/hub/Students-with-Aspergers-Syndrome-Tips-for-Teachers-and-Parents

Massachusetts General Hospital. (2006a). *Anxiety (generalized anxiety disorder)*. Retrieved from http://www2.massgeneral.org/schoolpsychiatry/info_anxiety.asp

Masten, A. S. (1994). Resilience in individual development: Successful adaptation despite risk and adversity. In M. C. Wang & E. W. Gordon (Eds.), *Educational resilience in inner-city America* (pp. 3–25). Hillsdale, NJ: Erlbaum.

National Crime Prevention Council. (n.d.). *Stop cyberbullying before it starts*. Retrieved from http://www.ncpc.org/resources/files/pdf/bullying/cyberbullying.pdf

National Dissemination Center for Children with Disabilities. (2010). *Autism spectrum disorders*. Retrieved from http://nichcy.org/wp-content/uploads/docs/fs1.pdf

National Dissemination Center for Children with Disabilities. (2012). *Attention-deficit/hyperactivity disorder (AD/HD)*. Retrieved from http://nichcy.org/wp-content/uploads/docs/fs19.pdf

National Society for the Gifted and Talented. (n.d.). *Giftedness defined–What is gifted & talented?* Retrieved from http://www.nsgt.org/articles/index.asp

Neufeld, K. (2004). *10 tips for helping your child fall asleep.* Retrieved from http://www.parents.com/kids/sleep/10-tips-for-helping-your-child-fall-asleep

Packer, L. E. (2002). *Accommodating students with mood lability: Depression and bipolar disorder.* Retrieved from http://www.schoolbehavior.com/Files/tips_mood.pdf

Smith, M., & Segal, J. (2011). *ADD/ADHD parenting tips.* Retrieved from http://helpguide.org/mental/adhd_add_parenting_strategies.htm

Stokes, S. (n.d.). *Children with Asperger's syndrome: Characteristics/learning styles and intervention strategies.* Retrieved from http://www.specialed.us/autism/asper/asper11.html

INTRODUCTION

This handout provides general guidelines for parents for working with children who have been bullied or cyberbullied or who have bullied other children. You are not expected to follow every suggestion, and some suggestions may not apply to your child. You should consider your child's age, sex, and language competency in applying these suggestions.

GENERAL SUGGESTIONS FOR PREVENTING AND DEALING WITH BULLYING

Talking to Your Child

1. Talk often with your child and listen to him or her carefully.
2. Ask about your child's school day, activities, and friends.
3. Ask whether your child feels safe and comfortable at school.
4. Help your child understand the meaning of good friends and, if necessary, help your child choose good friends.
5. Teach your child that we live in a very diverse world, where people are different in many ways.
6. Teach your child basic good manners and practice them yourself.
7. Help your child find and develop his or her personal talents.
8. Help your child choose TV, music, and video games that promote respect, kindness, and understanding.
9. Instill self-confidence in your child.
10. Help your child establish good social skills.
11. Teach your child to speak up for himself or herself.
12. Be clear with your child about your expectations for acceptable behavior.

Guiding Your Child About Bullying

1. Talk to your child about what bullying and cyberbullying mean. Several websites, such as StopbullyingNow.com, provide useful information.
2. Your child should know that the following forms of bullying may be against the law:
   - Bullying someone on the basis of his or her race, ethnicity, religion, disability, or sexual orientation (these may be forms of hate crimes)

   - Bullying in the form of hazing (usually a form of group bullying)
   - Bullying of a sexual nature in the form of, for example, stalking, assault, or harassing communications
3. Teach your child that bullying is unacceptable and can be dangerous. Discourage your child from bullying others, including making disparaging comments about other children.
4. Stop bullying when it happens at home.
5. Consistently discipline your child when he or she engages in hurtful teasing and/or bullying.
6. Encourage your child to tell you if he or she is being bullied.
7. If your child has been bullied at school, tell him or her to tell a member of the school staff—a teacher, mental health or other health specialist (for example, school psychologist, counselor, social worker, speech pathologist, or nurse), or school administrator (for example, principal or vice-principal).
8. Teach your child to tell a friend who has been bullied to talk to his or her parents, a trusted relative, another trusted adult, or a member of the school staff.
9. Be clear that your child should refuse to join in if he or she sees another child or children being bullied.
10. Make sure your child is prepared to speak up and offer support to a friend who is being bullied.
11. Tell your child that bullying behaviors that continue into adulthood can create serious personal and professional problems.
12. Tell your child that bullying can have a lifetime of negative consequences for the child who is bullied and for the bully as well (and even for some bystanders).

Getting Involved in Your Child's School

1. Stay in touch with your child's teacher.
2. Learn about the school's rules and sanctions regarding bullying and cyberbullying.
3. Participate in any training that the school offers regarding bullying.
4. As soon as you become aware of a bullying problem, report it to the school.
5. Accept help from the school with regard to bullying problems, whether your child is the target, the bully, or a bystander.
6. Become a part of bullying prevention efforts and programs at your school.

Helping Your Child Adjust to a New School

1. Recognize that going to a new school presents special challenges for your child, and talk with your child in advance about adjusting to this new setting.
2. Help your child think through how he or she will address social situations in the new school, such as finding peers to sit with at lunch and joining activities at recess. It may be helpful to ask members of the school staff or other families that have a child attending the school about school

routines before the school year begins. Visiting the school before the first day of school may also be helpful.

3. Once the school year begins, talk to your child about how he or she is getting along in the new school.

4. Observe whether there are any changes in your child's behavior. For example, is your child more anxious, worried, irritable, solemn, or withdrawn than he or she was in the former school? Has your child been having difficulty concentrating or falling asleep since he or she began at the new school? Has your child made friends at the new school, and, if so, have you met them?

5. If you want additional information about how your child is adjusting to the new school, contact his or her teacher.

Helping Your Child When He or She Is a Bystander to a Bullying Incident at School

1. Tell your child to seek immediate assistance from someone on the school staff if a child who has been bullied needs help.

2. Talk to your child about how to help defuse a bullying situation and how to help the victim of bullying without getting hurt. Your child might say, "Cool it! This isn't going to solve anything."

3. Tell your child to offer support to the victim of bullying, such as picking up the victim's books and handing them to him or her and offering words of kindness or condolence.

4. Tell your child not to join in during the bullying or to cheer the bully.

5. Tell your child to report the incident afterward if someone on the school staff has not been contacted.

6. Encourage your child to include children who are victims of bullying in his or her activities.

SUGGESTIONS FOR PREVENTING AND DEALING WITH CYBERBULLYING AND OTHER INTERNET ISSUES

Guiding Your Child About Appropriate Online Behavior

1. Remind your child that real people with real feelings are behind screen names and profiles.

2. Convey to your child how your family values relate to how he or she functions online.

3. Talk to your child about online manners. Teach your child to use courtesy and common sense in all forms of communication, regardless of where and how they take place.

4. Explain to your child that using all caps, long rows of exclamation points, or large bold fonts is the online equivalent of yelling and others may not appreciate receiving those types of communications.

5. Tell your child not to impersonate someone else online or create websites, web pages, or electronic posts that seem to come from someone else, like a teacher, a classmate, or someone that he or she made up.

6. Teach your child that online actions can reverberate. This means that the words he or she writes and the images he or she posts have consequences offline.

7. Teach your child to reply with care to electronic messages and think hard before sending a message to everyone on his or her contact list.

8. Inform your child that among the pitfalls of social networking sites, chat rooms, virtual worlds, and blogs are sharing too much information and posting pictures, video, or words that can damage another person's reputation or hurt his or her feelings.

9. Discuss with your child why it is important to post only information that he or she is comfortable with everyone seeing, as employers, college admissions officers, coaches, teachers, police, and other people may view his or her online posts.

10. Inform your child that once information is posted online, it can't be taken back. Even if he or she deletes private information from his or her profile, your child has little control over prior versions of the information that may exist on other people's computers and that circulate online.

11. Encourage your child to think before posting pictures or videos or altering photos posted by someone else. Tell your child never to send his or her picture to someone online unless you give your permission to do so.

12. Remind your child that cell phones also can be used to bully or harass others. He or she should apply the same good manners and ethics when using a cell phone as he or she does when on the Internet and in other situations.

13. Tell your child to use common sense when he or she is social networking.

14. Talk to your child about texting. Tell him or her to think about how a text message might be read and understood before sending it and to ignore text messages from people he or she does not know. Make sure your child knows how to block numbers from his or her cell phone.

15. Tell your child not to send or forward sexually explicit photos, videos, or messages from any device (known as "sexting"). Not only would he or she be risking his or her reputation and friendships, but he or she could be breaking the law by creating, forwarding, or even saving this kind of message.

Guiding Your Child About Cyberbullying

1. Tell your child to take Internet harassment seriously; it is harmful and unacceptable.

2. Make sure your child knows to tell you immediately if electronic bullying includes physical threats (including death threats). You should then immediately notify the police and the social networking site (if appropriate).

3. Let your child know that you want to know if he or she feels threatened by someone or uncomfortable because of something that is happening online.

4. Tell your child not to respond to anything online that he or she believes is wrong or that makes him or her uncomfortable and to tell you about his or her feelings.

5. Tell your child never to reply to harassing messages and to log out of a site immediately if he or she is being harassed.

6. If your child sees cyberbullying happening to someone else, encourage him or her to not engage in or forward anything and to report it to you so that you can notify the site or network.

7. Encourage your child to tell you if he or she is aware of others who may be the victims of cyberbullying.

8. Assure your child that you will not revoke his or her Internet privileges if he or she is cyberbullied.

9. Find out how to block a bully's messages and show your child how to do this, how to delete messages without reading them, and how to save them and forward them to your Internet or e-mail provider.
10. If someone on your child's "friends" or "buddies" list initiates bullying, work with your child to delete the bully from the list.

Guiding Your Child About Internet Privacy and Identity Theft

1. Tell your child never to share his or her Internet passwords with friends or anyone else except you and other trusted members of your family.
2. Talk to your child about using strong e-mail passwords. The longer and more complex the password, the harder it is to crack. Passwords that are not safe include those that contain personal information, your child's login name, or common words or that use adjacent keys on the keyboard.
3. Discuss with your child that communicating with strangers online is dangerous (just as talking to strangers in person is dangerous). Particularly, tell your child not to share personal information or talk about sex with anyone he or she does not know. Also, tell your child never to arrange to meet in person someone he or she has met online, unless you say that it is okay to do so.
4. Teach your child to maintain privacy and avoid identity theft by not replying to texts, e-mails, or pop-up messages that ask for his or her or others' personal or financial information—including his or her full name, address, telephone number, parents' names, school's name, social security number, or account numbers for bank or credit card accounts. Also tell your child not to click on any links in such messages or cut and paste a link from one of them into a web browser. (If your child wants to check a financial account, for example, he or she should type the web address of the bank directly into the browser window.) Personal information (except for social security numbers) can, however, be posted when ordering from a secure business website.
5. Tell your child not to give personal information on the phone in response to a text message. Some scammers send text messages that appear to be from a legitimate business and then ask the recipient to call a phone number to update the account or to obtain a "refund." If the recipient gives them personal information, the scammers use the information to run up charges in the recipient's name.
6. Tell your child to forward "phishing" e-mails (e-mails used by scam artists to send spam, pop-ups, or text messages to trick the recipient into disclosing personal, financial, and/or other sensitive information) to spam@uce.gov and to the company, bank, or organization impersonated in the phishing e-mail. You and your child may also want to report a phishing e-mail to the Anti-Phishing Working Group at reportphishing@antiphishing.org.
7. Tell your child to create a safe screen name and to think about the impression that screen name conveys. A good screen name won't reveal how old your child is, where your child lives, or your child's gender. Further, your child's screen name should not be the same as his or her e-mail address.

8. Tell your child to use security software and update it regularly.
9. Talk to your child about your expectations about who should be allowed to view his or her profile online. Make sure your child uses appropriate privacy settings to restrict who can access and post notes on his or her profile.
10. Talk to your child about setting high privacy preferences on his or her instant messaging (IM) and video calling accounts. (Most IM programs allow parents to control whether people on their child's contact list can see his or her IM status, including whether he or she is online. Some IM and e-mail accounts allow parents to determine who can send their child messages and block anyone not on the list.)
11. Tell your child not to forward (or even open) e-mail chain letters. Most recipients find chain letters a nuisance, and they may be scams or may carry viruses or spyware.
12. If your child finds a profile that was created or altered without his or her permission, work with your child to contact the company or group that runs the website, chat room, or message board to have it taken down.
13. Advise your child to use GPS technology installed on his or her cell phone only with friends he or she knows well and trusts, and not to broadcast his or her location to the world. (Your child should know that some carriers offer GPS services that allow parents to map their child's location.)
14. If your child is under 13 years of age, tell your child that he or she must have parental consent to post information to a website. The Children's Online Privacy Protection Act (COPPA), enforced by the Federal Trade Commission, requires websites to get parental consent before collecting or sharing information from children under 13.
15. Tell your child to avoid posting his or her cell phone number online.
16. Tell your child to read his or her regular mail and to carefully review printed (or e-mailed) credit card and bank account statements as soon as they arrive to check for unauthorized charges.

Supervising Your Child's Internet Use

1. Recognize that your child has Internet access not only through his or her computer at home, but also through cell phones and other mobile devices, friends' computers, computers at school, computers at the library, and computers at Internet cafes.
2. Talk regularly with your child about online activities that he or she is involved in. Spend time with your child while he or she is online.
3. If possible, keep your home computer in a place where you can see it, such as a family room or kitchen.
4. Closely supervise a young child who is beginning to use a computer. Choose appropriate websites for your young child to visit, and supervise your young child as he or she explores the sites. When your child is ready to explore on his or her own, continue to stay in close touch as he or she goes from site to site.
5. Tell your child that you may review his or her online communications if you think there is reason for concern. (Concerns for your child's safety may sometimes override privacy concerns.) You may want to check the web pages

your child has opened and his or her browser history from time to time to see what is there.

6. Consider using child-oriented search engines and monitoring software that alerts you to your child's online activity without blocking access.

7. Consider installing parental control filtering software and/or tracking programs, but don't rely solely on these tools. You should learn about tools that will allow you to filter and block certain sites, words, or images from websites, e-mails, chat rooms, and instant messages.

8. Help your child recognize which Internet sources and websites are trustworthy. You can do this by helping him or her understand the concept of "credibility." Your child needs to understand that not everything he or she sees on the Internet is true and that people on the Internet may not be who they appear to be.

9. Consider whether it may be best to turn off or at least limit certain features on your child's cell phone, such as Internet access.

10. Review your child's list of friends and talk to your child about limiting his or her online "friends" to people he or she actually knows.

11. Consider setting limits on how much time to allow your child to spend online.

12. Be careful about allowing your child to use a webcam. A webcam allows a possible predator to communicate face to face with your child. If your child does use a webcam, talk to him or her about its appropriate use.

13. Limit your child's use of chat rooms and message boards. Entering chat rooms or using message boards may place your child at risk.

POSSIBLE WARNING SIGNS THAT YOUR CHILD MAY BE A VICTIM OF BULLYING

PHYSICAL SIGNS

Your child

- Is hungry after school.
- Comes home in torn or damaged clothes.
- Tells you that possessions (for example, books, electronics, clothing, jewelry) have been "lost."
- Brings damaged possessions home from school.
- Has unexplained bruises, scratches, or cuts.
- Complains of illness (for example, pains, headaches, stomachaches).
- Complains of tiredness or fatigue.
- Has difficulty sleeping (for example, nightmares, bedwetting).

BEHAVIORAL SIGNS

Your child

- Acts differently than usual.
- Avoids certain places in the neighborhood.
- Does not want to go to school.
- Displays "victim" body language (for example, hangs head, hunches shoulders, avoids eye contact).
- Fears riding on the school bus or walking to and from school.
- Is getting poor grades in school for the first time.
- Has difficulty concentrating.
- Has little interest in schoolwork or other activities.
- Has unexplained absences from school.

- Asks you for additional lunch money.
- Stays late at school to avoid encounters with other students.
- Steals money from you.
- Takes some form of "protection" to school (for example, a stick, knife, gun).
- Takes an "illogical" route when walking to and from school.
- Talks about running away.
- Threatens violence against others.
- Talks about wanting to commit suicide.
- Doesn't want to be with his or her friends.

EMOTIONAL SIGNS

Your child

- Is irritable, anxious, fearful, or insecure.
- Shows evidence of (or expresses) feeling sad, hopeless, depressed, isolated, lonely, or trapped.
- Displays mood swings and cries easily.
- Shows evidence of (or expresses) feeling rejected, picked on, persecuted, or powerless.
- Has angry outbursts.
- Complains of flashbacks.
- Has self-doubt and low self-esteem.

SIGNS OF CYBERBULLYING IN PARTICULAR

Your child

- Is upset after being online or seeing text messages.
- Stops using his or her computer, cell phone, or smartphone unexpectedly.

GETTING THE FACTS ABOUT THE POSSIBLE BULLYING INCIDENT

1. Ask the following questions as needed.
   - What signs suggest that your child was a victim of bullying?
   - How is your child behaving?
   - What kind of bullying occurred? Was it physical, verbal, indirect (for example, by e-mail), or some combination of these?
   - How did your child react to the bullying?
   - When did the bullying take place?
   - Where did the bullying take place?
   - If the bullying is ongoing, how often does it take place?
   - If the bullying is ongoing, how long has it been going on?
   - How many children have been bullied?
   - How much has your child (and other children, if relevant) been harmed?
   - Who was the bully?
   - Did any onlookers contribute to the bullying? (If yes) Who were they and what did they do?
   - Were there any witnesses present? (If yes) Who were they and what did they see?
   - Did your child do anything to bring on the bullying? (If yes) What did your child do?
   - Did your child do anything to prevent or stop the bullying? (If yes) What did your child do?
   - If the bullying took place at school, did your child report it to anyone at the school? (If yes) To whom did your child report it? What did that person do?

2. Take pictures of any physical evidence of bullying (for example, bruises, cuts, damaged books, torn clothes).
3. Keep a written record of all the incidents that have occurred. Include as many details as possible, such as who was there, where it happened, when it happened, and what happened.
4. Praise your child for his or her willingness to discuss the bullying incident with you.

ACTIONS YOU SHOULD TAKE WHEN YOUR CHILD HAS BEEN BULLIED

Supporting Your Child

1. Find out all you can about bullying.
2. If your child tells you that he or she has been bullied, listen carefully.
3. Always respond to requests for help from your child.
4. Observe your child carefully. Look for signs of stress, including anxiety, sleep problems, depression, loss of appetite, temper tantrums, and suicidal thoughts or actions.
5. If your child shows signs of stress, determine how he or she is dealing with the stress. Consider the following questions:
   - Is your child turning to alcohol, cigarettes, or drugs?
   - Has your child joined a group whose values may be worrisome, such as a gang, a cult, or a hate group?
   - Is your child seeking help from a mental health specialist at school?
6. If your child is not seeing a mental health specialist at school, ask for a referral to a mental health specialist if you are concerned about how your child is dealing with the stress of being bullied.
7. Support your child in a way that helps him or her to regain self-control, to "save face," and to feel safe from retaliation. For example, assure your child that bullying is not his or her fault, and tell him or her that you want to work together to resolve the situation and protect him or her from further bullying. Also encourage your child to tell you about the good parts of his or her day and make sure that your child knows that you trust and believe him or her. Encourage your child to spend time with friends who are a positive influence, and to participate in clubs, sports, hobbies, or other enjoyable activities.
8. Make sure your child knows that it is okay to feel scared, upset, or anxious when he or she is bullied.
9. Think about your child's behavior and style of interaction and consider how you might help him or her handle these types of situations in the future. For example, you might teach your child basic social skills, such as how to invite a classmate to play a game or how to seek permission from a group of children to join in a play activity, or you might pair your child with a child who is socially competent and who can serve as a role model.
10. Tell your child to tell you or a trusted adult anytime he or she is bullied.
11. Work with other parents to stop bullying in the school and the community.

Reporting an Assault

1. Contact the police. Consider filing formal charges against the bully and seeking a restraining order.
2. If the assault happened at school, also contact the school authorities.

Reporting Bullying That Takes Place in School

1. Contact your child's teacher or another member of the school staff and ask for assistance.
2. Ask the teacher if he or she has observed any incidents of bullying involving your child.
3. Find out how the school intends to deal with the bullying.
4. Work collaboratively with the school to address the problem, knowing that the school must provide your child with a safe place to study and learn.
5. Even if you are not aware of a specific incident, if your child has to resort to unsafe measures (such as avoiding use of a bathroom all day) or is scared to go to school, take immediate action by requesting a meeting with a school administrator.

Talking to Your Child About How to Respond to the Bully

1. Suggest that your child try the following:
   - Act brave (even if he or she doesn't feel brave).
   - Firmly and clearly tell the bully to stop, then walk away (or run away if necessary).
   - Get help if pursued.
   - Ignore any hurtful remarks made by a bully, such as by acting uninterested or texting someone. Tell your child that ignoring the bully shows the bully that he or she doesn't care. Eventually, the bully might get bored and stop bothering him or her.
   - Try to change the subject or distract the bully. Doing so might make it harder for him or her to continue with the bullying.
   - Hold in his or her anger. It's natural to get upset by a bully, but that's what bullies thrive on; it makes them feel more powerful. Advise your child not to respond to a bully by losing his or her temper, fighting back, bullying back, or calling the bully names. This might make the situation worse. Similarly, keep the bully off guard by not crying or looking upset.
   - Adopt a "poker face" when he or she is bullied. Smiling or laughing might provoke the bully.
   - Practice a "cooling down" strategy such as counting to 10, taking deep breaths, or walking away.
2. Remind your child not to get others to gang up on the bully at another time and never to bring weapons to school to threaten the bully or to protect himself or herself from more bullying.

Talking to Your Child About Ways to Avoid Being Bullied

1. Recommend that your child use a buddy system whenever possible so that he or she does not have to walk alone. For example, your child should try to "buddy up" with a friend in the hallway, at recess, and on the bus.
2. Help your child figure out ways to avoid the bully whenever possible. Your child can do this by choosing an activity the bully might not choose, sitting at a table far from the bully at lunchtime, going to a part of the playground away from

the bully, using a different bathroom if the bully is nearby, using a hallway that the bully does not use (if possible), and moving to an area close to an adult who can keep an eye on what is going on.

3. Suggest to your child ways to remove incentives for the bullying. For example, if the bully is demanding his or her lunch money, your child should not bring lunch money to school and should instead start bringing his or her lunch. If the bully tries to get his or her possessions (cell phone or other electronics, jewelry, books), he or she should avoid bringing such items to school unless they are absolutely necessary.

4. Teach your child the following assertiveness skills:
   - How to maintain his or her composure
   - How to stand firm and continue to behave appropriately even when provoked
   - How to respond to taunts, insults, or teasing with a bland response ("Oh"; "That's your opinion"; "Maybe")
   - How to get away from a situation if he or she starts to get very angry
   - How to say "No" firmly and loudly if he or she doesn't want to do something that someone else says to do and to stand up straight and look the other person in the eye when he or she says it
   - How to refuse to be talked into doing something that he or she will be sorry for, even if someone dares him or her to do it

Particular Actions in Response to Cyberbullying

1. Investigate a report of cyberbullying immediately.
2. Tell your child *not* to respond to the cyberbullying. He or she should never reply to harassing messages but should log out of the site or otherwise disengage from the interaction immediately.
3. Do not delete bullying messages or pictures. Save these as evidence.
4. Try to identify the individual doing the cyberbullying. Even if the cyberbully is anonymous (for example, is using a fake name or someone else's identity), there may be a way to track him or her through your Internet service provider. If the cyberbullying is criminal (or if you suspect that it may be), contact the police and ask them to do the tracking.
5. As sending inappropriate language may violate the terms and conditions of e-mail or Internet service providers, websites, and cell phone companies, consider contacting the provider and filing a complaint. If the cyberbullying is coming through e-mail or a cell phone, it may be possible to block future contact from the cyberbully.
6. Contact your school if the cyberbullying is occurring through your school district's Internet system. School administrators have an obligation to intervene. Make your school administrators aware of the problem even if the cyberbullying is occurring off campus. They may be able to help you resolve the cyberbullying or to watch for face-to-face bullying.
7. Consider contacting the cyberbully's parents. They may put a stop to the cyberbullying when they learn about what their child has been doing. However, they may not like your contacting them, so proceed cautiously. If you decide to contact a cyberbully's parents, communicate with them in writing—not face to face. Present proof of the cyberbullying

(for example, copies of an e-mail message) and ask them to make sure that the cyberbullying stops.

8. Consider contacting an attorney in cases of serious cyberbullying. In some circumstances, civil law permits victims to sue a bully or his or her parents in order to recover damages.
9. Contact the police if cyberbullying involves any of the following:
   - Threats of violence directed toward your child, your family, your property, or your child's school and school teachers
   - Repeated insults or intimidating comments that cause fear for your child's safety, including obscene or harassing phone calls or text messages or any other form of harassment or stalking
   - Extortion
   - Negative comments about race, religion, or some other aspect of identity
   - Sharing of photos that invade your child's privacy
   - Communications that are sexually explicit or obscene, including child pornography

If you are uncertain whether the cyberbullying event violates the law, contact your local police department for advice.

ACTIONS YOU SHOULD *NOT* TAKE WHEN YOUR CHILD MAY BE A VICTIM OF BULLYING

1. Do not ask your child to solve a bullying problem by himself or herself. Because of the differences in power between your child and the bully, your child may suffer further. Bullying problems require adult intervention.
2. Do not advise your child to fight the bully. Fighting is in violation of school conduct codes, and your child might be seriously injured.
3. Do not try to mediate a bullying situation. Bringing together children who are bullied and those who do the bullying to "work out" the problems between them generally is not a good idea. It may set up a child who is being bullied for further bullying.
4. Do not blame either your child or the child who is a bully.
5. Do not confront the parent of the bully directly. However, in cases in which your child has been a victim of cyber-bullying, you might consider contacting the parents of the bully in writing.
6. Do not confront a teacher and insist that the bully be punished.
7. Do not threaten the school.

POSSIBLE WARNING SIGNS THAT YOUR CHILD MAY BE A BULLY

Your child
- Seeks to dominate and/or manipulate others.
- Appears to enjoy feeling powerful and in control.
- Is both a poor winner (boastful and arrogant) and a poor loser.
- Seems to derive satisfaction from others' fears, discomfort, or pain.
- Is good at hiding behaviors or doing them where adults can't notice—for example, by closing a program or turning off a computer, cell phone, or other electronic device when you enter the room.

- Is excited by conflicts between others.
- Blames others for his or her problems.
- Displays uncontrolled anger.
- Has a history of discipline problems.
- Displays a pattern of impulsive and chronic hitting, intimidating, and aggressive behaviors.
- Displays intolerance and prejudice toward others.
- Uses drugs or alcohol or is a member of a gang.
- Lacks empathy toward others.

Teachers report that your child does one or more of the following:
- Expresses physical superiority.
- Shows off in class.
- Is defiant and rude.
- Is disruptive in class.
- Makes fun of or disparages other students.
- Damages other students' schoolwork or property.
- Makes repeated threats (including threats of physical harm).
- Pushes, shoves, and/or hits other students.
- Blames other students for starting conflicts.
- Practices extortion (such as asking for or taking lunch money from other students).
- Ignores others or excludes others from his or her group.
- Posts slanderous notes about other students (or teachers or other people) in public places.
- Uses electronic means (such as the Internet or cell phones) to start rumors about other students (or teachers or other people), write derogatory comments about them, or show disparaging pictures of them.
- Encourages other students to be disruptive.
- Fails to engage fully in classroom activities.
- Repeatedly fails to turn in homework on time.

ACTIONS YOU SHOULD TAKE WHEN YOUR CHILD IS A BULLY

1. When you learn that your child is bullying others, take it seriously. Children who are bullies may have problems that will get worse as they grow older and even continue into adulthood. Now is the time when you can make a difference and try to change your child's behavior.
2. Get the facts:
   - What did your child do?
   - Was the child's action physical, verbal, indirect (for example, e-mailing others), or some combination of these?
   - How severe was the bullying?
   - When did the bullying take place?
   - Where did the bullying take place?
   - How long has the bullying been going on?
   - Who was there when the bullying took place?
   - What did they do or see?
   - Was your child provoked by the other child? (If yes) In what way?
   - If the bullying took place at school, was it reported to anyone at the school? (If yes) What did the school do?
3. Try to understand why the bullying behavior took place:
   - Was it because of some prejudice (for example, against a child from another ethnic group, a child of the opposite sex, or a child perceived as lesbian, gay, bisexual, or transgendered)?

   - Was it because of group pressure? (If yes) What group was it?
   - Was it due to a misguided sense of fun?
4. Find out about your child's feelings and the reasons for them:
   - Does your child behave in a bullying manner because he or she is frustrated or resentful for some reason? (If yes) What might be the reason for the frustration or resentment?
   - Is your child bored at school? (If yes) What might be the reasons for your child's boredom?
5. Make sure that your child realizes the serious harm that bullying behavior can cause.
6. Make sure that your child knows that bullying is *not* acceptable behavior.
7. Tell your child the penalties that you will invoke for bullying and be sure that you enforce them fairly and consistently.
8. Warn your child not to retaliate against anyone for telling you that he or she engaged in bullying or cyberbullying.
9. Tell your child that you will monitor all of his or her Internet activities at home by installing monitoring software until trust has been reestablished.
10. Use effective nonphysical discipline, such as loss of privileges. When your child needs discipline, explain why his or her behavior was wrong and how it can be changed.
11. Teach your child more appropriate behavior, and reward him or her for it.
12. Help your child develop new and constructive strategies for getting what he or she wants.
13. Discuss with your child how power can be achieved by doing good things.
14. Be a positive role model.
15. Show your child how to relate to others without teasing, threatening, or attacking them.
16. Help your child learn to treat others with respect.
17. Work out a way for your child to make amends for the bullying, such as by apologizing.
18. Help your child understand how the other child feels about being bullied.
19. Examine your family climate:
    - What is your family climate?
    - What is the relationship among the family members?
    - What kind of discipline do you and your spouse use with your child (and the other children, if relevant)?
    - Is your discipline fair and consistent, or is it harsh?
20. Find out about how your child is getting along with other children.
21. Find out about how your child is doing at school.
22. Seek help or counseling if your child's bullying behavior continues.
23. If contacted by the school, stay calm; try not to become angry or defensive. Remember that the school staff are concerned about the well-being of your child.

REFERENCES

Bully OnLine. (n.d.). *Bullying in the family*. Retrieved from http://bullyonline.org/related/family.htm

Kansas State Department of Education. (n.d.). *Definitions/characteristics of bullying*. Retrieved from http://www.education.com/print/definitions-characteristics-bullying

Massachusetts Medical Society. (2001). *Bullying—It's not O.K.* Retrieved from http://www.massmed.org/AM/Template.

cfm?Section=Home&TEMPLATE=/CM/HTMLDisplay.
cfm&CONTENTID=7365

National Crime Prevention Council. (n.d.). *Stop cyberbullying before it starts*. Retrieved from http://www.ncpc.org/resources/files/pdf/bullying/cyberbullying.pdf

OnGuard Online. (2009). *Net cetera: Chatting with kids about being online*. Retrieved from http://www.onguardonline.gov/pdf/tec04.pdf

Orpinas, P., & Horne, A. M. (2006). *Bullying prevention: Creating a positive school climate and developing social competence*. Washington, DC: American Psychological Association.

Quiroz, H. C., Arnette, J. L., & Stephens, R. D. (2006). *Bullying in schools: Fighting the bully battle*. Retrieved from http://www.dps.mo.gov/homelandsecurity/safeschools/documents/Discussion%20Activities%20for%20School%20Communities.pdf

Raskauskas, J., & Stoltz, A. D. (2007). Involvement in traditional and electronic bullying among adolescents. *Developmental Psychology, 43*(3), 564–575. doi:10.1037/0012-1649.43.3.564

Rigby, K. (2008). *Children and bullying: How parents and educators can reduce bullying at school*. Malden, MA: Blackwell.

Rivers, I., Duncan, N., & Besag, V. E. (2007). *Bullying: A handbook for educators and parents*. Westport, CT: Greenwood/Praeger.

U.S. Department of Health and Human Services. (2003b). *Take action against bullying*. Retrieved from http://download.ncadi.samhsa.gov/ken/pdf/SVP-0056/SVP-0056.pdf

The Washington Times. (2007, October 1). *Delete cyberbullying*. Retrieved from http://www.ncpc.org/programs/crime-prevention-month/newspaper-supplements/2007-cpm-newspaper-supplement.pdf

Willard, N. E. (2007). *Cyber-safe kids, cyber-savvy teens: Helping young people learn to use the Internet safely and responsibly*. Hoboken, NJ: Wiley.

Ylvisaker, M., & Feeney, T. (2008). Helping children without making them helpless: Facilitating development of executive self-regulation in children and adolescents. In V. Anderson, R. Jacobs, & P. J. Anderson (Eds.), *Executive functions and the frontal lobes: A lifespan perspective* (pp. 409–438). Philadelphia, PA: Taylor & Francis.

Handout K-3
Handout for Teachers: Instructional and Behavioral Support Strategies for Students with Special Needs

INTRODUCTION

The suggestions in this handout represent a wide range of educational and behavioral approaches and strategies for use with students who are struggling academically, who are suspected of having special needs, or who have been identified as having special needs. (Note that many of the suggestions in this handout represent effective pedagogical techniques that can be used with students in any classroom.) As many educators are aware, students with special needs may go unidentified, but these students still require additional academic and/or behavioral supports.

Generally, a student with a diagnosed disability that affects his or her ability to learn in the classroom will have an individualized education program (IEP) or a formal plan of special accommodations under Section 504 of the Rehabilitation Act of 1973 and a special education or 504 case manager. If a student does not have a diagnosed disability and you learn or suspect that he or she has special needs, you should follow the process that your school has developed for meeting the needs of students with academic or behavioral challenges. Most schools have prereferral or problem-solving teams that meet to identify any student's areas of need and to develop and monitor intervention plans. Depending on a student's response to the intervention that he or she is provided, the team may decide to increase the frequency with which the student receives the intervention or provide a different intervention. If the student's response to the intervention continues to be less than optimal, the school team may refer the student for a psychoeducational evaluation.

If the student is qualified to receive services under the Individuals with Disabilities Education Act (IDEA) or under Section 504 of the Rehabilitation Act, study the report written by the student's IEP team or by the 504 plan committee and implement it as faithfully as possible. If you have questions about working with a student who is receiving an intervention monitored by a school team or who has an IEP or a 504 plan, consult with the student's case manager. You should also consult with a specialist if you have questions about any student who is having problems learning. Specialists include school psychologists, clinical child psychologists, special education teachers, teachers of visually impaired students, orientation and mobility specialists, teachers of deaf and hard of hearing students, speech/language pathologists, and occupational therapists.

Note that some of the suggestions in this handout are applicable to students with almost any type of disability, whereas others are geared to students with a specific type of disability. Thus, every suggestion does not apply to every student. You should consider the student's age, sex, culture, language competency, type of disability, and severity of disability in applying these suggestions. Do not use any procedure described in this handout with a student with a diagnosed disability unless the procedure conforms to the student's educational plan or is approved by the student's case manager. Use your judgment in deciding on the appropriateness of each suggestion for a given student. Finally, you should always notify the student's parents and case manager if the student displays problematic behavior at school.

All students with disabilities are students first of all, each with his or her own individual history, needs, desires, and future goals and aspirations. Further, students with special needs face the same developmental challenges as other students of the same age and sex. However, they also have to cope with psychological issues associated with their disability. These issues may include poor self-esteem, anxiety, depression, loneliness, fatigue, and frustration. They may also have to master technologies and equipment needed to help them deal with their disability. Good teachers understand that each student is an individual first and an individual with special needs second.

Consult the student's school team or case manager (if he or she has one) about how to encourage the student to seek counseling or to enroll in a special program if the student appears likely to benefit from these services. (Of course, you or the student's case manager would need to gain permission from the student's parents for the student to start counseling or a special program.) Examples of special programs are social skills training programs, anger management and conflict management training programs, organizational skills training groups, study skills training programs, and coaching programs. If you are concerned that any of your students may be victims of bullying, ask the school psychologist for a handout titled "Strategies for Preventing and Dealing with Bullying, Cyberbullying, and Other Internet Issues" prepared by the author of this handout.

All students, including those with special needs, benefit when both teachers and students show respect for diversity and respect for honesty. Schools can help you perform your duties better by holding staff meetings at which you have the opportunity to discuss a particular student with other teachers and gain insight into strategies useful for working with the student. Recognize that students with special needs may show setbacks in their development. Be patient during these especially difficult times. Remember that setbacks are also opportunities for learning.

As has been pointed out by the United Nations Committee on the Rights of the Child (2001), "Education also must be aimed at ensuring that essential life skills are learnt by every student . . . such as the ability to make well-balanced decisions; to resolve conflicts in a non-violent manner; and to develop a healthy lifestyle, good social relationships and responsibility" (para. 9). And, as Sullivan and Keeney (2008) noted,

> The UN Committee on the Rights of the Child recognizes that schools must teach students how "to resolve conflict in a non-violent manner" and promote supportive approaches to discipline that reinforce positive social interaction. Good classroom management, conflict resolution, mediation and restorative practices in schools encourage students to take responsibility for their actions, consider the impact their behavior has on others, and work collaboratively with members of the school community to repair any harm done and prevent conflict from reoccurring. . . . Restorative practices involve students and staff in a process to repair the harm resulting from conflicts or misbehavior through fairness committees, community circles, and peer juries. (pp. 34, 36).

ACCOMMODATIONS FOR STUDENTS WITH SPECIAL NEEDS

Accommodations are practices and procedures that are intended to reduce the effects of a student's disability on performance in the classroom in order to maximize the student's chances of learning. Unlike instruction or interventions, accommodations themselves do not provide the student with any new information. Instead, they alter the environment in which the information is learned by providing alternative ways of conveying information and assessing learning. And they may also alter the amount of work the student needs to complete or the standards that the student is held to. Accommodations can also be provided as a component of an intervention plan for students who do not have a diagnosed disability but still appear to have a need for additional supports. Accommodations can be made in the presentation of material, in the ways students respond, in the setting, and in the timing and scheduling of presentations (Thompson, Morse, Sharpe, & Hall, 2005).

- *Presentation accommodations* refer to using alternative modes of presenting information—such as auditory, tactile, visual, and multi-sensory means—that allow students to access information in ways that do not require them to read.
- *Response accommodations* allow students to complete activities, assignments, and assessments using some type of assistive device or organizer.
- *Setting accommodations* permit changes in the location or the conditions in which a test or assignment is given.
- *Timing and scheduling accommodations* include increasing the allowable length of time to complete an assignment or a test and changing the schedule.

Suggestions for specific accommodations for testing, cognitive issues, behavioral issues, and perceptual issues are presented later in the handout.

Some accommodations may have the unintended consequence of reducing the student's opportunity to learn critical content and therefore should not be used. Examples are requiring the student to learn less material, revising assignments so that the student is required to complete only the easiest portions of the material, revising tests to make them easier, and giving the student hints or clues to correct answers on assignments and tests.

When you make accommodations, base them on the following principles:

- Accommodations are intended to allow the student to participate in educational programs, services, and activities.
- Accommodations should be based on documented individual student needs.
- Accommodations should not compromise the essential requirements of a course of study.
- Accommodations must not provide the student with an unfair advantage or interfere with the validity of tests.
- Accommodations should not distract other students. Thus, for accommodations that might disturb others, such as using a reader or scribe or allowing the student to read or think out loud or make noises, use an office setting.

Following are some questions that can guide you in selecting appropriate accommodations (Thompson et al., 2005, p. 18, with changes in notation).

General Questions for Selecting Appropriate Accommodations

1. Does the student have a physical disability, sensory disability, or learning disability (including difficulties with memory, sequencing, directionality, alignment, or organization) that can benefit from some type of accommodation? If so, what type of disability does the student have and what type of accommodation is needed?
2. What are the student's learning strengths and areas needing further improvement? This includes any learning needs that affect the student's ability to achieve at grade-level standards.
3. What specialized instruction (e.g., learning strategies, organizational skills, reading skills) does the student need in order to achieve grade-level content standards?
4. Can the student participate in activities in the same way as his or her peers? (If no) What are the student's limitations and how can they be addressed?
5. Does the student need specialized or adapted equipment? (If yes) Which ones?
6. Are there effective combinations of accommodations that can support the student?
7. Are accommodations needed to provide the student with structure and limits? (If yes) What are they?
8. Does the student require the same amount of feedback and practice as other students? (If no) What accommodations are needed?
9. Can the student manage independent assignments and teamwork as well as his or her peers? (If no) What accommodations are needed?

10. Can the student use the same kinds of books, tools, and instructional resources as other students? (If no) What accommodations are needed?
11. Can the student be evaluated in the same ways as his or her peers? (If no) How can he or she be evaluated?
12. Can the student work at the same tempo as other students? (If no) What accommodations are needed?
13. Does the student currently use any accommodations? (If yes) What are they? Are they effective? (If no) What changes are needed?

Specific Suggestions for Selecting Appropriate Accommodations

The following questions are grouped into four areas: presentation accommodations, response accommodations, setting accommodations, and timing and scheduling accommodations (adapted from Thompson et al., 2005, pp. 47–48, with changes in notation; a checklist form of these questions is available at http://www.cdl.org/resource-library/pdf/AccommodationsManual.pdf).

PRESENTATION ACCOMMODATIONS

1. Does the student have a visual impairment that requires large-type or Braille materials?
2. Is the student able to read and understand directions?
3. Can the student follow oral directions?
4. Does the student need to have directions repeated frequently?
5. Are assistive technology devices indicated on the student's IEP or 504 plan?
6. Does the student have a hearing impairment that requires an interpreter to sign directions?
7. Does the student have a hearing impairment that might benefit from a hearing aid?

RESPONSE ACCOMMODATIONS

1. Does the student have difficulty tracking from one page to another or maintaining his or her place when reading?
2. Does the student have special needs that affect his or her ability to record responses or copy material?
3. Can the student use a pencil or other writing instrument?
4. Does the student use a word processor to complete homework assignments or tests?
5. Does the student use a recording device to complete assignments or tests?
6. Does the student need the services of a scribe?
7. Does the student have special needs that affect his or her ability to spell?
8. Does the student have a visual or motor disability that affects his or her ability to perform math computations?

SETTING ACCOMMODATIONS

1. Do other students easily distract the student?
2. Does the student have difficulty remaining on task?
3. Does the student require any specialized equipment or other accommodations that may be distracting to others?
4. Does the student have visual or auditory impairments that require special lighting or acoustics?

5. Can the student focus on his or her own work in a setting with large groups of other students?
6. Does the student exhibit behaviors that may disrupt the attention of other students?
7. Do any physical accommodations need to be made for the student in the classroom?

TIMING AND SCHEDULING ACCOMMODATIONS

1. Can the student work continuously for the length of time allocated for standard test administration?
2. Does the student need additional time to complete tests?
3. Does the student tire easily because of health problems?
4. Does the student have a visual impairment that causes eyestrain, necessitating frequent breaks?
5. Does the student have a learning disability that affects the rate at which he or she processes written information?
6. Does the student have a motor disability that affects the rate at which he or she writes responses?
7. Does the student take any type of medication to facilitate optimal performance?
8. Does the student's attention span or distractibility require shorter working periods and frequent breaks?

Examples of Response Accommodations

Following are examples of response accommodations (adapted from Thompson et al., 2005, pp. 26–33).

1. *Scribe.* A scribe is someone who writes down what a student dictates by means of an assistive communication device, pointing, sign language, or speech. If a scribe is used, he or she should request clarification from the student about capitalization, punctuation, and spelling key words and should have the student review and edit what the scribe has written. The scribe's role is to write down, as precisely as possible, only what the student has dictated.
2. *Specialized word processors.* Specialized devices on a computer that can facilitate word processing include customized keyboards; mouth, headstick, or other pointing devices; sticky keys; touch screens; and trackballs.
3. *Speech-to-text conversion or voice recognition software.* Speech-to-text conversion software or voice recognition software allows a student to dictate text into the computer or give commands to the computer (e.g., open a program, pull down a menu, or save work).
4. *Notetaker.* Another student can take notes for the student or the student can use an electronic note-taking device.
5. *Audio recorder.* An audio recorder can be used to record class work or test responses when the student has difficulty writing his or her responses.
6. *Writing directly on test booklet.* The student might need to write directly on a test booklet rather than on an answer sheet (e.g., a scannable "bubble" sheet) when taking a test.
7. *Monitor.* A monitor can observe how the student fills out an answer sheet during a test to ensure that the student is responding to the intended question.
8. *Calculator or other assistive device.* A student may use a calculator or other assistive device (e.g., abacus, arithmetic table, manipulatives, or number chart) to work on arithmetic problems during class or on a test. Note that an assistive device can be useful if a student's disability affects

mathematics calculation but not reasoning. Special calculators may have large keys or voice output.

9. *Dictionary and spelling and grammar checker.* Use of a dictionary and a spelling and grammar checker may be helpful to the student.

10. *Visual organizer.* Visual organizers such as graph paper, highlighters, place markers, scratch paper, and templates may be helpful to the student.

11. *Graphic organizer.* A graphic organizer—a means of visually organizing thoughts before starting to write, such as a chart, diagram, or timeline—can help the student arrange information into patterns in order to organize his or her work, especially in writing reports and essays. Semantic mapping software can help the student understand a narrative story or elements of writing.

Evaluating Effectiveness of Accommodations

Following are some questions for evaluating accommodations.

1. How effective is the accommodation used by the student?
2. Was the student able to participate better in the activity because of the accommodation?
3. Was the student able to better learn the lesson because of the accommodation?
4. Did the accommodation help the student to feel that he or she belongs in the class?

SUGGESTIONS FOR EFFECTIVE PEDAGOGY

1. Learn about the student's disability. Consult relevant books and/or Internet sources, such as the *Diagnostic and Statistical Manual of Mental Disorders*, Fifth Edition (*DSM-5*; American Psychiatric Association, 2013), Centers for Disease Control and Prevention (http://www.cdc.gov), National Dissemination Center for Students with Disabilities (http://www.nichcy.org/), and *Merck Manual* (http://www.merck.com).
2. Learn about the student's strengths, competencies, and areas of interest.
3. Learn about effective methods of teaching the student, ways to adapt the curriculum, and how to address the goals listed in the student's IEP or 504 plan.
4. Consider the following questions about a student with special needs:
   - What are the student's preferences with respect to sensory input (auditory, visual, and kinesthetic), mode of expression (oral or written), environmental characteristics (room and workspace design, lighting and sound, temperature)?
   - Does the student function better alone or in a group?
   - What prerequisite skills does the student need for success in the course curriculum?
   - Which of these skills does the student have?
   - In what areas will the student need additional preparation or support?
   - How well can the student stay on track and adapt to routines and changes?
5. Talk to other teachers who have students with a similar disability about how they approach teaching.
6. If the student is acting out or shows side effects associated with a medication, send the student to the staff professional designated to handle such situations. The student may need to calm down, receive special help, and/or be moved to a place with reduced stimulation.

7. If the student is reluctant to attend school, determine the causes of his or her reluctance and address them. Work with the student's parents to get the student back to school as soon as possible. You may also need to consult with the school psychologist, school counselor, or social worker.
8. Do not expect the student to have immediate success; work for incremental improvements. If the student is not meeting objectives in his or her IEP or 504 plan, consult the student's case manager.
9. Try to anticipate classroom situations (including transitions to other rooms or places at school) in which the student might act out, and be prepared to deal with the acting out.
10. Apply the same classroom conduct rules to students with special needs as you do to the rest of the class, except when you need to make accommodations for the student's disability.
11. Compensate for absences by providing assignment sheets, lecture notes, worksheets, study aids, and other related materials.
12. Continually assess the student's progress. Don't wait until it's too late to discover that there is a problem or that the problem is getting worse.
13. Help the student develop healthy, realistic self-esteem, based on a clear understanding of his or her strengths and weaknesses.
14. Help the student become internally motivated and learn to set realistic goals.
15. To reduce a student's fear of failure (if that is an issue), help the student learn to accept his or her mistakes and recognize that he or she can learn from errors.
16. Help the student learn to accept help from others.
17. Help the student learn how to help others.
18. Help the student develop a sense of humor about himself or herself and events outside his or her control.

General Teaching Strategies

1. Provide the student with a daily schedule as needed.
2. Gain the student's attention before the lesson begins and maintain appropriate eye contact.
3. If appropriate, require the student to keep a daily assignment notebook and make sure that the student writes down all assignments correctly. If necessary, show the student how to use the assignment notebook.
4. Initial the notebook daily to signify completion of homework assignments. (Parents should also sign the notebook page.)
5. Allow all students to use a computer when appropriate for activities.
6. Review with the student how to proofread assignments and check answers on tests.
7. Establish peer tutoring programs to facilitate the student's learning. If possible, pair the student with a student who does not have special needs and who has well-developed social, behavioral, and academic skills and will accept the student. Encourage cooperative and collaborative learning.

Strategies for Presenting Class Lectures

1. Be sure that you have the student's attention before giving the lecture.

2. Maintain a brisk instructional pace.
3. Be sure that your words match your nonverbal behavior.
4. Talk distinctly at a moderate rate, without too many pauses.
5. Speak at a normal volume and check to make sure all students in the classroom can hear you.
6. Provide adequate time for the student to process the information and respond to questions.
7. Monitor the student's responses.
8. Take breaks as needed.
9. Give the student feedback about any incorrect responses.
10. If needed, ask questions to guide the student to give a correct response.
11. Watch for any signs that the student may need additional assistance.
12. Do not use puns or humor that the student will not understand (or any difficult words or concepts without explaining them).

Strategies for Teaching New Skills

1. Demonstrate the skill or strategy being taught in the lesson.
2. Provide sufficient practice and assistance at each stage of the lesson.
3. Observe the student as he or she performs each new skill or strategy.
4. Give the student opportunities to practice the new skill in different problems and situations, and assign homework related to the current lesson.
5. Teach the student study skills and learning strategies, and reinforce these regularly.
6. Learn about the areas in which the student is having difficulties and about the student's strengths and interests, and use this knowledge in your teaching.

Teaching Techniques

1. Start each assignment with a few questions you know the student can answer or activities you know the student can accomplish successfully.
2. Be consistent with all daily instructions.
3. Divide tasks into manageable segments.
4. Provide specific steps for each segment.
5. Provide examples for each step.
6. Set task priorities.
7. Establish fixed work periods.
8. Vary tasks to prevent boredom.
9. Alternate activities preferred by the student with those that are less preferred.
10. Help the student feel comfortable in seeking assistance.
11. Have realistic expectations for the student.
12. Be willing to try new ways of doing things.
13. Ask questions in a way that helps the student gain confidence. For example, use language that fits the student's ability level, phrase questions so that the student understands what type of response is expected (e.g., short or long), and ask both *convergent, or lower order, questions* (requiring only short answers recalled from memory and little reflection) and *divergent, or higher order, questions* (requiring longer answers and analysis or extrapolation of information recalled from memory). Also encourage responses from students who do not volunteer and encourage students to clarify, expand on, and support

their answers. Pause three to five seconds after you ask a question to give students time to think.
14. Actively involve the student during the lesson presentation.
15. Promote consistent study habits.
16. Promote a sense of responsibility for completing tasks.
17. Give the student positive feedback when appropriate.
18. Reward the student for each small success.

Strategies for Establishing Routines

1. Establish routines to help students know what is going to happen from the beginning to the end of the lesson (predictability), know what they are supposed to do (consistency), know what to get ready for (anticipation), and know that they can practice something that they have recently learned (practice).
2. Provide a clear signal to the student that the lesson is starting.
3. Present the steps of the lesson in the same sequence every time.
4. Perform each step in the same way each time (same materials, same person, same place).
5. Provide assistance as needed.
6. Pace the instruction throughout the lesson at an appropriate level.
7. Provide a clear signal to the student that the lesson is finished.

Strategies for Supplementing Traditional Lectures

1. Use multi-sensory approaches and stimulating tasks to help the student learn the material.
2. Use visual aids such as diagrams, charts, illustrations, graphic organizers, video clips, and demonstrations.
3. Use physical supports, prompts, and movement.
4. Use hands-on activities and computers, calculators, and audio recorders.
5. Teach the student to visualize information actively while listening and reading (e.g., in teaching vocabulary words, use a flash card with a photo of the object and the name of the object on the same side of the card or show the actual object).
6. Use a chalkboard or whiteboard, overhead projector, or computer with a projector for a PowerPoint presentation, as needed (e.g., for new or technical vocabulary).
7. Use small-group activities.

Strategies for Modifying Work Demands

1. Assign fewer problems for in-class and homework assignments.
2. Give the student additional time to complete assignments.
3. Allow the student to turn in only half of an assignment if he or she meets a specified criterion, such as 90% accuracy on the completed part.
4. Allow the student to dictate his or her work to a parent.
5. Instead of a written paper, allow the student to submit an audio recording of an assignment.
6. Break new tasks into small steps, demonstrate the steps, have the student do the steps one at a time, check to see whether the student understands the information, and provide assistance as needed.
7. Intersperse high-interest activities with more routine work activities to maintain motivation.

8. Use novel tasks.
9. Alternate activities involving sitting and standing.
10. If needed, use alternative activities or exercises that are easier for the student, but maintain your learning objectives.

Strategies for Introducing a New Lesson

1. Review information from prior lessons before starting a new lesson.
2. Provide an overview of the new lesson.
3. State the goals of the new lesson and describe what materials the student will need, what the student is expected to learn, and what behaviors are expected from the student.
4. Summarize the important segments of each presentation.
5. At the end of the lesson, review it and summarize the major points covered.

Strategies for Teaching Study Skills

1. Teach the student to set short-term goals.
2. Teach the student how to survey material before reading it.
3. Teach the student how to develop questions about the material.
4. Teach the student how to identify the pertinent facts about the material to be learned.
5. Teach the student how to review the material that he or she has learned.
6. Teach the student how to check his or her work.
7. Teach the student how to test himself or herself for an understanding of the material.

Strategies for Teaching Students with Reading Difficulties

1. Use commercial books on tape, have someone make a recording of a book, or read the text aloud. (Do not use this strategy on tests measuring reading skills.)
2. Provide the student with a card or frame to help him or her block out parts of the text and thus focus on the words.
3. Use assistive devices that translate text to speech, such as a reading pen, Kurzweil reader, or scanner with character recognition software.
4. Use interactive CDs or computer-assisted training with auditory and visual cues rather than written descriptions only.
5. Allow the student to use sticky notes or a highlighter to mark key points in the textbook.
6. Give the student a list of important vocabulary words with definitions.
7. Provide a study guide to help the student read independently.
8. Divide complex information into chunks or sections.
9. Provide alternative ways of learning abstract concepts or complex information, such as using hands-on activities, visual aids, pictures, or diagrams.
10. Choose books with clear syntax and passages with clear meaning.
11. Select readings that are organized by subheadings, as this aids in the flow of ideas.
12. If available, consider using companion versions of your textbooks written at lower reading levels.
13. Provide the student with chapter outlines or study guides that identify key points in the readings.

14. Give the student a version of the reading passage with the main ideas underlined or highlighted.
15. Provide clear photocopies of your notes and overhead transparencies.
16. Repeat or paraphrase test directions as needed.
17. Underline or highlight important words in the test directions.
18. Allow the student to read test items aloud to himself or herself during the test.

Strategies for Teaching Students with Listening Difficulties

1. Allow the student to borrow notes from a classmate or to use an audio recorder.
2. Introduce new vocabulary words prior to the lesson and provide a definition of each word.
3. Provide an overview of the lesson or an advance organizer (i.e., information presented prior to learning to help the student organize and interpret the upcoming new information).
4. Present materials in a logical manner, with explicit cues to shift from one part to the next.
5. Break down information into steps or key components.
6. Write important ideas on the chalkboard, whiteboard, or overhead transparencies, or show them on a projector.
7. Repeat and summarize important points, particularly at the conclusion of the lecture.
8. Provide organizers for note-taking, such as a copy of the overheads, an outline of the lecture, or a graphic organizer.
9. Provide copies of exemplary notes taken by other students in the class.
10. Record class lectures using an audio recorder.
11. Meet with the student after class to clarify any parts of the lesson or assignment that he or she did not understand.

Strategies for Teaching Students with Handwriting Difficulties

1. Encourage the student to use adaptive devices, such as pencil grips or special pen or pencil holders, erasable pens, or special paper with raised or color-coded line indicators.
2. Use worksheets and test answer sheets with ample space for writing answers.
3. Provide two copies of a worksheet—one to work on as a draft and one to use as a final copy.
4. Give the student graph paper to write on to help him or her align the numbers in computation problems or organize information.
5. Allow the student to use a word processor for written assignments.
6. Allow another student or a classroom aide to write down what the student dictates.
7. Allow for shorter assignments.
8. Allow the student to use an audio recorder or give oral reports.
9. Allow the student to mix cursive writing and printing.

Strategies for Teaching Students with Mathematical Difficulties

1. Use concrete materials and manipulatives or computer-based models to help the student understand abstract math concepts.

2. Allow the student to use a regular calculator, a talking calculator, or an on-screen computer calculator for computation tasks.
3. Provide the student with flowcharts to plan strategies for problem solving.
4. Assist the student with specialized mathematical vocabulary and mathematical symbols.
5. Provide additional examples and explanations as needed.
6. Allow the student to use graph paper or color coding to organize answers to math problems.
7. Review (or have an assistant review) with the student his or her understanding of each lesson within a day or two of the initial learning.
8. Have the student practice subskills related to new material.
9. Provide additional independent practice until the student has adequate mastery of the materials.

Strategies for Teaching Students with Expressive Language Difficulties

1. Allow the student to use a thesaurus to find words when writing or speaking.
2. Allow the student to use special word-processing software that anticipates what the student is trying to write.
3. Provide the student with a structured outline or graphic organizer to help him or her plan written assignments or presentations.
4. Allow the student to use demonstrations or video-recorded responses for classroom assignments.

Strategies for Teaching Students with Grammar and Spelling Difficulties

1. Allow the student to use a spelling dictionary or electronic spelling aid with speech capabilities.
2. Allow a peer or an assistant to help the student revise written assignments.
3. Grade content separately from grammar and spelling in written assignments.
4. Give the student an opportunity to correct spelling and grammar errors.

Strategies for Teaching Students Who Have Difficulty Following Directions

1. Outline each day's assignments.
2. Combine oral directions with pictures, words, or diagrams.
3. Repeat the directions.
4. Simplify the directions.
5. Give step-by-step instructions and outline the steps in writing or in picture sequences.
6. Allow another student to assist the student with special needs.

Strategies for Teaching Students Who Have Difficulty Initiating and Sustaining Effort

1. Divide assignments into parts with individual due dates.
2. Make a checklist that allows the student to check off each part of the assignment that he or she completes.
3. Use a reward system to motivate the student to complete assignments (e.g., let the student engage in an activity of choice following completion of an assignment).

4. Encourage the student to use resources and instructional materials outside of class, such as information obtained from Internet searches.
5. Use flexible scheduling practices.
6. Allow additional time for assignments and tests.
7. Give assignments ahead of time so that the student can get started early.

Strategies for Interacting with Students

1. Give the student your individual attention; have realistic expectations for him or her; be willing to try new ways of doing things; be patient, fair, and consistent in working with the student, but temper your consistency with flexibility; and aim to maximize the student's chances for success. Be aware that your body language and tone of voice play an important role in your communications. Your actions will serve as a model for the student.
2. Look for signs of stress and implement strategies to reduce stress.
3. Don't try to talk your student out of his or her symptoms, and avoid offering unsolicited advice.
4. Acknowledge any difficulties or emotional pain that the student is feeling, and try to understand or at least respect his or her feelings.
5. Try to stay calm even when the student is frustrated or experiencing intense emotions.
6. Keep lines of communication open with your student.
7. Don't let the student's emotional or physical disabilities bias your understanding of his or her mental abilities.
8. Recognize that the student may be hesitant to participate in extracurricular activities or join clubs because of fear of being rejected. Try to help the student diminish this fear.
9. Encourage the student to accept positions of responsibility in the school, such as class president, class secretary, or team captain, or to be in charge of some activity, when appropriate.
10. Encourage the student to interact with other students who do not have special needs.
11. Encourage all students to accept students with special needs, and discourage them from bullying, harassing, or teasing these students. If bullying does occur, follow your school's procedures for reporting bullying.
12. Encourage the student to keep a journal or diary if he or she is able to write.
13. Make sure that the student uses any assistive technology device that has been recommended for him or her. If the student refuses to use the device, contact the student's case manager and the student's parents, if appropriate.
14. When the student shows interest in a subject or activity, encourage the student to pursue further study of the subject.

Strategies for Maintaining a Positive and Constructive Classroom Environment

1. At the beginning of the year, actively engage your students in establishing a set of class rules.
2. Check in with your students at the start of each class to see what they want to get out of the class.
3. Make sure that your expectations for the student with special needs are consistent with those of other teachers in the school and with schoolwide procedures.

4. Make sure that the environment is consistently and clearly structured.
5. Adjust class schedules, as needed.
6. Change the student's seating, as needed.
7. Seat the student near a good role model or "study buddy."
8. Label objects and containers.
9. Post signs, schedules, lists, charts, calendars, and outlines.
10. Let the student know where things belong.
11. Let the student know what is expected of him or her in a specific situation.
12. Let the student know what to anticipate.
13. Use the chalkboard or whiteboard to present information.
14. Eliminate visual distractions such as excessive light, movement, reflection, or background patterns.
15. Eliminate auditory distractions such as noisy fans and loudspeakers.
16. Alter the location of personal or classroom supplies, if necessary for easier access or to minimize distractions.
17. Maintain appropriate room temperature.
18. Provide a designated quiet area where the student can go to relax.
19. Provide a safe place where the student can retreat from stressful situations.
20. Provide small-group instruction, as needed.
21. Consult with the student's case manager before you place the student in a new location or setting.

Strategies for Helping Students with Organizational Difficulties

1. Establish firm class routines that help the student organize his or her day.
2. Give the student a schedule indicating what will be done during each class period.
3. Prepare the student for the day's lesson by quickly summarizing the order of various activities planned.
4. Schedule academic subjects in the morning and nonacademic subjects in the afternoon, because the student's attention span may worsen over the course of the day.
5. Explain in advance when any change in the routine will be needed.
6. Tell the student in advance about any special event (e.g., assembly, field trip) and what to expect.
7. Make the transition from one activity to another in a brief and well-organized manner.
8. Develop a clear system for keeping track of completed and incomplete work. For example, arrange individual hanging files in which each student can place completed work, with a special folder for incomplete work.
9. Suggest organizational strategies to help the student complete his or her assignments and better control his or her behavior. For example, encourage the student to use the following:
   • Assignment logs
   • Memory strategies (see the later section "Problems with Memory and Learning")
   • Study strategies (see the earlier section "Strategies for Teaching Study Skills")

• A notebook with dividers to separate sections for lecture notes, assignments, appointments, phone numbers, and other materials
• Color-coded folders to organize assignments for reading, mathematics, social studies, science, and other subjects
• Highlighters and colored pens
• A checklist of the day's activities placed on the desk

10. To ensure that the student knows the homework assignments before he or she leaves school, do one or more of the following:
    • Give the student a homework assignment sheet.
    • Post assignments in the classroom and have the student copy them in his or her notebook.
    • Post assignments on the school's website, if one is available.
    • Have the student complete at least one item of each homework task before leaving school.
    • Encourage the student to e-mail the list of assignments to his or her home, if the school provides access to e-mail.
    • Tape a checklist to the student's desk.
    • Put a checklist in each subject folder/notebook that outlines the steps needed to complete a homework assignment (or an in-class assignment).

Strategies for Helping Students Who Take Medications

1. Make sure that the student is following all treatment instructions, including taking prescription medications, while at school.
2. If the student is taking medication, watch for any possible side effects, such as nausea, insomnia, anxiety, irritability, restlessness, dizziness, weight gain or loss, tremors, sweating, fatigue, dry mouth, diarrhea, constipation, headaches, stomach upset, depressed mood, anger, drowsiness, tics (abnormal movements, eye blinking, lip biting, arm jerking, vocal sounds), decreased appetite, or irregular heartbeat.
3. If the student shows any of these side effects, contact the student's case manager (if he or she has one), the school nurse, and/or the person at your school designated to contact the student's parents.
4. Make appropriate accommodations in the classroom for side effects associated with medications. Examples of possible accommodations include the following:
   • If the student has diarrhea, allow him or her to have a permanent pass to leave the classroom as needed.
   • If the student is frequently thirsty, allow him or her to have a water bottle.
   • If the student is excessively hungry, allow him or her to have snacks in school (perhaps at the nurse's office).
   • If the student has visual blurring, reduce the length of reading assignments or allow someone to read the material to the student and to write his or her answers for an assignment or test.
   • If the student has a sleep disturbance, allow him or her to arrive late or leave early, to walk around during class, to sit in a bright area of the room, or to take a short nap.
   • If the student occasionally seems to lose control, allow him or her to go for a walk or perform a vigorous activity (like cleaning the blackboard) to help him or her regain a sense of stability or balance.

5. If the nurse at your school oversees the administration of the medications, remind your student when he or she has to go the nurse.
6. Do not discuss the student's symptoms, treatment plan (including medications), or disability with anyone who is not authorized to have this information.

Strategies for Working with Parents

1. Involve the parents in the educational program.
2. Inform the parents of the goals you have set and the methods you are using to meet the goals.
3. Review the school's behavior policy with the parents.
4. Establish a home/school communication system for monitoring behavior. Regularly share information with the parents about how their child is doing at school and ask the parents to do the same about how the student is doing at home. Encourage the parents to communicate weekly with you.
5. Encourage the parents to write a contract with the student outlining expected behavior.
6. Encourage the parents to create a reward system for appropriate behavior at home. The system can be an extension of the reward system used in the classroom.
7. Encourage the parents to provide the student with a quiet, well-lit place to study and to establish set times and routines for study.
8. Encourage the parents to read with the student each evening.
9. Encourage the parents to have the student read magazines and/or books on topics of interest to him or her (such as sports, fishing, hunting, or fashion).
10. Encourage the parents to work with the student on "functional math" problems such as maintaining an allowance, calculating how much to save to buy a desired object, and calculating the correct change when making a purchase.
11. Encourage the parents to have the student explain homework to them prior to getting started.
12. Encourage the parents to implement an incentive or reward system for completing homework correctly.
13. Encourage the parents to secure a private tutor if needed. (Be sensitive to parents' financial situation, however; some parents will be unable to afford a private tutor.)
14. Encourage the parents to review the student's homework daily and sign and return to the teacher a daily log of the assignments and/or homework completed by the student.
15. Encourage the parents to participate in all teacher-parent meetings.
16. Encourage the parents to take the student to a public library weekly.
17. Encourage the parents to practice homework assignments with the student.
18. Encourage the parents to have the student attend school daily and be on time.
19. Encourage the parents to respond promptly to notes sent home by the teacher.
20. Encourage the parents to communicate with the school when family issues arise that may affect the student's behavior.
21. Encourage the parents to establish a routine for after-school and weekend activities.
22. Work together with the student's IEP team or 504 plan team and the student's parents to implement an educational plan tailored to meet the student's needs (and to suggest modifications as needed).
23. Make sure that knowledgeable staff members are available to answer the family's questions.

POSITIVE BEHAVIORAL SUPPORT TECHNIQUES

1. Use behavior management techniques such as modeling, physical prompts, visual cues, and reinforcement to encourage attention, imitation, communication, and interaction.
2. Look for the cause of any misbehavior and identify the situations in which the misbehavior arises. Look at what happened before the event (antecedents), what happened during the event (behavior), and what happened after the event (consequences).
3. Use age-appropriate reinforcers that are meaningful to the student:
   • Verbal praise
   • Points
   • Tokens
   • Free choice of an activity
   • Access to a classroom computer
   • Recognition
   • Time alone
   • Time to talk to a favorite staff member
   • A trip to the cafeteria
   • A walk
   • Playing with a favorite object
   • Playing in water
   • Performing a favorite routine
   • Spending time with objects that provide specific sensory stimulation
   • Sitting at a window
4. Use a reward system for appropriate in-school behavior, completion of schoolwork, and completion of homework.
   • Use small rewards frequently, rather than large rewards infrequently.
   • Reinforce both work quality and work quantity by using a system that involves translating points earned into "dollars" to be used for a silent auction at the end of the grading period.
   • Deliver rewards quickly after the desired behavior is exhibited and immediately praise any and all good behavior and performance (e.g., "I like how you wrote down all your assignments correctly").
   • Reward the student's behavior and communicate to the student the specific behavior that led to the reward (e.g., "Because you've been doing so well working independently for 15 minutes, you get to take a short break and take these books back to the library for me").
   • Use several carefully selected rewards to ensure that they are reinforcing to the student.
   • Use extrinsic rewards initially with a young student to reinforce appropriate behaviors (e.g., stickers, stamps on a chart, tokens in a jar, or extra time for preferred activities).
   • Gradually replace extrinsic rewards with more intrinsic, naturally occurring reinforcements that come from

positive academic and behavioral experiences (e.g., feeling satisfaction and pride in the work produced, enjoying working in a team and gaining friendships, and having fun while learning).

- Prevent access to reinforcing consequences for inappropriate behavior (e.g., if the student is avoiding a task, don't dismiss the student from the activity, but rather make adjustments to the setting or curriculum to help the student achieve success).
- Reward more than punish.
- Change rewards if they are not effective in motivating behavioral change. Provide a changing array of backup rewards or privileges so that the student does not become too accustomed to (and thus no longer motivated by) a particular reward or privilege.
- When necessary, develop contracts with the student and his or her parents to reinforce selected behaviors. Behaviors that could be monitored and reinforced by a behavioral contract include turning in papers on time, raising the hand to speak, staying seated during lectures, and following playground safety rules.

5. Implement classroom rules:
   - Establish clear, simple, and concrete rules and guidelines for appropriate classroom behavior.
   - Teach these classroom rules as needed with several examples.
   - Remind students of these classroom rules.
   - Enforce these classroom rules consistently.
6. To reinforce paying attention, set a timer, alarm clock, or audio recorder to make a sound at random intervals and reinforce the student if he or she is attending when the sound occurs.
7. Encourage the student to use self-monitoring techniques to record selected behaviors. For example, the student might record whether he or she is performing a specific behavior (e.g., is sitting in his or her seat) when a cell phone or other electronic device emits a random beep.
8. Monitor behavior frequently and direct the student to an appropriate behavior when needed.
9. Avoid ridicule, sarcasm, and criticism. Maintain student dignity by handling situations fairly, quietly, and calmly, without being accusatory. Remember that the student may have difficulty staying in control.
10. Devise a contingency plan with the student for replacing inappropriate responses with appropriate ones. Have pre-established consequences for misbehavior, remain calm, state the infraction of the rule, and avoid debating or arguing with the student.
11. Encourage positive self-talk (e.g., "I did very well remaining in my seat today"; "I'm proud of myself"). This helps the student to think positively about himself or herself.
12. Use time-out sessions when the student displays disruptive behavior so that he or she can cool off. Provide a break if the student needs one.
13. Avoid distracting stimuli. For example, place the student in a quiet area of the room rather than near an air conditioner, high traffic area, heater, door, or window.
14. Avoid publicly reminding the student who is on medication to take his or her medicine.
15. Increase the student's motivation by modeling enthusiasm and interest in the lesson.
16. Designate a buddy to help the student regain composure, regroup, and refocus when needed.
17. Consider establishing a fairness committee composed of teachers and students in order to allow students who misbehave to tell their side of the story and/or make amends as appropriate.

SUGGESTIONS FOR DEALING WITH VARIOUS BEHAVIORAL DIFFICULTIES

Note that several of the following suggestions have been previously covered in the handout.

General Suggestions

1. Teach the student how to gain your attention appropriately.
2. Help the student develop emotional awareness, responsibility, and self-regulation (e.g., the ability to cool down in an anger-provoking situation).
3. Help the student understand how to behave appropriately at school.
4. Break each behavioral skill down into concrete, teachable steps.
5. Model the skill and provide examples of its appropriate use.
6. Offer opportunities for guided and independent practice and role playing.
7. Prompt and cue the student about the use of the behavioral skill.
8. Give feedback about the student's performance and praise successful approximations of the skill.
9. Encourage the student to collect, record, and reflect on instances of his or her own behavior.
10. Work with the student to identify which behaviors are improving and which are not.
11. Reinforce the use of appropriate behavioral skills over time.
12. Gradually diminish prompts and rewards for displaying the skill.

Emotional Lability (sudden, frequent changes of mood and behavior)

1. Provide a structured environment.
2. Keep assignments short.
3. Reduce the student's course load so that the work does not become overwhelming.
4. Reduce stressful experiences, such as being required to take pop quizzes or to perform in front of the class.
5. Find ways to help the student calm down when frustrated, such as by giving the student extra time to respond to questions or by having the student take a deep breath.
6. Allow the student to rest as needed.
7. Be alert to any signs that the student is reaching his or her frustration level.
8. Understand that the student's outbursts are not deliberate and are not intended to embarrass anyone in class.
9. Don't let the student perform any actions that might hurt another student; instead, redirect the student to an acceptable activity.
10. Avoid overstimulating the student.
11. Avoid overloading the student with information.

12. Develop consistent routines. This helps the student know what to expect. If the routine is going to change, let the student know ahead of time.

Motor Restlessness

1. Plan extracurricular activities tailored to the student's physical and emotional capabilities and interests.
2. Encourage the student to stand while reading or performing other activities.
3. Give the student frequent opportunities to move around the classroom.
4. Assign the student active jobs in the classroom or allow the student to do errands at school (if appropriate).

Inattentiveness

1. Look at the student when you speak to him or her.
2. Speak in a clear soft voice.
3. Use the student's name when you ask him or her a question.
4. Guide the student to listen for specific information.
5. Speak slowly and distinctly.
6. Select simple tasks.
7. Present one task at a time.
8. Alternate physical and mental tasks.
9. Shorten assignments or work periods to coincide with the student's attention span.
10. Gradually increase the amount of information you present to the student.
11. Use frequent rest periods.
12. Keep assignments to a reasonable level and fitted to the student's ability level.
13. Be prepared for delays in the student's responses.
14. Provide the student with advance notice when schedule changes are to occur.
15. Alert the student to the upcoming activity ("I'm going to tell a story and then we'll discuss where it takes place").
16. Keep classroom distractions to a minimum.
17. Allow additional time to complete tests.
18. Teach self-monitoring strategies.
19. Modify instructions to improve the student's attention. For example, use short, specific, and direct instructions; use visual and auditory modes of presentation; repeat instructions as needed; and check to see whether the student comprehends the instructions.
20. Use short and simple instructions, both orally and in writing.
21. Write clearly and in large script.
22. Demonstrate what is to be done.
23. Alert the student to critical information by using key phrases (e.g., "This is important," "Listen carefully").
24. Encourage the student to ask you to repeat instructions if he or she doesn't understand them.
25. Confirm that the student understands instructions before proceeding to the task.
26. Paraphrase abstract concepts in more concrete terms.
27. Avoid idioms or jargon, figures of speech, double meanings, sarcasm, nicknames, and teasing.

Problems with Language Processing

1. Look at the student when you speak to him or her.
2. Make sure that you have the student's attention before you give him or her directions.
3. Speak slowly and distinctly.
4. Use simple, concrete language. Avoid figurative, idiomatic, ambiguous, ironic, or sarcastic language.
5. Guide the student to listen for specific information.
6. Gradually increase the amount of information that you give the student.
7. Learn to read the student's nonverbal cues.
8. Encourage the student to communicate clearly and to speak in complete sentences.
9. Establish a system of verbal or nonverbal signals to cue the student to attend, respond, or alter his or her behavior.
10. Accompany oral instructions with written instructions and, when possible, use visual cues along with verbal communications.
11. Increase communication activities gradually and systematically.
12. Break complex instructions down into small, specific steps, and give directions one step at a time. For tasks with many steps, give the student written directions.
13. Repeat instructions as needed.
14. Limit the number of choices that you give the student.
15. Allow the student to use a calculator, tape recorder, computer, and/or augmentative communication devices.

Problems with Memory and Learning

1. Give instructions one step at a time and use visual and verbal formats.
2. Slow the pace at which you present information, and pause frequently when you give classroom instructions.
3. Encourage the student to repeat instructions and explain what they mean.
4. Repeat instructions as needed.
5. Present information in a controlled and manageable fashion.
6. Determine the student's optimal rate of reception of information.
7. Use orientation and memory cues liberally.
8. Summarize frequently.
9. Encourage the student to overlearn the material.
10. Teach the student to use visual images to assist in memorizing terms.
11. Before your lecture, provide a brief outline of the lecture or a partially completed graphic organizer that the student can complete during the lecture.
12. Allow the student to use sticky notes to jot down information.
13. Encourage the student to make an outline of the main ideas after completing a reading assignment.
14. Encourage the student to use graphic organizers.
15. Encourage the student to write down every step in his or her calculations when solving math problems.
16. Offer the student practice tests and encourage him or her to take them.
17. Encourage (or require) the student to construct a test and then answer the questions. Having the student construct a

test will give you information about whether he or she knows what information to study.

18. Help the student develop cues when storing information. For example, the acronym HOMES can be used to represent the names of the Great Lakes—Huron, Ontario, Michigan, Erie, and Superior.
19. Prime the student's memory by preparing the student for an assignment. For example, present and define several vocabulary words that the student will encounter in a reading assignment, or use an advance organizer or CliffsNotes for a literature assignment.
20. Encourage the student to review material for a test shortly before going to sleep at night.
21. Encourage the student to make a weekly calendar.
22. Encourage the student to carry a written log of activities, a schedule of classes, a list of assignments and their due dates, and a list of classroom locations.
23. Take baseline measures of the student's performance in each academic area so that you can measure progress.
24. Focus on activities that the student likes, that are neither too easy nor too boring, and that can be completed successfully.
25. Use multimodal cuing (i.e., present cues in more than one sensory modality).
26. Allow the student as much time as he or she needs to complete assignments and tests.
27. Limit the amount of material you require the student to copy from the chalkboard or whiteboard.
28. Use repetition and drilling.
29. Present new information only after the student has mastered previously studied information.
30. Explicitly connect new information with previously learned information.
31. Reintroduce facts in several different contexts.
32. Record your lesson on an audio recorder for the student to replay later, thereby minimizing the need for note-taking.
33. Provide written handouts whenever possible.
34. Increase the student's use of word processing when possible to reduce the need for writing.
35. Alert the student to what you expect him or her to do shortly before you present the assignment. For example, you might say "In doing today's homework assignment, you may find some words in the reading passage that are unfamiliar to you. You can use an electronic dictionary or a print dictionary to look up the meaning of any difficult words."
36. Gradually introduce tasks that require the student to remember greater amounts of information.

Problems with Executive Functioning and Problem-Solving Skills

1. Select a classroom buddy to help the student with instructions, transitions, and assignments and to write for the student, if necessary.
2. Encourage the student to monitor his or her behavior.
3. Individualize the assignments and tests to accommodate the student's special needs.
4. Establish specific goals for the student.
5. Use positive reinforcement to increase desired behavior.
6. Encourage the student to participate in programs that may help him or her overcome limitations.
7. Explain the difference between the demands of new situations and those of old ones.
8. Give clear step-by-step instructions and pair oral instructions with written instructions.
9. Help the student develop systems for maintaining organization, such as checklists or "to do" lists.
10. Establish specific goals for the student.
11. Break down assignments into manageable parts.
12. Keep choices to a minimum.
13. Establish a subdeadline for each separate step in a long-term project.
14. Plan small-group activities to facilitate learning.
15. Use positive reinforcement to increase desired behavior.
16. Use true/false or multiple-choice questions rather than essay questions that require lengthy answers.

Problems with Social Skills

1. Teach the student about feelings and appropriate interpersonal behavior. For example, teach about (a) positive emotions associated with sharing, taking turns, and working together and (b) negative emotions associated with being teased, criticized, harassed, bullied, ignored, or interrupted.
2. Explain to the student at the beginning of the year that you want to help him or her feel comfortable in class and that you do not want to embarrass him or her.
3. Provide opportunities for the student to have meaningful contact with peers who behave appropriately.
4. Do not permit bullying in the classroom or anywhere else at school.
5. Arrange with other students to have the student chosen early for team games.
6. Pair the student with a buddy for nonacademic activities such as walking down the hall or playing on the playground.
7. Vary peer buddies from time to time and from one activity to another to prevent the student from becoming dependent on one peer.
8. Provide opportunities for the student to interact in a variety of environments where appropriate models and natural cues, stimuli, and reinforcers are available.
9. Teach independence and self-management skills by (a) having the student define a target behavior, identify reinforcers, and use an appropriate self-monitoring method (e.g., a wrist counter or stickers) and (b) gradually reducing the prompts that you give the student and increasing the time the student spends managing his or her own behavior.
10. Encourage the student to play games with other students that require taking turns.
11. Help the student learn to work and play quietly.
12. Help the student learn that losing a game is not always bad.
13. Encourage a socially anxious student to become more involved in class activities. If possible, call on him or her to speak in class. You may need to ask the student's permission ahead of time.
14. Help prepare the student to speak in class. Remind the student that speaking up in class will get easier with practice.
15. Help calm the student with anxiety reactions. Encourage him or her to find a place where he or she can be alone

briefly, listen to soothing music, participate in a favorite activity, exercise, or take prescribed medicines.

Thoughts of Suicide

1. Respond quickly if a student tells you that he or she is thinking about dying or committing suicide. It is important to evaluate the extent of the danger. Students at the highest risk for committing suicide in the very near future have a specific suicide plan, the means to carry out the plan, a time schedule for doing it, and an intention to do it. Signs of suicidal thinking include the following:
   * New or more thoughts of suicide
   * Talking overtly or obliquely about suicide
   * Trying to commit suicide
   * New or worsening signs of depression
   * New or worsening signs of anxiety
   * New or worsening signs of agitation
   * New or worsening signs of irritability
   * Aggressive, angry, or violent behavior
   * New or worsening signs of anger
   * Panic attacks
   * Giving away prized possessions
   * Sudden improvement in mood
   * Acting on dangerous impulses
   * Other unusual changes in behavior
2. If you notice any of the above signs of suicidal thinking, contact the designated person at your school who handles such issues. If there is no designated staff member, contact the student's case manager or, as needed, a school administrator, school counselor or psychologist, or school nurse. Also call the parents immediately (if there is no designated staff member to do this) and, if necessary, call 911.

SUGGESTIONS FOR PROVIDING ACCOMMODATIONS

Accommodations for Testing

1. Allow the student to take practice tests.
2. Explain to the student how the test is scored, particularly for short-answer and essay questions.
3. Provide the student with study guides, including a review of the knowledge and skills to be tested.
4. Avoid complicated language in exam questions.
5. Clearly separate items when spacing them on the exam sheet.
6. In creating fill-in-the blank questions, use direct statements that have a definitive answer, use only one blank per item, and place the blank near the end of the sentence.
7. Eliminate distractions while the student is taking exams; use screens to block out distractions, if needed.
8. Schedule the test at the time of day when the student is most alert.
9. Allow the student with reading or perceptual difficulties to have a proctor read the test items to him or her; to dictate, audio record, or sign answers to a test; or to write on the test itself instead of on the answer sheet.
10. Allow the student with writing difficulties to use a computer with specialized software with spell check, grammar check, and/or speech recognition capability; to have someone

write the answers for him or her; or to use an audio recorder to record his or her answers.
11. Make sure that the student comprehends the test instructions before beginning the test.
12. Make sure that you are testing knowledge and not attention span. For example, if the student is hyperactive, distracted, unable to follow the instructions, fidgeting, and/or squirming, try to calm the student before administering the test; reschedule the test if necessary.
13. Use alternative ways to test the student's mastery of the material. For example, allow the student to complete a project or make a poster instead of taking a test, take a multiple-choice test instead of a short-answer test, answer questions orally instead of in writing, take tests with extended time limits, use special software, or take tests in a separate quiet room with a proctor.
14. Provide constructive feedback after tests.
15. Encourage the student to evaluate his or her performance after the test by asking the student these questions:
    * Did you study the right things?
    * Did you make use of clues on the test?
    * Did you survey the test (particularly for an essay test), and plan your response?
    * Did you use the time allowed effectively?
    * Did you correct your mistakes?
    * Did you have to guess?

Accommodations for Cognitive Issues

1. If the student does not understand the task demands:
   * Provide clear, concrete instructions.
   * Show examples.
   * Model the task yourself.
2. If the student is unable to do an assigned task:
   * Simplify the task.
   * Provide additional training to allow the student to perform the task successfully.
   * Teach each step of the task separately.
   * Use "reverse chaining" to integrate the steps one at a time, beginning with the last step and working back toward the first.
3. If the student has difficulty prioritizing assignments, following a plan, or sequencing and completing steps to accomplish specific tasks:
   * Provide a model for the student of an appropriate sequence or order.
   * Help the student break up the task into manageable steps.
   * Provide examples and specific steps to accomplish the task.
   * Have the student set a clear timeline for accomplishing each step.
4. If the student cannot find the right words to express himself or herself, use structured play and manipulative activities to help the student develop concrete verbal strategies to compensate for word retrieval difficulties.
5. If the student has difficulty finding the main ideas in a paragraph:
   * Provide the student with a copy of the reading material with the main ideas underlined or highlighted.
   * Teach the student how to outline the main ideas.

- Provide the student with an outline of the important points.

6. If the student has difficulty understanding nonverbal cues:
   - Teach the student (e.g., by modeling) to understand nonverbal cues.
   - Have the student practice reading nonverbal cues.

7. If the student has difficulty with a memory task or forgets to do homework:
   - Present the assignment orally and in writing.
   - Combine seeing, saying, writing, and doing.
   - Teach memory techniques such as a study strategy, mnemonics, visualization, oral rehearsal, or repetition.
   - Develop with the student a daily written assignment sheet indicating dates and times when assignments are due.

8. If the student shifts from one uncompleted activity to another or has difficulty completing assignments:
   - List and say the steps needed to complete the assignment.
   - Arrange for the student to have a "study buddy" for each subject area.
   - Tell the student what the requirements are of a completed activity (e.g., "Your math is finished when all six problems are complete and corrected").
   - Instruct the student not to begin the next step until the previous one has been completed.

9. If the student habitually turns in work that is incomplete or of lower quality than what you would expect, have the student show you his or her work before he or she hands it in. If you see no glaring problems, allow the work to be handed in. If you see obvious problems, return the work for revision or completion.

10. If the student has poor self-monitoring skills (e.g., careless errors in spelling, arithmetic, and/or reading):
    - Teach the student specific methods of self-monitoring (e.g., stop-look-listen).
    - Teach the student how to proofread his or her finished work.

11. If the student has poorly developed study skills:
    - Teach the student study skills such as finding the main idea, mapping, outlining, skimming, and summarizing.
    - Teach the student note-taking skills.

12. If the student has difficulty taking tests:
    - Allow extra time.
    - Teach test-taking skills and strategies.
    - Allow the student to be tested orally.
    - Use clear, readable, and uncluttered test forms.
    - Use the test format that the student is most comfortable with.
    - Allow ample space on the test form for the student's responses.
    - Separate the test into sections and allow the sections to be taken over a period of days.
    - Allow the student to take breaks during the test.
    - Use lined sheets for essay or short-answer tests.
    - Provide extra examples for practice.
    - Use fewer questions that measure all required content and skills.
    - Grade separately for content and mechanics.
    - Allow for open book tests unless memorization of content is required.

- Allow for use of a calculator for computations if math reasoning is being tested.
- Give partial credit for answers that are only partly correct.
- Allow the student to use headphones that generate white noise (to reduce auditory distractions).
- Allow the student to take the test in a study carrel.

Accommodations for Behavioral Issues

1. If the student is inattentive, has difficulty sustaining attention to tasks, or is easily distracted by extraneous stimuli:
   - Actively involve the student in the lesson.
   - Give positive reinforcement for following class rules, for attending, and for timely accomplishments.
   - Allow the student to use headphones or to go to a study carrel or other quiet place to complete independent work.
   - Seat the student away from distractions such as windows, air vents, doors, resource areas, and other students who may disrupt the student.
   - Allow the student to take tests in a study carrel.
   - Allow the student to sit in the front of the classroom.
   - Get the student's attention before giving directions ("Look at me while I talk," "Watch my eyes when I speak").
   - Encourage the student to pay attention.
   - Ask the student to repeat the directions for each assignment.
   - Give the student a copy of rules and expectations.
   - Establish a hierarchy of consequences for rule infractions.
   - If possible, have a teacher's aide available who can help the student when you are busy.
   - Give the student short assignments.
   - Allow the student to get up and move.

2. If the student does not begin an assigned task on time:
   - Give the student prompts.
   - Reinforce each instance of initiative that the student shows, however minor.

3. If the student has difficulty sustaining effort and accuracy over time and is not motivated to complete assignments:
   - Make assignments more interesting.
   - Give the student a reward when he or she completes an assignment.
   - Reduce the length of assignments.

4. If the student has difficulty using unstructured time:
   - Structure the time by providing the student with a definite purpose ("The purpose of going to the library is to check out . . .," "The purpose of . . . is . . .").
   - Encourage the student to play games with other students.
   - Encourage the student to join a school group or club.

5. If the student makes poor use of time:
   - Give the student an appropriate hand signal.
   - Give the student a time limit for each assignment.
   - Give positive reinforcement for completing an assignment on time.
   - Encourage the student to use a self-monitoring procedure such as a timer to remind him or her to stay on track.

6. If the student is noncompliant, interrupts class, or violates rules:
   - Seat the student in the front of the room or in close proximity to where you sit.
   - Reward appropriate behavior.
   - Allow the student to use a study carrel.
   - Use a time-out procedure.
   - Ignore the student's behavior.
   - Inform the student that he or she must complete the assigned task, taking as much time as needed.
   - Alternate difficult tasks with easy tasks.

7. If the student talks excessively:
   - Teach the student the hand signals you will use to tell him or her when to talk and when not to talk.
   - Call on the student when it is appropriate and reinforce listening.

8. If the student inappropriately seeks attention:
   - Show the student how to properly gain another's attention.
   - Reward appropriate behavior.

9. If the student is careless about safety:
   - Set firm limits on the student's behavior.
   - Establish specific rules of behavior.

10. If the student argues and fights with peers on the playground:
    - Set firm limits on the student's behavior.
    - Select a buddy with whom the student gets along and encourage the buddy to be with the student during recess.
    - Work with the student in small groups to encourage cooperative behavior.

11. If the student has difficulty remaining seated:
    - Give the student frequent opportunities to get up and move around.
    - Reward the student when he or she remains seated.

12. If the student has difficulty making transitions:
    - Give advance warning of transitions ("Now we are completing the worksheet; next we will . . .").
    - Inform the student about the transition ("You will need . . .").
    - If needed, have a peer accompany the student during transitions.

13. If the student has low self-esteem and makes negative comments about himself or herself:
    - Allow opportunities for the student to show his or her strengths.
    - Give positive recognition to the student when appropriate.
    - Encourage the student to participate in group activities that he or she enjoys.
    - Have a peer spend some positive time with the student.

14. If the student shows signs of depression:
    - Contact the student's case manager.
    - Contact the student's parents or ask someone from the school staff to do so.
    - Encourage the student to stay active, because exercise can help relieve symptoms of depression.

15. If the student shows agitation under pressure or is overwhelmed by a situation:
    - Set up a procedure that allows the student to quickly exit from the situation and go to a safe place.

- Minimize stressful activities.

16. If the student is frequently involved in dangerous activities:
    - Anticipate any potentially dangerous situations, plan for them in advance, and talk to the student about appropriate behavior.
    - Stress stop-look-listen to the student.
    - Pair the student with a responsible peer and rotate the peers so that the student has greater social exposure and does not become dependent on one peer.

17. If the student is frequently messy or sloppy:
    - Teach organizational skills.
    - Provide the student with daily, weekly, and/or monthly assignment sheets.
    - Provide lists of materials needed daily.
    - Have a consistent way for the student to turn in and receive papers.
    - Reduce distractions in the classroom.
    - Reward neat notebooks and papers.
    - Establish a daily routine.
    - Arrange for a peer to help the student with organization.
    - Suggest that the student keep materials in a specific place (e.g., pencils and pens in a pouch).

SUGGESTIONS FOR WORKING WITH PRESCHOOL STUDENTS

1. Help the preschooler become familiar with the surroundings and people before his or her caregiver leaves.
2. Let the preschooler know that you appreciate how distressing it is to be separated from his or her caregiver, but do not dwell on the distress.
3. Never make fun of the preschooler's separation distress.
4. Focus on the positive activities that take place in the preschool and provide a positive activity as soon as possible.
5. If the preschooler is excessively anxious, ask the caregiver to stay until the preschooler is less anxious. Ask the caregiver to comfort the preschooler, especially if you cannot engage the preschooler in an appealing activity.
6. Speak slowly, use short sentences, emphasize key words, limit the length of your conversations, and give one direction at a time.
7. If the preschooler seems reluctant to speak,
   - Do not ask for verbal responses until he or she is more comfortable.
   - Play games, such as "Candy Land," that require minimal talking.
   - Tell the preschooler about your day and see if he or she will follow your example.
   - Kneel down to the preschooler's level when talking with him or her.
8. If the preschooler fails to bring a required object to school (e.g., a pencil), have the preschooler put a picture of the object (the pencil) on the cover of his or her notebook.
9. If the preschooler fails to bring an assignment to school, ask his or her parent to maintain a list of assignments to be completed at home.
10. Don't scold the preschooler if he or she fails to carry out a task.

11. Use pictures and words to provide information, especially when you are preparing a preschooler for a transition to a new activity or helping him or her perform a task that may not be enjoyable.
12. Limit the preschooler's exposure to sensory stressors such as noisy places, crowded places, and disliked food.
13. Encourage the preschooler to play under your supervision with peers who do not have special needs.
14. Incorporate any special interests that the preschooler has into a broader range of activities.

SUGGESTIONS FOR TEACHERS OF STUDENTS WITH DISORDERS OF WRITTEN EXPRESSION

Environmental Modifications

1. Use direct lighting (e.g., seat the child away from windows to avoid glare; place the child's seat with its back to the window to take advantage of natural lighting; reduce the amount of fluorescent lighting; increase natural lighting).
2. Reduce glare by using black print on cream-colored paper, rather than black print on white paper.
3. Minimize visual distractions (such as bright pictures or objects) around material to be copied and around posted directions.
4. Seat the child close to the chalkboard or whiteboard next to you, and keep the chalkboard or whiteboard clean.
5. To highlight information on the board, use different colors of chalk (or markers), draw lines beneath specific information, and use arrows to connect information.

Task Modifications

1. Encourage the child to practice letter formation with different writing implements (e.g., pencil, pen, felt-tipped pens of different types, markers, crayons, chalk, paint).
2. Give the child a slanted writing surface such as an easel or a sling board, if needed, to help with fine-motor control.
3. Use fill-in-the-blank tests, multiple-choice tests, or true-false tests to reduce writing demands; also allow the child to demonstrate mastery of the material orally.
4. Allow the child to highlight words or phrases on worksheets instead of copying the words.
5. Use large, bold type; paper with triple-spaced lines; paper with wide margins; and extra spacing between letters, words, and graphics.
6. To help the child stay within a defined writing space, use handwriting guides or templates, instruct the child to use every other line (if paper with triple lines is not used), or provide a writing space of a different color or shade on the paper.
7. Encourage the child to use his or her preferred method of writing (manuscript or cursive) and writing implements that are easy to grasp.
8. To help the child align numbers, have the child use graph paper, writing one number in each block.
9. Permit the child to begin each assignment early, shorten the length of assignments, reduce the number of assignments, allow additional time for the child to complete assignments as needed, and permit the child to complete homework during study hall periods.

10. To help the child form letters, use raised-line paper, sandpaper letters, or stencils as guides.
11. To help the child organize thoughts and information, use graphic organizers and outlining techniques.
12. Provide the child with both written and oral directions for an assignment (and a tape recording of directions and assignments if needed), and ask the child to repeat the directions orally.
13. Have the child make an assignment calendar book organized by subject.
14. Have available a telephone hotline and/or website that the child can use to review each day's assignments, if needed.

Instructional Modifications

1. Use a multisensory approach to teach letter formation. Have the child talk about the mechanics of writing as he or she writes, have the child write in the air, have the child use dot-to-dot techniques, or have the child write words in sand.
2. Encourage the child to leave a space between letters (and between words) about the size of his or her letter "o."
3. Encourage the child to examine the items in his or her notebooks, folders, and desk daily and to remove unneeded items. Check to see whether this has been done. Provide help as needed.
4. Encourage the child to ask questions about unclear directions.
5. Give the child a list of materials needed for each activity, ask the child to review the list before starting an activity, and assign a peer to check on whether the child has the proper materials for the activity.
6. Teach the child organizational strategies, including making a daily "to do" list and prioritizing assignments.
7. Encourage parents to help their child use organizational strategies at home.
8. With the child, develop a checklist of the steps needed to complete each assignment.
9. Develop short, clear objectives for written assignments; use a specific routine or sequence of tasks to structure the writing process; and gear written assignments to the child's level of readiness.
10. Allow the child to draw a line through errors instead of erasing them.
11. Brainstorm ideas for essay topics and journal entries with the child before he or she begins an assignment.
12. Give the child opportunities to read and write daily (especially to write about everyday activities).
13. Review and post the rules of punctuation and capitalization.
14. Give the child a checklist to help him or her edit drafts.
15. Use oral, pictorial, and written cues to help enrich the child's knowledge of word use and word order.
16. Encourage the child to use a dictionary and a thesaurus, and show him or her how to use these resources if necessary.
17. Encourage the child to make cards (or a personal spelling notebook) with words that he or she frequently misspells and to review these words daily.
18. Analyze the child's writing samples for content, organization, and spelling errors. Give the child prompt

feedback about his or her work, with appropriate reinforcements, and teach the child how to reduce errors.

19. Show the child how to check drafts of his or her written assignments and how to proofread.

20. Encourage the child to practice visualizing how words are spelled.

21. Develop with the child mnemonic strategies to assist in spelling.

22. Grade the content of the child's written assignment and not his or her handwriting, spelling (unless spelling is the focus of the assignment), or organization.

Assistive Technology Modifications

Use software to help the child learn to write more effectively. For example, use software with spelling and grammar checking features, outline/graphic organizer features, voice feedback, word prediction features, and templates to structure different writing tasks.

SUGGESTIONS FOR TEACHERS OF STUDENTS WITH BRAIN INJURY

(Note that the earlier section "Suggestions for Dealing with Various Behavioral Difficulties" applies also to students with brain injury.)

Using Direct Instruction

1. Gain the student's attention before the lesson begins.

2. Maintain a brisk instructional pace, require frequent responses from the student, provide adequate time for the student to process the information and to respond to questions, monitor the student's responses, and give the student feedback about incorrect responses.

3. Review prior lessons as appropriate.

4. State the goals of the current lesson.

5. Demonstrate the skill or strategy being taught.

6. Provide sufficient practice and assistance at each stage of the lesson.

7. Observe the student as he or she performs the new skill or strategy.

8. Have the student apply the new skill or strategy to different problems and situations.

9. Provide a cumulative review of the material before introducing new material.

10. Preview the next lesson for the student.

11. Assign homework related to the current lesson.

Handling Difficulties

1. If the student does not understand a task, provide clear, concrete instructions and, if necessary, model the task yourself.

2. If the student does not begin an assigned task, give the student prompts and reinforce the student's efforts.

3. If the student begins an assigned task but cannot complete it, simplify the task, teach each step of the task, and use "reverse chaining" to integrate the steps one at a time, beginning with the last step and working toward the first.

4. If the student cannot find the right words to express herself or himself, use structured play and manipulative activities. The goal is to help the student develop concrete verbal strategies to compensate for word retrieval difficulties.

5. If the student is not motivated to perform a task, try to find a way to make the task more interesting; also, give the student rewards when he or she completes the task.

6. If the student does not comply with assigned tasks, alternate difficult tasks with easy ones.

7. If the student complains about a task, inform the student that he or she should try to complete the task, taking as much time as he or she needs.

8. If the student refuses to do a task, use a time-out procedure.

9. If the student is careless about safety, set firm limits on the student's behavior and establish specific rules of behavior.

10. If the student argues and fights with peers on the playground, set firm limits on the student's behavior, select a buddy with whom the student gets along, encourage the buddy to be with the student during recess, and work with the student in small groups to encourage cooperative behavior.

11. If the student forgets to do homework, develop with the student a daily written assignment sheet indicating dates and times when assignments are due.

Working with the Family and Monitoring Progress

1. Involve the family in the educational program.

2. Inform the family of the goals that you have set and the methods that you are using to meet the goals.

3. Update the family about the student's progress.

4. Make sure that knowledgeable staff members are available to answer the family's questions.

5. Monitor the student's progress in order to make needed revisions in the educational program.

SUGGESTIONS FOR TEACHERS OF STUDENTS WITH ATTENTION DEFICIT/HYPERACTIVITY DISORDER (ADHD)

Rearranging Classroom Layout

1. Seat the student near your desk and preferably with quiet students, in order to reduce distractions, better monitor the student's behavior, and apply behavior management techniques. You may need to experiment to find the best seating arrangement.

2. Offer the student a study carrel if carrels are available. It is best to allow other children to use carrels as well so that the student with ADHD is not singled out.

3. Put desks in traditional rows or a large U-shaped arrangement, rather than the currently popular grouping into four, five, or six desks facing each other in "pods," which may not be ideal for children with ADHD.

Modifying Teaching Techniques

1. Use directed teaching with individual attention to improve learning and behavior. Use highly structured, step-by-step methods, with ample opportunities for practice. Check the student's understanding of the information that you presented. Maintain appropriate eye contact with the student.

2. Use multi-sensory approaches and stimulating tasks to help the student learn the material. Supplement traditional lectures with visual aids (diagrams, illustrations, graphic organizers), video clips, demonstrations, and small-group

activities; use physical movement and hands-on activities; use computers, calculators, and tape recorders. Teach the student to actively visualize information while listening and reading.

3. Modify work demands to increase the student's success rate. For example, assign fewer problems for in-class and homework assignments, allow the student to turn in half of an assignment if he or she meets a specified criterion (such as 90% accuracy on the completed part), divide tasks into manageable segments, set task priorities, establish fixed work periods, intersperse high-interest activities with regular work activities to maintain motivation, use novel tasks, alternate activities involving sitting and moving, promote consistent study habits, and promote a sense of responsibility for completing tasks.

4. Modify instructions to improve the student's attention. Use short and simple instructions, slow the rate at which instructions are presented, demonstrate what is to be done, alert the student to critical information by using key phrases (e.g., "This is important," "Listen carefully"), encourage the student to ask for instructions to be repeated if he or she doesn't understand them, and confirm that the student understands instructions before proceeding to the task.

5. If necessary, before the start of an activity, remind the student about behaviors that are expected during the activity.

6. Establish peer tutoring programs to facilitate the student's learning. Pair the student with a student who does not have ADHD and who has well-developed social, behavioral, or academic skills and will not exploit the student with ADHD.

Increasing Student Motivation

1. Increase the student's motivation by modeling enthusiasm and interest in the lesson.

2. To reinforce attending behavior, set a timer, alarm clock, or tape recorder to make a sound at random intervals and give the student reinforcement—such as verbal praise, points, tokens, free choice of an activity, or access to a classroom computer—if he or she is attending when the sound occurs.

Implementing Organizational Strategies

1. Suggest organizational strategies to help the student complete his or her assignments and better control his or her behavior. For example, encourage the student to use assignment logs; memory and study strategies; a notebook with dividers to separate sections for lecture notes, assignments, appointments, phone numbers, and so forth; color-coded folders to organize assignments for reading, mathematics, social studies, science, and other subjects; highlighters and colored pens; a checklist of the day's activities placed on the desk; and self-monitoring procedures.

2. Ensure that the student knows the homework assignments before he or she leaves school. Give the student a homework assignment sheet, post assignments in the classroom and have the student copy them in his or her notebook, post assignments on a classroom website or on the school's website, have the student complete at least one item of each homework task before leaving school, or encourage the student to e-mail the list of assignments to his or her home (if the school provides access to e-mail).

3. Establish firm class routines to help the student organize his or her day. Give the student a schedule indicating what will be done during each class period. Schedule academic subjects in the morning and nonacademic subjects in the afternoon, because the attention span of students with ADHD tends to worsen over the course of the day. Explain in advance when any change in the routine will be needed. Make the transition from one activity to another in a brief and well-organized manner.

4. Establish clear rules and guidelines for appropriate behavior. Teach these rules as needed, remind students of these classroom rules, and provide examples of students who are following the rules.

Using Alternative Testing Procedures and Offering Counseling and Special Programs

1. Use alternative ways to test the student's mastery of material. For example, allow the student to complete a project or make a poster instead of taking a test, take a multiple-choice test instead of a short-answer test, answer questions orally instead of in writing, take tests without the usual time limits, use special software, or take tests in a quiet room.

2. Encourage the student to seek counseling or to enroll in a special program (e.g., a social skills training program, an anger management or conflict management program, an organizational skills training group, a study skills training program, or a coaching program) if the student appears likely to benefit from these services. In a coaching program, an adult coach helps the student with ADHD develop better time management and study skills and organize assignments into meaningful, manageable tasks.

SUGGESTIONS FOR TEACHERS OF STUDENTS WITH VISUAL IMPAIRMENTS

The following suggestions should be implemented only if they are (a) in the student's IEP or 504 plan, (b) approved by the student's case manager, (c) approved by the student's teacher of the visually impaired (TVI) or orientation and mobility (O&M) specialist, or (d) approved by a school consultant for students with a visual impairment. Even for students with a visual impairment who do not have an IEP or 504 plan, it would be helpful to consult with a TVI or O&M specialist or a school consultant for students with visual impairments before implementing the suggestions. Check with your TVI or O&M specialist about how to obtain needed special equipment and for additional information about working with students who are visually impaired.

General Suggestions

1. If the student has a functional vision assessment report and/or a learning media assessment report, review the report(s) carefully. Consult with the student's case manager and/or TVI or O&M specialist if anything is unclear.

2. Check to be sure that the student is wearing (or using) any prescribed vision aids.

3. Help the student make sense of all the information that he or she may be receiving simultaneously.
4. Read aloud any material that you write on the chalkboard, show on a transparency, or present on a handout.
5. Ask a student without a visual impairment, a volunteer, or a paid reader to assist the student with texts, other materials, and library readings.
6. Encourage the student to take his or her own notes.
7. Use an auditory or tactile signal where a visual signal is normally used.
8. Allow more time for activities as needed.
9. Order in advance any needed specialized texts or other reading materials through the Talking Book Service, Recording for the Blind and Dyslexic, or other services or organizations.

Modifying Your Speech

1. State your name when you begin to talk to the student, and encourage other students and staff members to do the same.
2. Don't hesitate to use words like "see" and "look," as they are part of our vocabulary.
3. Give the student clear descriptions and explanations of class materials (e.g., charts, pictures, diagrams), and repeat them as often as needed.
4. Use descriptive words such as "straight," "forward," and "left" in relation to the student's body orientation.
5. Be specific in giving directions; avoid the use of vague terms such as "over there," "here," and "this."
6. Spell out new or technical words.
7. Describe in detail anything pertinent that happens in the classroom and anything you write on the chalkboard.
8. Use an overhead projector, chalkboard, graphs, or slides as you would normally, but provide more detailed oral descriptions, possibly supplemented with thermoforms where appropriate. (A *thermoform* is a molded plastic sheet that has raised line "pictures," diagrams, or graphs and, in addition, may have Braille labeling and dark print overprinting of the picture, diagram, or graph.)

Dealing with Environmental and Mobility Considerations

1. Seat the student close to the front of the room or in the part of the room that has the best light.
2. Offer your arm to the student if he or she asks you to do so. Tell the student whether he or she needs to step up or step down, let him or her know whether the door is on the left or right, and warn him or her of any possible hazards.
3. If the student has a guide dog, do not pet or touch the dog or allow other students or staff to do so. Guide dogs are working animals. It can be hazardous for the student if the dog is distracted.
4. Encourage the student to walk around the classroom and to learn to navigate the outdoor areas of the school.
5. Reduce excessive noise, both inside and outside the classroom.
6. Consider safety issues inside the classroom (e.g., cords, placement of furniture, steps) and outside the classroom (e.g., steps, placement of equipment, streets and sidewalks, and street crossings).

7. Keep cupboard doors completely closed (unless they are the sliding type) and room doors completely closed or open.
8. Have all students push their chairs in when they get up from their desks.
9. Place a strip of high-contrast colored tape on the floor before a ramp or step or other place where there is a change in surface level.
10. Provide work and storage space to accommodate any special equipment that the student has (e.g., large print books, Braille materials, optical devices).
11. Orient the student to the lunchroom, auditorium, gym, playground, and other facilities (or ask the O&M specialist to do so).

Implementing Strategies for Paper Text, Electronic Text, Auditory Access, and Tactile Access

Use the most appropriate assistive technology to help the student, as prescribed in the IEP or 504 plan and/or by a TVI or O&M specialist. Examples of assistive technology and electronic text strategies follow.

STRATEGIES FOR PAPER TEXT

1. *Adapted writing tools*, such as felt-tip pens and soft-lead pencils, are specialized tools useful for writing. A *low vision pen* has a special felt tip that produces highly visible lines of bold black ink that dries instantly
2. *Adapted paper* provides additional visual or tactile feedback to the writer. Examples include dark-line paper, Braille paper, colored paper, raised-line paper, and signature guides (plastic guides placed over an area that requires a signature, such as the signature line on checks).
3. *Video magnifiers* are closed-circuit televisions (CCTVs), with adjustable print size, color combinations, brightness, and contrast, that "project a magnified image of printed text or handwriting onto a video monitor or TV screen" (Special Education Technology British Columbia, 2008, p. 8). Models include flex-arm camera models, portable hand-held camera models, head-mounted display models, electronic pocket models, and digital imaging systems (Presley & D'Andrea, 2008).
4. A *manual Brailler* is a six-key machine, with keys corresponding to dot positions, that enables users to write Braille text on inserted paper. It is analogous to a manual typewriter.
5. A *Braille slate* is a hinged device made of metal or plastic; a *Braille stylus* is used to punch dots into paper inserted between the parts of the slate.
6. *Portable hand-held electronic magnifiers* are used to improve ability to read print and see small objects.
7. *Portable telescopes* are used to locate distant targets (e.g., scan a shopping center to find a particular store).
8. *Optical character recognition (OCR) software* allows a printed document to be scanned by a camera and converted into digitized characters, which then can be spoken aloud by a synthesizer.
9. *Large print* facilitates reading for students with some useful vision.
10. *Reading stands* are useful to promote the proper placement of reading materials and healthy posture.

11. *Increased spacing between items* and *reduced number of items per page or line* allow for easier reading.
12. *Highlighting* of key words or phrases in written materials gives additional cues to the student.
13. *Directed lighting on reading materials* helps to prevent glare and facilitates reading.
14. *Colored overlays* help to reduce glare for students with some useful vision.
15. A *large-print calculator* has large numbers and symbols on the buttons and a large readout.
16. A *talking calculator* sounds out answers.
17. A *Cranmer modified abacus* is an abacus that has been modified for individuals who are blind, with round beads and nonslip backing.
18. A *Brannan Cubarithm Slate* consists of a 16-by-16 grid of square cups. Plastic cubes with Braille markings are placed in the square cups, allowing the student to enter and manipulate numeric symbols.
19. A *hat or visor* helps to decrease the glare from overhead lights.
20. *Braille keyboard labels* are labels with Braille letters that can be placed on individual computer or typewriter keys. Alternatively, Braille dots can be glued directly on keys.
21. *Tactile locators* are stickers or other materials that can be placed in strategic spots on a keyboard to identify important keys and facilitate positioning for touch typing.

STRATEGIES FOR ELECTRONIC TEXT

1. *Word-processing software with speech* (*screenreader*) is useful for converting text on screen into speech output.
2. *Word-processing software with screen magnification* is useful for enlarging type and graphics and for enhancing color on computer screens.
3. *Word-processing software with speech and screen magnification* is useful for tracking words or sentences as they are read aloud, enlarging type and graphics, and enhancing color.
4. An *electronic Brailler* is a six-key machine, with keys corresponding to dot positions, that enables users to write and edit Braille text.
5. An *electronic Braille notetaker* is a small, portable device with either a Braille keyboard or a QWERTY keyboard for input and a speech synthesizer and Braille display for output.
6. *Word-processing software with refreshable Braille* has a hardware template (either a separate component or part of an integrated system) that displays Braille as it is being written. As each letter is typed, round-tip plastic pins corresponding to Braille dots pop up on the template to form Braille letters. The Braille display is refreshable because it can be altered as the text is changed and advanced letter by letter or line by line.
7. *Word-processing software with speech and refreshable Braille* is the same device as above with the addition of speech capabilities.
8. *Braille software translators* and *Braille embossers* enable users to print high-quality Braille documents from a computer. Software converts the screen display to Braille before it is sent to the Braille embosser to be printed. Braille embossers typically have blunt pins that punch dots into special heavy (100-pound-weight) paper.

STRATEGIES FOR AUDITORY ACCESS

1. *Digital and CD recorders and players* are useful for dictating reports, comments, and other material.
2. *Portable reading devices* are useful for downloading books, which are then read aloud in a synthesized voice by the devices.
3. A *talking global positioning system* (*GPS*) is a satellite-based navigation system that calculates the user's exact location anywhere in the world and then gives directions to one or more destinations; it can speak or display directions in Braille with special additional software.
4. *Other talking devices*, in addition to the ones described under Strategies for Electronic Text, include MP3 players, talking dictionaries, personal digital assistants, and talking compasses.

STRATEGIES FOR TACTILE ACCESS

1. Supplement auditory instructions with tactile presentation, as needed.
2. Use tactile graphic images, such as maps, charts, graphs, diagrams, and illustrations presented in a raised format (paper or thermoform), to convey information through the fingers instead of the eyes. The graphic material usually will need to be presented along with word descriptions.
3. Provide direct experiences for the student with actual objects. For example, let the student touch various objects in the room, and name the objects as he or she touches them. Help the student learn the objects' functions through touch.

Modifying Examinations

1. Present examinations in a form that takes into account the student's needs, following the IEP or 504 plan and recommendations of the TVI.
2. Use large print for test questions or present the test in Braille, if needed, and allow answers to be written in Braille, if needed.
3. Allow the student to write his or her answers directly on the test booklet rather than filling in "bubbles" on an answer sheet.
4. Be sure that the student uses any needed special equipment to take exams, such as a magnifier or magnifying machine.
5. Consider presenting the test questions orally and allowing the answers to be given orally.
6. Allow the student to digitally record answers for later verbatim transcription.
7. Allow a scribe to record the student's answers.
8. Administer the test in a location with minimal distractions, such as a study carrel.
9. Administer the test in a small group or individually.
10. Allow the student more time to complete the examination.

Teaching Independent Living Skills

Depending on the student's age, the skills he or she needs to become independent may include maintaining personal hygiene, feeding himself or herself, dressing, grooming, cooking, shopping, orienting himself or herself, and maintaining mobility. Here are some suggestions for teaching these independent living skills:

1. Recognize that the student may be hesitant to explore because of fear of the unknown, and your job is to diminish his or her fear.
2. Don't fall into the habit of doing everything for the student.
3. Give the student the time that he or she needs to complete tasks, remembering that it probably will take longer for him or her to complete tasks than it does for students who are sighted.
4. Remember that the student is likely to take longer to develop self-help skills, because these skills are often learned by watching others.
5. Encourage the student to follow proper social conventions when speaking to another person, such as turning toward the other person, maintaining face-to-face contact, and maintaining appropriate distance.
6. Encourage the student to play with other students. Remember that the student may have some difficulty interacting with other students because he or she misses subtle cues and facial expressions that are helpful in social interactions.
7. Include the student in all class activities unless the activity is inappropriate for the student.

SUGGESTIONS FOR TEACHERS OF STUDENTS WITH A HEARING LOSS

The following suggestions should be implemented only if they are (a) in the student's IEP or 504 plan, (b) approved by the student's case manager, (c) approved by the student's teacher of the deaf and hard of hearing (DHH), or (d) approved by a school consultant for deaf and hard of hearing students. If the student has a speech and language pathologist (SLP), consult with the SLP as well. Even for students with a hearing impairment who do not have an IEP or 504 plan, it would be helpful to consult with a DHH teacher, SLP, or school consultant for students with hearing impairments before implementing the suggestions.

1. Make sure that the student uses any appropriate assistive technology devices that have been recommended for him or her and that they are in good working order. In addition to hearing aids, consider (in consultation with a specialist) technology such as computer-aided realtime translation (CART), which uses a stenotype machine with a phonetic keyboard and special software. A computer translates the phonetic symbols into English captions almost instantaneously.
2. Allow the student to use an audio amplification device, in addition to a hearing aid, if needed to increase his or her ability to hear more clearly, especially when there is a great deal of ambient noise.
3. Seat the student close to you and use, as needed, an amplified microphone or sign language. Be sure that the student can read your lips (speech reading). Do not have the student sit near a projector or other equipment that makes noise or in a heavy traffic area.
4. Illuminate the room adequately so that the student can clearly see your face and hands (and those of the interpreter, if there is one).
5. Make sure that lights do not shine in the student's eyes or create a glare on the materials.

6. Avoid standing in front of windows or light sources that may silhouette your profile and hinder visual cues.
7. Present only one source of visual information at a time. Don't talk while the child's attention is directed elsewhere.
8. Arrange through the IEP team, 504 plan team, or DHH teacher to use a sign language interpreter, if needed.
9. Use captioned films, videos, and DVDs. If captioning is not feasible, arrange through the IEP team, 504 plan team, or DHH teacher for an interpreter to sign the audio portion of the film, video, or DVD. If possible, make the material available to the interpreter at least a day before your presentation.
10. Look at the student when you speak to him or her, and be sure that the student, in turn, is watching you (or the interpreter, if there is one). Keep your hands away from your face when speaking. Be sure that no obstructions block the student's view of your lips.
11. Also keep your face visible to the entire class when speaking before the class, repeating questions asked by other students, and summarizing classroom discussions.
12. Do not chew gum, put your hand on your chin, cover your mouth, or do anything else that might impede speech reading.
13. Maintain a pleasant facial expression.
14. Speak distinctly and slowly, without exaggerating or distorting your lip movements, particularly if the student has some hearing ability or speech-reading ability.
15. Use short, simple sentences.
16. Emphasize key words in your phrases.
17. If you need to repeat yourself, rephrase if at all possible.
18. Do not turn away from the student in the middle of a sentence.
19. Arrange students in a semicircle or circle for group discussions.
20. Make sure that only one student speaks at a time during group discussions, and gesture toward the speaker so that the student can see who is talking.
21. Maximize the use of visual materials.
22. Use written handouts listing assignments, due dates, exam dates, changes in the class schedule, dates of special events, and similar information.
23. Provide an outline of the lesson or activity to give to the student in advance.
24. Write all homework assignments, class instructions, and procedural changes on the chalkboard or whiteboard.
25. Do not talk while writing on the chalkboard or whiteboard.
26. Eliminate background noises. Sounds taken for granted and normally ignored by individuals who can hear are amplified by a hearing aid and may interfere with the hearing of a student who is hard of hearing.
27. Supplement audible alarm systems with simple visual alarms such as flashing lights.

SUGGESTIONS FOR TEACHERS OF STUDENTS WITH AN AUTISM SPECTRUM DISORDER

Engineering the Classroom

1. Adopt strategies for organizing the environment, such as labeling objects and containers; posting signs, schedules, lists, charts, calendars, and outlines; and using choice boards. Give the student a visual calendar for use at

school and at home so that the student knows about upcoming events and activities.

2. Give the student a daily visual schedule so that he or she knows what will be going on in the classroom. Laminate the daily schedule and place it on the student's desk or in the front of his or her binder. Mark any changes directly on the schedule, using water-soluble markers or sticky notes.

3. Use visual aids in the classroom, such as a large carpet or tape on the floor to mark the area for reading. Color-code the classroom materials, books, workstations, and other materials used for a particular subject by marking them all with the same color. Place the student's picture on materials that have been specifically chosen for him or her.

4. Reduce environmental distractions by placing the student away from high traffic spots (e.g., away from the classroom door and the teacher's desk).

5. Make sure that the environment is consistently and clearly structured, and use consistent classroom routines. For example, let the student know where things belong, what is expected of him or her in specific situations, and what to anticipate.

Teaching and Providing Directives

1. Speak slowly, use short sentences, and emphasize key words.

2. Limit the length of your conversations.

3. Provide one directive at a time.

4. Give written or visual directions or cues whenever possible to accompany oral directions. Use pictures and words to provide information, especially when you are preparing the student for transitions to new activities.

5. Incorporate any special interests that the student has into classroom activities.

6. Teach an augmentative communication system (e.g., a sign language or picture communication system) to a student who is nonverbal.

7. Use visual aids to convey information about classroom rules, to present directions for tasks and activities, to encourage social development, to manage challenging behaviors, to help develop self-control, and to teach abstract ideas.

8. Vary tasks to prevent boredom, take breaks as needed, and alternate preferred tasks with less preferred tasks.

9. Use age-appropriate reinforcers that are meaningful to the student, such as getting time to talk to a favorite staff member, making a trip to the cafeteria, going for a walk, playing with a favorite object, playing in water, performing a favorite routine, spending time with objects that provide specific sensory stimulation, or sitting at a window. Remember to change reinforcers regularly, as it is normal for students to cease being motivated by items or activities that were once reinforcing.

10. Use the student's special interests as a motivator to help him or her learn new material. For example, if a student loves trains, place a train sticker at the top of his or her worksheet or use train-related information in directions or assignments.

11. Establish connections between the student's interests and areas of study. For example, if the student is fascinated

with baseball, have him or her read a biography of a famous baseball player and write a report. Math skills could be taught by having the student look at baseball statistics.

12. Set aside specific times during the day for the student to discuss his or her interests. This discussion time can be included on the student's visual schedule.

13. Use modeling, physical prompts, visual cues, and reinforcement to encourage attention, imitation, communication, and interaction.

14. Introduce unfamiliar tasks in a familiar environment when possible.

15. Modify tests and assignments as needed. For example, allow additional time on tests, reduce written homework assignments, allow the student to dictate his or her work to a designated individual, modify testing arrangements (e.g., test in a separate room, allow oral instead of written answers, and use multiple-choice questions instead of essay questions).

16. Before repeating a question, give the student enough time to respond, especially if he or she has auditory processing difficulties. If you are not sure how long to wait, count slowly to five.

17. Use literal—rather than metaphorical or figurative—language, except when you are specifically working to increase the student's comprehension of figurative language, such as idioms, multi-meaning words, jokes, and teasing.

18. If the student is staring off into space or doodling, don't assume that he or she is not listening; doodling or staring may actually help the student focus on what you are presenting. Simply ask the student a question to find out whether he or she is listening.

19. If the student experiences difficulties focusing on the material, allow the student to record lectures, have a copy of another student's notes, or sit in a location where distractions are minimal.

20. To teach self-management skills, have the student define a target behavior, identify reinforcers, and use an appropriate self-monitoring method (e.g., a wrist counter or stickers). Also facilitate the student's independence by gradually reducing prompts and increasing the time the student spends managing his or her own behavior.

Organizing the Student's Material

1. Teach the student how to design a color-coding system for his or her daily planner to help keep track of due dates for assignments and activities. Use the same color-coding system for the various subjects as you do for material within the classroom (see "Engineering the Classroom" above).

2. Give the student a written checklist to keep him or her focused and "on task." Encourage the student to complete each step listed on the checklist in sequential order.

3. Modify worksheets as needed. For example, you may need to include fewer problems per sheet; larger, highly visual space for responding; and a box next to each question to be checked when the question has been completed.

4. Have the student make an "Assignments to Be Completed" folder as well as a "Completed Assignments" folder.

Addressing Sensory Considerations

1. Limit the student's exposure to auditory distractions such as noisy fans, loudspeakers, and rooms.
2. Eliminate visual distractions such as excessive light, movement, reflection, or background patterns. Have the student keep only necessary items on his or her desk.
3. Eliminate textures that seem to be aversive.
4. Make sure that the temperature in the room is appropriate.

Managing Stress

1. Watch for signs of anxiety and stress due to sensory or emotional overload. For example, notice if the student puts his or her hands over his or her ears, plugs his or her ears, squeezes a body part, or engages in repetitive behaviors, like rocking or hand/finger twisting.
2. Keep in mind that the student may engage in disruptive behavior as a reaction to aversive or overwhelming sensory stimuli. For example, the ticking of a clock can seem like the beating of a drum, the breeze from an open window can feel like a tremendous gust, the smell of food from the cafeteria can make the student feel sick, and the bright sunshine pouring through the windows may be almost blinding to the student. This sensory overload may make focusing difficult and frustrating. To cope with the frustration, the student might choose to tap a pencil on a desk repeatedly (or engage in some other disruptive behavior). What appears to be disruptive behavior may be a way for the student to cope with the sensory overload.
3. Create a "quiet space" where the student can go if he or she has an anxiety reaction, in order to decrease sensory overload and increase self-calming. The quiet space should be a specified location with objects that are calming to the student, such as Koosh balls, books, a bean bag chair, squeeze toys, a weighted blanket, headphones, or a music player. The student can listen to soothing music, do a favorite activity, exercise, or take prescribed medicines. For the student who moves to and from various classrooms, the use of a "home base" classroom as a safe place to go when he or she feels the need for calming is suggested.
4. Have a "fiddle basket" containing small items (e.g., small Koosh balls, Bend Bands, FiddleLinks, and clothespins) for the student to use when he or she is anxious.
5. Teach the student relaxation techniques to use when he or she is anxious, such as "Take a big breath" or "Count to 10." These steps could initially be written down on visual cue cards for the student to carry with him or her and refer to as needed.
6. Always remain calm and help the student regain his or her composure.
7. Ask an occupational therapist to perform a sensory inventory assessment, in which sensory aversions and interests are catalogued, and then to recommend activities that will compensate for the student's aversions and self-calming strategies based on the student's interests.
8. Use a color-coding system to help the student manage his or her behavior. For example, use a green card when the student is behaving appropriately, a yellow card when the student is behaving in a disruptive manner, and a red card when the student should leave the room.

9. If the student repeats the same question over and over, despite having heard the answer to the question, write the answer on a sheet of paper. Then when the student repeats the question, point to the paper with the written answer. This will help you avoid becoming involved in a repetitive verbal ritual.
10. If the student is fearful, remember that it may be because he or she is having difficulty controlling his or her environment or because the environment seems unpredictable. For example, the student may have difficulty with transitions (such as changing class periods, going to or from recess, or changing clothes for gym in the locker room) and get "stuck." To help the student, provide an environment with clear structure and routine. Post his or her daily schedule in an accessible area of the room, discuss upcoming activities, role play, and/or allow the student to transition a few minutes earlier or later than the other students.
11. Teach the student how to maintain eye contact and work at his or her pace, but don't insist that the student maintain eye contact with you.

Promoting Social Interaction and Play

1. Provide opportunities for meaningful contact with peers who have appropriate social behavior. Do not permit bullying in the classroom or in any other place at school, arrange team games so that the student is not always chosen last, and form cooperative learning groups in which the student's special skills are useful and appreciated by the other students.
2. If the student is awkward or poorly coordinated, try to steer him or her to activities on the playground that he or she may like.
3. Encourage the student to play with other students who do not have disabilities, including playing board games and card games, under your supervision.
4. Pair the student with a buddy for unstructured activities such as walking down the hall or playing on the playground.
5. Vary peer buddies from time to time and from one activity to another to prevent the student from becoming dependent on one peer and the buddy from feeling overwhelmed.
6. Provide opportunities for the student to interact in a variety of natural environments that offer appropriate models, natural cues and stimuli, and functional reinforcers.
7. Help the student learn how to take turns while playing games with other students. Also teach the student how to take turns in social conversations.
8. Help the student learn that losing a game is not always bad.

Promoting Acceptance

1. Use classroom situations to teach all students in the class about feelings and interpersonal relations, including positive emotions associated with sharing, taking turns, and working together and negative emotions associated with being teased, ignored, interrupted, rejected for a team, and criticized.
2. Help the student learn about appropriate social interactions. For example, discuss with the student how

words and actions affect other people. The student may need to be taught to recognize the effects of his or her actions on others. If he or she says something offensive, let him or her know that "words hurt, just like getting punched in the arm." Encourage the student to stop and think how another person might feel before he or she acts or speaks. However, because of possible idiosyncratic behavior and narrow interests, the student may have difficulty talking to others.

3. Recognize that the student has gifts as well as limitations and, while the student may be a challenge, he or she has much to contribute to society.

SUGGESTIONS FOR TEACHERS FOR DEALING WITH A POSSIBLE SUBSTANCE-INDUCED DISORDER

1. Maintain good communication with your student.
2. Be alert to signs of a substance-induced disorder (excessive alcohol or drug use), such as the following:

PHYSICAL AND HEALTH CHANGES

- Bloodshot eyes, extremely large or small pupils, watery eyes, blank stares, or involuntary movements of the eyeball (*nystagmus*)
- Deterioration in physical appearance, rapid weight loss, unexplained injuries such as cuts or bruises, unusual breath or body odors, slurred speech, unsteady gait, tremors, fast heart rate, extremely dry mouth, nausea or vomiting, complaints of *tinnitus* (ringing in the ears) or *paresthesias* (sensations such as prickling, burning), dramatic fluctuations in appetite
- Chronic coughing, sniffing, or black phlegm
- Needle tracks on various parts of the body or perforated nasal septum
- Skin boils, skin sores, or nasal bleeding

EMOTIONAL CHANGES

- Extremes of energy and tiredness, sleep difficulties or excessive sleep, or fatigue
- Changes in social activities or relationships with friends, ranging from extreme social confidence to lack of interest in things that used to provide pleasure
- Poor judgment
- Irresponsibility with money
- Restlessness, manic behavior, or panic attacks
- Feelings of depression, anxiety, or euphoria
- Emotional lability, decreased impulse control, violent behavior, or hyperactivity
- Marked distortion in sense of time, feelings of *depersonalization* (a sense that things around you are not real or that you're observing yourself from outside your body), paranoia, delusions, visual distortions, or hallucinations

FAMILY AND SCHOOL CHANGES

- Starting arguments with family members, breaking family rules, missing curfews, or withdrawing from interactions with family members (e.g., spending time alone behind closed doors)
- Decreased interest in school, negative attitudes toward school, drop in school grades, increased absences from school, or disciplinary problems in school

3. Notify the person at your school who is responsible for receiving reports from teachers about students who may have a substance-induced disorder.

SUGGESTIONS FOR TEACHERS OF STUDENTS WHO ARE GIFTED AND TALENTED

1. Include advanced content for grade level.
2. Encourage the student's enthusiasm and persistence.
3. Consider the student's learning style.
4. Avoid unnecessary repetition and drill.
5. Avoid redundancy.
6. Provide many opportunities for the student to ask questions.
7. Include critical-thinking and problem-solving activities.
8. Provide opportunities for the student to direct activities.
9. Encourage independent study.
10. Allow sufficient time for open-ended discussion.
11. Encourage creative-thinking skills, including fluency, flexibility, originality, and elaboration.
12. Involve the student in the design of lessons.
13. Use advanced technology when appropriate.
14. Encourage the student to develop and employ technological skills.
15. Give the student academic challenges so that he or she develops a strong sense that achievement comes with effort.
16. Encourage the student to pursue traditional as well as nontraditional goals and to select from a range of available options.

REFERENCES

Barkley, R. A. (1998). *Attention-deficit hyperactivity disorder: A handbook for diagnosis and treatment* (2nd ed.). New York, NY: Guilford.

Baron, I. S. (2000). Clinical implications and practical applications of child neuropsychological evaluations. In K. O. Yeates, M. D. Ris, & H. G. Taylor (Eds.), *Pediatric neuropsychology: Research, theory, and practice* (pp. 446–452). New York, NY: Guilford.

Busch, B. (1993). Attention deficits: Current concepts, controversies, management, and approaches to classroom instruction. *Annals of Dyslexia, 43*(1), 5–25.

Cardman, S. (1994). *More classroom tips for teachers of ADD ADHD students*. Retrieved from http://newideas.net/book/export/html/163

Center for Technology and Education. (1997). *Adapted pencils to computers: Strategies for improving writing*. Retrieved from http://cte.jhu.edu/adaptedpencils.pdf

Child Development Institute. (2010). *Suggested classroom accommodations for children with ADD & learning disabilities*. Retrieved from http://childdevelopmentinfo.com/learning/teacher.shtml

Cohen, S. B. (1991). Adapting educational programs for students with head injuries. *Journal of Head Trauma Rehabilitation, 6*(1), 56–63.

Dawson, P., & Guare, R. (1998). *Coaching the ADHD student*. North Tonawanda, NY: Multi-Health Systems.

DePompei, R., & Blosser, J. L. (1987). Strategies for helping head-injured children successfully return to school. *Language, Speech, and Hearing Services in Schools, 18*(4), 292–300.

DuPaul, G. J., Ervin, R. A., Hook, C. L., & McGoey, K. E. (1998). Peer tutoring for children with attention deficit hyperactivity disorder: Effects on classroom behavior and academic performance. *Journal of Applied Behavior Analysis, 31*(4), 579–592.

DuPaul, G. J., & Hennington, P. N. (1993). Peer tutoring effects on the classroom performance of children with ADHD. *School Psychology Review, 22*(1), 134–143.

DuPaul, G. J., & Stoner, G. (2003). *ADHD in the schools* (2nd ed.). New York, NY: Guilford.

Florida Department of Education. (2005). *Accommodations and modifications for students with disabilities in career education and adult general education.* Retrieved from http://cpt.fsu.edu/ESE/pdf/k12_05-59a.pdf

Howard, M. E. (1988). Behavior management in the acute care rehabilitation setting. *Journal of Head Trauma Rehabilitation, 3*(3), 14–22.

Johnson, J. A. (n.d.). *Students with Aspergers syndrome: Tips for teachers and parents.* Retrieved from http://hubpages.com/hub/Students-with-Aspergers-Syndrome-Tips-for-Teachers-and-Parents

Lerner, J. W. (1997). Attention deficit disorder. In J. W. Lloyd, D. J. Kameenui, & D. Chard (Eds.), *Issues in educating students with disabilities* (pp. 27–44). Mahwah, NJ: Erlbaum.

Martin, D. A. (1988). Children and adolescents with traumatic brain injury: Impact on the family. *Journal of Learning Disabilities, 21*(8), 464–470. doi:10.1177/002221948802100803

Mesibov, G. B., Shea, V., & Adams, L. W. (2001). *Understanding Asperger syndrome and high functioning autism.* Norwell, MA: Kluwer Plenum.

Myles, B. S. (2005). *Children and youth with Asperger syndrome: Strategies for success in inclusive settings.* Thousand Oaks, CA: Corwin Press.

National Dissemination Center for Children with Disabilities. (2010). *Autism spectrum disorders.* Retrieved from http://nichcy.org/wp-content/uploads/docs/fs1.pdf

National Dissemination Center for Children with Disabilities. (2011a). *Intellectual disability.* Retrieved from http://nichcy.org/wp-content/uploads/docs/fs8.pdf

National Dissemination Center for Children with Disabilities. (2011b). *Learning disabilities (LD).* Retrieved from http://nichcy.org/wp-content/uploads/docs/fs7.pdf

National Dissemination Center for Children with Disabilities. (2012a). *Attention-deficit/hyperactivity disorder(AD/HD).* Retrieved from http://nichcy.org/wp-content/uploads/docs/fs19.pdf

National Dissemination Center for Children with Disabilities. (2012b). *Traumatic brain injury.* Retrieved from http://nichcy.org/wp-content/uploads/docs/fs18.pdf

Packer, L. E. (2002). *Accommodating students with mood lability: Depression and bipolar disorder.* Retrieved from http://www.schoolbehavior.com/Files/tips_mood.pdf

Peters, S. J., & Gates, J. C. (2010). The teacher observation form: Revisions and updates. *Gifted Child Quarterly, 54*(3), 179–188. doi:10.1177/0016986210369258

Presley, I., & D'Andrea, F. M. (2008). *Assistive technology for students who are blind or visually impaired: A guide to assessment.* New York, NY: AFB Press.

Prigatano, G. P., Fordyce, D. J., Zeiner, H. K., Roueche, J. R., Pepping, M., & Wood, B. C. (1986). *Neuropsychological rehabilitation after brain injury.* Baltimore, MD: Johns Hopkins University Press.

Rich, D., & Taylor, H. G. (1993). Attention deficit hyperactivity disorder. In M. Singer, L. Singer, & T. Anglin (Eds.), *Handbook for screening adolescents at psychosocial risk* (pp. 333–374). New York, NY: Lexington Books.

Rief, S. F. (1993). *How to reach and teach ADD/ADHD children.* San Francisco, CA: Jossey-Bass.

Rief, S. F. (2003). *The ADHD book of lists.* San Francisco, CA: Jossey-Bass.

Roberts, M. A. (1999). Mild traumatic brain injury in children and adolescents. In W. R. Varney & R. J. Roberts (Eds.), *Mild head injury: Causes, evaluation, and treatment* (pp. 493–512). Hillsdale, NJ: Erlbaum.

Saskatchewan Education. (1999). *Teaching students with autism: A guide for educators, 1999.* Retrieved from http://www.education.gov.sk.ca/ASD

Schibsted, E. (2009). *How to develop positive classroom management.* Retrieved from http://www.edutopia.org/classroom-management-relationships-strategies-tips

Scruggs, T. E., & Mastropieri, M. A. (1992). Effective mainstreaming strategies for mildly handicapped students. *Elementary School Journal, 92*(3), 389–409.

Smith, M. (2004). *Joseph's coat: People teaming in transdisciplinary ways.* Retrieved from http://www.tsbvi.edu/Outreach/seehear/spring98/joseph.html

Sohlberg, M. M., & Mateer, C. A. (2001). *Cognitive rehabilitation: An integrative neuropsychological approach.* New York, NY: Guilford.

Special Education Technology British Columbia. (2008). *Writing strategies for students with visual impairments: A classroom teacher's guide.* Retrieved from http://www.setbc.org/Download/LearningCentre/Vision/Writing_Strategies_for_Visual_Impairments.pdf

Spungin, S., McNear, D., Torres, I., Corn, A. L., Erin, J. N., Farrenkopf, C., & Huebner, K. M. (2002). *When you have a visually impaired student in your classroom: A guide for teachers.* New York, NY: AFB Press.

Stokes, S. (n.d.). *Children with Asperger's syndrome: Characteristics/learning styles and intervention strategies.* Retrieved from http://www.specialed.us/autism/asper/asper11.html

Thompson, S. J., Morse, A. B., Sharpe, M., & Hall, S. (2005). *Accommodations manual: How to select, administer, and evaluate use of accommodations for instruction and assessment of students with disabilities.* Retrieved from http://www.ccsso.org/content/pdfs/AccommodationsManual.pdf

Thomson, J. B., & Kerns, K. A. (2000). Mild traumatic brain injury in children. In S. A. Raskin & C. A. Mateer (Eds.), *Neuropsychological management of mild traumatic brain injury* (pp. 233–253). London, England: Oxford University Press.

UN Committee on the Rights of the Child. (2001). *General comment no. 1, the aims of education, U.N. doc. CRC/GC/2001/1.* Retrieved from http://www1.umn.edu/humanrts/crc/comment1.htm

U.S. Department of Education, Office of Special Education and Rehabilitation Services, Office of Special Education Programs. (2008). *Teaching children with attention deficit hyperactivity disorder: Instructional strategies and practices.* Retrieved from http://www.ed.gov/rschstat/research/pubs/adhd/adhd-teaching-2008.pdf

Watkins, C. E., & Brynes, G. (2003). *Anxiety disorders in children and adults.* Retrieved from http://www.ncpamd.com/anxiety.htm

Weyandt, L. L., Stein, S., Rice, J. A., & Wermus, C. (1994). Classroom interventions for children with attention-deficit hyperactivity disorder. *The Oregon Conference Monograph, 6*, 137–143.

Ylvisaker, M. (1986). Language and communication disorders following pediatric head injury. *Journal of Head Trauma Rehabilitation, 1*(4), 48–56.

Handout K-4
Handout for Teachers: Strategies for Preventing and Dealing with Bullying, Cyberbullying, and Other Internet Issues

---

INTRODUCTION

This handout provides general guidelines for working with students who have been bullied or cyberbullied and students who have bullied other children. You are not expected to follow every suggestion, and some suggestions do not apply in every case. You should consider the student's age, sex, and language competency in applying the suggestions.

GENERAL SUGGESTIONS FOR PREVENTING AND DEALING WITH BULLYING

Emphasizing Positive School Values and Character Development

1. Establish a positive, friendly, and trusting relationship with each student.
2. Model desired attitudes and behaviors by applying classroom rules fairly and consistently.
3. Build character education into each school day and promote personal and social skill development.
4. Encourage positive peer relations and emphasize that no one has the right to make another person feel miserable, threatened, or afraid.
5. Teach students what it means to respect each other's differences, in part by recognizing cultural diversity as an influence on relationship, identity, and social issues.
6. Teach cooperative learning skills.
7. Teach children to be both confident and assertive, and point out differences between being assertive and being aggressive.
8. Foster student-shared responsibility for the classroom's social and physical environment.
9. Introduce the topics of courage, reasoning, fairness, justice, responsibility, citizenship, and collaboration into appropriate academic content and extracurricular activities.

Teaching Your Students About Bullying

1. Start by learning about bullying. Be aware of your attitudes toward bullying and realistic about your ability to recognize bullying when it occurs.
2. Educate students about bullies. Talk about common myths regarding bullying, such as the following:

- Being bullied is just a part of growing up.
- Bullying is child's play.
- Bullying always involves physical aggression.
- Bullying only happens on the way to and from school and on the playground.
- Bullying is confined to boys.
- Fighting back is a valid way to deal with bullies.

3. Explain to students the difference between playfulness and bullying or cruelty.
4. Emphasize the consequences of hurting others.
5. Let students know that bullying or making disparaging comments about other students is unacceptable and is against school rules (e.g., "Calling someone names is bullying and is against our school rules," "That was bullying; it is never okay for students to push or hurt each other that way").
6. Draft a list of clear rules and expectations for playground behavior. Use simple language for the list, and keep it short. If necessary, have classes recite it before they go outdoors.
7. Inform students about the penalties for bullying.
8. Enforce consistent and immediate consequences for bullying behaviors.
9. Tell students to immediately report any bullying, cruelty, or harassment they see or experience to a member of the school staff. The person should be someone they trust, such as a counselor, teacher, school psychologist, social worker, nurse, speech therapist, vice-principal, or principal. Even if he or she can't fix the situation immediately, the person may be able to offer some helpful suggestions, and sharing the problem may help students feel a little less alone. This person can also provide emotional support and connect students with someone who can help more directly to prevent further bullying.
10. Recommend to students that they also tell their parents about any bullying occurring at school.
11. Teach students about simple measures to lessen the likelihood of becoming the target of a bully, such as looking a bully in the eye, speaking up, and standing straight; these behaviors communicate self-confidence.
12. Use role-playing exercises (e.g., students can practice saying "Leave me alone" and walking away).
13. Encourage inactive bystanders to take a more active or prosocial role next time (e.g., "Maybe you weren't sure what to do. Next time, please tell the person to stop or get an adult to help if you feel you can't handle the situation").
14. Talk with all students about the harm caused by cyberbullying. Remember that cyberbullying that occurs off campus can become common knowledge among students and can affect how the students behave and relate to each other at school.
15. Create an environment in which students feel safe enough to report bullying, cyberbullying, cruelty, and harassment and to ask for help.
16. Develop a classroom action plan to ensure that students know what to do when they observe a bullying incident.

17. Emphasize the difference between tattling and telling on someone who is bullying another student. The goal of tattling is to get someone else in trouble or avoid blame, look good in someone else's eyes, or gain attention. The goal of telling is to keep someone else out of trouble or ensure someone's safety. If a student thinks that he or she or someone else may be in danger, that student should report the other student.

18. Give students the assurance that you or a member of the staff will step in when you learn about a bullying incident.

POSSIBLE WARNING SIGNS THAT A STUDENT MAY BE A VICTIM OF BULLYING

PHYSICAL SIGNS

A student

- Is hungry by the end of the school day.
- Brings damaged possessions to school.
- Complains of illness (e.g., pains, headaches, stomachaches).
- Complains of tiredness or fatigue.
- Reports that he or she has difficulty sleeping (e.g., nightmares, bedwetting) and looks sleepy.
- Has torn or damaged clothes.
- Has unexplained bruises, scratches, or cuts.
- Reports that possessions (e.g., books, electronics, clothing, jewelry) have been "lost."

BEHAVIORAL SIGNS

A student

- Acts differently than usual.
- Avoids classes or skips school.
- Displays "victim" body language (e.g., hangs head, hunches shoulders, avoids eye contact).
- Expresses fear of riding on a school bus or walking to and from school.
- Has deteriorating school performance.
- Has difficulty concentrating.
- Has little interest in school work or other activities.
- Expresses thoughts about suicide.
- Has unexplained absences.
- Requests additional money for lunch from school personnel.
- Eats little or nothing at lunch or avoids the lunchroom.
- Stays late at school to avoid encounters with other students.
- Steals money.
- Takes "protection" to school (e.g., a stick, knife, gun).
- Reports that he or she takes an "illogical" route when walking to and from school.
- Talks about running away.
- Threatens violence against others.
- Withdraws socially or has few or no friends.

EMOTIONAL SIGNS

A student

- Is irritable, anxious, fearful, or insecure.
- Displays mood swings and cries easily.
- Shows evidence of (or expresses) feeling isolated, lonely, or trapped.
- Shows evidence of (or expresses) feeling picked on, persecuted, or powerless.
- Shows evidence of (or expresses) feeling rejected and not liked.
- Shows evidence of (or expresses) feeling sad, hopeless, and depressed.
- Has angry outbursts.
- Complains of flashbacks.
- Has self-doubt and low self-esteem.

SIGNS OF CYBERBULLYING IN PARTICULAR

A student

- Is upset after being online or seeing text messages.
- Stops using his or her computer, cell phone, or smartphone unexpectedly.

ACTIONS YOU SHOULD TAKE IN RESPONSE TO BULLYING

General Suggestions

1. Intervene if you observe students expressing undesirable attitudes or displaying behaviors that could be "gateway behaviors" to bullying and harassment.
2. Watch for signs of bullying and investigate immediately.
3. Manage time and tasks so that students remain connected and productive and thus less likely to engage in undesirable behaviors.
4. Listen receptively to parents who report bullying, investigate reported circumstances immediately, and take appropriate action.
5. Report any bullying incidents to the school administration and follow all school guidelines and procedures, including policies about mediating a bullying situation.
6. Work with other teachers at your school to stop bullying in the school and the community.

Getting the Facts About the Bullying Incident

1. Ask each student involved in the incident (bully or bullies, victim or victims, bystanders) to tell you about what happened in his or her own words.
2. Ask the following questions as needed:
   - When did the bullying take place?
   - Where did the bullying take place?
   - What happened first?
   - What followed?
   - What specific events led up to the incident?
   - Who did the bullying?
   - What did he or she (or they) do?
   - What did the victim do when he or she was bullied?
   - Did the victim do anything to prevent or stop the bullying? (If yes) What did he or she do?
   - How long did the bullying go on?
   - How severe was the bullying?
   - Has this happened before? (If yes) Tell me about it.
   - Were any members of the school staff present? (If yes) Who was there? What did he or she (or they) do?
   - Is there anything else that you would like to tell me?
3. Take pictures of any physical evidence of bullying (e.g., bruises, cuts, damaged books, torn clothes).
4. Keep a written record of all the incidents that have occurred.

Assisting the Victim

1. Always respond to requests for help from victims.
2. Be calm, stand between the victim and the student who is doing the bullying (but consider whether doing so puts you in harm's way), and do not allow it to continue.
3. Use a matter-of-fact tone of voice to state what behaviors you saw and heard.
4. Support the victim in a way that helps him or her to regain self-control, to "save face," and to feel safe from retaliation. For example, listen to the student, assure him or her that bullying is not his or her fault, and tell him or her that you want to work together to resolve the situation and protect him or her from further bullying. Also encourage the student to tell you about the good parts of his or her day and make sure that the student knows that you trust and believe him or her. Encourage the student to spend time with friends who are a positive influence and with hobbies, and to participate in clubs, sports, or other enjoyable activities.
5. Make sure the victim knows that it is okay to feel scared, upset, or anxious when he or she is bullied.
6. Let the victim know that he or she does not have to face being bullied alone.
7. Ask the victim how he or she thinks the problem can be solved.
8. Discuss with the victim ways of responding to the student who is bullying him or her. Tell the victim to try the following:
   - Act brave (even if he or she doesn't feel brave).
   - Firmly and clearly tell the bully to stop, then walk away (or run away if necessary).
   - Ignore any hurtful remarks made by a bully, such as by acting uninterested or texting someone. Tell the victim that ignoring the bully shows the bully that he or she doesn't care. Eventually, the bully might get bored and stop bothering him or her.
   - Try to change the subject or distract the bully. Doing so might make it harder for him or her to continue with the bullying.
   - Hold in his or her anger. It's natural to get upset by a bully, but that's what bullies thrive on; it makes them feel more powerful. Advise the student not to respond to a bully by losing his or her temper, fighting back, bullying back, or calling the bully names. This might make the situation worse. Similarly, keep the bully off guard by not crying and not looking upset.
   - Adopt a "poker face" when he or she is bullied. Smiling or laughing might provoke the bully.
   - Practice a "cooling down" strategy such as counting to 10, taking deep breaths, or walking away.
9. Remind the student not to get others to gang up on the bully at another time and never to bring weapons to school to threaten the bully or to protect himself or herself from more bullying. Bringing weapons to school is dangerous.
10. Discuss ways the student can try to avoid being bullied again.
    - Use a buddy system whenever possible so that he or she does not have to walk alone. For example, the victim should "buddy up" with a friend in the hallway, at recess, and on the bus.
    - Avoid the bully whenever possible. The victim can do this by choosing an activity the bully might not choose, sitting at a table far from the bully at lunchtime, going to a part of the playground away from the bully, using a different bathroom if the bully is nearby, using a hallway that the bully doesn't use (if possible), and moving to an area close to an adult who can keep an eye on what is going on.
    - Remove incentives for the bullying. For example, if the bully is demanding his or her lunch money, the student should not bring lunch money and should instead start bringing his or her lunch. If the bully tries to get his or her possessions (cell phone or other electronics, jewelry, books), he or she should avoid bringing such items to school unless they are absolutely necessary.
11. If the victim resorts to drastic measures (e.g., avoiding use of a bathroom all day or skipping school), take immediate action by requesting a meeting with a school administrator.
12. Closely monitor the behavior of the victim.
13. If you need to discuss the bullying incident further, praise the victim for his or her willingness to discuss the incident with you and emphasize who will and will not be given the information.
14. Provide as much information as you can about your next steps, because information can help the victim regain a sense of safety and control.
15. Urge the victim to report any further incidents of bullying, whether they involve the same or different students.
16. Ask the victim whether he or she has discussed the bullying incident with his or her parents. If he or she has done so, find out what the parents suggested the student should do. If not, explore with the victim how his or her parents may be of help. (Depending on your school's policy, you or someone from the administrative staff may be obliged to notify the parents of both the victim and the bully when a confrontation occurs and seek to resolve the problem expeditiously.)
17. Make sure you follow up with the victim. Let the student know that you want to be supportive and that you plan to check in with him or her in the coming days and weeks.
18. Think about the victim's behavior and style of interaction and consider how you might help him or her handle these types of situations in the future. For example, you might teach the victim basic social skills, such as how to invite a classmate to play a game or to seek permission from a group of children to join in a play activity, or you might pair the victim with a socially competent student who can serve as a role model.
19. If needed, provide protection for the victim—such as by creating a buddy system whereby the victim has a buddy on whom he or she can depend and with whom he or she shares class schedule information and plans for the school day.
20. If needed, arrange pull-out services for the victim during non-free-time periods. These services might include seeing a psychologist, counselor, speech pathologist, physical therapist, or occupational therapist to help correct problems that might be affecting the child's ability to learn.
21. Enlist one or more adults in the school to spend time mentoring the victim, and encourage the victim to invite a friend to some of the activities with the mentor.

22. Encourage other students to make every effort to include the victim in their games.
23. Teach the victim assertiveness skills:
    - How to maintain his or her composure
    - How to stand firm and continue to behave appropriately even when provoked
    - How to respond to taunts, insults, or teasing with a bland response ("Oh"; "That's your opinion"; "Maybe")
    - How to get away from a situation if he or she starts to get very angry
    - How to say "No" firmly and loudly if he or she doesn't want to do something that someone else says to do and to stand up straight and look the other child in the eye when he or she says it
    - How to refuse to be talked into doing something that he or she will be sorry for even if someone dares him or her to do it
24. Refer the victim to an appropriate mental health specialist if you are concerned about how he or she is dealing with the stress of being bullied.

SUGGESTIONS FOR PREVENTING AND DEALING WITH CYBERBULLYING AND OTHER INTERNET ISSUES

General Considerations

1. Closely monitor students' use of computers at school.
2. Become familiar with cyberbullying, its dangers, and what to do if a student is the victim of cyberbullying.
3. Be sure that your school's anti-bullying rules and policies address cyberbullying.
4. Investigate a report of cyberbullying immediately.
5. Strongly encourage the victim *not* to respond to the cyberbullying.
6. Do not delete bullying messages or pictures. Save these as evidence.
7. Notify parents of the victims and parents of the cyberbullies (if known).
8. Contact the school administrator who is in charge of bullying incidents at the school and ask him or her to call the police immediately if the known or suspected acts of cyberbullying involve any of the following:
    - Threats of violence directed toward a student, school personnel, or school property
    - Repeated insults or intimidating comments that cause fear for a student's safety, including obscene or harassing phone calls or text messages or any other form of harassment or stalking
    - Extortion
    - Negative comments about a victim's race, religion, or some other aspect of identity
    - Sharing of photos that invade someone's privacy
    - Communications that are sexually explicit or obscene, including child pornography
9. As sending inappropriate language may violate the terms and conditions of e-mail or Internet service providers, websites, and cell phone companies, consider asking the school administrator responsible for handling cases of cyberbullying to contact the service provider and file a complaint. If the cyberbullying is coming through e-mail or

a cell phone, it may be possible to block future contact from the cyberbully.
10. Tell the victim that, if necessary, he or she could change contact details, getting a new user name and a new cell phone number and giving the new information only to his or her closest friends.
11. Try to identify the individual perpetrating the cyberbullying. Even if the cyberbully is anonymous (e.g., using a fake name or someone else's identity), there may be a way to track him or her through the school's Internet service provider.

Teaching Students About Appropriate Online Behavior

1. Remind students that real people with real feelings are behind screen names and profiles.
2. Talk to students about online manners. Teach students to use courtesy and common sense in all forms of communication, regardless of where and how they take place. Explain to students that using all caps, long rows of exclamation points, or large bold fonts is the online equivalent of yelling and others may not appreciate receiving those types of communications.
3. Tell students not to impersonate someone else online or create websites, web pages, or electronic posts that seem to come from someone else, like a teacher, a classmate, or someone that they made up.
4. Teach students that online actions can reverberate. This means that the words they write and the images they post have consequences offline.
5. Teach students to reply with care to electronic messages and think hard before sending a message to everyone on their contact lists.
6. Inform students that among the pitfalls of social networking sites, chat rooms, virtual worlds, and blogs are sharing too much information and posting pictures, video, or words that can damage another person's reputation or hurt his or her feelings.
7. Discuss with students why it is important to post only information that they are comfortable with everyone seeing, as employers, college admissions officers, coaches, teachers, and the police may view their online posts.
8. Inform students that once information is posted online, it can't be taken back. Even if they delete private information from their profiles, they have little control over prior versions of the information that may exist on other people's computers and that circulate online.
9. Encourage students to think before posting pictures or videos or altering photos posted by someone else. Tell students never to send their picture to someone online unless they have permission from their parents to do so.
10. Remind students that cell phones also can be used to bully or harass others. They should apply the same good manners and ethics when using cell phones as they do when on the computer and in other situations. They should use common sense when they are social networking from their phones.
11. Tell students not to reply to messages when they are angry or hurt, because when they feel this way they may do something that they will regret later.
12. Talk to students about texting. Tell them to think about how a text message might be read and understood before

sending it and to ignore text messages from people they do not know. They should learn how to block numbers from their cell phones.

13. Tell students not to send or forward sexually explicit photos, videos, or messages from any device (known as "sexting"). Not only would they be risking their reputation and friendships, but they could be breaking the law by creating, forwarding, or even saving this kind of message.

Teaching Students About Cyberbullying

1. Tell students to take Internet harassment seriously; it is harmful and unacceptable.
2. Make sure students know to tell their parents immediately if electronic bullying includes physical threats (including death threats). The parents should then immediately notify the police, the school, and the social networking site (if appropriate).
3. Tell students that you want them to let you and their parents know if they feel threatened by someone or uncomfortable because of something that is happening online.
4. Tell students not to respond to anything online that they believe is wrong or that makes them uncomfortable and to tell you about their feelings.
5. Tell students never to reply to harassing messages and to log out of a site immediately if they are being harassed.
6. If a student sees cyberbullying happening to another student, encourage him or her not to engage in or forward anything and to notify appropriate authorities as well as his or her parents.
7. Encourage students to tell you if they are aware of others who may be the victims of cyberbullying.
8. Find out how to block a bully's messages and show students how to do this, how to delete messages without reading them, and how to save them and forward them to their Internet or e-mail provider.
9. If someone on a student's "friends" or "buddies" list initiates bullying, work with the victim to delete the bully from the list.

Teaching Students About Internet Privacy and Identity Theft

1. Tell students never to share their Internet passwords with friends or anyone else except trusted members of their family.
2. Talk to students about using strong e-mail passwords. Long and complex passwords that contain letters, numerals, and symbols are hardest to crack. Passwords that are not safe include those that contain personal information, the student's login name, or common words or that use adjacent keys on the keyboard.
3. Discuss with students that communicating with strangers online is dangerous (just as talking to strangers in person is dangerous). Particularly, tell students not to share personal information or talk about sex with anyone they do not know. Also, tell students never to arrange to meet in person someone they have met online, unless their parents say that it is okay to do so.
4. Teach students to maintain privacy and avoid identity theft by not replying to texts, e-mails, or pop-up messages that ask for their or others' personal or financial information—including their full name, address, telephone number,

parents' names, school's name, social security number, or account numbers for bank or credit card accounts. Also tell students not to click on any links in such messages or cut and paste a link from one of them into a web browser. (If a student wants to check a financial account, for example, he or she should type the web address of the bank directly into the browser window.) Personal information (except for social security numbers) can, however, be posted when ordering from a secure business website.

5. Tell students not to give personal information on the phone in response to a text message. Some scammers send text messages that appear to be from a legitimate business and ask the recipient to call a phone number to update the account or obtain a "refund." If the recipient gives them personal information, the scammers can use the information to run up charges in the recipient's name.
6. Tell students to forward "phishing" e-mails (e-mails used by scam artists to send spam, pop-ups, or text messages to trick the recipient into disclosing personal, financial, and/or other sensitive information) to spam@uce.gov and to the company, bank, or organization impersonated in the phishing e-mail. Students (or their parents) may also want to report a phishing e-mail to the Anti-Phishing Working Group at reportphishing@antiphishing.org.
7. Tell students to create safe screen names and to think about the impression screen names convey. A good screen name won't reveal how old a person is, where he or she lives, or his or her gender. Further, screen names should not be the same as students' e-mail addresses.
8. Tell students to use security software and update it regularly.
9. Talk to students about their expectations about who should be allowed to view their profiles online. Recommend that they use appropriate privacy settings to restrict those who can access and post notes on their profiles.
10. Talk to students about setting high privacy preferences on their instant messaging (IM) and video calling accounts. (Students should know that most IM programs allow parents to control whether people on their children's contact list can see their IM status, including whether they are online. Some IM and e-mail accounts allow parents to determine who can send their children messages, and block anyone not on the list.)
11. Tell students not to forward (or even open) e-mail chain letters. Most recipients find chain letters a nuisance, and they may be scams and may carry viruses or spyware.
12. If a student finds a profile that was created or altered without his or her permission, work with the student (or have the student work with his or her parents) to contact the company or group that runs the website, chat room, or message board to have the profile taken down.
13. Advise students to use GPS technology installed on their cell phones only with friends they know well and trust, and not to broadcast their location to the world. (Students should know that some carriers offer GPS services that let parents map their locations.)
14. If your students are under 13 years of age, tell them that they must have parental consent to post information to a website. The Children's Online Privacy Protection Act (COPPA), enforced by the Federal Trade Commission,

requires websites to get parental consent before collecting or sharing information from children under 13.

15. Tell students to avoid posting their cell phone numbers online.

16. Tell students to read their regular mail and review printed (or e-mailed) credit card and bank account statements as soon as they arrive to check for unauthorized charges.

Supervising Internet Use

1. Recognize that students have Internet access not only through their computers at home, but also through cell phones or other mobile devices, friends' computers, computers at school, computers at the library, and computers at Internet cafes.

2. Talk regularly with students about their online activities. Spend time with students while they are online.

3. Closely supervise young students who are beginning to use a computer. Show them how to choose appropriate websites. A librarian may give you advice on selecting appropriate websites.

4. Help students recognize which Internet sources and websites are trustworthy. You can do this by helping them understand the concept of "credibility." Students need to understand that not everything they see on the Internet is true and that people on the Internet may not be who they appear to be.

5. Tell students to be careful about chat rooms and message boards; entering chat rooms or using message boards may place them at risk.

6. Talk to students about limiting their online "friends" to people they actually know.

POSSIBLE WARNING SIGNS THAT A STUDENT MAY BE A BULLY

A student
- Seeks to dominate and/or manipulate others.
- Appears to enjoy feeling powerful and in control.
- Is both a poor winner (boastful and arrogant) and a poor loser.
- Seems to derive satisfaction from others' fears, discomfort, or pain.
- Is good at hiding behaviors or doing them where adults can't notice—for example, by closing a program or turning off a computer when you enter the room.
- Is excited by conflicts between others.
- Blames others for his or her problems.
- Displays uncontrolled anger.
- Has a history of discipline problems.
- Displays intolerance and prejudice toward others.
- Uses drugs or alcohol or is a member of a gang.
- Lacks empathy toward others.
- Expresses physical superiority.
- Shows off in class.
- Is defiant and rude.
- Ignores requests to listen to the teacher.
- Ignores requests to stop misbehaving.
- Is disruptive in class.
- Makes fun of or disparages other students, including those who are different in some way or who have special needs (teases others about possessions, physical

appearance, clothes; calls others names; makes insulting remarks about others' ethnicity, size, religion, gender, sexual orientation).
- Takes items that belong to other students.
- Damages other students' school work or property.
- Makes repeated threats (including threats of physical harm).
- Pushes, shoves, and/or hits other students.
- Blames other students for starting conflicts.
- Has possessions that he or she (or his or her family) might not be able to afford.
- Practices extortion (such as asking for or taking lunch money).
- Ignores others or excludes others from his or her group.
- Posts slanderous notes in public places.
- Uses electronic means (such as the Internet or cell phones) to start rumors, write derogatory comments, or show disparaging pictures.
- Encourages other students to be disruptive or to bully others.
- Fails to engage fully in classroom activities.
- Repeatedly fails to turn in homework on time.

ACTIONS YOU SHOULD TAKE WITH THE BULLY

1. When you learn that a student is bullying other students, take it seriously. Students who are bullies may have problems that can get worse as they grow older and even continue into adulthood.

2. Try to understand why the bullying behavior took place:
   - Was it because of some prejudice (e.g., against a student from another ethnic group, a student of the opposite sex, or a student perceived as lesbian, gay, bisexual, or transgendered)?
   - Was it because of group pressure? (If yes) What kind of pressure?
   - Was it due to a misguided sense of fun?

3. Find out about the student's feelings and the reasons for them:
   - Does the student behave in a bullying manner because he or she is frustrated or resentful for some reason? (If yes) What might be the reason for the frustration or resentment?
   - Is the student bored at school? (If yes) What might be the reasons for the boredom?

4. Help the student understand how the victims feel about being bullied. Does the student realize the serious harm that bullying behavior can cause?

5. Make sure that the student knows that bullying is *not* acceptable behavior and that treating others badly online is inappropriate.

6. Tell the student the penalties for bullying, and be sure to enforce the penalties fairly and consistently.

7. Use effective nonphysical discipline, such as loss of privileges. When the student needs discipline, explain why his or her behavior was wrong and how it can be changed.

8. Work out a way for the student to make amends for the bullying, such as by apologizing.

9. Implement a behavioral contract.

10. Ask an adult to mentor the student.

11. Help the student learn alternative ways to deal with anger and frustration.
12. Teach the student more appropriate behavior, and reward the student's positive behaviors to reinforce them.
13. Help the student develop new and constructive strategies for getting what he or she wants.
14. Discuss with the student how power can be achieved by doing good things.
15. Be a positive role model.
16. Show the student how to relate to others without teasing, threatening, or attacking them.
17. Help the student learn to treat others with respect.
18. Refer the student to an appropriate mental health specialist if his or her bullying behavior continues or if the student has mental health issues, including anger control issues.
19. Warn the student not to retaliate against anyone for telling you that he or she engaged in bullying or cyberbullying.
20. Monitor the student's behavior as needed.

ACTIONS YOU SHOULD *NOT* TAKE IN RESPONSE TO BULLYING OR CYBERBULLYING

1. Do not ask a victim to solve a bullying problem himself or herself. If you do, the victim may suffer further because of the differences in power between him or her and the bully. Bullying problems often require adult intervention.
2. Do not advise the victim to fight the bully. Fighting is in violation of school conduct codes, and the victim might be seriously injured.
3. Do not try to resolve a bullying incident when you are angry or when the students are angry.
4. Do not require the bully to apologize or make amends in the heat of the moment, because everyone should have time to cool off. Have all involved take a time-out and agree to meet with you (and other school personnel, as appropriate) at a specific future time.
5. Do not blame either the victim or the student who is a bully.

RECOMMENDATIONS YOU CAN MAKE TO THE SCHOOL ADMINISTRATION ABOUT BULLYING AND CYBERBULLYING

1. Hold training sessions for all teachers, staff members, parents, and volunteers. Training sessions should cover the following topics:
   - Signs of bullying and cyberbulling
   - Ways to respond to incidents of bullying
   - Bullying prevention methods
   - The school's responsibility to provide students with a safe place to study, learn, and play
   - The school's anti-bullying policy and discipline code, which should include clear schoolwide and classroom rules about bullying and the consequences for bullying
   - How to encourage students to report bullying, such as by setting up a bullying hot line, creating a "bully box" (where students can drop a note to alert teachers and administrators about students who are bullies), and having teachers lead class discussions about why reporting bullying is heroic behavior rather than tattling
   - The school's method for tracking and coordinating responses to bullying reports (such as a notebook where staff members record incidents) and verifying that follow-up has occurred
   - The need to maintain confidentiality of reports of bullying whenever possible
   - Ways to improve communication among school administrators, teachers, parents, and students
2. Organize a cybersafety forum for school and community that involves students, parents, educators, local law enforcement officers, city and school officials, and local technology companies. Topics should include Internet safety awareness, threatening messages, and actions to take in cases of cyberbullying.
3. Develop a policy on limiting use of technology in school, such as having students turn off their cell phones and other personal electronic devices during the school day.
4. Post playground rules in visible places.
5. Because recess is one of the few times during the school day when students play, pursue activities, and interact with one another on relatively unstructured terms, give thoughtful attention to the physical environment of the playground, adult supervision, and activities.
   - Plan ahead for positive changes the school would like to make on the playground.
   - Draw a large map of the playground and plot on it visual barriers to supervision, locations that provide opportunities for bullying, and areas where students tend to get into conflicts.
   - Provide an adequate number of playground monitors (teachers, other staff members, or volunteers) to organize games, introduce activities, and help with social problem solving.
   - Offer students of all ages a range of activities, games, and equipment.
6. Monitor the cafeteria and other "hot spots" where bullying is likely to occur.
7. Develop peer mediation programs to help students learn to communicate better and to resolve issues among themselves.
8. Use filtering and tracking software on all computers, but don't rely solely on this software to screen out cyberbullying and other problematic online behavior.
9. Provide counseling to help bullies with anger control and the development of empathy.

REFERENCES

Bradshaw, C. P., Waasdorp, T. E., O'Brennan, L. M., & Gulemetova, M. (2011). *Findings from the National Education Association's nationwide study of bullying: Teachers' and education support professionals' perspectives.* Retrieved from http://www.nea.org/assets/docs/Nationwide_Bullying_Research_Findings.pdf

Bully OnLine. (n.d.). *Bullying in the family.* Retrieved from http://bullyonline.org/related/family.htm

California Department of Education. (2010). *Bullying frequently asked questions.* Retrieved from http://www.cde.ca.gov/ls/ss/se/bullyfaq.asp

Massachusetts Medical Society. (2001). *Bullying—It's not O.K.* Retrieved from http://www.massmed.org/AM/Template.cfm?Section=Home&TEMPLATE=/CM/HTMLDisplay.cfm&CONTENTID=7365

Olweus, D. (1993). *Bullying at school: What we know and what we can do.* Cambridge, MA: Blackwell Publishers.

Orpinas, P., & Horne, A. M. (2006). *Bullying prevention: Creating a positive school climate and developing social competence.* Washington, DC: American Psychological Association.

Quiroz, H. C., Arnette, J. L., & Stephens, R. D. (2006). *Bullying in schools: Fighting the bully battle.* Retrieved from http://www.dps.mo.gov/homelandsecurity/safeschools/documents/Discussion%20Activities%20for%20School%20Communities.pdf

Rigby, K. (2008). *Children and bullying: How parents and educators can reduce bullying at school.* Malden, MA: Blackwell.

Rivers, I., Duncan, N., & Besag, V. E. (2007). *Bullying: A handbook for educators and parents.* Westport, CT: Greenwood/Praeger.

Sullivan, E., & Keeney, E. (2008). *Teacher talk: School culture, safety and human rights.* New York, NY: National Economic and Social Rights Initiative.

U.S. Department of Health and Human Services. (n.d.a). *How to intervene to stop bullying: Tips for on-the-spot intervention at school.* Retrieved from http://safeschools.state.co.us/docs/SBN_Tip_4%20How%20to%20Intervene.pdf

U.S. Department of Health and Human Services. (n.d.b). *Providing support to children who are bullied: Tips for school personnel (and other adults).* Retrieved from http://safeschools.state.co.us/docs/SBN_Tip_18%20Providing%20Support.pdf

U.S. Department of Health and Human Services. (2003b). *Take action against bullying.* Retrieved from http://download.ncadi.samhsa.gov/ken/pdf/SVP-0056/SVP-0056.pdf

U.S. Department of Health and Human Services. (2009). *Cyberbullying.* Retrieved from http://www.stopbullying.gov/cyberbullying/what-is-it

The Washington Times. (2007, October 1). *Delete cyberbullying.* Retrieved from http://www.ncpc.org/programs/crime-prevention-month/newspaper-supplements/2007-cpm-newspaper-supplement.pdf

Willard, N. E. (2007). *Cyber-safe kids, cyber-savvy teens: Helping young people learn to use the Internet safely and responsibly.* Hoboken, NJ: Wiley.

Wright, J. (2004). *Preventing classroom bullying: What teachers can do.* Retrieved from http://www.jimwrightonline.com/pdfdocs/bully/bullyBooklet.pdf

Table L-1
Interview Techniques Checklist

INTERVIEW TECHNIQUES CHECKLIST

Name of interviewer: _____   Date of interview: _____

Name of interviewee: _____   Rater's name: _____

Directions: Please rate the interviewer on each item, using the rating key below. Circle one number for each item.

Rating Key

Excellent demonstration of this skill	Good demonstration of this skill	Adequate demonstration of this skill	Poor demonstration of this skill	Very poor demonstration of this skill	Not applicable
1	2	3	4	5	NA

Skill	Rating
1. Made a smooth transition from opening greeting to next topic	1 2 3 4 5 NA
2. Created a positive interview climate	1 2 3 4 5 NA
3. Showed respect for interviewee	1 2 3 4 5 NA
4. Gave undivided attention to interviewee	1 2 3 4 5 NA
5. Established an environment free from distractions	1 2 3 4 5 NA
6. Used good diction	1 2 3 4 5 NA
7. Spoke in a clear, audible voice with warmth	1 2 3 4 5 NA
8. Spoke in a modulated voice that reflected nuances of feeling	1 2 3 4 5 NA
9. Spoke at a moderate tempo	1 2 3 4 5 NA
10. Used appropriate vocabulary	1 2 3 4 5 NA
11. Formulated general questions	1 2 3 4 5 NA
12. Formulated open-ended questions	1 2 3 4 5 NA
13. Used nonleading questions	1 2 3 4 5 NA
14. Used relatively few yes-no questions	1 2 3 4 5 NA
15. Used few, if any, multiple-choice questions	1 2 3 4 5 NA
16. Used structuring statements	1 2 3 4 5 NA
17. Encouraged replies	1 2 3 4 5 NA
18. Used probes effectively	1 2 3 4 5 NA
19. Allowed interviewee to express feelings and thoughts in his or her own way	1 2 3 4 5 NA
20. Formulated follow-up questions to pursue issues	1 2 3 4 5 NA
21. Was attentive to interviewee's nonverbal behavior	1 2 3 4 5 NA
22. Conveyed a desire to understand interviewee	1 2 3 4 5 NA
23. Conveyed to interviewee an interest in obtaining relevant facts, not in confirming pre-existing hypotheses	1 2 3 4 5 NA
24. Rephrased questions	1 2 3 4 5 NA
25. Used reflection	1 2 3 4 5 NA
26. Used feedback	1 2 3 4 5 NA
27. Handled a minimally communicative interviewee appropriately	1 2 3 4 5 NA
28. Handled interviewee's resistance and anxiety appropriately	1 2 3 4 5 NA
29. Showed sensitivity to interviewee's emotional state	1 2 3 4 5 NA
30. Clarified areas of confusion in interviewee's statements	1 2 3 4 5 NA
31. Intervened when interviewee had difficulty expressing thoughts	1 2 3 4 5 NA
32. Handled rambling communications appropriately	1 2 3 4 5 NA

Table L-1 *(Continued)*

Skill	Rating					
33. Dealt with difficult behavior appropriately	1	2	3	4	5	NA
34. Used props, crayons, clay, or toys appropriately	1	2	3	4	5	NA
35. Timed questions appropriately	1	2	3	4	5	NA
36. Handled silences appropriately	1	2	3	4	5	NA
37. Used periodic summaries during the interview	1	2	3	4	5	NA
38. Asked questions about all relevant areas without avoiding potentially stressful ones	1	2	3	4	5	NA
39. Provided appropriate support to interviewee to minimize effects of discussing stressful topics	1	2	3	4	5	NA
40. Made clear transitions	1	2	3	4	5	NA
41. Paced the interview	1	2	3	4	5	NA
42. Self-disclosed only when necessary	1	2	3	4	5	NA
43. Evidenced appropriate sensitivity to interviewee's cultural identity	1	2	3	4	5	NA
44. Established and maintained eye contact	1	2	3	4	5	NA
45. Maintained facial expressions relevant to content	1	2	3	4	5	NA
46. Used nonverbal behavior to further the interview	1	2	3	4	5	NA
47. Demonstrated consistency between nonverbal and verbal behavior	1	2	3	4	5	NA
48. Responded in nonjudgmental manner (without moralizing, advising prematurely, persuading, criticizing, or labeling)	1	2	3	4	5	NA
49. Resisted distractions	1	2	3	4	5	NA
50. Avoided overreacting	1	2	3	4	5	NA
51. Avoided arguments	1	2	3	4	5	NA
52. Handled interviewee's questions and concerns appropriately	1	2	3	4	5	NA
53. Allowed interviewee to express remaining thoughts and questions at close of interview	1	2	3	4	5	NA
54. Arranged for post-assessment interview	1	2	3	4	5	NA
55. Used summary statements at the end of the interview as needed	1	2	3	4	5	NA
56. Used closing statements	1	2	3	4	5	NA

Comments: _____

_____

_____

Table L-2
Checklist for an Interviewee's Evaluation of an Interviewer

EVALUATING THE INTERVIEWER

Client's name: _____   Name of interviewer: _____

Date of interview: _____

Directions: Please rate the interviewer on each item. Circle Y for Yes, N for No, or ? if you are not sure of your answer. Be sure to respond to each item. Thank you.

Item	Rating			Item	Rating		
1. The interviewer saw me at approximately the scheduled time.	Y	N	?	10. The interviewer asked about my feelings and responded appropriately to them.	Y	N	?
2. The interviewer put me at ease during the interview.	Y	N	?	11. I was able to talk about problems and issues that were important to me.	Y	N	?
3. The interviewer greeted me in a way that made me feel comfortable.	Y	N	?	12. The topics covered by the interviewer were appropriate.	Y	N	?
4. The interviewer appeared interested in me.	Y	N	?	13. The interviewer seemed organized during the interview.	Y	N	?
5. The interviewer appeared to be confident.	Y	N	?	14. The interviewer was thorough in asking me relevant questions.	Y	N	?
6. The interviewer spoke clearly and was easily understood.	Y	N	?	15. The interviewer summarized the problems as he or she saw them.	Y	N	?
7. The interviewer asked questions in a way that allowed me time to think about my answers.	Y	N	?	16. The time spent with the interviewer was adequate for my needs.	Y	N	?
8. The interviewer asked relevant questions about my personal and social life.	Y	N	?	17. I felt nervous during the interview.	Y	N	?
9. The interviewer seemed to understand me.	Y	N	?	18. Overall, I felt satisfied with the interview.	Y	N	?

Any other comments are welcome.

_____

_____

_____

Source: Adapted from Brockway (1978).

From *Foundations of Behavioral, Social, and Clinical Assessment of Children* (Sixth Edition) by Jerome M. Sattler. Copyright 2014 by Jerome M. Sattler, Publisher, Inc. Permission to photocopy this appendix table is granted to purchaser of this book for personal use only (see copyright page for details).

Table L-3
Checklist of Risk Factors for Child Maltreatment

CHECKLIST OF RISK FACTORS FOR CHILD MALTREATMENT

Child's name: _____   Date: _____

Age: _____   Grade: _____

Examiner's name: _____   School: _____

Directions: Check Y (Yes) or N (No) for each item.

Signs of Possible Maltreatment
Child
Check one

1. Has developmental delays, as indicated by failure to reach expected developmental milestones ☐ Y ☐ N
2. Shows regressive behavior, such as losing skills already mastered ☐ Y ☐ N
3. Shows failure to thrive, as indicated by a growth pattern not in the healthy range ☐ Y ☐ N
4. Shows sudden changes in behavior or school performance ☐ Y ☐ N
5. Exhibits low self-esteem, anxiety, depression, or suicidal tendencies ☐ Y ☐ N
6. Has not received help for physical or medical problems brought to the parents' attention ☐ Y ☐ N
7. Has learning problems that cannot be attributed to specific physical or psychological causes ☐ Y ☐ N
8. Is always watchful and closely monitors parents, as though preparing for something bad to happen ☐ Y ☐ N
9. Lacks adult supervision ☐ Y ☐ N
10. Is overly compliant, an overachiever, or too responsible ☐ Y ☐ N
11. Comes to school early, stays late, and does not want to go home ☐ Y ☐ N

Parent
1. Shows little concern for the child, rarely responding to the school's requests for information, for conferences, or for home visits ☐ Y ☐ N
2. Denies the existence of—or blames the child for—the child's problems in school or at home ☐ Y ☐ N
3. Asks the classroom teacher to use harsh physical discipline if the child misbehaves ☐ Y ☐ N
4. Sees the child as entirely bad, worthless, or burdensome ☐ Y ☐ N
5. Demands perfection or a level of physical or academic performance that the child cannot achieve ☐ Y ☐ N
6. Looks primarily to the child for care, attention, and satisfaction of emotional needs ☐ Y ☐ N

Signs of Possible Maltreatment
Child and Parent Interaction
Check one

1. Child and parent rarely touch or look at each other ☐ Y ☐ N
2. Child and parent consider their relationship entirely negative ☐ Y ☐ N
3. Child and parent state that they do not like each other ☐ Y ☐ N
4. Parent shares dangerous drugs or alcohol with the child ☐ Y ☐ N

Signs of Possible Physical Abuse
Child
1. Has unexplained burns, bites, bruises, broken bones, or black eyes ☐ Y ☐ N
2. Has fading but noticeable bruises or other marks after an absence from school ☐ Y ☐ N
3. Has injuries that have occurred previously ☐ Y ☐ N
4. Seems frightened of the parents and protests or cries when it is time to go home from school ☐ Y ☐ N
5. Shrinks at the approach of adults ☐ Y ☐ N
6. Reports injury by a parent or another adult caregiver ☐ Y ☐ N

Parent
1. Offers conflicting, unconvincing, or no explanation for the child's injury ☐ Y ☐ N
2. Describes the child in a negative way, such as "evil" ☐ Y ☐ N
3. Uses harsh physical discipline with the child ☐ Y ☐ N
4. Delays getting medical care for the child's injury ☐ Y ☐ N
5. Has a history of being abused as a child ☐ Y ☐ N

Signs of Possible Neglect
Child
1. Has developmental delays, as indicated by failure to reach expected developmental milestones ☐ Y ☐ N
2. Shows regressive behavior, such as losing skills already mastered ☐ Y ☐ N
3. Shows failure to thrive, as indicated by a growth pattern not in the healthy range ☐ Y ☐ N
4. Is frequently absent from school ☐ Y ☐ N

(Continued)

Table L-3 (Continued)

Signs of Possible Neglect (Cont.)

	Check one
5. Is constantly hungry	☐ Y ☐ N
6. Begs for or steals food or money from classmates	☐ Y ☐ N
7. Lacks needed medical or dental care, immunizations, or glasses	☐ Y ☐ N
8. Is consistently dirty and has severe body odor	☐ Y ☐ N
9. Is inadequately clothed	☐ Y ☐ N
10. Abuses alcohol or other drugs	☐ Y ☐ N
11. States there is no one at home to provide care	☐ Y ☐ N

Parent

	Check one
1. Appears to be indifferent to the child	☐ Y ☐ N
2. Seems apathetic or depressed	☐ Y ☐ N
3. Behaves irrationally or in a bizarre manner	☐ Y ☐ N
4. Is abusing alcohol or other drugs	☐ Y ☐ N
5. Withholds food from the child	☐ Y ☐ N
6. Withholds medical attention from the child	☐ Y ☐ N
7. Isolates the child from society or normal friendships	☐ Y ☐ N
8. Keeps the child out of school	☐ Y ☐ N

Signs of Possible Sexual Abuse

Child

	Check one
1. Is reluctant to go to the bathroom	☐ Y ☐ N
2. Shows signs of discomfort or pain while sitting, urinating, or moving bowels	☐ Y ☐ N
3. Has pain or itching around genitals	☐ Y ☐ N
4. Has discharges from the vagina or penis	☐ Y ☐ N
5. Bleeds through his or her pants	☐ Y ☐ N
6. Has semen in an orifice, hickeys on face or neck, or other signs of sexual activity	☐ Y ☐ N
7. Has difficulty walking or sitting	☐ Y ☐ N
8. Has age-inappropriate awareness and knowledge of sex or sexual behavior	☐ Y ☐ N
9. Demonstrates knowledge of bizarre or unusual sexual behavior	☐ Y ☐ N
10. Suddenly refuses to change for gym or to participate in physical activities	☐ Y ☐ N
11. Becomes pregnant or contracts a sexually transmitted disease[a]	☐ Y ☐ N
12. Runs away	☐ Y ☐ N
13. Reports sexual abuse by a parent or another adult caregiver	☐ Y ☐ N
14. Has attempted suicide	☐ Y ☐ N

Signs of Possible Sexual Abuse

Parent

	Check one
1. Is unduly protective of the child or severely limits the child's contact with other children, especially those of the opposite sex	☐ Y ☐ N
2. Is secretive and isolated	☐ Y ☐ N
3. Describes marital difficulties involving family power struggles or sexual relations	☐ Y ☐ N

Signs of Possible Emotional Maltreatment

Child

	Check one
1. Engages frequently in rocking, head-banging, or other similar inappropriate acts	☐ Y ☐ N
2. Has little interest in what is going on around him or her	☐ Y ☐ N
3. Is not eager to try new activities	☐ Y ☐ N
4. Has inappropriate responses to pain, other people, or changes in his or her environment	☐ Y ☐ N
5. Avoids a parent or caregiver	☐ Y ☐ N
6. Acts overly fearful, angry, distressed, or anxious	☐ Y ☐ N
7. Performs poorly in school	☐ Y ☐ N
8. Injures self	☐ Y ☐ N
9. Shows delayed emotional development	☐ Y ☐ N
10. Has attempted suicide	☐ Y ☐ N

Parent

	Check one
1. Constantly teases, blames, belittles, or berates the child	☐ Y ☐ N
2. Constantly yells or screams at the child	☐ Y ☐ N
3. Is unconcerned about the child and refuses to consider offers of help for the child's school problems	☐ Y ☐ N
4. Threatens to harm the child	☐ Y ☐ N
5. Withholds love, affection, or attention from the child	☐ Y ☐ N
6. Embarrasses the child in public	☐ Y ☐ N
7. Sets up the child to fail	☐ Y ☐ N
8. Often makes the child feel ashamed or guilty	☐ Y ☐ N
9. Dresses the child in clothes of the opposite sex	☐ Y ☐ N
10. Places the child in dangerous situations	☐ Y ☐ N
11. Fails to be supportive of the child	☐ Y ☐ N
12. Shows no interest in the child	☐ Y ☐ N
13. Overtly rejects the child	☐ Y ☐ N

[a] Particularly likely to be a sign of sexual abuse if the child is under age 14.

Source: Adapted from Brown (2007), Prevent Child Abuse America (n.d.), and WebMD (2008).

From *Foundations of Behavioral, Social, and Clinical Assessment of Children* (Sixth Edition) by Jerome M. Sattler. Copyright 2014 by Jerome M. Sattler, Publisher, Inc. Permission to photocopy this appendix table is granted to purchaser of this book for personal use only (see copyright page for details).

Table L-4
Child Risk Factors Checklist

CHILD RISK FACTORS CHECKLIST

Child's name: _____   Date: _____

Age: _____   Grade: _____

Examiner's name: _____   School: _____

Directions: Check Y (Yes) or N (No) for each item.

Individual   Check one

1. Genetic vulnerabilities   ☐ Y   ☐ N
2. Prenatal exposure to viral strep
   infections   ☐ Y   ☐ N
3. Prenatal exposure to alcohol or harmful
   drugs   ☐ Y   ☐ N
4. Prenatal exposure to malnutrition   ☐ Y   ☐ N
5. Defects or complications at birth   ☐ Y   ☐ N
6. Insecure parent-child attachment   ☐ Y   ☐ N
7. Exposure to toxins   ☐ Y   ☐ N
8. Medical problems   ☐ Y   ☐ N
9. Chronic underarousal   ☐ Y   ☐ N
10. Mental illness   ☐ Y   ☐ N
11. Exposure to violence   ☐ Y   ☐ N
12. Aggressive and hostile behavior   ☐ Y   ☐ N
13. Antisocial attitudes or beliefs   ☐ Y   ☐ N
14. Antisocial behavior   ☐ Y   ☐ N
15. Cognitive deficits   ☐ Y   ☐ N
16. Poor problem-solving skills   ☐ Y   ☐ N
17. Anxiety   ☐ Y   ☐ N
18. Hyperactivity   ☐ Y   ☐ N
19. Restlessness   ☐ Y   ☐ N
20. Impulsivity   ☐ Y   ☐ N
21. Attention difficulties   ☐ Y   ☐ N
22. Concentration difficulties   ☐ Y   ☐ N
23. Shallow affect   ☐ Y   ☐ N
24. Risk-taking   ☐ Y   ☐ N
25. Victim of violence   ☐ Y   ☐ N
26. Exposure to considerable stress   ☐ Y   ☐ N
27. Depression   ☐ Y   ☐ N
28. Substance use   ☐ Y   ☐ N
29. Academic failure   ☐ Y   ☐ N
30. Learning difficulties   ☐ Y   ☐ N
31. Language deficits   ☐ Y   ☐ N
32. High truancy rates   ☐ Y   ☐ N
33. Low educational aspirations   ☐ Y   ☐ N
34. Failure to understand consequences of
    actions   ☐ Y   ☐ N
35. Maladaptive methods of handling stress   ☐ Y   ☐ N
36. Poor coping ability   ☐ Y   ☐ N

Family

1. Obstetrical complications   ☐ Y   ☐ N
2. Low socioeconomic status   ☐ Y   ☐ N
3. Unemployed parents   ☐ Y   ☐ N

Family *(continued)*   Check one

4. Poverty   ☐ Y   ☐ N
5. Parents with mental illness   ☐ Y   ☐ N
6. Parents with physical problems   ☐ Y   ☐ N
7. Parents who are antisocial   ☐ Y   ☐ N
8. Parents who are poorly educated   ☐ Y   ☐ N
9. Parents who are substance abusers   ☐ Y   ☐ N
10. Parents under considerable stress   ☐ Y   ☐ N
11. Parents who maltreat their child   ☐ Y   ☐ N
12. Parents who reject or neglect their child   ☐ Y   ☐ N
13. Parents who are uninvolved with their
    child   ☐ Y   ☐ N
14. Parents who use ineffective discipline   ☐ Y   ☐ N
15. Parents who use inconsistent, harsh, or
    permissive methods of parenting   ☐ Y   ☐ N
16. Parents who provide poor supervision   ☐ Y   ☐ N
17. Parents who have inappropriate
    expectations   ☐ Y   ☐ N
18. Disruptive family relationships   ☐ Y   ☐ N
19. Delinquent siblings   ☐ Y   ☐ N
20. Domestic violence   ☐ Y   ☐ N
21. Residential mobility   ☐ Y   ☐ N
22. Homelessness   ☐ Y   ☐ N
23. Large family size   ☐ Y   ☐ N
24. Single parent   ☐ Y   ☐ N
25. High turnover of caregivers   ☐ Y   ☐ N

School/Community/Environment

1. Inferior schools   ☐ Y   ☐ N
2. Inferior teachers   ☐ Y   ☐ N
3. Community disorganization and/or
   violence   ☐ Y   ☐ N
4. Easy access to firearms and drugs   ☐ Y   ☐ N
5. No access to health care and social
   services   ☐ Y   ☐ N
6. No mentors   ☐ Y   ☐ N
7. Rejection by peers   ☐ Y   ☐ N
8. Antisocial peers   ☐ Y   ☐ N
9. No supportive church community   ☐ Y   ☐ N
10. No leisure or sport facilities   ☐ Y   ☐ N
11. Racism   ☐ Y   ☐ N
12. Residential segregation   ☐ Y   ☐ N
13. Environmental toxins   ☐ Y   ☐ N
14. Recent natural disaster   ☐ Y   ☐ N
15. Economic recession   ☐ Y   ☐ N

Table L-5
Child Protective Factors Checklist

CHILD PROTECTIVE FACTORS CHECKLIST

Child's name: _____   Date: _____

Age: _____   Grade: _____

Examiner's name: _____   School: _____

Directions: Check Y (Yes) or N (No) for each item.

Individual	**Check one**		**Family**	**Check one**	
1. Close bond with primary caregiver	☐ Y	☐ N	1. Good prenatal care	☐ Y	☐ N
2. Good physical health	☐ Y	☐ N	2. Educated parents	☐ Y	☐ N
3. Emotional maturity	☐ Y	☐ N	3. Competent parents	☐ Y	☐ N
4. Good mental health	☐ Y	☐ N	4. Stable, cohesive, and well-adjusted family	☐ Y	☐ N
5. Positive, prosocial attitudes (e.g., values honesty, integrity, caring, responsibility)	☐ Y	☐ N	5. Warm, nurturing, or supportive relationship with at least one parent	☐ Y	☐ N
6. High self-esteem	☐ Y	☐ N	6. Other supportive and caring family members	☐ Y	☐ N
7. Good intellectual functioning	☐ Y	☐ N	7. Appropriate supervision and direction by parents, including promotion of prosocial values	☐ Y	☐ N
8. Good problem-solving skills	☐ Y	☐ N	8. Small family size	☐ Y	☐ N
9. Good social skills	☐ Y	☐ N	9. Financial stability	☐ Y	☐ N
10. Good academic performance	☐ Y	☐ N	10. Stable and attractive home environment	☐ Y	☐ N
11. Participation in positive leisure or sport activities	☐ Y	☐ N	11. Assigned chores	☐ Y	☐ N
12. High motivation to address problems	☐ Y	☐ N	**School/Community/Environment**		
13. No exposure to violence	☐ Y	☐ N	1. Good schools	☐ Y	☐ N
14. Good coping ability	☐ Y	☐ N	2. Good teachers	☐ Y	☐ N
15. Self-discipline	☐ Y	☐ N	3. Good neighborhood	☐ Y	☐ N
16. Adaptability	☐ Y	☐ N	4. Firearms and drugs not easily available	☐ Y	☐ N
17. Easy, engaging temperament	☐ Y	☐ N	5. Health care and social services available	☐ Y	☐ N
18. Special talent	☐ Y	☐ N	6. Mentors available	☐ Y	☐ N
19. Impulse control	☐ Y	☐ N	7. Peer acceptance and support	☐ Y	☐ N
20. Achievement motivation	☐ Y	☐ N	8. Supportive church community	☐ Y	☐ N
21. Persistence	☐ Y	☐ N	9. Adequate leisure and/or sport facilities	☐ Y	☐ N
22. Faith	☐ Y	☐ N	10. Tolerance of ethnic groups	☐ Y	☐ N
23. Internal locus of control (e.g., feels in control of what happens)	☐ Y	☐ N	11. Integrated neighborhood	☐ Y	☐ N
24. Intolerant attitude toward deviance	☐ Y	☐ N	12. Clean environment	☐ Y	☐ N
25. Understanding of consequences of actions	☐ Y	☐ N	13. No major natural disasters	☐ Y	☐ N
26. Ability to see things from other people's perspective	☐ Y	☐ N	14. Economic prosperity	☐ Y	☐ N
27. Involvement in community service	☐ Y	☐ N			

Table L-6
Checklist of Risk Factors for Child or Adolescent Suicide

CHECKLIST OF RISK FACTORS FOR CHILD OR ADOLESCENT SUICIDE

Child's or adolescent's name: _____   Date: _____

Age: _____ Sex: _____   Grade: _____

Examiner's name: _____   School: _____

Directions: Check Y (Yes) or N (No) for each item.

Historical-Situational Risk Factors	Check one	
1. Serious medical illness	☐ Y	☐ N
2. Chronic preoccupation with death	☐ Y	☐ N
3. Fantasies about being immune to death	☐ Y	☐ N
4. Romanticizing and glorifying death	☐ Y	☐ N
5. Inadequate coping mechanisms	☐ Y	☐ N
6. Repeated failures in school	☐ Y	☐ N
7. Family pressures to achieve	☐ Y	☐ N
8. Poor peer relations (e.g., isolation, bullying, humiliation)	☐ Y	☐ N
9. Dysfunctional family (e.g., severe marital discord) and/or parents with severe emotional distress (e.g., psychosis, suicidality, chronic depression)	☐ Y	☐ N
10. Family violence (e.g., spousal abuse, physical or sexual child abuse)	☐ Y	☐ N
11. Severe life stressor (e.g., death of a family member or friend, parental divorce, termination of a significant relationship, family economic hardship, suspension from school, failure to get into college)	☐ Y	☐ N
12. Previous deliberately dangerous behaviors	☐ Y	☐ N
13. Previous suicide attempts	☐ Y	☐ N
14. Exposure to the suicidal behavior of others, such as family members, peers, or media figures	☐ Y	☐ N

Physical and Psychological Risk Factors	Check one	
1. Depression or other mood disorders, which may be indicated by flat affect, loss of interest in everyday activities, limited energy, feelings of sadness, worry, poor attention and concentration, difficulty sleeping, feelings of guilt, excessive crying, or changes in appetite or weight	☐ Y	☐ N
2. Eating disorders (e.g., bulimia nervosa or anorexia nervosa)	☐ Y	☐ N
3. Substance abuse (e.g., alcohol or drug abuse)	☐ Y	☐ N
4. Other psychiatric disorders	☐ Y	☐ N
5. Feelings of hopelessness (e.g., saying he or she wants to die, looking for a way to kill oneself, wishing to be in heaven)	☐ Y	☐ N
6. Feelings of helplessness (e.g., talking about being a burden to others, lacking a sense of belonging)	☐ Y	☐ N
7. Feelings of not being in control of his or her life	☐ Y	☐ N
8. Severe anxiety, tension, or irritability (e.g., talking about being trapped or being in unbearable pain)	☐ Y	☐ N
9. Low self-esteem and poor self-image	☐ Y	☐ N
10. Changes in temperament and behavior (e.g., sudden displays of disruptive behavior, abrupt changes in school performance and attendance)	☐ Y	☐ N
11. Withdrawal from family and friends	☐ Y	☐ N
12. Suicidal plan[a]	☐ Y	☐ N
13. Final arrangements (e.g., saying goodbye with finality, giving away favored possessions, putting affairs in order, appearing unusually calm and contented)	☐ Y	☐ N

[a] A suicidal plan would consider availability and lethality of means of suicide and would suggest intent. The most common means, in decreasing order of lethality, are gunshot, carbon monoxide, hanging, drowning, suffocation with plastic bag, impact associated with jumping from a high place, fire, poison, drugs, gas, and cutting wrists.

Source: Adapted from DeSpelder and Strickland (1992); Fremouw, De Perczel, and Ellis (1990); and Haag-Granello and Granello (2007). From *Foundations of Behavioral, Social, and Clinical Assessment of Children* (Sixth Edition) by Jerome M. Sattler. Copyright 2014 by Jerome M. Sattler, Publisher, Inc. Permission to photocopy this table is granted to purchasers of this book for personal use only (see copyright page for details).

Table L-7
Indicators of Psychological or Physical Difficulties

INDICATORS OF PSYCHOLOGICAL OR PHYSICAL DIFFICULTIES

Name: _____   Date: _____

Sex: _____   Grade: _____   School: _____

Birth date: _____   Teacher: _____

Directions: Place a check mark in the box next to each appropriate item. (See Table L-8 for an explanation of the terms.)

Appearance
- ☐ 1. Atypical posture
- ☐ 2. Bad breath
- ☐ 3. Bizarre hair style
- ☐ 4. Body odor
- ☐ 5. Body piercing
- ☐ 6. Disheveled
- ☐ 7. Emaciated
- ☐ 8. Excessively thin
- ☐ 9. Inappropriate facial expressions
- ☐ 10. Inflamed eyes
- ☐ 11. Multiple tattoos
- ☐ 12. Outlandish dress
- ☐ 13. Obese
- ☐ 14. Poor teeth
- ☐ 15. Provocative dress
- ☐ 16. Rigid posture
- ☐ 17. Scars
- ☐ 18. Slumped posture
- ☐ 19. Soiled clothes
- ☐ 20. Watery eyes
- ☐ Other: _____
  _____

Attitude Toward Examiner
- ☐ 1. Avoids eye contact
- ☐ 2. Avoids talking
- ☐ 3. Clinging
- ☐ 4. Defensive
- ☐ 5. Demanding
- ☐ 6. Domineering
- ☐ 7. Evasive
- ☐ 8. Excessively dependent
- ☐ 9. Hostile
- ☐ 10. Indifferent
- ☐ 11. Ingratiating
- ☐ 12. Overcompliant
- ☐ 13. Provocative
- ☐ 14. Seductive
- ☐ 15. Suspicious
- ☐ 16. Unfriendly
- ☐ 17. Withdrawn
- ☐ Other: _____
  _____

Motor Behavior
- ☐ 1. Absence seizure
- ☐ 2. Astereognosis

- ☐ 3. Ataxia
- ☐ 4. Athetosis
- ☐ 5. Body asymmetries
- ☐ 6. Dyspraxia
- ☐ 7. Echopraxia
- ☐ 8. Extremely limited use of gestures
- ☐ 9. Extremely relaxed posture
- ☐ 10. Fine-motor coordination difficulties
- ☐ 11. Grand mal seizure
- ☐ 12. Graphesthesia
- ☐ 13. Gross excitement
- ☐ 14. Gross-motor coordination difficulties
- ☐ 15. Hemiplegia
- ☐ 16. Hyperactivity
- ☐ 17. Hypoactivity
- ☐ 18. Involuntary body movements
- ☐ 19. Mixed laterality
- ☐ 20. Motor difficulties
- ☐ 21. Motor retardation
- ☐ 22. Muscle tone difficulties
- ☐ 23. Nervous habits
- ☐ 24. Odd mannerisms
- ☐ 25. Restlessness or fidgetiness
- ☐ 26. Spastic contractions
- ☐ 27. Spastic gait
- ☐ 28. Squirming
- ☐ 29. Tense musculature
- ☐ Other: _____

Affect
- ☐ 1. Agitated affect
- ☐ 2. Angry affect
- ☐ 3. Anxious affect
- ☐ 4. Apathetic affect
- ☐ 5. Blunted affect
- ☐ 6. Depressed affect
- ☐ 7. Flat affect
- ☐ 8. Hypomanic affect
- ☐ 9. Incongruous affect
- ☐ 10. Irritable affect
- ☐ 11. Labile affect
- ☐ 12. Panicked affect
- ☐ 13. Perplexed affect
- ☐ 14. Restricted affect
- ☐ 15. Silly affect
- ☐ 16. Tense affect

- ☐ Other: _____
  _____

Vocal Production
- ☐ 1. Disfluency
- ☐ 2. Distractible speech
- ☐ 3. Dysarthria
- ☐ 4. Dysphonia
- ☐ 5. Dysprosody
- ☐ 6. Loud voice
- ☐ 7. Low voice
- ☐ 8. No speech or delayed speech
- ☐ 9. Rapid speech
- ☐ 10. Slow speech
- ☐ 11. Stutters
- ☐ 12. Unintelligible speech
- ☐ Other: _____
  _____

Language and Thought
- ☐ 1. Agnosia
- ☐ 2. Agrammatism
- ☐ 3. Alexia
- ☐ 4. Amnesia
- ☐ 5. Anomia
- ☐ 6. Anterograde amnesia
- ☐ 7. Aphasia
- ☐ 8. Aphonia
- ☐ 9. Apraxia
- ☐ 10. Asymbolia
- ☐ 11. Auditory agnosia
- ☐ 12. Auditory aphasia
- ☐ 13. Automatic speaking
- ☐ 14. Autotopagnosia
- ☐ 15. Blocking
- ☐ 16. Circumlocution
- ☐ 17. Circumstantiality
- ☐ 18. Clang association
- ☐ 19. Concrete thinking
- ☐ 20. Confabulation
- ☐ 21. Confusion
- ☐ 22. Constructional apraxia
- ☐ 23. Deja vu
- ☐ 24. Delusion
- ☐ 25. Denial
- ☐ 26. Depersonalization
- ☐ 27. Derailment
- ☐ 28. Derealization
- ☐ 29. Disorientation

Table L-7 *(Continued)*

Language and Thought *(Continued)*
- ☐ 30. Distortion of ideas
- ☐ 31. Distractible speech
- ☐ 32. Dysgraphia
- ☐ 33. Dyslexia
- ☐ 34. Echolalia
- ☐ 35. Embarrassing speech
- ☐ 36. Expressive aphasia
- ☐ 37. Expressive difficulties
- ☐ 38. Facial apraxia
- ☐ 39. Finger agnosia
- ☐ 40. Flight of ideas
- ☐ 41. Global aphasia
- ☐ 42. Hallucination
- ☐ 43. Homicidal ideation
- ☐ 44. Ideas of reference
- ☐ 45. Ideational agnosia
- ☐ 46. Ideational apraxia
- ☐ 47. Ideomotor apraxia
- ☐ 48. Illogicality
- ☐ 49. Illusions
- ☐ 50. Inappropriate grammar
- ☐ 51. Inconsistencies and gaps
- ☐ 52. Irrelevant language
- ☐ 53. Jamais vu
- ☐ 54. Lateral confusion
- ☐ 55. Letter reversal
- ☐ 56. Limited content
- ☐ 57. Loose association
- ☐ 58. Loss of train of thought
- ☐ 59. Malingering
- ☐ 60. Minimal insight
- ☐ 61. Mixed type of aphasia
- ☐ 62. Monomania
- ☐ 63. Multiple personality
- ☐ 64. Neologisms
- ☐ 65. Nonfluent aphasia
- ☐ 66. Paragrammatism
- ☐ 67. Paramnesia
- ☐ 68. Paraphasia
- ☐ 69. Perseveration
- ☐ 70. Phobias
- ☐ 71. Phonemic paraphasia
- ☐ 72. Poverty of speech
- ☐ 73. Poverty of thought
- ☐ 74. Prolongations of sounds
- ☐ 75. Pronoun reversal
- ☐ 76. Prosopagnosia
- ☐ 77. Rambling
- ☐ 78. Receptive aphasia
- ☐ 79. Repetitions
- ☐ 80. Ruminations
- ☐ 81. Self-reference
- ☐ 82. Somatic concerns
- ☐ 83. Stilted speech
- ☐ 84. Suicidal ideation
- ☐ 85. Tactile agnosia
- ☐ 86. Tangentiality
- ☐ 87. Telegraphic speech
- ☐ 88. Underproductive responses
- ☐ 89. Visual agnosia
- ☐ 90. Visual-spatial agnosia
- ☐ 91. Word approximations
- ☐ 92. Word salad
- ☐ Other: _____
  _____

Behavior and Attention
- ☐ 1. Attention difficulties
- ☐ 2. Automatism
- ☐ 3. Blank spells
- ☐ 4. Carelessness
- ☐ 5. Catalepsy
- ☐ 6. Compulsive rituals
- ☐ 7. Concentration difficulties
- ☐ 8. Disorganized behavior
- ☐ 9. Distractibility
- ☐ 10. Grimacing
- ☐ 11. Hearing difficulties
- ☐ 12. Hemianopsia
- ☐ 13. Immaturity
- ☐ 14. Impulsivity
- ☐ 15. Inappropriate behavior
- ☐ 16. Limited frustration tolerance
- ☐ 17. Limited stamina
- ☐ 18. Obsessive behavior
- ☐ 19. Perfectionism
- ☐ 20. Preoccupation with irrelevant details
- ☐ 21. Resistance to clarifying answers
- ☐ 22. Rigidity
- ☐ 23. Self-mutilation
- ☐ 24. Shifting difficulties
- ☐ 25. Slow reaction time
- ☐ 26. Staring
- ☐ 27. Temper tantrums
- ☐ 28. Unaware of failure
- ☐ 29. Unaware of time limits
- ☐ 30. Visual difficulties
- ☐ 31. Withdrawn behavior
- ☐ Other: _____
  _____

Table L-8
Explanation of Indicators of Psychological or Physical Difficulties from Table L-7

Attitude Toward Examiner

1. *Avoids eye contact*—Does not look at examiner; lowers eyes; closes eyes at times
2. *Avoids talking*—Is reluctant to speak; does not speak unless strongly encouraged to do so
3. *Clinging*—Clings to examiner; seeks physical contact; demands constant attention and direction
4. *Defensive*—Tries to protect self against criticism or exposure of shortcomings
5. *Demanding*—Demands examiner's attention; wants an immediate response to every request
6. *Domineering*—Tells examiner what to do and how to do it
7. *Evasive*—Is intentionally vague, ambiguous, or equivocal
8. *Excessively dependent*—Constantly asks for reassurance and feedback
9. *Hostile*—Is disrespectful, belligerent, or quarrelsome
10. *Indifferent*—Is apathetic; has no particular interest or concern
11. *Ingratiating*—Is calculatedly pleasing or agreeable
12. *Overcompliant*—Is passive; fails to assert self
13. *Provocative*—Deliberately attempts to anger examiner
14. *Seductive*—Behaves enticingly
15. *Suspicious*—Is wary, guarded, or distrustful of examiner
16. *Unfriendly*—Refuses to cooperate; makes guarded, evasive replies; remains silent; is manipulative or defiant
17. *Withdrawn*—Is preoccupied; avoids eye contact with examiner; acts aloof or distant; responds mechanically

Motor Behavior

1. *Absence seizure*—Has brief episodes of staring into space; jerks and twitches muscles (formerly referred to as *petit mal seizure*)
2. *Astereognosis*—Is unable to identify objects by touch
3. *Ataxia*—Displays jerky patterns of movement; has a lurching walk
4. *Athetosis*—Displays slow, recurring, writhing movements of arms and legs; makes facial grimaces
5. *Body asymmetries*—Displays drooping of one side of the face, weakness in one arm, or other body asymmetries
6. *Dyspraxia*—Displays uncoordinated movements
7. *Echopraxia*—Imitates others' movements and gestures
8. *Extremely limited use of gestures*—Fails to use gestures as would normally be expected, given his or her cultural background
9. *Extremely relaxed posture*—Slouches or acts inappropriately relaxed
10. *Fine-motor coordination difficulties*—Is unable to do precise fine-motor movements, such as those required for writing and drawing
11. *Grand mal seizure*—Has violent convulsions marked by muscle spasm and loss of consciousness
12. *Graphesthesia*—Is unable to recognize numbers, words, or symbols traced or written on her or his skin
13. *Gross excitement*—Throws things; runs; jumps around; waves arms wildly; shouts; screams
14. *Gross-motor coordination difficulties*—Displays awkward, stiff, or clumsy gross-motor movements; stumbles
15. *Hemiplegia*—Has paralysis on one side of the body
16. *Hyperactivity*—Is excessively active
17. *Hypoactivity*—Is lethargic or sleepy; moves little
18. *Involuntary body movements*—Displays *at-rest tremors* (tremors that appear when one is still), *choreiform movements* (jerky involuntary movements or spasms of short duration), *tics* (involuntary movements, usually of eyes, lips, or cheeks), *dyskinesias* (defects in voluntary movement), *dystonias* (disordered muscle tone and posture), or *intention tremors* (tremors that appear when one is asked to perform an action)
19. *Mixed laterality*—Tends to shift between dominance of left and right sides of the body when performing a particular action
20. *Motor difficulties*—Displays *akathisia* (motor restlessness indicated by muscular quivering and inability to sit still), *akinesia* (lowered level of muscle activity), *athetoid movements* (slow, recurring, writhing movements of arms and legs), or *deviant locomotion* (walking on toes, twirling, or running in small circles)
21. *Motor retardation*—Sits unusually still; is sluggish; has slow, feeble, or labored movements; walks slowly; performs movements after a delay
22. *Muscle tone difficulties*—Displays *atonia* (no muscle tone), *flaccidity* (slumps, lets arms dangle limply, has slack facial muscles), or *hypotonia* (low muscle tone)
23. *Nervous habits*—Taps or "drums" with hands or feet; grinds teeth; sucks tongue; bites lips, nails, hands, or cuticles; sucks body parts (fingers, hair, etc.); picks skin, scabs, or nose; twists hair
24. *Odd mannerisms*—Exhibits odd, stylized movements, postures, or actions (e.g., maintains uncomfortable or inappropriate postures of trunk or extremities, flaps or oscillates hands, wiggles fingers or positions them bizarrely); makes bizarre facial movements; engages in complex, usually idiosyncratic motor rituals; performs compulsive rituals (e.g., touching and counting things, folding arms in order to avoid germs); darts and lunges peculiarly; sits in one peculiar position for a long time; rocks; sways; bangs head; rolls head; engages in repetitive jumping; rubs hand round and round on head; nods head constantly
25. *Restlessness or fidgetiness*—Paces up and down; makes frequent unnecessary movements
26. *Spastic contractions*—Has sudden, violent, involuntary contractions of a muscle or a group of muscles
27. *Spastic gait*—Walks with a choppy and stiff gait
28. *Squirming*—Wriggles or shifts restlessly in chair
29. *Tense musculature*—Holds body taut or rigid; clenches jaw; grips arms of chair; has trembling hands

Table L-8 *(Continued)*

Affect

1. *Agitated affect*—Is unsettled, restless, and distressed
2. *Angry affect*—Is angry, hostile, antagonistic, touchy, or violent; erupts easily; throws things or threatens to throw things
3. *Anxious affect*—Is fearful, apprehensive, overconcerned, tense, or worried; speaks in a frightened tone of voice; has tremors; has sweaty palms
4. *Apathetic affect*—Is indifferent; has almost no interest in anything
5. *Blunted affect*—Has restricted range and intensity of emotional expression; has expressionless face and voice; has limited emotional responses to distressing topics
6. *Depressed affect*—Appears sad; has mournful facial expression; breaks into tears; speaks in a monotone; frequently sighs deeply; voice chokes on distressing topics
7. *Flat affect*—Displays almost no emotion
8. *Hypomanic affect*—Has an elevated mood, irritability, racing thoughts, grandiose thinking, and pressured speech
9. *Incongruous affect*—Displays affect not in keeping with content of his or her verbal communication
10. *Irritable affect*—Is easily annoyed, bad tempered, or crabby
11. *Labile affect*—Has rapid shifts from one emotion to another
12. *Panicked affect*—Displays a sudden, overpowering terror; is greatly agitated; is extremely fearful
13. *Perplexed affect*—Looks puzzled; cannot explain or understand experiences
14. *Restricted affect*—Shows limited variability of emotion
15. *Silly affect*—Engages in excessive clowning; is giddy or facetious; makes jokes or flippant remarks
16. *Tense affect*—Is edgy, fidgety, jittery, or jumpy

Vocal Production

1. *Disfluency*—Does not use complete words or phrases
2. *Distractible speech*—Changes the subject in the middle of a sentence in response to a stimulus (e.g., "I graduated from high school and . . . where did you get that picture?")
3. *Dysarthria*—Has a motor speech disorder characterized by poor articulation and poor control of tongue, throat, or lips
4. *Dysphonia*—Has speaking difficulty because of hoarseness or other phonation problems
5. *Dysprosody*—Uses question-like (rising) inflection when speaking; chants; uses sing-song inflection; has monotonic speech; exhibits other manneristic changes in pitch, intonation, stress, phrasing, or rhythm
6. *Loud voice*—Is boisterous; shouts; sings loudly; shrieks; squeals
7. *Low voice*—Has a weak, soft, whispering, monotonous, or almost inaudible voice
8. *No speech or delayed speech*—Has no speech or a delay of more than 1 year in the appearance of individual speech sounds
9. *Rapid speech*—Speaks very quickly
10. *Slow speech*—Leaves long pauses between words
11. *Stutters*—Has difficulty speaking; prolongs sounds
12. *Unintelligible speech*—Has slurred, mumbled, or heavily accented speech

Language and Thought

1. *Agnosia*—Cannot recognize, interpret, or comprehend the meaning of sensory stimuli, despite having no perceptual disability
2. *Agrammatism*—Has difficulty following grammatical rules while speaking, including rules governing word use, verb tense, and subject-verb agreement (e.g., says "Ah . . . Tuesday . . . ah, mom and Jim Rudy [referring to himself] . . . hospital")
3. *Alexia*—Is unable to read, despite adequate vision and intelligence
4. *Amnesia*—Has partial or total loss of memory for past experiences
5. *Anomia*—Has difficulty finding the right word when speaking (e.g., says "He, uh, just hurried along" for "He ran"; says "the thing you put in your mouth" for "the spoon")
6. *Anterograde amnesia*—Is unable to remember events that occurred after the onset of amnesia
7. *Aphasia*—Has difficulty comprehending spoken or written language or articulating ideas (formerly referred to as *dysphasia*)
8. *Aphonia*— Cannot speak
9. *Apraxia*—Is unable to perform purposeful movements, despite having no paralysis or sensory disturbance
10. *Asymbolia*—Is unable to comprehend the significance of signs or symbols
11. *Auditory agnosia*—Is unable to identify sounds
12. *Auditory aphasia*—Is unable to comprehend spoken language
13. *Automatic speaking*—Speaks without voluntary control
14. *Autotopagnosia*—Is unable to identify his or her own body parts
15. *Blocking*—Is unable to complete a train of thought; suddenly stops speaking
16. *Circumlocution*—Uses unnecessary words and indirect language; main point is never lost but rather accompanied by much nonessential information (e.g., the question "How do you tell time?" elicits "I wear it right here," pointing to his or her wrist)
17. *Circumstantiality*—Has unnecessary digressions in speech, eventually reaching the main thought; is excessively long-winded; speech is filled with tedious details and parenthetical remarks
18. *Clang association*—Uses words based on their sounds rather than on their meaning (e.g., "I want to say the play of the day, ray, stay, may I pay?")
19. *Concrete thinking*—Is unable to think in abstract terms; gives over-literal interpretations of events; talks only about specific ideas or things
20. *Confabulation*—Gives false and irrelevant information
21. *Confusion*—Is unable to make sense of the environment
22. *Constructional apraxia*—Is unable to construct objects
23. *Deja vu*—Expresses his or her sense that an event has already been experienced
24. *Delusion*—Has false beliefs
25. *Denial*—Is unable to acknowledge unpleasant or traumatic experiences

(Continued)

Table L-8 *(Continued)*

26. *Depersonalization*—Expresses feelings of being detached, unreal, and physically altered (e.g., describes out-of-body experiences, fears that body parts have been altered, feels cut off from other people)
27. *Derailment*—Displays loose or oblique associations related to the topic under discussion; makes illogical connections in speech (e.g., "Last week when I was at the lake, you know, the new movie, boy, it sure is hot near the refrigerator")
28. *Derealization*—Expresses feelings that the surroundings are unreal
29. *Disorientation*—Is confused as to time, place, or person
30. *Distortion of ideas*—Uses hyperbole or exaggeration; misrepresents facts
31. *Distractible speech*—Changes the subject when a nearby stimulus gains his or her attention
32. *Dysgraphia*—Has difficulty expressing ideas in writing
33. *Dyslexia*—Is unable to read either silently or aloud
34. *Echolalia*—Echoes others' words either immediately or after a delay (e.g., the question "How are you today?" elicits "Are you today?")
35. *Embarrassing speech*—Says things that make others uncomfortable
36. *Expressive aphasia*—Has difficulty speaking, writing, or using signs
37. *Expressive difficulties*—Has difficulty coming up with the right word; has halting speech
38. *Facial apraxia*—Is unable to execute facial movements on command (e.g., whistling, puckering lips, or sticking out tongue) but can do so spontaneously
39. *Finger agnosia*—Is unable to identify the individual fingers of his or her hands or the hands of others
40. *Flight of ideas*—Shifts rapidly from topic to topic when speaking
41. *Global aphasia*—Can neither express nor understand speech and other forms of communication (also called *total aphasia*)
42. *Hallucination*—Sees things in the absence of a physical external stimulus
43. *Homicidal ideation*—Talks about the possibility of killing someone
44. *Ideas of reference*—Believes that other people's statements or actions have special reference to him or her when they do not
45. *Ideational agnosia*—Is unable to state the function or purpose of an object when shown it
46. *Ideational apraxia*—Is unable to execute a series of acts, even though he or she can perform each step correctly
47. *Ideomotor apraxia*—Is unable to carry out an action on verbal command, even though he or she can perform the action automatically and despite having intact comprehension
48. *Illogicality*—Reaches illogical conclusions; uses non sequiturs; makes faulty inductive inferences
49. *Illusions*—Has erroneous perceptions of reality
50. *Inappropriate grammar*—Uses poor grammar
51. *Inconsistencies and gaps*—Has incomplete speech

52. *Irrelevant language*—Uses language unrelated to the matter being considered
53. *Jamais vu*—Has the impression of being unfamiliar with a person or situation that is very familiar
54. *Lateral confusion*—Is unable to distinguish left from right
55. *Letter reversal*—Reverses letters when reading
56. *Limited content*—Is unable to recognize when answers are correct or incorrect
57. *Loose association*—Says things that are either only distantly related or completely unrelated to one another
58. *Loss of train of thought*—Fails to follow a chain of thought through to its natural conclusion
59. *Malingering*—Fabricates or grossly exaggerates physical or psychological symptoms
60. *Minimal insight*—Displays limited understanding of his or her problems
61. *Mixed type of aphasia*—Has impaired expressive and receptive language
62. *Monomania*—Is intensely preoccupied with a single idea or subject
63. *Multiple personality*—Displays two or more distinct personalities (also called *dissociative disorder*)
64. *Neologisms*—Makes up nonsensical and unrecognizable words (e.g., says *plint* for *door*)
65. *Nonfluent aphasia*—Has better auditory comprehension than verbal expression
66. *Paragrammatism*—Uses verbs, clauses, or prepositional phrases incorrectly
67. *Paramnesia*—Recollects events that never occurred
68. *Paraphasia*—Substitutes incorrect words for intended words (e.g., says "The flower is up the garden" for "The flower is in the garden")
69. *Perseveration*—Has difficulty shifting from one strategy or procedure to another or repeatedly says the same sound, word, or phrase
70. *Phobias*—Has persistent fears of situations, objects, activities, or persons
71. *Phonemic paraphasia*—Substitutes one sound for another, primarily as a result of a breakdown in the retrieval of phonological word patterns (e.g., *pike* for *pipe*, *amihal* for *animal*)
72. *Poverty of speech*—Gives brief, concrete, and unelaborated replies to questions; is reluctant to give unprompted additional information
73. *Poverty of thought*—Speech is vague, empty, or stereotyped or contains multiple repetitions
74. *Prolongations of sounds*—Draws out sounds
75. *Pronoun reversal*—Reverses pronouns (e.g., refers to self as "you" and to other people as "I")
76. *Prosopagnosia*—Is unable to recognize familiar faces
77. *Rambling*—Digresses when speaking; has unrelated thoughts; talks aimlessly
78. *Receptive aphasia*—Is unable to understand spoken or written language, even though auditory and visual senses are intact (also referred to as *fluent aphasia*)
79. *Repetitions*—Repeats ideas or words
80. *Ruminations*—Has persistent and recurrent worries

Table L-8 *(Continued)*

81. *Self-reference*—Refers the subject under discussion back to self, even when someone else is talking (e.g., the question "How is your mother doing?" elicits "I did not sleep well last night")
82. *Somatic concerns*—Has concerns about his or her body
83. *Stilted speech*—Uses pompous, distant, overpolite, or formal speech (e.g., "The attorney comported himself indecorously")
84. *Suicidal ideation*—Has thoughts about killing self; is preoccupied with death and dying; appears to be preparing for death (e.g., giving away possessions, making funeral arrangements)
85. *Tactile agnosia*—Is unable to identify familiar objects placed in his or her hand without looking
86. *Tangentiality*—Replies to questions in an oblique or irrelevant way; constantly digresses to irrelevant topics and fails to arrive at main point (e.g., the question "What is your occupation?" elicits "Well, there are many jobs out there and I can do things like my father. You know, fix things.")
87. *Telegraphic speech*—Omits connectives, prepositions, modifiers, and refinements of language when speaking (e.g., says "Mother, father . . . making dogs" for "A mother and father are fixing hotdogs")
88. *Underproductive responses*—Does not answer questions fully; gives monosyllabic answers; has to be pressured for an answer
89. *Visual agnosia*—Is unable to recognize familiar objects by sight
90. *Visual-spatial agnosia*—Is unable to understand spatial details (e.g., follow directions, understand the floor plan of a house)
91. *Word approximations*—Uses words in new and unconventional ways; develops new words (e.g., says "His boss was a seeover" for "His boss was an overseer")
92. *Word salad*— Has incomprehensible speech in which real words are strung together in gibberish (e.g., the question "What should you do when it is cold outside?" elicits "Well, the new blue moon, silly will, come to me, let's read") (also referred to as *jargon aphasia*)

Behavior and Attention
1. *Attention difficulties*—Is unable to focus on a task
2. *Automatism*—Performs actions without conscious awareness
3. *Blank spells*—Has abrupt interruptions of attention lasting a few seconds or longer
4. *Carelessness*—Is indifferent to his or her performance; does not give sufficient attention to his or her work during the evaluation
5. *Catalepsy*—Has a sudden episode of muscle weakness triggered by strong emotions
6. *Compulsive rituals*—Displays rituals (e.g., checks work repeatedly, touches desk three times before beginning a task)
7. *Concentration difficulties*—Is unable to bring together thought processes or focus on a task for an extended time

8. *Disorganized behavior*—Is unable to solve tasks in an organized manner
9. *Distractibility*—Is unable to maintain attention when extraneous stimuli are present
10. *Grimacing*—Has expressions of pain, contempt, or disgust
11. *Hearing difficulties*—Does not respond to directions; leans forward to hear speaker; makes mistakes in carrying out spoken instructions
12. *Hemianopsia*—Is unable to see one half of the visual field
13. *Immaturity*—Acts younger than his or her age
14. *Impulsivity*—Acts quickly without thinking
15. *Inappropriate behavior*—Engages in peculiar or inappropriate behavior (e.g., passively lets objects fall out of his or her hand; flicks fingers at objects; feels, strokes, rubs, or scratches objects; is preoccupied with trivial specks, breaks, points, and the like in objects; uses objects ritualistically or in a bizarre, idiosyncratic manner; spins objects; remains preoccupied with the same object or activity; ignores objects; holds an object without paying attention to it; mouths or sucks objects; taps; stares at objects or at nothing in particular; engages in repetitive banging; cries inappropriately; is excessively slow or excessively quick in responding)
16. *Limited frustration tolerance*—Gives up easily when faced with difficult questions; fails to try; breaks into tears at times
17. *Limited stamina*—Has no energy
18. *Obsessive behavior*—Has unwanted ideas or impulses (e.g., persistent fears that he or she may be harmed, unreasonable fear of becoming contaminated)
19. *Perfectionism*—Attends to every possible detail; is self-critical even when answers are correct
20. *Preoccupation with irrelevant* details—Is preoccupied with details not relevant to the situation
21. *Resistance to clarifying answers*—Fails to elaborate on an answer when asked to do so
22. *Rigidity*—Is unyielding in a point of view even when it is no longer appropriate to maintain it
23. *Self-mutilation*—Deliberately inflicts harm on his or her body (e.g., bites, scratches, hits self, bangs head)
24. *Shifting difficulties*—Is unable to move easily from one task to another
25. *Slow reaction time*—Responds to questions slowly; has difficulty solving tasks quickly
26. *Staring*—Stares at examiner; fixates on a picture in the office
27. *Temper tantrums*—Acts out frustrations (e.g., screams, kicks, has fits of anger)
28. *Unaware of failure*—Does not seem to realize when items have been failed
29. *Unaware of time limits*—Does not seem to realize when time limits have been reached
30. *Visual difficulties*—Is unable to see objects clearly; squints or frowns when looking at something; has jerky eye movements
31. *Withdrawn behavior*—Is preoccupied; avoids eye contact; is aloof

Note: Table L-7 provides a checklist for the terms covered in this table.

Table L-9
Acculturative Stress Inventory for Children

ACCULTURATIVE STRESS INVENTORY FOR CHILDREN

Name: _____   Date: _____

Date of birth: _____   Age: _____   Sex: _____   Grade: _____   School: _____

Directions: Please read each item and check either Y (Yes) if the item generally describes how you feel or N (No) if the item does not generally describe how you feel.

	Check one
1. I often feel as if people who are supposed to help me are really not paying any attention to me.	☐ Y ☐ N
2. It bothers me when people force me to be like everyone else.	☐ Y ☐ N
3. Because of the ethnic group I am in, I don't get the grades I deserve.	☐ Y ☐ N
4. Many people believe certain things about the way people in my ethnic group act, think, or are, and they treat me as if those things were true.	☐ Y ☐ N
5. Because of the ethnic group I am in, I feel others don't include me in some of the things they do or games they play.	☐ Y ☐ N
6. I have more things that get in my way than most people do.	☐ Y ☐ N
7. It's hard for me to tell my friends how I really feel.	☐ Y ☐ N
8. I feel bad when others make jokes about people who are in the same ethnic group as I am.	☐ Y ☐ N
9. It's hard to be away from the country I used to live in.	☐ Y ☐ N
10. I don't feel at home in the United States.	☐ Y ☐ N
11. People think I'm shy, when really I just have trouble speaking English.	☐ Y ☐ N
12. I think a lot about my ethnic group and its culture.	☐ Y ☐ N

Source: Adapted from Suarez-Morales, Dillon, and Szapocznik (2007).
From *Foundations of Behavioral, Social, and Clinical Assessment of Children* (Sixth Edition) by Jerome M. Sattler. Copyright 2014 by Jerome M. Sattler, Publisher, Inc. Permission to photocopy this table is granted to purchasers of this book for personal use only (see copyright page for details).

Table L-10
Student Oral Language Observation Matrix (SOLOM)

STUDENT ORAL LANGUAGE OBSERVATION MATRIX (SOLOM)

Student's name: _____   Date: _____

Grade: _____   Teacher's name: _____

Class: _____   Language observed: _____

Directions:

Based on your observation of the student, circle the category that best describes the student's abilities.

Note. The SOLOM should be administered only by persons who themselves score at level 4 or above in all categories in the language being assessed.

	1	2	3	4	5
A. Comprehension	Does not understand simple conversation.	Has great difficulty following what is said. Can comprehend only social conversation spoken slowly and with frequent repetitions.	Understands most of what is said at slower-than-normal speed with repetitions.	Understands nearly everything at normal speed, although occasional repetition may be necessary.	Understands everyday conversation and normal classroom discussions.
B. Fluency	Speech is so halting and fragmentary that conversation is impossible.	Usually hesitant and often silent because of language limitations.	Speech in everyday conversation and classroom discussions is frequently disrupted by a search for the correct expression.	Speech in everyday conversation and classroom discussions is generally fluent with occasional lapses to search for the correct expression.	Speech in everyday conversation and classroom discussions is fluent and effortless and approximates that of a native speaker.
C. Vocabulary	Vocabulary limitations are so extreme that conversation is impossible.	Misuses words, has limited vocabulary, and has difficulty with comprehension.	Frequently uses wrong words. Conversation is somewhat limited because of inadequate vocabulary.	Occasionally uses inappropriate terms or must rephrase ideas because of language inadequacies.	Extent of vocabulary and usage of idiomatic words approximate those of a native speaker.
D. Pronunciation	Pronunciation problems are so severe that speech is unintelligible.	Hard to understand because of pronunciation problems. Must frequently repeat himself or herself in order to be understood.	Pronunciation problems necessitate concentration on the part of the listener and occasionally lead to misunderstanding.	Always intelligible, although the listener is conscious of an accent and occasional inappropriate intonation patterns.	Pronunciation and intonation approximate those of a native speaker.
E. Grammar	Errors in grammar and word order are so severe that speech is unintelligible.	Makes so many grammar and word errors that comprehension is difficult. Must often rephrase or restrict himself or herself to basic speech patterns.	Makes frequent errors of grammar and word order that occasionally obscure meaning.	Occasionally makes grammatical or word order errors, but these do not obscure meaning.	Grammar and word order approximate those of a native speaker.

Note. A total score of about 19 or 20 can be considered proficient.
Source: Adapted from San Jose Area Bilingual Consortium (n.d.). SOLOM is in the public domain.

Table L-11
Sentence Completion Technique

SENTENCE COMPLETION TECHNIQUE

Child's or adolescent's name: _____   Date: _____

Age: _____ Sex: _____   Grade: _____

Examiner's name: _____   School: _____

Directions: Say to the child or adolescent "I'm going to start a sentence. I'd like you to finish it any way you want. Here is an example. If I say 'A car . . . ,' you can say 'is fun to go in,' 'is nice to have,' 'is good when it works,' 'costs a lot of money,' or anything else that you can think of. OK? Let's try the first one."

1. My favorite TV show _____.

2. At night _____.

3. My teacher _____.

4. The scariest thing is when _____.

5. Mothers _____.

6. At school, I usually feel _____.

7. The thing that upsets me the most is _____.

8. When I wake up, I usually _____.

9. I dislike _____.

10. Fathers _____.

11. I am happiest when _____.

12. My favorite subjects are _____.

13. I worry about _____.

14. My friends _____.

15. I need _____.

16. My life would be better if _____.

17. I feel angry when _____.

18. My neighborhood is _____.

19. Animals are _____.

20. It is wrong to _____.

21. The best thing about being me is _____.

22. I like _____.

23. The saddest time is when _____.

24. The best thing about my home is _____.

25. My favorite book is _____.

26. I feel ashamed when _____.

27. My worst subjects are _____.

28. I am proud of _____.

29. If I could change one thing about my family, it would be _____.

30. (If appropriate) My sister(s) _____.

31. (If appropriate) My brother(s) _____.

Table L-12
Positive Reinforcement Sentence Completion

POSITIVE REINFORCEMENT SENTENCE COMPLETION

Child's name: _____   Date: _____

Age: _____ Sex: _____   Grade: _____

Examiner's name: _____   School: _____

Directions: Read all the sentence stems to the child, one at a time, following up on the child's responses as necessary. Then state all the reinforcers named by the child, and ask the child to rank them in order of their importance.

1. My favorite grown-up is _____.

2. My favorite thing to do with him [her] is _____.

3. The best reward anybody can give me is _____.

4. The two things I like best to do at home are _____.

5. The two things I like best to do at school are _____.

6. My favorite adult at school is _____.

7. My favorite friend at school is _____.

8. When I do something well, my parents _____.

9. I feel terrific when _____.

10. When I have money, I like to _____.

11. Something I really want is _____.

12. The person I would like most to reward me is _____.

13. I would like [person's name] to reward me by _____.

14. The thing I like best to do with my mom is _____.

15. The thing I like best to do with my dad is _____.

16. On the weekend, my favorite thing to do is _____.

17. My favorite thing to do with both my parents is _____.

18. The thing I like to do most is _____.

19. My two favorite TV programs are _____.

20. During my free time, I like to _____.

21. My favorite thing to do with friends is _____.

22. My favorite music to listen to is _____.

23. My favorite activity to do on the computer or phone is _____.

Child's Ranking of Reinforcers

_____

_____

_____

_____

_____

Source: Adapted from Tharp and Wetzel (1969).
From *Foundations of Behavioral, Social, and Clinical Assessment of Children* (Sixth Edition) by Jerome M. Sattler. Copyright 2014 by Jerome M. Sattler, Publisher, Inc. Permission to photocopy this table is granted to purchasers of this book for personal use only (see copyright page for details).

Table L-13
Informal Checklist of Adaptive Behavior

INFORMAL CHECKLIST OF ADAPTIVE BEHAVIOR

Name: _____   Date: _____

Age: _____   Sex: _____   Name of rater: _____

Directions: Use the key below to rate the examinee's behavior.

Key: **Y** (Yes) = Examinee can perform skill at a level appropriate for his or her age.
N (No) = Examinee cannot perform skill at a level appropriate for his or her age.
DK (Don't Know) = Don't know whether examinee can perform skill at a level appropriate for his or her age.
NR (Not Relevant) = Examinee is not expected to be able to perform this skill at his or her current age level.

Area	Check one			

Conceptual Skills (Ability to formulate ideas)

1. Comprehends a request	☐ Y	☐ N	☐ DK	☐ NR
2. Uses Internet to find information	☐ Y	☐ N	☐ DK	☐ NR
3. Spells	☐ Y	☐ N	☐ DK	☐ NR
4. Writes a letter	☐ Y	☐ N	☐ DK	☐ NR
5. Reads	☐ Y	☐ N	☐ DK	☐ NR
6. Answers questions about a story	☐ Y	☐ N	☐ DK	☐ NR
7. Knows basic math	☐ Y	☐ N	☐ DK	☐ NR
8. Identifies coins	☐ Y	☐ N	☐ DK	☐ NR
9. Makes change	☐ Y	☐ N	☐ DK	☐ NR
10. Tells time	☐ Y	☐ N	☐ DK	☐ NR
Other: _____	☐ Y	☐ N	☐ DK	☐ NR

Social Skills (Ability to engage in socially appropriate behavior)

1. Has friends	☐ Y	☐ N	☐ DK	☐ NR
2. Takes turns in interactions	☐ Y	☐ N	☐ DK	☐ NR
3. Demonstrates honesty, trustworthiness, and appropriate play	☐ Y	☐ N	☐ DK	☐ NR
4. Shows sympathy for others when appropriate	☐ Y	☐ N	☐ DK	☐ NR
5. Shows interest in the ideas of others	☐ Y	☐ N	☐ DK	☐ NR
6. Follows rules	☐ Y	☐ N	☐ DK	☐ NR
7. Obeys laws	☐ Y	☐ N	☐ DK	☐ NR
8. Avoids being a victim of fraud	☐ Y	☐ N	☐ DK	☐ NR
9. Demonstrates appropriate assertiveness and self-advocacy	☐ Y	☐ N	☐ DK	☐ NR
10. Assumes responsibility	☐ Y	☐ N	☐ DK	☐ NR
Other: _____	☐ Y	☐ N	☐ DK	☐ NR

Practical Skills (Ability to take care of oneself)

1. Dresses self	☐ Y	☐ N	☐ DK	☐ NR
2. Uses utensils properly	☐ Y	☐ N	☐ DK	☐ NR
3. Uses toilet appropriately	☐ Y	☐ N	☐ DK	☐ NR
4. Uses telephone	☐ Y	☐ N	☐ DK	☐ NR
5. Prepares meals	☐ Y	☐ N	☐ DK	☐ NR
6. Uses money correctly	☐ Y	☐ N	☐ DK	☐ NR
7. Shows caution around dangerous activities	☐ Y	☐ N	☐ DK	☐ NR
8. Uses public transportation	☐ Y	☐ N	☐ DK	☐ NR
9. Takes medicine by himself or herself	☐ Y	☐ N	☐ DK	☐ NR
10. Has appropriate work skills	☐ Y	☐ N	☐ DK	☐ NR
Other: _____	☐ Y	☐ N	☐ DK	☐ NR

Table L-14
Checklist of Symptoms Associated with Brain Injury

CHECKLIST OF SYMPTOMS ASSOCIATED WITH BRAIN INJURY

Name: _____   Date: _____

Physical	Y	N
1. Abnormal sensations	☐	☐
2. Awakening frequently	☐	☐
3. Balance problems	☐	☐
4. Bladder problems	☐	☐
5. Bowel problems	☐	☐
6. Coordination problems	☐	☐
7. Dizziness	☐	☐
8. Drowsiness	☐	☐
9. Fatigue	☐	☐
10. Genital problems	☐	☐
11. Grimaces	☐	☐
12. Head buzzing or tingling	☐	☐
13. Headaches	☐	☐
14. Hyperactivity	☐	☐
15. Loss of appetite	☐	☐
16. Motor or vocal tics	☐	☐
17. Muscle weakness	☐	☐
18. Nightmares	☐	☐
19. Overeating	☐	☐
20. Paralysis	☐	☐
21. Problems hearing	☐	☐
22. Problems seeing	☐	☐
23. Problems smelling	☐	☐
24. Problems speaking	☐	☐
25. Problems tasting	☐	☐
26. Psychomotor slowing	☐	☐
27. Refusal to go to bed	☐	☐
28. Seizures	☐	☐
29. Significant weight gain	☐	☐
30. Significant weight loss	☐	☐
31. Sleeping during the day	☐	☐
32. Slow reaction time	☐	☐
33. Somatic concerns	☐	☐
34. Stiffness	☐	☐
35. Swallowing problems	☐	☐
36. Vomiting	☐	☐

Affective	Y	N
1. Aggression	☐	☐
2. Agitation	☐	☐
3. Anger	☐	☐
4. Anxiety	☐	☐
5. Boastfulness	☐	☐
6. Depression	☐	☐
7. Difficulty inhibiting actions	☐	☐

Affective (Cont.)	Y	N
8. Difficulty modulating emotions	☐	☐
9. Guilt feelings	☐	☐
10. Impulsiveness	☐	☐
11. Inappropriate laughter	☐	☐
12. Indifference	☐	☐
13. Irritability	☐	☐
14. Marked apathy	☐	☐
15. Marked shifts in mood	☐	☐
16. Moodiness	☐	☐
17. Poor frustration tolerance	☐	☐
18. Poor self-control	☐	☐
19. Quick temper	☐	☐
20. Restlessness	☐	☐
21. Restricted emotions	☐	☐
22. Talkativeness	☐	☐
23. Verbal outbursts	☐	☐
24. Withdrawal	☐	☐

Cognitive	Y	N
1. Alteration in consciousness	☐	☐
2. Attention difficulties	☐	☐
3. Concentration difficulties	☐	☐
4. Confabulation	☐	☐
5. Confusion	☐	☐
6. Confusion when confronted with choices	☐	☐
7. Decreased intellectual efficiency	☐	☐
8. Deterioration of academic performance	☐	☐
9. Difficulties in understanding	☐	☐
10. Difficulties with spatial relationships	☐	☐
11. Difficulty anticipating predictable outcomes	☐	☐
12. Difficulty generalizing	☐	☐
13. Difficulty setting goals	☐	☐
14. Distractibility	☐	☐
15. Failure to learn from experience	☐	☐
16. Impaired judgment	☐	☐
17. Impaired organizational skills	☐	☐
18. Impaired orientation	☐	☐
19. Inability to plan ahead	☐	☐
20. Intrusive thoughts	☐	☐

Cognitive (Cont.)	Y	N
21. Irrelevant speech	☐	☐
22. Memory difficulties	☐	☐
23. Overly concrete thinking	☐	☐
24. Preoccupation with irrelevant details	☐	☐
25. Problems following directions	☐	☐
26. Rigid and inflexible thinking	☐	☐
27. Slow thought processes	☐	☐
28. Tangential communication	☐	☐
29. Unusual thought content	☐	☐

Social/Personality	Y	N
1. Bodily preoccupations	☐	☐
2. Coarse language	☐	☐
3. Denial of deficits	☐	☐
4. Difficulty accepting feedback	☐	☐
5. Difficulty in engaging in give-and-take conversations	☐	☐
6. Difficulty in respecting others' personal space	☐	☐
7. Impolite speech	☐	☐
8. Inaccurate insight and self-appraisal	☐	☐
9. Lack of concern for others	☐	☐
10. Limited initiative	☐	☐
11. Loss of interest in friends	☐	☐
12. Lying	☐	☐
13. Making unusual remarks	☐	☐
14. Misperception of intentions of others	☐	☐
15. Overdependence on parents	☐	☐
16. Performing crude bodily functions in public	☐	☐
17. Performing inappropriate actions	☐	☐
18. Poor table manners	☐	☐
19. Regressive behavior	☐	☐
20. Sexual offenses	☐	☐
21. Stealing	☐	☐
22. Suspiciousness	☐	☐
23. Truancy	☐	☐
24. Uncooperativeness	☐	☐
25. Unkempt and careless appearance (when previously fastidious)	☐	☐

Table L-15
Adolescent Brain Injury Symptom Checklist

ADOLESCENT BRAIN INJURY SYMPTOM CHECKLIST

Name: _____   Date: _____

Directions: Please read each item and circle one number in each column. Note that each column has a different scale. Use the description of each scale below to make your rating.

Scale		
Frequency	**Intensity**	**Duration**
1 = Not at all	1 = Not at all	1 = Not at all
2 = Seldom	2 = Vaguely present	2 = A few seconds
3 = Often	3 = Clearly present	3 = A few minutes
4 = Very often	4 = Interfering	4 = A few hours
5 = All the time	5 = Crippling	5 = Constant

Complaint	**Frequency** (Circle one)	**Intensity** (Circle one)	**Duration** (Circle one)
1. Headache	1 2 3 4 5	1 2 3 4 5	1 2 3 4 5
2. Dizziness	1 2 3 4 5	1 2 3 4 5	1 2 3 4 5
3. Nausea and/or vomiting	1 2 3 4 5	1 2 3 4 5	1 2 3 4 5
4. Sleep disturbance	1 2 3 4 5	1 2 3 4 5	1 2 3 4 5
5. Easily fatigued	1 2 3 4 5	1 2 3 4 5	1 2 3 4 5
6. Blurred vision	1 2 3 4 5	1 2 3 4 5	1 2 3 4 5
7. Easily upset by bright light	1 2 3 4 5	1 2 3 4 5	1 2 3 4 5
8. Aggravated by noise	1 2 3 4 5	1 2 3 4 5	1 2 3 4 5
9. Ringing in ears	1 2 3 4 5	1 2 3 4 5	1 2 3 4 5
10. Impaired smell and taste	1 2 3 4 5	1 2 3 4 5	1 2 3 4 5
11. Slurred speech	1 2 3 4 5	1 2 3 4 5	1 2 3 4 5
12. Impaired balance	1 2 3 4 5	1 2 3 4 5	1 2 3 4 5
13. Poor gross-motor control	1 2 3 4 5	1 2 3 4 5	1 2 3 4 5
14. Poor fine-motor control	1 2 3 4 5	1 2 3 4 5	1 2 3 4 5
15. Difficulty concentrating	1 2 3 4 5	1 2 3 4 5	1 2 3 4 5
16. Judgment problems	1 2 3 4 5	1 2 3 4 5	1 2 3 4 5
17. Frustrated or impatient	1 2 3 4 5	1 2 3 4 5	1 2 3 4 5
18. Anxiety	1 2 3 4 5	1 2 3 4 5	1 2 3 4 5
19. Depressed or tearful	1 2 3 4 5	1 2 3 4 5	1 2 3 4 5
20. Temper outbursts	1 2 3 4 5	1 2 3 4 5	1 2 3 4 5
21. Staring spells	1 2 3 4 5	1 2 3 4 5	1 2 3 4 5
22. Difficulty expressing ideas	1 2 3 4 5	1 2 3 4 5	1 2 3 4 5
23. Left/right confusion	1 2 3 4 5	1 2 3 4 5	1 2 3 4 5
24. Difficulty organizing things	1 2 3 4 5	1 2 3 4 5	1 2 3 4 5
25. Not able to understand jokes	1 2 3 4 5	1 2 3 4 5	1 2 3 4 5
26. Easily distracted	1 2 3 4 5	1 2 3 4 5	1 2 3 4 5

Table L-16
Worksheet for Writing a Neuropsychological Report for a Child of School Age

WORKSHEET FOR WRITING A NEUROPSYCHOLOGICAL REPORT FOR A CHILD OF SCHOOL AGE

Instructions: Insert applicable information in the spaces and cross out inapplicable phrases.

Reason for Referral

_____ is a _____ -year-old male/female who was born on _____. He/She was referred for a neuropsychological evaluation after a _____ on _____.

Tests Administered

The following records, tests, and assessment procedures were used [check appropriate ones]:

1. School records
2. Medical records
3. Interview with parents
4. Interview with child
5. Wechsler Intelligence Scale for Children–Fourth Edition (WISC–IV)
6. Wechsler Intelligence Scale for Children–Fourth Edition Integrated (WISC–IV Integrated)
7. Wechsler Adult Intelligence Scale–Fourth Edition (WAIS–IV)
8. Stanford-Binet: Fifth Edition
9. Woodcock-Johnson–Revised Tests of Cognitive Ability
10. Kaufman Assessment Battery for Children–Second Edition (KABC–II)
11. Bender Visual Motor Gestalt Test
12. Benton Visual Retention Test–Revised Fifth Edition
13. Wide Range Achievement Test–Fourth Edition
14. Halstead-Reitan Neuropsychological Test Battery for Older Children
15. Reitan-Indiana Neuropsychological Test Battery for Children
16. Luria-Nebraska Neuropsychological Battery–Children's Revision
17. Contributions to Neuropsychological Assessment Battery
18. NEPSY–II: A Developmental Neuropsychological Assessment
19. Bruininks-Oseretsky Test of Motor Proficiency
20. Purdue Pegboard
21. Grooved Pegboard Test
22. Token Test for Children
23. Reporter's Test
24. Raven's Progressive Matrices
25. California Verbal Learning Test–Children's Version
26. Children's Auditory Verbal Learning Test–Second Edition
27. Children's Memory Scale
28. Rey Auditory-Verbal Learning Test
29. Test of Memory and Learning–Second Edition
30. Wide Range Assessment of Memory and Learning–Second Edition
31. Delis-Kaplan Executive Function System (D-KEFS)
32. Behavior Rating Inventory of Executive Functions (BRIEF)
33. Comprehensive Executive Function Inventory (CEFI)
34. Informal tests: _____
35. Other tests: _____

History

The child has noticed/parents have reported the following problems since the accident/onset of symptoms:

1. _____
2. _____
3. _____
4. _____
5. _____

These problems appear to be improving/getting worse/ remaining the same.

The child is in the _____ grade and was performing at a satisfactory/an unsatisfactory level before the injury/onset of symptoms. Behavioral problems were/were not present before the injury/onset of symptoms. [If present, describe the behavioral problems: The child had difficulties in _____ _____.]

Birth was normal/abnormal. [If abnormal, describe what was abnormal:

_____.]

Achievement of developmental milestones was satisfactory/ delayed. [If delayed, describe what milestones were delayed.

_____.]

Behavioral Observations

When seen for testing, _____ was/was not alert and well oriented. Difficulties were/were not observed during the evaluation. [If present, describe the difficulties: These difficulties included _____

_____.]

Intellectual Functioning

The child achieved a Verbal Comprehension Index of_____ (_____ percentile), a Perceptual Organization Index of _____ (_____ percentile), a Working Memory Index of _____ (_____ percentile), a Processing Speed Index of _____ (_____ percentile), and a Full Scale IQ of _____ ± _____ on the WISC–IV. His/Her overall score suggests that current intellectual functioning falls within the _____ range and at the _____ percentile. The chances that the range of scores from _____ to _____ includes his/her true IQ are about _____ out of 100. The results appear/do not appear to be reliable.

The Full Scale IQ appears/does not appear to reflect the child's level of functioning before injury/onset of symptoms. This estimate is based on parents' and teacher's reports/prior psychological tests. Thus, there is/is no evidence of a general loss of intellectual functioning. [If present, describe the estimated loss: The loss appears to be of approximately _____ IQ points.]

(Continued)

Table L-16 *(Continued)*

Marked intellectual impairments were/were not noted on the subtests of the WISC–IV. There was/was no evidence of clinically significant scaled-score deviations. [If present, describe which subtest scores deviated significantly from the mean of each scale: Strengths were shown in _____

_____

Weaknesses were shown in _____

_____.]

Higher cognitive functions (comprehension, abstract thinking, and problem solving) appeared to be generally intact/impaired.

Educational Achievement
Reading skills are at the _____ grade level and the _____ percentile (standard score of _____), spelling skills are at the _____ grade level and the_____ percentile (standard score of_____), and arithmetic skills are at the _____ grade level and the_____ percentile (standard score of _____), as measured by the_____

_____.

These standard achievement scores are consistent with/ discrepant from _____'s level of scholastic attainment before injury/onset of symptoms. Writing ability was adequate/impaired and thus not indicative/indicative of dysgraphia. There is/is no evidence of a learning disability. [If present, describe the learning disability: The learning disability involves the child's reading/spelling/arithmetic, with difficulties in

_____

_____

_____.]

Motor Functioning
_____ demonstrated consistent right/left/mixed hand dominance. Gross-motor coordination was intact/impaired. Fine-motor coordination was adequate/impaired.
[Additional comments: _____

_____

_____.]

Auditory Perceptual Functioning
Auditory perceptual functioning was intact/impaired. _____ had no/had difficulty in differentiating between pairs of words.
[Additional comments: _____

_____

_____.]

Tactile Perceptual Functioning
Tactile perceptual functioning was relatively intact/impaired. There were no/some errors indicating finger agnosia, no/some errors in graphesthesia, and no/some errors in stereognosis.
[Additional comments: _____

_____

_____.]

Visuo-Spatial Functioning
Visuo-spatial functioning appeared to be adequate/impaired. Visuomotor speed was adequate/impaired.
[Additional comments: _____

_____

_____.]

Oral Language Ability
Language ability was intact/impaired with respect to reading, writing, listening, and talking. There was no/was evidence of dysarthria. Motor aspects of speech were intact/impaired, as there was no/was evidence of disturbance in articulation and repetition. Comprehension of speech was adequate/inadequate and thus not indicative/indicative of a receptive disorder. Word-finding fluency was intact/impaired and thus not indicative/ indicative of an expressive disorder.
[Additional comments: _____

_____

_____.]

Attentional Processes
_____'s primary auditory attention was intact/ impaired. _____'s capacity to manage complex attention (competing attention demands) was within normal limits/ impaired. There was no/was evidence of impairments on tasks that required sustained attention.
[Additional comments: _____

_____

_____.]

Memory Processes
_____'s immediate memory was intact/impaired. Recent memory, including the ability to learn both new verbal and new visual information, was adequate/impaired. Remote memory was satisfactory/impaired.
[Additional comments: _____

_____

_____.]

Behavior
Parental reports indicate that _____ has satisfactory/ unsatisfactory behavior patterns. [If unsatisfactory, include additional comments here: Parents report that _____

_____.]

School reports indicate that his/her behavior in school is satisfactory/unsatisfactory. [If unsatisfactory, include additional comments here: Teachers report that _____

_____

_____.]

Comments
[Include additional comments and recommendations here:

_____

_____

_____.]

Table L-17
Checklist for Accuracy and Completeness of an Assessment Report

CHECKLIST FOR ACCURACY AND COMPLETENESS OF AN ASSESSMENT REPORT

Examinee's name: _____   Report number: _____

Examiner's name: _____   Date of report: _____

Directions: Use this checklist to evaluate the accuracy and completeness of an assessment report. Place a checkmark in the box after you check the item in the report. Write "NA" next to items that are not applicable.

☐ 1. **Report Title**

2. **Identifying Data**
☐   a. Examinee's name
☐   b. Date of birth
☐   c. Age
☐   d. Sex
☐   e. School
☐   f. Grade
☐   g. Date(s) of assessment
☐   h. Date of report
☐   i. Examiner's name and title

☐ 3. **Names of Assessment Instruments Used**

☐ 4. **Reason for Referral**

5. **Background Information**
☐   a. Developmental history
☐   b. Health history
☐   c. Educational history
☐   d. Family history

6. **Observations During the Assessment**
☐   a. Appearance
☐   b. Attitude toward examiner
☐   c. Attitude toward test situation
☐   d. Attitude toward self
☐   e. Speech and language
☐   f. Behavior
☐   g. Affect
☐   h. Work habits
☐   i. Reaction to successes
☐   j. Reaction to failures
☐   k. Visual-motor abilities
☐   l. Motor abilities

7. **Assessment Results**
☐   a. Statement about reliability of test results
☐   b. Statement about validity of test results
☐   c. Scores included as appropriate
☐   d. Percentile ranks included as appropriate
☐   e. Confidence intervals included as appropriate
☐   f. Classification of scores included as appropriate
☐   g. Scores compared with those from previous evaluations, if any

8. **Clinical Impressions**
☐   a. All assessment information considered
☐   b. Reasonable diagnostic conclusion

9. **Recommendations**
☐   a. Clear
☐   b. Covering relevant areas
☐   c. Feasible

10. **Summary**
☐   a. Short (one or two paragraphs)
☐   b. At least one statement (e.g., an idea, thought, or theme) included from each section of the report

11. **Signature**
☐   a. Examiner's name and title typewritten at end of report
☐   b. Examiner's signature included at end of report

12. **Technical Qualities**
☐   a. Language understandable and free of technical jargon
☐   b. No spelling errors
☐   c. No punctuation errors
☐   d. No grammatical errors
☐   e. No errors in reporting test results

Table L-18
Executive Functions Checklist

EXECUTIVE FUNCTIONS CHECKLIST

Child's name: _____   Examiner's name: _____

Age: _____   Sex: _____   Grade: _____

School: _____   Date: _____

Directions: Check **Yes** if the child displays this ability appropriately. Check **No** if the child displays this ability inappropriately or does not display it at all. Check **DK** if you don't know.

	Check one		
Planning and Goal Setting	Yes	No	DK
1. Plans enough time to study before a test	☐	☐	☐
2. Completes tests within time limits	☐	☐	☐
3. Formulates steps to complete a task	☐	☐	☐
4. Sets goals for completing work	☐	☐	☐
5. Uses problem-solving strategies to work around obstacles and complete tasks	☐	☐	☐
6. Initiates activities	☐	☐	☐
Organizing			
1. Organizes information and ideas	☐	☐	☐
2. Arranges complex information in a logical, systematic, and strategic manner	☐	☐	☐
3. Organizes resources to complete tasks	☐	☐	☐
Prioritizing			
1. Knows what to begin first in order to complete a task	☐	☐	☐
2. Focuses on relevant themes and details	☐	☐	☐
3. Executes plans in the correct order	☐	☐	☐
4. Manages deadlines so that more pressing tasks are completed first	☐	☐	☐
Working Memory			
1. Holds and manipulates information temporarily for the purposes of guiding future responses and behaviors	☐	☐	☐
2. Relates concepts to other concepts in a meaningful way	☐	☐	☐

	Check one		
Shifting	Yes	No	DK
1. Shifts between different thoughts and actions according to changes in a situation	☐	☐	☐
2. Modifies plans if needed	☐	☐	☐
3. Uses feedback to improve work	☐	☐	☐
4. Generates concepts based on new knowledge	☐	☐	☐
5. Devises alternative problem-solving strategies	☐	☐	☐
6. Learns from mistakes	☐	☐	☐
7. Divides attention	☐	☐	☐
8. Processes information from multiple sources	☐	☐	☐
Inhibition			
1. Suppresses irrelevant or interfering information	☐	☐	☐
2. Inhibits impulses	☐	☐	☐
3. Thinks through an idea before acting on it	☐	☐	☐
4. Resists distraction by external stimuli	☐	☐	☐
Self-Regulation			
1. Regulates own behavior	☐	☐	☐
2. Monitors own thoughts and actions	☐	☐	☐
3. Attends selectively to specific stimuli	☐	☐	☐
4. Focuses attention for a prolonged period	☐	☐	☐
5. Identifies errors in his or her own work	☐	☐	☐

Table L-19
Checklist of Risk Factors for Potential Violence

CHECKLIST OF RISK FACTORS FOR POTENTIAL VIOLENCE

Name: _____ Date: _____

Sex: _____ Birth date: _____ Interviewer: _____

Directions: Place a check in the box next to each item that applies.

Early Warning Signs

- ☐ 1. Has irrational beliefs and ideas
- ☐ 2. Has made verbal or nonverbal threats
- ☐ 3. Shows fascination with weaponry and/or acts of violence
- ☐ 4. Is knowledgeable about weapons
- ☐ 5. Has a plan to hurt himself or herself or others
- ☐ 6. Externalizes blame
- ☐ 7. Has an unreciprocated romantic obsession
- ☐ 8. Takes up much of teacher's time with behavior problems
- ☐ 9. Other individuals are fearful of him or her
- ☐ 10. Family members are fearful of him or her
- ☐ 11. Shows drastic changes in his or her belief system
- ☐ 12. Displays unwarranted anger and tantrums
- ☐ 13. Experiences high level of stress at home
- ☐ 14. Experiences high level of stress at school
- ☐ 15. Is unable to take criticism
- ☐ 16. Has feelings of being victimized
- ☐ 17. Has bouts of intoxication from alcohol or other substances
- ☐ 18. Is fearful or anxious
- ☐ 19. Is frequently absent from school
- ☐ 20. Often fails to turn in assignments on time
- ☐ 21. Shows violence toward inanimate objects
- ☐ 22. Has stolen school equipment
- ☐ 23. Shows lack of concern for the safety of others
- ☐ 24. Appears to be a loner and has no close friends
- ☐ 25. Has a history of being bullied or teased
- ☐ 26. Has little concern for personal consequences

At-Risk Signs

- ☐ 1. Has a history of bringing a weapon to school
- ☐ 2. Has a history of being violent toward his or her peers
- ☐ 3. Has access to firearms and/or other weapons
- ☐ 4. Is involved in drinking alcohol and/or taking drugs
- ☐ 5. Has caregivers who have a history of drug/alcohol involvement
- ☐ 6. Has a peer group that reinforces antisocial behaviors
- ☐ 7. Accepts aggressiveness as "normal" and as an effective way to solve problems

- ☐ 8. Lives in a home with a high level of violence
- ☐ 9. Lives in a neighborhood with a high level of violence
- ☐ 10. Has a history of aggressive and disruptive classroom behaviors
- ☐ 11. Has a history of poor school achievement
- ☐ 12. Has a history of poor school attendance
- ☐ 13. Has a history of numerous school suspensions
- ☐ 14. Has poor social skills and peer relations
- ☐ 15. Experiences parental rejection at home
- ☐ 16. Has a history of being maltreated as a child
- ☐ 17. Has inconsistent discipline at home
- ☐ 18. Lacks supervision at home
- ☐ 19. Believes that he or she is being treated unfairly and broods over it
- ☐ 20. Thinks that he or she is being persecuted by others
- ☐ 21. Speaks in a threatening manner
- ☐ 22. Shows signs of agitation (e.g., pacing, clenching fists)
- ☐ 23. Displays signs of depression, hopelessness, or despair
- ☐ 24. Refuses to communicate with the staff

Imminent Warning Signs

- ☐ 1. Has episodes of serious physical fighting with peers and/or family members
- ☐ 2. Has recently engaged in acts of vandalism, fire setting, and/or animal cruelty
- ☐ 3. Shows severe rage for seemingly minor reasons
- ☐ 4. Has recently made detailed threats of lethal violence
- ☐ 5. Has engaged in self-injurious behavior and/or has made threats of suicide
- ☐ 6. Has presented a realistic, detailed plan to harm another person or persons
- ☐ 7. Carries a weapon and threatens to use it

Overall Rating of Risk for Potential Violence

- ☐ 1. Low level of risk for potential violence
- ☐ 2. Medium level of risk for potential violence
- ☐ 3. High level of risk for potential violence

Summary/Recommendations/Action Plan

_____
_____
_____
_____

(Continued)

Table L-19 *(Continued)*

LEVELS OF RISK FOR POTENTIAL VIOLENCE

Low Risk

Threat is vague—information is inconsistent, implausible, and/or lacks detail. The threat lacks realism, and the content of the threat suggests that the individual is unlikely to carry out a violent act. ***Action plan:*** Interview individual and obtain additional background information as needed; conduct follow-up interviews as needed.

Medium Risk

Threat is more direct and concrete. There is no strong indication that the individual has taken preparatory steps. However, there may be ambiguous evidence (for example, the individual made references to a book or movie that contains a violent act). There may be a specific statement seeking to convey that the threat is not empty. Lethality is unclear. ***Action plan:*** Interview individual and obtain additional background information and notify law enforcement.

High Risk

Threat is direct, specific, and plausible. The individual has taken concrete steps toward carrying out a potentially lethal act (for example, the individual has acquired or practiced with weapons and/or has one or more victims under surveillance). The individual poses an imminent and serious danger to the safety of others. ***Action plan: Contact law enforcement immediately.***

Table L-20
Ten-Item Personality Inventory (TIPI)

TEN-ITEM PERSONALITY INVENTORY (TIPI)

Name: _____   Date: _____

Directions: Here are a number of personality traits that may or may not apply to you. Please check one of the seven boxes opposite each statement to indicate the extent to which you agree or disagree with that statement. You should rate the extent to which the pair of traits applies to you, even if one characteristic applies more strongly than the other. Use the rating scale below.

Rating Scale:

1	2	3	4	5	6	7
Disagree strongly	Disagree moderately	Disagree a little	Neither agree nor disagree	Agree a little	Agree moderately	Agree strongly

I see myself as	**Check one**						
	1	2	3	4	5	6	7
1. Extraverted, enthusiastic	☐	☐	☐	☐	☐	☐	☐
2. Critical, quarrelsome	☐	☐	☐	☐	☐	☐	☐
3. Dependable, self-disciplined	☐	☐	☐	☐	☐	☐	☐
4. Anxious, easily upset	☐	☐	☐	☐	☐	☐	☐
5. Open to new experiences, complex	☐	☐	☐	☐	☐	☐	☐
6. Reserved, quiet	☐	☐	☐	☐	☐	☐	☐
7. Sympathetic, warm	☐	☐	☐	☐	☐	☐	☐
8. Disorganized, careless	☐	☐	☐	☐	☐	☐	☐
9. Calm, emotionally stable	☐	☐	☐	☐	☐	☐	☐
10. Conventional, uncreative	☐	☐	☐	☐	☐	☐	☐

Note. The TIPI is nonproprietary.

Biology gives you a brain. Life turns it into a mind.
—Jeffrey Eugenides (1960–), American author

The pessimist complains about the wind; the optimist expects it to change; the realist adjusts the sails.
—William Arthur Ward (1921–1994), American author

Goals and Objectives

This chapter is designed to enable you to do the following:

- Become familiar with the concept of executive functions

- Understand the primary executive functions

- Understand the relationship between executive functions and brain areas, intelligence, and academic tasks

- Understand how executive functions can be compromised

- Become familiar with the assessment of executive functions

- Understand how to improve deficits in executive functions

Executive functions are cognitive abilities that consist of several interrelated processes responsible for complex goal-directed behavior, adaptation to environmental changes and demands, and the development of social and cognitive competence and self-regulation of behavior. Executive functions enable individuals to modulate, control, organize, and direct cognitive, emotional, and behavioral activities by helping them make personal and social decisions, distinguish relevant from irrelevant material, follow general rules, and make use of existing knowledge in new situations (P. J. Anderson, 2008). Thus, executive functions are important for daily living, academic performance, work-related activities, and social relationships.

PRIMARY EXECUTIVE FUNCTIONS

Seven primary executive functions are usually cited in the literature (P. J. Anderson, 2008; Blair, Zelazo, & Greenberg, 2005; Howard, Anderson, & Taylor, 2008; Meltzer & Krishnan, 2007; Ylvisaker, Szekeres, & Haabauer-Krupa, 1998):

1. *Planning and goal setting* involves the ability to plan and reason conceptually, monitor one's actions, and set goals. Examples are devising a plan to complete an activity, setting a goal for a project, using problem-solving strategies to work around an obstacle, planning enough time to study before a test, and allocating time to answer all the questions on a test within the time limit. Deficits include difficulty setting appropriate goals, poor conceptual reasoning, inadequate planning ability, poor problem-solving ability, and inefficient problem-solving strategies.

2. *Organizing* involves the ability to organize ideas and information. Examples are organizing information and ideas in a way that others can understand and organizing resources that aid in the completion of tasks. Deficits include poor organizational ability and difficulty formulating organized plans.

3. *Prioritizing* involves the ability to focus on relevant themes and details. Examples are understanding what information is important to study and in what order, knowing what to do first in order to complete a task, executing plans in the correct order, and managing deadlines so that more pressing tasks are completed first. Deficits include difficulty knowing which information takes priority or should be emphasized.

4. *Working memory* involves the ability to temporarily hold and manipulate information in memory. Examples are focusing on material; holding, recalling, and manipulating information temporarily for the purpose of guiding future responses and behaviors; and relating concepts to other concepts in a meaningful way. Deficits include forgetfulness and difficulty holding in memory critical information about the subject matter. *Updating*, which is a component of working memory, involves monitoring and coding incoming information and updating the content of memory by replacing old items with newer,

more relevant ones (van der Sluis, de Jong, & van der Leij, 2007). *Short-term memory* is different from working memory and refers to the storage of information without manipulation or organization.

5. *Shifting* involves the ability to alternate between different thoughts and actions, to devise alternative problem-solving strategies, and to be cognitively flexible. Examples are responding to changes in a situation, modifying plans as needed, using feedback to improve work, generating concepts based on new knowledge, learning from mistakes, dividing attention between different tasks, and processing multiple sources of information. Deficits include difficulty transitioning from one task to another, difficulty multitasking, perseverating on thoughts or actions, difficulty adapting to new demands, and difficulty benefiting from feedback.

6. *Inhibition* involves the ability to inhibit thoughts and actions that are inappropriate for a situation. Examples are inhibiting impulsive remarks and decisions, suppressing irrelevant information, thinking through an idea before acting on it, and resisting distraction from external stimuli. Deficits include acting without thinking, making impulsive buying decisions, insulting others without intending to, and continuing actions even when they are inappropriate.

7. *Self-regulation* involves the ability to regulate one's behavior and monitor one's thoughts and actions. Examples are attending selectively to specific stimuli, focusing attention for a prolonged period, knowing when a project has been completed, knowing which strategies were successful and which were not, and identifying errors in one's work. Deficits include poor self-monitoring, failing to check one's work, and difficulty learning from past experiences.

THREE MODELS OF EXECUTIVE FUNCTIONS

At least three different models have been proposed to explain executive functions. Let's look at these models.

Two-System Model

The two-system model postulates that executive functions can be classified as either metacognitive or emotional/motivational (Ardila, 2013). *Metacognitive executive functions* (or, more broadly, *cognitive control functions*) include planning and goal setting, organizing, prioritizing, and working memory. *Emotional/motivational executive functions* (or, more broadly, *behavior*) include shifting, inhibition, and self-regulation. The two systems reside in different areas of the frontal lobes. Metacognitive executive functions are correlated with intelligence; emotional/motivational executive functions are not.

Three-System Model

The three-system model postulates that three components explain executive functions (Koziol & Lutz, 2013). One component, the *instrumental reward learning system*, allows individuals to learn about the relationship between their actions and consequences—behaviors followed by satisfying consequences tend to be repeated, while those followed by unsatisfying consequences tend not to be repeated. A second component, the *cerebellum*, assists in the automation of behavior by anticipating outcomes and adjusting behavior to environmental changes. The third component, which deals with higher-order processing and decision making, is referred to as the *cognitive control*, or *thinking*, *component*. The first component encompasses the entire cerebral cortex, the second component involves the cerebellum, and the third component resides in the frontal lobes.

Four-System Model

The four-system model postulates that the seven primary executive functions plus one additional general function (information processing) are part of a four-domain *executive control system* (P. J. Anderson, 2008). The system is a good example of a developmental model useful for understanding executive functions and is based on factor analytic and developmental neuropsychology studies. Although the four domains are considered to be independent, they are interrelated and function together as an overall control system. The nature of a specific task determines which domain or domains are needed. Figure M-1 shows examples of possible deficits associated with each domain.

DOMAINS OF THE EXECUTIVE CONTROL SYSTEM

1. *Attentional control* refers to the ability to attend to specific stimuli and ignore irrelevant or distracting stimuli (*selective attention*) and focus attention for prolonged periods (*sustained attention*). It "involves the regulation and monitoring of actions, so that plans are executed in the correct order, errors are identified, and goals are achieved" (P. J. Anderson, 2008, p. 16). The executive functions in this domain are prioritizing, self-regulation, and inhibition.
2. *Cognitive flexibility* refers to "the ability to shift between response sets, learn from mistakes, devise alternative strategies, divide attention, and process multiple sources of information concurrently; working memory is an integral part of the domain" (P. J. Anderson, 2008, p. 17, with changes in notation). The executive functions in this domain are shifting and working memory.
3. *Goal setting* refers to the ability to start an activity and devise a plan to complete it. It involves planning, anticipating future events, and formulating a goal and a sequence of steps in a logical, systematic, and strategic manner in order to achieve the goal. The executive functions in this domain are planning and goal setting and organizing.
4. *Information processing* refers to the ability to process information fluently, efficiently, and speedily. There are no specific primary executive functions involved in this domain.

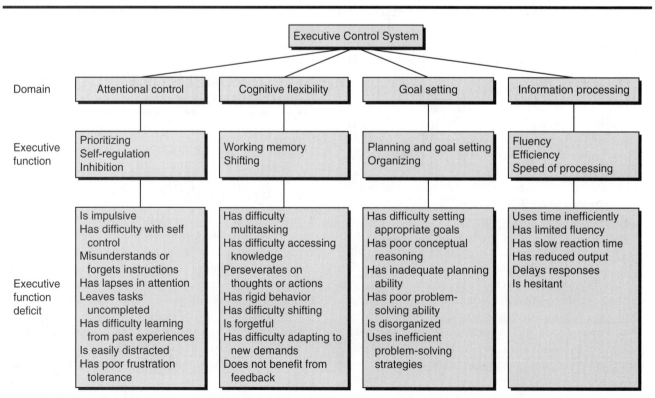

Figure M-1. Executive control system. Adapted from P. J. Anderson (2008).

DEVELOPMENTAL ASPECTS OF EXECUTIVE FUNCTIONS

Executive functions are most closely associated with the frontal lobes of the brain (Nyhus & Barcelo, 2009). Injury to the frontal lobes at an early age may impair executive functions and may hinder a child's ability to acquire and develop more advanced cognitive functions. Early deficits associated with injury to the frontal lobes may become more pronounced when children reach adolescence because of the increasing cognitive, emotional, and self-regulatory demands associated with this period (Eslinger & Biddle, 2008). In some cases, depending on where the damage is located, children with deficits develop compensatory behaviors that allow them to function at higher levels (Eslinger & Biddle, 2008). In other cases, diffuse brain injury impairs executive functions even without frontal lobe involvement (P. J. Anderson, 2008).

Maturational changes in brain structure and function and in social experiences govern the development of executive functions (Carlson, 2005). Although executive functions develop throughout childhood, growth is most robust from birth to 2 years, from 7 to 9 years, and from 15 to 19 years (Ardila, 2013). As children develop executive functions, they acquire *procedural knowledge* (knowledge that often remains unconscious and is obtained through the accomplishment of a task) and *semantic declarative knowledge* (knowledge about the world obtained through language; Koziol & Lutz, 2013). Acquiring both forms of knowledge is a slow, protracted process characterized by changing neuroanatomic underpinnings in large-scale brain networks, including the frontal lobes.

As Table M-1 shows, primitive executive functions begin to develop as early as 2 months of age in the form of self-exploration and an emerging understanding of volitional actions. By 1 year of age, working memory ability and the ability to detect another's attentional and intentional states enable the infant to have more meaningful interactions with others. Executive functions and related cognitive abilities continue to improve throughout development, as children experience

Table M-1
Average Milestones in the Development of Executive Functions from 2 Months to 18 Years

Age	Milestone	Age	Milestone
2 months	Engages in self-exploration Shows an emerging understanding of self-agency (i.e., subjective awareness that one is initiating, executing, and controlling one's own volitional actions in the world)	3 to 8 years *(Continued)*	Improves cognitive flexibility Displays planning ability and goal-directed behavior Develops more mature inhibitory skills Increases memory span Develops more elaborate cognitive strategies Begins to shift efficiently between ideas Holds and manipulates complex information
6 months	Distinguishes inanimate from animate objects Shows signs of greater self-exploration		
7 to 8 months	Shows first signs of working memory and inhibitory control	8 to 10 years	Improves complex continuous performance skills Improves ability to shift between sets, inhibit responses, control impulsive responding, and selectively attend Improves vigilance
12 months	Detects another person's attentional and intentional states based on the direction of his or her eye gaze (referred to as *joint attentional skills*) Improves working memory (e.g., correctly retrieves objects on a delayed response task when the delay is 9 seconds or less)		
		10 to 13 years	Improves capacity and efficiency of working memory Improves strategic thinking and fluency Increases goal-directed behavior and monitoring of behavior Increases flexibility Improves understanding of emotions, intentions, beliefs, and desires Deciphers metaphors and understands faux pas Reaches adult levels of ability to shift attentional sets
14 to 18 months	Actively follows a person's gaze to an object Uses information about objects obtained by observing the emotional reactions of others (referred to as *social referencing*)		
2 years	Has a simple understanding of emotions, intentions, desires, and their relationship to goals Distinguishes between reality and pretense Engages in imaginary play Improves working memory		
3 to 8 years	Improves inhibition and sustained attention Forms meaningful connections between temporally separated events	13 to 18 years	Improves working memory Improves inhibitory control Improves processing speed Improves strategic planning Improves problem solving

Source: Adapted from De Luca and Leventer (2008).

gains in working memory; strategic thinking and fluency; goal-directed behavior and monitoring of behavior; flexibility; understanding of emotions, intentions, beliefs, and desires; deciphering of metaphors and understanding of faux pas; processing speed; and problem solving. However, executive functions mature at different rates depending on the unique abilities of each individual child (Fischer & Daley, 2007). In addition, "There is no clear evidence that children who develop executive skills early will maintain that advantage over later developing children" (Golden & Hines, 2011, p. 261). It is best to conceive of the development of executive functions as having elements of uniformity—*common evolution across executive functions*—and elements of individuality and variation—*unique evolution across executive functions*.

INTELLIGENCE, ACHIEVEMENT, AND EXECUTIVE FUNCTIONS

Tests of intelligence correlate moderately (r_s about .40 to .60) with tests of executive functions, suggesting that both types of tests measure a similar general construct (Crinella & Yu, 1999; Floyd, Bergeron, Hamilton, & Parra, 2010; Friedman, Miyake, Corley, Young, DeFries, & Hewitt, 2006). For example, a factor analysis of the Delis–Kaplan Executive Function System and the Woodcock-Johnson, Third Edition showed that both tests generally load on a common factor (Floyd et al., 2010). Other research suggests that some aspects of executive functions are more related to intelligence than others. For example, working memory is more closely related to both fluid and crystallized intelligence than are inhibition and flexibility (P. J. Anderson, 2008; van der Sluis et al., 2007). One reason for the moderate correlation is that items on intelligence tests are presented one at a time and do *not* require (a) shifting between different tasks or between competing demands, (b) using self-regulation strategies to maximize long-term objectives, or (c) inhibiting less favorable responses (Huffcutt, Goebl, & Culbertson, 2012). Perhaps executive functions represent another broad component of intelligence along with fluid intelligence and crystallized intelligence.

Executive functions play a role in various achievement areas (Meltzer & Krishnan, 2007).

- Writing essays may require (a) planning and defining the first step, (b) rephrasing and paraphrasing one's own work and the work of others (cognitive flexibility), (c) organizing and prioritizing (crafting a complete thought and including an introduction, body, and conclusion in the essay), and (d) using accurate syntax.
- Reading to comprehend may require (a) planning what to read first and which sections to focus on most, (b) organizing the material mentally by its most important points, and (c) monitoring one's comprehension by summarizing material.
- Independent studying and completing homework and long-term projects may require (a) planning ahead (time

management), (b) acquiring materials and information (information processing), (c) setting long-term goals (completing tasks), (d) self-regulation (balancing needs), (e) self-monitoring (remembering to submit completed assignments by a specific time), and (f) cognitive flexibility (the ability to modify how one goes about doing projects).
- Test-taking may require (a) prioritizing and focusing on relevant themes (e.g., using cues from classroom lectures, textbooks, and notes to know which information is important to study) and (b) managing time (e.g., planning enough time to study before a test and allocating time to answer all the questions on a test within the time limit).

In higher grades, academic subjects require students to coordinate and integrate multiple skills (Meltzer & Krishnan, 2007). If students have deficits in executive functions, their performance is likely to be more impaired on general open-ended tasks (such as writing a term paper or completing a review of literature) than on discrete tasks (such as completing a series of arithmetic problems or answering multiple-choice questions).

HOW EXECUTIVE FUNCTIONS ARE COMPROMISED

Executive functions may be compromised by a mental disorder, brain injury, or learning disability or by attention difficulties, fatigue, anxiety, stress, depression, motivational deficits, or very low birth weight (Aarnoudse-Moens, Weisglad-Kuperus, van Goudoever, & Oosterlaan, 2009; Catale, Marique, Closset, & Meulemans, 2008; Fischer & Daley, 2007; Maricle, Johnson, & Avirett, 2010; Muscara, Catroppa, & Anderson, 2008; Ozonoff & Schetter, 2007; Robinson, Goddard, Dritschel, Wisley, & Howlin, 2009; Sesma, Slomine, Ding, & McCarthy, 2008; Yeates, 2010). For example, (a) children with an autism spectrum disorder may have deficits in planning and goal setting, inhibition, and self-regulation, (b) children with ADHD may have deficits in inhibition, organizing, shifting, and self-regulation, (c) children with traumatic brain injury may have deficits in working memory, inhibition, planning and goal setting, shifting, and self-regulation, and (d) children with learning disabilities may have deficits in planning and goal setting, organizing, prioritizing, shifting, and self-regulation.

Research indicates that executive functions in children with traumatic brain injury can be compromised by certain parenting styles and by stressors and lack of resources on the part of the family. One study reported that executive function difficulties at 12 and 18 months following moderate traumatic brain injury (but not severe brain injury) were greater among children whose parents had an authoritarian parenting style than among children whose parents had a permissive or authoritative parenting style (Potter, Wade, Walz, Cassedy, Stevens, Yeates, & Taylor, 2011). Further, regardless of the degree of injury (e.g., moderate or severe), children living in families with heightened stressors and fewer resources had more impaired executive functions than children living in families with fewer stressors and more resources. The results suggest that it may be valuable to assess parenting style and family resources when you evaluate a child with brain injury.

ASSESSMENT OF EXECUTIVE FUNCTIONS

Executive functions can be assessed by administering neuropsychological and psychological tests; conducting interviews with the child and his or her parents and teachers; observing the child at school, at home, and during the assessment; and analyzing samples of the child's schoolwork and written homework assignments (Bernstein & Waber, 2007). The test battery should cover cognitive, linguistic, perceptual, and motor domains. Table M-2 lists formal procedures for evaluating executive functions, Table M-3 lists informal procedures for evaluating executive functions, and Table L-18 in Appendix L shows a checklist for rating executive functions in older children. Interviews with the child, parent, and teacher can cover topics related to the child's executive functions, such as how the child gets ready for school, makes plans, organizes his or her free time and study time, completes homework assignments, and remembers household chores. We recommend that multiple measures be used to assess executive functions.

Table M-2
Formal Measures of Executive Functions

Test or Procedure	Description	Executive Function
Auditory Continuous Performance Test (ACPT; Keith, 1994)	Requires child to listen to single words presented on a tape and raise thumb when he or she hears the target word	Self-regulation
Beery-Buktenica Developmental Test of Visual-Motor Integration, Sixth Edition (Beery VMI; Beery, Buktenica, & Beery, 2010)	Requires child to copy up to 24 designs, draw spontaneously, and imitate the examiner's drawing of several lines	Planning and goal setting Organizing
Behavior Rating Inventory of Executive Function (BRIEF; Gioia, Isquith, Guy, & Kenworthy, 2000)	Asks parents and/or teachers to give information about a child's behaviors	Inhibition Shifting Working memory Planning and goal setting Organizing Self-regulation
Behavior Rating Inventory of Executive Function–Preschool Version (BRIEF–P; Gioia, Espy, & Isquith, 2003)	Asks parents, teachers, and/or day care providers to give information about a child's behaviors	Inhibition Shifting Working memory Planning and goal setting Organizing Self-regulation
Behavior Rating Inventory of Executive Function–Self-Report Version (BRIEF–SR; Guy, Isquith, & Gioia, 2004)	Asks an adolescent to give information about his or her behaviors	Inhibition Shifting Working memory Planning and goal setting Organizing Self-regulation
Behavioural Assessment of the Dysexecutive Syndrome (BADS; Wilson, Alderman, Burgess, Emslie, & Evans, 1996)	Requires individual (age 16 to 87 years) to perform various tasks, such as manipulate an object, adapt to a changing stimulus, or plan a course of action. The individual and a family member also complete a questionnaire about the individual's executive function abilities.	Shifting Inhibition Planning and goal setting Self-regulation
Behavioural Assessment of the Dysexecutive Syndrome in Children (BADS–C; Emslie, Wilson, Burden, Nimmo-Smith, & Wilson, 2003)	Requires child (age 8 to 16 years) to perform various tasks, such as manipulate an object, adapt to a changing stimulus, or plan a course of action. The child and a family member also complete a questionnaire about the child's executive function abilities.	Shifting Inhibition Planning and goal setting Self-regulation

(Continued)

Table M-2 *(Continued)*

Test or Procedure	Description	Executive Function
Bender Visual-Motor Gestalt Test (Bender, 1938)	Requires child to copy 9 geometric figures	Planning and goal setting Organizing
Bender Visual-Motor Gestalt Test, Second Edition (Bender-Gestalt II; Brannigan & Decker, 2003)	Requires child to copy 16 geometric figures	Planning and goal setting Organizing
Children's Behavior Questionnaire (CBQ; Rothbart, Ahadi, Hersey, & Fisher, 2001)	Asks caregiver to answer questions on child's reactivity and self-regulation (For a copy of the CBQ, see http://childcare. wceruw.org/pdf/1stgrade/childrens_behavior_questionnaire. pdf)	Self-regulation Inhibition
Children's Category Test (CCT; Boll, 1993)	Requires child to respond to feedback and clues and shift response sets to solve problems	Shifting
Clock Drawing Test (Freedman, Leach, Kaplan, Winocur, Shulman, & Delis, 1994)	Requires child to draw numbers in a circle in order to make the circle look like the face of a clock and then to draw the hands of the clock to read "10 after 11" (For a copy of the Clock Drawing Test, see http://www. healthcare.uiowa.edu/igec/tools/cognitive/clockdrawing.pdf)	Planning and goal setting Organizing
Comprehensive Executive Function Inventory (CEFI; Naglieri & Goldstein, 2013)	Asks parents, teachers, and/or the child to give information about how often the child performs various behaviors	Self-regulation Inhibition Organizing Planning and goal setting Working memory
Comprehensive Trail Making Test (CTMT; Reynolds, 2002)	Requires child to connect a series of numbers (expressed either as numerals or in word form) and letters in a specified order	Self-regulation Planning and goal setting Shifting
Conners' Continuous Performance Test II, Version 5 (CPT–II V.5; Conners & MHS Staff, 2004)	Requires child to press a space bar in response to all stimuli except the target stimulus	Self-regulation Inhibition
Controlled Oral Word Association Test (COWA; Benton, Hamsher, & Sivan, 1994)[a]	Requires child to produce as many words as possible beginning with the letter C in one minute. The procedure is then repeated for the letters F and L.	Self-regulation
Delayed response tasks, including A-not-B, delayed alternation, spatial reversal, color reversal, and self-control (Espy, Kaufman, McDiarmid, & Glisky, 1999; Lee, Vaughn, & Kopp, 1983)	Requires child to locate an object after it has been hidden from view under various conditions or requires child to inhibit himself or herself from taking a reward immediately in order to receive a larger reward later	Working memory Inhibition
Delis–Kaplan Executive Function System (D–KEFS; Delis, Kaplan, & Kramer, 2001)		
Trail Making Test	Requires child to scan letters and numbers and mark a number, connect numbers in ascending order, connect letters in alphabetical order, switch between connecting numbers and letters, and draw a line over a dotted line	Shifting
Verbal Fluency Test	Requires child to say words that begin with a certain letter and belong to a certain category and alternate between saying words from two different categories	Self-regulation Shifting
Design Fluency Test	Requires child to produce different designs from an array of dots	Self-regulation

Table M-2 (Continued)

Test or Procedure	Description	Executive Function
Color-Word Interference Test	Requires child to name colors, read words that denote colors, and state the color of the ink in which other color names are printed	Inhibition Shifting
Sorting Test	Requires child to sort cards into two groups by following certain rules and identify and describe the correct rules	Shifting Planning and goal setting
Twenty Questions	Requires child to identify 30 common objects with the fewest yes-no questions possible	Planning and goal setting Self-regulation
Word Context Test	Requires child to discover the meanings of made-up words, given a series of clues	Shifting
Tower Test	Requires child to move five disks across three pegs to build a tower with the fewest possible moves	Inhibition Planning and goal setting
Delis–Rating of Executive Function (D–REF; Delis, 2012)	Requires child, parent, and/or teacher to give information about the child's executive function abilities	Self-regulation Working memory Inhibition Planning and goal setting
Go-No Go (Luria, 1980) (See also KITAP below)	Requires child to respond in various ways to the tapping pattern of the examiner	Inhibition
Gordon Diagnostic System (Gordon, 1988)	Requires child to press a button every time a "1" is followed by a "9" presented on a microprocessor-based portable unit	Inhibition
Kaufman Assessment Battery for Children, Second Edition (KABC–II; Kaufman & Kaufman, 2004)		
Conceptual Thinking	Requires child to point to the picture that does not go with the other pictures presented with it	Self-regulation
Pattern Reasoning	Requires child to select the one stimulus that completes a pattern correctly	Shifting Self-regulation
Rover	Requires child to find the most efficient path in a route with obstacles	Planning and goal setting Self-regulation Inhibition
Triangles	Requires child to assemble triangles to match a picture	Planning and goal setting Organizing
KITAP–Test of Attentional Performance for Children (Zimmerman, Gondan, & Fimm, 2005)		
Alertness	Requires child to press a key every time a stimulus (witch) appears on the screen	Self-regulation Inhibition
Distractibility	Requires child to press a key when a target stimulus (sad ghost) appears on the screen, but ignore distractors	Working memory Self-regulation
Divided Attention	Requires child to simultaneously listen to a series of high and low owl sounds and watch for target stimuli (owls with closed eyes) and press a key either when a sound is repeated or when the target stimulus appears	Working memory Shifting Self-regulation
Flexibility	Requires child to alternate between identifying (by tapping one of two buttons) blue and green dragons that are presented on random sides of the screen	Working memory Self-regulation

(Continued)

Table M-2 *(Continued)*

Test or Procedure	Description	Executive Function
Go/No Go	Requires child to press a key when the target stimulus (a bat) is presented, but not when the nontarget stimulus (a cat) is presented	Inhibition Self-regulation
Sustained Attention	Requires child to press a key as quickly as possible when two ghosts of the same color appear on the screen sequentially or when two ghosts of any color appear in the same position on the screen	Self-regulation
Vigilance	Requires child to press a key as quickly as possible when the evil ghost appears on the screen, but not when the good ghost appears on the screen	Self-regulation
Visual Scanning	Requires child to scan a grid of 25 witches and press one key if all the witches are flying in the same direction and another key if one of the witches is flying in the opposite direction	Self-regulation
Koppitz–2: Koppitz Developmental Scoring System for the Bender Gestalt Test, Second Edition (Reynolds, 2007)	Requires child to copy 16 geometric figures	Planning and goal setting Organizing
Matching Familiar Figures Test (MFFT; Cairns & Cammock, 1978; Kagan, Rosman, Day, Albert, & Phillips, 1964)	Requires child to identify the exact duplicate of a given picture when presented with six images	Inhibition Working memory
NEPSY–II (Korkman, Kirk, & Kemp, 2007)		
Animal Sorting	Requires child to sort cards into categories using different sets of sorting rules	Shifting
Auditory Attention & Response Set	Requires child to listen to a series of words and touch the appropriate circle when he or she hears a target word	Self-regulation Inhibition Shifting
Clocks	Requires child to either draw a clock or read one without numbers	Planning and goal setting Organizing
Design Fluency	Requires child to generate unique designs by connecting dots in structured and random arrays	Shifting Planning and goal setting
Inhibition	Requires child to name shapes, the direction of arrows, and the opposite of what he or she sees, or to choose a name dependent on an object's color	Inhibition Shifting
Statue	Requires child to maintain a certain body position for 75 seconds and inhibit responding to auditory distractor stimuli	Inhibition
NIH Toolbox (National Institutes of Health and Northwestern University, 2012)		
Flanker Inhibitory Control & Attention	Requires child to focus on a given stimulus while inhibiting attention to other stimuli	Inhibition Self-regulation
Dimensional Change Card Sort Test	Requires child to match a series of test pictures to a target picture, first according to one dimension (e.g., color) and then according to the other dimension (e.g., shape)	Shifting
List Sorting Working Memory Test	Requires child to arrange pictures of foods and animals in order of size	Working memory

Table M-2 *(Continued)*

Test or Procedure	Description	Executive Function
Rey Complex Figure Test and Recognition Trial (RCFT; Meyers & Meyers, 1995)	Requires child to copy and then recall a complex geometric figure	Planning and goal setting Organizing Working memory
Rey-Osterrieth Complex Figure Test (ROCFT; Rey, 1941)	Requires child to copy a complex geometric figure	Planning and goal setting Organizing
SCAN–3 Tests for Auditory Processing Disorders for Children (SCAN–3:C; Keith, 2009)	Requires child to listen to tones and to indicate whether one or two tones were presented, and to listen to words under various background conditions and then repeat them	Self-regulation
Shape School (Espy, 1997)	Requires child to name stimulus items based on a given set of contingencies	Inhibition Self-regulation
Stroop Color and Word Test–Revised, Children's Version (Golden, Freshwater, & Golden, 2003)	Requires child to look at color names that are printed in different colors and to name the color of the presented words as quickly as possible. For example, if the word *BLUE* is printed in red ink, the correct response is "red."	Self-regulation Shifting Inhibition
Test of Everyday Attention for Children (TEA–Ch; Manly, Robertson, Anderson, & Nimmo-Smith, 1998)		
Sky Search	Requires child in the first part to find target items, a pair of identical spaceships, as quickly as possible on a sheet filled with pairs of identical and nonidentical spaceships (distractor spaceships) and in the second part circle the target items as quickly as possible on a sheet with target items only (to assess motor slowness).	Prioritizing Inhibition
Score!	Requires child to track specific stimuli, such as a target tone from an audiotape	Self-regulation Shifting
Dual Task, Sky Search Dual Task	Requires child to perform two tasks simultaneously	Self-regulation Shifting
Creature Counting	Requires child to switch between two relatively simple activities of counting upward and counting downward	Inhibition Self-regulation Shifting
Sky Search DT	Requires child to find spaceships (Sky Search) and to keep a count of sounds (Score!)	Self-regulation
Map Mission	Requires child to find target symbols on a map	Self-regulation
Score DT	Requires child to count sounds and to listen for an animal name	Self-regulation
Walk, Don't Walk	Requires child to take one step along a paper path (using a pen) after hearing a tone and stop when another tone is heard	Self-regulation Inhibition
Opposite Worlds	Requires child in one condition to name the digit that is shown and in the other condition to say "one" when he or she sees a 2 and "two" when he or she sees a 1	Self-regulation Inhibition
Tower of Hanoi (Simon, 1975; Welsh, Pennington, & Groisser, 1991)	Requires child to move three rings, one at a time, to achieve the examiner's model configuration (one variant is to use Playschool Rock-a-Stack rings)	Inhibition Planning and goal setting Organizing

(Continued)

Table M-2 *(Continued)*

Test or Procedure	Description	Executive Function
Tower of London DX, Second Edition (TOLDX; Culbertson & Zillmer, 2005)	Requires child to match a figure by moving the fewest pegs possible	Inhibition Planning and goal setting Organizing
Wechsler Intelligence Scale for Children–Fourth Edition (WISC–IV; Wechsler, 2003)		
Block Design	Requires child to use blocks to assemble designs	Planning and goal setting Organizing
Cancellation	Requires child to cross out certain stimuli	Self-regulation Inhibition
Coding	Requires child to copy symbols paired with other symbols or numbers	Self-regulation Planning and goal setting
Digit Span	Requires child to repeat a series of digits forward and backward	Working memory
Letter–Number Sequencing	Requires child to repeat a series of numbers and letters in a specified random order	Working memory
Wechsler Intelligence Scale for Children–Fourth Edition Integrated (WISC–IV Integrated; Kaplan, Fein, Kramer, Delis, & Morris, 2004)		
Elithorn Mazes	Requires child to draw a path through a specific number of dots in a maze on the way to an exit	Planning and goal setting Organizing
Visual Digit Span	Requires child to look at numbers on a card for a brief period of time and then repeat them in the order in which they were presented	Working memory
Spatial Span	Requires child to repeat a series of taps on ten different three-dimensional cubes after they are performed by the examiner, first in the same order and then in reverse order	Working memory
Letter Span	Requires child to repeat a series of nonrhyming and rhyming letters in the order given by the examiner	Working memory
Wechsler Preschool and Primary Scale of Intelligence–Fourth Edition (WPPSI–IV; Wechsler, 2012)		
Block Design	Requires child to use blocks to assemble designs	Planning and goal setting Organizing
Bug Search	Requires child to mark the bug in the search group that matches the target bug	Self-regulation
Picture Memory	Requires child to select one or more pictures previously shown from a group of pictures	Self-regulation Working memory
Cancellation	Requires child to cross out certain stimuli	Self-regulation Inhibition
Zoo Location	Requires child to place a card in a specific location after previously having seen the card in that location	Working memory
Animal Coding	Requires child to mark shapes that correspond to pictured animals	Self-regulation Planning and goal setting

Table M-2 *(Continued)*

Test or Procedure	Description	Executive Function
Wisconsin Card Sorting Test (WCST; Heaton, Chelune, Talley, Kay, & Curtiss, 1993)	Requires child to match cards by color, quantity, or design, using different principles for the matching	Shifting Self-regulation Working memory
Woodcock-Johnson III Normative Update Tests of Cognitive Abilities (WJ III NU; Woodcock, McGrew, & Mather, 2007)		
Executive Process Cluster	Requires child to formulate rules, categorize, scan, and reason	Inhibition Shifting Planning and goal setting
Broad Attention Cluster	Requires child to hold information in short-term memory, discriminate speech sounds, and sustain attention in a pair cancellation task	Self-regulation Working memory

[a] A subtest in the Multilingual Aphasia Examination, Third Edition.

The assessment of executive functions has several limitations:

1. Planning and goal setting, organizing, and self-regulation cannot be measured exclusively by tests of executive functions because such tests are administered in a distraction-free environment that does not mirror more fluid and natural environments. In addition, the tests may be too static to provide an accurate picture of how the child functions in the real world (Bernstein & Waber, 2007; Gioia, Isquith, & Kenealy, 2008).

2. Scores on tests of executive functions do not correlate highly with the ability to work independently or complete long-term projects (Meltzer & Krishnan, 2007).

3. Scores on performance-based measures of executive functions have low correlations with rater-based measures of executive functions (Isquith, Roth, & Gioia, 2013).

4. High reliabilities may be difficult to achieve on measures of executive functions because of children's variable attention and concentration (Espy, Bull, Kaiser, Martin, & Banet, 2008).

5. Test-retest reliabilities on measures of executive functions are often lower than acceptable for school-age and adolescent children; if, on the initial testing, they figure out how to perform the tasks, their performance on retest often improves (Golden & Hines, 2011; Strauss, Sherman, & Spreen, 2006).

6. Because tasks used to assess executive functions are not pure measures of executive functions, it is not always clear how best to interpret the test scores (Suchy, 2009). For example, poor scores on the Stroop test (see Table M-2) may reflect poor inhibitory control, poor speed of color naming, poor speed of word identification, or any combination of these.

The measurement of executive functions could be improved in several ways (Anderson, Anderson, Jacobs, & Smith, 2008; Koziol & Lutz, 2013; Sesma et al., 2008; Shaheen, 2013).

1. Traditional tests should be normed for children so that age-appropriate scores are available.

2. Tests with several parts should provide scores for each part as well as summary scores.

3. Tests of procedural learning need to be developed, normed, and validated. These tests could build on existing ones like the Trail-Making Test and Mazes (a test on prior forms of the Wechsler Scales). Administering multiple trials of these tests would provide an index of procedural learning (time for completion).

4. Tests of motor functions should be routinely administered. The tests should examine motor control, speed, rhythmicity, duration, smoothness, and freedom from overflow (unwanted movements that occur during a desired movement). Tests useful in assessing motor functions include the NEPSY–II, NIH Toolbox, and Bruininks-Oseretsky Test of Motor Proficiency, Second Edition (all of which are covered in the main text). Motor functions provide information about the cerebellum, which plays a key role in coordination, balance, equilibrium, and muscle tone in addition to its role in executive functions.

5. New child-friendly tests need to be designed and validated. Studies need to report detailed information about the research sample and how the findings relate to the characteristics of the sample (e.g., severity of brain injury, location of brain injury, and time since injury).

6. Longitudinal studies are needed that map developmental trajectories for individual children so that our understanding does not rely on cross-sectional studies exclusively.

7. Studies should compare results from tests of executive functions administered by examiners with those from tests administered by computers.

Table M-3
Informal Procedures for the Assessment of Executive Functions

---

Directions: Follow up on "yes" or "no" responses as needed with a comment such as "Tell me more about that."

Interviewing an Older Child

1. Do you make plans about things that you want to do in the future?
2. Do you set goals for yourself?
3. Tell me about your memory ability. (If needed) Do you use any memory strategies?
4. Do you anticipate the consequences of your actions?
5. Do you sometimes act without thinking?
6. Do you use time efficiently?
7. Can you do two things at one time?
8. Are you easily distracted when you are reading, working on the computer, or doing other things?
9. Can you follow multi-step directions?
10. Tell me how you study for a test.
11. Do you usually allow enough time to answer all of the questions on a test?
12. How do you arrange things so that you get to school on time?
13. Do you live for the moment?
14. Can you start and stop a conversation appropriately?
15. Do you usually adjust your voice to the noise level of the setting that you are in?
16. Do you usually adjust the words you use depending on the person you are talking to?
17. What chores do you do at home? (If child does chores) Do you do your chores without having to be reminded of them?
18. How do you express your emotions?
19. Do you think through an idea before you act on it?
20. Do you sometimes blurt out an answer before the teacher wants it?
21. Do you ever lose track of what you are doing?
22. Tell me about how your room is organized at home.
23. Do you review your completed homework before you turn it in?
24. Tell me about how you go about writing a composition or a term paper.
25. Do you usually learn from your mistakes?

Interviewing the Child's Parent

1. Does your child make plans about things he [she] wants to do in the future?
2. Does your child set goals for himself [herself]?
3. Tell me about your child's memory ability. (If needed) Does your child use any memory strategies?
4. Does your child anticipate the consequences of his [her] actions?
5. Does your child sometimes act without thinking?
6. Does your child use time efficiently?
7. Can your child do two things at one time?
8. Is your child easily distracted when he [she] is reading, working on the computer, or doing other things?
9. Can your child follow multi-step directions?
10. Tell me how your child studies for a test.
11. Does your child usually allow enough time to answer all of the questions on a test?

12. How does your child arrange things so that he [she] gets to school on time?
13. Does your child live for the moment?
14. Can your child start and stop a conversation appropriately?
15. Does your child usually adjust his [her] voice to the noise level of the setting he [she] is in?
16. Does your child usually adjust the words he [she] uses depending on the person he [she] is talking to?
17. What chores does your child do at home? (If child does chores) Does your child do his [her] chores without having to be reminded of them?
18. How does your child express his [her] emotions?
19. Does your child think through an idea before he [she] acts on it?
20. Does your child sometimes blurt out an answer before the teacher wants it?
21. Does your child ever lose track of what he [she] is doing?
22. Tell me about how your child's room is organized at home.
23. Does your child review his [her] completed homework before he [she] turns it in?
24. Tell me about how your child goes about writing a composition or a term paper.
25. Does your child usually learn from his [her] mistakes?

Analyzing Written Composition Assignments
Look at the child's ability to do the following:

1. Interpret the assignment correctly
2. Write with good motor control
3. Place written material on the page correctly
4. Use language appropriate for the intended audience
5. Introduce the topic clearly
6. Organize the content of the written material coherently
7. Retrieve textbook information
8. Arrive at an adequate conclusion
9. Use correct punctuation, spelling, and grammar
10. Express ideas clearly
11. Turn in completed homework on time

Analyzing Mathematics Assignments
Look at the child's ability to do the following:

1. Use self-correction when doing calculations
2. Use an organizing strategy in solving problems
3. Retrieve stored information
4. Execute appropriate steps in arriving at solutions

Observations During the Assessment
Observe the child's

1. Approach to starting each task
2. Problem-solving strategies
3. Persistence in completing tasks
4. Flexibility in switching from one task to another
5. Attention span
6. Memory ability (including recall of directions)
7. Organizational skills
8. Time management skills

Table M-3 (Continued)

Observations in the Classroom

Observe whether the child does the following (also see Table C-1 in Appendix C):

1. Observes classroom rules
2. Follows the teacher's directions
3. Brings homework to class
4. Has materials ready at the beginning of a lesson
5. Begins and ends working appropriately
6. Switches from one task to another task appropriately
7. Manages to avoid being easily distracted
8. Manages to avoid acting impulsively (e.g., thinks about an answer before responding)
9. Is considerate of others (e.g., recognizes that other children's feelings and ideas are as important as his or her own)
10. Writes well
11. Organizes his or her desk appropriately
12. Organizes his or her backpack appropriately
13. Completes assignments on time
14. Reads words fluently aloud
15. Understands the written material
16. Responds appropriately when called on by the teacher
17. Makes appropriate inferences when reading
18. Listens appropriately
19. Gleans needed information from the lecture
20. Notices similarities and differences
21. Knows where his or her possessions are

Observations on the Playground

Observe the child's ability to do the following (also see Table C-7 in Appendix C):

1. Follow playground rules
2. Follow teacher's directions
3. Interact with other children
4. Stay focused on an activity
5. Interact with adults
6. Converse with others, including speaking appropriately, understanding conversations, and starting and ending conversations appropriately
7. Be empathic
8. Adapt to new situations
9. Be a leader
10. Handle difficult situations

Source: The Teaching Research Institute–Eugene (n.d.).

IMPROVING DEFICITS IN EXECUTIVE FUNCTIONS

Children with executive function deficits may benefit from learning the following (Meltzer & Krishnan, 2007; NCLD Editorial Staff, 2010):

- Strategies for planning, prioritizing, memorizing, shifting flexibly, and checking their work. These strategies might include taking a step-by-step approach to studying or writing, using visual organizers, preparing a schedule each day and reviewing it several times a day, and planning and structuring transition times.
- Strategies for organizing their time and materials, developing their ideas, meeting deadlines, and reviewing completed work. These strategies might include estimating how long a task will take, creating "to do" lists, breaking long assignments into chunks, assigning a time frame to complete each chunk of work, and using a calendar to keep track of long-term assignments and due dates.
- How, when, and why specific strategies can be used for different academic tasks
- How to modify strategies to match their own learning style
- How to select and apply strategies to different academic tasks and settings
- How to develop self-monitoring skills, including identifying their most common mistakes
- How to recognize that "learning how to learn" is an important step in doing well in school

Also see Handout K-1 (for parents) and Handout K-3 (for teachers) in Appendix K for suggestions for working with children with various kinds of special needs.

Other methods of improving deficits in executive functions include use of stimulant medications (especially for children with attention-deficit/hyperactivity disorder; see Chapter 15); cognitive strategy instruction focused on teaching children how to observe, evaluate, monitor, and regulate any deficits in executive functions; computerized programs designed to address deficits in executive functions through repeated practice and reinforcement, with the aim of making changes in brain functioning; neurofeedback training to help children learn to normalize patterns of electrical activity in the brain; and multimodal procedures that include medication and behavioral interventions (Riccio & Gomes, 2013).

Following are some ways to enhance self-regulation in children (Ylvisaker & Feeney, 2008):

- Encouraging parents to provide a home environment that is stable, organized, and predictable
- Encouraging adults important in children's lives to form emotional attachments with the children
- Encouraging parents to provide adequate opportunities for their children to exercise control over events in their lives
- Encouraging parents to adopt an authoritative/responsive style of parenting (neither too permissive nor too authoritarian)
- Encouraging parents and teachers to reward self-regulation, autonomy, and personal responsibility

- Giving children opportunities to work with adults who actively use self-regulatory strategies for themselves and who foster self-regulatory skills in the children
- Giving children opportunities to develop effective language
- Giving children opportunities at home, at school, and in the neighborhood to develop a coherent sense of personal identity

THINKING THROUGH THE ISSUES

1. Why do you think there has been increased interest in the assessment of executive functions?
2. When would you use a test of executive functions?
3. How is the assessment of executive functions different from the assessment of intelligence?
4. How do you use executive functions in your own daily life?
5. How might you know if you had deficits in your own executive functions?
6. If you were to discover deficits in your own executive functions, what are some things that you could do in order to reduce these deficits or to function more adequately in spite of them?
7. How can we improve the assessment of executive functions?
8. Can there be a sound psychometric basis for the measurement of executive functions?

SUMMARY

1. Executive functions are cognitive abilities that consist of several interrelated processes responsible for complex goal-directed behavior, adaptation to environmental changes and demands, and the development of social and cognitive competence and self-regulation of behavior.
2. Executive functions enable individuals to modulate, control, organize, and direct cognitive, emotional, and behavioral activities by helping them make personal and social decisions, distinguish relevant from irrelevant material, follow general rules, and make use of existing knowledge in new situations.
3. Executive functions are important for daily living, academic performance, work-related activities, and social relationships.

Primary Executive Functions

4. Planning and goal setting involves the ability to plan and reason conceptually, monitor one's actions, and set goals.
5. Organizing involves the ability to organize ideas and information.
6. Prioritizing involves the ability to focus on relevant themes and details.
7. Working memory involves the ability to temporarily hold and manipulate information in memory.
8. Shifting involves the ability to alternate between different thoughts and actions, to devise alternative problem-solving strategies, and to be cognitively flexible.
9. Inhibition involves the ability to inhibit thoughts and actions that are inappropriate for a situation.
10. Self-regulation involves the ability to regulate one's behavior and monitor one's thoughts and actions.

Three Models of Executive Functions

11. The two-system model postulates that executive functions can be classified as either metacognitive or emotional/motivational.
12. The three-system model postulates that three components explain executive functions: the instrumental reward learning system, the cerebellum, and the cognitive control, or thinking, component.
13. The four-system model, referred to as the executive control system, postulates that four domains account for executive functions: attentional control, cognitive flexibility, goal setting, and information processing.

Developmental Aspects of Executive Functions

14. Executive functions are most closely associated with the frontal lobes of the brain.
15. Injury to the frontal lobes at an early age may impair executive functions and may hinder a child's ability to acquire and develop more advanced cognitive functions.
16. Early deficits associated with injury to the fontal lobes may become more pronounced when children reach adolescence.
17. Maturational changes in brain structure and function and in social experiences govern the development of executive functions.
18. Although executive functions develop throughout childhood, growth is most robust from birth to 2 years, from 7 to 9 years, and from 15 to 19 years.
19. As children develop executive functions, they acquire procedural knowledge and semantic declarative knowledge.
20. Executive functions and related cognitive abilities continue to improve throughout development.
21. Executive functions mature at different rates depending on the unique abilities of each individual child.
22. It is best to conceive of the development of executive functions as having elements of uniformity—common evolution across executive functions—and elements of individuality and variation—unique evolution across executive functions.

Intelligence, Achievement, and Executive Functions

23. Tests of intelligence correlate moderately (r_s about .40 to .60) with tests of executive functions, suggesting that both types of tests measure a similar general construct.
24. Working memory is more closely related to both fluid and crystallized intelligence than are inhibition and flexibility.
25. Perhaps executive functions represent another broad component of intelligence along with fluid intelligence and crystallized intelligence.
26. Executive functions play a role in various achievement areas.
27. If students have deficits in executive functions, their performance is likely to be more impaired on open-ended tasks than on discrete tasks.

How Executive Functions Are Compromised

28. Executive functions may be compromised by a mental disorder, brain injury, or learning disability or by attention difficulties, fatigue, anxiety, stress, depression, motivational deficits, or very low birth weight.
29. Children with an autism spectrum disorder may have deficits in planning and goal setting, inhibition, and self-regulation.

30. Children with ADHD may have deficits in inhibition, organizing, shifting, and self-regulation.
31. Children with traumatic brain injury may have deficits in working memory, inhibition, planning and goal setting, shifting, and self-regulation.
32. Children with learning disabilities may have deficits in planning and goal setting, organizing, prioritizing, shifting, and self-regulation.
33. Research indicates that executive functions in children with traumatic brain injury can be compromised by certain parenting styles and by stressors and lack of resources on the part of the family.
34. It may be valuable to assess parenting style and family resources when you evaluate a child with brain injury.

Assessment of Executive Functions

35. Executive functions can be assessed by administering neuropsychological and psychological tests; conducting interviews with the child and his or her parents and teachers; observing the child at school, at home, and during the assessment; and analyzing samples of the child's schoolwork and written homework assignments.
36. The test battery should evaluate cognitive, linguistic, perceptual, and motor domains.
37. We recommend that multiple measures be used to assess executive functions.
38. The assessment of executive functions has several limitations. Planning and goal setting, organizing, and self-regulation cannot be measured exclusively by tests of executive functions because such tests are administered in a distraction-free environment that does not mirror more fluid and natural environments.
39. Scores on tests of executive functions do not correlate highly with the ability to work independently or complete long-term projects.
40. Scores on performance-based tests of working memory have low correlations with rater-based measures of executive functions.
41. High reliabilities may be difficult to achieve on measures of executive functions because of children's variable attention and concentration.
42. Test-retest reliabilities on measures of executive functions are often lower than acceptable for school-age and adolescent children.
43. Because tasks used to assess executive functions are not pure measures of executive functions, it is not always clear how best to interpret the test scores.
44. The measurement of executive functions could be improved in several ways. Traditional tests should be normed for children so that age-appropriate scores are available.
45. Tests with several parts should provide scores for each part as well as summary scores.
46. Tests of procedural learning need to be developed, normed, and validated.
47. Tests of motor functions should be routinely administered.
48. New child-friendly tests need to be designed and validated.
49. Longitudinal studies are needed that map developmental trajectories for individual children so that our understanding does not rely on cross-sectional studies exclusively.
50. Studies should compare results from tests of executive functions administered by examiners with those from tests administered by computers.

Improving Deficits in Executive Functions

51. Children with executive function deficits may benefit from learning various strategies and from the use of stimulant medications, neurofeedback training, and multimodal procedures.

KEY TERMS, CONCEPTS, AND NAMES

Executive functions (p. 247)
Primary executive functions (p. 247)
Planning and goal setting (p. 247)
Organizing (p. 247)
Prioritizing (p. 247)
Working memory (p. 247)
Updating (p. 247)
Short-term memory (p. 247)
Shifting (p. 247)
Inhibition (p. 247)
Self-regulation (p. 247)
Three models of executive functions (p. 247)
Two-system model (p. 247)
Metacognitive executive functions (cognitive control functions) (p. 247)
Emotional/motivational executive functions (behavior) (p. 247)
Three-system model (p. 248)
Instrumental reward learning system (p. 248)
Cerebellum (p. 248)
Cognitive control component (thinking component) (p. 248)
Four-system model (p. 248)
Executive control system (p. 248)
Attentional control (p. 248)
Selective attention (p. 248)
Sustained attention (p. 248)
Cognitive flexibility (p. 248)
Goal setting (p. 248)
Information processing (p. 248)
Developmental aspects of executive functions (p. 249)
Procedural knowledge (p. 249)
Semantic declarative knowledge (p. 249)
Joint attentional skills (p. 249)
Social referencing (p. 249)
Common evolution across executive functions (p. 250)
Unique evolution across executive functions (p. 250)
Intelligence, achievement, and executive functions (p. 250)
How executive functions are compromised (p. 250)
Assessment of executive functions (p. 251)
Improving deficits in executive functions (p. 259)

STUDY QUESTIONS

1. Define executive functions and describe the purposes served by executive functions.
2. Discuss the seven primary executive functions.
3. Describe three models that have been proposed to explain executive functions.

4. Discuss developmental aspects of executive functions and the brain areas involved.
5. What is the relationship between intelligence and executive functions? Cite research findings in your discussion.
6. Discuss the role that executive functions play in various achievement areas.
7. How may executive functions be compromised?
8. Discuss the assessment of executive functions. Describe some limitations of assessment and give suggestions for improving the assessment of executive functions.
9. How would you go about helping children who have deficits in executive functions?

Bullying and Cyberbullying

Jamie Zibulsky and Jerome M. Sattler

When people hurt you over and over, think of them like sand paper. They may scratch and hurt you a bit, but in the end, you end up polished and they end up useless.
—Chris Colfer, American actor (1990–)

That girl you made fun of for crying . . . Her dad just died in the war.
The girl you tripped down the stairs . . . She broke her leg.
That boy you just called stupid . . . He's dieing of a brain disease.
The girl you laughed at for her mom cutting her hair . . . Her mother is blind.
Does it hurt you? Stop the bullying!
If you don't stop it, you are one!
—Bunny (pseudonym)

Goals and Objectives

This chapter is designed to enable you to do the following:

- Become familiar with the characteristics of bullying and cyberbullying

- Understand the characteristics of bullies and victims

- Understand the role of bystanders in bullying situations

- Become familiar with techniques for consulting about bullying with schools, children, and parents

- Become acquainted with federal laws that pertain to bullying and the role of the courts in cases of bullying

Bullying and cyberbullying are insidious problems that occur far too often on playgrounds and in schools, neighborhoods, parks, homes, and workplaces. Bullying not only affects the physical and mental health of the victim, but also has negative implications for the victim's peers and family, schools, the community, and society at large. It has both short- and long-term psychological, academic, and physical consequences for the victim and the perpetrator as well as for bystanders. Perpetrators, in particular, are at increased risk for more serious acts of aggressive and antisocial behavior. For example, one group of researchers interviewed a sample of children between the ages of 9 and 16 years ($N = 1,420$) who had been victims of bullying, bullies, or both (bully-victims) during their preadolescent and adolescent years and then interviewed them again when they were 19, 21, 24, 25, and 26 years old (Copeland, Wolke, Angold, & Costello, 2013). The researchers found that these children faced an increased risk of developing one or more mental disorders when they reached young adulthood. Victims of bullying were at increased risk for developing agoraphobia (the need to avoid situations that may cause panic, such as being in a public place), generalized anxiety, and panic disorder. Bullies were at increased risk for developing an antisocial personality disorder. And bully-victims were at increased risk for developing depression, panic disorder, agoraphobia (females only), and suicidality (males only). Bully-victims had the worst long-term effects.

Efforts to counteract bullying must focus on setting and enforcing rules that prevent bullying and promote bystander intervention. Training programs for teachers and school administrators need to focus on ensuring that a school's culture is not conducive to bullying. And parents need help in addressing bullying issues at home and in their community. Both in school and at home, children need to learn about the harmful effects of bullying, to build resiliency skills, and to increase their sense of self-efficacy and self-worth. As Secretary of Education Arne Duncan (2010) noted, "Bullying is part of that continuum of school safety. It is troubling in and of itself. But bullying is doubly dangerous because if left unattended it can rapidly escalate into even more serious violence and abuse. Just as you have gateway drugs, bullying is gateway behavior. Too often it is the first step down the road to one of the tragic incidents of school violence . . . ."

In face-to-face bullying situations, children can play various roles (Dixon & Smith, 2011). These include the (a) *bully* who takes the initiative, (b) *follower* who joins in, (c) *reinforcer* who encourages the bully or who laughs at the victim, (d) *intervener* who tries to stop the bullying, (e) *bystander* who looks on but does not participate, and (f) *victim* who is the object of the bullying. Many individuals can play a part in reducing bullying and cyberbullying, including children, parents, teachers, psychologists, counselors, nurses, school administrators, law enforcement personnel, and community members. Ideally, all of these groups should work together to decrease bullying perpetrated in face-to-face interactions and via the Internet, mobile phones, and other electronic media.

Bullying involves repeated harmful physical acts, verbal acts, or sexual acts that threaten, insult, dehumanize, or intimidate another individual who cannot properly defend himself or herself; when these acts are carried out by means of any electronic device, they constitute cyberbullying. Specific examples of these various forms of bullying are provided in Table N-1. There are many and varied reasons an individual may be unable to defend himself or herself against bullying, including obvious reasons such as size, strength, or being outnumbered

Table N-1
Types of Bullying

Physical Acts

Assaulting a child with a weapon

Defacing schoolwork or other personal property (e.g., clothing, locker, or books)

Destroying personal property (e.g., clothing, books, jewelry)

Hazing (e.g., imposing embarrassing initiation rituals on a new candidate for a fraternity or sorority)

Holding nose or making other insulting gestures

Making threatening gestures

Physical violence (e.g., burning, choking, hitting, tripping, pushing, shoving, punching, assaulting)

Playing mean tricks to embarrass someone

Stealing valued possessions, money, and/or schoolwork

Verbal Acts

Blackmailing a child

Blaming the victim for starting the conflict

Humiliating a child

Intimidating a child

Making demands for money or engaging in other forms of extortion

Making harassing phone calls

Name calling (e.g., using slurs directed against gender, sexual orientation, ethnicity, religion, skin color, national origin, socioeconomic background, social/family background, dialect, political beliefs, age, disability, or food allergies)

Daring another child to engage in dangerous behavior

Rejecting a child (including social exclusion)

Spreading rumors about a child

Teasing a child about possessions, clothes, or physical appearance

Terrorizing a child

Threatening a child to keep him or her silent: "If you tell, it will be a lot worse!"

Writing insulting graffiti or posting slanderous comments in public places

Sexual Acts

Initiating or engaging in unwanted sexual contact (e.g., touching, pinching, or grabbing someone in a sexual way)

Ostracizing a child based on perceived sexual orientation

Sexual harassment (e.g., repeated exhibitionism, voyeurism, and/or sexual propositioning)

Source: Sampson (2009).

as well as less overt reasons such as being less psychologically resilient (Sampson, 2009). Bullies attempt to control, dominate, and subjugate those who are bullied through the use of power (Bully Online, n.d.). A person can derive power from being (a) older, stronger, or bigger than others, (b) a member of a cohesive majority group, or (c) more socially competent and popular than others (Vaillancourt, McDougall, Hymel, & Sunderani, 2010). The actions of bullies are designed to disempower the victims by undermining their worth and status. *Thus, two key components of bullying are repeated harmful acts and an imbalance of power.*

CHARACTERISTICS OF BULLYING

Bullying stems from the interaction of several factors.

- *Individual factors* include children's temperaments and personalities.
- *Parental factors* include parents' temperaments and personalities, the nature of the family environment, and the parent-child relationship.
- *Peer group factors* include the nature of the peer group and the quality of friendships.
- *School factors* include the school climate, teacher-student interactions, and school and classroom policies about bullying.
- *Community and cultural factors* include the level of and tolerance for violence, safety factors in the community, the socioeconomic level of the community's inhabitants, the cohesiveness of the community, and the power distribution among the community's inhabitants.

Table N-2 describes these factors in more detail.

Some forms of bullying are *direct* (e.g., physical violence, name calling, destruction of property), while others are *indirect* (e.g., rumor spreading, isolation). The indirect forms of bullying, often referred to as *relational aggression*, are a type of psychological violence and leave no physical evidence (Crick & Grotpeter, 1996). Bullying behaviors fall on a continuum from those that are not considered to violate the law (name calling) to those that most likely are against the law (physical violence). Figure N-1 reviews several misconceptions about bullying.

Let's look at a case that illustrates various types of direct bullying:

I was a victim of bullying for two years in gym. Boys from the football team called me names like "lard ass, fat boy, and fag." They threw things at me in class and shoved me in the hall. One day they put my head in the toilet and gave me a "swirly." When I told the gym teacher he told me to "toughen up." I just stopped going to gym after that. (Raskauskas & Stoltz, 2007, p. 565)

This case demonstrates that verbal and nonverbal acts of bullying may co-occur and that the same bullying incident may affect a student's social status and cause him or her physical

---

Table N-2
Factors That May Lead to Bullying

Individual

Engages in substance use
Enjoys pushing, hitting, or teasing others
Fails to participate in school activities
Gets poor grades in school
Has a negative self-identity
Has an affinity for high-risk behaviors
Has little empathy for others
Has poor problem-solving skills
Has wide-ranging prejudices
Is aggressive, hostile, domineering, prone to lose temper, quick to anger, impulsive, devious, manipulative, spiteful, selfish, insincere, immature, depressed
Is physically stronger than victims

Parents

Are depressed or angry
Are indifferent to or overprotective of their child
Establish a negative family climate (e.g., yell, hit, neglect child)
Give direct or indirect permission for aggressive behavior
Give little emotional support to their child
Have a history of insecure attachment with their child
Have little empathy for their child
Provide poor role models for constructive problem solving
Provide poor role models for positive interpersonal relations
Show inconsistent discipline
Show little interest in monitoring their child's activities
Show little interest in their child's school
Show low involvement with or affection for their child

Peer Group

Has deviant norms and practices (e.g., engages in violent and delinquent behavior; uses tobacco, alcohol, or drugs; dislikes school)
Pressures others to engage in aggressive behaviors

School

Has a negative school climate
Has poorly developed or no policies against bullying
Has teachers who fail to encourage positive relationships among students and between students and teachers
Has teachers who have low expectations for their students
Has teachers who ignore or tolerate bullying
Has teachers who provide poor supervision

Community and Culture

Display high levels of violence in the media
Expose children to bullying and other forms of violence
Fail to create safe and respectful environments
Foster violence by allowing easy access to firearms
Have poor resources
Lack cohesion
Promote and encourage aggressive behavior

Source: Espelage and Swearer (2009), Georgiou (2008), Orpinas and Horne (2006), and Sampson (2009).

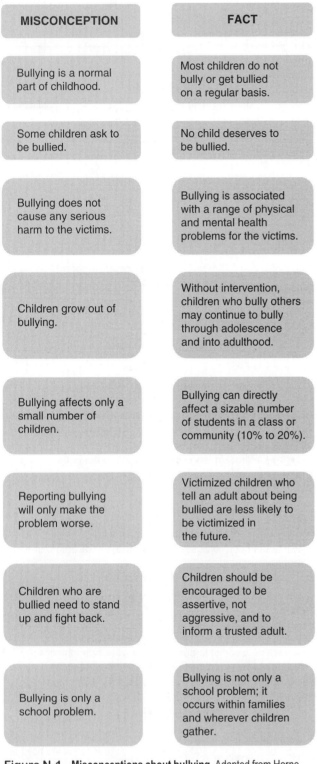

MISCONCEPTION	FACT
Bullying is a normal part of childhood.	Most children do not bully or get bullied on a regular basis.
Some children ask to be bullied.	No child deserves to be bullied.
Bullying does not cause any serious harm to the victims.	Bullying is associated with a range of physical and mental health problems for the victims.
Children grow out of bullying.	Without intervention, children who bully others may continue to bully through adolescence and into adulthood.
Bullying affects only a small number of children.	Bullying can directly affect a sizable number of students in a class or community (10% to 20%).
Reporting bullying will only make the problem worse.	Victimized children who tell an adult about being bullied are less likely to be victimized in the future.
Children who are bullied need to stand up and fight back.	Children should be encouraged to be assertive, not aggressive, and to inform a trusted adult.
Bullying is only a school problem.	Bullying is not only a school problem; it occurs within families and wherever children gather.

Figure N-1. Misconceptions about bullying. Adapted from Horne, Orpinas, Newman-Carlson, and Bartolomucci (2004); PREVNet (n.d.).

harm. Furthermore, it demonstrates that school personnel may fail to respond adequately to observed or reported acts of bullying. When adults do not reprimand students for engaging in bullying, perhaps ignoring name calling or not intervening when they witness an altercation, students may escalate bullying behavior. Teachers need to respond to all incidents of bullying and not ignore or make light of such behavior. Bullying is difficult to reduce because "the children or youth who bully often enjoy considerable status and power within the peer group, are seldom admonished by either peers or adults for their negative behavior, and are sometimes actively encouraged by a small but significant number of peers when behaving inappropriately" (Vaillancourt et al., 2010, p. 214).

CHARACTERISTICS OF CYBERBULLYING

With the increasing personal use of electronic media, children and adults have found new ways to engage in bullying behavior. *Cyberbullying* involves the use of any digital technology with the intent to hurt, defame, or embarrass another person. Examples include bullying via mobile phones (abusive calls, text messages, or picture/video clips) and bullying via the Internet (abusive e-mails, instant messages, websites, blog posts, or messages on social networking sites such as Facebook and Twitter, as well as behavior in chat rooms).

Instances of cyberbullying have been increasing over the last several years. Because most American teenagers use the Internet and social networking sites, there is the potential for teenagers to be particularly affected by cyberbullying (Jones, 2009). As the use of these technological tools continues to become more commonplace, younger children are at increased risk of being affected by cyberbullying as well. The impact of cyberbullying depends on such factors as the nature of the material (e.g., text message, pictures, video clips), the intended audience for the material, the extent of circulation, and the intent of the communication (e.g., planned or spontaneous, personal or impersonal, group or individual targeted).

Cyberbullying may take a number of forms (Bauman, 2011; Wikipedia, 2009, 2010; Willard, 2007, pp. 206–207):

1. *Flaming:* engaging in online "fights" by sending electronic messages with angry or vulgar language.
2. *Harassment:* repeatedly sending offensive, rude, or insulting messages, often including threats, sexual remarks, or pejorative labels (i.e., hate speech).
3. *Denigration:* sending or posting cruel gossip or rumors about a person to damage that person's reputation or friendships. Bullies may post false information about their victim on websites or set up their own websites, blogs, or user pages for this purpose. They may post allegations about their victim to newsgroups, chat rooms, or other sites that allow public contributions.
4. *Instigating and disclosing:* instigating others to gang up on a person by disclosing that person's personal data (e.g., real name and address or workplace/school) on a website or forum. To encourage others to harass the victim, bullies may claim that the victim harmed them or their family in

some way. They may even claim that the victim is harassing them.

5. *Impersonation:* breaking into someone's account, posing as that person, and sending messages designed to make the person look bad, get the person in trouble or danger, or damage the person's reputation or friendships. Bullies may order sex toys or subscriptions to pornography magazines and then have the goods or magazines delivered to their victim.

6. *Outing and trickery:* sharing someone's secrets or embarrassing information or images online; tricking someone into revealing secrets or embarrassing information, which is then shared online. Bullies may approach their victim's friends and family to obtain personal information; they may advertise for information on the Internet or hire a private detective. They may monitor their victim's online activities and attempt to trace the person's electronic address in an effort to gather more information about the victim.

7. *Exclusion:* intentionally excluding someone from an online group, such as a "buddy list."

8. *Attacking data and equipment:* trying to damage the victim's computer by sending viruses.

9. *Cyberstalking:* using electronic communication to stalk another person in a way that causes substantial emotional distress to that person and serves no legitimate purpose, including repeatedly sending messages that include threats of harm or that are highly intimidating. Cyberstalkers may eventually try to set up a meeting with their victim. Adult cyberstalkers sometimes pretend to be children. In addition to cyberstalking, they may make abusive or repetitive phone calls, solicit the victim for sex, assault the victim, or trespass on the victim's property.

Cyberbullying vs. Traditional Bullying

Cyberbullying differs from traditional bullying in several ways. Perhaps most importantly, cyberbullies can remain anonymous by assuming a screen name or stealing someone else's screen name; in addition, witnesses to the cyberbullying can remain anonymous. Being anonymous allows cyberbullies to avoid being judged or disciplined in the same way as they might for engaging in face-to-face bullying. In fact, some cyberbullies would be hesitant to say to another child's face what they say online or through wireless messages. The anonymity and ease with which children can access online and wireless technologies also makes it easy for cyberbullies to strike at a moment's notice and without premeditation.

Wielding their power from a distance, cyberbullies can attract an audience whose size is limitless. They can fan the flames of a conflict at all hours of the day and night simply by posting information online or texting a friend or group of friends. Because there is little regulation or supervision of the material posted online, damaging and hurtful information

may remain posted publicly for a long time. Children are often more technologically savvy than their parents and teachers, and their furtive online activity can be difficult to monitor.

Children who are cyberbullied may experience more distress and depression than children who are bullied in person (Wang, Nansel, & Iannotti, 2011). They may feel that they have no respite from bullying and that they cannot retaliate or stand up for themselves because the bullying is not face to face. They may feel hopeless, wonder what to do and why this is happening to them, and believe that there is no way that they can get out of the situation. They may not know who else has seen the negative posting and whether the bullying is being perpetrated by one child or a group of children. They may wonder whether each child whom they meet is the perpetrator and worry that other children can find the harassing content by using a search engine (Kowalski & Limber, 2007). And they may realize that they can avoid the harassment only by turning off a device that connects them with family and friends.

The imbalance of power in cyberbullying is "not in the bully's size or strength, but in the instrument the bully chose to use, bringing worldwide publication to vicious school gossip" (Sampson, 2009, p. 11). The following incident illustrates how a website was used to harass a student:

15-year-old Jacqueline was bullied at school and on the Internet. For Jacqueline, bullying began with name-calling on the bus and bullying in the hallway. Then, last month someone created a website posting her picture and poking fun at her lipstick and long black hair. Taking it a step further, they also added her home address, telephone number, and obscenity-laden descriptions about her. The website was posted for a month before the rumors and whispering led one of Jacqueline's friends to tell her about the website. When she learned about the posting on the website, her hands were shaking. She now refuses to go to school and says that she feels threatened. She and her mother say that the school officials are not taking the incident seriously enough. (Tench, 2003, p. B1, with changes in notation)

CHARACTERISTICS OF BULLIES

The families of bullies tend to be *less cohesive* (e.g., low parent-child involvement, warmth, and affection), *more conflictual* (e.g., angry, hostile parent-child interactions), and *less organized* than those of children who are not bullies. Thus, bullies may have learned their negative traits in their homes when interacting with their siblings or when witnessing altercations between their parents (Curner-Smith, Smith, & Porter, 2010; Stauffacher & DeHart, 2006). And both bullies and their victims are more likely than other children to come from disadvantaged families and communities (Due, Merlo, Harel-Fisch, Damsgaard, Holstein, Hetland, Currie, Gabhainn, de Matos, & Lynch, 2009; Hylton, 2008; Sampson, 2009). Students attending schools located in economically disadvantaged neighborhoods may experience less social cohesion and have fewer resources than students in other schools. Thus, these students are "at an increased risk for aggressive behavior, retaliatory attitudes, and diminished perceptions of safety" (Waasdorp,

Pas, O'Brennan, & Bradshaw, 2011, p. 117). Adults who work in disadvantaged schools and communities should be aware of the heightened need for bullying prevention and intervention. Bullying may also occur more frequently in schools where students are aggressive and group norms support bullying (Schwartz, Kelly, Duong, & Badaly, 2010).

Bullies may engage in both overt bullying and covert cyberbullying. They may bully others because they are bored, are jealous of others, want revenge, want to conceal shame or anxiety, or want to boost self-esteem. By demeaning others, they may feel empowered in the moment. Yet bullies may also be hurt by their acts of bullying (Quiroz, Arnette, & Stephens, 2006). They may lose the respect and trust of others and may be seen as mean and unpleasant.

Bullies may also engage in other forms of antisocial behavior, such as vandalism, shoplifting, fighting, and the use of drugs and alcohol (U.S. Department of Justice, 2001). And when they reach late adolescence and adulthood, their aggressive and antisocial behavior may continue in the form of violent crimes, assault, child maltreatment, domestic violence, or substance abuse (Bender & Lösel, 2011; Jiang, Walsh, & Augimeri, 2011; Kim, Catalano, Haggerty, & Abbott, 2011; Olweus, 2011; Renda, Vassallo, & Edwards, 2011; Ttofi, Farrington, Lösel, & Loeber, 2011).

When bullies are called to account for their actions, they may deny everything and counterattack with distorted or fabricated criticisms and allegations. For example, they may rationalize their bullying with a form of moral justification—they see the transgression as serving a higher end or moral purpose (e.g., it's all right to bully a child with special needs if he or she bothers others). They may abdicate their personal responsibility and view the transgression solely as a result of situational pressures or of other people's demands. They may try to disregard the negative consequences of their actions by not recognizing the extent of the victim's grief and suffering. Finally, they may even vilify the victim, blaming and devaluing him or her and viewing the victim as unworthy and unable to experience feelings as other people do.

Victims of bullying who themselves engage in bullying are referred to as *bully-victims*. Bully-victims tend to have behavior patterns associated with both victims and bullies (Swearer, Song, Cary, Eagle, & Mickelson, 2001; Totura, Green, Karver, & Gesten, 2009). For example, they may have a psychosocial profile characterized by anxiety, depression, loneliness, low self-esteem, and health problems together with poor peer relationships and high levels of dominance, aggression, and antisocial behavior. They may be at a higher risk for maladjustment and rejection by their peers than those who are only bullies or victims of bullying. The maladjustment may be evident in high levels of acting out and inattentive behavior and low levels of academic achievement (Burk, Armstrong, Park, Zahn-Waxler, Klein, & Essex, 2011; Copeland et al., 2013; Finkelhor, Turner, Hamby, & Ormrod, 2011).

If you need to interview a child who appears to have bullied another child, you can use the questions in Table B-19 in Appendix B. After the interview and your study of the incident, you will need to decide what actions to take, depending on the policies and procedures of your school. You can have the bully, for example, apologize to the victim, agree to go to mediation or counseling, sign an agreement not to continue with the bullying, agree to pay for damages, or agree to return money or the equivalent value of any property destroyed, or you can recommend to the school administration that the student be detained after school or suspended from school. You should caution the bully against taking revenge against the victim or against any other students whom the bully suspects may have provided information to teachers or the school staff, and you should set clear consequences for continued bullying behavior.

The bully and any other perpetrators involved in the bullying incident should be monitored. And, of course, a record should be kept of the interview, including your recommendations and the actions that you have taken.

CHARACTERISTICS OF VICTIMS

Some children are exposed to bullying in a limited fashion; if they are targeted for reasons that are unlikely to cause them to be bullied continually, they may suffer only short-term effects from this type of mistreatment. However, other children are frequent victims of bullying, and the effects of this prolonged mistreatment on their emotional well-being and academic engagement can be considerable. Even siblings are not immune from the effects of bullying. A national survey conducted in 2011 reported that children who were repeatedly attacked, threatened, or intimidated by their siblings were more likely to have increased levels of depression, anger, and anxiety than children who were not bullied by their siblings (Tucker, Finkelhor, Turner, & Shattuck, 2013). The findings point out that bullying among siblings should be taken as seriously as bullying among peers.

There is no one profile of a child who is likely to be bullied. However, a child who possesses one or more of the following characteristics may be at heightened risk of being bullied (Bontempo & D'Augelli, 2002; Lindsay, Dockrell, & Mackie, 2008; Guerra, Williams, & Sadek, 2011; Luciano & Savage, 2007; Young & Sweeting, 2004):

- Displays vulnerability or insecurity
- Dresses differently and doesn't conform to the norm
- Has learning, speech, or other physical or mental disabilities
- Has low self-esteem
- Has physical attributes that differ from the norm, including being overweight, underweight, very short, or very tall
- Has poor communication skills
- Has poor social skills, prefers not to socialize, or is withdrawn and solitary
- Is a member of an ethnic or religious group viewed as different
- Is bright, talented, or gifted
- Is clumsy or immature
- Is perceived to be lesbian, gay, bisexual, or transgendered
- Is new to the school

- Is nonassertive and refuses to fight
- Is physically weak
- Is annoying, provocative, or aggressive
- Is richer or poorer than the majority of classmates
- Is shy, reserved, timid, or submissive
- Is the smallest or youngest child in school

Being a victim of bullying may exacerbate children's social and academic difficulties and decrease their self-esteem. These effects may become even more severe if victims lack close friends, because friendships help to mitigate the trauma of being bullied (Schwartz et al., 2010) and having a defender likely means that the victim will be less victimized in the future (Sainio, Veenstra, Huitsing, & Salmivalli, 2011). Because being the victim of bullying tends to prevent children from having opportunities for positive social interactions with peers, their chances for developing stronger social skills are diminished. Thus, to keep a cycle from developing, school staffs must identify children who are at risk and help them build the skills they need to form positive peer relationships. Table N-3 gives first-person accounts of bullying, and Table N-4 shows the physical, behavioral, and emotional signs of distress displayed by victims of bullying. In addition to the signs in Table N-4, signs of cyberbullying include (a) appearing upset after being online or receiving text messages and (b) unexpectedly ceasing to use a computer, cell phone, or smartphone.

Sticks and stones may break your bones but mean words can tear holes in your spirit.

—Anonymous

Table N-3
Victims' First-Person Accounts of What Bullies Did to Them

Social Level
Got my friends to turn their backs on me
Deliberately excluded me from group work
Talked about me behind my back
Acted as if they could catch my fatness if they came too close
Dispersed as I approached
Ignored me
Did not respond to overtures of friendship

Physical Level
Threw my things away
Damaged my belongings
Stole my belongings
Kicked me
Made me take my clothes off and laughed at what I'd got
Forced me to eat things I hated
Pulled my hair
Bossed me about

Psychological Level
Blamed me for everything that went wrong
Criticized everything I did
Humiliated me by repeatedly telling me I was stupid
Blackmailed me to steal from my mother with threats of the devil
Threatened me to stop me telling on the bully
Called me names
Laughed at me
Picked me last for teams

Source: Adapted from Dixon (2006, pp. 18–20).

Table N-4
Signs of Distress Displayed by Victims of Bullying

Physical Signs
Is hungry after school
Brings damaged possessions to school or home
Complains of illness (e.g., pains, headaches, stomachaches)
Complains of tiredness or fatigue
Has difficulty sleeping (e.g., nightmares, bedwetting)
Has torn or damaged clothes
Has unexplained bruises, scratches, or cuts
Reports that possessions have been "lost" (e.g., books, electronics, clothing, jewelry)

Behavioral Signs
Acts differently than usual
Avoids certain places in the neighborhood
Avoids classes or does not want to go to school
Displays "victim" body language (e.g., hangs head, hunches shoulders, avoids eye contact)
Fears riding on the school bus or walking to and from school
Has deteriorating school performance
Has difficulty concentrating
Has little interest in schoolwork or other activities
Has unexplained absences
Requests additional money for lunch from school personnel
Shows changes in eating patterns at lunch (e.g., poor eating)
Stays late at school to avoid encounters with other students
Steals money
Takes "protection" to school (e.g., a stick, knife, gun)
Takes an "illogical" route when walking to and from school
Talks about running away
Talks about suicide
Threatens violence to self and/or others
Withdraws socially or has few or no friends

Emotional Signs
Is irritable, anxious, fearful, or insecure
Displays mood swings and cries easily
Expresses feeling isolated, lonely, or trapped
Expresses feeling picked on, persecuted, and powerless
Expresses feeling rejected and not liked
Expresses feeling sad, hopeless, and depressed
Has angry outbursts
Has flashbacks
Has self-doubt and low self-esteem

Source: Rivers, Duncan, and Besag (2007); and Sampson (2009).

Chronic victims of bullying are found most often in elementary school, followed by middle school and then high school (Sampson, 2009). Chronic victims of bullying tend (a) to be extremely passive, (b) to have low self-esteem, (c) to be anxious, insecure, fearful, less able than others to control their emotions, and socially withdrawn, and (d) to be unable to defend themselves adequately. They may suffer more than other victims of bullying. Those who are chronic victims of bullying and who inadvertently provoke bullying may be particularly difficult to help because they must make substantial changes in their behavior in order to stop the bullying. Chronic victims of bullying may even "return to bullies to try to continue the perceived relationship, which may initiate a new cycle of victimization. Chronic victims often remain victims even after switching to new classes with new students, suggesting that, without other interventions, nothing will change" (Sampson, 2009, p. 13).

Without interventions, children who are chronic victims of bullying may develop an intense dislike of school, may become truant, and may drop out of school (Sampson, 2009). If bullying is accompanied by rejection, victims may develop emotional numbness and lethargy and suffer decreased self-awareness. Some victims of bullying may even consider suicide (Heikkilä, Väänänen, Helminen, Fröjd, Marttunen, & Kaltiala-Heino, 2013). And when children who are chronically bullied become adults, their children are more likely to be victims of bullying than are children of adults who were not bullied as children (Sampson, 2009). If you need to interview a child who has been a victim of bullying, see the suggested questions in Table B-17 in Appendix B.

Following is a verse from "Welcome to My Life" by Simple Plan that expresses teenage angst.

No, you don't know what it's like
When nothing feels all right
You don't know what it's like
To be like me
To be hurt
To feel lost
To be left out in the dark
To be kicked when you're down
To feel like you've been pushed around
To be on the edge of breaking down
And no one's there to save you
No, you don't know what it's like
Welcome to my life

DIMENSIONS OF BULLYING

Ten dimensions of bullying can be delineated (Benenson, 2009):

1. *Intensity:* extremely intense versus mildly intense (e.g., displaying fury versus irritation when disparaging the victim)

2. *Frequency:* continual versus sporadic (e.g., making ongoing versus infrequent and erratic physical or verbal threats to the victim)

3. *Presence of victim:* present versus absent (e.g., making disparaging comments to the victim's face versus behind the victim's back)

4. *Clarity of intent to harm:* overt versus covert (e.g., hitting victim deliberately versus ostensibly accidentally)

5. *Emotion:* expressed versus not expressed (e.g., displaying anger or pleasure versus no emotion when disparaging victim)

6. *Physical contact:* present versus absent (e.g., hitting the victim versus threatening to hit the victim)

7. *Verbal message:* present versus absent (e.g., making versus not making disparaging comments while hitting the victim)

8. *Nonverbal gestures:* present versus absent (e.g., rolling eyes versus maintaining a straight face while making disparaging comments about the victim)

9. *Number of bullies:* one versus several (e.g., bullying the victim alone versus together with others)

10. *Goal of bully:* physical harm versus verbal harm versus social harm (e.g., intending to physically hurt versus belittle or ostracize the victim)

INCIDENCE OF BULLYING

Sound statistics on the extent of bullying are difficult to obtain because children who are victims are often reluctant to report bullying for the following reasons (Sampson, 2009, p. 5):

- Fearing retaliation
- Feeling shame at not being able to stand up for themselves
- Fearing they would not be believed
- Not wanting to worry their parents
- Having no confidence that anything would change as a result
- Thinking their parents' or teacher's advice would make the problem worse
- Fearing their teacher would tell the bully who told on him or her
- Thinking it would be worse to be thought of as a snitch

Despite the difficulty of obtaining accurate incidence figures, it is important to try to gain some sense of the incidence of bullying. In 2011, the Pew Research Center conducted a national survey of children ages 12 to 17 years on their use of the Internet, including incidents of bullying. The survey's results follow.

INTERNET USE
- 95% reported that they are online
- 80% reported that they are users of social media sites
- 65% reported that their peers are mostly nice online
- 20% reported that their peers are mostly unkind online

- 88% reported that they had witnessed someone who had been cruel to another person on a social media site
- 15% reported that when they were on a social media site they were the target of online meanness

BULLYING INCIDENTS

- 19% reported having been bullied in some way in the last 12 months
- 12% reported having been bullied in person in the last 12 months
- 9% reported having been bullied via text message in the last 12 months
- 8% reported having been bullied online (e.g., through email, a social networking site, or instant messaging)
- 7% reported having been bullied by calls over the phone

Another national survey of online harassment, conducted in 2010, found that 11% of children ages 10 to 17 years who used the Internet were harassed, with a majority (69%) of the victims being female (Jones, Mitchell, & Finkelhor, 2013). A similar survey conducted in 1999–2000 reported that only 6% of online users were harassed (Finkelhor, Mitchell, & Wolak, 2000). Thus, over a 10-year period, online harassment increased by about 83%. The increase in harassment reflects a rise in indirect harassment—someone posting or sending comments about an individual to others online. Incidents of harassment were likely to be perpetrated by a school friend or acquaintance and to occur on a social networking site. The findings suggest that "the increase in online harassment can likely be attributed to changes in how youth are using the Internet, especially a disproportional increase in online communication with friends by girls, providing more opportunity for offline peer conflicts to expand to this environment" (Jones et al., 2013, p. 53).

BYSTANDER RELUCTANCE TO REPORT BULLYING

It is often the case that although bystanders know that bullying is wrong, they are reluctant to report it. Bystanders may not want to invite the bully's wrath and become the next target and may fear that they will be thought of as tattletales or informers and possibly be rejected by their peers (Sampson, 2009). Some bystanders may wrongly believe that they are not responsible for stopping the bullying, or they may think that bullying is acceptable. Other bystanders may assume that school personnel don't care enough to stop the bullying or are unable to stop it (Quiroz et al., 2006). When bystanders fail to act, bullies are less likely to receive any punishment and may be reinforced for their actions, and the victim is less likely to be protected from future bullying.

Bystanders are not immune to the effects of bullying. They may feel unsafe in the classroom and on the playground. They may reduce their social contacts with victims for fear of lowering their own social status. They may feel powerless to report bullying, but also feel guilty for not reporting it. Bystanders who witness the victimization of their peers can experience heightened anxiety, depression, and/or substance abuse (Rivers, Poteat, Noret, & Ashurst, 2009). Some bystanders may become bullies themselves because they think that this is a way to become part of a group. Finally, bystanders may think that bullying is not so bad because adults don't seem to care if someone is being bullied. Bystander intervention is likely to increase when schools consistently enforce rules related to bullying.

Still, there are children who intervene and help victims of bullying or report incidents of bullying to authorities. These children may be friends with the victim, may know that their parents or teachers expect them to support victims, or may believe that it is the moral and proper thing to do. Children are most likely to intervene when they have the support of their peer group (Gini, Pozzoli, Borghi, & Franzoni, 2008). Victims of bullying who are supported by their peers suffer fewer negative effects as a result of being bullied than those children who do not receive peer support (Sainio et al., 2011).

Fostering a school climate in which children feel comfortable supporting their peers and reporting bullying may help children who are at risk find allies, which, in turn, may reduce incidents of bullying. Children who believe that children and teachers can work together to reduce bullying are more likely to intervene when their peers are bullied than those who do not hold this belief (Barchia & Bussey, 2011; Williams & Guerra, 2011). Bystander intervention needs to be taught in early school grades, and the education needs to be continued in later school grades, accompanied by programs that encourage peer support for victims of bullying. Research has shown that programs are effective in increasing bystander interventions in bullying situations (Polanin, Espelage, & Pigott, 2012). If you need to interview a child who has witnessed a bullying event, see the questions in Table B-18 in Appendix B.

The bully survives on your silence.

—Christine Farrell Crotty

Bystanders who are helpless in the presence of another student's victimization learn passive acceptance of injustice.

—Linda R. Jeffrey, DeMond Miller, and Margaret Linn

CORRELATES OF BULLYING

Let's look at the relationship between bullying and such factors as gender, age, and school, gleaned from research findings (Lacey & Cornell, 2011; Sampson, 2009):

- Male bullies tend to rely more on physical aggression, whereas female bullies tend to rely more on indirect forms of bullying, such as teasing, rumor spreading, exclusion, and social isolation.

- Males are more likely to bully than females, but males and females have similar rates of victimization.
- Bullying occurs with most frequency during elementary school years and less often during middle school years and the early years of high school.
- Bullying declines substantially after age 14 or 15 years.
- Schools with negative social climates or located in socially disadvantaged areas have higher rates of bullying than schools in more advantaged areas.
- Bullying occurs more often at school than on the way to and from school.
- Bullies operate alone in about 50% of the cases.
- Higher rates of bullying in schools negatively affect students' performance on standardized tests.
- The degree of a school principal's involvement in school programs designed to prevent bullying may help to determine the level of bullying at the school.

CONSULTATION

Consultation with Schools

The National Education Association reported that almost all educators at the schools they surveyed in 2010 were aware that it is their job to intervene and prevent bullying (Bradshaw, Waasdorp, O'Brennan, & Gulemetova, 2011). More than half of the educators sampled reported witnessing two or more bullying incidents in the past month. However, 46% had not received training on their district's bullying policy, 61% reported that they could benefit from more training in order to address bullying related to sexual orientation and gender expression, and 74% reported that they could benefit from more training in order to address cyberbullying. These findings indicate that school staffs may be receptive to training about bullying and cyberbullying. Handout K-4 in Appendix K provides strategies for teachers for preventing and dealing with bullying and cyberbullying.

Effective consultation about bullying in schools requires asking the right questions about a school's policies for dealing with bullying (see Table B-20 in Appendix B). Answers to the questions in Table B-20 will provide information about the incidence of bullying at the school, including hot spots, victims, and offenders, and give you leads for choosing an appropriate set of responses to deal with bullying (Sampson, 2009). Bullying in schools tends to occur in areas with limited or no adult supervision (e.g., cafeteria, schoolyard, bathroom, hallway, or stairwell). When bullying occurs in a classroom setting, however, it "may have more to do with the classroom management techniques a teacher uses than with the number of adult supervisors in the room" (Sampson, 2009, p. 10). If a school does not do anything about bullying, it risks (a)

gaining a reputation for being dangerous or unsafe, (b) not fulfilling its academic mission, (c) losing enrollment, and (d) being the subject of litigation (California Department of Education, 2010).

It is important for a consultant to help teachers and administrators recognize that combatting bullying needs to be a primary prevention activity in schools and strong universal supports must be in place for all students. In order to provide such supports, schools have increasingly adopted a model referred to as School-Wide Positive Behavior and Supports (SWPBS; Sugai & Horner, 2009). Working from this model, schools are prompted to develop three to five school-wide rules that are stated positively, can be implemented widely, and can be interpreted both broadly and specifically (e.g., be safe, be responsible, and be respectful). Students are then given the opportunity to define, observe, and practice the specific behaviors associated with each rule in both structured and unstructured school settings. For example, students may be taught that being safe in the classroom means sitting quietly and keeping one's hands to oneself and that being safe at recess means running only when in a particular fenced-in area. Engaging in direct and indirect bullying behaviors violates these school rules. Cultivating a school culture that values and rewards positive behavior will help diminish bullying (Ross, Horner, & Stiller, n.d.).

Teachers need to deal with bullying on the playground and in the classroom, lunchroom, and other places in school. Handout K-4 in Appendix K provides a list of suggestions to help them meet this challenge. School staffs must recognize that if they permit bullying, they are possibly contributing to an atmosphere of school violence (Quiroz et al., 2006). Bullying endangers the school's academic mission and compromises its safety mission. Finally, school staffs must recognize that if bullying is permitted on their campuses, parents may come to believe that schools provide an uncaring, irresponsible, and dangerous environment.

If parents fear for the safety of their children, they are more likely to advise their children to fight back when provoked, rather than encouraging them to report bullying behavior to school authorities. The school culture needs to diminish, rather than enhance, tendencies to act aggressively. To be successful, intervention programs must focus on helping school personnel accept the program, getting teachers to implement the program, and ensuring that teachers, students, and staff adopt an anti-bullying philosophy. In addition, intervention programs must take into consideration the types of bullying encountered in the school, the ages of the students, and their sex, ethnicity, socioeconomic status, and disabilities (if present). Exhibit N-1 highlights the philosophical underpinnings of effective bullying prevention programs and presents effective strategies to counter bullying in schools.

A meta-analysis of anti-bullying programs in several different countries reported that bullying behavior decreased by 20% to 23 % after the programs were implemented (Farrington & Ttofi, 2009). Components of effective intervention

Exhibit N-1
Characteristics of Effective Bullying Prevention Programs in Schools

Philosophical Underpinnings

1. *Basis in evidence.* The program should be built on scientific principles and supported by scientifically valid evidence of effectiveness. It should be replicable, amenable to evaluation, and open to modification based on research evidence.

2. *Buy-in.* The program should motivate participants and other stakeholders to believe that bullying is a serious and preventable problem, that this specific program will work, and that they themselves can make a difference.

3. *Shared vision.* The program and its supporting policy should promote a common understanding of the problem and ways to address it, clear roles and responsibilities, and ongoing communication among members of the school, parents, and community.

4. *Support for implementation.* The program should provide a systematic method for conveying information, including materials for training teachers, other members of the school staff, students, parents, and community members.

5. *User-friendliness.* The program should present strategies that are clear, relevant, and comprehensible to both teachers and students. In order to achieve a high degree of user-friendliness, the strategies should be developed and revised based on user feedback.

6. *Focus on regulating thoughts, feelings, and behaviors.* The program should change habitual patterns of thought and action that support bullying and teach appropriate social-emotional and interpersonal skills, including the following:
   - *Self-regulation skills:* how to control impulses and replace them with reflective decision making, sustain and shift attention, and become empathic
   - *Perspective taking skills:* how to appreciate similarities and differences among people, respect diversity, and recognize and identify feelings of others
   - *Emotion management skills:* how to identify one's own feelings, calm down one's emotions, understand that one's feelings are complex and can change, and manage stress and anxiety
   - *Problem-solving skills:* how to solve problems, resolve conflicts, and set goals
   - *Communication skills:* how to be assertive yet respectful and negotiate and compromise to arrive at workable solutions
   - *Pro-social skills:* how to make friends, cooperate with others, and meet group goals

7. *Practice.* The program should offer structured and repeated opportunities for students to apply and adopt new habits of thought and action—both during training sessions and at other times—through modeling, role-playing, and giving corrective feedback to oneself and others.

8. *Mutual commitment and responsibility.* The program and its supporting policy should call on all members of the school and community to redefine their shared commitment to and responsibility for reducing and eventually eliminating bullying. This commitment should include adopting a proactive bystander strategy, practicing the ideals of participatory democracy, and calling for an infusion (rather than a diffusion) of responsibility for everyone.

9. *Sustainability.* The program and its supporting policy should empower participants to broaden and sustain prevention activities—developing support systems at all levels and turning limited interventions into a broad, school-wide philosophy. Reminder sessions should be held periodically.

Strategies Effective in Countering Bullying

1. *Enlisting the school principal's commitment to creating a positive school climate, promoting effective teaching, and preventing bullying.* School principals can ensure a positive school climate in part by emphasizing that teachers and school staff must show respect for all students, regardless of their sex and sexual orientation, ethnicity, language, and socioeconomic status. Principals also need to be committed to having the best teaching possible and to investing resources in preventing and limiting bullying.

2. *Taking a multifaceted, comprehensive approach.* Such an approach encompasses the following actions:
   - Establishing a school-wide policy that addresses both indirect bullying (e.g., rumor spreading, isolation, social exclusion) and direct bullying (e.g., physical aggression)
   - Providing guidelines for teachers, other staff members, and students (including student bystanders) on specific actions to take if bullying occurs and ensuring that all reports of bullying are taken seriously
   - Raising awareness school-wide of the prevalence of bullying and cyberbullying and the consequences for both the victims and the bullies
   - Using focus groups to discuss ways to prevent bullying
   - Educating and involving parents so that they understand the problem of bullying, recognize its signs, and intervene appropriately
   - Adopting specific strategies to deal with individual bullies and victims, including meeting with the parents of the bullies and the victims and providing victims with immediate support services, including school counseling services, social services, and other mental health services
   - Ensuring that the strategies for dealing with bullies do not reinforce the bullying cycle by providing the bully with attention and/or power for inappropriate behavior
   - Encouraging students to report bullying when they witness it
   - Developing a comprehensive reporting system to track bullying that includes (a) recording the prevalence, location, and kind of bullying activities, (b) recording the names of the bullies, victims, and bystanders, (c) recording the actions taken by the staff after each incident of bullying, and (d) obtaining relevant reports from students, teachers, staff, and parents about the bullying incident
   - Encouraging students to help classmates who have been bullied

(Continued)

Exhibit N-1 (*Continued*)

- Developing tailored strategies to counter bullying in specific school hot spots by using environmental redesign, increasing supervision (e.g., by teachers, other staff members, parents, and volunteers), and employing monitoring equipment
- Conducting post-intervention surveys to assess the effectiveness of anti-bullying programs

3. *Increasing student reporting of bullying.* Schools should create an environment that encourages students to report bullying by doing the following:
    - Having clear school-wide and classroom rules about bullying, the consequences of bullying, and the necessity of supporting victims of bullying
    - Conducting class discussions about why reporting bullying is admirable behavior, not tattling
    - Setting up a bully hot line
    - Having a "bully box" in which students can drop a note to alert teachers and administrators about students who are bullies and to report incidents of bullying
    - Establishing an online reporting system, such as an email address for reporting incidents of bullying
    - Providing adults with training in taking bullying reports, emphasizing the need to listen attentively to the student's report, take action as needed, and provide timely follow-ups
    - Creating an environment where students feel safe reporting bullying by maintaining the reporting student's confidentiality whenever possible so that he or she will be protected from retaliation
    - Making sure that parents understand the importance of reporting bullying so that they will encourage their children to come forward or they will contact the school themselves

4. *Developing activities in less-supervised areas and increasing the amount of time students are supervised.* Teachers

(or adult monitors and volunteers) should be stationed in schoolyards, lunchrooms, hallways, and less-supervised areas and trained to spot bullying and initiate activities that limit opportunities for bullying.

5. *Staggering recess, lunch, and/or class release times.* Schools should minimize the number of younger and older students mingling together in a setting in order to reduce incidents of bullying.

6. *Assigning bullies to a particular location or to particular chores during release times.* Schools should separate bullies from their intended victims, give bullies constructive tasks to occupy them during release times, and monitor their activities.

7. *Posting classroom signs prohibiting bullying and listing the consequences for it.* Schools should post signs in each classroom that include age-appropriate penalties. This puts would-be bullies on notice and shows them the risks they take if they bully another student.

8. *Providing teachers with effective classroom management training.* Schools should ensure that all their teachers have effective classroom management training. Teachers must consistently enforce the rules if the rules are to have any meaning. Teachers in classes that contain students with behavioral, emotional, or learning problems may require additional tailored training in spotting and handling bullying.

9. *Having high-level school administrators inform late-enrolling students about the school's bullying policy.* Implementing this policy removes any excuse new students have for bullying and stresses the importance the school places on countering bullying.

10. *Maintaining school buildings and grounds.* Schools should ensure the safety of all teachers, other staff members, and students by having adequate lighting, heat, and air conditioning and maintaining cleanliness.

Source: Jones, Doces, Swearer, and Collier (2012); Kochenderfer-Ladd and Ladd (2010); Sampson (2009, pp. 19–23); and U.S. Department of Justice (2009).

Exhibit N-2
Bullying Prevention Programs, Social-Emotional Learning Programs, Workbooks and Exercises, and Useful Websites

Bullying Prevention Programs
- *KiVa* (www.kivakoulu.fi/there-is-no-bullying-in-kiva-school), a program developed in Finland, has been shown to be effective. Efforts are being made to translate the program into English.
- *Olweus Bullying Prevention Program* (http://www.olweus.org) has shown successful results in European countries, but results in the United States have been mixed.
- *Steps to Respect* (http://www.cfchildren.org/steps-to-respect.aspx), developed by the Seattle-based Committee for Children, has been shown to increase positive bystander behaviors in children and decrease physical bullying.

Social-Emotional Learning Programs
- Promoting Alternative Thinking Strategies (PATHS): http://www.prevention.psu.edu/projects/PATHS.html
- Roots of Empathy: http://www.rootsofempathy.org
- The RULER program: http://therulerapproach.org
- Second Step: http://www.cfchildren.org/second-step.aspx
- Tribes Learning Communities: http://tribes.com/about/a-model-program/caselselect-program
- WITS Programs: http://www.witsprogram.ca

Exhibit N-2 (*Continued*)

Workbooks and Exercises

- Beane, A. L. (2005). *Bully free classroom: Over 100 tips and strategies for teachers K–8*. Minneapolis, MN: Free Spirit Publishing.
- Beane, A. L. (2006). *How to be bully free workbook: Word searches, mazes, what-ifs, and other fun activities for kids*. Minneapolis, MN: Free Spirit Publishing.
- Bowen, J., Ashcroft, P., Jenson, W. R., & Rhode, G. (2008). *The tough kid bully blockers book*. Eugene, OR: Pacific Northwest Publishing.
- Brady, J. (2007). *101 bully prevention activities: A year's worth of activities to help kids prevent bullying*. Farmingville, NY: The Bureau for At-Risk Youth.
- Breakstone, S., Dreiblatt, M., & Dreiblatt, K. (2009). *How to stop bullying and social aggression: Elementary grade lessons and activities that teach empathy, friendship, and respect*. Thousand Oaks, CA: Sage.
- Centrone, T. (2007). *How not to be a bully target: A program for victims of childhood bullying*. Chapin, SC: Youthlight, Inc.
- Cook, J. (2010). *Bully B.E.A.N.S. activity and idea book*. Chattanooga, TN: National Center for Youth Issues.
- Drew, N. (2010). *No kidding about bullying: 125 ready-to-use activities to help kids manage anger, resolve conflicts, build empathy, and get along*. Minneapolis, MN: Free Spirit Publishing.
- Green, S. E. (2010). *Don't pick on me: Help for kids to stand up to and deal with bullies*. Oakland, CA: Instant Help Books.
- i-SAFE Inc. (2010). *i-SAFE internet safety activities: Reproducible projects for teachers and parents*. Hoboken, NJ: Wiley.
- Limber, S. P., Kowalski, R. M., & Agatston, P. W. (2009a). *Cyber bullying: A prevention curriculum for grades 3–5*. Center City, MN: Hazelden Publishing & Educational Services.
- Limber, S. P., Kowalski, R. M., & Agatston, P. W. (2009b). *Cyber bullying: A prevention curriculum for grades 6–12*. Center City, MN: Hazelden Publishing & Educational Services.
- Liptak, J. J., & Leutenberg, E. A. (2011). *Teen aggression & bullying workbook: Facilitator reproducible self-assessments, exercises, and educational handouts*. Duluth, MN: Whole Person.
- Lohmann, R. C., & Taylor, J. V. (2013). *The bullying workbook for teens: Activities to help you deal with social aggression and cyberbullying*. Oakland, CA: Instant Help Books.
- Meyers, R. E. (2006). *Respect matters: Real life scenarios provide powerful discussion starters for all aspects of respect*. Tucson, AZ: Good Year Books.
- Pownall-Gray, D. (2006). *Surviving bullies workbook: Skills to help protect you from bullying*. Weston, CT: Willoughby & Lamont Publications.
- Randall, K., & Bowen, A. A. (2008). *Mean girls: 101½ creative strategies for working with relational aggression*. Chapin, SC: Youthlight, Inc.
- Richards, M. (2006). *I didn't know I was a bully*. Champaign, IL: Research Press.
- Senn, D. (2007). *Bullying in the girl's world: A school-wide approach to girl bullying*. Chapin, SC: Youthlight, Inc.
- Sprague, S. (2008). *Coping with cliques: A workbook to help girls deal with gossip, put-downs, bullying, and other mean behavior*. Oakland, CA: Instant Help Books.
- Super Teacher Worksheets: http://www.superteacherworksheets.com/anti-bullying.html
- Wiseman, R. (2009). *Owning up™ curriculum: Empowering adolescents to confront social cruelty, bullying, and injustice*. Champaign, IL: Research Press.

Websites

- Broward County Public Schools, Office of Prevention Programs: http://www.browardprevention.org/anti-bullying/anti-bullying-classroom-activities
- Bully Free: https://sites.google.com/site/courageisfirebullyingissmoke/home
- Center for the Study and Prevention of Violence: http://www.colorado.edu/cspv/blueprints
- Centers for Disease Control and Prevention: http://www.cdc.gov/violenceprevention/pdf/BullyCompendiumBk-a.pdf
- Child Trends: http://www.childtrends.org/links
- Collaborative for Academic, Social and Emotional Learning (CASEL): http://casel.org/in-schools/selecting-programs
- Education World: http://www.educationworld.com/a_special/bully.shtml
- Find Youth Info: http://findyouthinfo.gov
- Massachusetts Department of Elementary and Secondary Education: http://www.doe.mass.edu/bullying/#4
- Promising Practices Network: http://www.promisingpractices.net/programs.asp
- Substance Abuse and Mental Health Services Administration (SAMHSA): http://nrepp.samhsa.gov
- Target Bullying: http://www.targetbullying.com
- U.S. Department of Education: http://ies.ed.gov/ncee/wwc
- U.S. Department of Justice (OJJDP): http://www.ojjdp.gov/mpg/search.aspx
- U.S. Department of Health & Human Services: http://www.stopbullying.gov/kids/webisodes
- World Health Organization's (WHO) Violence Prevention Alliance: http://www.preventviolence.info/evidence_base_complete.aspx

Source: Partially adapted from Jones, Doces, Swearer, and Collier (2012).

programs included adequate teacher and student training, improved supervision on the playground and in other unstructured areas, consistent and firm responses to bullying behavior, inclusion of parent training or outreach, and sufficient duration of the program. Another review of anti-bullying studies found that the most effective programs were designed to improve students' social and interpersonal skills and modify their attitudes and beliefs (Barbero, Hernández, Esteban, & García, 2012). By helping school districts implement and evaluate their chosen program, you will help school administrators and teachers adopt the best practices for preventing and reducing bullying. School staffs often are acutely aware of the negative impact that bullying can have and are searching for ways to more effectively address the problem. Exhibit N-2 lists bullying prevention programs, social-emotional learning programs, and workbooks and exercises, as well as websites useful for obtaining information about bullying.

Effective anti-bullying programmes should be promoted, and could be viewed as a form of early crime prevention.
—Maria M. Ttofi (British criminologist), David P. Farrington (British criminologist), Friedrich Lösel (German forensic psychologist), and Rolf Loeber (American psychologist)

Consultation with Children

As a result of being bullied (or sometimes as a result of bullying other children), children may show clinically significant levels of anxiety, depression, or other symptoms. Children who play both roles—perpetrator and victim—may have more internalizing symptoms than their peers (Özdemir & Stattin, 2011; Swearer et al., 2001). Children who experience bullying for several years may be especially at risk and therefore may need long-term interventions (Buhs, Ladd, & Herald-Brown, 2010). Also, the aggressive or withdrawal tendencies of children who are rejected by others may be exacerbated by bullying; therefore, in an intervention program you will need to consider whether victims of bullying have problems handling their aggressive or withdrawal tendencies.

Victims of bullying may benefit from various types of interventions, such as "anxiety management, social-skills training, coping-skills training, pleasant-events scheduling, assertiveness training, problem solving, and peer cooperativeness/mediation" (Swearer, Grills, Haye, & Cary, 2004, p. 78). Research is needed to evaluate the effectiveness of these interventions, singly and in combination.

It is a good procedure to have both the perpetrator and the victim meet individually with an appropriate school staff member to address an incident. In addition, perpetrators need training in developing more mature prosocial behavior and perhaps training in anger management. They need to learn to realize the harm that they cause their victims. They also need to give up self-justifying mechanisms, egocentric reasoning, and distorted ethics. Finally, they must understand that they have the ability and responsibility to engage in ethical behavior.

To better understand how children view bullying at their school, you might conduct a formal survey or interview children. Here are some Internet sites where you can obtain survey forms:

- Safe school and bullying surveys for students, parents, teachers, and school administrators, both in English and in Spanish, are available at https://sdfs.esc18.net/Sample_Surveys/SSM.asp
- English-language-only surveys are available at http://attorney general.delaware.gov/schools/bullquesti.shtml
- A compendium of surveys related to bullying, victimization, and bystander experiences is available at http://www.cdc.gov/violenceprevention/pdf/BullyCompendiumBk-a.pdf

Tables B-16–B-19 in Appendix B present interview questions designed to help you gather information about bullying from students who are in the upper grades in schools. Included are (a) general questions about bullying, (b) questions for victims of bullying, (c) questions for witnesses of bullying, and (d) questions for bullies. The questions can be modified to be more developmentally appropriate for elementary-aged populations.

Consultation with Parents

As noted earlier, children who bully may come from homes where they observe physical or verbal aggression. If you have any reason to suspect that a child is in danger of maltreatment, you should call Child Protective Services immediately. All parents should be encouraged to play an active role in reducing bullying behavior in their schools and neighborhoods. Thus, schools should give parents access to materials that can help them prevent and deal with bullying and cyberbullying. Parents can promote respectful and thoughtful behaviors in their children by following the suggestions in *Net Cetera: Chatting with Kids About Being Online* (OnGuard Online, 2009; free copies of the brochure are available at bulkorder.ftc.gov). It may also be helpful to have copies of Handout K-2 in Appendix K available in the main school office and on hand to distribute during parent-teacher conferences; the table lists strategies that parents can use in dealing with bullying or cyberbullying. Discussing bullying behaviors at PTA meetings and in other public forums is a good way to educate parents about their role in bullying prevention. We also recommend offering general classes on the nature of bullying for all parents and special classes for parents of victims of bullying and parents of bullies. School efforts to combat bullying, especially programs aimed at young children, may be more successful when parents are included (Leff, Thomas, Shapiro, Paskewich, Wilson, Necowitz-Hoffman, & Jawad, 2011).

LAWS TO PREVENT BULLYING

Federal Laws to Prevent Bullying

On October 26, 2010, the United States Department of Education issued a "Dear Colleague" letter to all elementary and secondary schools (and included a statement indicating that the same issues pertain to postsecondary educational institutions), reminding them that "some student misconduct that falls under a school's anti-bullying policy may also trigger responsibilities under one or more of the federal antidiscrimination laws enforced by the Department's Office for Civil Rights" (Ali, 2010) and that schools must respond to such events in accordance with the policies and practices developed by the Office of Civil Rights. Specifically, (a) Title VI of the 1964 Civil Rights Act prohibits discrimination on the basis of race, color, or national origin, (b) Title IX of the Education Amendments of 1972 prohibits discrimination on the basis of sex, (c) Section 504 of the Rehabilitation Act of 1973 prohibits discrimination on the basis of disability, and (d) Title II of the Americans with Disabilities Act of 1990 also prohibits discrimination on the basis of disability. The occurrence of any act of discrimination addressed by these federal laws requires that schools take immediate action to end harassment and prevent the reoccurrence of such behavior by, for example, providing services to the victim, intervening with the perpetrator, training the broader school community, and rewriting school policies. These federal statutes are designed to help protect students and provide schools with a baseline to use when creating their own anti-bullying policies.

The United States Department of Education issued another "Dear Colleague" letter on August 20, 2013 (Musgrove & Yudin, 2013), emphasizing that schools have the responsibility to ensure that students with disabilities who are subject to bullying receive a free appropriate public education under the Individuals with Disabilities Education Act (IDEA). Highlights of the letter follow.

Bullying of a student with a disability that results in the student not receiving meaningful educational benefit constitutes a denial of a free appropriate public education (FAPE) under the IDEA that must be remedied. Schools have an obligation to ensure that a student with a disability who is the target of bullying behavior continues to receive FAPE in accordance with his or her IEP. . . . If the IEP is no longer designed to provide a meaningful educational benefit to the student, the IEP Team must then determine to what extent additional or different special education or related services are needed to address the student's individual needs; and revise the IEP accordingly. . . . While it may be appropriate to consider whether to change the placement of the child who was the target of the bullying behavior, placement teams should be aware that certain changes to the education program of a student with a disability (*e.g.*, placement in a more restrictive "protected" setting to avoid bullying behavior) may constitute a denial of the IDEA's requirement that the school provide FAPE in the LRE [least restrictive environment]. . . . If the student who engaged in the bullying behavior is a student with a disability, the IEP Team should review the student's IEP to determine if additional supports and services are needed to address the inappropriate behavior. In addition, the IEP Team and other school personnel should consider examining the environment in which the bullying occurred to determine if changes to the environment are warranted.

No one federal law will prevent tragedies from happening. Most of the time, we have the laws on the books that we need. It's a commitment to teaching and mentoring, to being supportive and to being tough where we have to be, that can help.

—John Palfrey, Professor, Harvard Law School

State Laws to Prevent Bullying

In the late 1990s, and in the wake of highly publicized incidents of school violence such as the shootings at Columbine High School in Littleton, Colorado, states began to create laws to address bullying behavior. As of January 2013, 49 states plus Washington, D.C. (Montana being the exception) had passed anti-bullying laws designed to protect students from being harassed, threatened, or humiliated, although states' laws vary in scope and quality (see http://cyberbullying.us for updates on state laws). The website www.bullypolice.org provides links to relevant statutes in each state, as well as a rating of the adequacy of each state's laws.

Florida's anti-bullying law is a good example of a law that meets all important criteria (HB 669—School Safety; http://laws.flrules.org/files/Ch_2008-123.pdf). It requires school districts to adopt anti-bullying policies that also address cyberbullying, which is not an easy task because schools must balance students' protection against their free-speech rights. Although schools must focus primarily on protecting students while they are in school, teachers and staffs in Florida schools may become involved in off-campus activities when students post messages that disrupt the learning process at school or cause other students to avoid going to school out of fear. School districts are required to investigate reports of bullying, provide counseling to bullies and their victims, and report incidents of bullying to parents and law enforcement, when appropriate. Schools will lose funds if they do not comply with the law. Schools are advised to take action even if the bullying occurs off campus, through the Internet, or through other methods of telecommunication.

THE ROLE OF THE COURT IN CASES INVOLVING BULLYING AND CYBERBULLYING

Historically, in order for a school to discipline a student for an act of bullying, the act had to meet two criteria: (a) It had to occur on school grounds, immediately before or after school, or at a school-sanctioned event, and (b) the bullying act or its ramifications had to cause a substantial disruption to school activities. Several states have established or updated their laws to clarify that electronic acts occurring off campus can cause a substantial disruption to school activities and can be considered cause for suspension and expulsion (Hinduja & Patchin, 2011). Recent case law indicates that ambiguities exist in the way courts interpret federal and state laws dealing with bullying, cyberbullying, and discrimination and harassment.

The outcomes of several cases have suggested that schools can be held accountable when they do not have policies for preventing and dealing with bullying or when they fail to carry out adequately their own policies against bullying (e.g., *J.L. v. Mohawk Central School District et al.*, 2010a, b) and *T.K. and S.K. v. New York City Department of Education*, 2011). Cases of cyberbullying are complicated by the fact that acts of cyberbullying can be committed anywhere and at any time and can affect victims at a later time. The courts must determine when cyberbullying violates the law and when it falls under the doctrine of free speech. Additionally, because laws governing behavior when using electronic devices or the Internet are still being developed, courts may have difficulty finding a perpetrator guilty of any specific charges of cyberbullying (e.g., *J.C. v. Beverly Hills Unified School District et al.*, 2009; *United States v. Drew*, 2009). Still, courts have ruled that cyberbullies were guilty of violating the law (*D.C. et al. v. R.R. et al.*, 2010) or deserving of imposed school sanctions (*D.J.M. v. Hannibal Public School District*, 2011; *Kowalski v. Berkeley County Schools*, 2011). It is becoming widely recognized that acts perpetrated over electronic devices or the Internet can result in a substantial disruption in school activities, although schools remain limited in their capacity to respond to electronic acts of bullying.

CONCLUDING COMMENT

All children need to develop good cooperative and communication skills and learn how to be assertive when necessary. If they do not have them, children need to be taught these skills. Those who engage in bullying need help in developing empathy, learning acceptable social behaviors, decreasing their impulsive behavior, and developing anger control strategies (d'Escury & Dudink, 2010). Parents of bullies should be enlisted to help their children stop their bullying behavior, and parents of victims should be encouraged to support their children and help them cope with the stress of bullying.

Bullying will be averted only through the concerted efforts of parents, the public, state and federal governments, and policymakers who influence school culture and the culture at large. By implementing the strategies discussed in this chapter, schools can address bullying behavior more systematically. School administrators, teachers, school psychologists, clinical psychologists, school counselors, school social workers, and school nurses all can play an important role in preventing bullying in schools, in alleviating the distress experienced by victims of bullying, and in helping bullies recognize the pain that they are inflicting on others and begin to change their ways. Preventing bullying should be a priority for anyone working in the fields of education and mental health.

Before we leave this subject, we should consider the question posed by Porter (2013) about whether we are overusing the bully label. Here is an excerpt from her article:

We hear a lot about bullying—on the playgrounds, in schools, in the media. As a culture, we are infuriated with the bullies and terrified for the victims, and rightly so when it is appropriate. But the idea that childhood today is full of bullies is misleading. We do have a problem, but it's not with our children. It's with us, the adults. . . . We must admit that our approach to childhood aggression is flawed. Our children are not worse than they used to be, nor are they less resilient. But we adults seem to be. Instead of being so quick to label them, we much teach them how to deal with their aggression and pain appropriately and to develop compassion, impulse control and resilience in their relationships. And we must learn to do the same. (p. A19)

When they push you down "Stand back up,"
When they call you names walk by as if you can't hear them,
When they make everyone hate you, find someone who thinks that's wrong,
When you feel like nothing's going right, look in between the lines,
But when you give them what they want then yes, "You will fall."
So act like they're not there or else you're just letting them take over you, and talk to people that know the truth about you and even then still stand by your side because they're your real friends.

—Kasie Barentine

THINKING THROUGH THE ISSUES

1. Why has bullying received so much attention from the media, professional journals, and government agencies throughout the world?
2. What needs are children fulfilling when they engage in bullying behavior, and how can schools help them fulfill these needs more appropriately?
3. Why do you think more girls than boys are harassed on the Internet?
4. How can children protect themselves from being bullied and cyberbullied?
5. What must be done to make anti-bullying programs effective?
6. Are we overusing the bully label?

SUMMARY

1. Bullying and cyberbullying are insidious problems that occur far too often on playgrounds and in schools, neighborhoods, parks, homes, and workplaces.

2. Bullying not only affects the physical and mental health of the victim, but also has negative implications for the victim's peers and family, schools, the community, and society at large.

3. Efforts to counteract bullying must focus on setting and enforcing rules that prevent bullying and promote bystander intervention.

4. Training programs for teachers and school administrators need to focus on ensuring that a school's culture is not conducive to bullying.

5. Parents need help in addressing bullying issues at home and in their community.

6. Both in school and at home, children need to learn about the harmful effects of bullying, to build resiliency skills, and to increase their sense of self-efficacy and self-worth.

7. In face-to-face bullying situations, children can play various roles. These include the (a) bully who takes the initiative, (b) follower who joins in, (c) reinforcer who encourages the bully or who laughs at the victim, (d) intervener who tries to stop the bullying, (e) bystander who looks on but does not participate, and (f) victim who is the object of the bullying.

8. Many individuals can play a part in reducing bullying and cyberbullying, including children, parents, teachers, psychologists, counselors, nurses, school administrators, law enforcement personnel, and community members.

9. Ideally, all of these groups should work together to decrease bullying perpetrated in face-to-face interactions and via the Internet, mobile phones, and other electronic media.

10. Bullying involves repeated harmful physical acts, verbal acts, or sexual acts that threaten, insult, dehumanize, or intimidate another individual who cannot properly defend himself or herself; when these acts are carried out by means of any electronic device, they constitute cyberbullying.

11. There are many and varied reasons an individual may be unable to defend himself or herself against bullying, including obvious reasons such as size, strength, or being outnumbered as well as less overt reasons such as being less psychologically resilient.

12. Bullies attempt to control, dominate, and subjugate those who are bullied through the use of power.

13. The actions of bullies are designed to disempower the victims by undermining their worth and status.

14. Thus, two key components of bullying are repeated harmful acts and an imbalance of power.

Characteristics of Bullying

15. Bullying stems from the interaction of individual factors, parental factors, peer group factors, school factors, and community and cultural factors.

16. Some forms of bullying are direct, while others are indirect.

17. The indirect forms of bullying, often referred to as relational aggression, are a type of psychological violence and leave no physical evidence.

Characteristics of Cyberbullying

18. Cyberbullying involves the use of any digital technology with the intent to hurt, defame, or embarrass another person.

19. Instances of cyberbullying have been increasing over the last several years.

20. The impact of cyberbullying depends on such factors as the nature of the material, the intended audience for the material, the extent of circulation, and the intent of the communication.

21. Cyberbullying may take a number of forms: flaming, harassment, denigration, instigating and disclosing, impersonation, outing and trickery, exclusion, attacking data and equipment, and cyberstalking.

22. Cyberbullying differs from traditional bullying in several ways. Perhaps most importantly, cyberbullies can remain anonymous by assuming a screen name or stealing someone else's screen name; in addition, witnesses to the cyberbullying can remain anonymous.

23. Being anonymous allows cyberbullies to avoid being judged or disciplined in the same way as they might for engaging in face-to-face bullying.

24. In fact, some cyberbullies would be hesitant to say to another child's face what they say online or through wireless messages.

25. The anonymity and ease with which children can access online and wireless technologies also makes it easy for cyberbullies to strike at a moment's notice and without premeditation.

26. Wielding their power from a distance, cyberbullies can attract an audience whose size is limitless.

27. Children are often more technologically savvy than their parents and teachers, and their furtive online activity can be difficult to monitor.

28. Children who are cyberbullied may experience more distress and depression than children who are bullied in person.

Characteristics of Bullies

29. The families of bullies tend to be less cohesive, more conflictual, and less organized than those of children who are not bullies. Thus, bullies may have learned their negative traits in their homes when interacting with their siblings or when witnessing altercations between their parents.

30. Both bullies and their victims are more likely than other children to come from disadvantaged families and communities.

31. Students attending schools located in economically disadvantaged neighborhoods may experience less social cohesion and have fewer resources than students in other schools. Thus, these students are "at an increased risk for aggressive behavior, retaliatory attitudes, and diminished perceptions of safety" (Waasdorp et al., 2011, p. 117).

32. Bullies may engage in both overt bullying and covert cyberbullying.

33. Bullies may also engage in other forms of antisocial behavior, such as vandalism, shoplifting, fighting, and the use of drugs and alcohol.

34. When they reach late adolescence and adulthood, their aggressive behavior and antisocial behavior may continue.

35. When bullies are called to account for their actions, they may deny everything and counterattack with distorted or fabricated criticisms and allegations.

36. Victims of bullying who themselves engage in bullying are referred to as bully-victims.

37. Bully-victims tend to have behavior patterns associated with both victims and bullies.

Characteristics of Victims

38. There is no one profile of a child who is likely to be bullied. However, a child who possesses one or more of the following characteristics may be at heightened risk of being bullied: displays vulnerability or insecurity; dresses differently and doesn't

conform to the norm; has learning, speech, or other physical or mental disabilities; has low self-esteem; has physical attributes that differ from the norm, including being overweight, underweight, very short, or very tall; has poor communication skills; has poor social skills, prefers not to socialize, and is withdrawn and solitary; is a member of an ethnic or religious group viewed as different; is bright, talented, or gifted; is clumsy and immature; is perceived to be lesbian, gay, bisexual, or transgendered; is new to the school; is nonassertive and refuses to fight; is physically weak; is annoying, provocative, or aggressive; is richer or poorer than the majority of classmates; is shy, reserved, timid, or submissive; is the smallest or youngest child in school.

39. Being a victim of bullying may exacerbate children's social and academic difficulties and decrease their self-esteem.

40. Chronic victims of bullying are found most often in elementary school, followed by middle school and then high school.

41. Chronic victims of bullying tend (a) to be extremely passive, (b) to have low self-esteem, (c) to be anxious, insecure, fearful, less able than others to control their emotions, and socially withdrawn, and (d) to be unable to defend themselves adequately.

42. Without interventions, children who are chronic victims of bullying may develop an intense dislike of school, may become truant, and may drop out of school.

43. If bullying is accompanied by rejection, victims may develop emotional numbness and lethargy and suffer decreased self-awareness.

44. Some victims of bullying may even consider suicide.

45. When children who are chronically bullied become adults, their children are more likely to be victims of bullying than are children of adults who were not bullied as children.

Dimensions of Bullying

46. Ten dimensions of bullying can be delineated: intensity, frequency, presence of victim, clarity of intent to harm, emotion, physical contact, verbal message, nonverbal gestures, number of bullies, and goal of bully.

Incidence of Bullying

47. Sound statistics on the extent of bullying are difficult to obtain because children who are victims are often reluctant to report bullying for the following reasons: fearing retaliation, feeling shame at not being able to stand up for themselves, fearing they would not be believed, not wanting to worry their parents, having no confidence that anything would change as a result, thinking their parents' or teacher's advice would make the problem worse, fearing their teacher would tell the bully who told on him or her, and thinking it would be worse to be thought of as a snitch.

48. A 2011 Pew Research Center national survey of children ages 12 to 17 years reported that 95% of the sample were online and that 19% reported having been bullied in some way in the last 12 months.

49. Another national survey of online harassment, conducted in 2010, found that 11% of children ages 10 to 17 years who used the Internet were harassed, with a majority (69%) of the victims being female.

50. Over a 10-year period, online harassment increased by about 83%.

Bystander Reluctance to Report Bullying

51. It is often the case that although bystanders know that bullying is wrong, they are reluctant to report it.

52. Bystanders may not want to invite the bully's wrath and become the next target and may fear that they will be thought of as tattletales or informers and possibly be rejected by their peers.

53. Some bystanders may wrongly believe that they are not responsible for stopping the bullying, or they may think that bullying is acceptable.

54. Other bystanders may assume that school personnel don't care enough to stop the bullying or are unable to stop it.

55. When bystanders fail to act, bullies are less likely to receive any punishment and may be reinforced for their actions, and the victim is less likely to be protected from future bullying.

56. Bystanders are not immune to the effects of bullying.

57. There are children who intervene and help victims of bullying or report incidents of bullying to authorities. These children may be friends with the victim, may know that their parents or teachers expect them to support victims, or may believe that it is the moral and proper thing to do.

58. Fostering a school climate in which children feel comfortable supporting their peers and reporting bullying may help children who are at risk find allies, which, in turn, may reduce incidents of bullying.

Correlates of Bullying

59. Male bullies tend to rely more on physical aggression, whereas female bullies tend to rely more on indirect forms of bullying, such as teasing, rumor spreading, exclusion, and social isolation.

60. Males are more likely to bully than females, but males and females have similar rates of victimization.

61. Bullying occurs with most frequency during elementary school years and less often during middle school years and the early years of high school.

62. Bullying declines substantially after age 14 or 15 years.

63. Schools with negative social climates or located in socially disadvantaged areas have higher rates of bullying than schools in more advantaged areas.

64. Bullying occurs more often at school than on the way to and from school.

65. Bullies operate alone in about 50% of the cases.

66. Higher rates of bullying in schools negatively affect students' performance on standardized tests.

67. The degree of a school principal's involvement in school programs designed to prevent bullying may help to determine the level of bullying at the school.

Consultation

68. The National Education Association reported that almost all educators at the schools they surveyed in 2010 were aware that it is their job to intervene and prevent bullying.

69. Effective consultation about bullying in schools requires asking the right questions about a school's policies for dealing with bullying.

70. Bullying in schools tends to occur in areas with limited or no adult supervision.

71. If a school does not do anything about bullying, it risks (a) gaining a reputation for being dangerous or unsafe, (b) not fulfilling its academic mission, (c) losing enrollment, and (d) being the subject of litigation.

72. It is important for a consultant to help teachers and administrators recognize that combatting bullying needs to be a primary prevention activity in schools and strong universal supports must be in place for all students.

73. Teachers need to deal with bullying on the playground and in the classroom, lunchroom, and other places in school.

74. Bullying endangers the school's academic mission and compromises its safety mission.

75. School staffs must recognize that if bullying is permitted on their campuses, parents may come to believe that schools provide an uncaring, irresponsible, and dangerous environment.

76. If parents fear for the safety of their children, they are more likely to advise their children to fight back when provoked, rather than encouraging them to report bullying behavior to school authorities.

77. The school culture needs to diminish, rather than enhance, tendencies to act aggressively.

78. To be successful, intervention programs must focus on helping school personnel accept the program, getting teachers to implement the program, and ensuring that teachers, students, and staff adopt an anti-bullying philosophy.

79. Intervention programs must take into consideration the types of bullying encountered in the school, the ages of the students, and their sex, ethnicity, socioeconomic status, and disabilities (if present).

80. A meta-analysis of anti-bullying programs in several different countries reported that bullying behavior decreased by 20% to 23% after the programs were implemented. Components of effective intervention programs include adequate teacher and student training, improved supervision on the playground and in other unstructured areas, consistent and firm responses to bullying behavior, inclusion of parent training or outreach, and sufficient duration of the program.

81. Another review of anti-bullying studies found that the most effective programs were designed to improve students' social and interpersonal skills and modify their attitudes and beliefs.

82. By helping school districts implement and evaluate their chosen program, you will help school administrators and teachers adopt the best practices for preventing and reducing bullying.

83. As a result of being bullied (or sometimes as a result of bullying other children), children may show clinically significant levels of anxiety, depression, or other symptoms.

84. Children who play both roles—bully-victims—may have more internalizing symptoms than their peers.

85. Children who experience bullying for several years may be especially at risk and therefore may need long-term interventions.

86. The aggressive or withdrawal tendencies of children who are rejected by others may be exacerbated by bullying; therefore, in an intervention program you will need to consider whether victims of bullying have problems handling their aggressive or withdrawal tendencies.

87. Victims of bullying may benefit from various types of interventions, such as "anxiety management, social-skills training, coping-skills training, pleasant-events scheduling, assertiveness training, problem solving, and peer cooperativeness/mediation" (Swearer et al., 2004, p. 78).

88. It is a good procedure to have both the perpetrator and the victim meet individually with an appropriate school staff member to address an incident.

89. Perpetrators need training in developing more mature prosocial behavior and perhaps training in anger management.

90. If you have any reason to suspect that a child is in danger of maltreatment, you should call Child Protective Services immediately.

91. All parents should be encouraged to play an active role in reducing bullying behavior in their schools and neighborhoods.

92. Schools should give parents access to materials that can help them prevent and deal with bullying and cyberbullying.

93. We also recommend offering general classes on the nature of bullying for all parents and special classes for parents of victims of bullying and parents of bullies.

Laws to Prevent Bullying

94. The federal statutes designed to help protect students and provide schools with a baseline to use when creating their own anti-bullying policies are (a) Title VI of the 1964 Civil Rights Act, which prohibits discrimination on the basis of race, color, or national origin, (b) Title IX of the Education Amendments of 1972, which prohibits discrimination on the basis of sex, (c) Section 504 of the Rehabilitation Act of 1973, which prohibits discrimination on the basis of disability, and (d) Title II of the Americans with Disabilities Act of 1990, which also prohibits discrimination on the basis of disability.

95. As of January 2013, 49 states plus Washington, D.C. (Montana being the exception) had passed anti-bullying laws designed to protect students from being harassed, threatened, or humiliated, although states' laws vary in scope and quality.

The Role of the Court in Cases Involving Bullying and Cyberbullying

96. Historically, in order for a school to discipline a student for an act of bullying, the act had to meet two criteria: (a) It had to occur on school grounds, immediately before or after school, or at a school-sanctioned event, and (b) the bullying act or its ramifications had to cause a substantial disruption to school activities.

97. Several states have established or updated their laws to clarify that electronic acts occurring off campus can cause a substantial disruption to school activities and can be considered cause for suspension and expulsion.

98. The outcomes of several cases have suggested that schools can be held accountable when they do not have policies for preventing and dealing with bullying or when they fail to carry out adequately their own policies against bullying.

99. Cases of cyberbullying are complicated by the fact that acts of cyberbullying can be committed anywhere and at any time and can affect victims at a later time.

100. The courts must determine when cyberbullying violates the law and when it falls under the doctrine of free speech.

101. Additionally, because laws governing behavior when using electronic devices or the Internet are still being developed, courts may have difficulty finding a perpetrator guilty of any specific charges of cyberbullying.

102. It is becoming widely recognized that acts perpetrated over electronic devices or the Internet can result in a substantial disruption in school activities, although schools remain limited in their capacity to respond to electronic acts of bullying.

Concluding Comment

103. All children need to develop good cooperative and communication skills and learn how to be assertive when necessary. If they do not have them, children need to be taught these skills.

104. Those who engage in bullying need help in developing empathy, learning acceptable social behaviors, decreasing their impulsive behavior, and developing anger control strategies.

105. Parents of bullies should be enlisted to help their children stop their bullying behavior, and parents of victims should be encouraged to support their children and help them cope with the stress of bullying.

106. Bullying will be averted only through the concerted efforts of parents, the public, state and federal governments, and policymakers who influence school culture and the culture at large.

107. By implementing the strategies discussed in this chapter, schools can address bullying behavior more systematically.

108. School administrators, teachers, school psychologists, clinical psychologists, school counselors, school social workers, and school nurses all can play an important role in preventing bullying in schools, in alleviating the distress experienced by victims of bullying, and in helping bullies recognize the pain that they are inflicting on others and begin to change their ways.

109. Preventing bullying should be a priority for anyone working in the fields of education and mental health.

KEY TERMS, CONCEPTS, AND NAMES

Bully (p. 264)
Follower (p. 264)
Reinforcer (p. 264)
Intervener (p. 264)
Bystander (p. 264)
Victim (p. 264)
Bullying (p. 264)
Physical acts (p. 264)
Verbal acts (p. 264)
Sexual acts (p. 264)
Individual factors (p. 265)
Parental factors (p. 265)
Peer group factors (p. 265)
School factors (p. 265)
Community and cultural factors (p. 265)
Direct bullying (p. 265)
Indirect bullying (p. 265)
Relational aggression (p. 265)
Cyberbullying (p. 266)
Flaming (p. 266)
Harassment (p. 266)
Denigration (p. 266)
Instigating and disclosing (p. 266)
Impersonation (p. 267)
Outing and trickery (p. 267)

Exclusion (p. 267)
Attacking data and equipment (p. 267)
Cyberstalking (p. 267)
Cyberbullying vs. traditional bullying (p. 267)
Characteristics of bullies (p. 267)
Less cohesive families (p. 267)
More conflictual families (p. 267)
Less organized families (p. 267)
Bully-victims (p. 268)
Characteristics of victims (p. 268)
Dimensions of bullying (p. 270)
Intensity (p. 270)
Frequency (p. 270)
Presence of victim (p. 270)
Clarity of intent to harm (p. 270)
Emotion (p. 270)
Physical contact (p. 270)
Verbal message (p. 270)
Nonverbal gestures (p. 270)
Number of bullies (p. 270)
Goal of bully (p. 270)
Incidence of bullying (p. 270)
Bystander reluctance to report bullying (p. 271)
Correlates of bullying (p. 271)
Consultation with schools (p. 272)
Consultation with children (p. 276)
Consultation with parents (p. 276)
Federal laws to prevent bullying (p. 277)
State laws to prevent bullying (p. 277)
The role of the court in cases involving bullying and cyberbullying (p. 277)

STUDY QUESTIONS

1. Discuss the characteristics of bullying. Include in your discussion the dimensions of bullying and the incidence of bullying.

2. Discuss the characteristics of cyberbullying. Include in your discussion several forms of cyberbullying and the incidence of cyberbullying.

3. Compare and contrast the characteristics of bullies and victims of bullying.

4. Discuss the differences between bullying and cyberbullying.

5. Why are bystanders reluctant to report bullying?

6. Discuss effective consultation in the schools about bullying.

7. Discuss effective consultation with children and parents about bullying.

8. Discuss federal laws that pertain to bullying.

9. Discuss the role of the courts in cases involving bullying and cyberbullying.

CHALLENGES OF BEING AN EXPERT WITNESS

The quality of justice will be enhanced by experts who provide testimony that is ethical, moral, reliable, and relevant.
—Brian R. Clifford, British psychologist

Goals and Objectives

This chapter is designed to enable you to do the following:

- Understand the challenges of being an expert witness

- Testify in court, at a deposition, or at a due process hearing

- Know how to deal with the tactics of the cross-examining attorney during a cross examination

You may be called on to testify in court, at a deposition, or at a due process hearing in a school about a psychological or psychoeducational evaluation that you have conducted. When you testify, you are considered an *expert witness* because of your education, training, skill, and specialized knowledge in a particular subject (psychology) beyond that of the average person. You may be asked to give your opinion about a child's need for a special program or about a child's mental status, adaptive and social skills, and overall adjustment. Testifying in court or in court-like settings can be a difficult experience, because court procedures are radically different from those followed in mental health, medical, or school settings. An expert witness in court often is asked to respond to questions (e.g., "Isn't it true that . . . ?") with simple one-word answers and is afforded little opportunity to qualify responses, particularly during cross examination. In the courtroom, issues are framed in black-and-white terms; it is not typically a place where complex philosophical or educational issues are debated or resolved.

Your job as an expert witness is to present your findings and opinions clearly and accurately. It is not to seek justice, such as adequate compensation for a victim, an appropriate sentence for an offender, or anything else that you believe is warranted. Although you can, of course, hope that your testimony will contribute to a just outcome of the case, *your role is to be an expert, not an advocate*.

The goal of the mental health system is to promote mental well being, whereas the goal of the legal system is to promote justice. These differing goals may cause psychologists fundamental conflicts:

The rules of evidence demand that experts assist the trier of fact, the adversary system demands that experts serve the parties who retain them, and the ethical codes and guidelines demand that experts impartially assist the court, only in their area of competence. Psychological experts are left to sort out the competing demands, as well as their potential liability, while recognizing the importance of being persuasive. (Shuman & Greenberg, 2003, p. 219)

The mental health and legal systems, however, have similar underlying values (Melton, 1994). Both systems reject exploitive use of power. Both emphasize fairness, honesty, and competence in expert testimony. Both recognize limitations in current scientific knowledge. Finally, both systems stress the advancement of human welfare.

An expert witness may play a critical role in deciding the outcome of a case, including the amount of damages awarded to a client. The key to being an expert witness is to adhere closely to the assessment findings, to answer the referral question as clearly and succinctly as possible, to be familiar with current research findings in the field, and to make interpretations cautiously. In some cases, an expert witness may be asked about the method he or she used in formulating his or her opinions and conclusions.

FRYE STANDARD AND DAUBERT STANDARD

Judges determine what constitutes appropriate, relevant, and admissible expert testimony. Typically, they do this by applying the Frye standard or the Daubert standard. Federal courts are obligated to use the Daubert standard, whereas state courts can use either standard (or even another standard or method, as appropriate). Both standards are legal precedents set by the courts regarding the admissibility of an expert witness's testimony during legal proceedings.

The *Frye standard* was set by the District of Columbia Circuit Court in 1923 in *Frye v. United States*. To meet the Frye standard, an expert witness's testimony must be determined to be based solely on underlying principles of scientific evidence that have been sufficiently tested and accepted by the relevant scientific community. The court will evaluate both the quality and the quantity of the evidence offered by an expert witness. Under the Frye standard, when novel scientific evidence is presented by an expert witness, the court defers to scientific expertise about whether the evidence has gained general acceptance in the relevant field. This standard was established in an attempt to keep pseudoscience out of the courtroom.

The *Daubert standard* was set in 1993 by the U.S. Supreme Court in *Daubert v. Merrell Dow Pharmaceuticals*. The Supreme Court ordered federal trial judges to evaluate whether the testimony of an expert witness was reliable and relevant. Among the criteria for *reliable testimony* is the requirement that the expert witness's conclusions be reached through the scientific method—that is, that they be based on theories that have been empirically tested, peer reviewed, and published and on procedures that have a known actual or potential error rate, that other experts can replicate, and that have been accepted by a relevant scientific community. *Relevant testimony* is testimony that fits the facts of the case.

In the aftermath of Daubert, *Rule 702 of the Federal Rules of Evidence* was implemented. It states the following:

Rule 702. Testimony by experts

If scientific, technical, or other specialized knowledge will assist the trier of fact to understand the evidence or to determine a fact in issue, a witness qualified as an expert by knowledge, skill, experience, training, or education may testify thereto in the form of an opinion or otherwise, if (1) the testimony is sufficiently based upon reliable facts or data, (2) the testimony is the product of reliable principles and methods, and (3) the witness has applied the principles and methods reliably to the facts of the case.

Under both judicial standards, the court usually must decide whether an expert's testimony will assist the jury in understanding the evidence or facts in the case and whether a particular witness is qualified as an expert. When an expert's opinion is based solely on his or her personal experience and training, the opinion (e.g., that a defendant is incompetent) is not subject to either the Daubert standard or the Frye standard.

STANDARDS OF PROOF

Your testimony in both civil and criminal cases will help the court decide on the merits of the case. One of three standards of proof is applied, depending on the type of case.

- *Proof beyond a reasonable doubt* is the highest level of proof and is used mainly in criminal trials. This level of proof requires that the judge or jury believe that the conclusion is close to certain. It can be thought of as the level that has been met if there is no plausible reason to believe otherwise; however, it does not mean absolute certainty.
- *Clear and convincing evidence* is an intermediate level of proof and is used mainly in civil trials. This level of proof requires that the judge or jury believe that the conclusion is highly probable and substantially more likely to be true than not true.
- *A preponderance of evidence* is the lowest level of proof and is used mainly in civil trials. This level of proof requires that the judge or jury believe that the conclusion is more likely to be true than not true or that there is greater than a 50% chance that the conclusion is true.

These standards of proof refer to "the level of certainty by which the jury must be persuaded by evidence presented by the party shouldering the burden of proof" (Myers, 2009, p. 169). The standard requiring *reasonable certainty of your opinion* (or reasonable confidence in your opinion) applies to your testimony, as noted below.

REASONABLE CERTAINTY OF OPINION

As an expert witness, you should be reasonably certain of your opinion. Although "reasonable certainty" is not well defined in law, according to Myers (2009) it requires that the expert (a) have considered all of the relevant elements of a case in formulating his or her opinion, (b) have an adequate understanding of the pertinent clinical and scientific principles needed to function as an expert witness, (c) have used appropriate, reliable, and valid methods of assessment, and (d) have made reasonable assumptions and conclusions based on the assessment results.

Myers (2009) outlines other considerations related to being reasonably certain of your opinion:

the degree of certainty needed for expert testimony does *not* vary with the type of litigation. Thus, experts do not have to be more certain of their opinions in a criminal case, where the burden of proof is highest, than in a civil case. Regardless of the type of litigation—criminal or civil—experts should take all necessary steps to ensure the correctness of the opinion.

Occasionally, attorneys ask experts whether they are certain of their opinions beyond a reasonable doubt or by a preponderance of the evidence. An accurate response to such a question is:

"Counsel, when I reach an opinion, I do not employ the legal concepts of burden of proof. Burdens of proof are legal constructs, and are not used in psychology. Instead, I use clinical and scientific principles to reach my opinion. In reaching my opinion in this case, I took all the steps I could to ensure that my opinion is correct. I am reasonably certain of my opinion, and by reasonably certain I mean I am confident my opinion is correct." (p. 170)

TESTIFYING AS AN EXPERT WITNESS

Table O-1 presents suggestions for testifying as an expert witness. It emphasizes how to prepare for your testimony, how to conduct yourself in court, how to testify, and how to conclude your testimony.

Table O-1
Suggestions for Testifying as an Expert Witness

Preparation

1. Always make sure you are completely familiar with the facts related to the referral question(s) in the materials provided to you for your assessment. Use the most current empirical findings relevant to your opinions and conclusions. Also, if any pretrial conference material was provided to you, become familiar with any parts pertinent to your testimony. Adhere to the deadlines given to you by the retaining attorney.

2. Review information pertinent to the tests that you administered, including standardization, reliability, validity, standard error of measurement, and strengths and weaknesses.

3. Check that all computations are correct, that you used the correct entries from the norm tables, and that all of the data you placed in the report are correct. Also, check your notes for accuracy and record the date when you evaluated the child and the dates of subsequent contacts (e.g., telephone calls, emails, and letters).

4. Segregate your personal notes and work products from the case file. Don't show them to the cross-examining attorney without either the permission of the retaining attorney (or judge or some other entity like a government agency) or a court order. Discuss with the retaining attorney what files you want to bring to the stand to assist you with your testimony. Recognize that these files must be made

(Continued)

Table O-1 *(Continued)*

available to the cross-examining attorney, if requested, and that he or she may place them into evidence.

5. When preparing your testimony, avoid using professional jargon. Identify any difficult words, and use a thesaurus to find simpler and clearer nontechnical words that the judge and jury will understand.

6. Confer with the retaining attorney before the hearing or trial to learn what information is expected from you and to inform the attorney about the substance of your testimony if he or she is interested in this information. Tell the retaining attorney about what the findings mean and any potential problems with the assessment findings or possible pitfalls in your testimony. You may want to address these weaknesses directly when you testify. Clarify technical details so that the retaining attorney has a good understanding of the report. Review with the retaining attorney other cases in which you have given similar testimony, and discuss potential cross-examination questions and answers.

7. Provide the retaining attorney with a list of qualification and foundation questions—that is, questions the retaining attorney can ask to establish your credentials. An up-to-date resume of your professional credentials and educational background will help in this effort and may be entered into evidence.

8. Suggest to the retaining attorney that if the cross-examining attorney wants to accept your credentials without having them heard in court, the retaining attorney should at least try to present the highlights of your credentials.

9. Maintain a file of literature, including monographs, articles, and books, about the specialty area in which you will be offering expert testimony. Make the file available to the retaining attorney so that he or she can better understand the results of your assessment. Also, be sure that the retaining attorney is aware of anything you have written about the subject under litigation, including materials you have prepared for college courses, workshops, and Internet postings. The cross-examining attorney may elect to do a very thorough background check on your credentials and publications.

10. Avoid allowing depositions to take place in your office, where the cross-examining attorney would be able to see your books. The cross-examining attorney could then challenge you in court by referring to one of your own books. A conference room or an attorney's office is a more neutral place for your meeting.

11. When you arrive for a deposition with the cross-examining attorney, make sure you are fully prepared, know the facts of your case, have spoken to the retaining attorney (who will usually be present during the deposition), and have reviewed the relevant references in the professional literature.

12. At a deposition, have a "game plan" that you have discussed with the retaining attorney. For example, you may want to impress the cross-examining attorney with *all*

the facts that support your position in order to encourage settlement of the case. Another plan is to answer the questions honestly but narrowly if you expect the case to go to trial.

13. If you anticipate that the cross-examining attorney will be calling other expert witnesses, offer to help the retaining attorney prepare to deal with them. If the attorney accepts your offer, prepare a list of questions that the retaining attorney may use to cross examine the other expert witnesses. Usually, you can even sit with the retaining attorney in court and suggest areas of cross examination on the spot. Develop a written contract with the attorney for this aspect of your consulting work.

14. If you have given a deposition, reread it before you testify in court.

15. Recognize that the court usually will not allow you to testify about matters that are beyond your specialized knowledge and training.

16. Know what visual aids will be available in the courtroom for your use (e.g., blackboards, projectors) and whether you can use your laptop during your testimony.

17. Study the publications of the expert witnesses who are working for the cross-examining attorney to see if they have written anything that supports your position.

18. Remember that your conclusions need to have a reasonable degree of certainty, not absolute certainty.

19. You can't request a change in the transcript of your deposition unless the court reporter made a mistake; however, if you want to change or clarify any information you gave in the deposition, ask the retaining attorney to give you this opportunity when you testify. You will need to point out the reason for the change.

20. Practice giving your testimony to someone who is knowledgeable about testifying as an expert witness. Ask him or her to point out anything about your appearance, language, delivery, posture, mannerisms, or gestures that may detract from your testimony.

21. Be sure you know where the courtroom is, how to get there, and where to park, if necessary. On the court date, plan to arrive early.

22. Don't be surprised if you end up waiting to be called or recalled to testify. If possible, avoid filling your schedule too tightly with other activities on days when you must testify.

Courtroom Behavior

1. Wear professional and conservative clothing.

2. When you enter the courtroom, don't do anything that will draw attention to your behavior.

3. Before sitting down in the witness stand, make brief eye contact with the judge and jury. Adjust the chair and the microphone so that you don't have to lean forward to answer questions. Don't slouch on the chair.

4. Don't be afraid to express a moderate amount of emotion and empathy, as long as it is consistent with your style and

Table O-1 *(Continued)*

the content of your testimony; you don't want to come across as impersonal and devoid of feeling.

5. Avoid distracting behaviors such as eating mints, chewing gum, dangling noisy bracelets, or fumbling through a file.

6. Don't be afraid to look jurors in the eye. Jurors are naturally sympathetic to witnesses and want to hear what they have to say. Look at them most of the time and speak to them as frankly and openly as you would to a friend or neighbor.

7. Don't argue with the cross-examining attorney. He or she has every right to question you. The retaining attorney should object if the cross-examining attorney asks an inappropriate question. Don't answer a question with a question unless the question you are asked is not clear.

8. Don't lose your temper or become hostile, no matter how hard you are pressed, badgered, or harassed. Although it may be difficult to do, stay in control, remain polite, and answer all questions nondefensively and dispassionately. If you lose your temper, you have played right into the hands of the cross-examining attorney. However, if the cross-examining attorney is badgering you to an intolerable degree, let the judge know that you have answered the question as best you can.

9. Be courteous. Courtesy is one of the best ways to make a good impression on the judge and jury. Address the judge as "Your Honor."

10. Be aware that anyone you encounter in or around the courthouse may be a judge, juror, hostile witness, or cross-examining attorney, and always conduct yourself accordingly. Don't discuss the case in any public place, including hallways, restaurants, or restrooms. Don't chat informally with the cross-examining attorney or any other person on his or her staff or with another witness.

11. Always tell the truth, and strive to be fair and objective.

12. Don't offer comments about what other experts might say. You can provide only your opinion.

13. Don't criticize the opinions of other experts. Doing so may be looked on unfavorably by the judge or jury and will reduce your credibility. However, if another expert draws a conclusion based on either inadequate data or data that conflict with your own, you can say that.

14. Don't expect help from the retaining attorney or the judge when you are on the witness stand; you are responsible for your testimony.

15. If asked whether you have talked to the retaining attorney or to an investigator, admit it freely. If you are being paid a fee, admit without hesitation that you are receiving compensation. Appearing defensive about being paid or about the amount that you are being paid will create a negative impression.

16. If the cross-examining attorney objects to a portion of your testimony, stop talking until the judge responds. If the judge overrules the objection, continue with your testimony. If the

judge sustains the objection, don't continue to answer the question. If you continue, you likely will be admonished by the judge, which will detract from your value as an expert witness.

17. Always let the retaining attorney guide the trial strategy. In pre-trial conferences, you certainly can make suggestions, but once you are testifying, don't offer material that differs from what you agreed to present or try to lead the examination in a different direction. Don't second-guess the strategy of the retaining attorney.

18. Never bring actual tests, test booklets, or test manuals to court. You can describe items similar to the ones on the tests you used, but never describe the actual test items.

19. Be prepared to defend everything you testify about, even in the face of a hostile cross examination. If relevant, identify counter-positions or counter-arguments in your presentation.

20. Never alter or slant your findings, even if you are asked to. Doing so not only is ethically wrong, but would diminish your professional reputation if your actions were disclosed.

21. Speak as a professional—with clarity, with confidence, and in a calm tone of voice. Keep "ums" and long pauses to a minimum, although pauses to check your data or report are appropriate. Don't preface every remark with the words "I think" or "I believe." A trial is a serious matter: Avoid jokes, wisecracks, and condescending comments or tone of voice. Make an effort to avoid coming across as pretentious, smug, arrogant, argumentative, flippant, sarcastic, or "all-knowing." Be as natural and as calm as you can be, given the possibly trying circumstances.

22. Listen to each question carefully and don't start answering a question before the attorney is finished asking it. Speak loudly enough that everyone can hear you, yet softly enough that you can raise your voice to emphasize a point. Don't simply nod your head, even if the proceedings are being videotaped; say yes or no instead, as the court reporter is recording everything you say.

23. Don't get into a pattern of repeating either attorney's questions or words. You don't want to give the appearance of being uncertain or lacking in confidence.

24. Before answering each question, control the situation by consciously pausing. This allows the judge and jury to mentally shift from hearing the attorney's question to listening to your answer. For example:
Q: State your name and occupation.
[Three-count pause]
A: My name is _____ . I am a psychologist for the _____.
Q: How long have you been employed?
[Three-count pause]
A: I have been working there for _____ years.

25. Answer each question with a complete sentence rather than a word or phrase. The cross-examining attorney may want the judge and jury to hear only his or her question. By using the three-count pause and complete sentences and

(Continued)

Table O-1 *(Continued)*

looking directly at the jury, you will take psychological control away from the cross-examining attorney.

26. When answering questions, don't guess. If you don't know the answer to a question, say so—but don't let the cross-examining attorney trap you into answering question after question with "I don't know." For example, you might say, "The answer to that question is unknown because the results of research on that issue are conflicting [or there are no research findings on that issue]." That will keep you from appearing ignorant when a cross-examining attorney is asking you unanswerable questions.

27. Be sure you understand the question before you attempt to give an answer. If necessary, ask that it be rephrased. Or you can say, "Do you mean by that . . . ?" and then answer the question if the attorney agrees with your restatement. You can't possibly give a truthful and accurate answer unless you clearly understand the question.

28. Be alert for questions with a double meaning and questions that assume you have testified to a fact when you have not done so. Treat all questions and comments as important (both during a deposition and when you testify), no matter how brief they are or how insignificant they seem.

29. Directly answer each question you are asked, especially on cross examination. Don't volunteer information irrelevant to the question you are asked. You can give additional information, however, if you think that it will help the judge or jury understand the issue better.

30. Support your position by referring in your testimony to scholarly work and relevant research findings.

31. Be sure that what you say in court agrees with what you said in your report.

32. Use words that not only depict what happened but also convey the impression that you intend. Your choice of words is important. Here are some examples of positive, "soft" words, followed by negative, "hard" words in parentheses: *mother* (woman, respondent, abuser), *father* (subject, suspect, defendant), *child* (juvenile, youth), *cut* (laceration, open wound), *molest* (rape, sexually assault), and *bruise* (contusion). Note how the soft and hard words leave different impressions.

33. If you are asked to give a yes or no answer and you believe that an explanation is warranted, ask the judge if you may qualify your answer because a yes or no answer is inappropriate. In some states, you are required to answer yes or no but may then have the opportunity to explain your answer.

34. Think hard about questions involving distances or intervals of time. If you make an estimate, make sure that everyone understands that you are estimating, and be sure your estimates are reasonable.

35. Never offer an opinion on a subject outside of your area of expertise. If a question is about something outside of your area of expertise, just say that and don't answer the question.

36. Use diagrams, charts, and computer graphics when appropriate (e.g., to present profiles of test scores, to illustrate changes in test scores or changes in handwriting over time), as most people learn best visually. While standing at a blackboard, whiteboard, easel, or screen, turn and face the judge and jury and talk to them directly. Avoid making inaudible statements to the blackboard, whiteboard, easel, or screen.

37. If you decide while testifying to make a drawing, think before drawing anything (e.g., the brain, block design patterns). Don't start with the cliché "Well, I am not much of an artist." Draw in proportion, and never refer to "here" and "there." If you use vague terms, anyone reviewing a transcript or an audiotape of the proceedings (e.g., a judge of an appeals court) will not understand your testimony. Describe specifically what you draw, and number each representation.

38. Don't read aloud from notes unless absolutely necessary. If you must do so, state your reason—to refresh your memory, to make sure your statements are specific, or the like. Be aware that the cross-examining attorney will have the right to see any notes that you refer to and any documents that you take to the stand. That is why it is important that you tell the retaining attorney what materials you plan to bring to court.

39. Don't say that any particular article or book is "authoritative," as that may give the impression that you based your opinion primarily on this source. The cross-examining attorney may then take statements from this source out of context and confront you with them during the cross examination. (Of course, if you did base your opinion on one source only, indicate that if you are asked. However, you can add that the source is one of a number of important sources about this topic, and be prepared to cite other sources if asked.)

40. If the cross-examining attorney quotes from articles, books, other people's opinions, or things you have said, in an effort to show that your opinion is inconsistent with these other sources, ask to see the statements to which the cross-examining attorney refers. Read them, and compare what you read with what the cross-examining attorney has said. Often, you will find that the cross-examining attorney has misinterpreted something or taken it out of context. In such cases, you should be able to demonstrate not only that you are correct, but also how the source agrees with your statement.

Conclusion

1. When you have finished testifying, nod to the judge and jury and say, "Thank you."

2. After each appearance as an expert witness, ask the retaining attorney or others to critique your performance. Use the critique to improve the way you testify in the future. If there is a transcript of your testimony, obtain a copy to review and critique your testimony for yourself.

Source: Ackerman (2001), American Prosecutors Research Institute (1993), and Benedek (2002).

Deposition

During the *time of discovery*, the information-gathering period before trial, you may be asked to give a deposition. A *deposition* is the testimony of a witness who is placed under oath and then questioned by the cross-examining attorney. The retaining attorney will be present at the deposition. (The retaining attorney is usually the one who asked you to perform the evaluation or who is representing the agency for which you conducted the evaluation.)

Your deposition testimony is as critical to the case outcome as your court testimony, as deposition responses are recorded for possible use in court later. At the deposition, the cross-examining attorney will want to learn about your involvement in the case, your findings, how you arrived at your conclusions and recommendations, and additional related matters. The cross-examining attorney is likely to refer to your psychological or psychoeducational report and other relevant assessment materials. Questions at the deposition tend to be open-ended, allowing you to expand on your responses, whereas cross-examination questions at trial tend to be closed-ended, requiring brief, specific answers.

Before the deposition, the cross-examining attorney might request the following from the retaining attorney (DiCarlo, n.d.):

1. All documents reflecting or relating to any communication between you and the retaining attorney, including letters of engagement and communications with witnesses. (Letters of engagement are documents describing your exact duties as an expert witness and your fee schedule.)
2. All documents reflecting or relating to any preliminary opinions or conclusions.
3. All documents that you consulted or relied on in connection with your testimony, including those that you consulted or relied on in forming your opinions.
4. All documents relating to your educational, employment, and professional history and any other documents relating to your qualifications to testify.
5. Copies of your resume (vita) and professional publications. Be sure that you submit an up-to-date, accurate resume.
6. All documents, including transcripts, reflecting or relating to other cases in which you testified as an expert, including any that reflect the substance of your testimony, the terms of your engagement, the court in which the action was pending, or the outcome of the case.
7. All other documents relating to the engagement, the opinions you expect to give, or the opinions you were asked to consider giving.

Following are examples of questions that might be asked during a deposition:

- Who engaged you in this case?
- What did that person ask you to do?
- What did you do?
- What conclusions and opinions did you reach?
- What other information or assessments are still needed?

If you become aware of a mistake that you made during the deposition, correct it before the end of the deposition after conferring with the retaining attorney.

The purpose of a deposition is to allow the cross-examining attorney to gather information that will assist his or her client. Answer all questions during the deposition carefully, because your answers can be used later to impugn your trial testimony, especially if the deposition and trial answers are different. Depositions, in some sense, are "fishing expeditions"—attempts by the cross-examining attorney to gain any information that might conceivably be useful during a trial. During a deposition, the retaining attorney might object to one or more questions posed by the cross-examining attorney, for the record, but the expert witness still has to answer these questions. The judge will later decide whether the questions can be admitted. Sometimes depositions, either recorded by a stenographer or videotaped, are taken to be used in lieu of testimony in court; the same rules apply.

Direct Examination

When you are sworn in as an expert witness in court or at a due process hearing and answer the questions posed to you by the retaining attorney, you are under *direct examination*. At this time you will be asked to present your findings, recommendations, and opinions. It is the retaining attorney's responsibility to know a great deal about the case and ask open-ended questions skillfully so that you can present your findings in a clear, logical, and understandable manner.

When you testify as an expert witness, expect to answer questions similar to those asked at the deposition. However, the questions will be more focused in order to bring out the facts that you have been asked to testify about and to support the retaining attorney's case (see Table O-2). The direct examination usually will cover questions on the following topics:

- Your professional background and credentials
- Your publications and professional experience
- Your experience as an expert witness
- Your familiarity with the subject matter of the case
- Your research, if you have conducted any, on the subject matter of the case, including a review of literature
- Your evaluation of the child
- Your findings and recommendations
- Your compliance with the subpoena to produce records
- Your consideration of other materials relevant to the case

After you have answered questions from the retaining attorney about your qualifications (referred to as *voir dire*), the cross-examining attorney has the opportunity to cross examine you about your qualifications (Benedek, 2002). The cross-examining attorney may scrutinize your credentials, including your background and training, your history as an expert witness, any incidents that reflect negatively on you, and your

Table O-2
Questions That Might Be Asked of an Expert Witness

Background

1. Please state your name.

2. What is your present occupation?

3. For those unfamiliar with the term *psychologist*, please explain to us what a psychologist is.

4. How does a psychologist differ from other professionals, such as psychiatrists or social workers?

5. By whom and where are you employed?

6. How long have you been so employed?

7. What services are provided by your organization?

8. Do you have a particular specialty in your work?

9. What are your specific duties?

10. Describe your prior work history.

11. What education have you had to allow you to do this work? Tell me about your undergraduate degree and institution, graduate degree and institution, and specialized training in the field.

12. (If pertinent to testimony) Did you have to write a thesis or research paper to obtain your graduate degree?

13. What is a thesis?

14. What was the topic of your thesis?

15. How many hours of research were involved?

16. Was your thesis published?

17. (If yes) Where and when was it published?

18. Have you had any other specialized training in your field, such as postgraduate training, on-the-job training, seminars, workshops, or continuing education?

19. (If yes) Tell me about this specialized training.

20. How did this specialized training prepare you for your specialty?

21. Is the specialized training you received the normal way in which one obtains that training?

22. Why do you think that the specialized training you had was sufficient for your specialty?

23. Are you board certified?

Publications and Professional Experience

24. What are the licensing procedures for psychologists in the state where you reside?

25. Are you licensed in your state?

26. (If no) Why are you not licensed?

27. Have you published any books or articles related to your work?

28. (If yes) Please describe each publication, including title, topic, publisher, date of publication, length, and approximate amount of time spent on the publication.

29. Are you presently on the teaching staff of any college or university?

30. (If yes) What classes do you teach? How long have you been teaching? Do you have other teaching experience?

31. Have you presented any papers on the subject of [issue addressed by lawsuit or prosecution] to professional symposiums?

32. (If yes) When? Where? What specific aspects of the subject did your presentations address?

33. Are you a member of any professional organizations?

34. (If yes) What organizations? Have you ever served as an officer or in any special capacity for any of those organizations? (If yes) In what capacity did you serve?

35. Have you received any honors or awards for your work in the field of _____?

36. (If yes) Tell me about them.

37. Have you appeared on local or national television concerning your work in this area?

38. (If yes) Tell me about your appearances.

39. Have any newspaper or magazine articles been written concerning your efforts in the field of _____?

40. (If yes) Tell me about these articles.

41. Have you received any national recognition for your work?

42. (If yes) Tell me about that.

Experience as an Expert Witness

43. Have you previously testified as an expert in the courts of this state regarding [reason for lawsuit or prosecution]?

44. (If yes) Tell me about that.

45. Have you testified as an expert in the courts of any other states?

46. (If yes) Which states?

47. How many times have you testified as an expert on the topic of [issue addressed by lawsuit or prosecution]?

48. About how many times did you testify for the plaintiff and about how many times for the defendant (or the defense and prosecution)?

Familiarity with Subject Matter

49. Are you familiar with recent literature [articles, research] in the area of [issue addressed by lawsuit or prosecution]?

50. Do you subscribe to any professional journals that deal with [issue addressed by lawsuit or prosecution]?

51. (If yes) Which journals?

52. Do you routinely keep up with the literature in this field?

53. What is the present state of knowledge in your profession on the characteristics of children with [disability related to lawsuit or prosecution]?

54. Can you give any examples of important works on children with [disability related to lawsuit or prosecution]?

55. Do you devote all of your professional time to this area of psychology, or do you do work in other areas also?

56. (If other areas) Tell me about these other areas.

57. Please explain how you came to be involved in your area of expertise.

58. Can you estimate the number of children you have talked to who have had [disability related to lawsuit or prosecution]?

59. What services do you offer these children?

Research on Subject Matter

60. Have you participated in any research regarding children with [disability related to lawsuit or prosecution]?
(If yes, go to question 61; if no, go to question 81.)

61. In what way did you participate?

62. Was anyone else involved in this research? (If yes) Who?

63. What was the goal of your study?

64. How many children were involved in the study?

65. Did you use accepted scientific methodology in conducting your research?

66. Did you follow current ethical standards regarding your research?

67. Did you follow approved and established statistical methods in compiling your data?

68. Please explain those methods.

69. What procedures did you follow to ensure the reliability and validity of your data?

70. Have other similar studies been conducted?

71. Can you give us some examples?

72. Have you compared the information you gathered with information obtained by other experts in your field?
(If yes, go to question 73; if no, go to question 75.)

73. How do they compare?

74. Is their information consistent with yours?

75. What use is made of this information within your profession?

76. Are the procedures you used generally accepted in your profession?

77. How do you know that to be true?

78. Do members of your profession rely on the data you collected in forming opinions or in making inferences regarding the diagnosis and treatment of children with [disability related to lawsuit or prosecution]?

79. In your experience, is the information revealed by your studies and those of other researchers in your field known to the average person?

80. On what do you base that opinion?

Compliance with Subpoena

81. Have you complied fully with each and every element of the subpoena to produce material?

82. Were any of these documents altered in any way?

83. Were any of them recopied, erased, written over, enhanced, edited, or added to in any way since the time each was originally created?

84. Are the photocopies you gave me true and exact replicas of the original documents without any revision?

85. Have any documents falling within the scope of the subpoena or otherwise relevant to the case been lost, stolen, misplaced, destroyed, or thrown away?

86. Are any documents you made, collected, handled, or received that are within the scope of this subpoena or otherwise relevant to the case absent from the documents made available to me?

Evaluation of Child

87. How much time do you spend with a child during an evaluation?

88. How many times do you normally see a child during an evaluation?

89. Did you have an opportunity to evaluate [child's name]?

90. Who contacted you to evaluate [child's name]?

91. Before meeting with [child's name], what did you do to familiarize yourself with the case?

92. Before meeting with [child's name], did you talk with anyone?
(If yes, go to question 93; if no, go to question 96.)

93. With whom did you talk?

94. What type of information did you hope to obtain from [person talked with]?

95. Is meeting with an adult before talking with the child an accepted practice within your profession?

96. Did you look at any reports on this case before meeting with [child's name]?

97. (If yes) From whom did you get the reports?

98. How did you use any information obtained from sources other than the child?

99. How much weight did you give to information obtained from sources other than the child?

100. How long were your meetings with [child's name]?

101. Were your interviews of an acceptable length, considering the child's age and level of development?

102. How many times did you meet with [child's name]?

103. How much time would you estimate that you spent with [child's name] in total?

104. How much time would you estimate that you have spent on this case?

105. Where did your meetings with [child's name] take place?

106. What procedures do you typically use when evaluating a child for [reason for referral]?

107. Tell me about the procedures you use, such as their reliability, validity, norm group, and any other relevant information about them.

108. Why do you use these procedures?

109. Do you typically follow the same protocol for every evaluation?

110. Are the procedures you have just described an accepted means of assessment in your profession?
(If yes, go to question 113; if no, go to question 111.)

(Continued)

Table O-2 *(Continued)*

111. Which procedures are not accepted?

112. Why aren't they accepted?

113. How many children have you evaluated using this protocol?

114. Do you regularly keep records of what you find during your evaluation?
(If yes, go to question 115; if no, go to question 117.)

115. Please describe what information is kept in these records.

116. When are these records completed?

117. Is there any way to ensure that what a child is telling you is not something that was related to the child by a third person?

118. (If yes) Tell me about that.

119. Please describe how [child's name] appeared and behaved during your evaluation.

120. During the course of your evaluation, did [child's name] express any reluctance to talk about anything?
(If yes, go to question 121; if no, go to question 123.)

121. What was the child reluctant to talk about?

122. How did you respond to the child's reluctance?

123. Did you arrive at a diagnostic impression or a specific diagnosis?

(If yes, go to question 125; if no, go to question 124 and then question 128.)

124. Why didn't you arrive at a diagnosis?

125. What was it?

126. How confident are you of your diagnosis?

127. Would other evaluators have arrived at the same diagnosis? (If no) Why not?

128. Do you have any doubts about the reliability or validity of the assessment findings?

129. (If yes) Tell me about your doubts.

130. What recommendations did you make?

131. What was the basis for your recommendations?

132. Is there anything else you want to tell us about your findings?

133. (If yes) Go ahead.

134. After meeting with [child's name], did you offer him [her] any further services?

135. (If yes) What services did you offer the child?

136. Did you offer or suggest any referral services to [child's name] and his [her] family?

137. (If yes) What referral services did you recommend to the child and family?

Sources: Most of the first 80 questions are from *Investigation and Prosecution of Child Abuse* (2nd ed., pp. 353–395), by the American Prosecutors Research Institute of the National Center for the Prosecution of Child Abuse. Copyright 1993 by the American Prosecutors Research Institute. Adapted and reprinted with permission. Questions 81–86 adapted from Pope, Butcher, and Seelen (1993, pp. 140–142). Questions 87–122 and 136–137 adapted and reprinted with permission from *Using Expert Witnesses in Child Abuse and Neglect Cases* (pp. 28–29), by M. Zehnder, St. Paul, Minnesota, County Attorneys Association. Copyright 1994 by the Minnesota County Attorneys Association.

credibility. He or she may emphasize your weakest areas and may even attempt to discredit you (a tactic used in many cases). For example, the cross-examining attorney may attack you in the following areas:

- Your education (especially if you do not have a doctoral degree): "Isn't it true that a Ph.D. is the accepted degree for the practice of psychology?"
- Your certification: "Are you certified by the American Board of Professional Psychology?" If not, "Why aren't you board certified?"
- Your specialized training: "Have you ever had a course in co-morbid disorders?"
- Your experience: "You're not a medical doctor, are you?" If not, "Then how can you tell us about the effects of brain damage?"
- The amount of time you spent with the child: "Do you mean that you spent only three hours testing the child?"
- Your ability to make recommendations: "Do you think that you know the child well enough based on a three-hour evaluation to make a recommendation?"

- Your fee: "How much are you being paid for your work on this case?"
- Your ability to be unbiased: "How can you give an unbiased opinion when you are being paid for your services?"

Often, however, a cross-examining attorney skips the cross examination part of *voir dire*, because it gives an expert witness an opportunity to reemphasize his or her credentials.

The psychological or psychoeducational report probably contains the information that you will need in order to answer most of the questions you will be asked about the child. You will want to review your report, recommendations, and deposition transcript carefully prior to testifying in court. Make sure that you have considered in your report all sources of data, have not mixed data with expert opinion, have not suppressed disconfirming evidence, have not relied on unsubstantiated diagnoses or the expert opinions of others, have not addressed the wrong forensic issues, and have not allowed the retaining attorney to change your opinion (Wettstein, 2004). Ask the retaining attorney whether you should have a copy of your report with you when you testify.

As an expert witness, you can and should rely on notes or other materials for information that you cannot readily recall. Consulting such materials, called *refreshing recollection*, is an acceptable means of providing information to the court. However, don't read directly from your notes; rather, use them to verify facts or other information. Note that any materials that you refer to in your testimony can be inspected by the cross-examining attorney. Therefore, before bringing materials to court, show them to the retaining attorney for approval.

Your role as an expert witness is to provide information to the court (or the hearing officer) so that a judge, hearing officer, or jury can reach an appropriate decision. In your testimony, present a logical, carefully reasoned summary of your findings, the implications of the findings, and your conclusions. Describe what you have found in a way that makes the technical material understandable. Rely on facts, do not stretch the truth, and do not overstate your opinion. Answer aggressive questioning by the cross-examining attorney in a rational, logical, and unemotional manner. Doing so will give you more credibility than responding in kind. In some cases, the retaining attorney or a judge may ask you to provide an opinion about a child (or parent) and to answer questions like the following: "What psychological problems has the child developed as a result of the accident?" "Should the child be placed in a psychiatric ward of a hospital?" "What are the implications of your findings?" "Which parent should be given custody of the child?" "Is the child ready to return home?" "What kind of treatment does the child need?"

You may be asked whether a defendant is likely to engage in dangerous behavior in the future. Predicting risk of future violence is extremely difficult, yet courts often rely on psychological experts to assist them in this manner.

The goal of ethical practice is to provide the court with information on risk factors, describe whether or not those factors apply in the current context, describe and elaborate on the person's history of previous violent behaviors, relate those previous contexts to the person's current and reasonably estimated future situations, and suggest strategies that could reduce risk. (Tolman & Rotzien, 2007, p. 76, with changes in notation)

Evaluating the risk of future violence requires an understanding of applicable current research. Current findings suggest the following (Tolman & Rotzien, 2007):

- Unstructured clinical techniques are insufficient for risk assessment.
- Psychopathy—including poor self-regulation and sexual violence—is linked to violent recidivism.
- The impact of treatment on the rate of recidivism for violence is unclear.
- Little is known about the effectiveness of risk evaluations in cases of spousal abuse, stalking, and custody disputes.

Note that clinicians are not experts in the prediction of dangerous behavior. We cannot diagnose dangerousness; the best we can do is to discuss an individual's propensities for violent behavior directed toward others or self, based on the individual's past behavior.

Cross Examination

Prior to the *cross examination*, which follows the direct examination, the retaining attorney should familiarize you with the key premises of the opposition's case. During the cross examination, the cross-examining attorney will generally ask you questions to which he or she already knows the answers; this common strategy by the opposition is designed to give you no "wiggle room."

During the cross examination, the cross-examining attorney's inquiries will typically have three goals (DiCarlo, n.d.): to establish how you formed your opinions and reached your conclusions, to get you to support his or her position, and to attack your credibility. The cross-examining attorney may try to attack your credibility by implying that you do not have the expertise needed for the case, by arguing that the methodology you used to gather information is faulty, by claiming that you made errors in statements of fact, by noting that you made prior statements inconsistent with your current testimony, by portraying you as biased, or by attacking your character (Bank & Packer, 2007). These attacks are usually designed to diminish your credibility, rather than to disqualify you as an expert witness.

Cross-examination topics. The cross examination usually will focus on several of the following topics:

- The facts on which your opinions and conclusions were based
- Whether relevant alternative facts might have resulted in a different conclusion, and why or why not
- The degree of confidence you have in each of your opinions (an attempt on the part of cross-examining attorney to distinguish between firmly held conclusions and mere guesswork or speculation)
- The precise nature of any disagreements with the cross-examining attorney's expert witnesses and whether such differences of opinion are based on assumptions made by the cross-examining attorney's expert witnesses that differ from your own assumptions
- Whether you would change your opinions and conclusions if you accepted the same facts or assumptions as the cross-examining attorney's expert witnesses
- Whether there is more than one school of thought in the community of experts and, if so, whether you will admit that there is a substantial body of thought that supports the position of the cross-examining attorney's expert witnesses
- What documents you reviewed while you were preparing to testify, including personal notes
- How you used these documents to form your opinion
- Whether you know of any relevant documents that were not given to the cross-examining attorney

- Whether there are other documents related to the subject of your testimony that you did not review
- Any limitations in your qualifications and experience
- Any limitations or lack of confidence about the credibility of your opinions or assumptions about the case
- Any limitations in your assessment results
- Any damaging admissions concerning any issues in the case
- Inconsistencies in your testimony (elicited, in part, by comparing your present testimony with a position that you previously advocated)
- Any of your opinions or assumptions about the case that can be disproved or questioned
- Any sources of bias in your testimony (e.g., prior relationships with the parties involved in the litigation)
- Hypothetical opinions that support the cross-examining attorney's theory
- Admissions about the qualifications of the cross-examining attorney's experts and the reliability of these experts' sources, tests, methods, and findings
- Your incentives for testing: "You're a hired gun."
- Your choice of assessment procedures: "Isn't it true that you used an American-normed test, which is culturally biased?"
- Your character and past behaviors: "Isn't it true that you have received four speeding tickets?"
- Your testimony: "What you are saying now is not what you said during the deposition. Why is that?"
- Your publications: "Some of your publications are in nonrefereed journals. What good are they?" (The publication standards of *nonrefereed journals* are less rigorous than those of refereed journals. Nonrefereed journals do not have a panel of expert readers review manuscripts. Instead, manuscripts are usually screened only by a publications editor. Thus, some nonrefereed journals will accept almost anything submitted for publication.)

- Your lack of knowledge about the subject matter under dispute: "Isn't it true that on page 17 of his book *Children's Testimony*, Smith says that children are not reliable informants?"
- Your recommendations: "How can you be sure that the child should be placed in a public school classroom for children with learning disabilities rather than in a private school?"

Maintaining professional demeanor. Myers (2009) offers the following advice on how to maintain a professional demeanor:

The experienced expert refuses to be cajoled, dragged, or tricked into verbal sparring with the cross-examiner. The professional is at all times just that—professional. Given the aggression of some cross-examiners—aggression that is sometimes laced with error, insinuation, and even personal attack—it can be difficult to maintain a calm, professional demeanor on the witness stand. Yet, remember that the jury is looking to you for objective guidance and wisdom. The jury wants a strong expert but not someone who takes off the gloves and fights it out with the cross-examiner. This does not mean, of course, that the expert cannot use pointed responses during cross-examination. The expert should express confidence when challenged and should not vacillate or equivocate in the face of attack. On the other hand, the expert should concede weak points and acknowledge conflicting evidence. (p. 172)

Possible tactics of the cross-examining attorney. In order to maintain your composure and avoid the perception of being defensive or argumentative, be aware of a number of tactics (or ploys) that a cross-examining attorney might use to undermine your credibility during cross examination. Table O-3 presents a number of tactics or ploys, along with suggestions for dealing with each of them.

Sometimes a cross-examining attorney may have difficulty formulating simple or straightforward questions (Gutheil &

Table O-3
Tactics or Ploys Used by Cross-Examining Attorneys

Tactic	Explanation	Suggestion
Adopting a pleasant demeanor initially	To get you to relax, the cross-examining attorney may start out friendly and later attempt to catch you off guard.	Listen thoughtfully to each question and then answer it carefully.
Asking leading questions	To encourage you to agree with his or her propositions or to confront you with contrary facts or opinions, the cross-examining attorney may ask you leading questions.	Don't allow the cross-examining attorney to mold your opinion to fit his or her theory. Correct any questions that are based on faulty assumptions.
Feigning ignorance	To get you to open up, the cross-examining attorney may feign ignorance.	Don't be lulled into thinking that the cross-examining attorney changed sides or is unfamiliar with the facts. Many attorneys work hard to gain scientific expertise on the subject matter of their cases. By answering questions concisely and respectfully, you can avoid this trap.

Table O-3 *(Continued)*

Tactic	*Explanation*	*Suggestion*
Limiting your testimony	To box you in, the cross-examining attorney may ask you to agree to answer a series of yes or no questions. The aim is to prevent you from giving a complete answer or explaining anything.	Say, "Because this case is so complicated, I do not see how I could do that without misleading the jury." If the cross-examining attorney says, "Doctor, can you answer the previous question with a yes or no?" say, "I am afraid it would be misleading to the jury for me to be any more precise in my answer than I have already been" (Gutheil & Dattilio, 2008, p. 65).
Cutting off your answers	To stop you from saying something detrimental to his or her case, the cross-examining attorney may cut off your testimony.	Remain polite, but, if necessary, ask the judge whether you may finish your answer. If the judge says you may not, it is up to the retaining attorney to decide whether to give you the opportunity to give an extended answer on redirect examination.
Asking rapid-fire questions	To prevent you from having time to think about your answers, the cross-examining attorney may ask questions in rapid succession.	Answer questions with due deliberation. You might say, "I need a moment to think about my answer." You can also wait as long as you need to before answering or ask which question you should answer first. If you are not sure that a question is appropriate, wait about 5 seconds before answering to give the retaining attorney time to raise an objection.
Phrasing questions ambiguously	To confuse you, the cross-examining attorney may use language with double meanings or ask complicated or intentionally ambiguous questions.	Say that there are many parts to the question and that you can't answer it with one answer. Break the question into its component parts and answer each part separately. If the cross-examining attorney makes a speech but fails to ask a question, you might say, "I do not understand what question you are asking me."
Using slanted rephrasing	To reduce the impact of your testimony, the cross-examining attorney may rephrase or slightly alter your testimony so that it is less harmful to his or her client.	Listen carefully to any rephrasing of your testimony. If it is slanted, politely inform the cross-examining attorney that the rephrased testimony is not correct.
Asking misleading questions	To make the jury think that you are a "hired gun," the cross-examining attorney may ask, "How much you are being paid for your testimony?" or "You are a professional witness, right?"	Say, "I am being paid for my time, not for my testimony" or "I am always a professional, and today I am also a witness, but I am not a professional witness."
Using flattery	To bring out what may be perceived as self-promotion and arrogance, the cross-examining attorney may flatter you by saying, "You consider yourself to be one of the best, if not the best, assessment specialist in the region, correct?"	Don't allow the cross-examining attorney to lull you into making self-centered statements. If you agree with the cross-examining attorney's characterization of your reputation, his or her next question is likely to be "But you are not nationally board certified, are you?" or some other question intended to undermine your credibility. Focus on the facts of your credentials, and be modest.
Citing supposedly inconsistent testimony	To rattle you, the cross-examining attorney may say that your court testimony conflicts with your deposition testimony or with your previous writings, lectures, recordings, or testimony in similar cases. Often the material from your deposition or previous work is taken out of context.	Ask to read the passage in the deposition transcript or your previous work before you respond to the cross-examination question. If your opinion did change from the one you gave in the deposition or in your previous work, give the rationale for the change. (Remember to review beforehand your previous professional work and your previous testimony in similar cases, to try to determine how your past opinions differ from your present opinions.)

(Continued)

Table O-3 *(Continued)*

Tactic	Explanation	Suggestion
Asking obvious questions	To get you to struggle over or argue about obvious points, the cross-examining attorney may ask you questions that you should concede to outright. Examples: "Isn't it true that suicide can't be predicted with certainty?" "Isn't it true that you reviewed the case after the fact?" "Isn't it true that experts may disagree about a case?"	Say "yes" to each of these or similar questions.
Asking "isn't it possible" questions	To get you to say something favorable to his or her client, the cross-examining attorney may ask you questions that begin "Isn't it possible that . . . ?"	Say, "You're asking if it is *possible*, not *probable*—is that right?" and then answer the question. You want to highlight the intent of the cross-examining attorney's question.
Asking hypothetical questions	To weaken your testimony, the cross-examining attorney may ask you about a hypothetical set of facts that differs from the facts in the case. "If the hypothetical facts I presented to you turned out to be true, you would change your opinion, correct?"	Say, "If the facts that you presented were true, I would change my opinion, but your hypothetical facts were not the facts of the case I examined."
Asking "what is missing" questions	To diminish your impact, the cross-examining attorney may ask you questions about what you left out of your report.	Be prepared to give the rationale for leaving information out of the report.
Implying bias	To suggest that you may be biased, the cross-examining attorney may imply that you are testifying on behalf of the family.	Say, "I was retained by the family's attorney to conduct a psychological evaluation of their child and that is what I did."
Referring to an authoritative text	To diminish the importance of your testimony, the cross-examining attorney may refer to an authoritative book or article that presents an opinion that differs from yours.	Say, "I agree that this is an important book [article], but I do have some reservations about it" or "This book [article] has limited applicability in this case because . . . ." Alternatively, you can say, "I cannot comment without reading the entire passage [article] you selected. I'll be happy to comment if you will allow me to read the entire passage [article]." In some cases, the judge will allow the cross-examining attorney to give you a copy of the book or article; if so, carefully read the passage before you respond. Also, if you can cite a book, article, or viewpoint that contradicts the one the cross-examining attorney mentioned, do so.
Implying impropriety	To make you uncomfortable, the cross-examining attorney may imply that you have done something improper, such as talking to others about your forthcoming testimony.	Give the names of the people with whom you have spoken, because it is perfectly permissible to have spoken with the retaining attorney, the client, your supervisor, and others.
Personalizing questions	To diminish your effectiveness, the cross-examining attorney may personalize his or her questions. For example, he or she may ask, "Would you want your child to be in the same class as this child?"	Don't buy into these types of questions. You might say, "My examination and professional education did not address how the client and my child would get along."

Table O-3 *(Continued)*

Tactic	*Explanation*	*Suggestion*
Extrapolating findings	To try to get you to go beyond your findings and what you definitely know about the case, the cross-examining attorney may ask you questions that require you to extrapolate from the findings, such as "Do you think that this young woman can get a job as a police officer?"	Since you don't know exactly which skills are required of a police officer and likely have not assessed all of them, say, "I'm not familiar with the hiring practices of the police force or the skills needed to become a police officer so I am not able to answer that question."
Diminishing your expertise	To make you uncomfortable, the cross-examining attorney may ask you if you have ever been wrong or if you have ever made a mistake.	Admit that you have and, if the cross-examining attorney does not ask further questions about your past mistakes, make sure the retaining attorney asks you about past mistakes on the redirect examination.
Staring at you	To get you to react and possibly make a bad impression, the cross-examining attorney may stare at you after you answer a question.	Don't respond; simply wait for the next question. Take a sip of water if you want.
Putting the burden on you to come up with subjects	To increase your anxiety, the cross-examining attorney may ask you to give him or her all of your opinions about the case. "Doctor, if you haven't given me all your opinions about the case when I finish the deposition, please indicate what they are, OK?"	Say, "I can't anticipate all of the questions that you have not asked me, and therefore you are going to have to ask me the question that you want me to answer."

Source: Ackerman (2001), Barsky and Gould (2002), Benjamin and Gollan (2003), Brodsky (2004), Gutheil and Dattilio (2008), and Myers (2009).

Dattilio, 2008). He or she may pack a query with so many qualifiers that it becomes incomprehensible. In such cases, ask to have the question rephrased or say that you do not understand it; these tactics are better than trying to answer such a question. Similarly, if a cross-examining attorney asks a compound question, such as "Doctor, did you examine the client yourself and did you discuss with your attorney how you were going to present the findings in court?" say, "I believe that you are asking me two questions; which one do you want me to answer first?"

Remember that the retaining attorney is not *your* attorney but simply the person who retained you. You may need to point that out, as well as the fact that you presented the results of your evaluation as a professional and not according to anyone else's dictates.

The cross-examining attorney may do anything within the limits of legal courtroom procedure to impugn your testimony. Because court hearings are based on the adversarial process, they rarely turn on absolute truths; the outcome of a case often depends on which party presents a more convincing set of facts and arguments. However, no matter how shrewd a cross-examining attorney might be, you are the expert. Unless he or she has had training similar to your own, you know more than

he or she will ever know about your specialty. Remember that your goal is not to be an advocate, but to present your data and conclusions as best you can and let the trier of fact decide on the outcome. Finally, your findings are based on your own and your profession's well-established standards. Stay committed to these, no matter what attorney pressures you face (Brodsky, 2004).

Redirect and Recross Examinations

After the cross examination has been completed, the retaining attorney may keep you on the stand to answer additional questions; this is referred to as *redirect examination*. During the redirect examination, you will be able to clarify or explain any potentially damaging responses you may have given during the cross examination and to restate your opinion. Again, the retaining attorney will ask you open-ended, but not leading, questions. After the redirect examination, the cross-examining attorney then can conduct another cross examination; this is referred to as *recross examination*. It is not permissible to introduce new material during the redirect or recross examination phase of the trial.

EFFECTIVENESS AS AN EXPERT WITNESS

Jurors and the judge will form an impression of you and your testimony based on such factors as your credentials, apparent motives, extent of bias (if any), and presentational style, including clarity of communications and quality of reasoning (Bank & Packer, 2007). For example, they are likely to consider the following:

- Whether you appeared likable and trustworthy
- Whether you considered all of the relevant facts
- Whether you were confident of the accuracy of the facts underlying your opinion
- Whether you showed an adequate understanding of the clinical and scientific principles involved in the case
- Whether you used methods of assessment and analysis recognized as appropriate by professionals in your field or having adequate scientific support
- Whether the inferences you drew were logical, reasonable, and objective
- Whether your testimony was clear and understandable
- Whether you appeared to be strongly biased or "a hired gun"
- Whether you appeared arrogant or cocky

Try to customize your testimony so that it will be clearly understood by the jurors. Remember that you are providing answers primarily to the jury and not to the attorney asking the questions. To make your testimony most effective, identify which aspects of your findings are most critical to your formulation of the case. Before you include any test results, make sure that the psychological tests that you have administered are highly reliable and valid for the relevant population and have been administered and scored properly. Finally, emphasize the range and breadth of your education and clinical training to become a licensed psychologist. After you complete your testimony, ask yourself whether you protected the truth of your opinion from any manipulation by either attorney (Gutheil & Dattilio, 2008).

CONCLUDING COMMENT

Bank and Packer's (2007) conclusion in their chapter on expert witness testimony is a fitting way to end this section:

Legal systems have utilized expert witnesses for approximately 700 years. Experts have testified on everything from bloodletting to DNA analysis. The twenty-first century will witness experts testifying about issues we cannot presently envision. The rules governing expert testimony and the substance of expert testimony are works in progress because human nature and science are ever changing. What will not change is the need for assistance on topics beyond the knowledge of jurors and courts. As technology progresses, the disparity between lay and expert knowledge widens, and the need for expert witnesses increases.

Experts must always strive to formulate inferences as objectively as possible. It is incumbent on experts to prevent misuse or misrepresentation of their work. To accomplish this, it is appropriate for experts to persuasively advocate for their positions. To be persuasive, experts must appear credible. Expertise, trustworthiness, and presentational style synergistically blend to determine the expert's credibility. When called to court, the expert should leave his or her ego at home. Do not become arrogant during direct examination or defensive on cross-examination. Understand that attorneys, not experts, win and lose cases. Experts must remain within the boundaries of their competence and thoroughly prepare for clinical issues, ethical concerns, and legal matters relevant to each phase of the trial.

The clinical content and legal process associated with expert witness testimony will constantly evolve even though the goal of providing courts with specialized knowledge will remain immutable. Experts should participate in every case as if it will be appealed and the proffered testimony will be responsible for a change in law or court rules. The credibility of expert testimony depends on the credibility of everything done before testifying, such as reviewing relevant case law and scientific literature, accurately explaining the purpose of the interview and limitations of confidentiality, selecting an appropriate assessment methodology, and interpreting data properly. The credibility of our legal system depends on the credibility of its witnesses. (pp. 443–444)

THINKING THROUGH THE ISSUES

1. Given your personal history and training, what concerns you the most about your possible performance as an expert witness?
2. What aspects of testifying as an expert witness do you think you would handle well?
3. How could you prepare yourself for testifying as an expert witness?
4. For what aspects of being an expert witness do you believe you need additional training or support?
5. Whom would you consult in order to prepare yourself better for providing expert testimony?

SUMMARY

1. You may be called on to testify in court, at a deposition, or at a due process hearing in a school about a psychological or psychoeducational evaluation that you have conducted.
2. Testifying in court or in court-like settings can be a difficult experience because court procedures are radically different from those followed in mental health, medical, or school settings.
3. In the courtroom, issues are framed in black-and-white terms; it is not typically a place where complex philosophical or educational issues are debated or resolved.
4. Your job as an expert witness is to present your findings and opinions clearly and accurately.
5. Your job as an expert witness is not to seek justice, such as adequate compensation for a victim, an appropriate sentence for an offender, or anything else that you believe is warranted.
6. Although you can, of course, hope that your testimony will contribute to a just outcome of the case, your role is to be an expert, not an advocate.

7. The goal of the mental health system is to promote mental well being, whereas the goal of the legal system is to promote justice.

8. An expert witness may play a critical role in deciding the outcome of a case, including the amount of damages awarded to a client.

9. The key to being an expert witness is to adhere closely to the assessment findings, to answer the referral question as clearly and succinctly as possible, to be familiar with current research findings in the field, and to make interpretations cautiously.

Frye Standard and Daubert Standard

10. Judges determine what constitutes appropriate, relevant, and admissible expert testimony. Typically, they do this by applying the Frye standard or the Daubert standard. Federal courts are obligated to use the Daubert standard, whereas state courts can use either standard (or even another standard or method, as appropriate).

11. The Frye standard was set by the District of Columbia Circuit Court in 1923 in *Frye v. United States*. To meet the Frye standard, an expert witness's testimony must be determined to be based solely on underlying principles of scientific evidence that have been sufficiently tested and accepted by the relevant scientific community.

12. The Daubert standard was set in 1993 by the U.S. Supreme Court in *Daubert v. Merrell Dow Pharmaceuticals*. The Supreme Court ordered federal trial judges to evaluate whether the testimony of an expert witness was reliable and relevant.

13. Under both judicial standards, the court usually must decide whether an expert's testimony will assist the jury in understanding the evidence or facts in the case and whether a particular witness is qualified as an expert.

Standards of Proof

14. Your testimony in both civil and criminal cases will help the court decide on the merits of the case.

15. Proof beyond a reasonable doubt is the highest level of proof and is used mainly in criminal trials.

16. Clear and convincing evidence is an intermediate level of proof and is used mainly in civil trials.

17. A preponderance of evidence is the lowest level of proof and is used mainly in civil trials.

Reasonable Certainty of Opinion

18. As an expert witness, you should be reasonably certain of your opinion.

19. "Reasonable certainty" requires that the expert (a) have considered all the relevant elements of a case in formulating his or her opinion, (b) have an adequate understanding of the pertinent clinical and scientific principles needed to function as an expert witness, (c) have used appropriate, reliable, and valid methods of assessment, and (d) have made reasonable assumptions and conclusions based on the assessment results.

Testifying as an Expert Witness

20. During the time of discovery, the information-gathering period before trial, you may be asked to give a deposition.

21. A deposition is the testimony of a witness who is placed under oath and then questioned by the cross-examining attorney.

22. Your deposition testimony is as critical to the case outcome as your court testimony, as deposition responses are recorded for possible use in court later.

23. Before the deposition, the cross-examining attorney might request all of your documents related to the case.

24. The purpose of a deposition is to allow the cross-examining attorney to gather information that will assist his or her client.

25. Answer all questions during the deposition carefully, because your answers can be used later to impugn your trial testimony, especially if the deposition and trial answers are different.

26. When you are sworn in as an expert witness in court or at a due process hearing and answer the questions posed to you by the retaining attorney, you are under direct examination.

27. After you have answered questions from the retaining attorney about your qualifications (referred to as *voir dire*), the cross-examining attorney has the opportunity to cross examine you about your qualifications.

28. The psychological or psychoeducational report probably contains the information that you will need in order to answer most of the questions you will be asked about the child.

29. As an expert witness, you can and should rely on notes or other materials for information that you cannot readily recall. Consulting such materials, called refreshing recollection, is an acceptable means of providing information to the court.

30. Your role as an expert witness is to provide information to the court (or the hearing officer) so that a judge, hearing officer, or jury can reach an appropriate decision.

31. In your testimony, present a logical, carefully reasoned summary of your findings, the implications of the findings, and your conclusions. Describe what you have found in a way that makes the technical material understandable. Rely on facts, do not stretch the truth, and do not overstate your opinion.

32. Predicting risk of future violence is extremely difficult, yet courts often rely on psychological experts to assist them in this manner.

33. During the cross examination, the cross-examining attorney will generally ask you questions to which he or she already knows the answers; this common strategy by the opposition is designed to give you no "wiggle room."

34. During the cross examination, the cross-examining attorney's inquiries will typically have three goals: to establish how you formed your opinions and reached your conclusions, to get you to support his or her position, and to attack your credibility.

35. Be aware of a number of specific tactics (or ploys) that a cross-examining attorney might use to undermine your credibility during cross examination.

36. The cross-examining attorney may do anything within the limits of legal courtroom procedure to impugn your testimony.

37. Because court hearings are based on the adversarial process, they rarely turn on absolute truths; the outcome of a case often depends on which party presents a more convincing set of facts and arguments.

38. However, no matter how shrewd a cross-examining attorney might be, you are the expert.

39. After the cross examination has been completed, the retaining attorney may keep you on the stand to answer additional questions; this is referred to as redirect examination. During the redirect examination, you will be able to clarify or explain any potentially damaging responses you may have given during the cross examination and to restate your opinion.

40. After the redirect examination, the cross-examining attorney then can conduct another cross examination; this is referred to as recross examination.

Effectiveness as an Expert Witness

41. Jurors and the judge will form an impression of you and your testimony based on such factors as your credentials, apparent motives, extent of bias (if any), and presentational style, including clarity of communications and quality of reasoning.
42. To make your testimony most effective, identify which aspects of your findings are most critical to your formulation of the case.

KEY TERMS, CONCEPTS, AND NAMES

Expert witness (p. 284)
Frye standard (p. 284)
Daubert standard (p. 284)
Reliable testimony (p. 284)
Relevant testimony (p. 284)
Rule 702 of the Federal Rules of Evidence (p. 284)

Standards of proof (p. 285)
Proof beyond a reasonable doubt (p. 285)
Clear and convincing evidence (p. 285)
A preponderance of evidence (p. 285)
Reasonable certainty of opinion (p. 285)
Testifying as an expert witness (p. 285)
Time of discovery (p. 289)
Deposition (p. 289)
Direct examination (p. 289)
Voir dire (p. 289)
Refreshing recollection (p. 293)
Cross examination (p. 293)
Nonrefereed journals (p. 294)
Redirect examination (p. 297)
Recross examination (p. 297)
Effectiveness as an expert witness (p. 298)

STUDY QUESTIONS

1. Discuss the challenges of being an expert witness.
2. Provide several guidelines for testifying as an expert witness.

Glossary of Abbreviations and Acronyms

AAC. Augmentative and alternative communication.
AADB. American Association of the Deaf-Blind.
AAMR. American Association on Mental Retardation.
ABA. Applied behavioral analysis; American Bar Association.
ABDC. Association of Birth Defect Children.
ACCH. Association for the Care of Children's Health.
ACF. Administration on Children and Families.
ACYF. Administration on Children, Youth, and Families.
ADA. Americans with Disabilities Act; average daily attendance.
ADC. Adult disabled children.
ADHD. Attention-deficit/hyperactivity disorder.
ADL. Activities of daily living.
AE. Age equivalent.
AEP. Alternative education placement.
AFB. American Federation of the Blind.
AFDC. Aid to Families with Dependent Children.
AG. Annual goal.
AGA. Appropriate for gestational age.
AHA. American Hospital Association.
AIT. Auditory integration training.
ALJ. Administrative law judge.
AMA. American Medical Association.
AMI. Alliance for the Mentally Ill.
APA. American Psychological Association; American Psychiatric Association.
APD. Auditory processing disorder.
APE. Adaptive physical education.
APWA. American Public Welfare Association.
ARC. Association for Retarded Citizens.
ARD. Admission, review, and dismissal process.
AS. Asperger's syndrome.
ASA. Autism Society of America.
ASD. Autism spectrum disorder.
ASL. American Sign Language.
AT. Assistive technology.
AU. Autistic.

BD. Behavior disorder.
BIA. Bureau of Indian Affairs.
BIP. Behavioral intervention plan.
BL. Blind.
BP. Bi-polar.
BVI. Blind and visually impaired.

CA. Chronological age.
CAPD. Central auditory processing disorder.
CARF. Commission on the Accreditation of Rehabilitation Facilities.
CASA. Court-appointed special advocate.
CD. Conduct disorder.
CDB. Childhood disability benefit.
CDC. Centers for Disease Control and Prevention.
CDF. Children's Defense Fund.
CEC. Council for Exceptional Children.
CFR. Code of Federal Regulations.
CHADD. Children with Attention Deficit Disorder.

CHINS. Child in need of supervision.
CHIPS. Child in need of protection or services.
CMS. Children's medical services.
CNS. Central nervous system.
COBRA. Consolidated Omnibus Budget Reconciliation Act.
COHI. Crippled and other health impaired.
CPS. Child Protective Services.
CRS. Children's rehabilitative services.
CSHN. Children with special health needs.
CSN. Children with special needs.
CWLA. Child Welfare League of America.

D&E. Diagnosis and evaluation.
DB. Deaf/blind (also abbreviated D/BL).
DCP. Disabled Children's Program.
DD. Developmental disabilities.
DE. Department of Education.
DEC. Developmental evaluation clinic.
DF. Deaf.
DH. Developmentally handicapped.
D/HH. Deaf/hard of hearing.
DHHS. Department of Health and Human Services.
DHR. Department of Human Resources.
DIS. Designated instructional services.
DMH. Department of Mental Health.
DMR. Department of Mental Retardation.
DoDDS. Department of Defense Dependent Schools.
DOE. Department of Education.
DSA. Down Syndrome Association.
DSM-5. *Diagnostic and Statistical Manual of Mental Disorders (Fifth Edition).*
DVR. Department of Vocational Rehabilitation.
Dx. Diagnosis.

ECI. Early childhood initiative.
ECSE. Early childhood special education.
ED. Department of Education; emotionally disturbed.
EDGAR. Education Department General Administrative Regulations.
EFA. Epilepsy Foundation of America.
EH. Emotionally handicapped.
EHA. Education for the Handicapped Act.
EI. Early intervention.
ELL. English language learner.
EMH. Educable mentally handicapped.
EPSDT. Medicaid Early Periodic Screening, Diagnosis and Treatment Program.
ERIC. Educational Resources Information Center.
ESA. Educational service agency.
ESEA. Elementary and Secondary Education Act.
ESL. English as a second language.
ESOL. English as a second or other language.
ESY. Extended school year.

FAE. Fetal alcohol effects.
FAPE. Free appropriate public education.
FAS. Fetal alcohol syndrome.

FBA. Functional behavioral assessment.
FC. Facilitated communication.
FEOG. Full educational opportunity goal.
FERPA. Family Educational Rights and Privacy Act (also known as the Buckley Amendment).
FMLA. Family Medical Leave Act.
FOIA. Freedom of Information Act.
FPCO. Family Policy Compliance Office.
FR. Federal Register.
FSA. Family Support Act.
FTE. Full-time equivalent.
FTT. Failure to thrive.

GAL. Guardian ad litem.
GE. Grade equivalent.
GED. General Educational Development Diploma.
GEPA. General Education Provisions Act.
GT. Gifted/talented.

HB. House bill.
HCFA. Health Care Financing Administration.
HCY. Healthy Children and Youth Program.
HFA. High functioning autism.
HH. Hearing handicapped.
HHS. Department of Health and Human Services.
HI. Hearing impaired.
HMO. Health Maintenance Organization.
HO. Hearing officer.
HOH. Hard of hearing.
HRO. Hearing review officer.
HT. Home teaching.

I&R. Information and referral.
IAES. Interim alternative educational setting.
IASA. Improving America's Schools Act.
ICF/MR. Intermediate care facility for the mentally retarded.
ICRC. Infant care review committee.
ICWA. Indian Child Welfare Act.
ID. Intellectual disability.
IDEA. Individuals with Disabilities Education Act.
IDEIA. Individuals with Disabilities Education Improvement Act.
IDELR. Individuals with Disabilities Education Law Reporter.
IDT. Interdisciplinary team.
IEE. Independent educational evaluation.
IEP. Individualized Education Program.
IEU. Intermediate educational unit.
IFSP. Individualized Family Service Plan.
ILC. Independent Living Center.
IRC. Instructional Resource Center.
ISP. Individualized service plan.
ITP. Individualized treatment plan; individual transition plan.
IWEN. Individual with exceptional needs.

LAS. Language and speech program.
LBW. Low birthweight.
LD. Learning disability.
LDA. Learning Disabilities Association.
LEA. Local educational agency.
LEP. Limited English proficiency.
LFA. Low-functioning autism.
LLD. Language-based learning disability.

LoF. Letter of Finding issued by the Office for Civil Rights.
LRE. Least restrictive environment.

MA. Mental age.
MBD. Minimum brain dysfunction.
MCH. Maternal and child health.
M-D. Manic depression.
MDD. Major depressive disorder.
MDE. Multidisciplinary evaluation.
MDT. Multidisciplinary team.
MH. Multiple handicapped.
MHA. Mental Health Association.
MHLP. Mental Health Law Project.
MI. Mentally ill.
MPD. Multiple personality disorder.
MR. Mental retardation.
MR/DD. Mental retardation and developmental disabilities.
MRRC. Mental Retardation Research Center.

NAMI. National Association for the Mentally Ill.
NASDSE. National Association of State Directors of Special Education.
NASP. National Association of School Psychologists.
NBD. Neurobiological disorders.
NCCA. National Center for Child Advocacy.
NCCAN. National Center on Child Abuse and Neglect.
NCES. National Center for Education Statistics.
NCLB. No Child Left Behind Act of 2001.
NCLD. National Center for Learning Disabilities.
NH. Nonhandicapped.
NIC. National Information Clearinghouse for Infants with Disabilities and Life-Threatening Conditions.
NICHCY. National Information Center for Children and Youth with Disabilities.
NIH. National Institutes of Health.
NLD. Nonverbal learning disability.
NOS. Not otherwise specified.
NPND. National Parent Network on Disability.
NPRM. Notice of proposed rulemaking.
NVLD. Nonverbal learning disability.

OCD. Obsessive-compulsive disorder.
OCR. Office for Civil Rights.
ODD. Oppositional-defiant disorder.
OH. Orthopedically handicapped.
OHDS. Office of Human Development Services.
OHI. Other health impairment.
OMB. Office of Management and Budget.
OMRDD. Office of Mental Retardation and Developmental Disabilities.
ORT-OHI. Orthopedically handicapped and other health impaired.
OSC. Order to show cause.
OSEP. Office of Special Education Programs.
OSERS. Office of Special Education and Rehabilitative Services.
OT. Occupational therapist.

P&A. Protection and advocacy.
PASS. Plan for achieving self-support.
PBIS. Positive behavioral interventions and supports.
PCA. Personal care assistant.
PDD. Pervasive developmental disorder.

PDDNOS. Pervasive developmental disorder not otherwise specified.

PE. Physical education.

PH. Physically handicapped.

PI. Physically impaired.

PINS. Person in need of supervision.

PL. Public law.

PLAAFP. Present levels of academic achievement and functional performance.

PLEP. Present levels of educational performance.

PLOP. Present levels of performance.

PMH. Profoundly mentally handicapped.

PMR. Profoundly mentally retarded.

POHI. Physically or otherwise health impaired.

PPRA. Protection of Pupil Rights Amendment.

PS. Partially sighted.

PSM. Problem solving model.

PT. Physical therapy.

PTA. Posttraumatic amnesia.

PTI. Parent Training and Information center.

PTSD. Posttraumatic stress disorder.

REI. Regular education initiative.

RRC. Regional resource center.

RSP. Resource specialist program.

RSPT. Resource specialist program teacher.

RST. Resource specialist teacher.

RT. Recreational therapy.

RTI. Response to intervention.

SB. Senate bill.

SCAN. Suspected child abuse and neglect.

SDC. Special day class.

SDD. Severe developmental disabilities.

SEA. State educational agency.

Sec (§). Section.

SED. Seriously emotionally disturbed.

SGA. Small for gestational age.

SH. Severely handicapped.

SIB. Self-injurious behavior.

SID. Sensory integration dysfunction.

SLD. Specific learning disability.

SLP. Speech-language pathologist.

SNF. Skilled nursing facility.

SP. Speech impaired.

SPED. Special education.

SPEDLAW. Special Education Law.

SQ. Social quotient.

SSA. Social Security Administration.

SSDI. Social Security Disability Income.

SSI. Supplemental Security Income.

STD. Sexually transmitted disease.

SWD. Students with disabilities.

TA. Technical assistance.

TANF. Temporary Aid to Needy Families Law.

TAPP. Technical Assistance to Parents Program.

TASH. The Association for Persons with Severe Handicaps.

TBI. Traumatic brain injury.

TDD. Telecommunication device for the deaf.

TEACCH. Treatment and Education of Autistic and Related Communication-Handicapped Children.

TMH. Trainable mentally handicapped.

TMR. Trainable mentally retarded.

TPR. Termination of parental rights.

TRO. Temporary restraining order.

TT. Text telephone.

TTD. Teletypewriting device.

TTY. Teletypewriter.

UCPA. United Cerebral Palsy Association.

USC. United States Code.

VH. Visually handicapped.

VI. Visually impaired.

VLBW. Very low birthweight.

VR. Vocational rehabilitation.

WIC. Women, Infants, and Children Program.

WPN. Written prior notice.

Glossary of Legal Terms and Concepts

Abandonment. The failure or refusal of a parent, caregiver, or legal guardian to support his or her child physically, emotionally, or financially. An abandoned child is one who is left without provision for reasonable and necessary care or supervision or whose parent has failed to maintain a reasonable degree of interest, concern, or responsibility for his or her welfare.

Accessory. A person who contributes to or aids in the commission of a crime, either before or after it is committed.

Accomplice. A person who knowingly assists the primary perpetrator in a crime.

Acquittal. The finding in a criminal case that a defendant is not guilty of the crime with which he or she has been charged.

Action. A lawsuit brought by one or more individuals seeking redress for or prevention of a wrong or protection of a right.

Adjudicated father. A male determined by the court to be a child's father, usually through a court action and genetic testing. See also *Paternity*.

Adjudication. A decision made by a court or administrative agency with respect to a case.

Adjudication hearing. A trial in juvenile court to determine whether allegations are true and whether they indicate a need for the court to intervene.

Admissible evidence. Evidence determined by a court to satisfy rules and laws about what a judge or jury may take into consideration.

Admission. A voluntary statement that something is true.

Admonition. Advice, instruction, or caution by a judge to jury members about what is and is not admissible, about their duties or conduct, or about alternative verdicts; a warning by a judge to a defendant or convicted felon of the consequences of future misconduct; a caution or reprimand of an attorney by a judge.

Adversarial system. A trial process whereby a judge or jury listens to the plaintiff and the defendant (or their attorneys) argue their cases and then decides which side has proven its claim.

Adversary parties. Individuals or groups in litigation whose interests are opposed to each other.

Adverse witness. A witness for the opposing party.

Advocate. An individual who is not an attorney but who assists individuals in their dealings with other entities—for example, helping parents negotiate with the school district regarding a child's special education program.

Affidavit. A written statement of facts that is formally confirmed by oath or by affirmation.

Affirm. To confirm a judgment. In affirming, an appellate court says that the decision of the trial court is correct.

Aggravating circumstance. A factor that tends to increase the sentence given a defendant.

ALI rule. A rule, proposed by the American Law Institute Model Penal Code and widely adopted in the United States, stating that a person is not responsible for criminal conduct if, at the time of the crime, as a result of mental disease or defect, the person lacked substantial capacity to appreciate the criminality (wrongfulness) of the act or to conform his or her conduct to the requirements of the law.

Allegation. A charge or complaint that is to be judged true or false at a hearing or trial.

Amicus curiae. "Friend of the court"; a person or organization that has an interest in a lawsuit and is granted permission to appear in court, file briefs, and present oral arguments, even though this person or organization is not party to the action.

Answer. The defendant's response to a plaintiff's allegations.

Appeal. A procedure in which a party seeks to reverse or modify a judgment or final order of a lower court or administrative agency, usually on the grounds that the lower court misinterpreted or misapplied the law, rather than on the grounds that it made an incorrect finding of fact.

Appeals court. A court that hears an appeal after a trial court has made a judgment.

Appellant. The party who initiates an appeal to a higher court.

Appellee. The party in a lawsuit against whom an appeal is made.

Appointed counsel. An attorney appointed by a court to render legal assistance to a person unable, for any of various reasons, to obtain counsel.

Arraignment. The process of bringing persons accused of crimes before a court to be advised of the charges against them and of their rights and, in certain cases, to give them an opportunity to state their answers to the charges (to plead guilty or not guilty); also known as *first appearance* or *initial appearance*.

Arrest. The process of taking a person into custody. Peace officers must have probable cause to arrest individuals.

Attorney-client privilege. A legal doctrine that permits a person to refuse to disclose, and to prevent others from disclosing, communications between the person and his or her attorney (or the attorney's agent) that are made during the course of their professional relationship.

Bail. The security, usually money, given to the court in exchange for the release of an arrested person. Designed to ensure that the person will appear in court on a specified date, bail is generally provided by a bail bondsperson, who thereby becomes responsible for the released person's return.

Bailiff. A court official who keeps order in a courtroom.

Bench trial. A trial with no jury, in which the judge renders the final verdict.

Beyond a reasonable doubt. See *Proof beyond a reasonable doubt*.

Bifurcated. Divided into two parts or sections. A hearing held in two parts, with separate issues decided at each hearing, is called a bifurcated hearing.

Bind over. To find that there is the probable cause needed to initiate grand jury or trial proceedings.

Brief. A written argument filed in court by an attorney.

Burden of proof. The standard a party has to meet to demonstrate to the court that the weight of the evidence in a legal action favors his or her side, position, or argument. See *Clear and convincing evidence, Preponderance of evidence, Proof beyond a reasonable doubt*.

Case law. Law established by previous cases decided by courts rather than by statute.

Cert. denied. The expression used by a superior court—usually the United States Supreme Court—to indicate that the court has declined to review a lower court's decision.

Certiorari. A discretionary writ giving a superior court the right to review the decision of a lower court.

Child in need of supervision (CHINS). A juvenile who has committed a delinquent act and has been found by a children's court judge to require further court supervision, often through probation or transfer of custody to a relative or public or private welfare agency for a period usually not to exceed one year; known as *person in need of supervision (PINS)* or *minor in need of supervision (MINS)* in some states.

Child neglect. See *Neglect.*

Child Protective Services (CPS). Public social services agency designated, in most states, to receive and investigate reports of child maltreatment and to provide rehabilitation services to children and families experiencing child maltreatment problems.

Circuit Court of Appeals. The intermediate appeals court in the federal system.

Circumstantial evidence. Fact from which a conclusion can reasonably be inferred. For example, a parent's possession of a broken appliance cord may be circumstantial evidence connecting the parent to the infliction of wounds on a child's body.

Civil action. See *Civil proceeding.*

Civil complaint. A legal document submitted to the court by the plaintiffs, in which they inform the court and the defendants that they are bringing a lawsuit and set out the reasons they are suing and the relief they want.

Civil proceeding. Any legal action other than a criminal prosecution; also known as *civil action.* Parties bringing a civil proceeding need not meet the standard of providing proof beyond a reasonable doubt, as is required in criminal proceedings; the standard is a preponderance of evidence. Juvenile and family court cases are considered civil proceedings.

Civil rights. Rights guaranteed to all citizens by the U.S. Constitution and relevant acts of Congress.

Class action. A lawsuit filed by one or a few people on behalf of a larger number of persons with a grievance against the same party.

Clear and convincing evidence. Evidence sufficient to persuade a judge or jury that the allegations against a defendant are very likely true. This is the intermediate burden of proof—more than a preponderance of evidence, but less than proof beyond a reasonable doubt.

Closing argument. An attorney's final statement to the court, summing up the case and the points proven, as well as those points not proven by opposing counsel; also known as a *final argument.*

Commission, act of. Willful or volitional act.

Commitment. In juvenile law, a court order placing a delinquent, neglected, dependent, or uncared-for child in a mental health facility or correctional facility.

Common law. Body of law based on judicial decision, precedents, customs, and usages.

Commutation. A reduction in punishment—as, for example, from a death sentence to life imprisonment.

Compensatory damages. Remuneration awarded to a party to compensate for an actual loss suffered, such as medical expenses.

Competency. The capacity to perform a given function with a degree of rationality, the requisite degree depending on the function to be performed.

Complainant. The party who initiates the complaint in an action; also known as the *plaintiff* or the *petitioner.*

Conciliation court. A civil court, found in many states, that helps resolve marital disputes and provides counseling services for couples considering divorce.

Confession. An admission of guilt by a person who committed a criminal act.

Confidential communication. A statement made under circumstances indicating that the speaker intended the statement only for the person addressed. If a communication is made in the presence of a third party whose presence is not reasonably necessary for the communication, it is not confidential. See also *Privileged communication.*

Confidentiality. Ethical obligation of a professional not to reveal, without specific consent, information obtained through professional contact with a client. It protects the client from unauthorized disclosure of information given in confidence to a professional. Confidentiality must be broken when the client threatens another person, talks about abusing children or about having been abused, or says he or she wants to harm himself or herself. See also *Tarasoff v. Regents of University of California.*

Consent decree. An agreement reached out of court by the parties to a lawsuit and then formally approved by the court.

Contempt. An act calculated to inhibit, hinder, or affront the court in the administration of justice; obstruction of the court's work. Disobedience of a judge's order is one type of contempt.

Continuance. A court order that postpones legal action, such as a court hearing, until a later time.

Contract action. A lawsuit based on the breach of an oral or written contract.

Court-appointed special advocate (CASA). An individual (usually a volunteer) whose responsibility is to ensure that the needs and best interests of a child are fully protected in judicial proceedings. See also *Guardian ad litem.*

Court diversion. An order by the court that a youth who has come before the court must make restitution, engage in community service, or complete a designated court-sponsored or -approved program.

Credibility. The degree to which a person appears to be worthy of belief; a quality of witnesses that makes their testimony believable.

Criminal complaint. A legal document that initiates a criminal proceeding; a written statement by the investigating officer(s) outlining the facts in a particular criminal violation and charging a suspect with the crime.

Cross examination. Questioning of an opposing party's witness who has already been questioned through direct examination by that party's attorney.

Custodial confinement. Placement in a secure facility, ordered by a court for the rehabilitation of a juvenile delinquent.

Custodial parent. Parent who has the physical control, care, and custody of a minor child.

Custody. The right to care for and control a child; the duty to provide food, clothing, shelter, ordinary medical care, education, and discipline for a child.

Custody evaluation. An investigative procedure in which facts about a family are gathered and analyzed for the purpose of making a recommendation to the court regarding child custody and/or visitation. A custody evaluation may be initiated by order of the court or by stipulation of the parties involved, pursuant to local court rules.

Custody hearing. A legal process, usually in family or juvenile court, to determine who will be awarded legal or physical custody of a minor. A custody hearing may involve one parent against the other, a parent against a third party, or a parent against a social services agency seeking protective custody in juvenile court.

Damages. Monetary compensation awarded by a court in a civil action to an individual who has been injured through the wrongful conduct of another party.

Daubert v. Merrell Dow Pharmaceuticals (509 U.S. 579, 1993). A case in which the U.S. Supreme Court set a two-pronged test for the admissibility of expert witnesses' testimony during legal proceedings: Federal trial judges must evaluate expert witnesses to determine whether their testimony is both *relevant* and *reliable.*

Declaration of parentage. A judicial decision stating who the parents of a child are.

Declaratory judgment. A statement in which a judge establishes the involved parties' rights or expresses an opinion on a legal question without ordering that anything be done.

De facto. "In fact"; a phrase used to describe a past action or a state of affairs that must be accepted for all practical purposes but is not necessarily legal or legitimate.

Default. Failure to meet a deadline or put in an appearance, causing a defendant to lose the legal right to challenge.

Defendant. A person against whom civil or criminal action is brought.

De jure. "In law"; a phrase used in contrast to *de facto.*

De minimus. "Insignificant"; a phrase used to designate a matter not sufficiently important to be dealt with judicially.

Dependency/neglect petition. A request on the part of Child Protective Services, filed by the county or district attorney, to remove a child from an allegedly abusive home for a period longer than the initial 48-hour emergency period.

Dependent child. A child who is homeless, destitute, or without proper care or support through no fault of his or her parent, guardian, or custodian; who lacks proper care or support because of the mental or physical condition of his or her parent, guardian, or custodian; or whose condition or environment warrants the state to assume guardianship in the child's interest.

Deposition. The questioning of a party or witness, under oath, outside of the courtroom by an attorney; also, the answers given in response to the questions. A deposition is usually taken in the office of an attorney representing one of the litigants.

Detention center. A place where a juvenile is held in custody while awaiting an adjudication hearing, disposition, or commitment placement. Placement in a detention center may also be used as "timeout" in domestic violence cases and for post-adjudicatory punishment.

Detention hearing. In juvenile court, the bail hearing.

Direct evidence. Information offered by witnesses who testify about their own knowledge of the facts.

Direct examination. Initial courtroom questioning of a witness testifying on behalf of the party who called the witness to the stand. This questioning is usually done by the attorney of the party who called the witness.

Discovery. Pretrial procedures that enable the parties involved in a court proceeding to find out about the evidence supporting the positions taken by the other parties, including facts that those parties believe support their positions.

Discretionary filing to try a minor as an adult. A request, filed by a state, to criminally prosecute a juvenile of 14 years of age or older in adult court for a serious, violent, or chronic offense.

Dismissal. An order by a judge dismissing a case. Cases can be dismissed with or without prejudice. Cases dismissed with prejudice cannot be filed again. Cases dismissed without prejudice can be filed again if certain circumstances change—for example, if additional evidence is obtained.

Disposition. The court's final determination of the outcome of a lawsuit or criminal charge. In child protection matters, the disposition is the order of a court, issued at a hearing, stating whether a minor already found to be delinquent or in need of protection or services should remain in or return to the parental home, be under a particular type of supervision, or be placed out of home (and, if so, in what kind of setting).

Divided custody. See *Joint custody.*

Due process of law. A person's right to be treated with fairness in legal proceedings. This right includes the right to adequate advance notice of a hearing, the right to notice of allegations of misconduct, the right to the assistance of an attorney, the right to confront and cross examine witnesses, and the right to refuse to give self-incriminating testimony. In public education, due process of law encompasses the educational rights of students under relevant local, state, and federal law.

Durham rule. A principle of criminal law stating that, in order for an insanity defense to be valid, the accused person must have been suffering from a defective mental condition at the time of the alleged offense and the alleged offense must have been caused by the defective mental condition. See also *Irresistible impulse rule* and *M'Naghton rule.*

Educational neglect. Failing to provide for a child's educational needs by not enrolling the child in school or tolerating truancy.

Emancipated minor. A minor who, as a result of exhibiting adequate control over his or her life, is found by a court to no longer require the care or custody of his or her parents or guardians and is thus accorded the rights of an adult.

Emancipation. An action by a court that grants independence to a minor who has not yet reached the age of majority defined by that state (usually 16 or 18 years). Several states do not grant emancipation.

Emergency custody. See *Protective custody.*

Emergency hearing. In juvenile and family court, a hearing held to determine the need for emergency protection of a child who may have been a victim of maltreatment.

Emotional abuse. A form of child maltreatment in which parents or other persons repeatedly convey to the child that he or she is worthless, unwanted, or of value only in meeting another's needs; also known as *emotional/psychological maltreatment* or *psychological abuse.* The abuse may include serious threats of physical or psychological violence.

Emotional neglect. See *Neglect.*

Enjoin. To issue a court order commanding a person to perform or abstain from performing a specified act.

Equal protection of the law. The constitutional guarantee that no person or class of persons shall be denied the legal protection that is enjoyed by other persons or other classes in like circumstances.

Evidence. Any sort of proof submitted to a court in support of an allegation or argument. See also *Circumstantial evidence, Direct evidence, Hearsay, Physical evidence.*

Evidentiary standards. Guidelines used to determine whether evidence was legally collected, whether it is factual, and whether it legally proves or is relevant to the case being heard. See also *Clear and convincing evidence, Preponderance of evidence, Proof beyond a reasonable doubt.*

Exculpatory. Clearing or tending to clear someone of guilt; excusing.

Exhibit. An item, produced during a trial or hearing, that is related to the case before the court and that, upon acceptance by the court, is marked for identification and made a part of the case.

Ex parte. "Involving only one party." An *ex parte* judicial proceeding is one brought by one party, without notice to or opportunity for challenge by the opposing party, in order to protect rights that could not otherwise be adequately protected. The judge's decision in such a proceeding will usually be subject to review at a subsequent proceeding, in which the opposing party will have the opportunity to participate.

Expert witness. An individual who, by reason of education or specialized experience, possesses extensive knowledge of a subject and is therefore determined by a court to be qualified to give an opinion in that subject area. Expert witnesses assist the jury in understanding complicated and technical subjects not within the realm of the average lay person.

Expunge. To delete from a court record. Expungement may be ordered by the court after a specified number of years or when a juvenile, parent, or defendant applies for expungement and shows that his or her conduct has improved. Expungement may also apply to removal of an unverified report of abuse or neglect that has been made to a central registry.

Ex rel. "On behalf of"; a term used in the title of a case when one party is bringing an action on behalf of another party.

Family court. A civil court, found in some states, that combines the functions of domestic relations, juvenile, and probate courts.

Family law. Field of law involving family issues, such as divorce, paternity, guardianship, dependency, adoption, and domestic violence.

Family preservation/reunification. The philosophical principle, established in law and policy and followed by social service agencies, that children should remain in their own families if their safety can be ensured.

Felony. A serious crime for which the punishment may be lengthy imprisonment and/or a significant fine.

Fifth Amendment to the U.S. Constitution. Amendment providing that no person will be compelled to present self-incriminating testimony, required to answer for crimes without an indictment or grand jury decision, tried twice for the same crime, or deprived of life, liberty, or property without due process of law.

Final argument. See *Closing argument.*

Finding. Determination of fact by a court, based on the evidence presented.

Forensic. Relating to courts of law. Forensic psychology refers to psychological methods or knowledge applied to resolve legal disputes. A forensic evaluation is a medical or psychological evaluation that interprets or establishes the facts in a civil or criminal case.

Forensic interview. An interview used to gather information from a possible victim, defendant, witness, or offender for the purpose of informing the court.

Frye standard. A standard regarding the admissibility of procedures, principles, or techniques presented by expert witnesses during legal proceedings, set in *Frye v. United States* (293 F. 1013 DC Cir 1923) by the District of Columbia Circuit Court: Trial judges must decide whether the evidence presented to the court is "generally accepted" by a meaningful segment of the relevant scientific community.

Gault decision. The ruling by the U.S. Supreme Court in *In re Gault* (387 U.S. 1, 1967) that juveniles are entitled to the same due process rights as adults.

Guardian ad litem (GAL). "Guardian at law"; an attorney, mental health professional, or (in some states) lay person, appointed by the court, who represents a child's best interests in juvenile or family court. In a civil legal proceeding, this person may perform a variety of roles on behalf of the child who is legally incapable of doing so on his or her own, including acting as an independent investigator, advocate, advisor, and guardian for the child. See also *Court-appointed special advocate.*

Guardianship. Legal responsibility of a person to provide for the protection, care, and management of a person considered unable to take care of his or her own affairs.

Habeas corpus. "[We command that] you have the body." A writ of habeus corpus requires that a person be brought before a court or a judge. It usually alleges that the person is illegally imprisoned.

Hearing. A judicial or legal examination of issues of law and fact disputed between parties; a formal proceeding at which evidence is taken for the purpose of determining an issue of fact and reaching a decision on the basis of that evidence.

Hearsay. Statements by someone who is not in court and therefore not subject to cross examination; second-hand evidence. Such evidence is usually excluded because it is considered unreliable and because the person making the original statement cannot be cross examined.

Hostile witness. A witness who is subject to cross examination by the party who called him or her because he or she antagonized that party during direct examination.

Hypothetical question. A question based on assumed facts, often asked of an expert witness to elicit an opinion.

Immunity from prosecution. Exemption from legal prosecution provided to certain individuals or categories of individuals. For example, a person who reports child abuse or neglect is immune from civil lawsuits and criminal prosecution as long as the report is made in good faith.

Impeachment. Calling into question a witness's truthfulness or credibility.

In camera. "In chambers"; taking place in a judge's chambers or another location where the public is not allowed to be present.

Incest. Sexual relations between persons who are closely related by blood and who are forbidden by law to marry. The most common form of incest is between fathers and daughters.

Indeterminate sentence. A prison term, imposed on a defendant convicted of a crime, that is stated in terms of a range of time, such as "5 to 10 years," rather than a specific period of time or a release date.

Indictment. A report of a grand jury charging an adult with criminal conduct. The process of indictment by a grand jury bypasses the filing of a criminal complaint and the holding of a preliminary hearing, so prosecution begins immediately.

Informed consent. Consent to a treatment that is based on adequate knowledge about the risks and benefits of the treatment, is voluntary, and is given while the individual is competent to make a decision.

Infra. "Later."

Injunction. A court order to act or abstain from a specific act.

Injunctive relief. A court-ordered remedy forbidding or requiring some action by the defendant.

In loco parentis. "In the place of a parent." A guardian or other nonparental custodian or authority acts *in loco parentis*.

In re. "In the matter of"; a term often used in the title of a court case.

Intake hearing. In juvenile court, a preliminary hearing to determine the appropriate disposition of a case in which a child is charged with a status offense (an action that is an offense only when performed by a minor). Dispositions range from diversion from the juvenile court system to adjudication (trial).

Inter alia. "Among other things"; a term used to make clear that an issue is only one of several involved.

Interlocutory. Temporary; provisional; not final.

Interrogation. An emphatic investigative interview, often with the goal of obtaining a confession from a person believed to have committed a crime.

Interrogatories. Written questions in a civil action that must be responded to with a truthful answer or with an explanation of why they cannot be answered.

Interstate compact re children. Agreement among a number of states governing interstate placement of children, defining state financial and supervisory responsibilities, and guaranteeing certain constitutional protections for children.

Investigation. A process of close examination or systematic inquiry.

Investigative interview. In child maltreatment, an interview designed to obtain information about possible maltreatment. It is perhaps the most stringent type of interview with a child and may play an important role in the criminal indictment of another individual.

Involuntary client. A person who has been referred for services, often through court order, but who has not asked for help.

Involuntary placement. Court-ordered assignment of custody to an agency for placement of a child, often against the parents' wishes, after a formal court proceeding; the taking of emergency or protective custody of a child, against the parents' wishes, preceding a custody hearing.

Irreparable harm. Any damage or wrong, resulting from a violation of a legal right, for which monetary damages would be inadequate compensation. The threat of irreparable harm may require some form of intervention, such as an injunction.

Irresistible impulse rule. A legal standard for insanity in some states, stating that even if a person knew that the act he or she was committing was wrong, the person cannot be held criminally responsible if he or she was driven by an irresistible impulse to perform the act or had a diminished capacity to resist performing the act.

Joint custody. A custodial arrangement in which both parents share the rights and responsibilities to make decisions regarding the health, education, and welfare of a child. See also *Joint physical custody*.

Joint physical custody. A custodial arrangement in which a child spends significant periods of time with each parent.

Judgment. An order by a court after a verdict has been reached; a judicial decision.

Jurisdiction. The realm in which a particular court has the power and authority to hear and determine cases, usually defined in terms of certain categories of persons or allegations.

Jury. A group of adult citizens who serve as fact finders, judging the truth of allegations made in a legal proceeding.

Juvenile. In a majority of states, a youth under the age of 18 years; a minor.

Juvenile court. A court with jurisdiction over minors. A juvenile court usually handles cases involving suspected delinquency, suspected child maltreatment, and termination of parental rights.

Juvenile court judge. The presiding officer in a juvenile court.

Juvenile delinquent. A minor who has been determined by a court to have violated a federal, state, or local criminal law.

Leading case. Precedent often cited as an authoritative or controlling guide in subsequent cases.

Leading question. A question that leads a witness toward a conclusion that supports the argument of the attorney asking the question. Leading questions are usually prohibited during direct examination.

Least restrictive alternative. The concept that, when the government is authorized to infringe on individual liberty, it must do so in the least drastic manner possible.

Litigation. The process that follows the filing of a lawsuit in court. Litigation includes such proceedings as the review of evidence, hearings before a judge, and the trial itself.

Malfeasance. Commission of an act in violation of legal duty. For example, a mental health professional who breaches confidentiality commits an act of malfeasance. See also *Nonfeasance*.

Malingering. Conscious fabrication or gross exaggeration of physical or psychological symptoms in pursuit of a recognizable goal.

Mandamus. "We command." A writ of mandamus is an order from a superior court to a lower court or other body commanding that a specified act be done.

Mandated reporters. In child maltreatment, persons legally required to report suspected cases of child maltreatment to the mandated agency. Mandated reporters are usually professionals (such as physicians, nurses, school personnel, social workers, psychologists, and clergy) or their delegates who have frequent contact with children and families.

Material. A legal term meaning relevant.

Mediation. A voluntary dispute resolution process involving intermediaries.

Minor in need of supervision (MINS). See *Child in need of supervision*.

Miranda warning. Warning given by police to advise suspects of their rights: "You have the right to remain silent. Anything you say may be used as evidence against you. You have the right to consult with an attorney and to have an attorney present during questioning. If you cannot afford an attorney, one will be appointed for you prior to any questioning, if you desire." A suspect's statement or confession is usually inadmissible as evidence in court proceedings if the suspect was not informed of these rights before the confession was made. The name "Miranda" comes from the U.S. Supreme Court case of *Miranda* *v. Arizona* (384 U.S. 436), in which the Court established the four-part warning.

Misdemeanor. A relatively minor offense punishable by a small fine or a short jail sentence.

Mistrial. A trial that is declared invalid, usually because of procedural errors.

Mitigating circumstance. A factor that tends to reduce the severity of the sentence given a defendant.

M'Naghton rule. The legal standard for insanity in many states, stating that someone who is guilty of committing a crime cannot be held criminally responsible if, at the time the crime is committed, he or she suffered from a disease of the mind that prevented him or her from knowing right from wrong.

Modification. Changing of a prior order of a court.

Motion. An application made to a court for an order or ruling.

Multidisciplinary team. A group of individuals from various disciplines who work together at all levels; also known as a *transdisciplinary team.*

Negligence. Failure to use the degree of care and skill that a prudent person would use in the same circumstances.

Neglect. Failure of a parent or caregiver to provide for a child's basic needs and a proper level of care with respect to food, shelter, hygiene, medical attention, and/or supervision. *Emotional neglect* refers to passive or passive-aggressive inattention to a child's emotional needs, nurturing, and/or emotional well-being. *Physical neglect* refers to failure to provide for a child's basic survival needs, such as food, clothing, shelter, and/or supervision, such that the child's health or safety is threatened.

Nolo contendre. "I will not contest it." A plea of *nolo contendre* in a criminal action has the same legal effect as a plea of guilty relative to the proceeding at hand. However, a *nolo* plea cannot be used against the defendant in a later civil suit regarding the same issues.

Nonfeasance. Failure to complete an act that is part of a legal duty. A mental health professional who fails to act to protect a third party from imminent danger from a patient may be guilty of nonfeasance in some states.

Nonoffending parent. A parent of an abused child who is not involved in the abusive act.

Objection. Contention by a party to a court proceeding that a question asked by the opposing attorney is improper.

Objection overruled. The expression used by a judge to signify that an objection is without legal basis.

Objection sustained. The expression used by a judge to indicate that an objection was appropriate and that the judge has ruled in favor of the party making the objection.

Omission, act of. In child maltreatment, failure of a parent or caregiver to provide for a child's physical and/or emotional well-being, due to unwillingness or inability.

Omnibus hearing. A hearing held in criminal court to resolve certain issues before trial (such as whether evidence is admissible) so as to ensure a fair and expeditious trial and avoid a multiplicity of court appearances.

Opening statement. An argument made by an attorney at the start of a trial or at the beginning of his or her presentation in court, summarizing what he or she plans to prove and the evidence to be presented.

Opinion. A formal written decision by a judge or court, containing the legal principles and rationale behind the ruling.

Order to show cause (OSC). An order to appear in court and present reasons why a particular action should not be taken. If the party receiving the order fails to appear or to give sufficient reasons why the court should desist, the court will take the action in question.

Out-of-home care. Child care, foster care, or residential care provided to children who are separated from their families, usually under the jurisdiction of juvenile or family court.

Parens patriae. "Parent of the country." A state's authority to act on behalf of persons who cannot act in their own interests, such as minors, persons who are incompetent as a result of mental illness, and some developmentally disabled persons.

Party. Any person involved in a lawsuit—the person who filed the suit or the person against whom the suit was filed.

Paternity. Being the father of a child. The law presumes that a man is a child's father under specified circumstances. See also *Adjudicated father.*

Pedophile. An adult who prefers to obtain sexual gratification through contact with children.

Pedophilia. Sexual behavior by an adult directed toward a prepubescent child.

Peremptory challenge. The right of an attorney, during jury selection, to remove a prospective juror from consideration without stating a valid reason. Each side can exercise a limited number of peremptory challenges.

Perjury. Lying under oath. Being convicted of perjury, which is a felony, can deprive a citizen of the right to vote, hold office, and hold a professional license.

Petition. A formal written application to a court for judicial action on a matter, stating allegations that, if true, form the basis for court intervention.

Petitioner. See *Complainant.*

Physical abuse. Physical harm inflicted on a child intentionally by his or her parents or caregiver.

Physical custody. A person's right to have a child reside with him or her and to make the day-to-day decisions regarding the child's care.

Physical evidence. Any tangible piece of proof, such as a document, an x-ray, a photograph, or a weapon used to inflict an injury. See also *Exhibit.*

Physical indicators of child maltreatment. Broken bones, burns, rashes, bites, and other signs suggestive of physical injuries or neglect.

Physical neglect. See *Neglect.*

Plaintiff. The party bringing a lawsuit.

Plea bargaining. In criminal cases, negotiation between a prosecutor (on behalf of the state) and a defendant of a mutually agreed-on disposition of the case, which is then submitted to the court for approval.

Pleadings. Statements, in logical and legal form, of each side of a case.

Precedent. Prior court decisions invoked in analyzing similar legal problems subsequently.

Preponderance of evidence. Evidence sufficient to persuade a judge or jury that it is more likely true than not true that the facts necessary to prove the plaintiff's case are as alleged by the plaintiff. This is the level of proof required to prevail in most civil cases.

Presentence investigation report. A document that details the subject's prior legal entanglements and other relevant factors and recommends a particular disposition or sentence. Such a report is prepared by a probation officer for the court's consideration at the time of disposition or sentencing in a case.

Presumption. An assumption of fact based on another fact or group of facts. A presumption is either conclusive (not subject to opposition) or rebuttable (capable of being rebutted by presentation of contrary proof).

Pretrial diversion. A decision of a district or county attorney's office not to file charges in a criminal case even though the charges would likely be provable. The decision is usually made on the condition that the defendant agree to participate in rehabilitative services.

Prima facie. "On the first appearance"; a term used to describe a fact presumed to be true unless it is disapproved.

Privileged communication. A disclosure made by a client to a professional, such as a psychologist, social worker, marriage and family counselor, attorney, clergyperson, psychiatrist, or other physician, that cannot be revealed during legal proceedings without the client's informed consent. See also *Confidentiality*.

Probable cause. Reasonable grounds, based on solid evidence, for the belief that an accused person should be subject to arrest or to the issuance of a warrant.

Probation. A sentencing alternative in which a convicted criminal defendant or a juvenile found to be delinquent is allowed to remain at liberty, generally under the supervision of a probation officer and under the threat of imprisonment if he or she fails to meet certain conditions.

Pro bono. "For the public good"; a term used to describe attorneys' or other professionals' services rendered at no charge.

Proceeding. Events comprising the process by which administrative or judicial action is initiated and resolved.

Proof beyond a reasonable doubt. Evidence that does not leave any significant doubt in the judge's or jury's mind as to the guilt of the accused. The judge or jury must be fully satisfied that the evidence is factual and that the facts proven establish guilt. This is the most stringent standard, which must be met in criminal cases to prove that the alleged offender violated the law.

Pro se. "For self"; a term used to describe representing oneself without assistance of legal counsel.

Prosecutor. Attorney for the local, state, or federal government in a criminal case.

Protection order. A court order generally issued in an emergency to protect a child from someone who might harm him or her.

Protective custody. Detainment of a child on an emergency basis until a written detention request can be filed; also known as *emergency custody*.

Psychological abuse. See *Emotional abuse*.

Psychological autopsy. A profile developed after an individual's death, from a retrospective analysis of the individual's writings and interviews with family members and friends.

Quash. To annul; to suppress—as, for example, a subpoena.

Quid pro quo. "Something for something." A *quid pro quo* exists when parties to a contract or agreement exchange something for something else.

Reasonable cause. Plausible suspicion that a crime is being committed or is being planned. This is a much lower standard than probable cause, the standard used in criminal matters. See also *Probable cause*.

Reasonable doubt. Doubt that would occur to a reasonable or prudent person. A judge or jury that has reasonable doubt must acquit a defendant.

Reasonable efforts. Plausible attempts by Child Protective Services or a similar agency to keep a family together or, if a child has already been removed, to reunite the family.

Reasonable medical judgment. A determination made by a prudent physician who is knowledgeable about the cause of an illness and its possible treatments.

Rebuttal. Refuting of statements made and evidence introduced; the stage of a trial during which such refuting is appropriate.

Recidivism. Repetition of a criminal act by the same offender.

Recommendation conference. A hearing at which a judge and attorneys review the recommendations of a custody evaluator and try to reach a settlement.

Records. Any written documents, audio or video recordings, or other tangible items that contain information related to a lawsuit.

Recross examination. Questioning of a witness by the party who previously cross examined the same witness.

Redirect examination. Questioning of a witness by the party who previously questioned the witness on direct examination.

Refreshing recollection. See *Refreshing the memory.*

Refreshing the memory. Reading documents in order to remember details related to one's testimony; also known as *refreshing recollection.*

Regulations. Rules of law created by government agencies (as opposed to statutes passed by state or federal legislatures).

Relevancy. The degree to which evidence addresses the issue before a court. Evidence not relevant to the issue before the court is usually not admissible.

Relief. A remedy requested by a plaintiff for some legal wrong. Relief is granted by a court or jury against a defendant. Examples include monetary damage, performance of a contractual obligation, a temporary restraining order, and a preliminary injunction.

Remand. An order from an appellate court sending a lawsuit back to a lower court with specific instructions on how to handle it.

Reporting laws. In cases of child maltreatment, laws that require specified categories of persons, such as professionals involved with children, to notify public authorities of cases of suspected child maltreatment. All 50 states have reporting laws.

Res ipsa loquitur. "The thing speaks for itself"; a legal doctrine, applicable to negligence law, under which no proof is needed other than the incident itself.

Respondent. The person who answers a petition.

Restraining order. A court order prohibiting a party from committing particular acts, either until a hearing can be held (temporary) or for a specific period of time.

Reversal. An appellate court's decision that the judgment of a lower court or other body should be set aside, vacated, or changed.

Review hearing. A hearing held in juvenile or family court (usually every 6 months) to reexamine earlier dispositions and determine whether to keep a child in out-of-home care and/or maintain the court's jurisdiction over the child.

Risk assessment. A process for determining whether a child is in danger of maltreatment and needs to be removed from the home or needs protective services. Risk assessment is usually done by Child Protective Services workers or law enforcement personnel.

Sanctions. Penalties imposed by a judge on witnesses who ignore a judge's orders to participate in the proceedings in an appropriate manner as dictated by law. Sanctions may include incarceration or a fine.

Sealing. In juvenile or criminal court practice, closing court records to inspection by all but the subject of the records.

Search warrant. A written order by a magistrate or a judge giving authorization to search a specific premise for specific items.

Sentencing. The last stage of criminal prosecution, in which a convicted defendant is imprisoned, fined, ordered to pay restitution, or granted a conditional release from custody. Sentencing is the equivalent of disposition in a juvenile case.

Settlement. Determination of a disputed matter by agreement of all parties. Settlement sometimes requires approval by the court, resulting in a court order outlining the parties' agreement.

Sexual abuse. Contacts or interactions between a child and an adult in which the adult uses the child for sexual stimulation and has power or control over the victim.

Sexual assault. Forcible sexual actions committed against a person's will; criminal sexual conduct.

Sexual exploitation. Involvement of children and adolescents in sexual activities that they do not usually fully comprehend, to which they are unable to give informed consent, and that violate social taboos.

Show cause. See *Order to show cause.*

Situational child abuse and neglect. A form of child maltreatment caused by problems over which the parents have little control, such as limited or no income.

Sodomy. Anal or oral intercourse between people or any sexual relations between a human being and an animal, punishable as a criminal offense.

Split custody. A custodial arrangement in which each parent has physical custody of at least one child of the marriage and specific visitation rights with the other child or children.

Standard of proof. See *Burden of proof.*

Stare decisis. "Let the decision stand"; the policy of the courts of following legal precedent.

Status offense. An action that is a crime only if the perpetrator is a minor. Examples are consumption of alcohol by a minor, underage driving, underage sexual activity, truancy, incorrigibility, and delinquency.

Statute. Law established by a legislature.

Statute of limitation. Time limit within which a lawsuit must be commenced.

Statutory laws. Written laws enacted by legislative bodies.

Statutory right. A right based on a statute passed by a unit of federal, state, or local government.

Stay. To stop, hold, or restrain; to suspend a case or part of it.

Stipulate. To agree.

Stipulation. A statement, either oral or written, that establishes certain facts agreed on by all parties in a court case.

Subpoena. A court order requiring a person to appear at a certain time to give testimony in a specified case. Failure to obey a subpoena may subject the person to contempt proceedings.

Subpoena duces tecum. "Under penalty you shall bring with you"; a court order requiring a person to bring specified records in her or his control or possession to the court.

Substantiated. Determined to be supported by credible evidence; also known as *founded.* An allegation of abuse or neglect may or may not be substantiated.

Substantive right. A right usually granted by statutes and constitutions.

Summary judgment. A decision made by a trial court based on written documentation submitted before any trial occurs. Summary judgments may be granted only when a case involves no genuine issues of material fact.

Summons. A document issued by a court clerk and usually delivered by a process server or law enforcement officer, notifying a person of the filing of a lawsuit against him or her and of the deadline for answering the suit.

Supervised visitation. An arrangement under which a court allows a parent to visit a child only in the presence of a designated third person.

Supra. "Before."

Tarasoff v. Regents of University of California [17 Cal.3d 425, 551 P.2d 334, 131 Cal. Rptr. 14 (1976)]. A landmark California case holding that a therapist is responsible for taking steps, such as warning others, to prevent his or her patient from harming another person.

Temporary restraining order (TRO). An emergency remedy of brief duration, issued by a court under exceptional circumstances, to protect a potential victim from the alleged behavior of another person until a hearing can be held on the matter.

Termination of parental rights. A formal judicial proceeding that permanently or indefinitely severs legal rights and responsibilities for a child. The parent's rights are no longer legally recognized, and the state assumes legal responsibility for the care and welfare of the child.

Testimony. Statements made by a witness, usually under oath in court. See also *Expert witness.*

Tort. Any legally recognized private injury or wrong, other than one that is litigated as a breach of contract.

Transcript. A verbatim copy of the record of a trial or hearing.

Transfer hearing. A hearing to decide whether a juvenile should be tried in an adult court; also called a *waiver hearing.*

Trial. A judicial examination and determination of issues of law and fact disputed by parties to a lawsuit.

Trial court. A local court that initially hears all cases in dispute. If an attorney or party believes that a trial court judge has exceeded judicial authority or inappropriately applied the law, an appeal can be made to an appeals court.

Undue influence. Any wrongful insistence, maneuvering, or threats used by one person to overpower another's free will and coerce him or her to perform acts against his or her own wishes.

Unsubstantiated. Determined not to be supported by credible evidence; also known as *unfounded.* In child maltreatment, any report of suspected abuse or neglect that the mandated agency is unable to confirm on investigation is deemed unsubstantiated.

Vacate. To rescind a decree or judgment.

Venue. The particular district, county, or state where a case may be heard and decided.

Verbatim. "Word for word; in the same words." The statements of sex offenders, sexual abuse victims, and principal parties must be recorded verbatim in order to avoid misunderstandings caused by interpretations that change the facts.

Verdict. A decision by a judge or jury in favor of one side or the other in a case.

Verification of maltreatment. A finding that maltreatment occurred, following an investigation of a suspected case by mandated agency workers or law enforcement officers.

Voir dire. "To speak the truth"; the procedure whereby attorneys question prospective jurors to determine their biases, competencies, and interests; the procedure whereby the court or attorneys question witnesses regarding their interests and qualifications before they give testimony.

Volitional insanity defense. See *Irresistible impulse rule.*

Voluntary placement. The voluntary relinquishing of custody of a child by a parent without a formal court proceeding.

Waiver. An intentional and voluntary relinquishment of a known right.

Wanton. With reckless disregard for consequences and the safety and welfare of others; malicious or immoral; undisciplined, unruly, or unjustified.

Ward of the court. A person (such as a minor child or someone who is psychotic) who, by reason of incapacity, is under protection of a court, either directly or through a court-appointed guardian.

Warrant. A document issued by a judge, authorizing a peace officer to arrest or detain a person or search a place and seize specified items.

Witness. A person whose declaration under oath is received as evidence. See also *Expert witness.*

Writ. A court order requiring performance of a specified act.

Glossary of Measurement Terms

Ability testing. The use of a standardized test to evaluate an individual's current performance in a defined domain of cognitive, psychomotor, or physical functioning.

Accommodations. Modifications in the way assessments are designed or administered, to permit their use with students with disabilities.

Achievement test. A test that measures educationally relevant skills or knowledge in a subject such as reading, writing, or mathematics.

Adaptive testing. A sequential form of individual testing in which successive test items are chosen based both on their psychometric properties and content and on the individual's responses to previous items.

Age-equivalent score. A score reflecting the age group in the standardization sample that obtained the same average raw score (also known as *test age* or *age equivalent*). Thus, if individuals 10 years, 6 months of age have an average raw score of 17 on a test, a person with a raw score of 17 is said to have an age-equivalent score of 10–6.

Age norm. A value representing the average performance of individuals in an age group.

Age-scale format. A test design in which norms (expressed in units of years and months) are used to evaluate an individual's performance and scores are expressed in units of age.

Alternate forms. Two (or more) forms of a test with different items that are considered interchangeable in that they measure the same constructs, are intended for the same purposes, and are administered using the same directions.

Alternate forms reliability. The degree to which two (or more) forms of a test, designed to meet the same item specifications, have similar means and variances and are correlated (also referred to as *parallel forms reliability* or *equivalent forms reliability*).

Alternative assessment. Assessment based on an examination of an individual's performance, through such means as journals, portfolios, demonstrations, and investigations (also referred to as *authentic assessment* or *performance assessment*). Alternative assessment requires individuals to actively accomplish tasks, bringing to bear prior knowledge, recent learning, and relevant skills to solve problems.

Aptitude test. A standardized measure of an individual's ability to profit from further training or experience in an occupation or skill.

Arithmetic mean. A measure of the average or central tendency of a group of scores, computed by dividing the sum of the scores by the number of scores.

Assessment. Any systematic method of obtaining evidence from tests, examinations, questionnaires, surveys, and other sources in order to draw inferences about characteristics of people or groups.

Attenuation. A decrease in the magnitude of the correlation between two measures, such as a test and a criterion measure, caused by unreliability in the measures.

Authentic assessment. See *Alternative assessment.*

Average. A statistic that indicates the central tendency or most typical score of a group of scores. Most often, average refers to the arithmetic mean, which is the sum of a set of scores divided by the number of scores in the set.

Basal level. The level on an ability test at which an individual passes all (or most) items.

Base rate. The rate at which a condition exists in the population prior to any treatment.

Battery. A group of tests administered to an individual or group.

Benchmark. A standard (or specific level of performance) against which an individual's performance is measured.

Bias. Any one of several factors that lead to inaccurate scores.

Biased sample. A sample that gives a distorted picture of a group.

Bimodal distribution. A frequency distribution with two modes reflecting equal or nearly equal frequencies.

Biserial correlation coefficient (r_b). A correlation coefficient that measures the relationship between a dichotomous variable (i.e., one that has only two possible values, such as 1 or 0) and a continuous variable (i.e., one that has an infinite number of possible values, such as 51, 52, 53, . . .).

Bivariate analysis. Statistical analysis of the relationship between two variables.

Breadth. The comprehensiveness of the content of a measure.

Ceiling. The highest score attainable on a test. A test with a low ceiling does not have a sufficient number of difficult items.

Classical test theory. The view that an individual's observed score on a test is the sum of a true score component plus an independent measurement error component.

Closed-ended question. A question that requires an individual to choose one of several possible responses given by the examiner or interviewer.

Coefficient alpha (α). An internal consistency reliability coefficient based on the number of parts into which a test is partitioned (e.g., items, subtests, or raters), the interrelationships of the parts, and the total test score variance (also called *Cronbach's coefficient alpha* or, for dichotomous items, *KR-20*).

Coefficient of determination (r^2). The square of the correlation coefficient showing the strength of association between two variables. It indicates the amount of the variance in one variable that can be predicted or explained by the other variable.

Coefficient of equivalence. The type of reliability coefficient obtained when parallel forms of the same test are administered to the same individuals.

Coefficient of stability. See *Test-retest reliability coefficient.*

Cohen's d. A measure of effect size, computed by obtaining the difference between two means divided by the standard deviation. See also *Effect size.*

Cohort. Any group of people with a common classification or characteristic.

Common factor. In factor analysis, a factor on which two or more variables load.

Common variance. Variation shared between two or more tests.

Communality (h^2). The proportion of a variable's variability accounted for by common variance; reliability minus specificity.

Composite score. A score calculated by combining two or more scores.

Concurrent validity. The degree to which results of a test correlate with those of other similar tests taken at the same time.

Confidence interval. A band or range of scores around an individual's obtained score that likely includes the individual's true score.

Confidence level. A statistical "degree of certainty" (e.g., 68, 95, or 99 percent) indicating the probability that an obtained value represents the population (or true) value.

Confirmatory factor analysis. A factor analysis performed for the purpose of confirming an established theory.

Confounding variable. An extraneous variable that was not controlled for, causing a particular "confounded" result to be observed. For example, if investigators found a positive relationship between children's weight and a country's gross domestic product over time and concluded that a higher gross domestic product caused weight gain in children, they would be ignoring the confounding variable of time, which is the real cause of both gains in weight and gains in gross domestic product.

Construct. The complex idea or concept, synthesized from simpler ideas, that a test is designed to measure.

Construct domain. The set of interrelated attributes (e.g., behaviors, attitudes, values) included in a construct.

Construct validity. The degree to which a test measures a specified psychological construct or trait.

Content analysis. A systematic, objective, and quantitative method of studying and analyzing a test's content or an individual's communication, in order to measure the frequency with which certain terms, ideas, or emotions are expressed.

Content domain. The set of behaviors, knowledge, skills, abilities, attitudes, and/or other characteristics measured by a test.

Content validity. The degree to which a test measures what it is supposed to measure.

Continuous variables. Variables (e.g., temperature, age, height) characterized by an infinite number of possible values.

Control group. A group of participants in an experiment that is comparable to the experimental group, except that it is not given the treatment or otherwise exposed to the independent variable.

Convergent validity. The degree to which measures of the same domain in different formats correlate positively.

Correction for attenuation. A correction that results in an estimate of what the correlation between two variables would be if both variables were perfectly reliable.

Correlation coefficient (r). An index of the strength and direction of the relationship between two variables.

Criterion. A standard against which a test may be validated.

Criterion-referenced test. A test designed to measure how well a learner has mastered a specific skill.

Criterion-related validity. The degree to which test scores and some type of criterion or outcome (such as ratings, classifications, or other test scores) correlate positively.

Cronbach's coefficient alpha. See *Coefficient alpha.*

Cross-validation. Assessment of the validity of a model by applying it to new data.

Curvilinear relationship. A relationship between two variables that can be portrayed better by a curve than by a straight line.

Cut-off score. A point on a scale at or above which scores are interpreted differently than they are below that point.

Database. A collection of data.

Data matrix. A rectangular arrangement of raw data on *n* cases over *m* variables. Most commonly, rows are used for the cases and columns for the variables.

Dependent variable. A measure of behavior that the experimenter observes but does not manipulate or control.

Derived score. A score resulting from the conversion of a raw score to a percentile rank, standard score, or other type of score.

Descriptive statistics. Statistics that summarize data obtained about a sample of individuals.

Deviation from the mean. The distance of a single score from the mean of the distribution from which the score was derived.

Deviation score. The difference between the mean of a distribution and an individual score in that distribution. Deviation scores are always found by subtracting the mean from the score; a positive value indicates a score above the mean, and a negative value indicates a score below the mean.

Diagnostic test. An achievement test composed of items in a number of subject areas and designed to diagnose an individual's relative strengths and weaknesses in those areas.

Dichotomous variable. A variable that can have only one of two values.

Difference score. The difference between a score on a test and a score on another administration of the same test or an equivalent test.

Differential item functioning (DIF). A statistical procedure that reveals whether test items function differently in different groups.

Differential validity. The degree to which a test predicts one criterion better than another criterion.

Difficulty index. The proportion or percentage of individuals passing a given test item. The larger the index, the easier the item is.

Discrete variables. Variables (e.g., gender, color, number of children in a family) characterized by separate, indivisible categories, with no intermediate values.

Discriminant validity. The extent to which measures of performance in different domains do not correlate with each other.

Discrimination index. An index that indicates how well an item discriminates between low and high scores on some criterion.

Dispersion. The variability of scores in a set or distribution of scores.

Distracter. An answer to a multiple-choice test item that is not the correct answer.

Distribution. A tabulation of scores that shows the frequency of each score.

Divergent validity. See *Discriminant validity.*

Documentation. The body of literature (test manuals, manual supplements, research reports, user's guides, etc.) made available by publishers and test authors to support test use.

Domain-referenced test. A test designed to measure a well-defined set of tasks or a body of knowledge.

Domain sampling. The process of selecting test items to represent a specified domain of performance.

Double-barreled question. A question that combines two or more issues.

Ecological validity. The extent to which assessment findings generalize to behaviors that occur in natural settings.

Effect size. A statistical index often based on standard deviation units, independent of sample size; often used to evaluate the strength of a relationship between variables in a study.

Eigenvalue. The variance in a set of variables explained by a factor or component; the sum of squared values in the column of a factor matrix, denoted by λ (lambda).

Empirical keying. Using empirical relationships between individual test items and the criterion of interest as the basis for test scoring. Items are weighted according to an external criterion, such as responses of people who belong to a certain group.

Equity. Freedom from bias or favoritism.

Equivalent forms reliability. See *Alternate forms reliability.*

Error of measurement. The difference between an observed score and the corresponding true score.

Error score. The score associated with the unreliability of a test.

Error variance. The proportion of variance attributable to random error, such as sampling error or experimental error. In factor analysis, error variance is assumed to be independent of common variance; it is a component of a variable's unique variance.

Examiner reliability. See *Interrater reliability.*

Exploratory factor analysis. Factor analysis used to explore the underlying structure of a collection of variables, when there are no a priori hypotheses about the factor structure.

Extrapolation. The process of extending norms to scores not actually obtained by the standardization sample.

Face validity. The extent to which test items appear to measure what the test is supposed to measure.

Factor. In factor analysis, a statistically derived, hypothetical dimension that accounts for part of the intercorrelation among tests.

Factor analysis. A statistical technique used to explain the pattern of intercorrelations among a set of variables by deriving the smallest number of meaningful variables or factors.

Factor loadings. The factor pattern coefficients or structure coefficients in a factor analysis.

Factor matrix. A matrix of coefficients in which the factors are presented in the columns and the variables are presented in the rows.

Factor scores. Linear combinations of variables that represent factors.

Fairness. The extent to which the items on a test are a representative sample of what individuals have been exposed to.

First unrotated factor. In factor analysis, a general factor on which most variables have high loadings.

Five percent level. A statistical level indicating that the obtained results would be expected to occur 5 percent of the time or less by chance alone. It is a common threshold for statistical significance.

Floor. The lowest score attainable on a test.

Frequency distribution. The frequencies of occurrence of a set of scores, arranged from lowest to highest.

Functional equivalence. The degree to which a test translated into another language measures the same functions as the original test.

g. General intelligence.

Gaussian distribution. See *Normal distribution.*

General factor. A factor on which all the variables in a factor analysis load.

Grade-equivalent score. A score reflecting the grade at which students in the standardization sample obtained the same average raw score. Thus, if students at the middle of the 6th grade have an average raw score of 21 on a test, a person with a raw score of 21 is said to have a grade-equivalent score of 6.5.

Grade norm. A value representing the average performance of students in a given grade.

Group factor. In factor analysis, a factor present in more than one test in a set of tests but not present in all tests. Examples of group factors are verbal abilities, spatial abilities, memory abilities, and visual-motor abilities.

Group test. A test that may be administered to a number of individuals simultaneously.

High-stakes test. A test whose results have important, direct consequences for individuals, programs, or institutions involved in the testing.

Independent variable. A variable manipulated by the experimenter.

Individual test. A test that is administered to one individual at a time.

Inferential statistics. Statistics that permit one to make inferences about a population based on a sample of the population.

Informal test. A nonstandardized test designed to provide information about an individual's level of ability.

Internal consistency reliability. The degree to which the scores from a single test administration are consistent in their measurement.

Interpolation. The process of estimating a value between two given values or points.

Interrater reliability. The degree to which raters agree (also referred to as *examiner reliability* or *scorer reliability*).

Interval measurement scale. A scale that has equal intervals and an arbitrary zero point and that classifies and orders.

Inventory. A questionnaire designed to obtain information about one or more specific areas of interest.

Ipsative method. Comparison of an individual's responses on an assessment measure to other responses of that individual, rather than to the responses of other individuals.

Item. An individual question in a test.

Item analysis. A general term for procedures designed to assess the usefulness of test items. See also *Difficulty index, Discrimination index.*

Item characteristic curve (ICC). A line representing the relationship between the probability of passing an item and an individual's position on the construct being measured.

Item difficulty. See *Difficulty index.*

Item discrimination. See *Discrimination index.*

Item gradient. The ratio of raw score to standard score; the number of raw-score points required to earn one standard-score point.

Item pool. The aggregate of items from which test items are selected during test development.

Item response theory (IRT). A theory that provides useful information about the relationships between the attribute being measured and test responses through the use of three parameters: item discrimination, item difficulty, and a "guessing" parameter, which corresponds to the probability that a correct response will occur by chance (also known as the *latent trait model*).

Kuder-Richardson formula 20 (KR-20). A formula for estimating the internal consistency reliability of a test based on a single administration of the test. See *Coefficient alpha.*

Latent trait model. See *Item response theory.*

Latent variable. A theoretical variable hypothesized to influence a number of observed variables.

Leading question. A question that suggests a certain answer.

Likert scale. A scale designed to measure attitudes, usually with five or seven points (e.g., from "strongly agree" to "strongly disagree").

Linear equation. An equation describing a relationship between two variables that can be represented on a graph by a straight line.

Linear relationship. A relationship between two variables that can be represented on a graph by a straight line.

Loadings. See *Factor loadings.*

Local norms. Norms based on a local school or school system and used in place of or in addition to national norms.

Longitudinal study. A study in which data on the same group of individuals are collected repeatedly over a period of time.

Main diagonal. The elements in a square matrix running in a diagonal line from the upper left to the lower right corner. Communality estimates are inserted in the main diagonal of a correlation matrix when a factor analysis is performed. When a principal component analysis is performed, the main diagonal of the correlation matrix will contain 1s.

Mastery test. A test designed to indicate whether an individual has mastered some domain, knowledge, or skill.

Mean. See *Arithmetic mean.*

Measurement error variance. That portion of the observed score variance attributable to one or more sources of measurement error.

Measure of central tendency. A single score that in some way best describes the scores in a data set (e.g., the mean, the median, the mode).

Median. The middle point in a set of scores arranged in order of magnitude.

Meta-analysis. A procedure in which rigorous research techniques (including quantitative methods) are used to summarize a body of similar studies for the purpose of integrating their findings.

Midpoint of an interval. The value located halfway between the upper and lower limits of an interval.

Mode. The score that occurs most frequently in a set of scores.

Moderator variables. Variables, such as sex, age, race, social class, and personality characteristics, that affect the relationship (correlation) between two other variables.

Multi-factor test. An instrument that measures two or more constructs that are less than perfectly correlated.

Multiple-choice test. A test in which several possible answers are given and individuals select one.

Multiple correlation coefficient (*R*). A measure of the overall degree of relationship between several predictor variables and a single criterion variable. The coefficient may range from 0.00 to +1.00.

Multiple regression. A statistical technique that allows one to make predictions about performance on one variable or measure (called the *criterion variable*) based on performance on two or more other variables (called the *predictor variables*).

National norms. Norms based on a national sample.

Naturalistic observation. Observation conducted in a real-world setting such as a playground, classroom, job site, or home.

Negative correlation. A relationship in which scores on two variables move in opposite directions.

Nominal measurement scale. A scale consisting of a set of categories that do not have a sequential order and that are each identified by a name, number, or letter. The names, numbers, or letters are merely labels or classifications and usually represent mutually exclusive categories, which cannot be arranged in a meaningful order.

Normal curve. The bell-shaped curve that results when a normal frequency distribution is graphed.

Normal curve equivalents (NCEs). Standard scores with a mean of 50 and a standard deviation of approximately 21.

Normal distribution. A distribution of scores that forms a bell-shaped curve (also called a *Gaussian distribution*).

Normalized scores. Scores that have been transformed to approximate a normal distribution.

Norm-referenced measurement. A type of measurement in which an individual's performance is compared with the performance of a specific group of individuals, referred to as a *norm group* or a *standardization sample.*

Norms. The scores of a sample of individuals that provide the standards for interpreting test scores.

Objective test. A test that can be scored objectively because there is a definitive correct answer to each question.

Oblique factors. In factor analysis, correlated factors.

Oblique rotation. In factor analysis, a rotation in which the factor axes are allowed to form acute or obtuse angles so that the factors can be correlated and a second- or third-order factor extracted.

Obtained score. See *Raw score.*

Odd-even reliability. The correlation between scores on the odd-numbered items and the even-numbered items on a test, corrected by the Spearman-Brown reliability formula. See also *Split-half reliability.*

One percent level. A statistical level indicating that the obtained results would be expected to occur 1 percent of the time or less by chance alone.

Open-ended question. A question that allows individuals to respond in their own words.

Ordinal measurement scale. A scale that ranks or orders—for example, into first, second, etc.

Orthogonal factors. In factor analysis, uncorrelated factors.

Orthogonal rotation. In factor analysis, a rotation that maintains the independence of factors—the axes are at right angles and the factors are therefore uncorrelated.

Outlier. A number that deviates extremely from the other numbers in a distribution; an atypical number.

Parallel forms reliability. See *Alternate forms reliability.*

Partial correlation. The correlation between two variables when the influence of a third variable is removed.

Pearson product-moment correlation coefficient. The correlation coefficient suitable for continuous variables.

Percentage agreement. The percentage of items on which two or more raters give the identical rating to the behavior or criterion being judged.

Percentile. See *Percentile rank.*

Percentile band. A range of percentile ranks, each with a certain probability of containing an individual's true score on a test.

Percentile norms. Norms expressed in terms of the percentile standings of individuals on a test.

Percentile rank. A point in a distribution at or below which the scores of a given percentage of individuals fall.

Performance assessment. See *Alternative assessment.*

Performance test. A test composed of nonverbal items.

Personal documents. Anything written, photographed, or recorded by an individual.

Phi coefficient. A correlation coefficient suitable for two dichotomous variables.

Pilot test. A preliminary test administered to a representative sample of individuals to determine the test's properties.

Point-biserial coefficient. A correlation coefficient suitable for one dichotomous variable and one continuous variable.

Point-scale format. A test design in which each item is assigned a point value and the individual's performance is rated on the basis of the total number of points earned.

Population. A complete group or set of cases.

Portfolio assessment. An assessment of a collection of a student's work (usually classroom work).

Positive correlation. A relationship in which scores on two variables move in the same direction.

Power test. A test with ample time limits (as opposed to one that requires speed).

Practice effects. Effects, seen on retest, that are associated with having had previous experience taking the test.

Precision of measurement. A general term for a measure's reliability or its sensitivity to measurement error.

Predictive power. A special type of predictive validity that assesses the accuracy of decisions made on the basis of a given measure.

Predictive validity. The extent to which results from a test correlate with a criterion measure taken at a later time.

Premorbid level. The level at which a trait or an ability was present before an injury, disease, or disability.

Principal axes or factors. In factor analysis, the main factors obtained.

Principal components analysis (PCA). A method of factoring aimed at determining the set of factors that can account for all common and unique variance in a set of variables, without estimating communalities.

Principal factor analysis (PFA). A method of factoring aimed at determining the smallest set of factors that can account for the common variance in a set of variables, taking into account prior communality estimates.

Product-moment correlation coefficient. An index of the relationship between two variables.

Psychological assessment. The process of administering a psychological test, evaluating and integrating test results and collateral information, and writing a report.

Psychological testing. Any procedure that involves the use of tests or inventories to assess particular psychological constructs in an individual.

Psychometrics. The branch of psychology that deals with the design, administration, and interpretation of quantitative tests that measure psychological variables such as intelligence, aptitude, and personality traits.

Quartile. A percentile that is an even multiple of 25. The 25th percentile is the first quartile, the 50th percentile is the second quartile (as well as the median), and the 75th percentile is the third quartile.

Random error. Any unsystematic error; a quantity (often observed indirectly) that appears to have no relationship to any other variable.

Random sample. A sample in which every person in the sample had an equal chance of being selected for the sample.

Range. The difference between the highest and lowest scores in a distribution.

Rank-order correlation (ρ). A correlation suitable for ranked data (also referred to as *Spearman's rho*).

Rasch scaling. An item scaling method in which the probability of a correct response is assumed to depend on two independently estimated parameters: the extent to which the item elicits the latent trait and the degree to which the individual possesses the latent trait.

Rating scale. A scale used by a rater to estimate the magnitude of a trait or quality being rated.

Ratio IQ. An intelligence quotient obtained by dividing the mental age obtained on an intelligence test by the individual's chronological age and multiplying by 100.

Ratio measurement scale. A scale with a true zero point, equal intervals between adjacent units, and equality of ratios.

Raw score. The unconverted score on a test (e.g., the number of correct answers or the number of correct answers minus incorrect answers).

Reactivity. An alteration in performance that occurs when people are aware of participating in a study or of being observed.

Readiness test. A test that measures the extent to which an individual possesses the skills and knowledge necessary to learn a complex subject, such as reading or writing.

Reading age. A score that indicates an individual's reading ability in terms of the age of the group in the standardization sample at that level.

Recognition item. A test item that requires recognizing the correct answer in a list of possible answers.

Reference group. The norm group that serves as the comparison group for computing standard scores, percentile ranks, or related statistics.

Regression effect. Tendency for a retest score to be closer to the mean than the initial test score (also referred to as *regression artifact, regression to the mean,* or *statistical regression*).

Regression equation. An equation for predicting a score on one variable, given a score on another variable.

Reliability. The degree to which a test is consistent in its measurements. See also *Alternate forms reliability, Internal consistency reliability, Split-half reliability.*

Reliability coefficient. An index from .00 to 1.00 that expresses the degree of consistency in the measurement of test scores.

Representative sample. A group drawn from a population and considered sufficiently representative of that population that conclusions based on the group also will be valid for the population.

Response bias. See *Response set.*

Response set. The tendency to respond to test items in a specific way, regardless of the content of the items (also referred to as *response bias*). Examples are agreeing with items regardless of content and endorsing items because it is socially desirable to do so. Response sets tend to distort the validity of a measure.

Restriction of range. Reduction in the observed score variance of a sample.

Rotation of factors. In factor analysis, a transformation of the principal factors or components in order to approximate a simple structure.

Rotation of figures. Changing the orientation of figures such as designs or letters.

Sample. A subset of the population.

Sampling. The process of drawing a sample from a population.

Scale. A system for assigning values or scores to some measurable trait or characteristic.

Scaled score. A type of standard score earned on subtests within an ability test. Subtests typically have scaled scores with $M = 10$ and $SD = 3$.

Score. Any specific number resulting from the assessment of an individual.

Scorer reliability. See *Interrater reliability.*

Screening test. A test used to quickly and efficiently identify individuals who meet a certain criterion level.

Semi-interquartile range (Q). Half the distance between the first and third quartiles in a frequency distribution.

Significance. The likelihood that a result did not occur by chance or as a result of random factors alone.

Simple structure. In factor analysis, the set of factors, arrived at through rotation, that produces the simplest solution.

Skewness. The degree of asymmetry of a frequency distribution.

Social desirability response set. The tendency for an individual to provide answers that are socially desirable.

Spearman-Brown formula. See *Split-half reliability.*

Spearman's rho. See *Rank-order correlation.*

Special ability tests. Tests that measure special abilities, such as mechanical, clerical, musical, or artistic ability.

Specific factor. A factor on which only one variable loads.

Specificity. The proportion of a variable's variability accounted for by specific variance rather than measurement error or common factors.

Specific variance. Variance associated with a specific test, in contrast to the variance the test has in common with other tests; in factor analysis, the component of unique variance that is reliable but not explained by common factors.

Specimen set. A sample set of testing materials available from a commercial test publisher.

Split-half reliability. An internal consistency coefficient obtained by using half the items on a test to yield one score and the other half of the items to yield a second, independent score and then adjusting for length using the Spearman-Brown formula.

Spread. See *Dispersion.*

Stability coefficient. See *Test-retest reliability coefficient.*

Standard deviation. A measure of how much scores vary, or deviate, from the mean.

Standard error of estimate. A measure in a regression equation of the accuracy of an individual's predicted score.

Standard error of measurement. An estimate of the amount of error associated with an obtained score.

Standardization. Administering a test to a large, representative sample of people under standard conditions for the purpose of determining test norms.

Standardization sample. See *Norm-referenced measurement.*

Standardized test. A test, administered under standard conditions, that has norms and reliability and validity data.

Standard score. A raw score that has been transformed so that it has a predetermined mean and standard deviation. Standard scores express an individual's distance from the mean in terms of the standard deviation of the distribution. *T* scores, IQs, *z* scores, and stanines are all standard scores.

Stanine. A standard score on a scale consisting of the scores 1 through 9, with a mean of 5 and a standard deviation of 2.

Statistic. Any value that represents the end result of statistical manipulation of other values.

Statistical inference. The process of making use of information from a sample to draw conclusions or inferences about the population from which the sample was taken.

Statistical significance. See *Significance.*

Sten score. A linearly transformed standard score on a scale consisting of the scores 0 through 9, with a mean of 5.5 and a standard deviation of 2.

Stratified sample. A sample in which cases are selected so that they closely match the population in terms of some specified characteristics such as geographical region, community size, grade, age, sex, or ethnicity.

Systematic error. A component of a score not related to test performance.

Test age. See *Age-equivalent score.*

Test of significance. A statistical procedure that determines whether variations observed under various treatment conditions are due to changes in conditions or to chance fluctuations.

Test-retest reliability coefficient. A reliability coefficient obtained by administering the same test a second time to the same group after a time interval and correlating the two sets of scores (also called *coefficient of stability*).

Tetrachoric correlation. The correlation between two dichotomized measures. Computation is based on the assumption that the underlying variables are continuous and normally distributed.

Thurstone scale. An attitude scale consisting of several statements, each representing a different degree of favorableness or unfavorableness toward a topic, arranged to form a continuum with equally spaced levels.

Traits. Distinguishable, relatively enduring ways in which one individual differs from another.

True score. The hypothetical score that measures an individual's true knowledge of the test material. In test theory, an individual's true score on a test is the mean of the distribution of scores that would result if the individual took the test an infinite number of times.

True variance. That part of the difference in test scores that is due to true differences in the characteristics under consideration.

***T* score.** A standard score with a mean of 50 and a standard deviation of 10.

Uniqueness. The proportion of a variable's variability that is not shared with a factor structure; 1 minus communality.

Unique variance. In factor analysis, the proportion of variance in a variable not explained by common factors. Unique variance is composed of specific variance and error variance.

Validation. The process of gathering evidence that supports inferences made on the basis of test scores.

Validity. The extent to which a test measures what it is intended to measure and, therefore, is appropriately used to make inferences.

Variability. The amount of dispersion in a set of scores.

Variable. A condition or characteristic that can take on different values or categories.

Variance. A measure of the amount of variability of scores around the mean—the greater the variability, the greater the variance.

Varimax rotation. In factor analysis, the orthogonal rotation that maximizes the variance of the squared elements in the columns of a factor matrix. Varimax is the most common rotational criterion. It produces factors that have the minimum correlation with one another.

Verbal test. A test in which the ability to understand and use words plays a crucial role in determining performance.

Weighted scoring. A method of scoring a test in which the number of points awarded for a correct response is not the same for all items on the test.

***z* score.** A standard score with a mean of 0 and a standard deviation of 1.

References

Aarnoudse-Moens, C. S. H., Weisglas-Kuperus, N., van Goudoever, J. B., & Oosterlaan, J. (2009). Meta-analysis of neurobehavioral outcomes in very preterm and/or very low birth weight children. *Pediatrics, 124*(2), 717–728. doi:10.1542/peds.2008-2816

Abikoff, H., & Gittelman, R. (1985). Classroom observation code: A modification of the Stony Brook Code. *Psychopharmacology Bulletin, 21*, 901–909.

Ackerman, M. J. (2001). *Clinician's guide to child custody evaluations* (2nd ed.). Hoboken, NJ: Wiley.

Adams-Wells Special Services Cooperative. (n.d.). *Systematic Behavior Observation Form*. Retrieved from http://awssc.k12.in.us/educators.htm

Adrien, J. L., Ornitz, E., Barthelemy, C., Sauvage, D., & LeLord, G. (1987). The presence or absence of certain behaviors associated with infantile autism in severely retarded autistic and nonautistic retarded children and very young normal children. *Journal of Autism and Developmental Disorders, 17*(3), 407–416.

Ali, R. (2010, October 26). [Dear Colleague Letter]. U.S. Department of Education Office of the Assistant Secretary. Retrieved from http://www2.ed.gov/about/offices/list/ocr/letters/colleague-201010.pdf

Allen, K. D., & Matthews, J. R. (1998). Behavior management of recurrent pain in children. In T. S. Watson & F. M. Gresham (Eds.), *Handbook of child behavior therapy* (pp. 263–285). New York, NY: Plenum.

Allington, R. L. (1979). Diagnosis of reading disability: Word prediction ability tests. *Academic Therapy, 14*(3), 267–274.

American Prosecutors Research Institute. (1993). *Investigation and prosecution of child abuse* (2nd ed.). Alexandria, VA: Author.

American Psychiatric Association. (2013). *Diagnostic and statistical manual of mental disorders (DSM-5)* (5th ed.). Washington, DC: Author.

Anderson, P. J. (2008). Towards a developmental model of executive function. In V. Anderson, R. Jacobs, & P. J. Anderson (Eds.), *Executive functions and the frontal lobes: A lifespan perspective* (pp. 3–21). Philadelphia, PA: Taylor & Francis.

Anderson, V., Anderson, P. J., Jacobs, R., & Smith, M. S. (2008). Development and assessment of executive function: From preschool to adolescence. In V. Anderson, R. Jacobs, & P. J. Anderson (Eds.), *Executive functions and the frontal lobes: A lifespan perspective* (pp. 123–154). Philadelphia, PA: Taylor & Francis.

Ardila, A. (2013). Development of metacognitive and emotional executive functions in children. *Applied Neuropsychology: Child, 2*(2), 82–87. doi:10.1080/21622965.2013.748388

Austega's Gifted Service. (n.d.). *Characteristics checklist for gifted children*. Retrieved from http://austega.com/gifted/9-gifted/22-characteristics.html

Bacon, E. H., & Rubin, D. C. (1983). Story recall by mentally retarded children. *Psychological Reports, 53*(3 Pt 1), 791–796.

Bagley, C. (1992). Development of an adolescent stress scale for use by school counsellors: Construct validity in terms of depression, self-esteem and suicidal ideation. *School Psychology International, 13*(1), 31–49. doi:10.1177/0143034392131003

Bank, S. C., & Packer, I. K. (2007). Expert witness testimony: Law, ethics, and practice. In A. M. Goldstein (Ed.), *Forensic psychology: Emerging topics and expanding roles* (pp. 421–445). Hoboken, NJ: Wiley.

Barbero, J. A. J., Hernández, J. A. R., Esteban, B. L., & García, M. P. (2012). Effectiveness of antibullying school programmes: A systematic review by evidence levels. *Children and Youth Services Review, 34*(9), 1646–1658. doi:10.1016/j.childyouth.2012.04.025

Barchia, K., & Bussey, K. (2011). Predictors of student defenders of peer aggression victims: Empathy and social cognitive factors. *International Journal of Behavioral Development, 35*(4), 289–297. doi:10.1177/0165025410396746

Barkley, R. A. (1998). *Attention-deficit hyperactivity disorder: A handbook for diagnosis and treatment* (2nd ed.). New York, NY: Guilford.

Baron, I. S. (2000). Clinical implications and practical applications of child neuropsychological evaluations. In K. O. Yeates, M. D. Ris, & H. G. Taylor (Eds.), *Pediatric neuropsychology: Research, theory, and practice* (pp. 446–452). New York, NY: Guilford.

Barsky, A. E., & Gould, J. W. (2002). *Clinicians in court: A guide to subpoenas, depositions, testifying, and everything else you need to know*. New York, NY: Guilford.

Bauman, S. (2011). *Cyberbullying: What counselors need to know*. Alexandria, VA: American Counseling Association.

Beane, A. L. (2005). *Bully free classroom: Over 100 tips and strategies for teachers K–8*. Minneapolis, MN: Free Spirit Publishing.

Beane, A. L. (2006). *How to be bully free workbook: Word searches, mazes, what-ifs, and other fun activities for kids*. Minneapolis, MN: Free Spirit Publishing.

Beavers, W. R., & Hampson, R. B. (1990). *Successful families: Assessment and intervention*. New York, NY: Norton.

Beery, K. E., Buktenica, N. A., & Beery, N. A. (2010). *Beery-Buktenica Developmental Test of Visual-Motor Integration, Sixth Edition (Beery VMI)*. San Antonio, TX: Pearson.

Bender, D., & Lösel, F. (2011). Bullying at school as a predictor of delinquency, violence and other anti-social behaviour in adulthood. *Criminal Behaviour and Mental Health, 21*(2), 99–106. doi:10.1002/cbm.799

Bender, L. (1938). A Visual Motor Gestalt Test and its clinical use. *American Orthopsychiatric Association Research Monograph, No. 3.*

Benedek, E. P. (2002). Testifying: The expert witness in court. In D. H. Schetky & E. P. Benedek (Eds.), *Principles and practice of child and adolescent forensic psychiatry* (pp. 33–43). Washington, DC: American Psychiatric Publishing.

Benenson, J. F. (2009). Sex differences in aggression from an adaptive perspective. In M. J. Harris (Ed.), *Bullying, rejection, and peer victimization: A social cognitive neuroscience perspective* (pp. 171–198). New York, NY: Springer.

Benjamin, G. A. H., & Gollan, J. K. (2003). Phase 2: First clinical interview. In G. A. H. Benjamin & J. K. Gollan (Eds.), *Family evaluation in custody litigation: Reducing risks of ethical infractions and malpractice* (pp. 49–64). Washington, DC: American Psychological Association.

Benton, A. L., Hamsher, K., & Sivan, A. B. (1994). *Multilingual Aphasia Examination* (3rd ed.). Iowa City, IA: AJA Associates.

Bernstein, J. H., & Waber, D. P. (2007). Executive capacities from a developmental perspective. In L. Meltzer (Ed.), *Executive function in education: From theory to practice* (pp. 39–54). New York, NY: Guilford.

Biller, J., Glassman, L. S., Roosa, L., Schneller, J., & Venezia, M. (2008). *Threat assessment, revised edition: Procedures manual.* Retrieved from http://www.broward.k12.fl.us/studentsupport/psychologicalservices/pdf/Revised%20Threat%20Assessment%20(Edition)%202.pdf

Billingsley, B. S. (1998). Writing: Teaching assessment skills. *Academic Therapy, 24*(1), 27–35.

Blair, C., Zelazo, P. D., & Greenberg, M. T. (2005). The measurement of executive function in early childhood. *Developmental Neuropsychology, 28*(2), 561–571. doi:10.1207/s15326942dn2802_1

Boll, T. (1993). *Children's Category Test.* San Antonio, TX: Pearson.

Bontempo, D. E., & D'Augelli, A. R. (2002). Effects of at-school victimization and sexual orientation on lesbian, gay, or bisexual youths' health risk behavior. *Journal of Adolescent Health, 30,* 364–374. doi:10.1016/S1054-139X(01)00415-3

Bowen, J., Ashcroft, P., Jenson, W. R., & Rhode, G. (2008). *The tough kid bully blockers book.* Eugene, OR: Pacific Northwest Publishing.

Boyse, K. (2004). *Non-verbal learning disability (NLD or NVLD).* Retrieved from http://www.med.umich.edu/1libr/yourchild/nld.htm

Boyse, K. (2009). *ADHD: What parents need to know.* Retrieved from http://med.umich.edu/yourchild/topics/adhd.htm

Boyse, K. (2010). *Sleep problems.* Retrieved from http://www.med.umich.edu/yourchild/topics/sleep.htm

Bradley, L. (1980). *Assessing reading difficulties: A diagnostic and remedial approach.* London, England: MacMillan.

Bradshaw, C. P., Waasdorp, T. E., O'Brennan, L. M., & Gulemetova, M. (2011). *Findings from the National Education Association's nationwide study of bullying: Teachers' and education support professionals' perspectives.* Retrieved from National Education Association website: http://fjuhsd.edlioschool.com/ourpages/auto/2012/4/23/46192893/1_NEA%20Bullying%20Findings%202011.pdf

Brady, J. (2007). *101 bully prevention activities: A year's worth of activities to help kids prevent bullying.* Farmingville, NY: The Bureau for At-Risk Youth.

Brannigan, G. G., & Decker, S. L. (2003). *Bender Visual-Motor Gestalt Test, Second Edition.* Itasca, IL: Riverside Publishing.

Breakstone, S., Dreiblatt, M., & Dreiblatt, K. (2009). *How to stop bullying and social aggression: Elementary grade lessons and activities that teach empathy, friendship, and respect.* Thousand Oaks, CA: Sage.

Brockway, B. S. (1978). Evaluating physician competency: What difference does it make? *Evaluation and Program Planning, 1*(3), 211–220.

Brodsky, S. L. (2004). *Coping with cross-examination and other pathways to effective testimony.* Washington, DC: American Psychological Association.

Bromwich, R. M. (1981). *Working with parents and infants: An interactional approach.* Baltimore, MD: University Park Press.

Brown, W. K. (2007). *Understanding child abuse and neglect.* Retrieved from http://www.williamgladdenfoundation.org/images/Image/user/Abuse.doc

Buhs, E. S., Ladd, G. W., & Herald-Brown, S. L. (2010). Victimization and exclusion: Links to peer rejection, classroom engagement, and achievement. In S. R. Jimerson, S. M. Swearer, & D. L. Espelage (Eds.), *Handbook of bullying in schools: An international perspective* (pp. 163–171). New York, NY: Routledge/Taylor & Francis Group.

Bully OnLine. (n.d.). *Bullying in the family.* Retrieved from http://bullyonline.org/related/family.htm

Burk, L. R., Armstrong, J. M., Park, J., Zahn-Waxler, C., Klein, M. H., & Essex, M. J. (2011). Stability of early identified aggressive victim status in elementary school and associations with later mental health problems and functional impairments. *Journal of Abnormal Child Psychology, 39*(2), 225–238. doi:10.1007/s10802-010-9454-6

Busch, B. (1993). Attention deficits: Current concepts, controversies, management, and approaches to classroom instruction. *Annals of Dyslexia, 43*(1), 5–25.

Cairns, E., & Cammock, T. (1978). Development of a more reliable version of the Matching Familiar Figures Test. *Developmental Psychology, 14*(5), 555–560. doi:10.1037/0012-1649.14.5.555

California Department of Education. (2010). *Bullying frequently asked questions.* Retrieved from http://www.cde.ca.gov/ls/ss/se/bullyfaq.asp

Cardman, S. (1994). *More classroom tips for teachers of ADD ADHD students.* Retrieved from http://newideas.net/book/export/html/163

Career Special Technical Populations. (n.d.). *Classroom management checklist.* Retrieved from http://ctsp.tamu.edu/videos/videos07/toolbox/accommodations/classroom%20management%20checklist.pdf

Carlson, S. M. (2005). Developmentally sensitive measures of executive function in preschool children. *Developmental Neuropsychology, 28*(2), 595–616. doi:10.1207/s15326942dn2802_3

Catale, C., Marique, P., Closset, A., & Meulemans, T. (2008). Attentional and executive functioning following mild traumatic brain injury in children using the test for attentional performance (TAP) battery. *Journal of Clinical and Experimental Neuropsychology, 31*(3), 331–338. doi:10.1080/13803390802134616

Center for Technology and Education. (1997). *Adapted pencils to computers: Strategies for improving writing.* Retrieved from http://cte.jhu.edu/adaptedpencils.pdf

Centrone, T. (2007). *How not to be a bully target: A program for victims of childhood bullying.* Chapin, SC: Youthlight, Inc.

Child Development Institute. (2010). *Suggested classroom accommodations for children with ADD & learning disabilities.* Retrieved from http://childdevelopmentinfo.com/learning/teacher.shtml

Cohen, S. B. (1991). Adapting educational programs for students with head injuries. *Journal of Head Trauma Rehabilitation, 6*(1), 56–63.

Conners, C. K., & MHS Staff. (2004). *Conners' Continuous Performance Test II Version 5 (CPT II V.5).* North Tonawanda, NY: Multi-Health Systems.

Cook, J. (2010). *Bully B.E.A.N.S. activity and idea book.* Chattanooga, TN: National Center for Youth Issues.

Copeland, W. E., Wolke, D., Angold, A., & Costello, E. J. (2013). Adult psychiatric outcomes of bullying and being bullied by peers in childhood and adolescence. *JAMA Psychiatry, 70*(4), 419–426. doi:10.1001/jamapsychiatry.2013.504

Crick, N., & Grotpeter, J. (1996). Children's treatment by peers: Victims of relational and overt aggression. *Development and Psychopathology, 8*(2), 367–380. doi:10.1017/S0954579400007148

Crinella, F. M., & Yu, J. (1999). Brain mechanisms and intelligence. Psychometric g and executive function. *Intelligence, 27*(4), 299–327. doi:10.1016/S0160-2896(99)00021-5

Culbertson, W. C., & Zillmer, E. A. (1998). The Tower of London (DX): A standardized approach to assessing executive functioning in children. *Archives of Clinical Neuropsychology, 13*(3), 285–301.

Curner-Smith, M. E., Smith, P. K., & Porter, M. (2010). Family-level perspective on bullies and victims. In E. M. Vernberg & B. K. Biggs (Eds.), *Preventing and treating bullying and victimization* (pp. 75–106). New York, NY: Oxford University Press.

Daubert v. Merrell Dow Pharmaceuticals., Inc., No. 92-102, 509 U.S. 579 (1993).

Dawson, P., & Guare, R. (1998). *Coaching the ADHD student.* North Tonawanda, NY: Multi-Health Systems.

D.C. et al. v. R.R. et al., B207869 (CA. Ct. App. 2010).

Delaware Attorney General. (n.d.). *Bully worksheet questionnaire.* Retrieved from http://attorneygeneral.delaware.gov/schools/bullquesti.shtml

Delis, D. C. (2012). *Delis–Rating of Executive Function (D–REF).* San Antonio, TX: Pearson.

Delis, D. C., Kaplan, E., & Kramer, J. H. (2001). *The Delis–Kaplan Executive Function System.* San Antonio, TX: The Psychological Corporation.

De Luca, C. R., & Leventer, R. J. (2008). Developmental trajectories of executive functions across the lifespan. In V. Anderson, R. Jacobs, & P. J. Anderson (Eds.), *Executive functions and the frontal lobes: A lifespan perspective* (pp. 23–56). Philadelphia, PA: Taylor & Francis.

DePompei, R., & Blosser, J. L. (1987). Strategies for helping head-injured children successfully return to school. *Language, Speech, and Hearing Services in Schools, 18*(4), 292–300.

d'Escury, A. L. C., & Dudink, A. C. M. (2010). Bullying beyond school: Examining the role of sports. In S. R. Jimerson, S. M. Swearer, & D. L. Espelage (Eds.), *Handbook of bullying in schools: An international perspective* (pp. 235–248). New York, NY: Routledge/Taylor & Francis Group.

Deshler, D. D., Ellis, E. S., & Lenz, B. K. (1996). *Teaching adolescents with learning disabilities: Strategies and methods.* Denver, CO: Love.

DeSpelder, L. A., & Strickland, A. L. (1992). *The last dance: Encountering death and dying* (3rd ed.). Mountain View, CA: Mayfield.

DiCarlo, V. (n.d.). *How to attack and defend expert witnesses.* Retrieved from http://www.dicarlolaw.com/ExpertWitnesses.html

Dixon, R. (2006). A framework for managing bullying that involves students. *Deafness and Education International, 8*(1), 11–32. doi:10.1002/dei.16

Dixon, R., & Smith, P. (2011). *Rethinking school bullying: Towards an integrated model.* New York, NY: Cambridge University Press.

D.J.M. v. Hannibal Public School District, 647 F. 3d 754 (2011).

Drew, N. (2010). *No kidding about bullying: 125 ready-to-use activities to help kids manage anger, resolve conflicts, build empathy, and get along.* Minneapolis, MN: Free Spirit Publishing.

Due, P., Merlo, J., Harel-Fisch, Y., Damsgaard, M. T., Holstein, B. E., Hetland, J., Currie, C., Gabhainn, S. N., de Matos, M. G., & Lynch, J. (2009). Socioeconomic inequality in exposure to bullying during adolescence: A comparative, cross-sectional, multilevel study in 35 countries. *American Journal of Public Health, 99*(5), 907–914. doi:10.2105/AJPH.2008.139303

Duncan, A. (2010, August). *The myths about bullying.* Remarks presented at the Federal Partners in Bullying Prevention Summit, Washington, DC. Retrieved from http://www.ed.gov/news/speeches/myths-about-bullying-secretary-arne-duncans-remarks-bullying-prevention-summit

Dunn, R., & Dunn, K. (1977). *How to raise independent and professionally successful daughters.* Englewood Cliffs, NJ: Prentice Hall.

DuPaul, G. J., Ervin, R. A., Hook, C. L., & McGoey, K. E. (1998). Peer tutoring for children with attention deficit hyperactivity disorder: Effects on classroom behavior and academic performance. *Journal of Applied Behavior Analysis, 31*(4), 579–592.

DuPaul, G. J., & Hennington, P. N. (1993). Peer tutoring effects on the classroom performance of children with ADHD. *School Psychology Review, 22*(1), 134–143.

DuPaul, G. J., & Stoner, G. (2003). *ADHD in the schools* (2nd ed.). New York, NY: Guilford.

Emslie, H., Wilson, F. C., Burden, V., Nimmo-Smith, I., & Wilson, B. A. (2003). *Behavioural Assessment of the Dysexecutive Syndrome in Children (BADS–C).* San Antonio, TX: Pearson.

Eslinger, P. J., & Biddle, K. R. (2008). Prefrontal cortex and the maturation of executive functions, cognitive expertise, and social adaptation. In V. Anderson, R. Jacobs, & P. J. Anderson (Eds.), *Executive functions and the frontal lobes: A lifespan perspective* (pp. 299–316). Philadelphia, PA: Taylor & Francis.

Espelage, D. L., & Swearer, S. M. (2009). Contributions of three social theories to understanding bullying perpetration and victimization among school-aged youth. In M. J. Harris (Ed.), *Bullying, rejection, and peer victimization: A social cognitive neuroscience perspective* (pp. 151–170). New York, NY: Springer.

Espy, K. A. (1997). The Shape School: Assessing executive function in preschool children. *Developmental Neuropsychology, 13*(4), 495–499.

Espy, K. A., Bull, R., Kaiser, H., Martin, J., & Banet, M. (2008). Methodological and conceptual issues in understanding the development of executive control in the preschool period. In V. Anderson, R. Jacobs, & P. J. Anderson (Eds.), *Executive functions and the frontal lobes: A lifespan perspective* (pp. 105–121). Philadelphia, PA: Taylor & Francis.

Espy, K. A., Kaufman, P. M., McDiarmid, M. D., & Glisky, M. L. (1999). Executive functioning in preschool children: Performance on A-Not-B and other delayed response format tasks. *Brain and Cognition, 41*(2), 178–199.

Farnan, N., & Kelly, P. (1991). Keeping track: Creating assessment portfolios in reading and writing. *Journal of Reading, Writing, and Learning Disabilities International, 7*(3), 255–269. doi:10.1080/0748763910070308

Farrington, D. P., & Ttofi, M. M. (2009). *School-based programs to reduce bullying and victimization.* Submitted to the U.S. Department of Justice for publication. Retrieved from http://www.ncjrs.gov/pdffiles1/nij/grants/229377.pdf

Ferholt, J. D. L. (1980). *Clinical assessment of children: A comprehensive approach to primary pediatric care.* Philadelphia, PA: Lippincott.

Filipek, P. A., Accardo, P. J., Baranek, G. T., Cook, E. H., Jr., Dawson, G., Gordon, B., Gravel, J. S., Johnson, C. P., Kallen, R. J., Levy, S. R., Minshew, N. J., Prizant, B. M., Rapin, I., Rogers, S. J., Stone, W. L., Teplin, S., Tuchman, R. F., & Volkmar, F. R. (1999). The screening and diagnosis of autistic spectrum disorders. *Journal of Autism and Developmental Disorders, 29*(6), 439–484.

Finkelhor, D., Mitchell, K. J., & Wolak, J. (2000). *Online victimization: A report on the nation's youth.* Alexandria, VA: National Center for Missing & Exploited Children. Retrieved from http://www.unh.edu/ccrc/pdf/jvq/CV38.pdf

Finkelhor, D., Turner, H., Hamby, S., & Ormrod, R. (2011). *Polyvictimization: Children's exposure to multiple types of violence, crime, and abuse*. Retrieved from https://www.ncjrs.gov/pdffiles1/ojjdp/235504.pdf

Fischer, K. W., & Daley, S. G. (2007). Connecting cognitive science and neuroscience to education. In L. Meltzer (Ed.), *Executive function in education: From theory to practice* (pp. 55–72). New York, NY: Guilford.

Florida Department of Education. (2005). *Accommodations and modifications for students with disabilities in career education and adult general education*. Retrieved from http://cpt.fsu.edu/ESE/pdf/k12_05-59a.pdf

Floyd, R. G., Bergeron, R., Hamilton, G., & Parra, G. R. (2010). How do executive functions fit with the Cattell-Horn-Carroll model? Some evidence from a joint factor analysis of the Delis-Kaplan Executive Function System and the Woodcock-Johnson III Tests of Cognitive Abilities. *Psychology in the Schools, 47*(7), 721–738. doi:10.1002/pits.20500

Ford, B. G., & Ford, R. D. (1981). Identifying creative potential in handicapped children. *Exceptional Children, 48*(2), 115–122.

Freebody, P., & Byrne, B. (1988). Word-reading strategies in elementary school children: Relations to comprehension, reading time, and phonemic awareness. *Reading Research Quarterly, 23*(4), 441–453.

Freedman, M. I., Leach, L., Kaplan, E., Winocur, G., Shulman, K. J., & Delis, D. C. (1994). *Clock Drawing: A neuropsychological analysis*. New York, NY: Oxford University Press.

Fremouw, W. J., De Perczel, M., & Ellis, T. E. (1990). *Suicide risk: Assessment and response guidelines*. Elmsford, NY: Pergamon.

Friedman, N. P., Miyake, A., Corley, R. P., Young, S. E., DeFries, J. C., & Hewitt, J. K. (2006). Not all executive functions are related to intelligence. *Psychological Science, 17*(2), 172–179. doi:10.1111/j.1467-9280.2006.01681.x

Frye v. United States, 293 F. 1013 (D.C., Cir. 1923).

Gathercole, S. E., & Adams, A. (1993). Phonological working memory in very young children. *Developmental Psychology, 29*(4), 770–778.

Geary, D. C. (2004). Mathematics and learning disabilities. *Journal of Learning Disabilities, 37*(1), 4–15. doi:10.1177/00222194040370010201

Georgiou, S. (2008). Bullying and victimization at school: The role of mothers. *British Journal of Educational Psychology, 78*(Pt. 1), 109–125.

Gilandas, A., Touyz, S., Beumont, P. J. V., & Greenberg, H. P. (1984). *Handbook of neuropsychological assessment*. New York, NY: Grune & Stratton.

Gini, G., Pozzoli, T., Borghi, F., & Franzoni, L. (2008). The role of bystanders in students' perception of bullying and sense of safety. *Journal of School Psychology, 46*(6), 617–638. doi:10.1016/j.jsp.2008.02.001

Gioia, G. A., Espy, K. A., & Isquith, P. K. (2003). *Behavior Rating Inventory of Executive Function–Preschool Version (BRIEF–P)*. Odessa, FL: Psychological Assessment Resources.

Gioia, G. A., Isquith, P. K., Guy, S. C., & Kenworthy, L. (2000). *Behavior Rating Inventory of Executive Function (BRIEF)*. Odessa, FL: Psychological Assessment Resources.

Gioia, G. A., Isquith, P. K., & Kenealy, L. E. (2008). Assessment of behavioral aspects of executive function. In V. Anderson, R. Jacobs, & P. J. Anderson (Eds.), *Executive functions and the frontal lobes: A lifespan perspective* (pp. 179–202). Philadelphia, PA: Taylor & Francis.

Giordano, G. (1987). Diagnosing specific math disabilities. *Academic Therapy, 23*(1), 69–74.

Golden, C. J., Freshwater, S. M., & Golden, Z. (2003). *Stroop Color and Word Test—Revised, Children's Version*. Wooddale, IL: Stoelting.

Golden, C. J., & Hines, L. J. (2011). Assessment of executive functions in a pediatric population. In A. S. Davis (Ed.), *Handbook of pediatric neuropsychology* (pp. 261–273). New York, NY: Springer.

Gordon, M. (1988). *The Gordon Diagnostic System*. Dewitt, NY: Gordon Systems.

Gouvier, W. D., Cubic, B., Jones, G., Brantley, P., & Cutlip, Q. (1992). Post-concussion symptoms and daily stress in normal and head-injured college populations. *Archives of Clinical Neuropsychology, 7*(3), 193–211. doi:10.1016/0887-6177(92)90162-G

Grandin, T. (2002). *Teaching tips for children and adults with autism*. Retrieved from http://www.autism.org/temple/tips.html

Green, S. E. (2010). *Don't pick on me: Help for kids to stand up to and deal with bullies*. Oakland, CA: Instant Help Books.

Guerra, N. G., Williams, K. R., & Sadek, S. (2011). Understanding bullying and victimization during childhood and adolescence: A mixed methods study. *Child Development, 82*(1), 295–310. doi:10.1111/j.1467-8624.2010.01556.x

Guralnick, M. J., & Groom, J. M. (1988). Friendships of preschool children in mainstreamed playgroups. *Developmental Psychology, 24*(4), 595–604.

Gusinger, P. (2009). *Self-monitoring*. Columbus, OH: Ohio Resource Center for Mathematics, Science, and Reading. Retrieved from http://ohiorc.org/adlit/strategy/strategy_each.aspx?id=000010

Gutheil, T. G., & Dattilio, F. M. (2008). *Practical approaches to forensic mental health testimony*. Philadelphia, PA: Lippincott Williams and Wilkins.

Guy, S. C., Isquith, P. K., & Gioia, G. A. (2004). *Behavior Rating Inventory of Executive Function–Self-Report Version (BRIEF–SR)*. Lutz, FL: Psychological Assessment Resources.

Haag-Granello, D., & Granello, P. F. (2007). *Suicide: An essential guide for helping professionals and educators*. Boston, MA: Pearson.

Hallahan, D. P., & Mercer, C. D. (2002). Learning disabilities: Historical perspective. In R. Bradley, L. Danielson, & D. P. Hallahan (Eds.), *Identification of learning disabilities: Research to practice* (pp. 1–67). Mahwah, NJ: Erlbaum.

Heaton, R., Chelune, G., Talley, J., Kay, G., & Curtiss, G. (1993). *Wisconsin Card Sorting Test manual: Revised and expanded*. Odessa, FL: Psychological Assessment Resources.

Heikkilä, H., Väänänen, J., Helminen, M., Fröjd, S., Marttunen, M., & Kaltiala-Heino, R. (2013). Involvement in bullying and suicidal ideation in middle adolescence: A 2-year follow-up study. *European Child & Adolescent Psychiatry, 22*(2), 95–102. doi:10.1007/s00787-012-0327-0

Hinduja, S., & Patchin, J. W. (2011). *State cyberbullying laws: A brief review of state cyberbullying laws and policies*. Retrieved from http://www.cyberbullying.us/Bullying_and_Cyberbullying_Laws.pdf

Horne, A. M., Orpinas, P., Newman-Carlson, D., & Bartolomucci, C. L. (2004). Elementary school bully busters program: Understanding why children bully and what to do about it. In D. L. Espelage & S. M. Swearer (Eds.), *Bullying in American schools: A social-ecological perspective on prevention and intervention* (pp. 297–325). Mahwah, NJ: Erlbaum.

Howard, K., Anderson, P. J., & Taylor, H. G. (2008). Executive functioning and attention in children born preterm. In V. Anderson, R. Jacobs, & P. J. Anderson (Eds.), *Executive functions and the frontal lobes: A lifespan perspective* (pp. 219–241). Philadelphia, PA: Taylor & Francis.

Howard, M. E. (1988). Behavior management in the acute care rehabilitation setting. *Journal of Head Trauma Rehabilitation, 3*(3), 14–22.

Huffcutt, A. I., Goebl, A. P., & Culbertson, S. S. (2012). The engine is important, but the driver is essential: The case for executive functioning. *Industrial and Organizational Psychology: Perspectives on Science and Practice, 5*(2), 183–186. doi:10.1111/j.1754-9434.2012.01428.x

Hylton, H. (2008, October 14). *Which kids are most vulnerable to bullying?* Retrieved from http://www.time.com/time/health/article/0,8599,1850405.00.html

i-SAFE inc. (2010). *i-SAFE internet safety activities: Reproducible projects for teachers and parents*. Hoboken, NJ: Wiley.

Isquith, P. K., Roth, R. M., & Gioia, G. (2013). Contribution of rating scales to the assessment of executive functions. *Applied Neuropsychology: Child, 2*(2), 125–132. doi:10.1080/21622965.2013.748389

Ives, M., & Munro, N. (2001). *Caring for a child with autism: A practical guide for parents*. London, England: Jessica Kingsley.

J.C. v. Beverly Hills Unified School District et al., CV 08-03824 SVW (CWx) (2009).

Jiang, D., Walsh, M., & Augimeri, L. K. (2011). The linkage between childhood bullying behaviour and future offending. *Criminal Behaviour and Mental Health, 21*(2), 128–135. doi:10.1002/cbm.803

J.L. v. Mohawk Central School District et al., No. 09-CV-943-DNH-DEP (N.D. NY., Amended Complaint, 2010a).

J.L. v. Mohawk Central School District et al., No. 09-CV-943-DNH-DEP (N.D. NY., Stipulation and Settlement Agreement, 2010b).

Johnson, D. J. (2000). *Helping young children with learning disabilities at home*. Retrieved from http://www.ldonline.org/article/Helping_Young_Children_with_Learning_Disabilities_at_Home

Johnson, J. A. (n.d.). *Students with Aspergers syndrome: Tips for teachers and parents*. Retrieved from http://hubpages.com/hub/Students-with-Aspergers-Syndrome-Tips-for-Teachers-and-Parents

Jones, L. M., Doces, M., Swearer, S., & Collier, A. (2012). *Implementing bullying prevention programs in schools: A how-to guide*. Retrieved from http://cyber.law.harvard.edu/sites/cyber.law.harvard.edu/files/ImplementingBullyingPrevention.pdf

Jones, L. M., Mitchell, K. J., & Finkelhor, D. (2013). Online harassment in context: Trends from three Youth Internet Safety Surveys (2000, 2005, 2010). *Psychology of Violence, 3*(1), 53–69. doi:10.1037/a0030309

Jones, S. (2009). *Generations online in 2009*. Retrieved from http://pewresearch.org/pubs/1093/generations-online

Kagan, J., Rosman, B. L., Day, D., Albert, J., & Phillips, W. (1964). Information processing in the child: Significance of analytical and reflective attitudes. *Psychological Monographs, 78*(1), 1–37.

Kansas State Department of Education. (n.d.). *Definitions/characteristics of bullying*. Retrieved from http://www.education.com/print/definitions-characteristics-bullying

Kaplan, E., Fein, D., Kramer, J., Delis, D., & Morris, R. (2004). *Wechsler Intelligence Scale for Children–Fourth Edition, Integrated (WISC–IV Integrated)*. San Antonio, TX: The Psychological Corporation.

Kaufman, A. S., & Kaufman, N. L. (2004). *Kaufman Assessment Battery for Children, Second Edition (KABC–II)*. San Antonio, TX: Pearson.

Kavale, K. A., & Forness, S. R. (1996). Social skill deficits and learning disabilities: A meta-analysis. *Journal of Learning Disabilities, 29*(3), 226–237. doi:10.1177/002221949602900301

Keith, R. (1994). *The Auditory Continuous Performance Test*. San Antonio, TX: The Psychological Corporation.

Keith, R. W. (2009). *SCAN–3 Tests for Auditory Processing Disorders for Children (SCAN–3:C)*. San Antonio, TX: Pearson.

Khan, N. A., & Hoge, R. D. (1983). A teacher-judgment measure of social competence: Validity data. *Journal of Consulting and Clinical Psychology, 51*(6), 809–814.

Kim, M. J., Catalano, R. F., Haggerty, K. P., & Abbott, R. D. (2011). Bullying at elementary school and problem behaviour in young adulthood: A study of bullying, violence and substance use from age 11 to age 21. *Criminal Behaviour and Mental Health, 21*(2), 136–144. doi:10.1002/cbm.804

King, N. S. (1996). Emotional, neuropsychological, and organic factors: Their use in the prediction of persisting postconcussion symptoms after mild head injuries. *Journal of Neurology, Neurosurgery, and Psychiatry, 61*(1), 75–81.

Kinston, W., & Loader, P. (1984). Eliciting whole-family interaction with a standardized clinical interview. *Journal of Family Therapy, 6*(3), 347–363. doi:10.1046/j.1467-6427.1984.00655.x

Knight, J. R., Shrier, L. A., Bravender, T. D., Farrell, M., Vander Bilt, J., & Shaffer, H. J. (1999). A new brief screen for adolescent substance abuse. *Archives of Pediatrics and Adolescent Medicine, 153*(6), 591–596.

Kochenderfer-Ladd, B., & Ladd, G. W. (2010). A child-by-environment framework for planning interventions with children involved in bullying. In E. M. Vernberg & B. K. Biggs (Eds.), *Preventing and treating bullying and victimization* (pp. 45–74). New York, NY: Oxford University Press.

Korkman, M., Kirk, U., & Kemp, S. (2007). *NEPSY–II: Clinical and interpretive manual*. San Antonio, TX: The Psychological Corporation.

Kottmeyer, W. (1959). *Teacher's guide for remedial reading*. St. Louis, MO: Webster.

Kowalski v. Berkeley County Schools, 652 F.3d 565 (2011).

Kowalski, R. M., & Limber, S. P. (2007). Electronic bullying among middle school students. *Journal of Adolescent Health, 41*, S22–S30. doi:10.1016/j.jadohealth.2007.08.017

Koziol, L. F., & Lutz, J. T. (2013). From movement to thought: The development of executive function. *Applied Neuropsychology: Child, 2*(2), 104–115. doi:10.1080/21622965.2013.748386

Lacey, A., & Cornell, D. (2011). *The impact of bullying climate on schoolwide academic performance*. Retrieved from http://curry.virginia.edu/uploads/resourceLibrary/8-11_Lacey_The_Impact_of_Bullying_Climate_-_APA_2011_Poster.pdf

Lee, M., Vaughn, B. E., & Kopp, C. B. (1983). Role of self-control in the performance of very young children on a delayed-response memory-for-location task. *Developmental Psychology, 19*(1), 40–44. doi:10.1037/0012-1649.19.1.40

Leff, S. S., Thomas, D. E., Shapiro, E. S., Paskewich, B., Wilson, K., Necowitz-Hoffman, B., & Jawad, A. F. (2011). Developing and validating a new classroom climate observation assessment tool. *Journal of School Violence, 10*(2), 165–184. doi:10.1080/15388220.2010.539167

Lerner, J. W. (1997). Attention deficit disorder. In J. W. Lloyd, D. J. Kameenui, & D. Chard (Eds.), *Issues in educating students with disabilities* (pp. 27–44). Mahwah, NJ: Erlbaum.

Lerner, J. W. (2003). *Learning disabilities: Theories, diagnosis, and teaching strategies*. Boston, MA: Houghton Mifflin.

Lichtenstein, R., & Ireton, H. (1984). *Preschool screening: Identifying young children with developmental and educational problems.* Orlando, FL: Grune & Stratton.

Limber, S. P., Kowalski, R. M., & Agatston, P. W. (2009a). *Cyber bullying: A prevention curriculum for grades 3–5.* Center City, MN: Hazelden Publishing & Educational Services.

Limber, S. P., Kowalski, R. M., & Agatston, P. W. (2009b). *Cyber bullying: A prevention curriculum for grades 6–12.* Center City, MN: Hazelden Publishing & Educational Services.

Lindsay, G., Dockrell, J. E., & Mackie, C. (2008). Vulnerability to bullying in children with a history of specific speech and language difficulties. *European Journal of Special Needs Education, 23*(1), 1–16. doi:10.1080/08856250701791203

Liptak, J. J., & Leutenberg, E. A. (2011). *Teen aggression & bullying workbook: Facilitator reproducible self-assessments, exercises, and educational handouts.* Duluth, MN: Whole Person.

Lohmann, R. C., & Taylor, J. V. (2013). *The bullying workbook for teens: Activities to help you deal with social aggression and cyberbullying.* Oakland, CA: Instant Help Books.

Luciano, S., & Savage, R. S. (2007). Bullying risk in children with learning difficulties in inclusive educational settings. *Canadian Journal of School Psychology, 22*(1), 14–31. doi:10.1177/0829573507301039

Luria, A. R. (1980). *Higher cortical functions in man.* New York, NY: Basic Books.

Maehler, C., & Schuchardt, K. (2011). Working memory in children with learning disabilities: Rethinking the criterion of discrepancy. *International Journal of Disability, Development and Education, 58*(1), 5–17. doi:10.1080/1034912X.2011.547335

Manly, T., Robertson, I. H., Anderson, V., & Nimmo-Smith, I. (1998). *Test of Everyday Attention for Children (TEA–Ch).* San Antonio, TX: Pearson.

Maricle, D. E., Johnson, W., & Avirett, E. (2010). Assessing and intervening in children with executive function disorders. In D. C. Miller (Ed.), *Best practices in school neuropsychology: Guidelines for effective practice, assessment, and evidence-based intervention* (pp. 599–640). Hoboken, NJ: Wiley.

Martin, D. A. (1988). Children and adolescents with traumatic brain injury: Impact on the family. *Journal of Learning Disabilities, 21*(8), 464–470. doi:10.1177/002221948802100803

Massachusetts General Hospital. (2006a). *Anxiety (generalized anxiety disorder).* Retrieved from http://www2.massgeneral.org/schoolpsychiatry/info_anxiety.asp

Massachusetts Medical Society. (2001). *Bullying—It's not O.K.* Retrieved from http://www.massmed.org/AM/Template.cfm?Section=Home&TEMPLATE=/CM/HTMLDisplay.cfm&CONTENTID=7365

Masten, A. S. (1994). Resilience in individual development: Successful adaptation despite risk and adversity. In M. C. Wang & E. W. Gordon (Eds.), *Educational resilience in inner-city America* (pp. 3–25). Hillsdale, NJ: Erlbaum.

Mather, N., & Gregg, N. (2003). "I can rite": Informal assessment of written language. In S. Vaughn & K. L. Briggs (Eds.), *Reading in the classroom: Systems for the observation of teaching and learning* (pp. 179–220). Baltimore, MD: Brookes.

Mazzocco, M. M. M., Feigenson, L., & Halberda, J. (2011). Impaired acuity of the approximate number system underlies mathematical learning disability (dyscalculia). *Child Development, 82*(4), 1224–1237. doi:10.1111/j.1467-8624.2011.01608.x

McClellan, D. E., & Katz, L. G. (2001). *Assessing young children's social competence.* Retrieved from http://ceep.crc.uiuc.edu/eecearchive/digests/2001/mcclel01.pdf

McMahon, R. J., & Forehand, R. (1988). Conduct disorders. In E. J. Mash & L. G. Terdal (Eds.), *Behavioral assessment of childhood disorders* (2nd ed., pp. 105–153). New York, NY: Guilford.

Melton, G. B. (1994). Doing justice and doing good: Conflicts for mental health professionals. *The Future of Children, 4*(2), 102–118.

Meltzer, L., & Krishnan, K. (2007). Executive function difficulties and learning disabilities. In L. Meltzer (Ed.), *Executive function in education: From theory to practice* (pp. 77–105). New York, NY: Guilford.

Mesibov, G. B., Shea, V., & Adams, L. W. (2001). *Understanding Asperger syndrome and high functioning autism.* Norwell, MA: Kluwer Plenum.

Meyers, J. E., & Meyers, K. R. (1995). *Rey Complex Figure Test and Recognition Trial (RCFT).* Lutz, FL: Psychological Assessment Resources.

Meyers, R. E. (2006). *Respect matters: Real life scenarios provide powerful discussion starters for all aspects of respect.* Tucson, AZ: Good Year Books.

Michigan Association of Secondary School Principals. (2008). *Risk Assessment Checklist.* Retrieved from http://mymassp.com/files/Risk%20Assessment%20Checklist.pdf

Muscara, F., Catroppa, C., & Anderson, V. (2008). The impact of injury severity on executive function 7–10 years following pediatric traumatic brain injury. *Developmental Neuropsychology, 33*(5), 623–636. doi:10.1080/87565640802171162

Musgrove, M., & Yudin, M. K. (2013, August 20). [Dear Colleague Letter]. U.S. Department of Education, Office of Special Education and Rehabilitation Service. Retrieved from http://www2.ed.gov/policy/speced/guid/idea/memosdcltrs/bullyingdcl-8-20-13.pdf

Myers, J. B. (2009). Expert psychological testimony in child sexual abuse trials. In B. L. Bottoms, C. J. Najdowski, & G. S. Goodman (Eds.), *Children as victims, witnesses, and offenders: The psychological science and the law* (pp. 167–187). New York, NY: Guilford.

Myles, B. S. (2005). *Children and youth with Asperger syndrome: Strategies for success in inclusive settings.* Thousand Oaks, CA: Corwin Press.

Naglieri, J. A., & Goldstein, S. (2013). *Comprehensive Executive Function Inventory.* North Tonawanda, NY: Multi-Health System.

National Crime Prevention Council. (n.d.). *Stop cyberbullying before it starts.* Retrieved from http://www.ncpc.org/resources/files/pdf/bullying/cyberbullying.pdf

National Dissemination Center for Children with Disabilities. (2010). *Autism spectrum disorders.* Retrieved from http://nichcy.org/wp-content/uploads/docs/fs1.pdf

National Dissemination Center for Children with Disabilities. (2011a). *Intellectual disability.* Retrieved from http://nichcy.org/wp-content/uploads/docs/fs8.pdf

National Dissemination Center for Children with Disabilities. (2011b). *Learning disabilities (LD).* Retrieved from http://nichcy.org/wp-content/uploads/docs/fs7.pdf

National Dissemination Center for Children with Disabilities. (2012a). *Attention-deficit/hyperactivity disorder (AD/HD).* Retrieved from http://nichcy.org/wp-content/uploads/docs/fs19.pdf

National Dissemination Center for Children with Disabilities. (2012b). *Traumatic brain injury.* Retrieved from http://nichcy.org/wp-content/uploads/docs/fs18.pdf

National Institutes of Health and Northwestern University. (2012). *NIH Toolbox: For the assessment of neurological and behavioral function.* Retrieved from http://www.nihtoolbox.org/Pages/default.aspx

National Society for the Gifted and Talented. (n.d.). *Giftedness defined–What is gifted & talented?* Retrieved from http://www.nsgt.org/articles/index/asp

NCLD Editorial Staff. (2010). *What is executive function?* Retrieved from http://www.ncld.org/ld-basics/ld-aamp-executive-functioning/basic-ef-facts/what-is-executive-function

Neufeld, K. (2004). *10 tips for helping your child fall asleep.* Retrieved from http://www.parents.com/kids/sleep/10-tips-for-helping-your-child-fall-asleep

Nyhus, E., & Barcelo, F. (2009). The Wisconsin Card Sorting Test and the cognitive assessment of prefrontal executive functions: A critical update. *Brain and Cognition, 71*(3), 437–451. doi:10.1016/j.bandc.2009.03.005

Olweus, D. (1993). *Bullying at school: What we know and what we can do.* Cambridge, MA: Blackwell Publishers.

Olweus, D. (2011). Bullying at school and later criminality: Findings from three Swedish community samples of males. *Criminal Behaviour and Mental Health, 21*(2), 151–156. doi:10.1002/cbm.806

OnGuard Online. (2009). *Net cetera: Chatting with kids about being online.* Retrieved from http://www.onguardonline.gov/pdf/tec04.pdf

Oregon Social Learning Center. (1992). *Lift Observer Impressions–Playground Code.* Retrieved from http://www.oslc.org/resources/codemanuals/playgroundobsimp.pdf

Orpinas, P., & Horne, A. M. (2006). *Bullying prevention: Creating a positive school climate and developing social competence.* Washington, DC: American Psychological Association.

O'Toole, M. E. (2000). *The school shooter: A threat assessment perspective.* Retrieved August 24, 2002, from http://www.fbi.gov/publications/school/school2.pdf

Özdemir, M., & Stattin, H. (2011). Bullies, victims, and bully-victims: A longitudinal examination of the effects of bullying-victimization experiences on youth well-being. *Journal of Aggression, Conflict, and Peace Research, 3*(2), 97–102. doi:10.1108/17596591111132918

Ozonoff, S., & Schetter, P. L. (2007). Executive dysfunction in autism spectrum disorders: From research to practice. In L. Meltzer (Ed.), *Executive function in education: From theory to practice* (pp. 133–163). New York, NY: Guilford.

Packer, L. E. (2002). *Accommodating students with mood lability: Depression and bipolar disorder.* Retrieved from http://www.schoolbehavior.com/Files/tips_mood.pdf

Peters, S. J., & Gates, J. C. (2010). The teacher observation form: Revisions and updates. *Gifted Child Quarterly, 54*(3), 179–188. doi:10.1177/0016986210369258

Pfeffer, C. R. (1986). *The suicidal child.* New York, NY: Guilford.

Phares, V., & Renk, K. (1998). Perceptions of parents: A measure of adolescents' feelings about their parents. *Journal of Marriage and the Family, 60*(3), 646–659.

Polanin, J. R., Espelage, D. L., & Pigott, T. D. (2012). A meta-analysis of school-based bullying prevention programs' effects on bystander intervention behavior. *School Psychology Review, 41*(1), 47–65.

Pope, K. S., Butcher, J. N., & Seelen, J. (1993). *The MMPI, MMPI–2, and MMPI–A in court: Assessment, testimony, and cross-examination for expert witnesses and attorneys.* Washington, DC: American Psychological Association.

Porter, S. E. (2013, March 15). Overusing the bully label. *The Los Angeles Times,* p. A19.

Potter, J. L., Wade, S. L., Walz, N. C., Cassedy, A., Stevens, M., Yeates, K. O., & Taylor, H. (2011). Parenting style is related to

executive dysfunction after brain injury in children. *Rehabilitation Psychology, 56*(4), 351–358. doi:10.1037/a0025445

Pownall-Gray, D. (2006). *Surviving bullies workbook: Skills to help protect you from bullying.* Weston, CT: Willoughby & Lamont Publications.

Presley, I., & D'Andrea, F. M. (2008). *Assistive technology for students who are blind or visually impaired: A guide to assessment.* New York, NY: AFB Press.

Prevent Child Abuse America. (n.d.). *Recognizing child abuse: What parents should know.* Retrieved from http://www.preventchildabuse.org/publications/parents/downloads/recognizing_abuse.pdf

PREVNet. (n.d.). *Bullying: Facts and myths.* Retrieved from http://prevnet.ca/Bullying/FactsandMyths/tabid/121/Default.aspx

Prigatano, G. P., Fordyce, D. J., Zeiner, H. K., Roueche, J. R., Pepping, M., & Wood, B. C. (1986). *Neuropsychological rehabilitation after brain injury.* Baltimore, MD: Johns Hopkins University Press.

Purdue University, School of Education. (2002). *Student Teacher Observation Form.* Retrieved from http://www.edci.purdue.edu/gunstra/496/evaluation/observation/downloads/evalform.xls

Quiroz, H. C., Arnette, J. L., & Stephens, R. D. (2006). *Bullying in schools: Fighting the bully battle.* Retrieved from http://www.dps.mo.gov/homelandsecurity/safeschools/documents/Discussion%20Activities%20for%20School%20Communities.pdf

Randall, K., & Bowen, A. A. (2008). *Mean girls: 101½ creative strategies and activities for reducing relational aggression.* Chapin, SC: Youthlight, Inc.

Raskauskas, J., & Stoltz, A. D. (2007). Involvement in traditional and electronic bullying among adolescents. *Developmental Psychology, 43*(3), 564–575. doi:10.1037/0012-1649.43.3.564

Renda, J., Vassallo, S., & Edwards, B. (2011). Bullying in early adolescence and its association with anti-social behaviour, criminality and violence 6 and 10 years later. *Criminal Behaviour and Mental Health, 21*(2), 117–127. doi:10.1002/cbm.805

Rey, A. (1941). L'examen psychologique dans les cas d'encephalopathie traumatique [Psychological examination of traumatic encephalopathy]. *Archives de Psychologie, 29,* 286–340.

Reynolds, C. R. (2002). *Comprehensive Trail Making Test.* Austin, TX: Pro-Ed.

Reynolds, C. R. (2007). *Koppitz–2: Koppitz Developmental Scoring System for the Bender Gestalt Test, Second Edition.* Austin, TX: Pro-Ed.

Riccio, C. A., & Gomes, H. (2013). Interventions for executive function deficit in children and adolescents. *Applied Neuropsychology: Child, 2*(2), 133–140. doi:10.1080/21622965.2013.748383

Rich, D., & Taylor, H. G. (1993). Attention deficit hyperactivity disorder. In M. Singer, L. Singer, & T. Anglin (Eds.), *Handbook for screening adolescents at psychosocial risk* (pp. 333–374). New York, NY: Lexington Books.

Richards, M. (2006). *I didn't know I was a bully.* Champaign, IL: Research Press.

Rief, S. F. (1993). *How to reach and teach ADD/ADHD children.* San Francisco, CA: Jossey-Bass.

Rief, S. F. (2003). *The ADHD book of lists.* San Francisco, CA: Jossey-Bass.

Rigby, K. (2008). *Children and bullying: How parents and educators can reduce bullying at school.* Malden, MA: Blackwell.

Rivers, I., Duncan, N., & Besag, V. E. (2007). *Bullying: A handbook for educators and parents.* Westport, CT: Greenwood/Praeger.

Rivers, I., Poteat, V. P., Noret, N., & Ashurst, N. (2009). Observing bullying at school: The mental health implications of witness status. *School Psychology Quarterly, 24*(4), 211–223. doi:10.1037/a0018164

Roberts, M. A. (1999). Mild traumatic brain injury in children and adolescents. In W. R. Varney & R. J. Roberts (Eds.), *Mild head injury: Causes, evaluation, and treatment* (pp. 493–512). Hillsdale, NJ: Erlbaum.

Roberts, M. A., Milich, R., & Loney, J. (1984). *Structured Observation of Academic and Play Settings (SOAPS)*. Unpublished manuscript, University of Iowa at Iowa City.

Robins, D., Fein, D., Barton, M., & Green, J. (2001). The Modified Checklist for Autism in Toddlers (M-CHAT): An initial study investigating the early detection of autism and pervasive developmental disorders. *Journal of Autism and Developmental Disorders, 31*(2), 131–144.

Robins, L. N., & Marcus, S. C. (1987). The Diagnostic Screening Procedure Writer: A tool to develop individualized screening procedures. *Medical Care, 25*(12), S106–S122.

Robinson, C. C., Mandleco, B., Olsen, S. F., & Hart, C. H. (1995). Authoritative, authoritarian, and permissive parenting practices: Development of a new measure. *Psychological Reports, 77*(3 Pt 1), 819–830. doi:10.2466/pr0.1995.77.3.819

Robinson, S., Goddard, L., Dritschel, B., Wisley, M., & Howlin, P. (2009). Executive functions in children with autism spectrum disorders. *Brain and Cognition, 71*(3), 362–368. doi:10.1016/j.bandc.2009.06.007

Roedell, W. C. (1980b). Programs for gifted young children. In W. C. Roedell, N. E. Jackson, & H. B. Robinson (Eds.), *Gifted young children* (pp. 66–89). New York, NY: Teachers College Press.

Roffman, R. A., & George, W. H. (1988). Cannabis abuse. In D. M. Donovan & G. A. Marlatt (Eds.), *Assessment of addictive behaviors* (pp. 325–363). New York, NY: Guilford.

Rosner, J., & Simon, D. P. (1971). The Auditory Analysis Test: An initial report. *Journal of Learning Disabilities, 4*(7), 384–392. doi:10.1177/002221947100400706

Ross, S., Horner, R., & Stiller, B. (n.d.). *Bullying prevention in positive behavior support*. Retrieved from http://www.pbis.org/common/pbisresources/publications/bullyprevention_ES.pdf

Rothbart, M. K., Ahadi, S. A., Hersey, K. L., & Fisher, P. (2001). Investigations of temperament at three to seven years: The Children's Behavior Questionnaire. *Child Development, 72*(5), 1394–1408. doi:10.1111/1467-8624.00355

Sainio, M., Veenstra, R., Huitsing, G., & Salmivalli, C. (2011). Victims and their defenders: A dyadic approach. *International Journal of Behavioral Development, 35*(2), 144–151. doi:10.1177/0165025410378068

Sampson, R. (2009). *Bullying in schools*. Retrieved from http://www.cops.usdoj.gov/files/RIC/Publications/e07063414-guide.pdf

San Jose Area Bilingual Consortium. (n.d.). *Student Oral Language Observation Matrix (SOLOM)*. Retrieved from http://www.cal.org/twi/evaltoolkit/appendix/solom.pdf

Saskatchewan Education. (1999). *Teaching students with autism: A guide for educators, 1999*. Retrieved from http://www.education.gov.sk.ca/ASD

Schibsted, E. (2009). *How to develop positive classroom management*. Retrieved from http://www.edutopia.org/classroom-management-relationships-strategies-tips

Schreibman, L. E. (1988). *Autism*. Newbury Park, CA: Sage.

Schwartz, D., Kelly, B. M., Duong, M. T., & Badaly, D. (2010). A contextual perspective on intervention and prevention efforts for bully-victim problems. In E. M. Vernberg & B. K. Biggs (Eds.), *Preventing and treating bullying and victimization* (pp. 17–44). New York, NY: Oxford University Press.

Scruggs, T. E., & Mastropieri, M. A. (1992). Effective mainstreaming strategies for mildly handicapped students. *Elementary School Journal, 92*(3), 389–409.

Seligman, M., & Darling, R. B. (1989). *Ordinary families, special children: A systems approach to childhood disability*. New York, NY: Guilford.

Senn, D. (2007). *Bullying in the girl's world: A school-wide approach to girl bullying*. Chapin, SC: Youthlight, Inc.

Sesma, H. W., Slomine, B. S., Ding, R., & McCarthy, M. L. (2008). Executive functioning in the first year after pediatric traumatic brain injury. *Pediatrics, 121*(6), e1686–e1695. doi:10.1542/peds.2007-2461

Shaheen, S. (2013). Motor assessment in pediatric neuropsychology: Relationships to executive function. *Applied Neuropsychology: Child, 2*(2), 116–124. doi:10.1080/21622965.2013.792668

Shuman, D. W., & Greenberg, S. A. (2003). The expert witness, the adversary system, and the voice of reason: Reconciling impartiality and advocacy. *Professional Psychology: Research and Practice, 34*(3), 219–224. doi:10.1037/0735-7028.34.3.219

Siegler, R. S. (1998). *Children's thinking* (3rd ed.). Upper Saddle River, NJ: Prentice-Hall.

Silver, L. B. (1992). *Attention-deficit hyperactivity disorder: A clinical guide to diagnosis and treatment*. Washington, DC: American Psychiatric Press.

Silverman, L. K. (1997). Family counseling with the gifted. In N. Colangelo & G. A. Davis (Eds.), *Handbook of gifted education* (pp. 382–397). Boston, MA: Allyn & Bacon.

Simon, H. A. (1975). The functional equivalence of problem solving skills. *Cognitive Psychology, 7*(2), 268–288. doi:10.1016/0010-0285(75)90012-2

Singh, S. K., Singh, R. K., & Singh, D. K. (2011). A comparative study of personality traits of children with learning disability and normal school going children. *Indian Journal of Community Psychology, 7*(2), 411–417.

Smith, M. (2004). *Joseph's coat: People teaming in transdisciplinary ways*. Retrieved from http://www.tsbvi.edu/Outreach/seehear/spring98/joseph.html

Smith, M., & Segal, J. (2011). *ADD/ADHD parenting tips*. Retrieved from http://helpguide.org/mental/adhd_add_parenting_strategies.htm

Sohlberg, M. M., & Mateer, C. A. (2001). *Cognitive rehabilitation: An integrative neuropsychological approach*. New York, NY: Guilford.

Special Education Technology British Columbia. (2008). *Writing strategies for students with visual impairments: A classroom teacher's guide*. Retrieved from http://www.setbc.org/Download/LearningCentre/Vision/Writing_Strategies_for_Visual_Impairments.pdf

Sprague, S. (2008). *Coping with cliques: A workbook to help girls deal with gossip, put-downs, bullying, and other mean behavior*. Oakland, CA: Instant Help Books.

Spungin, S., McNear, D., Torres, I., Corn, A. L., Erin, J. N., Farrenkopf, C., & Huebner, K. M. (2002). *When you have a visually impaired student in your classroom: A guide for teachers*. New York, NY: AFB Press.

Stanovich, K. E., Cunningham, A. E., & Cramer, B. B. (1984). Assessing phonological awareness in kindergarten children: Issues of task comparability. *Journal of Experimental Child Psychology, 38*(2), 175–190.

Stauffacher, K., & DeHart, G. B. (2006). Crossing social contexts: Relational aggression during early and middle childhood. *Journal of Applied Developmental Psychology, 27*(3), 228–240. doi:10.1016/j.appdev.2006.02.004

Stokes, S. (n.d.). *Children with Asperger's syndrome: Characteristics/learning styles and intervention strategies.* Retrieved from http://www.specialed.us/autism/asper/asper11.html

Stone, W. L., & Hogan, K. L. (1993). A structured parent interview for identifying young children with autism. *Journal of Autism & Developmental Disorders, 23*(4), 639–652.

Strauss, E., Sherman, E., & Spreen, O. (2006). *A compendium of neuropsychological tests: Administration, norms, and commentary.* New York, NY: Oxford University Press.

Suarez-Morales, L., Dillon, F. R., & Szapocznik, J. (2007). Validation of the Acculturative Stress Inventory for Children. *Cultural Diversity and Ethnic Minority Psychology, 13*(3), 216–224. doi:10.1037/1099-9809.13.3.216

Suchy, Y. (2009). Executive functioning: Overview, assessment, and research issues for non-neuropsychologists. *Annals of Behavioral Medicine, 37*(2), 106–116. doi:10.1007/s12160-009-9097-4

Sugai, G., & Horner, R. H. (2009). Responsiveness-to-intervention and school-wide positive behavior supports: Integration of multi-tiered system approaches. *Exceptionality, 17*(4), 223–237. doi:10.1080/09362830903235375

Sullivan, E., & Keeney, E. (2008). *Teacher talk: School culture, safety and human rights.* New York, NY: National Economic and Social Rights Initiative.

Swearer, S. M., Grills, A. E., Haye, K. M., & Cary, P. T. (2004). Internalizing problems in students involved in bullying and victimization: Implications for intervention. In D. L. Espelage & S. M. Swearer (Eds.), *Bullying in American schools: A social-ecological perspective on prevention and intervention* (pp. 63–83). Mahwah, NJ: Erlbaum.

Swearer, S. M., Song, S. Y., Cary, P. T., Eagle, J. W., & Mickelson, W. T. (2001). Psychosocial correlates in bullying and victimization: The relationship between depression, anxiety, and bully/victim status. *Journal of Emotional Abuse, 2*(2–3), 95–121. doi:10.1300/J135v02n02_07

The Teaching Research Institute–Eugene. (n.d.). *School-based assessment of executive functions.* Retrieved from http://www.brainline.org/content/2010/06/school-based-assessment-of-executive-functions.html

Tench, M. (2003, January 21). Web tangle. Schools struggling to stop tech-savvy bullies who have taken their taunting to cyberspace. *Boston Globe*, p. B1.

Tharp, R. G., & Wetzel, R. J. (1969). *Behavior modification in the natural environment.* New York, NY: Academic Press.

Thompson, S. J., Morse, A. B., Sharpe, M., & Hall, S. (2005). *Accommodations manual: How to select, administer, and evaluate use of accommodations for instruction and assessment of students with disabilities.* Retrieved from http://www.ccsso.org/content/pdfs/AccommodationsManual.pdf

Thomson, J. B., & Kerns, K. A. (2000). Mild traumatic brain injury in children. In S. A. Raskin & C. A. Mateer (Eds.), *Neuropsychological management of mild traumatic brain injury* (pp. 233–253). London, England: Oxford University Press.

T.K. and S.K. v. New York City Department of Education, 779 F.Supp. 2d 289 (2011).

Tolman, A. O., & Rotzien, A. L. (2007). Conducting risk evaluations for future violence: Ethical practice is possible. *Professional Psychology: Research and Practice, 38*(1), 71–79. doi:10.1037/0735-7028.38.1.71

Totura, C. M. W., Green, A. E., Karver, M. S., & Gesten, E. L. (2009). Multiple informants in the assessment of psychological, behavioral, and academic correlates of bullying and victimization in middle school. *Journal of Adolescence, 32*, 193–211. doi:10.1016/j.adolescence.2008.04.005

Trapani, C., & Gettinger, M. (1996). Treatment of students with learning disabilities: Case conceptualization and program design. In M. A. Reinecke, F. M. Dattilio, & A. Freeman (Eds.), *Cognitive therapy with children and adolescents: A casebook for clinical practice* (pp. 251–277). New York, NY: Guilford.

Ttofi, M. M., Farrington, D. P., Lösel, F., & Loeber, R. (2011). The predictive efficiency of school bullying versus later offending: A systematic/meta-analytic review of longitudinal studies. *Criminal Behaviour and Mental Health, 21*(2), 80–89. doi:10.1002/cbm.808

Tucker, C. J., Finkelhor, D., Turner, H., & Shattuck, A. (2013). Association of sibling aggression with child and adolescent mental health. *Pediatrics, 132*(1) 79–84. doi:10.1542/peds.2012-3801

UN Committee on the Rights of the Child. (2001). *General comment no. 1, the aims of education, U.N. doc. CRC/GC/2001/1.* Retrieved from http://www1.umn.edu/humanrts/crc/comment1.htm

United States v. Drew, No. 2:08-cr-582-GW (D.C. Central District of CA, 2009).

U.S. Department of Education, Office of Special Education and Rehabilitation Services, Office of Special Education Programs. (2008). *Teaching children with attention deficit hyperactivity disorder: Instructional strategies and practices.* Washington, DC: Author. Retrieved from http://www.ed.gov/rschstat/research/pubs/adhd/adhd-teaching-2008.pdf

U.S. Department of Health and Human Services. (2003a). *15+ make time to listen, take time to talk . . . about bullying.* Retrieved from http://store.samhsa.gov/product/15-Make-Time-To-Listen-Take-Time-To-Talk-About-Bullying/SM08-4321

U.S. Department of Health and Human Services. (2003b). *Take action against bullying.* Retrieved from http://download.ncadi.samhsa.gov/ken/pdf/SVP-0056/SVP-0056.pdf

U.S. Department of Health and Human Services. (2009). *Cyberbullying.* Retrieved from http://www.stopbullying.gov/cyberbullying/what-is-it

U.S. Department of Health and Human Services. (n.d.a). *How to intervene to stop bullying: Tips for on-the-spot intervention at school.* Retrieved from http://safeschools.state.co.us/docs/SBN_Tip_4%20How%20to%20Intervene.pdf

U.S. Department of Health and Human Services. (n.d.b). *Providing support to children who are bullied: Tips for school personnel (and other adults).* Retrieved from http://safeschools.state.co.us/docs/SBN_Tip_18%20Providing%20Support.pdf

U.S. Department of Justice. (2001). *Addressing the problem of juvenile bullying.* Retrieved from http://www.ncjrs.gov/pdffiles1/ojjdp/fs200127.pdf

U.S. Department of Justice. (2009). *Guide for preventing and responding to school violence* (2nd ed.). Retrieved from http://www.ojp.usdoj.gov/BJA/pdf/IACP_School_Violence.pdf

Vaillancourt, T., McDougall, P., Hymel, S., & Sunderani, S. (2010). Respect or fear? The relationship between power and bullying behavior. In S. R. Jimerson, S. M. Swearer, & D. L. Espelage (Eds.), *Handbook of bullying in schools: An international perspective* (pp. 211–222). New York, NY: Routledge/Taylor & Francis Group.

van der Sluis, S., de Jong, P., & van der Leij, A. (2007). Executive functioning in children, and its relations with reasoning, reading, and arithmetic. *Intelligence, 35*(5), 427–449. doi:10.1016/j.intell.2006.09.001

Vellutino, F. R., Fletcher, J. M., Snowling, M. J., & Scanlon, D. M. (2004). Specific reading disability (dyslexia): What have we learned in the past four decades. *Journal of Child Psychology and Psychiatry, 45*(1), 2–40.

Waasdorp, T. E., Pas, E. T., O'Brennan, L. M., & Bradshaw, C. P. (2011). A multilevel perspective on the climate of bullying: Discrepancies among students, school staff, and parents. *Journal of School Violence, 10*(2), 115–132. doi:10.1080/15388220.2010.539164

Wang, J., Nansel, T. R., & Iannotti, R. J. (2011). Cyber and traditional bullying: Differential association with depression. *Journal of Adolescent Health, 48*(4), 415–417. doi:10.1016/j.jadohealth.2010.07.012

The Washington Times. (2007, October 1). *Delete cyberbullying.* Retrieved from http://www.ncpc.org/programs/crime-prevention-month/newspaper-supplements/2007-cpm-newspaper-supplement.pdf

Washton, A. M., Stone, N. S., & Hendrickson, E. C. (1988). Cocaine abuse. In D. M. Donovan & G. A. Marlatt (Eds.), *Assessment of addictive behaviors* (pp. 364–389). New York, NY: Guilford.

Watkins, C. E., & Brynes, G. (2003). *Anxiety disorders in children and adults.* Retrieved from http://www.ncpamd.com/anxiety.htm

WebMD. (2008). *Child abuse and neglect—Symptoms.* Retrieved from http://www.webmd.com/parenting/tc/child-maltreatment-symptoms?page=2&print=true

Wechsler, D. (2003). *Wechsler Intelligence Scale for Children–Fourth Edition.* San Antonio, TX: The Psychological Corporation.

Wechsler, D. (2012). *Wechsler Preschool and Primary Scale of Intelligence–Fourth Edition.* San Antonio, TX: The Psychological Corporation.

Weinberg, W. A., Rutman, J., Sullivan, L., Penick, E. C., & Dietz, S. G. (1973). Depression in children referred to an educational diagnostic center: Diagnosis and treatment. *Journal of Pediatrics, 83*(6), 1065–1072.

Welsh, M., Pennington, B., & Groisser, D. (1991). A normative-developmental study of executive function: A window on prefrontal function in children. *Developmental Neuropsychology, 7*(2), 131–149. doi:10.1080/87565649109540483

Wettstein, R. M. (2004). The forensic examination and report. In R. I. Simon & L. Gold (Eds.), *Textbook of forensic psychiatry* (pp. 139–164). Washington, DC: American Psychiatric Press.

Weyandt, L. L., Stein, S., Rice, J. A., & Wermus, C. (1994). Classroom interventions for children with attention-deficit hyperactivity disorder. *The Oregon Conference Monograph, 6,* 137–143.

Whitebread, D., Coltman, P., Pasternak, D. P., Sangster, C., Grau, V., Bingham, S., Almeqdad, Q., & Demetriou, D. (2009). The development of two observational tools for assessing metacognition and self-regulated learning in young children. *Metacognition and Learning, 4*(1), 63–85. doi:10.1007/s11409-008-9033-1

Wikipedia. (2009). *Cyber-bullying.* Retrieved from http://en.wikipedia.org/wiki/Cyber-bullying

Wikipedia. (2010). *Cyberstalking.* Retrieved from http://en.wikipedia.org/wiki/Cyberstalking

Wilhelm, J. D. (2001). *Improving comprehension with think-aloud strategies.* New York, NY: Scholastic, Inc.

Willard, N. E. (2007). *Cyber-safe kids, cyber-savvy teens: Helping young people learn to use the Internet safely and responsibly.* Hoboken, NJ: Wiley.

Williams, K. R., & Guerra, N. G. (2011). Perceptions of collective efficacy and bullying perpetration in schools. *Social Problems, 58*(1), 126–143. doi:10.1525/sp.2011.58.1.126

Wilson, B. A., Alderman, N., Burgess, P. W., Emslie, H., & Evans, J. J. (1996). *Behavioural Assessment of the Dysexecutive Syndrome (BADS).* San Antonio, TX: Pearson.

Wilson, P. H., Spence, S. H., & Kavanagh, D. J. (1989). *Cognitive-behavioral interviewing for adult disorders: A practical handbook.* London, England: Routledge.

Wing, L. (1976). Assessment: The role of the teacher. In M. P. Everard (Ed.), *An approach to teaching autistic children* (pp. 15–30). New York, NY: Pergamon.

Wiseman, R. (2009). *Owning up™ curriculum: Empowering adolescents to confront social cruelty, bullying, and injustice.* Champaign, IL: Research Press.

Witt, J. C., & Elliott, S. N. (1983). Assessment in behavioral consultation: The initial interview. *School Psychology Review, 12*(1), 42–49.

Woodcock, R. W., McGrew, K. S., & Mather, N. (2007). *Woodcock Johnson III Normative Update Tests of Cognitive Abilities.* Rolling Meadows, IL: Riverside Publishing.

Wright, J. (2004). *Preventing classroom bullying: What teachers can do.* Retrieved from http://www.jimwrightonline.com/pdfdocs/bully/bullyBooklet.pdf

Yeates, K. (2010). Traumatic brain injury. In K. O. Yeates, M. D. Ris, H. G. Taylor, & B. F. Pennington (Eds.), *Pediatric neuropsychology: Research, theory, and practice* (2nd ed., pp. 112–146). New York, NY: Guilford.

Ylvisaker, M. (1986). Language and communication disorders following pediatric head injury. *Journal of Head Trauma Rehabilitation, 1*(4), 48–56.

Ylvisaker, M., & Feeney, T. (2008). Helping children without making them helpless: Facilitating development of executive self-regulation in children and adolescents. In V. Anderson, R. Jacobs, & P. J. Anderson (Eds.), *Executive functions and the frontal lobes: A lifespan perspective* (pp. 409–438). Philadelphia, PA: Taylor & Francis.

Ylvisaker, M., Szekeres, S. F., & Haarbauer-Krupa, J. (1998). Cognitive rehabilitation: Executive functions. In M. Ylvisaker (Ed.), *Traumatic brain injury rehabilitation: Children and adolescents* (Rev. ed., pp. 221–265). Boston, MA: Butterworth-Heinemann.

Yopp, H. K. (1995). A test for assessing phonemic awareness in young children. *Reading Teacher, 49*(1), 20–29.

Young, R., & Sweeting, H. (2004). Adolescent bullying, relationships, psychological well-being, and gender-atypical behavior: A gender diagnosticity approach. *Sex Roles, 50*(7–8), 525–537.

Zehnder, M. M. (1994). *Using expert witnesses in child abuse and neglect cases.* St. Paul, MN: Minnesota County Attorneys Association.

Zimmerman, P., Gondan, M., & Fimm, B. (2005). *KITAP–Test of Attentional Performance for Children.* Herzogenrath, Germany: PsyTest.

Name Index

Subject Index